Theological Education
in the Catholic Tradition

THEOLOGICAL EDUCATION
IN THE
CATHOLIC TRADITION:

CONTEMPORARY CHALLENGES

Edited by
Patrick W. Carey
and
Earl C. Muller, S.J.

A Crossroad Herder Book
The Crossroad Publishing Company
New York

1997

The Crossroad Publishing Company
370 Lexington Avenue, New York, NY 10017

Copyright © 1997 by Patrick W. Carey and Earl C. Muller

Printed in the United States of America

Library of Congress Cataloging-in-Publication Data

Theological education in the Catholic tradition : contemporary
   challenges / edited by Patrick W. Carey and Earl C. Muller.
      p.   cm.
   "A Crossroad Herder book."
   Selected papers presented at a national symposium, Marquette
University, Aug. 1995.
   Includes bibliographical references and index.
   ISBN 0-8245-1672-9 (pbk.)
   1. Theology--Study and teaching--Catholic Church--Congresses.
2. Catholic Church--Education--United States--Congresses.
I. Carey, Patrick W., 1940-   .   II. Muller, Earl C., 1947-   .
BX905.T43 1997
230' .07'32--dc21   96-51970
                                                                   CIP

Contents

Part Four: GRADUATE AND RESEARCH PROGRAMS

Part Five: SEMINARY PROGRAMS

Part Six: INSTITUTIONAL AND ECCLESIAL CONTEXTS
FOR THEOLOGICAL EDUCATION

Part Seven: INTEGRATION AND INCULTURATION IN THE THEOLOGICAL CURRICULUM

Acknowledgments

In August of 1995, Marquette University hosted a national symposium entitled "Theological Education in the Catholic Tradition." This book is a collection of selected papers from that conference. Neither the conference nor the book would have been possible without a generous grant from Ms. Erica John, president of the Archdiocese of Milwaukee Supporting Fund. We express our gratitude and that of the conference participants for this support. We also thank the many theologians who attended, the seventy-five who delivered stimulating papers at the conference, and the contributors to this volume who have allowed us to publish their papers. We are grateful, moreover, to Sr. Emmanuel Luckman, O.S.B., Mr. Ian Levy, and Mr. Steven Bridge who either helped organize the conference or contributed to the production of this book, and to Ms. Aldemar Hagen who copy edited the text and Ms. Joan Skocir who provided layout, indexing, and final preparation of the book for publication. Finally, we thank Dr. James Le Grys of The Crossroad Publishing Company for encouraging us to publish this volume.

List of Abbreviations

A.C.E.	American Council on Education
ATS	Association of Theological Schools
CA	Catholic Action
CARA	Center for Applied Research in the Apostolate
CCD	Confraternity on Christian Doctrine
CDF	Congregation for the Doctrine of the Faith
CHSI	Catholic Home Study Institute
CTSA	Catholic Theological Society of America
DS	H. Denzinger and A. Schönmetzer, *Enchiridion Symbolorum* (Freiburg, 1965)
DTC	*Dictionnaire de théologie catholique*
FADICA	Foundations and Donors Interested in Catholic Activities
GE	*Gravissimum educationis* (Vatican II's *Declaration on Christian Education*)
J.E.A.	Jesuit Educational Association
NCCB	National Council of Catholic Bishops
NCE	*New Catholic Encyclopedia*
NCEA	National Catholic Educational Association
SCCTSD	Society of Catholic College Teachers of Sacred Doctrine
USCC	United States Catholic Conference
YCS	Young Catholic Students

Introduction

Patrick W. Carey

Theological education in the Catholic tradition has changed significantly since the end of the Second Vatican Council in 1965, creating opportunities and problems that need current systematic reflection and national attention. It is the purpose of this book to raise questions about the contemporary theological enterprise and to suggest ways to improve theological education at the college, seminary, and graduate levels. Although colleges, graduate schools, and seminaries have quite different educational missions—one to provide a basic liberal education where theology is part of a total humanities and science education; another to prepare academic researchers and professional teachers, and seminaries to provide for the spiritual formation as well as academic preparation of persons who will serve ecclesiastical ministries—they all participate in the Catholic tradition of theological scholarship and education.

In the United States, the Catholic tradition of theological education is relatively short, developing in response to various intellectual and cultural movements in the Church and society, new institutions, philosophies of education, and to changing paradigms of theology itself. Formal theological education had its origin in 1791 when French Sulpicians established at Baltimore the first seminary in the United States. Throughout the nineteenth century theological education was centered in the seminaries, receiving at the Third Plenary Council of Baltimore (1884) a thorough systematic structure and course of studies that lasted into the early 1960s.[1] The first attempt to develop theological education at the university level took place in 1889, when the Catholic University of America was established with the explicit purpose of providing a comprehensive graduate level education in theology—a vision, however, that was limited exclusively to the education of the clergy. Theology as a discipline within the undergraduate curriculum of the Catholic colleges and universities developed gradually throughout the twentieth century. Under-

---

[1] On the history of seminary education, see the helpful and comprehensive study by Joseph White, *The Diocesan Seminary in the United States: A History from the 1780s to the Present* (Notre Dame, Ind.: University of Notre Dame Press, 1989).

graduate theology had its origin as a distinct discipline in the 1920s at the Catholic University of America. But it was not until about 1940 that a national debate erupted on the aims of what was then called college theology.[2]

Prior to the 1960s most Catholic theology was taught by ordained clergy. The universal language of clerical theologians was Latin. In the seminaries a teacher could presume that his students had a considerable philosophical education in Thomism. Dialogue partners for theological discussion tended to be other Catholic theologians. Undergraduate theology departments in colleges and universities were often staffed by priests who taught other subjects and who had no theological education beyond the seminary. Catechetical programs for pre-college students were well established, and, if not reaching all Catholics, at least served to create a critical mass of Catholics who had basic information about their faith.

Major theological and cultural changes in the 1960s, and particularly after the Second Vatican Council, greatly affected theological education at all levels. The profile of the faculty and students, the theological programs, and the relationship between the Church and the theologian changed rather dramatically.

A profile of contemporary theological faculties reveals some significant changes in the past thirty years. Greater numbers of laity, for example, have become professional theologians. A number of the younger theologians, clerical as well as lay, have received much of their theological education in American secular and/or ecumenical institutions where attention to the Catholic tradition is not the central focus of attention. Latin has faded as the professional language of the discipline to be superseded by modern languages, Thomism has been replaced by widespread use of other philosophical systems, and a variety of modern critical methodologies have been embraced. The theological discipline, moreover, has been increasingly diversified by the emergence of specialization, a tendency created in part by the modern university conception of professionalism. Many theologians, furthermore, teach theology and do their research from an ecumenical perspective. Their dialogue partners in their theological and educational work are Protestants and/or members of other religious traditions as well as other Catholic theologians. These changes in the profile of the theological faculties since the Second Vatican Council have intensified significantly pluralism within the discipline itself.

Students, too, have changed over the past thirty years. In many Catholic colleges and universities the student body is more ecumenical and socially diverse than in the past. Undergraduate, seminary, and graduate students, faculties complain, are also not as prepared for a theological education as they should be. Undergraduates, like many others in the society at large,

---

[2]On the origins and historical debates on college theology, see Rosemary Rodgers, "The Changing Concept of College Theology: A Case Study" (Ph.D. dissertation, The Catholic University of America, 1973) and Pamela C. Young, "Theological Education in American Catholic Higher Education, 1939-1973" (Ph.D. dissertation, Marquette University, 1995).

have little or no basic religious literacy; many seminary students have minimal catechetical or philosophical background for the study of theology and ministry; graduate students do not have the requisite linguistic skills nor an adequate philosophical and historical foundation—tools necessary to enable original research into the primary sources of the tradition. The complaint is sometimes heard that graduate schools are now preparing a new generation of theologians who will be unable to engage the Church's theological tradition.

In many places the theological educational programs have not been fashioned to meet the basic needs of these students. Adequate institutional and financial resources, moreover, have not been supplied to enable faculty and students to remedy these weaknesses. As already indicated, a diverse, ecumenical, and specialized faculty have produced manifold benefits and advantages for theological education; however, theological programs, reflecting the pluralism among the theologians themselves, have become highly specialized and have produced an unintegrated elective system. These developments make it difficult to provide students with an introduction to theology as a discipline and to give them a sense of its unity.

Recent lamentations in Protestant as well as Catholic circles about the fragmentation and disintegration of theology as a discipline have generally been followed by calls for reconstruction and reform of the discipline. In fact the complaints have unleashed the self-corrective and creative impulses that have been a characteristic of Christian theology since its beginnings.

In the midst of these general problems in theological education, problems which are widely shared in the American theological academy, there are the specifically Catholic issues of religious identity in institutions of higher learning and the relationship between academic theology and the Church's magisterium. Highly controversial and public institutional disputes over academic freedom, especially with reference to theologians, have brought to the fore the issues of ecclesial communion, ecclesial authority, and a legitimate freedom for theological research and reflection.

In addition to the internal programmatic and ecclesial issues are issues related to the level of institutional and financial support for carrying out the mission of theological education in the Catholic tradition. The resolution of some significant problems (e.g., more language study, more financial support for theological research, the creation of focused national centers of theological research) will demand greater levels of financial resources from local institutions and from national funding agencies than has been customary in the past.

The diversity of the faculty, the lack of preparedness on the part of the students, the movement toward elective fragmentation in theological education, the relationship between communion with the Church and freedom for the theological enterprise, and the levels of institutional support are issues that have received national attention and have prompted a number of educators to call for a re-examination of theological education in Catholic schools of higher learning.[3]

The Marquette Conference on Theological Education in the Catholic Tradition was convoked to address many of the issues that had surfaced in the national journals of public opinion. The conference hoped to identify more systematically than in the past the problems, needs, and resources in theological education, and to propose solutions and future directions for programs and institutions. This book hopes to accomplish these same goals.

The book is divided into seven areas of investigation, each chapter identifying problems or proposing solutions to difficulties in contemporary theological education. The first section introduces the major topics to be covered in subsequent chapters, outlines the historical context in which theological education developed in twentieth-century America, and focuses upon the Catholic identity of the institutions in which academic theology is taught. Avery Dulles, S.J., sets the tone, outlining the issues that theologians face in communicating the Catholic tradition to their students. He points out that the very success of the developing theological tradition in the United States is manifested most recently in the many lamentations about the state of the discipline. Insisting that theology presupposes faith, he calls for a renewal of the theological task and theological education to meet the new problems that have emerged in society and in the schools during the last thirty years. Philip Gleason places theological education within the historical development of Catholic higher education in the twentieth century, arguing that Neo-Scholasticism dominated as the intellectual context during the pre-conciliar era and that after the breakup of the Neo-Scholastic synthesis Catholic educators have been without major agreement on what constitutes the intellectual core of the Catholic educational experience. Joseph A. Komonchak raises a crucial issue of the inherent link between the Catholic identity of a college, theology's role in it, and the college's redemptive mission in the world, contending that the christological heart of Catholic identity is intrinsically related to a college's "world-embracing and world-redemptive apostolic mission." For him it is impossible, theologically, to separate, as some have done, a distinctive identity from a mission to the world.

The relationship between catechesis and theology is the focus of the second section. There is near unanimous agreement that many students in colleges and seminaries do not possess a basic catechetical knowledge of Catholic doctrine, life, and culture. Some would blame poor catechesis for such a

---

[3]See, for example, James Tunstead Burtchaell, "The Decline and Fall of the Christian College (II)," *First Things* 13 (May 1991): 30-38; Matthew L. Lamb, "Will There Be Catholic Theology in the United States?" *America* 162 (May 26, 1990): 523-34; Gerald O'Collins, "Catholic Theology (1965-1990)," *America* 162 (February 3, 1990): 86-105; Thomas F. O'Meara, "Doctoral Programs in Theology at U.S. Catholic Universities," *America* 162 (February 3, 1990): 79-103; George P. Schner, *Education for Ministry* (Kansas City: Sheed & Ward, 1993); Katarina Schuth, *Reason for the Hope: The Futures of Roman Catholic Theologates* (Wilmington, Del.: Michael Glazier, 1989); Robert J. Wister, "The Teaching of Theology 1950-1990: The American Catholic Experience," *America* 162 (February 3, 1990): 88-109.

state of affairs, but Berard L. Marthaler, O.F.M.Conv., maintains that catechesis has been misunderstood; it has its own integrity and should not be perceived simply as a propaedeutic to theology. He suggests, moreover, that graduate and seminary programs introduce courses on catechesis into their curriculum and summons theologians to rethink how their own enterprise relates to other forms of the ministry of the Word.

The third section examines undergraduate programs in theology with special attention given to the introductory course and the development of a major in theology. Monika K. Hellwig introduces this section by raising a number of critical questions about what is being done at the undergraduate level. She proposes a corrective course for the discipline and invites colleges to rethink the content of their core curricular requirements. She advocates, for example, that the curriculum be restructured to include more doctrinal content to meet the needs of a student body that lacks appropriate formation in the tradition. Arthur L. Kennedy analyzes the most difficult of undergraduate courses in theology, the introductory courses, and offers a theological analysis of the postmodern culture and intellectual context in which such courses exists today. He indicates how students who come to college with a weakened catechetical background might be introduced or awakened to the mystery of Christian reality in a world that is suspicious of all institutional mediations of meaning and truth. Lawrence S. Cunningham discusses the creation of a strong major within the undergraduate curriculum. He outlines the historical development of undergraduate theology, demonstrates how the University of Notre Dame built a successful undergraduate major, and delineates the aims and content of that major.

University graduate and research programs are analyzed in the fourth section. Matthew L. Lamb challenges the graduate programs in theology to make the Catholic intellectual tradition the heart of higher education. He proposes that graduate education in the third millennium integrate the first millennium's search for divine wisdom with the second millennium's movement toward science and critical thinking. Graduate programs, moreover, need to bring together the two major forces at the Second Vatican Council, the *ressourcement* and the *aggiornamento* traditions. William M. Shea enumerates many of the contemporary problems in graduate theological education; examines postmodernism, professionalism, and ecclesial conflict as the intellectual context in which these programs currently exist; and suggests that graduate theology in the future must be comparative, rigorously theoretic, identifiably Catholic, and research-oriented to prepare students for the professional tasks they must assume as theologians. John C. Haughey, S.J., invites readers to consider how the Catholic identity of an institution might affect a faculty's research decisions and agenda. Neither descriptive nor prescriptive, he proposes how institutions and faculty might envision what he calls a "spirituality of research." The chapter is a Jesuit-inspired examination of how discernment of one's choices might be put into practice.

Seminary programs are the subject of the next section of the book. Robert J.

Wister introduces theological education in the seminary within the historical context of the reforms of the Council of Trent (1564), the Third Plenary Council of Baltimore (1884), and the Second Vatican Council, emphasizing the almost universal agreement in ecclesiastical documents on the necessity of integrating spiritual, intellectual, and pastoral concerns in the theological education of future priests. He examines, too, a number of major problems (e.g., the declining numbers of seminarians) in contemporary seminaries and indicates the challenges that must be met in the third millennium. Katarina Schuth, O.S.F., analyzes the different institutional structures of seminaries, presents a sociological profile of the students and faculty, and dissects an opinion survey of seminary faculty. She underlines concretely the bases for hope and the emerging crises that seminaries are facing and will continue to face in the future.

The sixth section explores the institutional context in which theological education takes place and the inherent ecclesial dimension of the theological discipline. James L. Heft, S.M., presses the need to articulate and to share a common vision of the distinctiveness of Catholic higher education. That shared vision should guide a university's or a college's allocation of time and resources for theological education within the institution. Thomas R. Kopfensteiner describes the pedagogical, curricular, and faculty resources that provide the institutional support for theological education in seminaries. He proposes that friendship is the most appropriate metaphor for illuminating the tasks that are inherent in teaching theology. Such a metaphor can be used to bring together into a synthetic whole in a way that other metaphors do not the educational tasks of acquiring practical skills, obtaining knowledge, using experience, and applying critical methods.

This section also examines the much-discussed relationship between Catholic theologians and the bishops. Using the philosophical insights of Josiah Royce, Bishop Francis E. George, O.M.I., asserts that one must always include the body of believers in any examination of the relationship between bishops and theologians. In his view theologians develop doctrine, the believing laity develop devotion, and the bishops exercise interpretation. All three exist in a triadic synthetic relationship where mutual support and criticism are possible and necessary for the good of the whole Church. Robert P. Imbelli, too, insists upon the ecclesial context of the roles of bishops and theologians and points to the very concrete and historically specific nature of the relationship between these two distinct roles in the Church. He argues for an "ecclesial-transformative" approach to theology which he believes provides solid theological grounds for the common commitments, distinct charisms and responsibilities, and inevitable tensions that characterize the relationship between bishops and theologians in the context of their mutual participation in the mystical element in the Church.

Archbishop Oscar H. Lipscomb, and Bishops John J. Leibrecht and Donald E. Pelotte, S.S.S., also analyze the ecclesial context in which theological education takes place. Archbishop Lipscomb argues that the truth of the faith is normative in the activities and roles of both bishops and theologians providing the common ground in which discussion and tension occurs. Bishop Leibrecht offers some concrete examples of how theologians and bishops have cooperated effectively within the diocesan church, and suggests ways in which the investigative scholar and teacher can contribute to the intellectual and cultural life of the local and national church. Bishop Pelotte demonstrates the necessity of theological inculturation and acculturation, and describes how theological education informed by these sensitivities can address the needs of a poverty-stricken diocese where basic intellectual and institutional resources are not readily available.

The last section focuses upon integration and inclusiveness in theological programs and curricula. The development of a legitimate diversity in theological methods as well as the development of specializations in theology (biblical, historical, and systematic) have influenced the curriculum in ways that have made integration and inclusiveness problematic. Many times students see the diversity in contemporary curricular arrangements but they cannot see the unity of the discipline. Lawrence E. Boadt, C.S.P., presents the issue of integration from the side of biblical theology. Biblical theology, he suggests, needs to communicate to students not only modern critical skills for interpreting the Scriptures but also an understanding of the vital role the Scriptures play and have played in the daily life of the Church through liturgy, personal prayer, catechesis, doctrine, and theology. Such an approach will necessarily modify the critical methods (i.e., by placing them within an ecclesial context of interpretation) and provide grounds for a common discussion between biblical and systematic theology. Joseph T. Lienhard, S.J., describes the relatively recent development of historical theology within American Catholic theological education. He, too, calls for an integration of biblical, historical, and systematic theology and suggests that the common rigid distinction between historical and systematic theology may not be beneficial for understanding the nature and functions of theology as a discipline. Susan K. Wood, S.C.L., argues that the Church's liturgy is itself the integrative center of the theological disciplines. She perceives all theology as doxology but such a doxological view of theology cannot dispense with the various historical and critical methods that have developed within the discipline in the modern period.

The integral relationship between theology and spirituality is the focus of two essays by Keith J. Egan and Austin C. Doran. Egan describes the origin and development of the separation of the study of spirituality from that of theology and suggests ways in which the relationship may be strengthened to the mutual benefit of both in colleges and universities. Doran identifies the problems and opportunities that seminaries face in trying to integrate spiritual growth and theological study. The entire seminary ambiance, he contends, should foster the idea that profound study can itself become a source of spiritual development and maturation.

The last two chapters raise the question of the relationship of religious and cultural experience in theological education and construction, concentrating in particular on what the African American and Hispanic Catholic experiences and culture can contribute to theology. M. Shawn Copeland urges departments of theology to educate more African American Catholics as theologians and to take seriously the African American experience in their theological education. She maintains that theologians themselves, if they are to develop their own Catholic theological vision and to prepare a new generation of African American Catholic theologians, must learn something of the African American culture and indeed integrate that cultural experience into their theological constructions and styles of educating. Roberto S. Goizueta points out that the future of the Catholic Church in the United States will be closely linked to the fortunes of the Hispanic community because of the size and growth of that community. In the past theologians as well as other American Catholic educators have largely ignored the Hispanic religious culture. Theologians, he insists, neglect the epistemological and anthropological implications of the Hispanic experience to the detriment of theology and theological education. Theologians need to expand their catholicity by inclusion of the Hispanic experience in their theology and methods of education.

Earl Muller, S.J., the primary organizer of the Marquette conference, has the last word. He draws out themes that transcend individual essays, makes explicit some issues that were only indirectly attended to in the papers, and focuses upon the Enlightenment problematic of contemporary theology.

A selected bibliography of studies on and proposals for theological education in the United States between 1881 and 1995 is added by Pamela C. Young, C.S.J. The bibliography provides resources for future study of theological education in the United States.

I
OVERVIEWS

1

Theological Education in the Catholic Tradition

Avery Dulles, S.J.

The Present Situation

The development of higher education in theology is one of the great success stories of the Catholic Church in the United States in the second half of the twentieth century. At the present time there is a record number of more than 600,000 students enrolled in American Catholic colleges and universities, nearly all of which require some study of theology or religion on the undergraduate level. At least eight Catholic universities offer doctoral programs in theology.[1] Catholic faculty members teach theology with distinction at many secular universities and nondenominational divinity schools. In addition there are innumerable Catholic biblical, catechetical, and pastoral institutes and programs for adult education and, of course, a large number of seminaries and houses of formation for religious orders. Although the center of gravity has seemed to be shifting in recent years toward the universities, many seminaries and theologates remain very vital, perhaps more so than in the first half of the century.

It would be a mistake, therefore, to begin with a wail of lamentation. The current disputes about Catholic identity, goals, and methods may be seen as by-products of the success story rather than as signs of disorientation and decline. Yet this conference would not have been convened unless there were serious problems, widely perceived.

Some of these problems are, or at least seem to be, merely technical in character. There are pedagogical questions regarding teaching methods, such as the use of lectures, reading, and field work in courses. There are problems about credit hours, including the number and sequence of required courses and electives. The number and quality of doctoral programs cause concern, as does the exact relationship between undergraduate and graduate theol-

[1] Boston College, Catholic University, Duquesne, Fordham, Loyola in Chicago, Marquette, Notre Dame, and St. Louis. See John W. Padberg, "Taking Theology Seriously," *Conversations on Jesuit Higher Education* 5 (spring 1994): 3.

10

ogy. There are problems of a financial character, such as the funding of the department itself, the funding of research, and the availability of stipends and scholarships. Unless practical problems such as these can be solved, the options will be severely limited. On examination it often turns out that the deep-seated differences of opinion about procedural questions are rooted in disagreements of a theoretical character.

At the other end of the spectrum are theoretical questions about the nature of theology. The very use of the term "theology" in the title of this conference seems to imply that we are dealing with something other than a confessionally neutral program of "religious studies." According to views that have become commonly accepted in most circles, theology is a discipline that begins in faith and seeks to serve faith by scholarly research and reflection. If this notion of theology is operative at the present conference, it may be easier to talk about theology in the Catholic tradition. But the definition of theology as a distinct discipline should not be taken as demanding that all courses be taught from a purely dogmatic perspective, with the documents of the magisterium as sources for major premises in syllogistic proofs. As we know from the practice of biblical and historical theology, apologetics and ecumenism, theology can pursue inductive and dialogical as well as dogmatic and deductive methods. Even within the field of systematics there is a reciprocity between reason and faith, between inquiry and response. Theology can speak to the *intellectus quaerens fidem* without forsaking its character as *fides quaerens intellectum*.

Recent Changes

The problematic areas have been surveyed in a multitude of books and articles. The problems are often identified by descriptions of the contrast between the period before Vatican II and the contemporary situation.[2] Before the Council it would not have occurred to anyone to say, as some prominent educators have recently done, that the theology department is the heart of the Catholic university.[3] Courses in theology offered on the college level scarcely went beyond the level of catechesis, and graduate courses for the laity were practically unknown. The professors, almost without exception, were Roman Catholic priests who had studied their theology in Neo-Scholastic manuals. Lacking any doctoral degree, they were considered equipped to teach theology by virtue of their four-year seminary course. What they passed on was in effect a diluted version of what they had learned in the seminary. It was taken for granted that the students were Roman Catholics. The majority

[2] For example, John C. Haughey, "Theology and the Mission of the Jesuit College and University," *Conversations* 5 (spring 1994): 5-6.

[3] "The Catholic university must be an institution, a community of learners or a community of scholars, in which Catholicism is perceptibly present and effectively operative. In the Catholic university this operative presence is effectively achieved first of all and distinctively by the presence of a group of scholars in all branches of theology"—Land O'Lakes Statement: "The

of them, I would suppose, were graduates of Catholic elementary schools and high schools.

Today the variety is much greater. Catholic departments and schools of theology include an increasing ratio of lay men and lay women and a diminishing number of priests and religious. The faculty have doctoral degrees obtained from European or American Catholic universities and, in growing proportions, from secular universities or Protestant or nondenominational divinity schools. No longer having a serviceable command of Latin, many younger faculty members, not to mention graduate students, are cut off from much of the Western theological tradition of the past fifteen hundred years. The majority of the professors, even though they be Catholic, have studied some Protestant authors and, very likely, some non-Christian religions. In many cases they are as familiar with Bultmann, Tillich, and Pannenberg as with classical or modern Catholic theologians. Scholastic method has been all but abandoned. Protestants are hired in increasing numbers to teach on Catholic faculties.[4]

These changes in faculty are paralleled to some degree by changes in the student body. Catholic students often come in with very little understanding of the elements of their faith. To an increasing degree members of other churches and religions elect to study in Catholic universities and even to enroll in Catholic graduate programs. This fact has an inevitable influence on the programs offered.

Remarkable changes have occurred in the curriculum. In an interesting study of a few typical Catholic universities (located in Boston, New York, and Washington, D.C.) Frank D. Schubert has documented what he describes as the "decatholicizing" and "secularization" of the Catholic religious curriculum.[5] He delineates three periods. From 1955 to 1965 the field was dominated by what Schubert calls the Catholic sacred order, reflected in course offerings on the Trinity, Christology, sin, grace, redemption, Church, sacraments, and the like. Sacred history was sharply distinguished from secular history. Everything was taught from an unequivocally Roman Catholic perspective.

In the second period, from 1965 to 1975, the course descriptions no longer make specific claims for sacred history, sacred doctrine, and sacred polity. Catholicism is introduced as one point of view—dominant but no longer su-

---

Nature of the Contemporary Catholic University," reprinted in Alice Gallin, ed., American Catholic Higher Education: Essential Documents, 1967-1990 (Notre Dame, Ind.: University of Notre Dame Press, 1992), 7-8.

[4] The danger that these changes in faculty development present to the maintenance of the Catholic tradition in Catholic institutions is explained by Thomas F. O'Meara in his "Doctoral Programs in Theology at U.S. Catholic Universities," *America* 162 (February 3, 1990): 79-84 and 101-3, and by Matthew L. Lamb in his "Will There Be Catholic Theology in the United States?" *America* 162 (May 26, 1990): 523-25 and 531-34.

[5] Frank D. Schubert, *A Sociological Study of Secularization Trends in the American Catholic University: Decatholicizing the Catholic Religious Curriculum* (Lewiston, N.Y.: The Edwin Mellon Press, 1990).

preme—and is considered in relation to the outlooks of other churches, other religions, and other ideologies. The catalogues announce courses in biblical theology, ecumenism, and comparative religion, and courses on revelation in relation to the modern world. The Catholic sacred order is still adverted to, but always in comparison with something else, which is also considered worthy of study. It is implied that Catholics might have something to learn from other religious and cultural traditions.

In the third period, from 1975 to 1985, the majority of the course offerings contain no reference to any sacred order. The titles are such that the courses could be taught by agnostics as well as by believers. One finds titles such as "Affirmation and Doubt in Modern Thinkers," "Science, Technology and Religion," "The Resurrection: Myth or Reality?" "Women and Religion," "Global Ethics," and "Classical Literature of World Religions." The range of the courses goes not only beyond Roman Catholicism (as in the second period), but beyond theism as a whole. The methodology is no longer distinctively theological. In order to achieve integration it is necessary to rely on secular disciplines such as history, sociology, psychology, anthropology, and literary criticism.

In summary, Schubert contends that the move has been from theology to religious studies and beyond. Theology, as he defines it, is the study of the tenets of a religion from within a particular sacred order. Theology in this sense is infrequently taught in Catholic colleges and universities in this country today. Religious studies deal with a multiplicity of sacred orders, but no longer from the point of view of their sponsors. After attempting to balance the claims of different sacred orders in ecumenical and interreligious studies, Catholic universities have been moving toward a study of the phenomenon of religion on the basis of secular disciplines. When this shift is made, theology loses whatever vestiges of its identity it may have retained in the interreligious approach.

Schubert's sampling is admittedly limited. He limits his analysis to a few East Coast metropolitan universities, and does not go beyond the year 1985. He takes over the idea of sacred orders from nineteenth-century sociologists. Although theologians may wish to differ from him on some points, they should find in his study much material for serious reflection.

Influence of Vatican II

As a justification for recent curricular changes some authors appeal to Vatican II. Unquestionably, one of the main purposes of the Council was to bring the Church out of its ghetto-like isolation and to situate it in the modern world. In abandoning its posture of isolation, the Church at Vatican II sought to enter into dialogue with other churches, other religions, and other ideologies, treating them as respected partners. The Council may be said to have embraced, though with notable reservations, the Enlightenment principles of freedom and equality that underlie the modern democratic state. It encouraged the laity to seek a theological education and to contribute positively to the development of doctrine.

Except in its *Decree on the Formation of Future Priests*, which is inapplicable to secular colleges and universities, Vatican II did not prescribe any method for the teaching of theology. Even for priests, the council recommended a biblically centered method that was a far cry from Neo-Scholasticism.[6] In many of its most significant documents the Council shied away from a strictly dogmatic approach. In its *Constitution on Revelation* and its *Decree on Ecumenism*, it adopted a biblical perspective that was highly ecumenical in tone. The *Declaration on Non-Christian Religions* begins with a presentation of the phenomenon of religion, and then proceeds to affirm the principles of tolerance and fellowship among different faith communities. The *Declaration on Religious Freedom* sets out from an affirmation of the emergence of the concept of human dignity in recent history. The *Pastoral Constitution on the Church in the Modern World*, addressed to the whole of humanity, opens with a phenomenology of the modern world. These documents, without abandoning the traditional insistence on the inviolability of magisterial teaching, locate that teaching within a larger context, seeking to make the Catholic point of view intelligible to a broader public.

It would be a mistake, however, to think that Vatican II intended to call any Catholic dogmas into question. The new methods may indicate, on the contrary, that the Church had become sufficiently self-confident to relinquish its defensive posture and to engage other constituencies in open dialogue. Dialogue is not seen as an alternative to evangelization but as a necessary phase of evangelization.

Thanks to the example set by the Council itself, many convinced Catholics hold that theology courses need not be overtly dogmatic. For some purposes, they believe, a more dialogical or phenomenological approach has definite advantages. It can show forth more clearly the credibility and significance of the Church's doctrines, and is almost the only approach that can be successful with non-Catholic students or marginal Catholics. Besides, a certain reticence regarding faith and the supernatural on the part of theologians may be motivated by an understandable concern to gain respectability from colleagues in other departments.

Pluralism in Debate

A few professors and administrators, going beyond this methodological strategy, hold that Church teaching should be subjected to deliberate doubt and affirmed only to the extent that it meets the criteria of autonomous reason. Although this view is not common among theologians, a few seem to be moving in this direction. For example, William Shea, who chairs the depart-

---

[6]See *Optatam totius*, 16. The *Declaration on Christian Education* (GE 10-11) encouraged higher education in the sacred sciences, but abstained from any concrete proposals regarding method.

ment of theological studies at St. Louis University, describes Roman Catholic theology as his "slice of the humanities pie."[7] Calling for "a public and universal theology critical of and responsible to the elements of our heterogeneous culture,"[8] he declares that pluralism of beliefs is a blessing, not a curse, and that loyalty to the human community should transcend loyalty to the Church. Shea speaks of himself as a theologian with a dual loyalty—both to his Catholic tradition and to a culture that has arisen apart from, and even in opposition, to the Church. In the past the Church has continually absorbed and baptized foreign cultures, but it is only recently, Shea concedes, that the Church is being asked to adopt overtly alien systems of thought. Does the gospel prohibition against serving two masters forbid a Christian to profess loyalty to secular systems of this kind? After raising several objections to his own dual loyalty, Shea responds by saying that he no longer shares the theology out of which the objections arise.[9]

The point of view represented by Dr. Shea gives one possible justification for the kind of curricular changes that Schubert notes in his survey of the years since 1975. But it is precisely this justification that convinces others that the new methods contain unacceptable threats to Catholic integrity. Catholic theology, they insist, can only be done by those who accept the Catholic faith and are personally committed to it. Robert Imbelli, for example, puts to Shea the question: "Among the loyalties of the Christian, is there not a paramount, indeed identity-founding loyalty: to Christ and his gospel, as proclaimed by the church?"[10] Another author, Bernard D. Green, expresses a similar view. "To be a Catholic," he writes, "means to be a committed member of a community of faith with its own specific beliefs, practices, and institutional disciplines." While making room for a search within faith, he insists that the Catholic is not a mere searcher. "Once the decision for the Church has been made, the Catholic stands committed to a body of religious truth to which he is even willing to witness."[11] To subject that body of truth to real doubt or denial, or to adhere to contrary systems, is to cease to speak as a Catholic; it is to opt out of the Catholic theological enterprise.

This faith-centered outlook provides a better rationale for the place of honor given to theology in the Catholic university. If the professors challenge and undermine the settled doctrine of the Church, it begins to be doubtful whether the department of theology is serving the purposes for which it was erected and whether it is meeting the legitimate expectations of those who make financial sacrifices to attend a Catholic college or university. Students

[7] William M. Shea, "Intelligence Shaped by Affection," *Conversations* 5 (spring 1994): 19.

[8] William M. Shea, "Pluralism and the Challenge to Catholic Higher Education," *American Catholic Issues: A Newsletter* (spring 1994): 1.

[9] William M. Shea, "Dual Loyalties in Catholic Theology Finding Faith in Alien Texts," *Commonweal* 119 (January 31, 1992): 14.

[10] Robert P. Imbelli, "Dual Loyalties in Catholic Theology," *Commonweal* 119 (April 24, 1992): 21.

[11] Bernard D. Green, "Catholicism Confronts New Age Syncretism," *New Oxford Review* 61 (April 1994): 19.

who sign up for courses in Catholic theology normally and, I think, legitimately expect to hear it presented from the perspective of faith. The bishops and the religious who have established most of the Catholic institutions of higher education, and the benefactors who support these institutions, presumably intend that theology courses be taught from a recognizably Catholic point of view.

Conflicts within Catholicism

More and more, the problems are moving beyond the limits of theology and touching on the very heart of Christian and Catholic existence. Catholics in this country are deeply divided by discordant outlooks and allegiances. For one group, still probably the largest, the Catholic stands committed to a body of revealed truth and is bound to bear witness to that truth. For this group experience is to be interpreted, enriched, and transformed in the light of the Church's heritage of faith, which becomes the decisive norm. For a second group religious truth is fashioned out of one's own experience, which then becomes the supreme criterion for judging all Catholic doctrines and practices.

The differences between these groups become especially manifest in ecclesiology. For members of the first group, who may be called traditional Catholics, the Church is the Body and the Bride of Christ and the mediator, under Christ, of grace and salvation. They accept the Church of Christ as a visible structured society, subsisting in the Roman Catholic Church of today. The pope and the bishops, they believe, are commissioned by the Lord himself to safeguard the heritage of faith, to teach with his authority, and to celebrate the sacraments as his faithful ministers. Membership in the Church, and acceptance of its doctrines, are not matters of personal preference but strict obligations binding on all who are capable of recognizing the Church for what it is. All of these theses, traditional though they be, are demonstrably in line with the Second Vatican Council.

For the other group, more in tune with the prevailing democratic culture and the reigning consumerist mentality, the Church is an ad hoc assembly of persons who happen to share a common outlook and who agree on common programs. The doctrines of the Church, they hold, can be revised according to the changing convictions of the members. The liturgy is, or should be, designed to provide emotionally satisfying experiences. Christians, on this view, are free to move from one church to another for the sake of emotional fulfillment or the attainment of their career goals, as they might move to a new business for the sake of getting a better job. Some adherents of this second group do not hesitate to organize their own alternative liturgies. They could easily be impelled to establish their own churches if their separatist policies ceased to be tolerated. The Church, for them, is a producer that must adapt its product to the tastes of the consumers, or else lose their patronage.

The leading religious rival of Catholic faith in the United States is no longer

the Protestantism of the Reformation or even the rationalism of the Enlightenment. At the edges of traditional Christianity proponents of New Age religion are promoting a new syncretism. They depict religion as a product of
peak experiences which put us into contact with a deeper reality, articulated
in different ways in different religions. In this framework Jesus Christ is no
longer acknowledged as the only Savior but only as one of a number of Savior
figures projected by the religious imagination. In some centers of spirituality,
Catholics are not only appropriating ideas and practices drawn from a multitude of spiritual traditions—Asiatic, African, and Native American—but doing so, apparently, without any serious effort to discriminate their truth or
validity in the light of Catholic faith. While one may be an experientialist
without buying into the New Age religion, any theology that subjects the dogmas of the faith to the test of autonomous experience is, I think, defenseless
against the onslaughts of this new syncretistic religiosity.

The New Age religion is no doubt an extreme case, but it is a glaring
example of a pervasive weakness in American Catholicism since the Second
Vatican Council. Many Catholics, including students in our universities, rely
primarily on their feelings. And yet, in typical cases, they hesitate to renounce
the vision of the Church as a divinely founded and supernatural society. They
need to be further instructed in the Catholic tradition in order to overcome
their ambivalence and find the strength to adhere to Catholic orthodoxy in a
climate of secular consumerism. A good academic introduction to Catholic
doctrine could be crucial for their continued adherence to the faith.

Among Catholic intellectuals the tensions between these opposed attitudes are resulting in a kind of spiritual schism. To an increasing degree, the
two parties attend different liturgies, join different professional societies, publish and read their own journals, and even set up their own educational institutions. Dr. Shea says quite frankly: "There is little communion, not to say
discussion, between Right and Left. We are witnessing a breakdown of ecclesial
life."[12] Walter Burghardt, several years earlier, commented on the growing
lack of communication. "I am afraid that the picture we intellectuals present
to our fellow Americans is a huge house hopelessly divided against itself. Do
we actually have a Catholic intellectual community?"[13] Bernard D. Green, an
English priest whom I have cited above, expressed astonishment at what he
found in this country. "I see a perilous amount of contentiousness, polarization, and fragmentation in the American Church," he wrote. He put this question: "I wonder: Are American Catholics any longer united around a fundamental set of beliefs and values such that they can recognize each other as
being in the same body? Furthermore, can they recognize that body as being
part of the universal Catholic Church with its center in Rome?"[14]

[12] Shea, "Dual Loyalties," 11.

[13] Walter J. Burghardt, "Intellectual and Catholic? Or Catholic Intellectual?" *America* 160
(May 6, 1989): 424.

[14] Bernard D. Green, "Tremors in the Foundation of the U.S. Catholic Church," *New Oxford
Review* 60 (October 1993): 16, 11.

What renders the situation so difficult is the virtual abandonment of rational argument, the normal resource of theology. Instead of engaging in civil discussion, the two groups resort to slogans and even to personal abuse. They form coalitions, go to the press with strident manifestos, and engage in heated letter-writing campaigns.

As the disputants drift further apart, it becomes increasingly difficult to find any common ground on which a rational debate could be conducted. There are few, if any, common principles. A decade or two ago, it would have been possible to settle disputes by an appeal to the teaching of the canonical Scriptures, the creeds, and the dogmas of popes and councils. But these sources are no longer accepted as peremptory authorities. Critical Catholic theologians often declare that the biblical canon was erroneously drawn up according to the biases of the hierarchical leaders in the early Church. Some Catholic scholars are buying into the liberal Protestant idea that the great trinitarian and christological dogmas of the early councils were unwarranted Hellenizations of the gospel. Confident of their own insights, they frequently seethe with hostility toward the pope and the Roman Congregations, who are ardently supported by Catholics of the opposite tendency. Lacking a common language, common goals, and common norms, theology seems to be in a state of chaos.

Theological Reconstruction

The crisis has not been produced by theology alone and will not be solved simply by better theology. But theology must not bury its head in the sand, acting as though the problems were merely academic. Theologians bear a share of the responsibility for the crisis and must make a contribution to its solution.

Although certain extremists on both sides will never be satisfied, it may be possible for a large body of Catholic educators to agree on some basic principles of theological method. All Catholic theology, I believe, must begin with the redemptive revelation of God in Jesus Christ or, in other words, with the gospel. It must recognize the Catholic Church as the primary bearer of the gospel. If this christological and ecclesial foundation is ignored or rejected, Catholic theology cannot even get underway.

The main division among the schools seems to depend on whether one recognizes some other norm in addition to revelation as mediated by the Church. Those who admit this may be called correlationists, whereas those who submit all other norms to the Church's faith may be called, in the terminology of David Tracy and Joseph Komonchak, epiphanic theologians.[15]

Correlation theology, as I understand it, accepts two poles, one of which

---

[15] The reflections in the next few paragraphs are inspired by my reading of Joseph A. Komonchak, "Recapturing the Great Tradition: In Memoriam Henri de Lubac," *Commonweal* 119 (January 31, 1992): 14-17.

may be described as the Christian texts. This pole includes the canonical Scriptures, and for Catholics it would have to include tradition, especially as articulated in the solemn teachings of ecumenical councils and popes. These biblical and ecclesial texts are viewed as normative for any theology that is entitled to be called Christian and Catholic. The second pole is usually depicted as some form of contemporary experience, a common human experience shared by believers and nonbelievers alike. The theologian has the task of interpreting the sacred texts so that they speak to the contemporary situation, and interpreting the situation so that the texts can be seen as relevant.

The method of correlation has shifted over the years. In a sense Thomas Aquinas already practiced such a method, since he accorded a certain autonomy to human reason and systematized the data of revelation according to a schema derived from philosophical sources. Paul Tillich, who gave the method its name, proposed that the questions of theology should arise out of the human situation and that the answers be given by the divine self-manifestation. But he recognized that the questions and the answers are to some degree interdependent. The experiences are modified by the revelation, accepted in faith, but the manifestation of the divine is conditioned by the situation into which it is received.[16] Although there is a risk that the divine manifestation will be adulterated by the application of an alien norm, that risk cannot be entirely avoided if the faith is to be made intelligible and meaningful for contemporary audiences.

Since the days of Tillich the correlationalist school has focused increasingly on the believer's subjectivity. Some representatives minimize the authority of the Christian texts, treating them no longer as criteria of truth but only as a criteria of appropriateness within a given tradition. The truth-value of the apostolic faith is more commonly measured by its adequacy to contemporary experience.[17] Furthermore, the objective meaning of the Christian texts is thrown open to question or practically dissolved by certain representatives of modern deconstructionist hermeneutics. The texts become subject to radical reinterpretation by every individual. Although these difficulties must be acknowledged, the method of correlation, in some form or other, can still be serviceable in Catholic theology.

A second theological approach, as Komonchak points out, is the epiphanic. It begins with a determinate revelation, and seeks to interpret, even to transform, experience in the light of that revelation. Although one of course needs human experience and culture to arrive at any interpretation, these human sources are not used critically against the deposit of faith. Rather, they are to be criticized in its light. The word of God exists, and has no rival. Theology retains the posture of faith, which demands a total submission of the mind and will to the divine as it reveals itself.

---

[16] Paul Tillich, *Systematic Theology* (Chicago: University of Chicago Press, 1951) 1:60-61.

[17] This seems to me to be the tendency of David Tracy in his *Blessed Rage for Order* (New York: Seabury/Crossroad, 1975), 64-75.

From the standpoint of theological education both methods have their advantages. But, as Komonchak points out, the method of correlation, as it has been practiced in the past generation, "has been conspicuously unsuccessful in transmitting the essential Christian faith."[18] For this reason, he believes, the epiphanic approach exemplified by de Lubac, von Balthasar, and Ratzinger has become increasingly popular in recent years.

As Komonchak also says, the difference between the two approaches should not be exaggerated. A sane use of correlation respects the integrity of the faith-tradition and seeks to put it into relationship to contemporary experience or whatever the second pole might be. On the one hand, "there can be no correlation or confrontation unless there is something that stands over and against the contemporary context with a life and substance of its own."[19] On the other hand, the manifestation of the divine, however sacred, always has to be understood in relation to some human fact or situation. The most epiphanic theology that can be imagined cannot get beyond the duality of the revealed datum and the human subject who receives the revelation and reflects upon it from a position in the world. Hence we cannot simply choose between the two methods.

I believe that theologians can understand and explain what they are doing on the basis of some combination of the epiphanic and correlational methods. If they can do so, we can hope that authentic theology may be reinvigorated in those Catholic institutions where it has been virtually displaced or seriously threatened by the encroachments of nonconfessional religious studies or secular methodologies.

Modalities of University Theology

Catholic theology, as I have described it, presupposes Catholic faith. It is exercised within the Catholic Church by someone who accepts the Church's normative sources and doctrinal standards. Such theology can be taught in the dogmatic mode, giving a central place to the teaching of the magisterium. But, as I have already indicated, it can also be taught with more direct attention to Scripture and tradition, adverting only occasionally to the magisterium where it has made important interventions. Theology can be taught apologetically for the benefit of inquirers or dialogically for the sake of fruitful conversation with other Christians or adherents of non-Christian religions. In none of these cases should the Catholic theologian feel under pressure to abandon the posture of faith. In fact, apologetics and interchurch or interfaith dialogue presuppose that the practitioner is a committed believer entering into conversation with those having a different perspective. If the faith-perspective is abandoned the whole point of the apologetics or the dialogue is removed.

In a Catholic university, I believe, special efforts should be made to open

[18] Komonchak, "Recapturing the Great Tradition," 17.
[19] Ibid.

up the minds of students to the riches of the Catholic tradition. As Walter Burghardt has reminded us, Catholic students often come to the university "utterly ignorant of their rich tradition."[20] Unless they can see the present moment against the background of the past, they will be at a loss to advance into the future. They can profit immensely from gaining a sense of how Catholicism continually builds upon its past, finding new things and old as it draws upon its heritage. As Monika Hellwig has said, Catholics should not succumb to the habit of moving, as some Protestants do, directly from the Scriptures to contemporary reflection, or even leaping from Augustine to Luther.[21] The Scriptures should be studied as inspired sources, but not as giving the definitive answers to all theological questions, which they were never intended to do. Catholicism can be effectively taught through the medium of Church history.[22]

The ecclesiastical magisterium is for Catholics the authoritative living interpreter of the Christian sources. Relationships between university theologians and the magisterium have at times been uneasy. A certain tension is to be expected because the two kinds of teaching proceed by different methods and have distinct but overlapping goals. The tension becomes particularly acute when either of the parties fails to respect its proper limits. It is not for the hierarchical magisterium to settle internal theological disputes, even at the urging of theologians, unless it finds a given theological system to be truly incompatible with Catholic faith. The magisterium in the seventeenth century did well in refusing to endorse or condemn any of the current theories about the relationship between grace and free will. Perhaps the magisterium should have exercised greater caution in speaking about certain other questions of a technical or scientific character that have arisen in the course of time, such as the authorship and dating of biblical books.

On the other hand, theologians should not try by themselves to establish the doctrine of the Church. They speak as private persons within the Church. When they are troubled by some pronouncement of the magisterium, they may indeed ask questions and express their difficulties, but they should be on guard against seeming to set themselves up as a kind of opposition party, a parallel magisterium.

If these rules are observed, it may be possible to develop a better working relationship between the theologians and the hierarchical magisterium. The bishops can be of great assistance in maintaining or restoring the discipline of university theology, which is under considerable pressure in the secular climate of the day. Even in Catholic universities, colleagues from other disci-

[20] Burghardt, "Intellectual and Catholic?" 424. He goes on to say: "During a half century of theology I have watched our incredibly rich tradition pass slowly but surely into museums or, at best, into the hands of appreciative Protestant brothers and sisters."

[21] Monika K. Hellwig, "Twenty-Six Years of Undergraduate Theology," *Conversations* 5 (spring 1994): 18.

[22] A brief indication of how this may be done is given in J. William Harmless, "Theology as Hard-Won Wisdom," *Conversations* 5 (spring 1994): 20.

plines frequently fail to appreciate the distinctive characteristics of theology, and are disposed to challenge its centrality in the mission of the university. Those who today urge university theologians to declare their independence from the magisterium may soon take the next logical step by demanding that theology be converted into some kind of scientific study of religion. Eventually they or their successors may insist that the residual functions of theology be absorbed by purely secular disciplines such as philosophy and the social sciences.[23]

When the status of theology is at stake, the influence of the ecclesiastical hierarchy upon the Catholic university may prove crucially important. The Holy See and the bishops share with theologians a deep concern for the integrity and transmission of the faith. Because of their lively sponsorship of Catholic higher education, the hierarchical leaders are the natural allies of university theologians in the struggle to prevent theology as a sacred discipline from being drowned in the rising tide of secularity.

[23] The antipathy of many academics toward theology has not been appeased by statements such as that of Land O'Lakes, which asserted that "the Catholic university must have true autonomy and academic freedom in the face of authority of every kind, lay or clerical, external to the academic community itself" (in Gallin, *American Catholic Higher Education*, 7). If this statement is true, it must be interpreted in the light of the statement of John Paul II that bishops "should not be seen as external agents but as participants in the life of the Catholic university" (Apostolic Constitution *Ex corde Ecclesiae*, 28; text in Gallin, ibid., 422). The precarious position of theology on the American academic scene is detailed in David J. O'Brien, *From the Heart of the American Church* (Maryknoll, N.Y.: Orbis, 1994), 157-86.

2

Catholic Higher Education as Historical Context for Theological Education[1]

PHILIP GLEASON

At an early point in James T. Farrell's depressing trilogy, the adolescent Studs Lonigan is reviewing with his friends their exploits while playing hooky from school. He chuckles to himself as he recalls the habitual reaction of the neighborhood druggist. Whenever Studs and his fellow truants entered the drugstore, the proprietor would call out to his clerk, "Ope lookat! . . . here comes the higher Catholic education! Lock up the candy cases!"

I fear your reaction now may be: "Look out! Here comes a discourse on the history of Catholic higher education! Get out the no-doze!" Especially since I plan to concentrate on the preconciliar period when it is well known that nothing of any conceivable interest was going on.

The reason behind this perverse decision is that I have studied the period up to the late 1960s in detail. From that time on, I have only a participant observer's knowledge of Catholic higher education in general. Concerning theological education, I know even less. Even so, I believe that several of the themes Catholic theologians have explored in the past three decades are relevant to this topic.

There is, for example, the heightened sensitivity to history, story, narrative, and experience—all of that is obviously relevant. The development of women's colleges, and eventually of theological study by women, might serve as background to the more recent emergence of feminist theology. But *inculturation* is the theme I want to apply to this essay—inculturation as it relates to Catholic colleges and universities between the 1920s and the 1960s.

---

[1] For documentation and substantiation of the arguments presented here, see Philip Gleason, *Contending with Modernity: Catholic Higher Education in the Twentieth Century* (New York: Oxford University Press, 1995).

I won't try to cover the seminaries, where theology was then much more effectively sealed off from general educational developments than it has been since the 1960s.

First, a word about inculturation as such. The concept as I understand it involves both adaptation of the gospel to the configuration of a particular culture, *and* the leavening influence of the Christian message upon the culture in question. The term was not available to Catholic educators of the period we are considering here, but they aimed at the same goal. For they realized they had to accommodate the prevailing American practice in higher education, while at the same time they struggled to maintain a distinctive religious identity and to exert a shaping influence on the national culture. Moreover, they were at least subliminally aware of the dialectical nature of the problem posed by inculturation. That is, they understood that an uncritical acceptance of prevailing cultural norms could be fatal, but that the opposite distortion—i.e., too rigid an insistence on maintaining distinctively Catholic ways—could be equally stultifying. True, those who pointed out these dangers usually focused on only half of the dialectical pair, with conservatives warning against uncritical acceptance, and liberals pointing out the folly of rigid inflexibility. But that no doubt sounds familiar.

In any case, accommodation to American norms did take place. Why did even conservatives accept it? Because they had to—it was forced on them by events, market forces, the needs of their clientele. The process entered a critical phase at the turn of the century. Its underlying cause was a set of interlinked changes in the American educational environment that affected schooling at the secondary, collegiate, and graduate levels. But for Catholics, the college was the crucial problem and we must begin there.

The College and Inculturation

The essence of the college problem was that when the century opened, the typical Catholic college still combined secondary and collegiate work in the same institution. This was not just a matter of academic inferiority; it reflected a distinctive history. The old-time Catholic college—like the minor seminary—derived from the same European model as the French *lycée* or German *Gymnasium*. That is, it was intended to combine in one institution what Americans regarded as properly belonging to two different kinds of schools, the academy and the college. But since most American colleges in the nineteenth century had their own "preparatory departments," the boundary between secondary and collegiate work was fuzzy everywhere, and Catholic colleges were less of an anomaly than what I have just said might suggest.

What brought on the crisis late in the century was the rapid growth of free public high schools, a similar expansion of both state and private universities, and an explosive increase of enrollments at both levels. These developments, along with the introduction of many new subjects and areas of specialization, intensified the problem of articulation—that is, the need to clarify where secondary education left off and collegiate education began and how the two levels were to be linked together.

To address the problem, American educators in the middle 1890s launched a movement to specify the kind of education high schools should provide, and how the colleges could be sure it had been imparted to those who applied for entry as first year students. The initial focus on college entrance requirements soon broadened into a drive for what was called "standardization." That is, the problem of articulation was solved by making a sharp distinction between high school and college, and by establishing verifiable criteria, or "standards," that both kinds of schools had to meet. To ease the work of verification, which was carried out by what we now call accrediting associations, the key standards were quantitative rather than qualitative. Thus, a "standard college" was a strictly post-secondary institution; it had to have at least eight "departments" and one hundred full-time students; only those who had already completed sixteen high-school "units" could be accepted as freshmen; they must accumulate 120 semester hours to graduate, and so on.

Familiar as all this seems to us today, it constituted a radical challenge to Catholic educators a century ago. Since it mandated complete separation of high school from college, and since Catholic colleges were heavily dependent on their prep enrollments, standardization meant that many of them had to drop down to academy status—or simply go out of business. But there were also genuine pedagogical issues. Especially among the Jesuits, the combined secondary-collegiate structure was inseparably linked to the ideal of a liberal arts education—by which Jesuits really meant the prescribed classical curriculum as embodied in their venerable *Ratio Studiorum*.

This seems perhaps impossibly conservative, but champions of the liberal arts were quite correct in pointing out that the reformers had substituted purely bureaucratic measures of control for the older belief that a college education had identifiable substantive content and its own internal principle of curricular unity. Accepting electivism, which gave students greater freedom of choice in their studies, and departmentalization, which was demanded by the increasing specialization of knowledge, were, indeed, necessary reforms. But they also represented an accommodation to fragmenting tendencies of modernity—tendencies whose effect on the undergraduate curriculum we have still not brought under control.

Despite the resistance of the conservatives, Catholic colleges accepted standardization. We cannot enter into the details of the process, but the new system was well in place by the early 1920s. In a sense, they had little choice—it was reform or die. However, the leading Catholic reformers understood that the old system really was outmoded. They recognized that the circumstances of the day demanded something like standardization, and they appreciated the positive values it embodied. Moreover, they insisted that the traditional goals of Catholic education could be realized as well under the new arrangement as under the old. Since they were advocating adjustments that would make it possible for Catholic schools to carry on their special mission, it seems justifiable to apply the term "inculturation" to what they were doing.

But what was the positive element of their inculturation strategy? Standardization itself was unquestionable *acculturative*—a matter of adjusting to the norms and practices of the surrounding secular culture. How was the distinctively Christian (which in those days meant uniquely Catholic) dimension to be embodied in the new system and inserted into that culture? The answer to that question was clear by the late twenties: more systematic and intensive teaching of Neo-Scholastic philosophy would serve this purpose.

Several factors played a role in this development. For one thing, philosophy had long been taught in Catholic colleges as part of the traditional liberal arts curriculum. With the decline of the classical languages, it seemed appropriate to lay greater emphasis upon it, and the newly adopted organizational system made it easy to do so simply by increasing credit-hour requirements. Thomism had been adopted as the Church's official philosophy almost a half-century earlier; it constituted an authoritative reconciliation of faith and reason and thus provided a distinctively Catholic intellectual perspective. It attained new professional visibility in this country with the organization of American Catholic Philosophical Association and the appearance of *The Modern Schoolman* and *The New Scholasticism*, all of which happened in the middle 1920s. The emergence of outstanding figures like Jacques Maritain and Étienne Gilson confirmed the key role of Neo-Scholasticism in what was soon to be called the "Catholic Renaissance."

But why philosophy rather than theology? The short answer is that when the new system took hold in the 1920s, theology simply wasn't in the picture. It was strictly a seminary subject, which had never been taught to collegians. All they had traditionally gotten was the catechism for an hour a week. Religion, many Catholic educators held, was not an academic subject at all—it was a way of life. That view was implicit in the widely reported activities of John O'Hara, C.S.C., Notre Dame's perfect of religion, who eschewed the classroom in favor of a high-pressure campaign to promote frequent Holy Communion. On the other hand, Catholic educators, Jesuits in particular, reacted vehemently to the suggestion that the supplemental religion courses offered by Catholic chaplains at secular universities adequately filled the spiritual needs of undergraduates. Religion must permeate the entire educational experience, they insisted.

Moreover, the man who did the most to make religion a regular academic subject in Catholic colleges—Fr. John Montgomery Cooper of the Catholic University of America—strongly opposed teaching theology. The only kind available—seminary theology—was, he maintained, entirely unsuitable for lay students living in the secular world. Cooper worked hard to create more appropriate teaching materials, but the whole enterprise of inserting the academic study of religion in the curriculum was just getting under way in the 1920s. It gained ground in the next decade, but as late as 1937 only three Catholic colleges out of eighty-four surveyed offered an academic major in religion. Two years later, philosophy's hegemonic role was challenged for the first time by the suggestion that theology was properly the queen of the sciences and should therefore "integrate" the curriculum of the Catholic college.

We will return to the debate that challenge set off. Before doing so, however, let us look briefly at the *praxis* side of the question—that is, the activities that followed from, or were related to, the inculturative strategy just described.

The most immediate form of praxis was, of course, classroom instruction in Neo-Scholastic philosophy. That was laid on in heavy doses, even in Catholic women's colleges, which typically required twelve to fourteen hours of philosophy despite the widespread feeling that women were temperamentally unsuited to its study. By the mid-fifties, some 2,400 Notre Dame students were enrolled in philosophy classes every semester; ten years later, Georgetown still required eighteen hours of philosophy for the A.B. degree.

Besides providing a rational grounding for the individual student's religious worldview, instruction in Neo-Scholasticism was related to a broader aspect of inculturative praxis—the goal of building a Catholic culture through Catholic Action. These terms—Catholic culture and Catholic Action—became buzzwords around 1930, just after philosophy had established itself as the crucial theoretical element of inculturation. As such, it furnished the natural law principles for building a properly ordered Catholic culture. Understanding these principles was crucial to forming "apostles." The point was most obvious in connection with sexual morality and family life, but Catholic Action militants, from the promoters of the Legion of Decency to the founders of the Catholic Worker Movement, understood themselves to be working within the Neo-Scholastic framework. The Jocist inspired Young Catholic Students (YCS) was the most significant Catholic Action (CA) movement actually centered in the colleges. But the apostolic ethos permeated Catholic campuses and inspired many idealistic young people to devote themselves to volunteer service in Houses of Hospitality or movements like the Grail.

How did the larger cultural context affect these Catholic developments? In the 1930s, the depression in this country and the rise of totalitarian movements in Europe testified to the existence of a genuine cultural crisis. Catholic educators, conscious of the palpable revival of intellectual and spiritual energies in the Church, believed that they understood its causes, and could prescribe a cure. World War II confirmed the existence of a crisis, which many commentators diagnosed as fundamentally spiritual. In these circumstances, the mentality and outlook of the Catholic intellectual revival carried over strongly into the postwar era. So strongly, in fact, that Protestant leaders reacted bitterly to Catholic "aggressiveness," and Paul Blanshard wrote a book to show that Catholic power was incompatible with American freedom. The resulting controversies gave thoughtful Catholics pause. But less obvious crosscurrents set in motion or strengthened by war also helped to shift the direction of Catholic thought and feeling.

Acculturation and Early Symptoms of Strain

World War II was a key turning point. On the practical level, a number of developments brought Catholic institutions into the mainstream of American higher education and required them to interact more intensively with "outsiders." The service programs (V-12 and ASTP) did this in the war itself, and the GI Bill did afterward. Over the longer term, the war encouraged the growth of sponsored research, more systematic fund-raising, and various forms of academic and administrative professionalization.

On the more explicitly ideological side, the wartime emphasis on democracy as the polar opposite to totalitarianism made Catholics more sensitive to core American values such as freedom, equality, and tolerance for diversity. The war, for example, put racial integration on the agenda of Catholic educators. The colleges' lamentable record in this area, and resistance to reform efforts, played a direct role in inspiring Fr. George Dunne's famous *Commonweal* article of September 21, 1945, "The Sin of Segregation," which did so much to popularize the notion that racial integration was a *moral* imperative.

Significant Catholic participation in the non-denominational National Student Association, organized in 1947, reflected a new appreciation of American pluralism and a desire to break away from self-enclosure. The importance of issues like this could not be ignored when unfriendly critics charged the Church with being inherently un-American and pursuing dangerously divisive policies. John Courtney Murray, S.J., was the leading Catholic thinker to address these issues. The solution he proposed can be called *acculturative* in tendency. That is, Murray's solution to the explosive church/state question brought Catholic teaching into line with American expectations, not the other way around. I am not suggesting that the accommodation was illegitimate—only that it was basically acculturative in character.

Joseph Clifford Fenton and his conservative allies did, of course, charge that Murray accommodated too much. The bitter controversy that developed was the most obvious symptom of strain in the internal unity of which Catholics had earlier boasted. It was not, however, the only symptom. Another of particular interest here was the theology-vs-religion debate.

As noted earlier, the proposal was made in 1939 that theology rather than philosophy should serve as the intellectual capstone of the college curriculum. Now Catholic philosophers did not deny that theology was, *in principle*, the true queen of the sciences. But they were by no means prepared to vacate the curricular territory they already held. And in practical terms, the theologians were not capable of dislodging them because they lacked teaching materials appropriate for collegians. Indeed, they could not even agree on the *kind of materials* collegians should study.

John Courtney Murray identified the key problem at the same meeting where teaching theology was first proposed. In remarks headed "Necessary Adjustments to Overcome Practical Difficulties," Murray made the same point John Montgomery Cooper had been making since the early twenties—seminary theology wouldn't do for collegians. But Murray was the only one to call the alternative he proposed "theology" rather than "religion," and since he was too preoccupied by other matters to give it much attention, the ensuing debate was billed as between theology (meaning seminary theology) and religion (Cooper's term). This gave an enormous advantage to the champions of theology, because it was said to be "scientific," and thus appropriate to the intellectual level at which higher education should operate. "Religion," on the other hand, was merely homiletic in character—suitable for catechetical instruction, but not for young adults who needed to grasp the cognitive dimension of their faith.

In the vast postwar expansion of higher education, "religion," "theology," and eclectic mixtures of the two approaches coexisted in a confusing melange. However, theoretical skirmishing on the religion-vs-theology question did not abate until 1954, when a kind of detente was reached. It took the form of a new Catholic professional society, organized to meet the needs of classroom teachers of religion/theology, who either did not qualify for membership in the seminary-based Catholic Theological Society of America or did not feel at home there. This was the Society of Catholic College Teachers of Sacred Doctrine whose mouth-filling title papered over a fissure at the deepest level of Catholic intellectual unity.

Graduate Studies and the Onset of Collapse

A much broader source of strain was the postwar expansion of graduate studies. This kind of education was still a relative novelty in Catholic institutions. The opening of the Catholic University of America in 1889 was a crucial early landmark, but graduate work did not really establish itself in other Catholic universities until the 1920s. Before World War II, it was overwhelmingly a masters' level operation, usually concentrated in summer sessions or other part-time arrangements. Only after the war did full-time doctoral work begin to characterize graduate programs at a number of Catholic institutions. And, that did not happen in the case of theology until the 1960s, when Marquette University played a pioneering role.

Progressive Catholic educators had understood since the twenties that high quality doctoral work was the distinguishing mark of a true university. They strove to meet that standard, but without abandoning the conviction that Catholic institutions of higher learning had their own distinctive intellectual position, according to which various areas of knowledge could be ordered into an intelligible unity. That ambition was in serious tension with the research ethos of graduate education, which was inherently specialized, emphasized scholarship over teaching, and prized discovery of new truth over the systematic ordering of what was already known.

In 1938, Fr. George Bull, S.J., chairman of Fordham's philosophy department, warned that Catholic graduate schools simply *could not accept* research as their primary aim. It was an activity whose built-in fragmentizing tendency would inevitably destroy the Catholic intellectual synthesis and the culture it inspired. More progressive educators dismissed this kind of pessimism. *Improving* Catholic graduate education was, in their view, the key to *more effective presentation* of Catholic truth to the learned world. And they could point to damning evidence of the need for improvement. The first comprehensive survey of graduate education, published by the American Council on Education in 1934, listed only six departments at Catholic institutions (5 at Catholic University of America; 1 at Notre Dame) as capable of offering the Ph.D. degree.

The problem was that improving Catholic graduate education meant accepting the standards and practices of the pace-setting research universities. It will perhaps seem old-fashioned to refer to such institutions as "secular," but the term is accurately descriptive of the intellectual outlook that dominated them. Religion was simply not to be taken seriously as a form of knowledge. Indeed, theology was not even included among the fields of specialization covered in the A.C.E.'s 1934 survey of graduate education. Still less could anything like the alleged Neo-Scholastic synthesis be taken seriously. In this sense, Bull's warning was prescient: acculturating to the prevailing graduate school ethos could not help but undermine the intellectual system that constituted the positive element of Catholic educators' strategy of inculturation.

Evidence that the process was actually taking place mounted after World War II. As Catholic universities moved more decisively into graduate work, they were increasingly affected by the supposedly value-free research ethos that permeated the larger university world. This form of academic acculturation, though not confined to, was perhaps most conspicuous among, the laypersons, many trained in leading secular graduate schools, who greatly outnumbered religious on the faculties of Catholic universities by the 1950s. Though most of them were deeply committed Catholics, these lay faculty members chafed under the regime of strict clerical control that still obtained in Catholic universities. Many were conscious of the low standing of their institutions in terms of academic prestige, and believed it was time for the American church to abandon its "siege mentality" and break out of its ghetto.

The growing spirit of dissatisfaction prepared the way for the almost volcanic eruption of "self-criticism" set off by John Tracy Ellis's celebrated critique of American Catholic intellectual life, published in 1955. Ellis proclaimed in effect that his subject (i.e., Catholic intellectual life) could barely be said to exist and had no discernible influence whatsoever on American culture in general. The overwhelming majority of those who joined in what was called a "great debate" endorsed the harsh verdict Ellis passed on the Catholic record as a whole and on Catholic institutions of higher education in particular.

Ellis, I hasten to add, did not think there was anything wrong with the *content* of the Catholic intellectual tradition. On the contrary, he called it "the oldest, wisest and most sublime of learning that the world has ever known." The problem, in his view, was that Catholic academics had not lived up to it because they were too lazy, too timid, and too much isolated by a "self-imposed ghetto mentality." As a solution, he urged them to work harder and, above all, to mingle more freely with their non-Catholic colleagues—which could certainly be taken as a prescription for more thoroughgoing academic acculturation.

The sequel demonstrated, however, that criticism could not continue indefinitely without calling into question the substance of the tradition. In a 1958 follow-up to Ellis's critique, Thomas F. O'Dea identified five negative features of the Catholic tradition that militated against intellectualism—namely, formalism, authoritarianism, clericalism, moralism, and defensiveness. That prompted Daniel Callahan to observe that whereas Ellis had shown that "the real culprit" was "the American Catholic mentality," O'Dea opened up "a far broader spectrum of questions" about the Catholic tradition.

Another follow-up to Ellis—this one by Gustave Weigel, S.J.—zeroed in on the teaching of Neo-Scholastic philosophy as a glaring weakness. His strictures on the subject, which were widely quoted, contributed significantly to the spectacular reversal of Neo-Scholasticism's fortunes that occurred in the 1950s. Utterly hegemonic in the American Catholic intellectual world when the decade opened, it was barely holding on ten years later, and had all but disappeared by the mid-sixties.

A multitude of factors contributed to the collapse. The very enterprise of classroom instruction on the massive scale of the preconciliar years inevitably vulgarized the system, highlighted its weaknesses, and reinforced the impression that it was nothing but an "official ideology," the teaching of which amounted to little more than "indoctrination in the 'party line.'" Disagreements among various schools of Neo-Scholastics also played a role, as did the increasing acceptance of non-Scholastic approaches—for example, phenomenology in philosophy; the scriptural perspective among theologians. After Vatican II, the general reaction against everything associated with "Tridentine Catholicism" put a definitive end, if not to Thomism as such, certainly to the role Neo-Scholasticism had played in Catholic higher education since the 1920s.

Conclusion

Obviously, much more could be said about how all this happened. Rather than that, however, let us look more carefully at the strengths and weaknesses of Neo-Scholasticism as the key element of the preconciliar inculturation strategy. It had, I would say, five strong points.

(1) It was faithful to the Church's contemporary self-understanding, being, after all, its officially chosen system.

(2) It was a highly elaborated rational system which claimed to show that the existence of God could be affirmed on the basis of natural reason. This made it especially attractive to educators existing in an academic culture permeated by naturalistic assumptions and skeptical about, if not hostile to, religion.

(3) It claimed to show how knowledge could be ordered into an organic

unity. Admittedly, the "synthesis" existed at a high level of abstraction, and its outlines were never fully mapped. Even so, the vision was tremendously appealing to Catholics who were struggling to preserve the commitment to "wholeness" intrinsic to liberal education.

(4) It was presented, not just as an academic subject, but as a "philosophy of life." Its study was thus assimilated to Catholic Action as the centerpiece of the "intellectual apostolate"; for if students in Catholic colleges appropriated Neo-Scholasticism in a personal way, and acted upon it in their daily lives, they would thereby help to renew "all things in Christ."

(5) Moving from the micro- to the macro-level of *praxis*, the doctrine of natural law offered guidelines for attacking social, political, and cultural problems in the broadest terms. This gave cognitive substance to Catholic reform efforts ranging from family life to international peace, and buttressed the belief that Catholicism must be presented to students, not simply as a creed, code, and cult, but as a culture, a comprehensive way of life.

But as an inculturative strategy, Neo-Scholasticism also had serious weaknesses, both theoretical and practical. As to the former, it seemed to all but its Catholic adherents, a relic of the past, unsuited to modern ways of thinking, and out of touch with the modern world. It was further discredited by the decisive role played by ecclesiastical authority in imposing it, and non-Catholic thinkers tended to regard it as religious orthodoxy masquerading as philosophy, a problem exacerbated in the 1950s, when some Catholic philosophers began calling Thomism a "Christian philosophy." Polemical battles between Scholastics and naturalistic philosophers like John Dewey reinforced the institutional isolation of Catholic academics and created emotional barriers that militated against Thomism's being accepted in the non-Catholic world. Evidence of this effect—and of how long it lasted—is the fact that as late as 1973 a prominent American philosopher felt free to characterize Jacques Maritain as a mere "technician . . . in the pay of an institutionalized religion."

As to *praxis*, the problems associated with teaching it on a vast scale have already been noted. For many Catholic collegians, philosophy was mostly "memory work" that had little connection with the rest of their studies and none at all to their "felt needs" as young persons. Beyond the classroom, there was another problem of *praxis*. The policy we can call "Catholic mobilization"—that is, effort to bring Catholic influence to bear by means of specialized organizations and movements—had the paradoxical effect of separating Catholics from others in American society. So obvious had this become by mid-century that Catholic liberals took to calling such groups "ghetto organizations" that functioned as cocoons designed to shield Catholics from competition with, or contamination by, outsiders. This charge, though understandable, was rather unfair, since the founders of such societies typically wanted to *enhance* Catholic participation in the areas concerned.

From the viewpoint of inculturation theory, the critics of ghettoism were pointing to one side of its built-in dialectical problem—the stultification resulting from an articulation of the Christian message that may be faithful to the Catholic tradition, but does not make effective contact with the culture to be evangelized. What they wanted was greater "openness"—that is to say, more thoroughgoing acculturation, fuller acceptance of the premises and practices of the larger society. Ellis's essay of 1955 turned the spotlight on higher education, and the torrent of self-criticism that followed added immensely to acculturative pressures in that area. Particularly decisive was the critique of Neo-Scholasticism which discredited precisely what Catholic educators had previously regarded as the foundation of their distinctive cognitive stance and their point of entry for substantive intellectual dialogue with others.

By the mid-sixties, postconciliar enthusiasm led the most radical Catholic critics to draw what seemed to them the appropriate conclusion: Catholic institutions of higher education had no valid reason for being. John Cogley said they were as obsolete as the papal states, and a faculty committee at the University of Dayton recommended outright secularization. But these were extreme positions. More characteristic—and more revealing of the basic problem—was the question asked by Catholic academics still committed to the idea, "What is it that makes a Catholic university Catholic?" At the time, people called this an "identity crisis." That phrase has lost most of its currency, but there is still no consensus on how the question it reflects is to be answered.

So long as the identity question remains unanswered, Catholic educators will lack the essential positive element for a strategy of inculturation—consensus about how to articulate the gospel leaven to be inserted into the culture to which they have adapted themselves. Lacking that understanding renders them susceptible to the other negative potential in the dialectic of inculturation—the possibility of the salt's losing its savor, accommodation that overwhelms the leaven of the gospel.

I am not sure just when the theologians began talking about inculturation. But it is safe to say that it happened in the context of the identity problem just described. My intention has been to show how that identity crisis itself grew out of the collapse of an earlier inculturation strategy. Since Catholic theologians as a group did not constitute a significant presence in Catholic universities until that inculturation strategy was already in tatters, they were not involved in the story in a directly institutional way. Now, however, they are much more part and parcel of the same institutional fabric, which means that they will be more deeply involved in whatever inculturation strategy for Catholic higher education is ultimately worked out—assuming one is!

That means at least two things. Positively, theologians constitute a new resource for meeting the task. Negatively, they are more exposed than they were in the past to the assimilative forces of the mainstream academic world that did so much to undermine the previous strategy. I hope that what I have said may help in some small way to meet both the positive and negative dimensions of the challenge.

3

Mission and Identity in Catholic Universities

JOSEPH A. KOMONCHAK

I was moved to start thinking about the identity and mission of our Catholic colleges and universities by reading John Courtney Murray's 1944 essays in *Theological Studies* on theology for lay people.[1] Two things struck me about them: first, the simple assumption that our institutions were about something different from other colleges; and, second, Murray's articulation of that purpose in terms of preparing students to contribute to the Catholic response to what he called "the spiritual crisis in the temporal order."

This was language which Murray had already been using for some time. Soon after returning from studies in Rome and in the midst of the crisis that was exploding as the Second World War, he began to think, lecture, and write about the crisis of world-civilization and what the Church could contribute to meeting it. Because he knew that the Church could not meet the crisis by itself, he encouraged inter-religious cooperation. From many Protestants his proposals encountered suspicion of darker motives (a Catholic take-over); from many Catholics they met fears of indifferentism, which Murray took to be symptomatic of a reluctance to leave the Catholic subculture.

In the essays on a theology for the laity, Murray was addressing a mainly Catholic audience, and his purpose was to promote what was then called the "lay apostolate," the engagement of a corps of lay people who would be well educated and trained, committed to the tasks of thinking hard about the state of the world and how to redeem it, and eager to undertake the activities needed to do both. Murray's aim was "the irradiation of the Christian spirit into the secular order, the penetration of the ideals of the gospel into all the relations between men and nations, the vitalization and stabilization of the institutional forms of human society by the truths which are their 'natural' (and hence

---

[1] John Courtney Murray, "Towards a Theology for the Layman: The Problem of its Finality," *Theological Studies* 5 (March 1944): 43-75; "Towards a Theology for the Layman: The Pedagogical Problem," ibid. (September 1944): 340-76.

Christian) inspiration, or, in Cardijn's phrase, 'the social flowering of Catholicism.'"[2] A theology for this task could not be a watered-down version of what priests were receiving, but one that focused precisely on the living of the Christian life in the world and for the sake of the world. But Murray's vision was not simply "naturalistic" or "horizontal," it was trinitarian, christological, biblical, ecclesial, and liturgical; his footnotes reveal how well aware he was of various movements of renewal in the Church which had picked up steam in the 1930s. This is his definition of the theology he wished to communicate to lay students: "That intelligence of faith, especially in its relation to human life and the common good of mankind, which is required in order that the laity of the Church may be able effectively to collaborate with the hierarchy in accomplishing the renewal and reconstruction of the whole of modern social life."[3]

In a later essay, Murray provided a useful summary of what he thought a college religion course might seek to accomplish:

> In most general statement the aim of the course would be "education unto religious adulthood, in intelligence, character, and sentiment." Adulthood in religious intelligence involves (1) a movement from the surface (Catholic practices, devotions, etc.) to the center, which is Christ, viewed in his full living reality; (2) an insight into Catholicism, in its doctrines, laws, liturgy, etc., as an organic whole, whose principle of unity is again Christ; (3) a personal possession of the whole truth of Christ, through a personal "discovery" of it; (4) a grasp of the relationship of Catholic truth to all other truth, and to the whole of life and all its problems; (5) the development of the faculty of Christian judgment on all that is secular. . . .
>
> More specifically, I should state the finality of the course as follows: (1) The theological instruction and religious formation (2) of the Catholic high school graduate, (3) that will leave him conscious of and equipped for, his Christian responsibilities as a layman, and as a member of an élite among the laity, (4) in our contemporary world, in which the Church has assigned to such men a definite, imposing mission.[4]

For all the qualifications that one might have about Murray's argument today (his description of what clerical theology should be is particularly dated), at least they represent a model of how one might go about thinking about the role of the Catholic college today and about the place of theology in it. One is especially struck by the intrinsic link he forged between Catholic identity and world mission. The relation between identity and mission is again back on

[2]Murray, "Theology for the Layman" (September 1944): 341-42.

[3]Murray, "Theology for the Layman" (March 1944): 75.

[4]John Courtney Murray, "On the Idea of a College Religion Course," *Jesuit Educational Quarterly* (October 1949): 80-81.

the agenda and has been intelligently addressed in David O'Brien's recent book.[5] O'Brien's preference is to focus on the mission of the Catholic university. Two remarks addressed to graduating classes at Catholic institutions and cited by O'Brien can point to the issue. Msgr. George Higgins urged that "the real test of a university's success in promoting justice for the poor and disadvantaged and for the minorities in our society is not what its professors say in the classroom and publish in learned tomes, but what its alumni and alumnae do as free and committed citizens directly involved in shaping the policies of the republic."[6] Cesar Jerez Garcia, arguing from a Central American perspective, proposed a similar challenge:

> Do you plan to use your degree for your own profit, be it profit in the form of money or power, status or respect? Will you end up with General Motors or Morgan Trust, with Chase Manhattan or Abbott Laboratories, with Goodyear or Boeing? . . . Will you become people who use your knowledge for the furtherance of justice . . . or live the good life of manipulated, unconcerned people in suburbia who grant honorary degrees to people from the Third World but refuse to join them in the fight for justice and liberty for the poor of the world?[7]

The two quotations are rather good in describing in general terms an important part of what many would like our graduates to be and to do after they leave our institutions. The snippets O'Brien has provided are less clear on why we would like them to undertake the task and how we might wish not only to train them but also to motivate them to do so. On this Murray was much clearer: he actually thought that Catholic theology, argued from its christological center, had this finality. For him a quite distinctive Catholic identity had a world-embracing and world-redemptive apostolic mission. Murray's distinctively Christian humanism was not sectarian but catholic in all the senses of that adjective.

O'Brien's book does not entirely avoid giving the impression that we have to choose between distinctive identity and worldly mission. He is nervous about all the talk today concerning Catholic distinctiveness. Even in the version adopted by Pope John Paul II and Michael Buckley, he fears that it is "sectarian and restorationist," serving "ecclesiastical interests and subcultural preoccupations."[8] I find myself greatly puzzled by my friend's argument here. I frankly do not see how either the Pope or Buckley can be fairly charged with promoting a sectarian agenda. The ecclesiology and the ideal of a university set out in *Ex corde Ecclesiae* is the opposite of sectarian. It proposes a view of the Church as existing for the redemption of the whole of humanity in

---

[5] David J. O'Brien, *From the Heart of the American Church: Catholic Higher Education and American Culture* (Maryknoll, N.Y.: Orbis, 1994).

[6] Ibid., 87.

[7] Ibid., 187-88.

[8] Ibid., 118.

both its personal and collective dimensions. And what should have been apparent even in Buckley's Georgetown talk is the explicit theme of his speech at the University of St. Thomas on "The University and the Concern for Justice: The Search for a New Humanism."[9]

O'Brien's remark about "ecclesiastical interests" seems related to his fear of "restorationism," apparently the effort to establish or restore papal or episcopal control. It is reflected in a comment he made at the Georgetown symposium on *Ex corde Ecclesiae*, where he asked that we give "more, not less, attention to the apostolic rather than the institutional dimensions of our identity."[10] To the degree that this is aimed at efforts to reassert Catholic identity, again as illustrated both by the Pope and by Buckley, I think it misses the point. When at the same conference, Michael Buckley and I urged that the Pope's document posed a challenge to us with regard to the *substantively* Catholic character of our colleges, we found that it was nearly impossible to generate a serious discussion of the issue among the participants. Nearly everyone, administrators and faculty alike, wanted to concentrate on the questions of institutional autonomy and academic freedom, with regard to which they saw in the document only a threat. It was they, not those urging reflection on Catholic identity, who were haunted by the institutional questions.

I wonder if there is something wrong with the posing of the question if identity and mission, substance and institution, institution and apostolate are thought to be in contradiction or even in tension with one another. The problem of integrating them is made even worse when the question of the Church is addressed in terms of different "models" or "images" of the Church, such as the three that O'Brien proposes ("institution," "community," "servant to humanity").[11] O'Brien's book is the latest example of the view that one must begin one's reflection on the Church with the choice of some governing image from which a model is derived and by reference to which all aspects of the

[9] The talk was largely concerned with a redefinition of classical humanism to include the effort to make for a more humane world. But it ended with a brief discussion of the theological dimensions of the issue: "It is here that the solemn teaching of the Church meets the humane concerns of the university. What Christ preaches and embodies is the Kingdom of God—that God might permeate and direct the understanding and the affectivity of human beings. From the time of the great Hebrew prophets, the Kingdom of God embodies a just social order, while the influence of sin lives in its negation. The university moves against injustice as it does against the inhumane. The Church moves against injustice as it does against sin and the denial of God. In the conjunction of both is found that purpose which the great Spanish humanist, Juan Luis Vives, used as a definition of the 'arts of humanity' and with which he shaped the Renaissance's reform of Christian liberal education: the humanities are, he wrote, 'those branches of learning (*disciplinae*) by means of which we separate ourselves from the way of life and customs of brutes and are restored to our humanity and are raised towards God Himself.' That is not a bad statement for the humane concerns and skills, for the sensitivities, the critical powers and the theological orientation—in a word, for the meaning and the value of what is to be done in a Catholic university."

[10] See his "Comment" on Philip Gleason's paper in *Catholic Universities in Church and Society: A Dialogue on Ex corde Ecclesiae*, ed. John P. Langan (Washington: Georgetown University Press, 1993), 26.

[11] O'Brien, *From the Heart*, 83-88.

Church are rendered intelligible. The common effect of this method, as O'Brien's book illustrates, is that elements that ought to be interrelated instead wind up in tension, as if to speak of the institution is to threaten community and to define community identity is to downplay mission.[12] I do not think that this is the only way, or even an effective way, to do ecclesiology. Ecclesiology should yield a vision of the Church as a whole, in which all images are integrated and no dimensions are neglected. It should show, to use O'Brien's three images, how the Church is an institutionally articulated community that exists in and for the sake of the world.

Consider O'Brien's preference for "the apostolic rather than the institutional dimensions of our identity." In one sense, this should go without saying: the institutional dimensions exist for the sake of the apostolic dimensions. But notice the dimension that is missing in this twofold schema, even though it is prominent in much discussion of the Catholic identity of our colleges. I refer to the constitutive community of faith, hope, and love that makes the Church the Church, that is, a distinctive human community in the larger society. The absence of this dimension is surprising given the fact that O'Brien's profound Catholicism is everywhere visible in the book, and he is quite clear that he thinks that Catholics can and ought to make a distinctive contribution to society and history. But he gives very little attention to the effort that a Catholic college must make to communicate the faith-grounds on which that Catholic contribution must rely and by which it ought to be inspired. In fact, he paints a far rosier picture of the situation of theology in our colleges than I would.[13]

I suspect that the unresolved tensions of a models approach to ecclesiology are also implied in another way in which the question of the relation between the Catholic college and the Church is sometimes posed: that is, whether the Catholic college is a "part" of the Church, an "arm" or "instrument" of the Church. Those who think it is tend to think of the college as existing "in" the Church. On the other hand, there are those who want to stress the "institutional autonomy" of the college, are nervous about thinking of it as existing and acting "in" the Church, and prefer rather to say that the Church exists "in" the college, whose educational project is an essentially "secular" enterprise.

What is often not asked (or perhaps the question has already been asked and answered in terms of one or another "model" of the Church) is what is meant by the word "Church," what it means to be "in" the Church, or what it means for something to be a "part" or an "instrument" of the Church. Is it

---

[12] The *reductio ad absurdum* of this approach was the graduate student who, investigating the ecclesiology of several catechisms, found one which he thought self-contradictory because it had questions both about the hierarchy and about the Mystical Body!

[13] The two things missing here are the considerable ignorance of their faith and tradition that many students bring to their college studies and the fact that the requirements in theology have been so drastically reduced and can often be met by courses in what is called "religious studies."

possible, for example, for something to be "in" the Church and even to be a "part" and "instrument" of the Church and yet to be institutionally autonomous? I think the answer is yes, but it is clear enough that there are large numbers of people who think the answer is no.

The remainder of this essay will be devoted to defending a notion of the Church and of the Catholic college that underlies my answer. (Notice that I did not call it a "model.") I will begin with a particular moment, a real one, that dramatically illustrates what it can mean for there to be a Church in the world.

About twenty years ago, racial tensions were high in a Bronx parish because of the murder of a white Catholic teen-ager by a black teen-ager, the second such tragedy in a few months. Grief and anger abounded, and there were racist calls for whites to respond in kind. Picture yourself as the priest who has to preach at the white boy's funeral. What is at stake in this funeral, at which the Christian church—his family, friends, neighbors—gathers? Is it not, beyond the question of surrendering the dead boy into the arms of a merciful God from whom we pray that he might have eternal life, also the question of what sort of history will be created in that portion of the Bronx? Will a future historian have to report that the funeral was the occasion for an intensification of racial hatred, that after the burial of the boy, white Catholics went on a rampage against blacks in the area? This prospect is not far-fetched: we have all watched funeral processions in the former Yugoslavia, in northern Ireland, in Africa, in the Middle East, which became moments at which tensions became worse, not better, and the wheel of violence was oiled for another turn.

Or will the future historian have to report that the funeral was the occasion on which whites and blacks, Catholics and non-Catholics, began to look for ways of ending the racial animosity? Suppose the preacher at the boy's funeral recalls another unjust and stupidly early death, the death of Jesus of Nazareth; suppose he reminds the congregation that Christ's dying words were of forgiveness for those who crucified him; suppose he reminds them of the Sermon on the Mount; suppose he reminds them that St. Paul summed up Christ's mission as a work of reconciliation, breaking down the wall of separation; suppose he reminds them that in a few minutes they will all, white and black, come up to receive from the altar-table the bread that was broken because of their sins and the blood poured out for their forgiveness, and that when they receive that Body they become that Body, and that in that Body there can be neither Jew nor Greek, nor slave nor free, nor male nor female, nor black nor white, but they are all one person in Christ; suppose he tells them that if they don't believe that they do not recognize the real Body of the Lord. Suppose he were to say something like all that. Would that not be a call back to the most central, defining, essential elements of the Church? Would it not be a call for the Church to be the Church? And would not the Church's being faithfully the Church make the world different? Because there is a faithful, authentic Church, the world is different than what it would be were there no such Church. Now the number of people following the *lex talionis*, "an eye for an eye, and a tooth for a tooth," is smaller. Now the number of people trying to forgive as they have been forgiven is larger. That world is different because an authentic Church has been born again, even on that dark day. At least in one small part of the world, among one portion of humanity, history—what human beings do with their freedom—is different, and the difference is attributable to Jesus Christ, the difference is the existence of an authentic Church.

That is how concretely to think of the Church. It is the portion of humanity that believes in Jesus Christ. It is the portion of the world that knows it has been reconciled to God by him and that the reconciliation that is the gift it has received is the task it must undertake. It does not need a second moment, after it has put itself together, in order to go out and find something to do in the world. It does not exist except as in the world, and its very self-constitution in faith and love is an event in the world's self-constitution, one of the events that makes the world what it is.

There never is a Church except in the world, in a world. The very decision of faith is an act in the world, a way of being in and with reference to the world. It is also a distinctive way of being in the world, one that is derived from and centered around Jesus Christ. But this distinctiveness should not be purchased at the price of a withdrawal from the world, but should rather be a distinctive way of being in and for the sake of the world. What the world of the Bronx needed on that day was the message of forgiving reconciliation that is also the heart of being a Christian, of being a Church. What most distinguishes the Church is what most immediately and directly relates it to the world. What rescues the world is what makes the Church the Church.

By the Church here, of course, I mean the community of men and women who believe that "God was in Christ reconciling the world to himself." That is one of the earliest definitions of the Church: it is the *congregatio fidelium*, the assembly of believers. It arose when a group of men and women first became convinced that God had made both Lord and Christ this Jesus who had been crucified. The Church that then arose was the only difference in the world before Jesus of Nazareth lived and after he died. The emergence of the Church is part of the very event of Jesus Christ, and without the Church he is not a historically significant figure. The Church is the difference Jesus Christ has made in human history and the means by which he continues to have an effect upon human history.

The genesis of the Church everyday continues to be what it was at its first genesis. It still arises out of the event of communication beautifully summarized in the first verses of the First Epistle of John: "What we have seen and heard we proclaim to you so that you may have communion with us, and our communion is with the Father and with his Son, Jesus Christ. And we write these things to you so that our joy may be complete" (1 John 1:3-4). Something was seen and heard—"the word of life," the author called it—and it gave communion with God and Christ. An urgency compels those who share this communion to bring it to others; their own joy in it will not be complete unless they proclaim to others what they have seen and heard. And from those first witnesses, that is how the communion with God and with his Son has been spread across two millennia and all across the globe until it has been offered to us, who today represent and embody whatever difference such communion with God can make in human affairs, in constructing and directing human history. The Church remains the community by which Jesus Christ is historically significant.

Over the centuries that reconciled and redemptive communion has been articulated in Scripture and tradition, in liturgy and devotion, in offices and roles, in dogmas and theologies; and it has taken concrete form in people and communities living in and attempting to redeem specific worlds at specific times, creating groups and institutions and movements for these purposes. This vast collective project called the Catholic Church is a historical movement ever in process. It is never exactly the same, having differed in first-century Palestine, in third-century Persia, in thirteenth-century Paris, in sixteenth-century China, in seventeenth-century Argentina, differing today in twentieth-century Milwaukee, Managua, Mombasa, Manila, Melbourne, and Moscow. For all the differences, however, one can still recognize one's brothers and sisters in Christ: the same *communio fidei, communio sanctorum*, across the centuries and across the cultures.

Among the institutions these believers have created have been various kinds of schools. We may think of the catechetical schools of Alexandria and Edessa, of the monastic and cathedral schools of the early Middle Ages, of the universities which succeeded them, of the Catholic universities and colleges founded in the United States in the last two centuries. In establishing all of these, the Church—believers, individually and communally—has repudiated Tertullian's simplistic dichotomy and sought an integration of Jerusalem and Athens, of the Church and the Academy, of faith and philosophy or science. In other words, these institutions have been one of the articulations of the redemptive process that is the Christian Church, one of the ways in which it has sought to express some of the implications of what was seen and heard in Jesus Christ.

These educational institutions have not and do not now need to be founded by popes or bishops to be articulations of the redeemed and redemptive community that is the Church. They can be fitted under what today are called "voluntary associations," which Vatican II and the new Code assures us the faithful have a right to found and to belong to. If they have been founded because of Jesus Christ and for his sake, they can be said to exist "in" the Church, even to be one of the articulations of the Church in the sense of that vast historical communion and movement that originates out of the communication of what was seen and heard in Jesus Christ and exists to share that communion with others. They are a particular kind of articulation of the Church, of course, not a grammar school, not a seminary, not a prayer group. They are privileged places for the adult appropriation of the faith, for education in critical thinking, for acquiring needed skills, for the vast collaborations without which serious problems cannot be adequately addressed, for motivating people to attempt to redeem the world by promoting progress and reversing decline. No other institutions in the Church attempt all this, and to attempt it they have their own required and characteristic features which assimilate them to other similar efforts, where many of the same things may be attempted but not because of and for the sake of Jesus Christ.

I do not know why one should be apologetic about such a distinctive way of being a college or university. Perhaps it would be useful if we were to imagine that we had the financial resources, whether as individuals or as a group or as a religious order, that would enable us to found a Catholic college. Why might we want to do that? What would we want it to do that other colleges are not doing? What sorts of students would we like to graduate? What kind of persons, doing what sorts of things, would we like them to be in, say, twenty or thirty years? What difference in the world would we like them to be making? What kind of structure and curriculum would be needed to produce such students for the sake of such goals? Perhaps the thought-experiment would be worthwhile, rather than starting from the situation of a college founded long ago and now required, for financial and other reasons, to give so much attention to other factors. What would an ideal Catholic college look like, exist for?

Let me urge three ways in which we might begin approaching an answer. The first is drawn from an essay by Murray in which he described what he called the "Ultimate Questions" a society and culture should address:

> What is the rank of man within the order of being, if there is an order of being? Is the nature of man simply continuous with the nature of the cosmic universe, to be understood in terms of its laws, whatever they may be? Or is there a discontinuity between man and the rest of nature, in consequence of the fact that the nature of man is spiritual in a unique sense? What is man's destiny, his *summum bonum*? Is it to be found and fulfilled within terrestrial history, or does it lie beyond time in "another world"? What is the "sense" of history, its direction and meaning and finality? Or is the category of "finality" meaningless? What can a man know? What do you mean when you say, "I know"? What manner of certitude or certainty attaches to human knowledge? Is knowledge a univocal term, or are there diverse modes and degrees of knowledge, discontinuous one from another? Can man's knowledge—and also his love—reach to realities that are transcendent to the world of matter, space, and time? Is there a God? What is God—a Person, a Power, or simply a projection of man's own consciousness? Does God have a care for man? Has God entered the world of human history there to accomplish a "redemption"? Is the theological concept of "salvation" only a reassuring ambiguity? Or has it a content that is at once mysterious and intelligible? What mental

equivalents attach to all the words that have been currency of civilized discourse—freedom, justice, order, law, authority, power, peace, virtue, morality, religion?[14]

These questions appear at the beginning of an essay on the place of religion in state universities. Murray recognized that in our society, pluralism means precisely disagreement about all those Big Questions (which, by the way, he also saw as already indicative that we are living in a "post-modern" world), but he urged that the state universities provide opportunities for students to address them in religion courses taught by believing representatives of all the great religions represented in the student body. He did not think that the university could attempt "to reduce modern pluralism to unity"; what it could do was contribute to a different task: "the reduction of modern pluralism to intelligibility."[15] Everything he wrote about Catholic education did imply, however, that its institutions were to be devoted to the transmission of the Catholic responses to these Ultimate Questions.

In these questions is outlined, of course, the tasks involved in constructing a general world view. Murray contrasted this to what Newman called "viewiness," superficial knowledge in several or even in all areas; he idealized "a universal knowledge, founded on a broad basis of fact, integrated by a philosophic view, this view itself being then vitally related to the organic body of Christian truth."[16] If the Catholic viewpoint could be communicated on the great questions, students would have a critically grounded basis on which to resist scientism and relativism.

My two other examples derive from the Christian conviction that God does have "a care for man" and has effected a redemption within our history. Bernard Lonergan outlined a theology of redemption as a theory of human history, a contemporary restatement of Aquinas's dialectic of nature, sin, and grace. Lonergan described three principles of movement in human history: progress, whose principle is intelligence; decline, whose principle is bias or sin; redemptive recovery through faith, hope, and love undoing the effects of bias and restoring the possibility of progress. In the course of his argument Lonergan set out careful dialectical analyses of other theories of human development, from Freud to Marx, and invoked the central Christian doctrines of the missions of the Son and of the Spirit in word and grace, not as accessory doctrines to a basically philosophical analysis but as central to a critical analysis of concrete human history. For him a philosophy of history had to be a theology, and the theology of history had something to say about the realms of human history studied by psychology, sociology, economics, and history.

[14] John Courtney Murray, "The Making of a Pluralistic Society—A Catholic View," in *Religion and the State University*, ed. Erich A. Walter (Ann Arbor: The University of Michigan Press, 1958), 14.

[15] Ibid. , 23.

[16] Murray, "The Christian Idea of Education," in *The Christian Idea of Education*, ed. Edmund Fuller (New Haven: Yale University Press, 1957), 162.

Similarly, Johann Baptist Metz has had the rare courage to ask a question that many theologians prefer to leave unexplored: the relationship between the vast program of human self-emancipation undertaken by the Enlightenment and the Christian doctrine of redemption by God in Jesus Christ. How could the two claims as to how human beings are liberated be reconciled? At a certain point Metz began to place them in tension, as when he began to speak about "the dangerous memory of Jesus Christ," dangerous because God's redemptive work took the form of the Cross, an option for a method discredited by the Enlightenment and for those most often left behind and forgotten in the movement of enlightened progress. Here too the central doctrine of Christianity grounds a critique of taken-for-granted modern assumptions.

These are only two examples of how what is most distinctive about Christianity—the message about Jesus Christ—was shown to be what is most pertinent to the dynamics of general human history. This is not a separated theology. Nor is it a view that can be left to departments of religion or theology to explore, while other departments go their own way, simply following the criteria for their disciplines in common use in the society and culture. For both Lonergan and Metz Christology, soteriology, and Christian anthropology are concrete disciplines: that is, they address the common human predicament described by sin and grace, and so they are directly pertinent to a broad range of disciplines and have something to say about the methods by which they ought to be undertaken.

To bring this down to earth a bit, let me refer to an incident at the Georgetown symposium on *Ex corde Ecclesiae*. During one of the discussions, David Hollenbach held up a half-page advertisement that had appeared in *The New York Times*. It included the large-print announcement: *DARWIN WAS RIGHT!* The suggestion was that if you wanted to learn how to be among the fittest who survive in the Wall Street jungle, you should come to the Fordham Business School. Everyone laughed, and most people seemed to acknowledge that the ad was somehow inappropriate: one would like to think that a Catholic college's business school tries to teach something loftier than Social Darwinism.

Why did people laugh at the thought that a Catholic business school could advertise itself in terms of Social Darwinism? I do not think the laughter arose from a learned conviction on the part of participants that Manchester liberalism had long since been refuted on purely economic grounds; there were few, if any, experts in economic theory there. It more probably came from a sense that human society should not be considered on the analogy of the jungle or measured by criteria that may apply in natural selection; it derived also from a more communitarian view of human interrelations than the possessive individualism underlying Social Darwinism. And these in turn derived also from a respected tradition in modern Church social teaching that condemned both liberalism and collectivism. In other words, Social Darwinism struck us as incompatible with a basic view of the common human life that has both philosophical and theological roots.

Now if, in part at least on the basis of our faith, we Catholics have a different basic view of so important an area of human life as economics, what does that say about how we set up a program in business? What implications does that basic view have for setting goals, for designing curriculum, for the hiring of faculty, for evaluating results? In what way can the basic Christian view of human solidarity be brought into critical conversation with various theories of economic life? Are the issues merely ethical, met simply by a course or two on the ethics of business? Do we envisage as one of the purposes intended by our programs the transformation of the economic landscape, national and international? Do judgments about what economic justice and equality enter into our thinking and planning?

The example urges that a measure of the difference that a Catholic university might make is what its graduates will be doing ten, twenty, or thirty years after they leave the institution. It is a criterion that asks not only what they will be doing but also what the world they are constituting and constructing will be like. Is it a world less like the jungle of natural selection, one where there is more freedom, less poverty, more justice, a securer peace? If these describe criteria for evaluating what we are "producing" in our graduates and effecting in our world, what are the grounds that legitimize the criteria themselves? What is their relationship with the faith? How does one work out a theory of economics that seeks to make the world less unlike the Kingdom of truth and life, of holiness and grace, of justice, of love, and of peace that we celebrate in the preface to the Mass of Christ the King?

And what would the effort be like to construct a curriculum that would give students the ability to think through all that needs to be thought through for economics to serve this vision of the Kingdom? Suppose one wanted to construct a program in economics that reflected the tradition of Catholic social thought as outlined, say, in the U.S. Bishops' pastoral letter on the U.S. economy or in the commitment to justice and freedom urged by Jerez Garcia, and then, on the basis of this finality, to construct a curriculum and to generate criteria for hiring faculty. Would this be legitimate? Or would this from the beginning sectarianize the program? threaten its academic integrity and freedom? Would it be considered permissible, by general academic agreement, not to hire Social Darwinists? Or is this the imposition of an orthodoxy?[17]

The point is not that other institutions should not be asking certain questions, but that, whatever may be the case at them, certain questions should

---

[17]Perhaps the example could be generalized. I recently asked a professor in a law school at a Catholic university how her program's curriculum might differ from that at a secular university. She said that she was not sure she could point to anything distinct. More specifically, she did not think that there was a course on ethics or anywhere where the relation between positive law and natural law was addressed. The incident suggests the need for comparative curriculum-studies. And then there is the case of a self-consciously Catholic scholar engaged in political science who fears that his work will be simply dismissed by his colleagues because of the religious questions he is asking.

certainly be asked at Catholic institutions. Why? Well, one could provide reasons or motives that are grounded in more proximate theories—and in fact, of course, there are some urgent questions that were in fact raised first at other institutions—but I think ultimately it is because of the implications for the business of human living, both individual and collective, that derive from the event of Jesus Christ. In other words, the Catholic institution's commitment to certain views of the whole human project—its mission, if you will—derives from an identity grounded in faith.

One of the reasons why we need institutions such as colleges and universities is precisely that to derive the implications of the Christ-event for everyday human living requires serious thought. It is not possible to derive a Christian view of the human psyche or of human society directly from the Bible or from conciliar or papal teachings. More technically, the primary religious categories of sin and grace are not adequate for the task, which requires also an elaboration of a critical notion of human nature. And it is no accident that the most successful past effort to undertake this task—that of Thomas Aquinas—was undertaken, not in a monastery or a seminary, but at a university and in regular conversation with the exciting encounter with the new world represented by Aristotelian philosophy and Arabic science.

I suppose that what I am asking for is that Catholic colleges and universities consider whether they could not become the privileged places where those integrated human studies could be undertaken that Bernard Lonergan called for in the last chapter of his *Method in Theology*. Here Lonergan spoke of the Church as "a process of self-constitution occurring within worldwide human society." He located the substance of that process in "the Christian message conjoined with the inner gift of God's love and resulting in Christian witness, Christian fellowship, and Christian service to mankind." But he went on immediately to insist that "the church is an out-going process. It exists not just for itself but for mankind. Its aim is the realization of the kingdom of God not only within its own organization but in the whole of human society and not only in the after life but also in this life." It is a redemptive process, whose central message "tells not only of God's love but also of man's sin. Sin is alienation from man's authentic being, which is self-transcendence, and sin justifies itself by ideology. As alienation and ideology are destructive of community, so the self-sacrificing love that is Christian charity reconciles alienated man to his true being, and undoes the mischief initiated by alienation and consolidated by ideology." And "this redemptive process has to be exercised both in the church and in human society generally." Lonergan then reminds us that it is time for the Church to become "a fully conscious process of self-constitution," and this has consequences directly relevant to our discussion:

> But to do this it will have to recognize that theology is not the full
> science of man, that theology illuminates only certain aspects of human reality, that the church can become a fully conscious process of

self-constitution only when theology unites itself with all other relevant branches of human studies.[18]

Lonergan here was addressing theologians and this is probably why he urged the need for them to seek an integration with other human sciences so that the Church may "remove from its action the widespread impression of complacent irrelevance and futility." His comment perhaps needs restatement in a day when some people are inclined so strongly to distinguish theology from religious studies as to suggest that the latter are not necessary to an adequately concrete theology. But I wonder whether in fact today, there is not an equal need to urge on the other branches of human studies that they too need to look beyond the narrow scope of their several disciplines to the broad question of the ongoing process of worldwide human self-constitution, that is, to what human beings have made and are now making of themselves. If these disciplines are not simply to be confirmations of the status quo, they will also need to engage in something like dialectics that will seek not only to uncover the basic differences within the social sciences but also to study the concrete dialectics at work in social situations and in social process. And at this point, at least in a Catholic university, one would like to think that the question would also be raised as to the pertinence of the central Christian message of alienating sin and reconciling redemption.

The urgency of the task is clearer today when human studies are concrete and empirical, no longer content, as in Aristotelian science, to study the human in abstract and universal terms. This entails a double concreteness. Not only is what is being studied—the whole complex human phenomenon—under the dialectic of sin and grace, but so are the scholars who study it. This recognition seems to me to offer a promising situation. There is scarcely a single discipline in the sciences, both physical and social, that is not the subject of serious methodological controversy today. One does not have to be an enthusiast for postmodern iconoclasm to recognize that contemporary science has lost its naiveté. In such a circumstance, departments of human studies at our universities cannot simply seek to duplicate "mainstream" science, and we ought to be less worried if we find that our faith-commitments lead us to promote such studies from different perspectives, by different methods, and for different purposes than are at work elsewhere.

This would also suggest that Catholic colleges and universities ought at least to foster interdisciplinary courses. If in fact we cannot count on theologians being adequately versed in the other disciplines nor other scholars and scientists to be adequately versed in theology, then interdisciplinary courses would seem to be required.[19] It is perhaps necessary to indicate that these

---

[18] Bernard Lonergan, *Method in Theology* (New York: Herder and Herder, 1972), 361-67.

[19] This may also suggest the need for greater communication among faculty members themselves. In the welcome renewal of the dialogue between theologians and physical scientists, for example, the ignorance, sometimes on both sides, of the sorts of distinctions between the First Cause and secondary causes that Aquinas worked out is striking: God is often thought of as an

courses would not be exhausted simply by courses in professional ethics. Religion is not simply ethics. Their point would be to provide opportunities for students intelligibly to relate their faith, appropriated as adult theology, to their other studies and vice versa.

I have argued that from a distinctive Christian identity can be derived a perspective that can contribute to a distinctive Christian mission, Christian role, in the common process of human self-constitution. Christian faith is not just for the Church; it is a message that is supposed to be redemptive of all of human history, through the overcoming of alienation and ideology. Theology cannot mediate, translate, that message into a redemptively effective concrete process without integration with the other human sciences, but neither can an effective redemption be achieved concretely without the word and grace of God. This is the sort of integrated thinking that ought to be going on in our universities, and it describes a sufficiently serious and difficult task to justify the existence and role of Catholic colleges and universities.

older, bigger, and more powerful secondary cause! And I have seen the relation between modern biology and neuro-psychology discussed as if the Christian view of the soul were that of Plato or of Descartes.

II

CATECHESIS
AND
THEOLOGY

4

Catechesis Isn't
Just for Children Anymore

BERARD L. MARTHALER, O.F.M.CONV.

Whatever one's views regarding the need for and the contents of the *Catechism of the Catholic Church*, there is no denying it has commanded widespread attention both within and without the Church. The circumstances surrounding its compilation and publication, a process that lasted almost seven years, has been duly chronicled elsewhere.[1] The prominent role played by theologians, bishops, cardinals, and the pope himself has brought the discussion of the nature and mission of catechesis back to center stage.

Theologians and biblical scholars who followed the evolution of the *Catechism* from when it was first proposed by Bernard Cardinal Law at the Extraordinary Assembly of the Synod of Bishops in 1985, commemorating the twentieth anniversary of the end of the Second Vatican Council, through the provisional text made available in 1990 to the bishops of the world, to the publication of the French text in 1992, acknowledge it is an unparalleled exercise of the ordinary magisterium. Whatever its relationship to the Second Vatican Council, future generations, not taking the time to read the conciliar documents, will interpret the Council through the pages of this *Catechism*.

I. Given the importance of catechesis in the Catholic tradition, why has it been held in low esteem in theological circles?

I offer four reasons: catechesis is regarded as child's play; it had little if any place in the seminary curriculum; it was widely regarded as women's work; and the catechetical revival was tied to *la nouvelle théologie*.

---

[1] See Joseph Ratzinger, "The *Catechism of the Catholic Church* and the Optimism of the Redeemed," *Communio* 20 (fall 1993): 469-84. Berard L. Marthaler, *The Catechism Yesterday and Today. The Evolution of a Genre* (Collegeville, Minn.: The Liturgical Press, 1995), chap. 14.

Child's Play

When I first became associated with the Department of Religious Education at the Catholic University of America during the years of Vatican II, it
was common for clergy and laity alike to think of the *Baltimore Catechism* as
the beginning and end of catechesis. It was almost universally accepted that
Baltimore's 499 questions and answers presented an adequate summary of
Catholic teaching and practice. Children were introduced to it as soon as
they were able to read. The same questions with slightly expanded answers
were incorporated into *Baltimore No. 3* which served as the basis for adult
instruction. If there was any discussion of catechetics at all, it focused on
method. (One priest-student in the canon law department described catechesis
as "scissors and paste theology.")

Few laity, religious, or clergy knew anything of the history of the *Baltimore Catechism*, even that the *Baltimore Catechism* of the 1950s was not the
same as the one approved by the U.S. bishops in 1884. Fewer still knew anything of the debate over catechisms that took more time at the First Vatican
Council than the discussion over infallibility. The significance for pastoral
ministry of the reforms instituted by Pope Pius X at the beginning of this
century was (is?) not fully understood or appreciated. The promulgation of
Sacra Tridentina Synodus (1905), the decree recommending more frequent reception of Holy Communion, was to have extensive repercussions on pastoral practice and the catechetical ministry. At the time it was already foreseen
that more frequent reception of the Eucharist would result in less frequent
confession.[2]

The implications of the decree *Quam singulari*, issued by the Sacred Congregation of the Sacraments in 1910 that corrected the practice of postponing
First Communion until ten, twelve, and even fourteen years of age, have never
been fully examined.[3] The resistance to admitting small children to the Table
of the Lord was gradually overcome, but it took a generation for the American Church to realize that sacramental preparation could not be the same for
six year olds as it had been for young adolescents. Six year olds could not
read the *Baltimore Catechism*, and the devotional prayer books that nurtured
the eucharistic piety of young adolescents had to be simplified for small children. But more than a revision of printed texts and catechetical materials was
at stake.

Quam singulari undid the catechetical structures that had gradually
evolved over time. In the post-Tridentine era, the catechism was the center of
catechesis. By the end of nineteenth century, a step-by-step catechesis, mod-

[2] Linda Gaupin, "More Frequent Communion, Less Frequent Confession," *The Living Light*
20 (March 1984): 254-60.
[3] See Linda Gaupin, "First Eucharist and the Shape of the Catechesis since *Quam Singulari*"
(Ph.D. dissertation, The Catholic University of America, Washington, D.C., 1986); Sylviane
Gresillon, "De la Communion solennelle aux fêtes de la foi," in *La Première Communion. Quatre
siècles d'histoire*, sous la direction de Jean Delumeau (Paris: Desclée de Brouwer, 1987), 217-52.

eled on the Sulpician method, was widespread not only in France but also in North America. According to this European practice, children began memorizing the questions and answers of the catechism about the age of seven. They were gradually introduced to the sacrament of penance, first making infrequent confessions until they made a general confession in immediate preparation for First Communion, sometime about twelve to fourteen years of age. Around the time that youngsters made their First Communion, they were ready to enter the work force, and what formal catechesis there was came to an end. Those who continued in school under Catholic auspices continued to study Christian doctrine. When the age for First Communion was pushed back to seven years, the change had consequences for the catechesis in preparation for the sacraments of penance and confirmation that have yet to be satisfactorily resolved. On the negative side, however, *Quam singulari* further reinforced the notion that catechesis is chiefly a ministry to children.

Closed Seminaries

The caricature of catechesis as scissors and paste theology is traceable to a web of misconceptions that were by-products of pre-Vatican II seminary education. According to the 1917 Code of Canon Law pastors had the primary responsibility for the religious instruction of children, but, in the words of Gerard S. Sloyan, "as a nation, by and large, the United States has scarcely known the priest in the role of catechist." The religious sister and lay catechist carried on the week-to-week task of catechizing youngsters, while "the priest gradually became the administrator of catechetical activity and 'examiner' of children's fitness to receive the various sacraments." A number of factors created this state of affairs, one of which, again in Sloyan's words, was "the modest attention that was given to catechetical preparation in theological seminaries."[4]

Although they were a far cry from the medieval universities, American seminaries continued to exalt theology as the queen of the sciences. Faculty members engaged in the theological disciplines were the royalty, and even in their ranks there was a pecking order. The dogmatic theologians stood at the pinnacle, the moral theologians a notch down, and so on through biblical studies, canon law, and the "auxiliary disciplines" like church history, patristics, liturgy, and pastoral theology. (Later, James Michael Lee, a critic of seminaries and a leading religious educator in the 1960s, labeled the hauteur of theologians "theological imperialism.")[5] The course in catechetics, if taught at all, focused on the *Baltimore Catechism*. I am old enough to remember the clerical gatherings of the pre-Vatican II years where we were regaled with stories of

---

[4] "The Good News and the Catechetical Scene in the United States," an essay appended to the American edition of Joseph Jungmann's *The Good News Yesterday and Today*, trans. (abridged) and ed. Wm. A. Huesman (New York: W. H. Sadlier, 1962), 211-12.

[5] James Michael Lee, *The Shape of Religious Instruction* (Dayton: Pflaum, 1971), 242-43, 247.

seminary life, the point of the anecdote often exposing the incompetence of the professor teaching catechetics. As commentary on human foibles, the stories were humorous; in the context of professional training they were a terrible indictment of the seminary system. I had my seminary training in Rome (as have many bishops) and do not recall having had a class in catechetics. My confreres who were pressed into service to teach the catechism for a semester or two did it without supervision and were ordained without a formal course in catechetics. And thus was created the "strange anomaly" of the pre-Vatican II Church that was described by Sloyan as follows:

> The non-catechizing cleric has taken the lead in writing catechisms and setting catechetical policy, though in any comparable field he would be thought to suffer a disabling handicap. The practicing catechist has been led to believe, as a result of this almost perfect vacuum of theory, that an important work of the Church needs to be carried on in the spirit of the catechism and aid books that exist, simply because they do exist.[6]

Early in the century, a few seminary professors like Joseph J. Baierl of St. Bernard's Seminary in Rochester, Rudolph G. Bandas of St. Paul Seminary in Minnesota, and Anthony N. Fuerst of St. Mary's Seminary in Cleveland had recognized the importance of catechesis in pastoral ministry. Baierl who did his seminary studies in Germany, introduced the Munich Method into the United States (a method, it might be noted, that was developed by *priest-catechists*). Bandas and Fuerst modified and helped popularize the method as a way of making religious instruction more than rote memorization of the catechism text. Their notion of a theory of catechetics, nonetheless, focused on method and technique, and it was only later that questions about content and specific goals of the catechetical ministry would arise.

In retrospect, we now realize that neither the *Baltimore Catechism* nor improved catechetical methods of themselves account for the vitality of the American church in the years before Vatican II. What success there was in the handing on of the faith must be attributed to the cohesiveness of the Catholic community, the zeal of dedicated catechists and school teachers, and the environment of Christian homes in the early part of the century.

Women's Work

Not only was catechesis thought of as ministry to children, but in the United States catechetical instruction was delegated to women. By the beginning of the twentieth century sisters staffed the schools, but they had little formal training in catechetics, let alone biblical studies, liturgy, or theology.

---

[6] Ibid.

A running dispute that continued for several years at the annual meetings of the [National] Catholic Educational Association illustrates the issue. In 1910 at one of the early meetings of the Association, the Reverend Edmund F. Gibbons, superintendent of parish schools in the Diocese of Buffalo, delivered an address, "Christian Doctrine in Our Schools. Who Teaches It? How Should It Be Taught?"[7] In answering the first part of his query, Father Gibbons sketched the profile of three classes of schools: (1) "schools in which the grade teachers; Brothers, Sisters, or seculars are expected to do all the teaching of Christian Doctrine",[8] (2) schools "in which grade teachers do practically no thorough catechetical work . . . but are restricted to hearing recitation of the catechism, and perhaps some very superficial verbal exposition of it, teaching prayers and other little practices of devotion."[9] In these schools religious instruction is almost entirely in the hands of parish priests; and (3) between these two extremes, a third class of schools in which there is a division of labor and cooperation.[10]

The reasons cited by Gibbons to justify the practice in the second class of schools today would be labeled "sexist." "It is sometimes urged," said Gibbons, "that for the most part our grade teachers are women, good women to be sure, but after all, women, in whose hands religious instruction is liable to be characterized and weakened by emotionalism and sentimentality."[11] He cited St. Paul's injunction, "Let women keep silent in the churches" (1 Cor. 14:34). In its mission to teach religion the school is only an extension of the pulpit, of the Church. Women teachers, therefore, have no more right to act as instructors in religion in the classroom than they have to "ascend the pulpit and enlighten the faithful therefrom."[12]

To his credit, Gibbons found these reasons "unsound," but they explain in part the lack of formal training of the sisters in religious studies. There was no place for women in seminaries and even the Catholic University of America, the home of the only graduate faculty in theology, was closed to them. But it was not just a Catholic problem. Mainline Protestant seminaries did not admit women, despite the fact that women were at the forefront in Christian education, especially in missionary countries. The Protestant answer was to create schools of Christian education adjacent to established seminaries: Auburn at Union Theological Seminary in New York; Scaritt at Vanderbilt in Nashville. As the seminaries opened their doors to women, these once prestigious schools of Christian education gradually disappeared. Only the Presbyterian School of Christian Education, adjacent to Union Theological Seminary in Richmond, Virginia, continues to be freestanding.

[7] Rev. Edmund F. Gibbons, "Christian Doctrine in our Schools, Who Teaches it? How Should it be Taught?" *The Catholic Association Bulletin* 7 (November 1910): 309-27.

[8] Ibid., 312.

[9] Ibid., 314.

[10] Ibid., 315.

[11] Ibid., 314.

[12] Ibid., 315.

Thomas Shields, a priest of the diocese of St. Paul, Minnesota, attempted a similar solution at the Catholic University of America. In 1911 he established Catholic Sister's College. It was a self-contained enclave of classrooms, library, and convents which included dormitories, discreetly situated in a clump of trees, separated from the University's main campus by railroad tracks.[13] It was only with World War II that the Catholic University like most other Catholic institutions of higher education became coeducational in its undergraduate schools. Up to that time, women religious took classes at Sister's College.

In her autobiography Sr. Madeleva Wolff, C.S.C., long-time president of St. Mary's College, Notre Dame, Indiana, reports that Frank Sheed "said bluntly, and more than once, 'There is no place in the United States where a layman can study Theology.'" "Even worse," she adds, "the courses of religion that were offered in our colleges were the dullest and the most poorly taught . . . We had no graduate schools in which to prepare young teachers of Theology on levels equal to their preparation in profane subjects." As early as 1942 the National Catholic Educational Association declared that "the preparation of teachers of religion in college constituted our biggest problem."[14] Sheed's statement gave Sister Madeleva no peace until she was able, about 1952, to bring into being a graduate program in "Sacred Theology and Scripture." Cardinal Newman's *The Idea of a University* supplied the inspiration, St. Thomas's *Summa Theologiae* provided the content.

The New Theology

It was only in 1966 that the School of Theology at the Catholic University of America opened its doors to women. Before that date, women, religious and lay, as well as lay men, who wanted to pursue graduate work in religious studies enrolled in the Department of Religious Education. In the years of Vatican II when similar programs for catechists and religion teachers and the laity in general were established at universities like Notre Dame, Marquette, Fordham, and San Francisco, they attracted students who had only a nodding acquaintance with scholastic philosophy. Modeled on the other M.A. and Ph.D. programs in these universities, the new programs in theology differed greatly in methodology, course requirements, and clientele from the traditional theological sequence in seminaries.

Despite the fact that these faculties recruited scholars with appropriate academic credentials the programs were not recognized by seminary faculties, and in some circles were held suspect because they abandoned Neo-Scholasticism which had the blessing of the magisterium. "Denzinger theology," the staple of seminary theology, under attack by Karl Rahner and others, had

---

[13] C. Joseph Nuesse, *The Catholic University of America. A Centennial History* (Washington: The Catholic University of America Press, 1990), 172-74.

[14] Sr. M. Madeleva Wolff, *My First Seventy Years* (New York: Macmillan, 1959), 114-15.

little place in the curriculum.[15] The faculty themselves were reading, and encouraging the students to read, works by Henri de Lubac, Yves Congar, Karl Rahner, Bernard Häring, John L. McKenzie, and Roderick MacKenzie, instead of manualists like Tanquerey, Pesch, Hervé, Noldin-Schmidt, and the decrees from the Biblical Commission.

The theologians of *la nouvelle théologie*, a term coined by their adversaries, worked to bring Catholic tradition into dialogue with the modern world. In Joseph Komonchak's words, they sought "to bring theology back from its cultural exile."[16] The approach of these new programs, biblically based and concerned with contemporary issues, appealed to a generation which, imbued with democratic ideals of government and authority, was grappling with the demise of colonialism, an evolutionary world view, socio-economic issues, and new technologies. The works they read were written in the vernacular, not Latin. They focused on liturgy, not sacramental theology; ecclesiology, not canon law. With greater interest in the social sciences than philosophy, they emphasized religious experience and historical consciousness. Issues like these were topics of study and research in psychology, philosophy, and other disciplines and could not be ignored by theology once it entered the mainstream of American intellectual life.

The Second Vatican Council rehabilitated Jungmann, Congar, de Lubac, and Rahner. The "new theology" had a significant role in shaping the conciliar documents. Young clergy, in Rome during the years of the Council, brought the new theology home, but many seminaries resisted change. Faculty members, trained in the old methods, looked with skepticism, if not disdain, on the university departments of theology and religious studies which were training the new generation of college teachers and catechists.

II. What happened to change the image of catechesis?

Just as events within and without the Church interacted to redefine the scope, task, and methodology of theology, they also clarified the catechetical mission and ministry. The factors that contributed to this change are many and complex, but among those that exercised the most direct influence seven deserve particular mention: the Confraternity of Christian Doctrine; the liturgical movement; the "flap" over kerygmatic theology; the International Study Weeks; the *General Catechetical Directory*; the *Order of Christian Initiation of Adults*; and Vatican II's *Decree on the Bishops' Pastoral Office in the Church*.

[15] Karl Rahner, "The Prospects for Dogmatic Theology," *Theological Investigation*, vol. 1. (Baltimore: Helicon Press, 1961), 3, n. 2.

[16] Joseph Komonchak, "Theology and the Culture at Mid-Century: The Example of Henri de Lubac," *Theological Studies* 51 (1990): 580.

The Confraternity of Christian Doctrine

The Confraternity of Christian Doctrine (CCD) was largely a lay movement. It recruited parochial school teachers and volunteers to teach the catechism to children who did not attend Catholic schools and also worked with adults. In the early years the CCD had a missionary outreach that stretched into the mining towns of Pennsylvania, the barrios of Los Angeles, and rural areas of the upper Midwest, where churches and priests were scarce, through the promotion of the Confraternity by the National Catholic Rural Life Conference. In a few dioceses, priests were assigned to assist the volunteers and help in catechist training. With the establishment of an episcopal committee of the CCD in 1933 and a National Center of Religious Education in 1935, the parish became the home base for the Confraternity. The National Center provided leadership and services, especially in the area of teacher and catechist training. These became the centerpiece in every well-run program.[17]

Bishop Edwin Vincent O'Hara of Great Falls, Montana (and later of Kansas City, Missouri), used his position as Executive Director of the Confraternity of Christian Doctrine to promote any number of causes that would provide opportunities for religious women and laity to study theology and improve the status of theology in the U.S. church. Sister Madeleva tells how O'Hara "authorized" the opening of a School of Sacred Theology at St. Mary's College.[18] He was the driving force behind the National Center of Religious Education that planned the National CCD Congresses held annually 1935-41 and, after World War II, every five years until 1971. O'Hara's biographer compares them to the German "Catholic Days" that gather thousands of priests, religious, and laity in meetings, theological discussions, reflections on pastoral ministry, exhibits of books and catechetical materials.[19] O'Hara sparked the revision that led to the 1941 edition of the *Baltimore Catechism* and organized the first meetings of Catholic biblical scholars that later developed into the Catholic Biblical Association.[20] The Confraternity provided the incentive for undertaking a revision of the Douai-Rheims-Challoner New Testament for use in catechesis. The Confraternity Edition of the New Testament, after several metamorphoses, was the beginning of the New American Bible, the first translation of the Bible by Catholics in English from the original languages. In the end, however, the chief contribution of the Confraternity of Christian Doctrine was the part it played in situating catechesis in the context of pastoral ministry and encouraging Catholic laity to see themselves as teachers.

[17] Jos. B. Collins, "Religious Education and CCD in the United States: Early Years (1902-1935)," *American Ecclesiastical Review* 169 (1975): 48-75 [reprinted in *Source Book for Modern Catechists*, ed. Michael Warren, (Winona, Minn.: St. Mary's Press, 1983): 158-75].

[18] *My First Seventy Years*, 115.

[19] Timothy M. Dolan, *Some Seed Fell on Good Ground. The Life of Edwin V. O'Hara* (Washington: The Catholic University of America Press, 1992), 148-49.

[20] Jos. B. Collins, "Bishop O'Hara and a National C.C.D.," *American Ecclesiastical Review* 169 (1975): 237-55 [reprinted in M. Warren, *Source Book*, pp. 176-92. Dolan, *Some Seed Fell*, 126-55].

The Liturgical Movement

Bishop O'Hara also did much to advance the liturgical movement. Early in the century, liturgics was a subject that, if present at all, was marginalized in the seminary curriculum. Thus, when the liturgical movement got underway in the U.S., its pioneers made common cause with catechetical leaders. The legendary Dom Virgil Michel of St. John's Abbey, Collegeville, Minnesota, recognized that for the movement to flourish it would be necessary to prepare teachers who were sympathetic and knowledgeable about the liturgy. For him catechesis held the key to raising up a new generation of Catholics that would take an active part in the Church's worship and sacramental life. For Michel the liturgy had a principal role in religious formation. He collaborated with the Dominican Sisters of Grand Rapids in producing the *Christ-Life Series* (Macmillan, 1935), a series of textbooks for elementary schools, grounded on biblical themes and targeted at involving school children in the prayer life of the Church. The changes advocated by Michel represented a break with the traditional concepts and methods of the catechism that most teachers of the time found too abrupt. Few had the background to assimilate the new method or the imagination to appreciate Michel's vision.

Gradually the liturgical movement and the renewal of catechesis, moving in tandem, won out. Together they presented a holistic vision of pastoral ministry, and returned the paschal mystery, the work of the Holy Trinity, to its rightful place at the center of Catholic life. They retrieved the formative-transformative power of symbols and highlighted forms of sacramental practice that are communal and experience-based.

Kerygmatic Catechesis

About the time that Dom Virgil was promoting liturgy-based catechesis in this country, in Austria, Joseph Jungmann, S.J., was calling for a pastoral renewal rooted in biblical theology and a revitalization of the liturgy and catechesis. Jungmann exposed the weaknesses in the current mode of using scientific theology as a basis for teaching religion in *Die Frohbotschaft und Unsere Glaubensverkündigung* (1936).[21] Jungmann urged that the catechism be replaced by a lucid presentation of the kerygma, that is, a proclamation of the gospel message revealed in the person and teachings of Christ. In posing the question why preaching and catechesis had lost its fire and focus, he "fingered"

---

[21] Because of the controversy that it stirred because of its criticisms of Scholastic theology and its advocacy of a "kerygmatic" approach, an English translation of *Die Frohbotschaft* did not appear until 1962 under the title *The Good News Yesterday and Today* (New York: W. H. Sadlier). In the course of the controversy Jungmann distanced himself from those who advocated a "special theology" for preachers. See Appendix III to his *Handing on the Faith* (New York: Herder and Herder, 1959), 398-405 [reprinted in M. Warren, *Source Book*, 207-12]. See also J. Jungmann, "Theology and the Kerygmatic Teaching," *Lumen Vitae* 5 (1950): 258-63.

Scholastic theology as one of the culprits:

> Is not the very reason why our proclamation has lost its cohesive unity and dynamic impact to be found right here, in the intellectualistic dissection and refinement of the great integrated whole of the Christian message, whatever be its validity as a development of this vital core. Was not Scholasticism the deceptive road that would surely lead to a separation between religious knowledge and religious life?[22]

Jungmann was not alone in criticizing the Neo-Scholastic theology of the time, and like some of the others he was accused of advocating two theologies, one for the professional theologians and one for the ordinary faithful.[23] Jungmann's position was more nuanced, but he did urge that theology be imbued with a historical sense and unified in the person of Jesus Christ. Jungmann's scholarly reputation rested more on his magisterial studies of the Roman liturgy than on his pastoral and catechetical works but, in his mind at least, they were closely related. His name and research helped to establish catechetics as something more than the study of methods and techniques. For Jungmann as for Virgil Michel the issue in catechesis was less the method used than its focus and content.

International Study Weeks

One of Jungmann's pupils, Johannes Hoffinger, S.J., the founder of the East Asian Pastoral Institute in Manila, inspired by his mentor's vision of kerygmatic theology, organized a series of International Study Weeks. The Study Week at Nijmegen was an outgrowth of the 1956 Assisi congress on pastoral liturgy, and the missionary character of catechesis was the dominant theme at Eichstätt, Katigondo, and Bangkok. They explored how catechesis, evangelization, and inculturation related to one another. The early Study Weeks fed into Vatican II, notably, the *Constitution on the Sacred Liturgy* and the *Decree on the Church's Missionary Activity*. The Study Weeks at Manila and, more particularly, at Medellín flowed from the Council. In the words of Michael Warren, "their international focus runs counter to the caricature of catechesis as provincial, with its scope narrowed to the drilling of children in 'church,' in-house concerns."[24] Today catechetical leaders throughout the world and official Church documents, inspired by the Study Weeks, recog-

---

[22] *The Good News Yesterday and Today*, 27-29.

[23] Some of the more noted advocates of the *Verkündigungstheologie* were Jungmann's Innsbruck colleagues, Hugo Rahner, F. Lakner, F. Dankner, and J. B. Lotz. See Domenico Grasso, "The Good News and the Renewal of Theology," *The Good News Yesterday and Today*, 201-10. L. De Coninck, "La théologie kérygmatique," *Lumen Vitae* 3 (1948): 103-20.

[24] *Source Book*, 24. See Luis Erdozaín, "The Evolution of Catechetics: A Survey of Six International Study Weeks on Catechetics," *Lumen Vitae* 25 (1970): 7-13 [reprinted in M. Warren, *Source Book*, 86-109].

nize that the missionary emphasis of catechesis is essential to evangelization wherever it takes place.

The General Catechetical Directory

The Study Weeks shaped the *General Catechetical Directory* which continues, even after the publication of the *Catechism of the Catholic Church*, to be the foundational reference defining the nature and principles of catechesis.[25] The *Directory* describes catechesis as a dimension of the Church's pastoral mission and presents it, along with evangelization, liturgical preaching, and theology, as a form of the ministry of the word.[26] The *Directory* acknowledges that although they are distinct forms, each governed by its own laws, they are closely bound together "in the concrete reality of the pastoral ministry." Pierre-André Liégé, O.P., whose writings influenced the *Directory*, used the classic distinction between *fides quae* and *fides qua* to explain how theology and catechesis relate to one another.[27] Theology concentrates on the former, the objectivity of the contents of faith and the orthodoxy of its assertion. Evangelization-catechesis concentrates on the latter, the act of faith conversion and commitment. Liégé held that in the life of individuals and the community, theology and catechesis do not follow one another as if they were successive stages in the *augmentum fidei*, but relate to one another in a continuous dialectic that leads to maturity of faith.

The influence of Liégé on the *Directory* can also be seen in the emphasis it puts on maturity of faith. According to the *Directory*, catechesis is "that form of ecclesial action which leads both communities and individual members of the faith to maturity of faith."[28] It is in this context that the *Directory* instructs "shepherds of souls" to

> remember that catechesis for adults, since it deals with persons who are capable of an adherence that is fully responsible, must be considered the chief form of catechesis. All the other forms, which are indeed always necessary, are in some way oriented to it.[29]

---

[25] *Catechesi tradendae* (Washington, D.C.: USCC, 1980): 50. José T. Sánchez, "Inculturation of the Catechism at the Local Level is Necessary," *Reflections on the Catechism of the Catholic Church*, comp. James P. Socias (Chicago: Midwest Theological Forum, 1993), 103-10.

[26] *General Catechetical Directory* (Washington, D.C.: USCC, 1971), 17.

[27] "The Ministry of the Word: From Kerygma to Catechesis," *Lumen Vitae* 17 (1962): 21-36 [reprinted in M. Warren, *Source Book*, pp. 313-28]. See Frank C. Sokol, *The Mission of the Church and the Nature of Catechesis in the Writings of Pierre-André Liégé* (1921-1979) (Ph.D. dissertation, The Catholic University of America, Washington, D.C., 1983).

[28] *General Catechetical Directory*, 21.

[29] Ibid., 20.

The Christian Initiation of Adults

A year after the publication of the *Directory*, the Congregation for Divine Worship promulgated the *Order of Christian Initiation of Adults* (1972). It restored catechesis to its primitive situs in the celebration of the initiation rites. Liturgy and catechesis take the catechumen on a spiritual journey that leads to Christ. The new *Order of Christian Initiation of Adults* and the restoration of the catechumenate confirmed (1) the importance of adult catechesis and (2) emphasized that catechesis is both the responsibility and the ministry of the local church community as a whole.

The Pastoral Office of Bishops

The *Decree on the Bishops' Pastoral Office in the Church* that mandated the *Directory* began a new chapter in the modern catechetical revival. Post-Vatican II bishops recognized that catechesis was central to the mission of the Church; it could not be defined in terms of method and means; and it was not just for children.

The 1974 assembly of the Synod of Bishops was the background for Pope Paul VI's apostolic exhortation *Evangelii nuntiandi* that presented catechesis as an important means of evangelization.[30] Pope Paul declared, "to evangelize must therefore very often be to give this necessary food and sustenance to the faith of believers, especially through a catechesis full of Gospel vitality and in a language suited to people and circumstances."[31] Catechesis became the central theme of the synod in 1977 and was the subject of Pope John Paul II's apostolic exhortation *Catechesi tradendae* in which he affirmed, "Catechesis cannot be dissociated from the Church's pastoral and missionary activity as a whole." Later in the same paragraph he adds,

> there is no separation or opposition between catechesis and evangelization . . . Instead, they have close links whereby they integrate and complement each other . . . Catechesis is one of these moments, a very remarkable one, in the whole process of evangelization.[32]

Further on he is even more explicit:

> To put it more precisely: within the whole process of evangelization, the aim of catechesis is to be the teaching and maturation stage, that is to say, the period in which the Christian, having accepted by faith the person of Jesus Christ as the one Lord and having given him complete adherence by sincere conversion of heart, endeavors to know better this Jesus to whom he has entrusted himself: to know his "mys-

[30] Ibid., 44.
[31] Ibid., 54.
[32] Ibid., 18.

tery," the Kingdom of God proclaimed by him, the requirements and promises contained in his Gospel message, and the paths that he has laid down for any one who wishes to follow him.[33]

The furor over the *Dutch Catechism* in the years immediately following Vatican II was as much about the nature of catechesis as it was about the contents of the book. The hierarchy of the Netherlands stated in the foreword that it was their hope "to present anew to adults the message which Jesus of Nazareth brought into the world, to make it sound as new as it is."[34] Inspired by the Council, they anticipated the *Directory* in targeting adults as their primary audience.[35] In 1985 the German bishops and in 1991 the French bishops published catechisms for adults. The bishops of Belgium, in response to the call of Pope John Paul II for a "new evangelization," issued a briefer but similar work. Further, John Paul has made a point of advertising the *Catechism* as a work by bishops for bishops.[36]

III. What do these changes and shifts in emphasis, and the factors that brought them about, mean for theological education?

The underlying hypothesis of this essay is that until seminary and graduate programs make catechetics an integral part of the curriculum catechesis will continue to be misunderstood and held in low esteem. Theologians in their turn will continue to patronize catechists rather than appreciate them for what they are, partners in the enterprise of bringing Christian communities and individual faithful to maturity of faith. By way of conclusion I propose a syllabus for an introductory course that can be a first step in correcting misunderstandings about the catechetical ministry.

As a whole, students engaged in the study of theology today are a very different lot from the seminary population of the pre-Vatican II days. They cover a broader age span and bring more diversified life experiences to the classroom. They include a large percentage of women, some among the most talented and pastorally experienced in the class. They bring a very different experience of Church community. Even seminarians who try to retrieve the past by wearing soutaine and biretta are ignorant of many popular devotions, practices, have never heard of many saints lionized in another era, and are not well grounded in Church history. They are innocent of distinctions such as "sacraments of the living and sacraments of the dead," and the moral

---

[33] Ibid., 20.

[34] *A New Catechism* (New York: Herder and Herder, 1969): V.

[35] Marthaler, *The Catechism Yesterday and Today*, 123-27. See Leo Alting von Geusau and Fernando Vittorino Joannes, *Il dossier del catechismo olandese* (Verona: Arnoldo Mondadori, 1968).

[36] See the apostolic constitution *Fidei depositum* that prefaces the *Catechism of the Catholic Church*, (St. Paul, Minn.: Wanderer, 1994): 1-6. See John E. Pollard, "The Collegial Character of the *Catechism of the Catholic Church*," *The Living Light* 30 (summer 1994): 61-74.

imperatives well known to users of the *Baltimore Catechism*. From the point of view of pre-Vatican II Catholics, students studying theology today are not well "catechized." From a post-Vatican II perspective, however, many are well catechized in the sense that they focus more on the person of Christ Jesus, are interested in understanding the gospel message, and are better informed about the Church's social teaching. In the tradition of the adult catechisms published in recent years, they are seeking not information but understanding. They put a higher priority on spirituality than they do on doctrine and the data of positive theology.

The new generation, however, is no different from the old in that each one's notion of catechesis is shaped by his or her own experience. For the most part the pre-Vatican II generation thought of catechesis in terms of the *Baltimore Catechism* or a graded textbook based on it. The generation of the sixties and early seventies remembers catechesis as lacking substance and during the high school years degenerating into "rap-sessions" that seemed to have little connection with Catholic tradition.[37] Only time will tell what memories the present generation will have of catechesis.

The image of the catechetical ministry is modeled by the catechist, whether the busy classroom teacher who approaches religion as another subject that must be fitted into the day's schedule, the volunteer catechist who more often than not is well intentioned but ill trained for the task, or the youth minister more taken up with the challenges of adolescence than presenting the Church's teachings. Few see the high school teacher, the college professor, and even the parish priest as catechists, probably because these do not see themselves as catechists. All are engaged in pastoral ministry but few think themselves engaged in evangelization and catechesis, the forms of ministry of the word that lead to maturity of faith and build the Christian community.

The popular caricature of catechesis and the catechist is a far cry from the image that appears in Church documents. The *Directory* insists that "ecclesiastical authorities regard the formation of catechists as a task of the greatest importance." It cites the help that parents and catechists need in "the initial and occasional catechesis for which they are responsible" and then continues:

> This formation is meant for deacons, and especially for priests . . . Indeed, in individual parishes the preaching of the word of God is committed chiefly to the priests, who are obliged to open the riches of Sacred Scripture to the faithful, and to explain the mysteries of faith and the norms of Christian living in homilies throughout the course of the liturgical year (cf. SC, 51, 52). Hence it is of great importance that a thorough catechetical preparation be given students in seminaries and scholasticates, which should be completed afterwards by the continuing formation mentioned above.[38]

[37] Peter A. Ritzer, "In Anticipation of the *Catechism of the Catholic Church*," *The Living Light* 30 (summer 1994): 49-60.

[38] *General Catechetical Directory*, 110.

The *Directory* adds:

> It is highly desirable that in this area of formation there be genuine cooperation between the various apostolic activities and catechesis, because they are performing, although under different aspects, a common task, that of communicating the Christian message.[39]

One of the latest Church documents to address the catechetical ministry, the *Guide for Catechists* published by the Congregation for the Evangelization of Peoples (1993), presents a synthesis of official statements beginning with the documents of Vatican II.[40] Its emphasis is on the full-time, lay catechist (corresponding to the Director of Religious Education in the U.S.), but its description of the catechetical ministry has universal validity. The concern of the Congregation for the Evangelization of Peoples for catechists is another indication that in the current understanding of missiology, evangelization and catechesis are inseparably linked. The document begins by remarking how Pope John Paul II "makes use of every opportunity to stress the importance and relevance of the work of catechists as a *fundamental evangelical service*."[41]

The catechist plays several important roles in the Church's missionary activity. Citing the *Catechism*, the *Guide* says:

> Apart from the explicit proclamation of the Christian message and the accompaniment of catechumens and newly baptized Christians on their road to full maturity in the faith and in sacramental life, the catechist's role comprises presence and witness, and involvement in human development, inculturation and dialogue.[42]

In Chapter three of Part I, the *Guide* presents a detailed outline of what is involved under each of these headings: presence and witness, human development, and ecumenical dialogue. It recognizes that there are many groups in the community—catechumens and the baptized, children and adults, women and men, workers and students—that require the services of catechists, and each group requires specialized skills and training. It compiles a list of directives, including an appreciation for popular piety, to guide the catechist in his or her efforts to plant the gospel in the soil of the local culture. In explaining the catechist's responsibility for human development, the *Guide* quotes Pope John Paul's encyclical *Redemptoris missio* and singles out for special comment the promotion of justice and the preferential option for the poor. In a spirit of ecumenism catechists should collaborate and give common witness with catechists and leaders of other churches. And catechists should be

---

[39] Ibid., 115.
[40] Both English and Spanish editions are available from the Office for Publishing and Promotion Services of the USCC, Washington, D.C.
[41] *Guide for Catechists* (Washington, D.C.: USCC, 1993): 1.
[42] Ibid., 3.

open to interreligious dialogue because it "forms part of the Church's evangelizing mission."[43]

My point is, catechesis has it own integrity. It is not simply propaedeutic to theology, nor does theology plus pedagogical method constitute catechesis. Parents, catechists, and parish clergy will continue, more or less adequately, to initiate a new generation in the faith, but to become more effective, less discouraged, and more focused, the popular image of catechesis must change. To do this we must rethink the curriculum of our seminary and graduate programs to make room for at least one course, an introduction that describes the goals of catechesis and relates it to other forms of the ministry of the word.

What would a syllabus for such a course look like?

I would begin with an analysis of the Emmaus story in Luke 24 that many have suggested is the archetype of all catechesis in the context of the ministry of the word and its relationship to evangelization. It is the story of a journey, an encounter, that evokes a liturgical setting: the liturgy of the word which "beginning with Moses" interprets the "law and the prophets" in light of the paschal mystery; and the recognition of the Lord in the breaking of the bread. (One recalls that Pope John Paul called for a catechism that gave a presentation of the Church's teaching that would be both biblical and liturgical.)

The story of Emmaus is an appropriate introduction to the *Didache*, the earliest of the post-New Testament writings, which in turn leads to the development of the catechumenate and a broad survey of sacramental practice in the Church. The case can be made that the pastoral ministry of the Church in the West into the fifth century focused on the sacraments of initiation. With the advent of infant baptism and the mass-baptisms of the Celts and Germanic tribes, evangelization and conversion came after baptism. The catechumenate disappeared, and catechesis focused on the sacrament of penance. It is only within our own time after the eucharistic reforms set in motion by Pius X that the primary focus of catechesis has swung back to the sacraments of initiation.

The third topic would present an introduction to recent Church documents that define the mission and goals of catechesis: the *Directory* (1972) and the National Catechetical Directory, *Sharing the Light of Faith* (1979); Pope John Paul's *Catechesi tradendae*; Book III of the 1983 *Code of Canon Law*, "The Teaching Office of the Church"; and finally, the *Guide for Catechists* published by the Congregation for the Evangelization of Peoples.

The fourth part would be an overview of catechetical literature. I have already made explicit mention of the *Didache* and implicit mention of Cyril of Jerusalem's instructions for catechumens. Here I would introduce the works that serve mystagogy—the ongoing catechesis that nurtures the faith of the community and individuals with a more in-depth presentation of the Christian mystery. There is Gregory of Nyssa's "Great Catechism" and Augustine's *Enchiridion* (*Faith, Hope and Charity*). In the medieval period I would cite St.

---

[43] Ibid., 15.

Thomas's well-known catechetical instructions on the creed, commandments, and the Lord's Prayer as examples of "initial catechesis," but spend more time on Dante Alighieri's *Divine Comedy* as an example of mystagogy for adult Christians.

Something should be said about the development of the catechism genre and the use of catechisms by the early missionaries to the Far East and Latin America as a means of evangelization and inculturation. Time permitting, I would delve further into inculturation, not in terms of abstract principles, but by way of examples of popular piety, devotions, and role models. From the earliest days of the Church, the lives of the saints had an important part in catechesis, first the martyrs, then bishops, monks, missionaries, and now more and more lay men and women. Sacramentals and devotional practices have over the centuries served as pedagogical tools by providing insights into the mysteries of the faith adapted to concrete situations and the culture of people at a given place and time.

Finally, the course would be incomplete without a general introduction to the *Catechism*, but it should be presented only as the latest chapter in the history of catechisms and situated in the broader context of Pope John Paul's vision of "new evangelization" and the revival of catechesis.

The syllabus I propose will be criticized as unrealistic, having too much material to cover in a semester or two. From my perspective it is easier to live with that criticism than not take catechesis seriously and allow it to continue to be marginalized in graduate theology programs and seminary curricula. A serious course, asking serious questions about evangelization and pastoral ministry, could not but command the attention of theologians and force them to rethink how their own enterprise relates to other forms of the ministry of the word.

III

UNDERGRADUATE PROGRAMS

5

Theological Education in the Undergraduate Core Curriculum

Monika K. Hellwig

Th>here is a history underlying the present theological component of undergraduate core curricula at U.S. Catholic colleges and universities. Both the present shape of that component and any evaluation leading to proposals for change can only be understood in the light of that history and of the broader context of undergraduate programs. This essay will look first at the present situation of the undergraduate programs. It will then attempt some assessment of the present state of theology/religious studies departments, reflect on desirable content for core courses, and conclude with some tentative proposals.

Situation of the American Catholic College

The very existence of the American Catholic college is seen by many as a paradox. It is integrated into the American system of higher education—a system which has developed within the philosophy and expectations of the Enlightenment. That philosophy places reason clearly and explicitly above authority and tradition in the pursuit of learning and wisdom. The expectation of the Enlightenment is that all ideas may be discussed, that all voices have a right to speak in the public forum, and that all opinions may be debated.[1] Every teaching from the past is subject to review and revision, be-

---

[1] This problem of conflicting goals for church-related colleges has been examined astutely and in depth in two essays by Richard T. Hughes of Pepperdine University, "Christian Culture and the Culture of American Higher Education" and "What Can the Church of Christ Tradition Contribute to Christian Higher Education? Assets and Liabilities," both in a forthcoming volume, *Christian Culture and the Culture of American Higher Education*, to be published by Eerdmans, and dealing with the goals and actual histories of institutions of higher education in seven Christian denominations. How Enlightenment ideology took over from Christian philosophies of education in the course of the past two centuries has been demonstrated with extensive historical documentation by George M. Marsden, *The Soul of the American University. From*

cause it is expected that experiment, study, comparison, and reflection will yield an improved understanding, a better society, a freer and more humanly fulfilled way of life. No questions are barred from theoretical or practical debate. No established teaching or explanation is privileged. To realize how little those expectations have been met, and how inadequately they have been realized in the life of the society, one need only remember the McCarthy era, the history of slavery, the massacre of Kent State. But the history of such failures has not dampened the impact which the ideals of the Enlightenment continue to have on expectations in higher education.

On the other hand, the Catholic colleges which form part of this network have been sponsored by Catholic bodies, for the most part religious orders and congregations, as an apostolic and church-building outreach. Educating young people in the tradition of their Church has seemed so central in the whole Christian project that great numbers of men and women have dedicated their lives to it, seeing it as integral to the redemptive mission of Christ in the world. There is no doubt that at the level of higher education the hope is to treasure and share and further explore and develop the intellectual and spiritual heritage of the Catholic community. Such a commitment carries the assumption that the Catholic intellectual and spiritual heritage enjoys a privileged place in the intellectual and communal life of the institution. It implies that the Catholic identity of the institution includes some normative principles and that all opinions are not equal in such matters either in classroom teaching or in persuasive oratory on campus.[2] Moreover, it was clearly the intent of the founders of Catholic institutes of higher education that there should be reflection on the various academic disciplines and professional fields within the horizon of a faith-shaped Catholic world view and practical wisdom.

It is clear, therefore, that there is a certain internal conflict in the very foundation of the institutions, even when a determined effort is made not to see the inconsistency of purpose in combining Enlightenment and Catholic ideals. What is concretely evident is the impact of various accreditations, federal funding, licensing examinations of professional bodies, fair hiring laws, the patterns of specialization of the graduate schools, the kind of scholarly work appreciated and rewarded in journals and conventions of academic professional societies, and in the appraisals of external referees for promotion and tenure. The more prestigious the institution, the more keenly the pressures from these sources are felt. It is true that regional accrediting associa-

---

Protestant Establishment to Established Nonbelief (New York: Oxford University Press, 1994), parts II and III.

[2] Reflections on such purposes are to be found, e.g., in Theodore Hesburgh, ed., *The Challenge and Promise of a Catholic University* (Notre Dame, Ind.: University of Notre Dame Press, 1994); *Catholic Universities in Church and Society*, ed. John P. Langan (Washington, D.C.: Georgetown University Press, 1993); *Statement on the Catholic and Marianist Identity of the University of Dayton* (Dayton: University of Dayton, 1990); *Ignatian Identity: Questions for Conversation with Documents for Reading and Study* (Scranton, Pa.: University of Scranton, 1994).

tions for the institutions have tended to be not only favorable but urgently exigent about the specific character and tradition of religiously sponsored colleges. Yet the impact of groups accrediting major programs, for instance in the sciences, has been such as to crowd the curriculum, leaving less and less time for philosophy and theology, or indeed for the humanities in general. Effective acquaintance and integration cannot really take place in the context of a quick dabble in each field.

These pressures are felt not only in relation to the undergraduates' major fields, but also in the professional advancement of the professors. Current developments in most academic disciplines reward narrow specialization in peripheral topics on which less has already been written. To achieve publication in refereed journals it is frequently necessary to concentrate attention away from the broad overview that would be more helpful to undergraduate teaching, and would also be more helpful toward intellectual exchange across disciplines among faculty. Where this kind of exchange is not possible, the appreciation, transmission, and contemporary engagement of the Catholic intellectual heritage is unlikely to take place. A further problem related to this is the contemporary trend to value method above content in the academic endeavor. This is a logical extension of the Enlightenment conviction that reason stands above authority and tradition, and that all ideas have a right to be heard, debated, and tried. This conviction, combined with the exponential increase in published material, scientific experimentation, accumulation of data, rapid worldwide communication, electronic storing and indexing of information, and its retrieval with unimaginable rapidity, tends to discourage the kind of education that introduces the learner to a thorough acquaintance and savoring of a small but discerningly culled selection of the wisdom of past ages. However, such treasuring, savoring, and handing on of the cumulative wisdom of the Christian past is a distinctive feature of the Catholic mode of Christian life and discipleship.

Current assumptions and practices in the recruitment of both students and faculty are also causes of tension in establishing the goals and objectives of Catholic undergraduate education. There is an obvious benefit in building a heterogeneous student body and faculty. As an education for life and leadership in the world of the future, it is critical to grow beyond prejudices based on race, sex, culture, language, economic status, and so forth. No thoughtful person would want to eliminate the experience of plurality and differences from a Catholic college education. While there are still colleges whose student body is overwhelmingly Catholic, the trend is away from this even outside the great cosmopolitan centers. It is well developed in the more prominent Catholic universities.

However, this plurality of backgrounds makes the transmission of the tradition that is normative for the university much more problematic. When to the plurality in the student body is added increasing plurality in the composition of the faculty, interest in and concern for the particular religious tradition of the institution will disappear unless deliberately and strenuously cultivated. The tendency is to give respectful reverence to all religious traditions and observances, but no privileged position in the affairs and curricula of the institution to the Catholic tradition.[3] So far this is more of a trend than an established fact. Indeed there are signs that this trend has also become a matter of concern in seminars, workshops, conferences, and conventions addressing the task of keeping our Catholic colleges and universities within the tradition and communion which they are supposed to be serving. Nevertheless, we have the example of the Protestant church-related colleges before us as a warning of the inexorable forces of secularization of higher education in our culture at our time.[4] It has frequently been remarked that the analogy of the Catholic and Protestant colleges is not close in terms of their foundation and sponsorship, in terms of their denominational affiliation patterns, and in terms of their relationship to the dominant culture and the public sphere. But it should be noted that it is precisely in these respects that the Catholic colleges and universities are moving closer to their Protestant counterparts.

There is a further factor with which we must reckon in the situation of the Catholic colleges and universities. This is the need and conditions for obtaining federal funding. The increasing cost of maintaining competitive institutions with the latest technology necessitates applications for federal funding. But the prevailing contemporary interpretation of separation of church and state makes this difficult, and Catholic institutions of higher education seem often to be reduced to an uncomfortable compromise. On the one hand they are persuading funding authorities that they are in no way using educational institutions to promote Catholicism. But on the other hand they are trying to fulfill the purpose of a separate and distinctly Catholic higher education, namely, to bring the wisdom and vision of the faith into engagement with the various academic and professional fields. This not only puts theology departments into a strange no-man's land, but can easily lead to all manner of equivocation at all levels of the institution's administration and teaching, not to mention research.

The Present State of Theology in the Catholic Colleges

In view of this context it is not surprising that in the quarter century since the end of the Second Vatican Council there has been a trend transforming religion and theology departments both in name and in fact into departments of religious studies. A brief survey of the departments going by any of these names in Catholic institutions bears this out.[5] In the theological component

---

[3] Robert J. Wister, "The Teaching of Theology 1950-90: the American Catholic Experience," *America* (February 3, 1990): 86-106; John C. Haughey, "Theology and the Mission of the Jesuit College and University," *Conversations* 5 (spring 1994); and David J. O'Brien, *From the Heart of the American Church* (Maryknoll, N.Y.: Orbis Books, 1994), chap. 9.

[4] Marsden, *The Soul.*

[5] A copy of the questionnaire is attached as an appendix. It was sent out to about forty institutions of varying size, type and locale, and elicited twenty-seven responses. In addition I asked the same questions *viva voce* at various colleges I had occasion to visit and of various

of undergraduate core curricula (as in undergraduate major concentrations) most Catholic institutions, though not all, include some Christian content in required courses, but very few include specifically Catholic content, and even fewer offer creedal content. In some cases specifically "confessional" content is excluded from core requirements on principle, even as one option within the offering of core courses.[6]

About half of the departments who responded to the survey question-naire stated that such policies were set by the departments themselves, and the other half responded that the policies had been set by the institution. More significant, however, is the frequency of the answer that within large bound-aries content was largely left to individual professors to decide, which raises an urgent question about the ways in which these professors hold themselves accountable.[7] In response to a question in the survey about the overriding concern in selecting content for the core curriculum theology component, the answers were interesting. Some focused almost exclusively on the student's need to confront fundamental questions about God, faith, and religion. Some (which were nine credit rather than the more usual six credit requirement programs) proposed the double aim of meeting the student's need to con-

colleagues at the other institutions whom I met during the time I was working on this paper. The survey was not scientifically constructed, the sample of schools was not random in the statistical sense, and I make no statistical claim for it. It was simply an attempt to make sure that reflections were based on a wider experience than the author's own campus.

[6] Some Jesuit schools are still following the recommendations of the Denver Report, *Guide-lines for Jesuit Higher Education: the Consensus Statements, Recommendations and Committee Reports of the J.E.A. Denver Workshop on Jesuit Universities and Colleges: Their Commitment in a World of Change* (Washington, D.C.: JEA, 1969). The statement on the role of theology in that document includes the thesis that "every student in the course of his [sic] college years should take courses touching upon the religious dimension of man [sic]. This may be studied in two kinds of courses, both of which contribute to the liberal education of the student." The document then describes one kind of course on "the phenomena of religious experience and religious belief" in such a way that it does not presuppose religious faith on the part of the student. This kind of course may be required of every student. "The second kind of course presumes and focuses upon the particular religious belief of the student . . . The second kind of course should not be required of any student." This is supported in the document by statements on religious freedom of Vatican II.

There seems to be an underlying assumption that a course on the subject matter of the student's own faith tradition ipso facto presumes the student's faith and adherence in this tradi-tion. As one who regularly offers a course entitled Introduction to Catholic Theology to an undergraduate class which frequently contains Protestants, Jews, Muslims, Hindus, and others, I find the link between Catholic subject matter and the assumption of Catholic faith in the stu-dent out of touch with the present reality in our classrooms. I also find that the assessment of student experience and attitude which supported the Denver Report's recommendations is an assessment badly in need of current review and updating in the light of all that has happened in the North American Catholic community since 1970.

[7] The rationale for this seems to be the logic of the position maintaining that the study of religion belongs to a liberal education as such and is not an effort to promote Catholic faith. Underlying the position, however, is also the memory from the middle sixties of queues of students outside deans' offices, offering to sign statements that they were no longer Catholics and were therefore entitled to be exempt from the theology courses then being required only of Catholic students. On the issue of accountability of faculty for the content of their courses, see Haughey, "Theology and Mission."

front basic religious questions, and also offering something of the Christian tradition. Others were clear that their concern in the core curriculum is to offer a post-Enlightenment foundational theology largely concerned with the possibility of religious faith at all, in any tradition or in personal isolation.

Though this was in no way a scientific survey, some general observations are warranted. It seems that in theology departments as in other academic fields there has been a drift away from content and towards method as the criterion and focus in the constructing of programs. Biblical studies may be one exception to this: although it is clear that in any Scripture course offered there must be attention to hermeneutics, it seems that the students do read the Bible. But beyond this there is no sense that there is either any classic body of literature or any classic formulation of creedal content or even any intelligent grasp of the community's traditions of worship which is assumed to be integral to the intellectual formation of a college-educated Catholic. Students coming to our colleges now (and for some decades already) do not bring from their secondary schools or parish programs anything to replace the common vocabulary and formulations of the pre-Vatican II catechisms, though they may have had a better introduction to Scripture, some reflection on moral principles and values clarification, and a preliminary acquaintance with the characteristics of other religions of the world. If they pass through our colleges acquiring more of the same, they will bring very little of the rich Catholic intellectual heritage into the encounter with secular learning and professional skills. There has been much discussion to the effect that it is not the task of the colleges to offer "remedial catechesis," but the question is yet to be explored as to the relationship between catechesis, adult assimilation and understanding of the intellectual and cultural heritage, theology in the strict sense, and religious studies as an outsider's scrutiny of religious phenomena and ideas.

Some students do, of course, pursue their religious studies beyond the core requirement. Even here, however, they will tend to understand the discipline in the way in which it has been introduced to them. If they have experienced an introduction to an essentially nonconfessional reflection on religious questions in modern life, related to the intellectual life of the academy as found in the graduate schools, but unrelated to any specific believing and worshiping community, they will tend to pursue their studies with that understanding. Moreover, there is always a great attraction in courses in other religions, offering entry to the esoteric, and in courses focusing on emotionally laden contemporary issues, both of which are likely to draw potential students away from a sequence that would give them a more thorough acquaintance with their own tradition. In addition to this, prevailing hiring patterns do not favor the use of Catholic sources or the discussion of Catholic concerns. It is generally taken for granted that a good faculty is drawn from a variety of graduate schools. But in the case of Catholic universities and more advantageously placed colleges, there is a tendency to hire if possible from Ivy League schools and other institutions with a worldwide secular reputation for scholarship. At the early stages of such a trend the cross-fertilization of scholarship and traditions is an immense benefit. But there comes a point at which we must ask whether we are losing the critical mass which makes the institution authentically Catholic. This is crucial in theology departments and has important implications for the core curriculum offerings. Even those professors who are themselves Catholic have for some decades been coming from graduate departments which are not. For the furtherance of their own academic careers they are under pressure to continue to work within the general range of subject matter which they studied in their doctoral programs. It is unlikely that those programs would have given a central place to the Catholic theological tradition, and it is even more unlikely that they would have given much attention to any magisterial formulations later than Chalcedon as reference points in theological discussion.

My informal survey turned up no Catholic undergraduate program without some requirement in theology or religious studies. All the schools that answered had made their requirements for all students, not for Catholic students only. While there are many good reasons for this, it does place a restraint on the structure of the core requirements. The requirements range from three to nine credits, therefore from one to three one-semester courses. Some schools have only the distribution pattern that requires students to take one or two courses in the theology or religious studies department, without further determining which courses in that department fulfill the core requirement. Other schools have a limited range of options at freshman, sophomore, and occasionally at junior level. One example of this is a course in theological foundations at first level, a choice of religious tradition (that is, Christianity or Judaism or Islam) at second level, and something in the area of ethics and applied religion at third level. Another design offers one course in foundational theology, followed by a wide choice to fill the second requirement. A variation of this is one course in Scripture followed by a wide choice. Some few schools have returned to more specifically Christian content in two one-semester core courses. At least one school, now rethinking its entire undergraduate core curriculum in all fields, has for some time had a standard core requirement of an introduction to the Bible at first level and an introduction to Christian theology at the second level. The student body in this case is overwhelmingly Catholic and almost one hundred percent Christian.

While these answers have no statistical value, they do indicate the range of what is taught in the core curricula of the various schools, and therefore the range of what reaches all our undergraduates. They indicate that the content is by no means uniform, that it is often left to the choice of the student as to course or section, and within the courses and sections it is often left largely to individual professors as to subject matter, approach, and texts read. This is in line with the practice of most of the other academic departments (except in the hard sciences) where the emphasis is more on the acquisition of specified critical skills at each level than with gaining acquaintance with a specified body of literature or information. In relation to theology and religious studies departments it leaves us with searching questions about whether the goals of Catholic higher education are being met, and whether they might be met better. This in turn entails the problem of balancing the needs and interests of the students at this stage of their personal and intellectual development with the expectations of the larger academy on the one hand, and on the other hand with the expectations and future needs of the Church for lay leadership. The present balance seems to lean towards seeing the student as consumer in a market economy in which the supply adjusts to the demand.

Desirable Content
for the Core Curriculum Theology Requirement

The content of all our offerings must relate to the goals and objectives of our undergraduate education. What we hope to achieve in a liberal arts college education is, I believe, as follows: we hope to direct the formation of persons of vision, integrity, competence, and confidence, who will be ready to assume responsibility, discernment, and leadership in all aspects of human society. What we hope to achieve in a Catholic liberal arts college is that the vision will be a faith-filled one, whether or not the graduate's faith is Catholic. And what we hope for our students of Catholic background and family is that they will find the vision and integration of their lives in their own Catholic tradition and will not need to seek further afield for a visionary and integrating faith and loyalty. We certainly do not want to pre-empt their freedom and their faith journey, but we really ought to be throwing a little light on their path from the resources of our own Catholic tradition. And in order to reach all, this must somehow be accommodated within the core curriculum.[8]

The debate that has haunted many Catholic colleges in the past few decades is whether a respectably academic department can call itself and be a theology department or whether it must be one of detached religious studies. Some have tried to lay the problem to rest by calling their departments "theology and religious studies," but the question is substantive, not cosmetic. As I understand the import of the terms, theology assumes a faith commitment within a living tradition of worshipers and believers, even when it is being explained or discussed before people who may not have made that commitment. Religious studies differentiates itself precisely by assuming a scientific detachment, standing outside the phenomena it observes and analyzes. It is true that there are some who use the term religious studies simply as an umbrella term to include biblical studies, church history, courses on other traditions, as well perhaps as catechetics and other fields of a practical nature. But this usage by some should not be allowed to obscure the fact that there is a

---

[8] "*Ex corde Ecclesiae*: The Apostolic Constitution on Catholic Universities," *Origins* 20 (4 October, 1990): 265-76. General Norms Art. 4, #5. See also the argument provided by Thomas F. O'Meara, O.P., "The Department of Theology at a Catholic University," in Hesburgh, *Challenge and Promise*, 248-56.

real issue involved in the more common use of the term, sometimes stated explicitly and sometimes contained in the terms as a hidden agenda.

Related to the question of naming the department is that of accountability. There is a strong sense on the part of many faculty members that their accountability is threefold: to the academy for competent methods of analysis and knowledge of the literature in the field; to the student for competent teaching, fair grading, and availability in office hours; and to their own consciences for honest work to justify their salaries. There is a very strong prejudice against any accountability to a living faith community for the transmission of its intellectual heritage to future generations, and even stronger prejudice against any accountability to a church *magisterium*. If my reading of the goals and objectives of Catholic liberal arts colleges is correct, there is a head-on collision of purpose here.

The two most common arguments for a faith-detached, critical-scientific academic department at the undergraduate level are that support for the faith of students belongs to campus ministry, and that catechesis should have taken place in pre-college education. To the first one might answer that intellectual matters are taken seriously if they are in the curriculum, and to the second that the identification of specifically Catholic subject matter with catechesis is false, though the boundary line between adult catechesis and theological reflection on the tradition is not as sharp as is implied in the argument. Information about the tradition, the issues in which it has been engaged, the normative formulations which have emerged, and so forth, are certainly integral both to catechesis and to theology. Without adequate information no serious reflection can begin. The fact is clear that today's Catholic students do not arrive on campus with a knowledge of Catholic beliefs, moral teachings, liturgical and private prayer practices, Church history, and so forth, that we might have expected thirty years ago. Even a faith-detached analysis of Western religious phenomena ought to begin with a thorough descriptive account presented as sympathetically as possible from within the tradition, just as we would certainly do in courses on Hinduism, Buddhism, or Islam. Without such a descriptive basis there is a primitive level of discussion resting on the student's untaught personal experience. We do not teach mathematics or science or history or political theory this way. In all other fields we benefit from the cumulative experience, reflection, and wisdom of the past.

Besides the intent of the sponsoring bodies, and the general arguments that may be brought forward, we must at this stage relate the task of undergraduate theology and its role in the core curriculum to the philosophy and expectations of the Apostolic Constitution *Ex corde Ecclesiae*.[9] The Constitution calls for reflection on human knowledge in the light of Catholic faith,[10] involving the search for an integration of knowledge, dialogue between faith

---

[9] The reference here to *Ex corde Ecclesiae* is not intended to imply any position on the questions surrounding the *mandatum* but rather to focus on those sections of the document bearing on questions about curriculum.

[10] *Ex corde Ecclesiae*, 13.

and reason, ethical concerns, and the providing of an explicitly theological perspective in various fields of study.[11] Quite specifically the General Norms of the Apostolic Constitution include the statement, "Courses in Catholic doctrine are to be made available to all the students."[12] Moreover, the Constitution repeatedly refers to the responsibilities of a Catholic university to prepare its graduates for an integration of their professional life with Christian principles,[13] and to provide that its teaching of Catholic theology will inculcate "an awareness of gospel principles to enrich the meaning of human life and give it a new dignity."[14]

The shape of higher education in this country is such that at the graduate level there is an intense narrowing of focus within the disciplinary specialization. If courses in Catholic doctrine are to be made available to all, and if the students are to have any foundation for the kind of integration envisaged here, a beginning at least must take place in the core curriculum at the undergraduate level. Likewise, if integration of research and teaching in other disciplines is to take place in the light of faith as envisaged in *Ex corde Ecclesiae*,[15] we must ask whence these theologically knowledgeable scientists, economists, political theorists, and others are to come if they have not received at least the beginnings of an intelligent grasp of Catholic doctrine and its evolution in their college years. At present we still have in our Catholic colleges and universities professors who are specialists in other disciplines and who fill this role. These are people who have a good philosophical foundation from their college years and, if they do not have theological training in any technical sense, they have a very thorough knowledge of Catholic doctrine and a sense of its intellectual worth. With retirements each year such professors become fewer and fewer. The question that becomes progressively more urgent is how long we shall continue to have any such professors at all in the future in the light of what we are offering at the undergraduate level at our colleges and universities in the present.

Some Proposals

Given the demands and the present constraints it is urgent to consider what can be done. Most colleges have a six-credit requirement, some still have nine, though with every core curriculum revision the pressure is felt to reduce even further. It seems to me that with only six credits available, basic questions belonging to philosophy of religion should be covered in the philosophy core courses, while theology core courses ought to be in Scripture at the first level. At the second level they should offer ample sections of an introduction to Catholic theology or an introduction to Catholic tradition with

[11] Ibid., 14, 15.
[12] Ibid., 4, 5.
[13] Ibid., 31, 32.
[14] Ibid., 20.
[15] Ibid., 16, 17.

doctrinal content, while also offering courses with demanding doctrinal subject matter in one or more other traditions for those students (whether Catholic or other) who are unwilling to study the Catholic tradition. This would present the Catholic course as the norm for Catholic students while allowing them an option if it is repugnant for any reason. Some will levy the charge that this is sheer indoctrination and does not belong in a college curriculum, but whether it is indoctrination or a proper element of a liberal arts education depends on how it is taught. It does not seem reasonable to hold that a pure exposition or historical treatment of Buddhism is properly academic but that such a presentation of Catholicism in a Catholic college is not academic.

A nine-credit requirement offers considerably more scope. In addition to the two levels mentioned it might offer at least the option of principles of Christian life, covering moral foundations and traditions of moral reasoning within Catholicism, and alternative offerings on worship and sacramental theology. In fact in my survey some programs reported a third three-credit course as a "swing" course which could be taken either in the theology or in the philosophy department, but in either case would focus on ethical foundations. This seems a good idea if the professors in the philosophy department are known to "recognize and respect the distinctive Catholic identity of the institution,"[16] or at least not to be hostile to that identity. Given the decentralized hiring patterns of the past two or three decades in larger institutions, combined with the overriding concern to attract known names from prestigious graduate schools, this cannot be taken for granted.

If these proposals seem to be limiting student options too much, three points should be remembered. First, for students in most undergraduate major programs there are plenty of free slots for electives, which could be used to pursue particular interests. Second, at the stage at which core courses are offered students do not know enough about the subject matter to make well-informed, authentically personal choices. Third, a well-planned sequence in the core curriculum will give both students and professors in later courses a common base on which to build, so that they need not begin with the same basic material in every course because there are always some students who have not covered it before. Students can have a much greater sense of achievement and satisfaction in their studies when they can experience each course building on the last and know that they are getting some sense of direction and "at-homeness" in the discipline.

The problem at this point in the development of Catholic undergraduate programs is not so much the resistance of students to change in requirements. Freshmen, for instance, seldom know what the requirements were in the previous year, and arrive with open minds to discover what courses are offered and required. The problem is rather the resistance of faculty members to change of any kind, and to change in this direction in particular. Where, for instance, hiring for several decades has been with an eye to a deliberately

[16] Ibid., Gen. Norms, Art.4, #4.

"nonconfessional" introductory course required of all students at the first level (therefore typically occupying two-thirds of the course slots of two-thirds of the professors), the research and publishing interests of those who applied for these positions tend to be in the area of the philosophy of religion, or with those foundational questions more concerned with the possibility of faith at all than with the credibility and coherence of any particular faith. These professors may have come largely from graduate programs which gave little attention or respect to theological discourse on creedal content within the boundaries of a denominational commitment. They may be not only unprepared and unwilling but also deeply insulted at the suggestion that they might be party to such a project.

Assuming that it is desirable to implement the vision of *Ex corde Ecclesiae*, the question therefore arises whether in the present situation it is actually possible. It may be easier under present circumstances to provide intellectually stimulating and substantive courses in Catholic thought, tradition, and doctrine through the Newman clubs on secular campuses than in the undergraduate programs of our Catholic institutions. This gives pause for thought. It suggests that the goals of our institutions will not be met by coasting along and doing what comes naturally. To meet those goals will involve long-range planning with active participation of the upper echelons of the administration. Such planning will have to include an intensive stock-taking of present resources and directions, analysis of faculty needs and a coherent hiring plan, tough decisions and countercultural moves. It will not be easy, but it is still possible, and much in the future of our undergraduate schools will depend on it.

Appendix

QUESTIONNAIRE ON UNDERGRADUATE CORE CURRICULUM THEOLOGY REQUIREMENTS

Name of Institution:

Approximate undergraduate enrollment:

Are all undergraduates required to take a course /courses in your department?

If not, are all Catholic undergraduates so required?

How many credits are mandatory?

Is there a single, specified introductory course required?

    or does the student have an option?

Please give title/ titles of required course/courses.

Does this course (or do any of these courses) have specifically Christian content?

    Catholic content?

    Catholic doctrinal (creedal) content?

or is it deliberately non-confessional?

    or dependent on teacher of each section as to all the above

        content specifications?

In this matter, do you follow a policy set by

    your department?

    your institution?

    another policy making body?

    If yes, please identify.

How would you identify the over-riding concern in your department in selecting content for core curriculum theology/religious studies course(s)?

How long has your present policy been in effect?

6

Introduction of Theology in the Catholic Tradition

ARTHUR L. KENNEDY

Context of the Question

In a letter written in July, 1959, to his former student, Hannah Arendt, Karl Jaspers, amidst comments about Bundespraesident Konrad Adenauer's statements on East Germany and Berlin, and on Arendt's trip to Hamburg where she was to receive the Lessing Prize, remarked that he was working "on preparing a new version of my *Universitätsidee*."[1] He added to the typed letter some handwritten remarks about the effort of a Dr. Martin, a member of the Foreign Policy Committee of the Bundesrat "to begin a journal dealing with university issues."[2] Jaspers noted that some people had in fact purchased the *Deutsche Universitätszeitung* and that an editorial board was being assembled. He hoped that Arendt would agree to serve on the board. Yet in an expression of concern about such a project, Jaspers notes his apprehension:

> One asks, what politician: what is his real motivation? I don't know
> . . . Perhaps he is grooming himself for the post of federal minister of
> culture, which will probably be created soon. (I personally favor state
> administration of the universities. If the federal government contrib-
> utes a lot of money, it will also want to have a say in things—that's
> not good.)[3]

---

[1] Lotte Kohler and Hans Saner, eds., *Hannah Arendt - Karl Jaspers Correspondence, 1926 - 1969*, trans. Robert and Rita Kimber (New York, San Diego, London: Harcourt Brace Jovanovich, 1992), 372.

[2] Ibid.

[3] Ibid., 373. For a fuller analysis of Arendt's treatment of the dilemma in education and its relationship to contemporary breakdowns in political order and culture, which she identifies as "a crisis in authority" and "a crisis in tradition," see "The Crisis in Education," *Between Past and Future: Six Exercises in Political Thought* (Cleveland, Ohio and New York: World, 1954), 173-96.

After some further asides on the relationships of education, economics, and government, he refers to his own prior efforts to analyze the university in the twentieth century. He notes:

> I have already begun on a revision of my *Universitätsidee*, the first version of which was, unfortunately, miserably written. Now this project is coinciding with my interest in this journal. When I read all the nonsense that is written about the German university and when I look at the present reality of the university, I think more often than not that we are fighting for a lost cause. That would be honorable enough in itself. But you can never know![4]

Arendt's response came in August. Expressing her anxiety about the control by governments both of education and the university, she wiggled out of accepting Jaspers's invitation to serve on the editorial board, while indicating a willingness to send the editor an essay, if she had something to say. Then she speaks about Jaspers's rethinking the place of the university in Western society.

> I am glad that you have decided to prepare a new edition of your *Universitätsidee* . . . Things can't go on as they are, neither in Europe nor in America. The Princeton experience in particular made that very clear to me. The whole educational system needs radical reform. As a young secondary school teacher from Germany who visited me here said, it simply won't do anymore . . . a great deal will depend on how we go about educational reform.[5]

It is important to consider how Arendt and Jaspers were concerned about the dialectical tensions of the various institutions of civil society, and to attend ourselves to the institutional context of education in relationship to the social and cultural backgrounds in which it is constituted when examining and making proposals for the introduction of theology in a Catholic university. Arendt and Jaspers are certainly not the only ones to have raised foundational questions about modern Western universities and their institutional responsibilities for teaching the foundations of cultural order. Whatever needs to be acknowledged about the general concerns about institutional meaning

---

[4] Kohler, *Hannah Arendt*, 373. Jaspers had written three essays on the role of the university in the transmission of learning and the advancement of research. The first edition, *Die Idee Der Universität* (Berlin: J. Springer, 1923); the second edition, (Berlin and Heidelberg: J. Springer, 1946). English translation:*The Idea of the University*, trans. H. A. T. Reiche and H. F. Vanderschmidt with a preface by Robert Ulich (Boston: Beacon Press, 1959); the third edition, *Die Idee Der Universität. Für die gegenwartige Situation entworfen von Karl Jaspers und Kurt Rossmann* (Berlin, Gottingen, Heidelberg: J. F. Springer, 1961).

[5] Kohler, *Hannah Arendt*, 374.

in universities does not disappear when considering Catholic universities; nor do questions about the institutional order of disciplines and sciences change when the discipline of theology is considered. Nor is the introduction of students to theology unaffected by the viewpoint of Catholic universities as social and cultural institutions. The relationship of theology to a Catholic university has a unique role to play in constituting what such a university ought to be, and it is understood to have a significant role in offering students a wisdom for considering a way both to learn and live. Indeed the relationship of Christian faith and academic life in American Protestant universities has been studied recently by scholars such as James Tunstead Burtchaell, George M. Marsden, and William G. Ringenberg. In different manners and institutions they have shown how these universities have been institutionally transformed and truncated by the manner in which theology cut itself off from its religious traditions and communities, and lost its ability as an academic discipline to mediate Christian claims with those of other disciplines.[6]

Related to similar concerns, the Apostolic Constitution on Catholic Universities, *Ex corde Ecclesiae*, identifies the clear importance of universities to both church and culture. As Pope John Paul II notes in his preamble,

> I turn to the whole church, convinced that Catholic universities are essential to her growth and to the development of Christian culture and human progress. For this reason, the entire ecclesial community is invited to give its support to Catholic institutions of higher education and to assist them in their process of development and renewal.[7]

The Constitution continues by noting a number of characteristics about a Catholic university, its commitment to teaching and research, and its institutional mediation of a Christian presence within the academic world and an institutional mediation of Church and culture.[8]

This matter of institutional mediation is assuredly one which continually lies behind so much of the concern about what has happened to many Protestant universities. Indeed as the writers noted above affirm, it was the theological discipline that ironically turned to deforming and destroying the identity of the university and its ability to engage that variety of institutional mediations of meaning and truth which are necessary for the creation and sustenance of any culture.

In addition to this problem, there is in the postmodern culture a suspicion

---

[6] James Tunstead Burtchaell, "The Decline and Fall of the Christian College" (I & II), *First Things* 12 (April and May 1991): 16-29; 30-38; George M. Marsden, *The Soul of the American University* (New York: Oxford University Press, 1994); William G. Ringenberg, *The Christian College: A History of Protestant Higher Education in America* (Grand Rapids, Mich.: William B. Eerdmans, 1984).

[7] John Paul II, "*Ex corde Ecclesiae*: The Apostolic Constitution of Catholic Universities," *Origins* 20 (4 October 1990): 267.

[8] Ibid., pars. 12, 267.

of most forms of institutional mediation and their role in cultural life. On the one hand, given the reduction of institutions to systems of power, there is the danger that all institutional control of meaning and truth will be passed over to the state, creating in the process a tyranny that can paralyze all institutional modes of truth and order. On the other hand, there is the Romantic, or Rousseauvian, suspicion of institutions which fills the modern American imagination with anguish in its portrayal of the imperfections of institutions such as families, schools, governments, religions, and cultures. This latter condition seeks to replace institutional mediation with the life of the private individual, especially witty or clever personalities who are supposed to carry, correct, or replace the vast range of claims and differentiations that were developed over time through institutional appropriations of meaning and truth. However, since the vast interstices of knowledge and wisdom are too large for any private individual, or subgroup, to sustain, there arises the danger that cultural meanings will be unable to be maintained and that the collapse of the institutional controls of meaning will lead, in the long run, to the disappearance of those differentiations which have often been added to "the public fund of knowledge" only at great cost.

Given this situation, a problem arises for both theology and Catholic universities. Any self-correcting tradition, which strives to balance private persons and public institutions, is either weakened or is no longer acceptable in addressing the substantive questions of human nature and persons, because such a tradition, read through the romantic suspicion, does not achieve the desired goal of instant perfection, as that is proposed by the clever, if not cynical, personality.

These perspectives about institutional mediation and control of meaning have great influence in all areas of the postmodern American society and most certainly in the context of teaching. It is important for us to know this, because one of the contemporary issues for Catholic colleges and universities and for the discipline of theology is that, in different manners, both involve not only ultimate questions and answers about personal life, but also about the institutional meanings of which they themselves are carriers and by which they are, in part, constituted. Both need to address other institutional claims—whether they are antagonistic and hostile, or supportive and complimentary.

Some Clues from within the Tradition

Within this context, there arises the issue of introducing the study of theology to contemporary undergraduates. Reflection on this question is not new, but is of greater significance now for a number of reasons. In attempting to develop some analytic reflections on this, it seems valuable to examine prior procedures of our tradition, and then to reconsider critically those procedures in the light of our concrete cultural conditions.

From the tradition then, theology is clearly related to two different spheres of knowledge. The first sphere is that of revelation, faith, and Church; this is a sphere of catechesis. Its goal is to teach what has been revealed for the purpose of educating persons about the presence and agency of God in history, the mystery of God as Triune, the formation of the Church, and the divine plan of overcoming or redeeming evil with good.

The usual order of teaching faith, and about faith, began in catechesis as instruction through the spoken word and the development of a conversation, or dialogue, that involved the mutual self-presence of a teacher and learner. (Cf. Luke 1:4; Acts 25:25—Apollo is noted as "instructed in the way of the Lord." In Paul, Gal. 6:6 and 1 Cor. 14:19.) While such instruction appears similar to Socratic dialogues, it is rather inherited from the Hebraic mode of teaching in three different contexts: domestic, educational, and synagogal. Proselytes were instructed before being admitted to faith; children began to move from the domestic to the more institutional instruction at age twelve, as is manifested in the story of Christ in the temple, sitting in the midst of the doctors—"hearing them and asking them questions" (Luke 2:46-47).

As John the Baptist presented his hearers a moral catechesis with its relationship to prayer and repentance as a necessary preparation for knowing the presence of the Messiah, so Christ extended the messianic knowledge of his person to the Apostles, instructing them to "teach all nations, instructing them to observe all things as I have commanded to you" (Matt. 28:19). Acts reveals the details of the apostolic catechesis that is both doctrinal and moral (Acts 2-3 by Peter; 6-7 by Stephen; 8 by Philip the deacon). The primary materials of catechesis are the Scriptures, the liturgies and sacraments, and the didache. Then Justin's *Apologies* and Clement's *Letters* begin to draw upon new insights drawn from the ancient secular *paideia* for instruction of those both belonging to and beginning to study the Christian mysteries.

During the early times of persecution, care was exercised in differentiating stages of both knowledge and participation in liturgical life. Thus people were identified as inquirers and as open to elementary and advanced tracts of catechesis. The classification of Cyril of Jerusalem's *Catechetical Discourses* provided twenty-four chapters differentiated into four stages of knowledge from *"Proto-catechesis"* to *"Catechesis Mystagogicae."*

St. Augustine's *De catechizandi rudibus* has twenty-seven chapters differentiated into theory (1-14) and practice (15-27). Written about A.D. 400 it benefits from Augustine's reflection on his own journey to Christian conversion and the role of intelligence in his own journey. Augustine's own psychology and theology, as well as his memory of St. Ambrose's lessons, remind him of the great importance of developing a proper catechesis both for those seeking the basics of faith, and for those who have undergone conversions but whose hearts remain restless. Speaking to the educator who is wearied of spending a life treating the same topics month after month, year after year, he encourages him to remember that this knowledge is for the benefit of the student. The story and truth is not as familiar to the student as it is to the teacher. The speaker should imagine himself in the place of the learner. In so doing the teacher seeks to know the intention of the student so that one may discern the motives of divine calling as well as recognizing those led by mere curiosity. Augustine draws on his own experiences and transformation of his own life as a teacher imitating the One Teacher.

Following on his encouragements, Augustine outlines the substance of the catechesis: of the need for retelling God's actions in the world, in nature, in the soul, and in history. The Scriptures are to be recovered and the two covenants are shown in their relationship to each other: *in veteri testamenti est occultatio novi, in novo testamenti est manifestatio veteris*. The next task is to teach the doctrine of the resurrection of the body, the last judgment with reward and punishment. The student needs to be warned about scandals both within and outside the Church, and to learn of love and grace that flows to him without human merit. For questioners who are more learned, these and other themes should be expanded in a deeper, yet briefer account.

In chapters ten to fourteen the vocation of the teacher is addressed psychologically and theologically as those who are called to follow God's will and to take on themselves the humility which Christ took on himself, "the form of a servant." In chapters sixteen to twenty-five, Augustine presents the biblical knowledge with a hermeneutic and points to the articles of the Creed, the life and death of Christ, the doctrine of the Church and the sacraments.

Already by the time of Augustine, elements of the second source of theological knowledge, *paideia* had already entered into the catechetical order for the purpose of engaging different interpretations of those more educated in both the Christian teaching and the achievements of human intelligence in the secular culture.

In its secular form, *paideia* was the Greek creation which sought to pass on, maintain, and increase a civil human order, and through this active engagement to create a culture grounded in intelligence and natural virtue. As Christopher Dawson pointed out,

> A common educational tradition creates a common world of thought with common moral and intellectual values and a common inheritance of knowledge, and these are the conditions which make a culture conscious of its identity and give it a common memory and a common past.[9]

Paideia was thus the precondition necessary for creating a political community, which for Athens was the most important form of institutional mediation of meaning; it depended on an institutional manner of providing for an "inculturation."[10] It is not surprising that *paideia* is central in Plato's

---

[9] Christopher Dawson, *The Crisis of Western Education* (Steubenville, Ohio: Franciscan University Press, 1989), 5. On the importance of culture, the apostolate of the Jesuits and certain sociological analyses of cultural systems, cf. Carl F. Starkloff, S.J., "Inculturation and Cultural Systems (Part One)," *Theological Studies* 55 (March 1994): 66-81.

[10] Ibid., 150.

Republic and Aristotle's *Laws*.[11] In *The Politics*, Aristotle remarks that it is a common education alone which turns a multitude toward a common bond and draws it into becoming a polis.[12]

The tension that arose in the Church when catechesis met *paideia* is well known through Tertullian's rhetorical question, "What does Athens have to do with Jerusalem?" But the forms of *paideia* had been entering into Christian knowledge through the Greek gentile converts who previously had been educated by the secular academy. Furthermore, it had become of considerable importance through the use of differentiated intelligence by Irenaeus in confronting the greatest cultural threat to Christian teaching, Gnosticism. By this time, there was a recognition that the secular knowledge was both preparatory to evangelization, or proto-evangelical, and was of assistance in clarifying the catechesis. Thus there developed in the teachings connected with Irenaeus *en kuklo paideia* and it made possible the growth not only of theology, but of the liberal learning that would mark the classical connection of faith and culture in the West. In different times the unity of catechesis and *paideia* allowed for the development of doctrine and learning, sometimes with ease and other times with great tension.[13]

The Present Dialectic

The present tension is constituted by the long history of the transpositions from classical to modern science and by the gradual entry into the society and culture of the development of the empirical sciences and the emergence of the human sciences. These developments are linked profoundly to the questions of new methods of human knowing and new sciences and scholarship for examining the structures of human order. In addition, the various foundational struggles which have emerged in this vast body of learning have slowly entered into the concrete social expressions of the age and into the larger cultural institutions through the scholarly debates and conflicts. For example the methodological base on which modern culture has defined and shaped much of the use of imagination has been guided by the Cartesian split of consciousness and body.[14]

The importance of modern methodology and the debates about their groundings have left the modern *paideia* in a condition which is deeply problematic. The difficulties arise over the fact that much contemporary scholar-

---

[11] *Republic*, 2.376c - 4.445a and 7.518b - 541b; *Laws*, 1.641b-2.674c and 4.722b - 9.880e.

[12] *The Politics*, 2.2.10; cf. also his remarks on the importance of the regime as defining the meaning of the unity.

[13] On the history and the proper requirements for the Church to live in the tension of learner and teacher see Frederick E. Crowe, S.J., "The Church as Learner: Two Crises, One Kairos," *Appropriating the Lonergan Idea*, ed. Michael Vertin (Washington, D.C.: The Catholic University of America Press, 1989.)

[14] Elizabeth Sewell, "The Death of the Imagination, a Research into the Collapse of the Body-Mind Problem," *Thought* 28 (1953): 413-44.

ship has grounded itself in some form of instrumental rationality, thus the prevailing methodologies used in the education and inculturation of students are positivist. Now these methodologies are passed through to students by the material to be learned and the process of learning which governs their educational life from the earliest days. Furthermore, the formation, legitimation, and maintenance of positivist methodologies has been the work of the academy. This was Jaspers's concern about Heidelberg and Basle, and Arendt's about Princeton.

The fact that this is a fundamental issue for all of Western culture was recognized by thinkers as different as Eric Voegelin, Christopher Dawson, Paul Valery, and Carl Boggs.[15] Voegelin identified the problem in his criticism of positivism and its influences on the conclusions about the reality of "race" as studied and taught by natural scientists in the early part of this century. His opening remark in *Die Rasenidee in der Geistesgeschichte* reads: "The knowledge of man has come to grief."[16] Later in his study on the need for creating a political science that will not be dominated by modern gnostic forms of positivism, he reminds the reader of the "thorniest question" of our culture, namely, how there can be vast progress in the world of material life, as that is governed by the technologies related to positivism, while at the same time there is a continuing truncation of the soul with its loss of God and all transcendence, which is replaced with a form of self-redemption. That is the "thorny question . . . how a civilization can advance and decline at the same time."[17] It is clear how well the methodological confusion has entered the mainstream of American common sense as faculty and students hear the postmodern television therapists console the worried soul with promises of self-forgiveness and self-redemption.

For those who would consider the introduction of theology in the modern Catholic university, and within the context of this difficult and confused *paideia*, one needs to attend to the manner in which this instrumentalization of meaning and knowledge has not only taken over many of the social disciplines taught in the university, but the secular model of what a university, Catholic or otherwise, ought to be. In his examination of what might be called the growth of the "thorny question" among intellectuals, professional academics, and university administrators, Carl Boggs notes the new model of the university as developed by Clark Kerr, president of the University of California in 1963.

---

[15] Valery thought that the West was caught in a spiritual crisis of relativity which was eroding and impoverishing the meaning of life, and that this was primarily a consequence of the "disorder of mind." Cf. "The Crisis of Mind," *The Outlook for Intelligence*, trans. Denise Foliot and Jackson Mathews, ed. Jackson Mathews (New York: Harper and Row, 1962), 25-36.

[16] Eric Voegelin, *Die Rasenidee in der Geistesgeschichte von Ray bis Carus* (Tübingen: Fischer, 1933), 1.

[17] Eric Voegelin, *The New Science of Politics: An Introduction* (Chicago and London: University of Chicago Press, 1987), 128-29.

Kerr's thesis embodied perhaps the clearest expression of the intellectual-cum-technocratic professional, and he articulated it from the vantage point of directing the largest and richest university complex in the world. Kerr argued that the multiversity stands at the center of a pluralistic network of interests that require servicing by the knowledge industry.[18]

He goes on to quote from Kerr's analysis of the fact that a professor's life has become "a rat race of business and activity, managing contracts and projects, guiding teams of assistants, bossing crews of technicians, making numerous trips, sitting on committees for government agencies and engaging in other distractions necessary to keep the whole frenetic business from collapse."[19]

Within this vision of the university as a corporation, with administrators as the CEO's, faculty as the managers and sales personnel, and students as customers, the university is a mere collection of bureaucracies lacking any moral, intellectual, or religious commitment. As Boggs notes, in this university "virtually all forms of scholarship are saturated with a positivist world view corresponding to this highly rationalized system."[20]

In this contemporary condition, the teaching of theology is going to need to be explicitly and dialectically engaged in the methodology which will allow it to be true to its sources, able to converse with the modern *paideia*, and aware of the traps which would seek to replace courses in theology with humanistic disciplines which may be dominated by positivism. Fortunately in the works of Karl Rahner, S.J., and Bernard Lonergan, S.J., Catholic theology has been given the foundations for both the coherent intelligibility of the discipline in its historical and cultural development and its ability to be critical in the academic tasks of teaching and research. In both thinkers a transcendental anthropology and its historical expression of the foundations for human knowledge are opened onto the mystery of God in the divine self-communication revealing the fundamental realities which enlighten the origin and purpose of human existence in its relationship to the trinitarian life.[21] The knowledge of transcendental method engages the mutual mediation of revealed and secular knowledge as well as the dialectic of conflicting meth-

[18] Carl Boggs, *Intellectuals and the Crisis of Modernity* (Albany: State University of New York Press, 1993), 109.

[19] Ibid., 110.

[20] "Deconstructing the University," a revision of the 52nd Annual Frederick William Reynolds Lecture (Salt Lake City: Division of Continuing Education, University of Utah, 1991). Article also appears in *Communio* 19 (summer 1992): 226-53.

[21] Karl Rahner, "Reflections on Methodology in Theology," *Theological Investigations*, vol. 11 (New York: Seabury, 1974), 87. Here Rahner speaks of method as providing the foundations for all acts of knowledge. "A transcendental line of enquiry, regardless of the particular area of the subject-matter in which it is applied, is present when and to the extent that it raises the questions of the conditions in which knowledge of a specific subject is possible in the knowing subject himself."

ods with the contemporary exercise of a *paideia* and so allows for theology to explain its knowledge within both a transcendental and a historical development. In this way the methodology can retrieve and transpose the crucial insights of the classical *paideia* and allow students to engage these insights as they begin to study, in an ordered manner, the range of theological questions. The emergence of the transcendental method and its collaborative integration arose in a series of empirical examinations of human knowledge, and its ordering in the university and the several acts which constitute both the tasks of teaching and learning.[22]

In Lonergan's formulation of a method that is grounded both in the revelation of the Christian mystery and of the appropriation of the operations of human consciousness, the different objects of the whole of the theological discipline, there is an exponential advance of the role of theology for the Catholic vision of truth given an earlier approximation by Newman. The functional specializations that organize the data of theological knowledge, the conversions which are invited by the activity undertaken in research, interpretation history, and dialectic, become foundational for religious interiority and spirituality, doctrines, systematics, and communication. When one can appropriate the fact that the transcendental method is also a general empirical method, one has an extraordinary, differentiated principle for collaboration with the range of academic disciplines which both acknowledges and accounts for each discipline in its proper objects and fields and yet allows for the different fields of knowledge to enter into collaboration with the knowledge of the Christian mystery of redemption.

Finally, it is evident today that most students are unfamiliar with the most important teachings about Catholic faith and that the expectations among college faculty regarding prior catechesis has been accordingly weakened. The testimonies to this ignorance abound, and it is the experience remarked on by some parents after their children depart Catholic high schools as well as by faculty who teach in colleges. The culture's vision and behavior is so bereft of meaning and truth that it is able in its instrumentalism to inculture the young into a suspicion about all the claims of truth presented through the whole of the Christian mystery. This suspicion is not just a viewpoint that happens here or there and is able to be engaged with the kindliness of people telling each other about their particular faith. This is an institutional crisis of both the university and the discipline. The Apostolic Constitution also sees this crisis as a very important moment for the Church as well as for Catholic universities.

In fact the Constitution proposes an issue of great value, in that it calls for recovering the tension between the university and the Church and of both, in

---

[22] Cf. Bernard Lonergan, *Method in Theology* (New York: Herder and Herder, 1972); *Collected Works of Bernard Lonergan* vol. 10, ed. Robert Doran and Frederick Crowe (Toronto, Buffalo, London: University of Toronto Press, 1993); cf. "The Role of a Catholic University in the Modern World," *Collection: Papers by Bernard Lonergan, S.J.* (Montreal: Palm, 1967), 114-20.

their different manners, with the culture. This recovery would open the possibility that a *paideia* rightly transformed will once again become the condition for a *preambula fidei* and so for the renewal of a catechesis that will benefit from the institutional addressing of the methodological conflicts that have penetrated into all aspects of modern culture. In addition, such an achievement for theology will allow the academic scholarship of the human sciences to find greater roles in teaching both theology and the Church about matters historical, economic, political, and sociological.

Proposals for Beginning

If the teaching of theology, at present, must depend on only a weakened catechetical background and if it must communicate to students who have been more or less successfully inculturated into a vision of personal and social meaning derived from the prevailing positivist methodologies, what is one to do? How might theology, in its early engagements, prepare the way for the awakening of students to the mystery of the Christian reality? How can the fundamentals be presented in a way that allows for a steady acquisition of religious knowledge? How can a modern student enter into the minds of those scholars of the classical tradition who had studied and explored the depths of Christian reality? How can students learn to read the moderns who seek to articulate the rightful tensions among theologians themselves, and between Church and academy?[23] Finally, how can students appropriate the sacramental, moral, and intellectual tradition which will allow them to transform the present problems?

Much of what can be done in theological preparation will depend on individual departments, but some suggestions lie within the scope and testing of the tradition. As noted in part II, the consideration of St. Augustine's *De catechizandi rudibus*, with its recommendation of selecting certain theological themes and the gradual adding and integrating of additional themes, seems to allow for an ordinary pedagogy, and also to leave room for the methodological conflicts which need to be addressed in enunciating the concrete issues. It is important, given the present conditions, that a theology faculty needs to raise for itself the matter of developing a unified introductory course which all students will take. Such a course has the benefit of providing students with a common base by which they can both understand certain foundational topics and enter into conversations with most of their fellow classmates. Such a course allows the faculty to know what all the students actually have been taught, and one hopes, learned. This in turn, allows for a reasonable sequencing of later courses where faculty do not have to "begin" again because they can assume a prior common body of knowledge. Obviously

---

[23] For a brief discussion of the problems noted here cf. Mary Collins, O.S.B., "Theological Excellence in the Catholic University," *Current Issues in Catholic Higher Education* 12 (summer 1991): 57-60.

this would allow theology to proceed in a manner similar to other academic disciplines and sciences. For the present I would like to discuss the programs which have been developed over the past five years in the Theology Department at the University of St. Thomas in St. Paul and Minneapolis. While concerns about the teaching of theology had been discussed by the faculty for some years, it was in the context of a larger review of the general requirements of the undergraduate college that the department assembled a major revision in the teaching of the three theology courses within those requirements. In the process of clarifying for itself, for the faculty of other disciplines in the general requirements, the theology courses have been thought out in the integrative context called "Faith and the Catholic Tradition."

The department spent five years discussing, trying out, revising, and trying again, a general introductory core course. Primary discussions developed around a carefully limited set of major theological themes which would be traced within a historical set of ongoing theological reflections. In addition, a collaboration in the college-wide development of the skills of reading, writing, and critical thinking was incorporated into this core course. The themes chosen for the theological introduction are revelation, God, creation, Jesus Christ, and the Church.

The selection of common readings (70 percent of all the texts) was the second step for developing the core course, and as can be imagined this created a very large set of discussions.[24] A specific "classical" text was needed either to introduce a topic, or to carry forward as much as possible a particular advance in understanding the topic. Obviously important was the selection of the scriptural texts, with their concrete details, complex histories, and literary forms, revealing in various manifestations of revelational self-consciousness, the mystery of Christian reality. Nor could one leave unattended their clues into the activity of teaching and learning itself, as both proceed from the known to the unknown, as in Peter's confession of faith and his subsequent rejection of Christ's revelation of the Messianic mission; or as biblical books recover what was revealed in an earlier time and expand on it by reinterpreting it in the light of later events and knowledge, as Jesus does with the disciples on the road to Emmaus.

Ex corde Ecclesiae understands the Church as the primary institution for teaching the Catholic truth; in the Catholic university, the beginning of theology will be clear about this to the degree that, in practice, it introduces students to the central sources of the tradition of faith seeking, and using, understanding. Such a beginning will also manifest that human intelligence, which is not deformed by ideology, will seek ultimate truth and so be open to the revealed truth. Theology in the university will be concerned to help students, from the beginning, "to a greater love for truth itself."[25]

In the core course there are two overarching issues that underpin the five

---

[24] See the list of readings in the Appendix I at the end of this chapter.
[25] *Ex corde Ecclesiae*, pars. 17, 268.

themes; these two are anthropology and redemption. By means of the first, one is able to engage students in examining the relationship of knowledge and faith. Furthermore, in the longer run, the unity of truth requires a type of anthropology which awakens students to the transcendental acts and objects which constitute the human self, human nature, and community. The study of anthropology opens up the questions for understanding, for truth and for virtue or good and seeks to show how such questions are answered. It examines how to unify the true good into our living; what constitutes an act of belief, its purpose and structure; the importance of imagination, and its primary mode of integrating diverse experiences and conditions. It explores the difference between meanings as achieved and those given as gifts, how one differentiates the two and knows the affect on the soul; the connection of imagination, affection, friendship, and virtue; the act of faith and its relationship to knowledge; the relationship of self to societies and polities; the experience of suffering; the yearning of the human subject to be loved and its openness to such a gift; the confusion of the lover and the rejection, indeed hatred of the lover's attention and call; the seeking out of a Divine Lover for his beloved and the promise of fidelity which calls forth a spiritual mutuality of presence.

This last concern, of God's seeking out humans, provides the second overarching issue, namely, that of redemption. Thus along with the engaging of students in the natural unity of truth, one leads them to discuss the supernatural purpose, or telos, of the whole of Christian faith and all of the theological themes. With such foundations the theological themes are identified first, in the biblical narratives as they make evident the gifts of nature and of history, and then are studied in various later analyses within the theological tradition.

In the introductory level, faculty have the opportunity to help students begin to address the certain methodological issues, such as the ordinary positivist ways of seeing that they will usually have brought with them. There are obviously many strategies for addressing this; because of the common use of this method in reading the Bible it can be helpful to contextualize the difference between nonrevelational expression of issues such as creation and evil, and the Old Testament account of existence and its corrections of the nonrevealed accounts. The methodological matters would also be important in the matter of faith, intelligence and Gnosticism in the New Testament; the interrelationship of statements made in the descriptions of biblical narrative and the technical language of doctrinal affirmations.

Also of importance is the connection of scriptural narratives to the anthropological studies and to their mediation in the properly theological issues. So for example, in St. Augustine's *Confessions*, the series of tensions of knowledge and faith, of love and prayer, of achievements and grace, of intellectual and Christian conversion, etc., are helpful in sketching the wealth of the tradition. In encountering Augustine in this way students often find a connection with experiential issues of faith and theology. Thus experiences are not just presented in the usual context of positivist affirmations of one's own immediacy as normative, but one's experience is presented in its fullness, because it is mediated by a tradition of critical intelligence.

The doctrinal context is important for an introduction because it raises the issues of faith and culture, the shift in the theological context from descriptive to explanatory contexts, and the role of the Church in the work of theology. It provides a considerable help to catechesis in terms of understanding both the importance and the necessity of creedal formulas with their differentiated statement of the Christian mystery.

The medieval achievements invite insight into the development of theology as a *scientia* with its integrative intellectual analysis of the mysteries of faith and the fuller connection of theology back to the anthropological and methodological issues. In addition it picks up from the Augustinian discussions on the spiritual appropriation as well as the interiority of theologians and students in engaging theological realities grounded in a life that is unified with the Trinity. This aspect of the tradition also suggests the possibility that students are called to be both participants in the Christian redemption and to be agents mediating its truth and effects into their personal and public lives.[26]

The Reformation and Counter Reformation contexts invite discussions about the relationships of faith and intelligence, grace and freedom, and Scripture and Church. It also provides an important realization that the process of learning theology cannot be done properly by being either a nominalist or a conceptualist, and so it adds to the importance of confronting modern positivism by inviting a knowledge of students acknowledging their interiority.

The modern period presents the continuing development of theology in helping to understand all those themes which have been previously introduced and in particular the contemporary theological insights which were of benefit to the whole Church in Vatican II. In our case we especially focus on the constitutions on *Divine Revelation* and *The Church in the Modern World*.

In developing the full program—three courses—of "Faith and the Catholic Tradition," once a core introduction was established, there remained a need to establish the integrative sequence for the remaining two courses. For the second course we identified four themes constituting a common body of knowledge which would build on the introductory course, and then asked the faculty in different theological subdisciplines to develop courses which would fulfill the criteria for the sequence. The primary concern was to deepen some themes previously addressed, and to add both new themes and a more explicit treatment of methodological developments.

In the second course, the themes developed from those introduced at the first level are revelation in history as expression of divine self-disclosure; theological anthropology; worship and spirituality as responses to God's presence; and the Church's appropriation, critique and transformation of culture.

---

[26] On the relationship of theology and spirituality see Carla Mae Streeter, O.P., "Aquinas, Lonergan, and the Split Soul," *Theology Digest* 32 (winter 1985): 327-40.

The theological topics are grace, virtues, and sacraments. The methodological component may include the rise of world historical consciousness, the role and place of scientific methods, the role of critical theory in humanities and social sciences, and the relationship of theory and praxis. The theological areas in which these criteria are presently being developed are biblical, historical, moral, and systematic theology.

The third and final course of the general requirement, continues to build on the common knowledge of the earlier two; here students are allowed to select a wider variety of courses—in systematics, history, moral, biblical, and liturgical areas. All courses are related to the general theme "Faith and Culture." Here the task is to find a variety of courses from which students may elect their final requirement. In this we mean by culture not a specific field which guides the meanings of history, but in a wider sense of those issues which give expression to the aspirations of the human spirit. This study of faith and culture is also related, in some courses, to other religious traditions, to other cultures, and to principles of modern culture which have their impact on the Christian tradition.

From within these three courses of the general curriculum, students may major or minor in theology. And now, in addition to the whole general theological requirement receiving a new context for understanding theology, there is a new major and minor in Catholic studies which seeks to relate the theological tradition to those other disciplines which share, from different scholarly fields, the issues of Christian wisdom and culture. The intention of this program is to integrate the theology and other disciplines in the humanities and the social sciences. Presently, those are philosophy, literature, art history, history, and psychology. Conversations are now underway to provide similar courses in sociology and political science. Finally, there is the intention to develop a minor in Catholic Studies which would relate various professions to the vocation of the Christian; given our own context the first plan is to develop a program related to work and business.

Given the importance of theology as an integrating discipline as that has been understood consistently in the Catholic tradition,[27] the theology department has an important role to play in helping to foster programs which bring that integrity into focus. Among the variety of ways in which this can be done is to engage in substantive conversations with faculty in other fields. In our own situation the department, along with the members of the Committee on Catholic Identity, developed summer seminars for the faculty which were supported and funded by the Faculty Development Office.[28] The first, di-

---

[27] *Ex corde Ecclesiae*, pars. 17, 19.

[28] The summer seminars are planned to take place over five years. The themes which they address are as follows: (1) The Idea of the Catholic University (1994); (2) The Catholic University and the Curriculum (1995); (3) The Role of Faculty—Catholic and non-Catholic—in the Catholic University (1996); (4) The Catholic University and Academic Freedom (1997); and (5) The Catholic University and American Culture (1998).

rected by Professor Brian Daley, S.J., was held in July 1994; the second directed by Professor Janine Langan was held in July 1995. These seminars have provided an opportunity for sustained reading and discussion that has been very beneficial to the larger university. This program, when joined to the revision of the curriculum as noted above, has provided significant articulation of the role of theology in leading

> the search for a synthesis of knowledge as well as in the dialogue of faith and reason. It serves all other disciplines in their search for meaning . . . by helping them to investigate how their discoveries will affect individuals and societies . . . and by bringing a perspective and an orientation not contained within their own methodologies.[29]

Parallel to the seminars for sustained faculty study, the department, and now the Catholic Studies Program, bring to the campus Catholic and Christian scholars, scientists, and cultural essayists who are known as excellent translators of the tradition, who have offered public lectures and lead small discussion sessions for a wide variety of students and faculty. These programs, supported by the Faculty Development Office, have been very fruitful in promoting faculty conversation, as well as interest among an increasingly larger number of students, Catholic or not. The role for theology in helping to shape the identity of a Catholic university is not only related to learning, researching, and communicating the knowledge of the tradition, but also to being a catalyst for seeking the unity of knowledge in itself, and even more importantly, the unity of knowledge and living.[30]

There is considerable talk today about college students being educated to become responsible citizens and to take their place in the modern context of *paideia*. But in addition to this, there is something else at stake in Catholic universities. There must be a hope and an intention of such universities that their graduates will become strengthened in faith, intelligence, and virtue; that they will be able to mediate its wisdom into the various professional and public tasks of the culture; and finally that among those graduates there will be some persons who increasingly undertake the tasks of catechesis.[31] Theology, even in its beginning, flourishes with the hope that some of those who have taken the intellectual and loving unity with the Divine Logos into their hearts and minds will become the theological scholars of the future.

---

[29] Ibid., par. 19.

[30] For a perceptive and critical analysis of how these concerns relate to the entire cultural dimension of our society and the role of a Catholic university within it, see Joseph Flanagan, S.J., "The Jesuit University as a Counter-Culture," *Method: Journal of Lonergan Studies* 10 (fall 1992): 127-45.

[31] On the variety of forms of catechesis for the Church see *Catechism of the Catholic Church* (Liguori, Mo.: Liguori, 1994), pars. 1697, 422-23.

Appendix

CORE LIST OF PRIMARY TEXTS

Biblical Section

    Genesis 1-11
    Genesis 12, 15, 17, 22
    Exodus 1-20
    2 Samuel 7-12
    Isaiah 52-53, 58

    Mark
    Matthew 5-7
    John 1-4
    Galatians

Historical Section

    Augustine, *Confessions*, bk. 1-2, 7-8
    Julian of Norwich, *Showings*, chap. 1, 58-63

    Thomas Aquinas, *Summa* I.1.1
    Reformation Period: Martin Luther, *Freedom of the Christian*, first half
    Reformation Period: Excerpts from Council of Trent

    Optional, but included in the packet of readings:
        Didache and Irenaeus, *Against Heresies*, bk. 1, pref.; bk. 3, pref.
        Thomas Aquinas, *Summa* I.1.3; III.1.2; excerpt from the commentary
            on Matthew
        Martin Luther, excerpts from *On the Babylonian Captivity*

Modern Section

    Excerpts from Vatican II Documents—Instructors choice. Recommenda-
    tions include *Dei Verbum; Gaudium et Spes; Lumen Gentium*, chap. 2;
    Decree on Ecumenism

7

The Undergraduate Theology Major

Lawrence S. Cunningham

General Observations

This essay will focus on the undergraduate major in theology in a Catholic college or university. These reflections derive from my own experience as the former undergraduate director of theology at the University of Notre Dame and my current position as chair of the same department. I stipulate those autobiographical facts only to provide a frame of reference for what follows. In other words, circumstances, institutional history, curricular demands, and the like may make many of my observations only partially applicable for the needs or desires of other institutions. Nonetheless, my experience may provide some help for those who, in fact, wish to strengthen (or initiate) an undergraduate major since we have had some success in this over the past years.

When I came to Notre Dame in 1988 there were less than twenty undergraduates who had declared first or second majors in theology although a fair number had enough theology credits to have declared minors. In the spring of 1995 we had roughly one hundred and thirty majors/second majors with the good prospect of at least a dozen more (since many do not make firm declarations of the major until well into their sophomore year). How we increased our majors by fivefold in a relatively short period of time will be explained later, but some preliminary observations first need to be made.

We might begin with a hard but not often commented upon fact; before the Second Vatican Council there were no undergraduate majors in theology; indeed, apart from a smattering of offerings in apologetics and/or marriage and the family, most undergraduates did not have a menu of choices in theology.

The reason why there was no theology undergraduate major forty years ago is easy enough to explain. Undergraduate education was understood to be an education in the liberal arts and the liberal arts were considered to be the necessary prerequisite for the study of theology. In other words, one first got a liberal education and only then did one embark on a theological education, which is considered to be a postgraduate enterprise.

The reason for this situation is deeply embedded in Christian history. Augustine's influential *De doctrina Christiana*, for example, argued for the legitimacy of employing pagan rhetorical learning to the study of Scripture, but Augustine's underlying assumption was that one must have an education in the *Artes* before undertaking the study of Scripture. In the monastic tradition, as Jean Leclercq massively demonstrated in his now classic work *The Love of Learning and the Desire for God*, young monks first trained in the liberal arts as a prelude to the serious study of the Bible. With the rise of the universities in the twelfth century this sequence became institutionalized: first, the study of the *Artes*, then work on philosophy and, finally, theology. In the post-Reformation period, this pattern received further codification. For example, the Jesuit Constitutions (1556) stipulate the steady progress of studies from the liberal arts through philosophy and then on to theology. Seminary education in this country, patterned on the *Ratio Studiorum* sanctioned by the Tridentine reforms, followed the same agendum. After high school, one studied the classics for two years and finished the bachelor's curriculum with a degree in philosophy; this was then followed by four years in theology. In the first four years there were no courses that could be called, in any strict sense of the term, theological.

The rationale for this academic procession of first the *Artes* and only then theology is not all that mysterious. Traditionally, theology was thought of as reflection on the *Sacra Pagina*. When the medieval theologian was given the triple duty of "reading, disputing, and preaching" (*legere/disputare/predicare*) the unsupplied but necessary object of the verbs was Sacred Scripture. It was thought obvious that one could not do this with anything approaching competence without a thorough grounding in the right use of language. It is worthwhile remembering that part of the Renaissance revival of the ancient classics was to provide a philological instrument for Church reform by a sophisticated retrieval of the authentic sources. Without the *Artes*, in short, one could not be a serious theologian.

The conclusion that one draws from the above historical fact when thinking about the undergraduate major in theology is this: We no longer *presuppose* that one has a solid liberal education when one begins the study of theology. Indeed, the matter is quite different, almost revolutionary; theology is now seen as one more option in the menu of possible liberal arts majors.

The rise of the theology major for undergraduates in the mid-1960s received an impetus from another important factor in higher education in the United States—the explosive growth of departments of religious studies in state and private schools as a result of Supreme Court decisions in the early 1960s allowing the teaching *about* religion as a constitutionally protected right. Indeed, one could say that many Catholic institutions did not (and still have not) sorted out the tangles of what, in fact, they possess—a department of theology or a department of religious studies or a *tertium quid*. Indeed, one institution where I taught for a year as a visitor in 1980-81, the Jesuit sponsored University of Scranton, called its program the "Department of Religious Studies/Theology." I suspect more than one institution has settled for that rather ambiguous use of the "slash."

One interesting question that does arise from the current state of affairs is this: What is the *telos* of the undergraduate major? In the older order, this was a question easily answered. With rare exceptions, persons studied theology in order to be ordained for the priesthood. The *telos* of the study of theology was, in effect, to produce priests. This fact determined both the curriculum in general and the way things were taught in particular. Thus, the older tradition of moral theology was designed to equip the potential confessor in his role as *medicus et judex* with a strong emphasis on his judicial role in the confessional. That is hardly the aim of theology today in the undergraduate curriculum.

The goal of undergraduate theology, moreover, must to some extent be determined by the students' qualifications and capabilities. Does the very fact that a student today can begin the study of theology without any classical language, with small acquaintance of history, and no background in philosophy necessarily determine what the curriculum is and what it cannot hope to be? In other words, what is the context assumed when one begins the study of theology as an undergraduate? Whatever the deficiencies of the older model might be (I myself am a product of the seminary curriculum)—and they were many—one thing was sure: students at least knew the names of the players; that, for instance, Anselm lived after Augustine and before Aquinas and that Descartes and Kant often showed up on the list of intellectual adversaries. They also had the philosophical vocabulary to recognize issues in the works of theologians.

So, then, what is the aim of the undergraduate theological curriculum?

Apart from those who would see it as an apologetic grounding in the "truths" of the faith or as a kind of advanced catechesis (which would basically mean that theology has no authentic function within a true university curriculum) one would have to answer the question of *telos* by shaping a theology curriculum taking stock of the following facts and aspirations. First, if students are going to get the required "tools" for advanced theological education they are going to have to do so in tandem with their major in theology and not before it. Therefore, one should have a fairly clear idea of what besides theology courses students should be required to take.

Next, departments are going to have to decide whether they are in the business of theology or religious studies. At the center, this is an easy decision to make once one has decided whether or not their department is committed to critical reflection from within the community of faith or not. At the edges, however, the issue becomes enormously complicated. Think of a possible hire in biblical studies—does one demand that a candidate, trained in exegetical and philological issues, also have theological interests? Must the methodology of the person in historical studies focus on theology or would someone, say, in patristics, whose main interest is in social history, suffice? Would a hire in comparative theology be satisfied if the person, an expert, say, in Buddhist studies, happened to be a Catholic or would training *ex professo* in theology be necessary?

Third, it seems eminently reasonable that an undergraduate major in theology will have to stand alongside other majors in the Arts faculty. If one grants that, then a number of things begin to fall into place which helps determine the shape of the curriculum. I would single out the following:

(1) The recognition that Catholic theology has a history and constitutes an intellectual tradition. Therefore, every major should have at least some broad sense of the history, sweep, and shape of that tradition.

(2) Next, and closely allied to the historical issue, is the fact that theology is an intellectual discipline which, variously, presupposes some kind of method for intellectual inquiry. Therefore, either as a free-standing course(s) or, as a presupposition in courses, some attention must be given to how a theologian theologizes and with what data and according to what criteria.

(3) From its beginnings, theology has had, at its foundation, an encounter with Sacred Scripture. Students must be introduced not only to exegesis but how exegesis interacts with the discipline of theology itself.

(4) Within this general framework of history, methodology, and exegesis there is then a wide area of flexibility that needs to be settled: Are the courses to be fashioned according to the older paradigm of the classical tractates of God, Christology, sacraments, etc.? How does theological ethics fit into this schema? What does one do about the emerging fields of spirituality, the spectrum of liberation theologies, etc.? How does one do justice to the need to fashion offerings that take account of the *de facto* situation of ecumenical and interreligious dialogue?

(5) Finally, how does one take into account the nexus between theological studies and other cognate fields represented in the liberal arts curriculum? Must theological studies take into account the philosophical disciplines? Can it ignore the relationship of theology to the more general issue of human culture represented, say, by the area of belletristics, art history, etc.? What about theology and the human sciences of social theory, anthropology, and psychology? The very fact that theology is now part of the Arts curriculum demands that these latter questions be taken into account. This fact does not even take into account the proliferation (for better or for worse) and increasing popularity of "area studies"—such interdisciplinary programs would find, in most cases, various theological courses congenial to their purposes.

Obviously, one cannot generalize a curricular model that takes into account all of the questions I have raised above because the exigencies and opportunities of a given college/university derive curricula in quite specific ways. Even allowing for that particularity, however, I do think that the core of history, method, critical reflection, and exegesis should serve as constants in the fashioning of the curriculum.

One last point may not be out of order here: We do have an obligation to find out *why* a student elects theology as a major in order to aid students in shaping the best program for their needs. If a student, for example, intends to go on to graduate school in some area of theology that student needs to begin, early enough, the requisite round of language preparation and/or those cognate subjects (i.e., philosophy) without which graduate education seems an unlikely endeavor. The same would hold true for those who intend to go on for a professional education or a Church-related education. Those who elect theology simply as a liberal arts degree with the intention of later venturing outside the area (into law, for instance) may not require the same kind of track as those who intend to stay inside the field. One strategy that we have adopted at Notre Dame to cover many bases was to design and offer a full double major in philosophy and theology but with this added obligation, to wit, that any student who elects the full double major must take at least one year of a classical language, preferably Greek. That program of the double major is relatively new at Notre Dame but has attracted some of the very brightest students in the college and proved to be an immensely attractive preparation for both graduate school and/or professional graduate education for Church-related work.

Building the Undergraduate Major

Every student at the University of Notre Dame is required to take two theology courses as part of the university's general education requirement for graduation. The first course is a broad survey of the Old and New Testament with a further trajectory into the early Church period. The second course focuses on a particular theological theme or topic considered both historically (as a natural sequence following on the first course) and systematically. The topic of the second course is left to the interest of the individual instructor as long as it fits into the broad understanding we have about the need to build on the trajectory of the first course.

One thing we learned from some informal inquiries directed to both teachers and students is that students, by and large, very much liked the study of theology and had a high degree of appreciation for their teachers (with two exceptions all of our nearly forty faculty members teach "across the board"— i.e., from undergraduate surveys to doctoral seminars). Few students in the past, however, elected theology as a first or second major because, frankly, the idea of a theology major seemed odd to them and, more importantly, they did not know what they could do with such a major, i.e., how would they earn a living? Students with a tentative inclination for theology also met frequent resistance either from parents who saw no economic future in the area or peer persuasion that theology was too odd a major to elect.

We saw our first task to be one of education. We emphasized the new reality about theology, which is to say, that it was a major like any other major in the liberal arts. Thus, if one wanted a general liberal arts education it made as much sense to elect theology as it did English or history since both would teach one how to read texts carefully, how to write analytically, and how to learn about our Western intellectual tradition. We had the admitted advantage of having a number of excellent teachers who also happened to be well-known scholars so we could argue, with understandable pride, that students would be studying with well-known professors in a "flagship" department of the university.

It is one thing to say that but quite another thing to get that message out to the students we most wanted to attract to the department. Our short-term strategy to provide a critical mass of excellent majors (who could serve as a "word of mouth" network among other students) was rather simple. We asked each teacher in the first course to give us, near the end of the term, the names of the top two or three students in their class. To each of those students we issued a letter of invitation to sign up for a special "by invitation only" course taught the following term by one of our very best faculty members who, in turn, were asked to encourage students to take more courses in theology as they finished their requirements. We pointed out the availability of a "second major" that could go along with their other majors in, e.g., pre-med or mathematics or whatever.

Second, we attempted, with fair success, to build into the major ways to encourage students to acquire some sense of community as students of theology. We did this through a double effort: by curricular design and by informal nonacademic developments.

In terms of the curriculum, we would put into place a two-semester required core course that ran through the junior year. Theology 395 (fall) and 396 (spring) surveyed the history of theology from the early patristic period down to the present with the break between the two courses geared to finishing the medieval period in the fall and beginning the Reformation in the spring. This required sequence served two purposes. First, it gave every major a sense of the sweep of the tradition as well as providing them the names and vocabulary to help them when they took more specialized courses in their senior year on topics in historical, moral, and systematic theology. Second, and more importantly for our purposes, it put theology students in the same class for a year where they would get some sense of what their peers were doing and how they might work together on various projects or research topics. The Theology 395/396 sequence, in short, was a painless way of giving students a sense of common purpose and a spirit of community.

Along with that curricular core, we also built up some informal traditions for the students. Each term we try to have at least one extracurricular "intellectual" event either in the form of a lecture or a discussion or a presentation. In addition, we now have a series of informal events. Before Christmas there is always a brunch for all majors and faculty at the home of a faculty member. In March, during "Junior Parents Weekend" we hold a reception for all majors and their families where we meet socially and have the faculty present. Finally, on the morning of Commencement we have a brunch for all those graduating and their families at which faculty also attend. It is always amazing to us (and a source of some satisfaction) that these small gestures of sociability are wonderfully well received by students.

As a final strategy we attempt to keep in contact with our alumni/alumnae both by informal means (welcoming them back to campus, writing to them in response to their letters, etc.) and keeping (imperfectly, alas!) a mailing list in order to send them our newsletter. We have discovered that this kind of networking also works to aid the "word of mouth" publicity for students already in school to know about the workings of the theology department.

Through this informal network we have been able to get some sense, impressionistic though it might be, of what our students have done after completing their education. Our unscientific research yields the following:

(1)   A significant number of our majors take a year or two to do volunteer work with Church-related groups like the Holy Cross volunteers or the similar groups sponsored by the Jesuits, Vincentians, etc. This is a much encouraged practice at Notre Dame in general (roughly 10 percent of graduating seniors do such volunteer work) but a particular goal of many majors.

(2)   A fair number of our students go on to teach theology in secondary schools with the intention to further their theological education at least at the level of the M.A.

(3)   A small number of male students go on to study for the ordained ministry but, with one exception, I know of only one woman who was a major in the past eight years who entered religious life. There are a similar small group of both men and women who go on for M.Div. degrees to do lay ministry in the Church.

(4)   A number of students go on for graduate education in theology either by staying on at Notre Dame for the M.A. or going to similar institutions. In turn, from this group, a number go on for the Ph.D.

(5)   Perhaps the simple majority of our graduates go into the work force in various capacities or go on to study for advanced degrees either in other fields of the liberal arts (e.g., history) or in professional education (law school).

The one important conclusion from our informal tracking is this: students who major in theology tend, in large numbers, to pursue vocational choices which are in the service of the Church. This is an important fact to recognize when considerations about a theology department are discussed either within the department or in the institution at large. Colleges and universities concerned with the "Catholic character" question should realize that an enthusiastically supported department of theology serves not only the exigent needs of the curriculum but also provides a long-term service to the Church at large. In that sense, theology departments are *seminaria*—seedbeds for ministries in the Church.

Concluding Reflections

Given the relative youthfulness of theology departments for undergraduates and given the sea change which is occurring in the post-Vatican II Church, what can we say about the future of undergraduate theological education for those who wish to study theology as the major concentration of their academic interest?

A number of observations as well as a few educated guesses may not be out of order as we conclude this essay. In the first place, we still have not thought through the implications of the fact that undergraduates do, in fact, elect majors in theology. The unexamined implications cluster around the issue I mentioned early in these reflections: Theology is now one of the options in the liberal arts; it is not what one studies after one has finished the arts curriculum. What are the ramifications of this fact in itself and what are the ramifications for those who intend to go on to advanced study in theology either for the professional training of a M.Div. program or for the research Ph.D.? Have we, in fact, tailored our curriculum to fit those needs or have we, in fact, examined the curriculum at all?

Second, what responsibility does the undergraduate theology program have vis-à-vis the ministry of the Church? To put the matter in another way, how much of our curriculum should be given over to experiential learning, field work, and the like? Are we reluctant to provide a spectrum of such courses because we fear the charge of having a "soft" major? Or, is it legitimate to say that such emphases are not the proper milieu of the major unless we stipulate *ex professo* that we are training people for ministry?

The answers to both the first and second questions depends, of course, on who is electing the major and for what reason. Alas, it is also true that tailoring the curriculum in one specific fashion or another may preclude some students from electing theology because they do not see that they will get what they want.

I do not have an easy answer to the much-debated question about theology versus religious studies (or if one should even frame the question in such a polarized fashion). Some Catholic schools have opted for one or the other while others seem to have a curriculum that from the outsider's point of view seems a marriage of both. Notre Dame has clearly opted for a theological model while attempting to give some attention to the other religious traditions of the world. It is worthwhile to note, however, that the methodologies of the study of religion(s) are not necessarily the same as those for the study of theology; and as much as we might wish to eschew long methodological battles, the approaches of how we teach and from what perspective are a neuralgic point especially if some faculty are not committed to a theological world view. It does seem clear, however, that those who opt for theology must take into account the postconciliar reality of ecumenism and interreligious dialogue just as religious studies orientations must give some account of the Catholic theological tradition if departments are set within the context of a Catholic school. There is, after all, a certain expectation deriving both from the character of the school itself and the legitimate expectations of both the students and their families who support the students.

Finally, we must think hard about the relationship of the theology department to cognate areas within the Arts curriculum. This means that theology cannot throw up barriers against other disciplines or against the rise of "area studies" whether those latter be somewhat traditional (e.g., medieval studies concentrations) or newer areas which fight for recognition within academe like "Women's Studies." How those interdisciplinary strategies work out in practice depend a good deal on the shape, flexibility, and demands of the larger curriculum.

A Final Word

What is set out above reflects the experience of one teacher at one school. It does not pretend either to prescribe for other schools whose ethos, tradition, and exigent realities are different from mine. It also presupposes a relatively homogeneous student body (i.e., largely Catholic) which may not be true of other schools in other settings. The only claim that I would advance is that any school with a willing faculty and certain expenditures of time and energy can attract students to the serious study of theology if there is a conviction that theology is a worthwhile path of inquiry to follow.

Many of the ideas that are expressed above were tested in presentations I have made at various schools. The excellent cut and thrust of those discussions has helped clarify my own ideas. Those same discussions have also convinced me that there is still much to think about, modify, and more deeply examine. In other words, this essay is near completion but the work is hardly done.

Which then leads me, finally, to express my appreciation to the faculty (and graduate students in some schools) of the following theology/religious studies departments who offered me hospitality and helpful clarifications (and demurrers!) over the past few years: Marquette University in Milwaukee, Wisconsin; St. John Fisher College in Rochester, New York; Siena College in Loudonville, New York; and St. Louis University in St. Louis, Missouri. In addition, I have learned much from my own colleagues, Joseph Wawrykow and Thomas O'Meara, O.P., who co-direct the undergraduate theology program at Notre Dame.

IV

GRADUATE
AND
RESEARCH PROGRAMS

8

Challenges for Catholic Graduate Theological Education

Matthew L. Lamb

The Catholic Church has the longest intellectual tradition of any institution in the contemporary world . . . The best service Catholic education can perform for the nation and all education is to show that
the intellectual tradition can again be made the heart of higher education.

Robert M. Hutchins

What does it mean to make the intellectual tradition the heart of
higher education? I shall explore this challenge from the eminent Professor Hutchins, contextualizing my remarks on graduate theological education within this larger issue. The preparation and outcome of graduate theological education raises the issue of the
culture in which the education takes place. To put it bluntly, graduate theological education in the United States is in crisis, perhaps especially at Catholic universities.

The crisis is of interest to more than theologians. It is part of an epochal
crisis in higher education and advanced commercial cultures generally. The
crisis is not just one of faith; it is also an intellectual crisis. Let me first sketch
the secular dimensions of this larger crisis, what I call the Janus-crisis of specialization and fragmentation. It was in part this crisis which worried Hutchins
earlier this century. Then I shall outline the two millennia intellectual tradition of Catholicism which might help us understand the particular *kairos* or
time of decision facing Catholic higher education today. Finally, I shall conclude with important contributions graduate theological education in the
Catholic tradition can make to the task of restoring the intellectual tradition
to the heart of higher education.

In effect, since Vatican II Catholic higher education has concentrated upon
the task of updating or *aggiornamento*. It is now time to integrate the genuine
gains from the specialization of this updating with the other task mentioned
at the Council, that of retrieving the many sources of wisdom, goodness, and

108

holiness through a *ressourcement*. If the first millennium of Catholic higher education concentrated upon the quest for wisdom and holiness, and the second millennium upon science and scholarship, then the third millennium should find new ways of integrating wisdom and science.

The Janus-Crisis of Specialization and Fragmentation

Roman Catholicism has generally flourished in the United States. Within four generations Catholics built up the largest independent school system and health care system in world history. Such unique institutional achievements occurred in a very unique post-Enlightenment culture. Only in the United States of America have Enlightenment liberal documents so coincided with the founding of the nation and the constituting of a national memory. With the exception of the Native Americans, the United States has no indigenous population whose collective memory predates the Enlightenment. Immigration was to a *novus ordo saeclorum* that broke with England, so that both conservatives and progressives would politically appeal to a very liberal set of documents: the Declaration of Independence and the Constitution. Education and health care are two major foundations in the Enlightenment edifice. The institutional success of Catholics, motivated by a zeal for the corporal and spiritual works of mercy, with scarce financial resources, was possible only by the dedication of thousands of celibate women and men whose motivation was spiritual rather than fiscal. We are now in the midst of the growing professionalization and laicization of these health care and educational institutions. Will they maintain their Catholic identity? The answer to this question is of interest to more than Catholics. For Catholicism has much to offer American culture if it maintains its specific Catholic identity.

The Catholic university in America today is challenged to engage in an intellectual apostolate. This apostolate is both a mission based upon the deepest human desires for understanding and knowledge, and a mission inspired by a faith that transcends all human achievement in the pure gift of the Triune God who loves into existence the universe and all the human race. This intellectual task has its own integrity. It is to be differentiated (but not separated, let alone set in opposition to) the moral task of promoting human goodness, and the religious task of cultivating holiness and worshiping the sacred.

The intellectual task facing Catholic universities is one they share with all other universities at this juncture of human history: the Janus-crisis of specialization and fragmentation. Janus was the god of beginnings and doorways, depicted with two faces looking in opposite directions. The intellectual task is to discern how to promote the good of increased scientific, scholarly, and professional specialization, while collaborating in overcoming the resulting fragmentation of everyday life.

In one direction, scientific and scholarly specialization results from a marvelous expansion of human inquiry into ever new and diverse phenomena. The veritable explosion of scientific and scholarly knowledge since the

Enlightenment is extraordinary. A reversal of the resulting fragmentation is intimated in the dynamics of interdisciplinary collaboration and research projects involving widely divergent sciences and scholarships. Yet one cannot renounce or lessen the importance of specialization. It is so difficult to understand even the simplest of things. The benefits of this specialization are evident, not only in the daily advances in knowledge but also in the transformation of daily living through ever more advanced technologies.

Looking in the opposite direction, if there is an overriding theme throughout twentieth-century Western cultures, it is a theme of fragmentation and a resulting disorientation in a historical world lacking any sense of wholeness. Wherever one turns in philosophy or cultural and social theory one finds the recurrence of concern for the fragmentation in both human knowledge and, more dramatically, human living. The theme runs from Neo-Kantianism and pragmatism, through phenomenology and existentialism, to poststructuralism and postmodernism. It is a well-worn complaint of educators that the university is in fact a fragmented multiversity, as scientific, scholarly, and professional specialization proliferates. Faculty and students have no coherent sense of the whole, only of fragmented parts managed by academic administrators who adjudicate which parts are going to satisfy credit requirements.

Sciences and technologies specialize and fragment into so many subspecialties and areas that the quest for intelligibility underlying the entire scientific enterprise is not itself intelligible to human beings. This theoretical crisis is terribly practical. The fragmentation of the natural sciences has led to an inability to understand how nature is a whole, how this application of physics, or that chemical compound, can have devastating effects on the environment, or poison food chains. Similarly in the human sciences, there is such a fragmentation of scientific and scholarly specialties that deconstructionists announce the disappearance of human nature, and others can point to the threats to human health from iatrogenic diseases, to dangers in unwise applications of genetic engineering, and to the harm done to human children from the disintegration of stable family life.

Catholic universities share with other universities in this Janus-crisis. Why are they so like their secular counterparts? In 1955 Msgr. John Tracy Ellis published "American Catholics and the Intellectual Life." The essay had immediate impact. The whole tenor of the essay was that Catholics in America, as an immigrant group, were failing to measure up to the standards of scholarly and scientific progress exemplified in the best universities of the country. Although he quoted Robert Hutchins, he never explored just what is the intellectual tradition of Catholicism. Indeed, Ellis did not seem to perceive how Hutchins was counseling a very different task for Catholic universities than that being advocated by Ellis himself. While Hutchins was pleading with Catholic universities to deepen the appropriation of their own intellectual traditions, Ellis was encouraging them to take as their models the great American universities. Although Ellis complained that Catholics betrayed their own resources by failing to recover their own scholastic traditions, he offered no intrinsic reasons for this complaint. Instead, it looked like another instance of the general theme of Ellis's essay, because he remarked how scholars at the universities of Chicago and Princeton were engaging in such a scholastic revival.[1] Forty years later Catholic universities, having followed Ellis's advice and modeled themselves on their American counterparts, are better able to return to Hutchins's challenge to make the intellectual life the heart of higher education.

Another historian has recently advanced just such a challenge. James Turner described well the crisis of knowledge which lies

> scattered around us, in great, unconnected pieces, like lonely mesas jutting up in a trackless waste. That this fragmentation has impoverished public discourse is a more or less common lament; that it has emaciated education, both undergraduate and graduate, is too painfully obvious to dwell on. So as we try . . . to navigate through waves of uncertainty from one disciplinary island to another, all universities, not just Catholic ones, face the challenges and dilemmas of remapping the world of learning.

Drawing upon Cardinal Newman's differentiation of the university from the Church, Turner properly sees this as a human problem which Catholicism has important intellectual resources to address. Now that institutions of secular knowledge are acknowledging a disorientation and confusion in a fragmented historical world, Turner poses the question: "How can the Catholic university reconstruct itself to bring the resources of Catholic tradition to bear on our common task of rebuilding the house of learning."[2]

What are some of the resources upon which we can draw in this intellectual apostolate of rebuilding the house of learning? By posing the Janus-crisis as one of specialization and fragmentation, the work of that eminent Jesuit philosopher and theologian Bernard Lonergan comes to mind. His work, being published in twenty-two volumes by the University of Toronto Press, offers a discovery of intelligence and understanding which, as he was fond of reminding us, issues an invitation to understand what understanding is, because this understanding provides a fixed base, an invariant pattern, with which we may begin to integrate the many specialized advances of human understanding.

To understand Lonergan's work adequately, or that of other prominent twentieth-century philosophers and theologians like Karl Rahner and Hans Urs von Balthasar, one has to study the texts they studied. One has to enter, as they so profoundly did, into the conversations which constitute the

---

[1] John Tracy Ellis, "American Catholics and the Intellectual Life," *Thought* 30 (autumn 1955): 351-88.

[2] James Turner, "The Catholic University in Modern Academe: Challenge and Dilemma," paper presented at a conference on "The Storm over the University" at the University of Notre Dame, October 13, 1992, unpublished.

history of philosophy and theology down the centuries.[3] This act of listening attentively to the tradition is essential if we are going to collaborate effectively with others in constructing a home for learning. We also need the ancient wisdom if we are going to do justice to the concerns for justice raised by the poor, women, minorities, and the environment.

The First Millennium and Catholic Education: Institutionalizing the Quest for Wisdom

Taking a cue from John Paul II's masterful *Tertio Millennio Adviente*, the *kairos* of the Catholic university on the edge of the third millennium is to appropriate and continue the work of centuries. We need a long view of such a monumental task. The major challenge, one Catholics have unique resources to meet, is to reintegrate the first millennial quest for wisdom and holiness with the second millennial quest for science and scholarship.

Learning is not easy, it has to be institutionalized. For us the word "institutionalized" connotes something bad. We use it of criminals or of the insane. Such an attitude about institutions is provincially modern, as if institutions contracted our individualist freedom. In fact, and in classical and Catholic history, institutions are patterns of human cooperation. Learning and the cultivation of intelligence are impossible except as cooperative enterprises down the ages. Cooperation down the centuries is tradition (another suspect word for moderns). The languages, words, and ideas which we learn all come to us from others. There are no Robinson Crusoes or Cartesian universal doubters in the realm of mind. As Newman and Lonergan so astutely observed: René Descartes could write what he did about universal doubt only because he steadfastly refused to doubt, and instead believed, the meanings of words and ideas he had learned. So setting up institutions of learning and traditions are crucial, not just for believers, but for all human learners. Belief and knowledge are symbiotically cooperative.[4]

During the first millennium of Christianity the task of nurturing learning and intelligence found a stable home or institution in the thousands of monasteries and cathedral schools where hundreds of thousands of men and

---

[3] C. S. Lewis in his introduction to St. Athanasius's *On The Incarnation* (Crestwood, N.Y.: St. Vladimir's Orthodox Theological Seminary, 1989), 3-4, where he counsels reading two ancient texts for each modern text read in order to grasp the full import of the theological conversation down the ages. To read only moderns, Lewis writes, is like coming into a conversation in the late afternoon that has been going on since early morning. To understand the moderns we need the ancients. Mistaken readings of modern theologians such as von Balthasar, Lonergan, or Rahner can be traced to an ignorance, on the part of the reader, of the patristic and medieval theologians these theologians studied.

[4] Bernard Lonergan, *Insight: A Study of Human Understanding* (Toronto: University of Toronto Press, 1992), 433-36; there are also the famous debates between Hans-Georg Gadamer and Jürgen Habermas, along with Karl Otto Apel, on the relation between tradition and critical reason, see Georgia Warnke, *Gadamer: Hermeneutics, Tradition and Reason* (Stanford: Stanford University Press, 1986).

women kept alive the sacred word of Scripture, the writings of the Fathers and Mothers of the Church, as well as the classic literature of East and West. Learning, as Jean Leclercq and others have shown, was integrated within the orientations of the monks, nuns, clerics, and lay students towards wisdom and holiness.[5]

Wisdom is both gift and task. As gift wisdom is a participation in the very wisdom of God, the Holy Spirit. Such wisdom is the love of God poured forth in our hearts by the Spirit who is given us (Rom. 5:5). It is this wisdom which guides the Church as it carries forward through history the missions of the Word and Spirit, cherishing the Word of the Father revealed in the Scriptures and worshiped in the liturgy. Such gifted wisdom from above evokes a cultivation of wisdom as a task. The monastic and cathedral schools not only cherished prayer and worship, but also study and reading and work. Divine gifts neither deny nor denigrate human abilities. For these human capacities are themselves the gifts of God's creative love. So the theological virtues called forth, or evoked, the journey of acquiring the human intellectual and moral virtues.

The Christian institutionalization of the love of learning and quest for wisdom had learned, thanks to the efforts of so many great teachers such as Athanasius, Augustine, Basil, Cassian, and the Gregories, from the intellectual and moral tragedies of Greece and Rome. Indeed, the history of empires and countless tribal lords had painfully revealed how lethal was the derailment of intelligence by pride. The lovers of wisdom, the philosophers, who genuinely sought the truth were always, it seemed, trumped by sophists and others who used intelligence for personal and political gain. More dramatically, the fall of the Greco-Roman empire illustrated how the intellectual and moral virtues, no matter how laboriously acquired, were unequal to the tasks set them by human vice and sin. As Augustine sketches in *The City of God*, faced with the violence of sinful history, the intellectual virtues cherished by the great lovers of wisdom declined into an academic cynicism, while the moral virtues retreated into an apathetic stoicism. The philosophers had to seek an elite wisdom that basically consigned the many to the passions of the powerful.

With the fall of the Roman empire, the Catholic institutionalization of learning in monasteries and cathedral schools sought to integrate the intellectual virtues of wisdom, science, understanding, and prudence with the moral and theological virtues. Wisdom was a gift to be gratefully received in faith, hope, and agapic love, to be reverenced as the Word of God, worshiped and listened to in the *lectio divina*. And this Word revealed how God had created the universe and humankind in his own image and likeness. The gift of re-

<hr>

[5] Jean Leclercq, O.S.B., *The Love of Learning and the Desire for God* (New York: Fordham University Press, 1982); Christopher Dawson, *The Making of Europe* (New York: Sheed & Ward, 1945); Pierre Riché, *Éducation et culture dans l'Occident barbare, 6e—8e siécles* (Paris: Editions du Seuil, 1962); L. D. Reynolds and N. G. Wilson, *Scribes and Scholars: A Guide to the Transmission of Greek and Latin Literature* (Oxford: Clarendon Press, 1991), 44-121.

demption enabled these lovers of wisdom to appreciate the gifts of human intelligence and will. They understood how the revealed wisdom of divine faith perfects, but neither abolishes nor substitutes for, the need to acquire intellectual and moral virtues. In books five through eight of his *Confessions* Augustine had dramatized how the grace of his conversion to Christ involved intellectual and moral dimensions. He narrates his personal and experiential discoveries of his own mind and heart as restless orientations into the loving mystery of the divine Triune Reality.[6] The expression "blind faith" is a modern concoction which came in only after faith was opposed to reason.

The light of divine wisdom in faith heals and strengthens—and in no way abolishes—the light of human wisdom acquired by the practice of the intellectual and moral virtues. So, from the apostolic times, with the sons and daughters of the covenant, through the ages of faith, down to our own day, the quest for holy wisdom as an integration of religious holiness, moral goodness, and intelligence continues in monastic and seminary institutions. In prayer, asceticism, and study the whole of life is oriented toward attending to the divine reality of the Triune God, who is more intimate to each human being than each of us are even to ourselves. Attention to the Father, Son, and Spirit involves the highest dimensions of the human mind and heart, so it is not surprising that the monastic quest for mystical and spiritual wisdom was also appreciative, as is evident in John Damascene and Anselm, of the exercise of the "ratio superior" in philosophical and metaphysical wisdom.[7]

As both the Greek and Latin fathers make abundantly clear, the differentiation of Christian dogmas or doctrines from the Scripture was not a separation or opposition. Doctrines confess the Word of God as *true*. It is only within liturgical prayer and worship that the truth of God's Word is confessed and the genuine nature of Catholic doctrine or dogma is appropriated. Wretched from this matrix, these dogmas can be misunderstood and twisted into the categories of power politics. This, as Athanasius saw so well, is to destroy the beauty of the doctrinal/dogmatic sanctuary. It is to betray the cross by the sword.

Nor was this attention to the sacred and the eternal neglectful of the secular and the temporal. Modern dichotomies between "other-worldly" and "this-worldly," as in general the modern misreading of monasticism, are in need of correction. All the skills, trades, and cooperative habits required by cities had

---

[6] St. Augustine's *Confessions* books 5-7; note how modern historians tend to miss the full impact of the intellectual conversion and its specifically Christian character. So Peter Brown misinterprets it as basically a "career" change from being a rhetorian to becoming a philosopher, cf. his *Augustine of Hippo: A Biography* (Berkeley: University of California Press, 1967), 101. This process of intellectual conversion in Augustine is what is often overlooked in many modern interpretations of Augustine and other ancient and medieval theologians. Appeals to wisdom without this noetic conversion usually miss the import of the wisdom tradition rather dramatically.

[7] On "ratio superior" and "ratio inferior" as diverse and complementary orientations of mind toward wisdom and toward science, cf. St. Thomas Aquinas and his references to Augustine in his *Summa Theologiae* I.79.9.

to a great extent been lost in the barbarian invasions and collapse of Rome. The evangelization of these tribes was by and large accomplished, not through the sword, but by the hundreds of thousands of men and women who peopled the monasteries and who over generations, often suffering persecution and death, converted the tribes to Christ. Again, over generations, it was these monasteries and cathedral schools which provided the nucleus for the re-learning of the skills and trades required for prosperous agrarian and city living. So, the quest for mystical wisdom, within the monastic and seminary tradition, are in no way inimical to the quest for metaphysical wisdom and the quest for the practical wisdom or prudence, needed to guide the practical sciences and skills. The first millennium might be characterized, as far as the love of learning was concerned, as the monastic millennium.[8]

The Second Millennium and Catholic Education: From Differentiation to Opposition

Soon after the beginning of the second millennium the *studia generalia* emerged within flourishing urban centers. They were communities of scholars and students from different countries, and the "universities" originally referred to communities of scholars from specific regions or countries. Already in the debates between Bernard and Abelard a concern surfaces that the legitimate differentiation of science and scholarship from wisdom could lead to a separation of science from wisdom. The universities soon institutionalized the quest for science and scholarship in ways that were decidedly secular in comparison with the routines of the monastic or cathedral schools. Indeed, some of the earliest accounts of student life at Paris, Bologna, Oxford narrate both growing tensions between and within faculties of theology, philosophy, medicine, and law, as well as the rather rough and tumble life of the students. Some describe the life as resembling more a miner's camp than a library, with its combination of hard study and, unfortunately by many students, harder drinking.[9] This contributed to the fateful absence of women from the new major universities; while a few did attend Salerno, Montpelier, and Salamanca, the institutions welcoming women continued to be monastic and convent schools.[10]

These wisdom-oriented schools soon were eclipsed by the growing and

---

[8] Cf. Matthew Lamb, "Die Offenheit der Geschichte und die Dialektik von Gemeinschaft und Herrschaft," in E. Arens, ed., *Anerkennung der Anderen* (Freiburg: Herder, 1995), 167-92 and references given there.

[9] Hastings Rashdall, *The Universities of Europe in the Middle Ages* (Oxford: Clarendon Press, 1937) vol. 1, 308-43; vol. 3, 339-464, esp. 419-41.

[10] This rough and tumble style of life contributed to the fact that far fewer women had access to the new universities. They continued to be sent to monastic and convent schools. See Prudence Allen, *The Concept of Woman: The Aristotelian Revolution 450 BC - 1250 AD*, 1st ed. (Montreal: Eden Press, 1985). On pages 416-17 she narrates how the executor of Hildegaard of Bingen traveled to Paris in 1214 to bring her work to the attention of the new masters. Blanche of Castille, the Queen-Regent of France, was a strong woman and played a role in the begin-

vibrant universities as centers of learning. The second millennium of Christianity witnessed the increased influence of the universities in setting the cultural agenda. It was in the universities that the differentiation of theology as an effort at a systematic understanding of sacred doctrine developed. Theology and philosophy were still dedicated to wisdom, but the emphasis was now on the scientific or systematic exploration of all the questions which arose regarding God, being, and nature. In the minds of such great teachers as an Aquinas or Bonaventure, the integral practice of prayer, worship, and the theological virtues assured that the differentiation of wisdom and science, doctrine and systematic understanding, expressed the divinely gifted unity of the intellectual quest for truth, the moral quest for goodness, and the religious quest for the sacred and holy.

Where the monasteries institutionalized the quest for wisdom and holiness, so the universities institutionalized the quest for science and scholarship. As with any process of differentiation, there is the danger of a failure at appropriation. Cut off from the appropriate exercises of a love-informed faith and wisdom, the human learning of Scripture can be distorted into a mere literalism or fundamentalism; the doctrinal differentiation can be distorted into a propositionalism and authoritarian dogmatism; the systematic differentiation, severed from a living wisdom, can be distorted into an arrogant and arid conceptualism. The key to preserving the differentiation, not letting it slip into a separation and opposition, was to maintain the intellectual, moral, and religious conversion processes narrated by Augustine. Without all three of these, along with the spiritual and intellectual practices and exercises they engender, the integral development of wisdom and science was threatened.

By the end of the fifteenth century scant attention was paid in university life to the intellectual exercises and practices which would cultivate the highest dimensions of human intelligence. What is sometimes called "decadent scholasticism" spread. There was the growing eclipse of wisdom in the displacement of metaphysical questions by logical analysis, in the spread of nominalism, in the conceptualism of deductivist philosophies and theologies. The ancient organs of intelligence that once pulsed with a vibrant understanding and living wisdom hardened into merely dominant organs of power and privilege. Philosophers and theologians measured up less and less to the achievements of their wise and intelligent predecessors. The universities lost the unifying vision a more serious exercise of philosophical wisdom would have afforded. The beginnings of the multiversity are evident in the nominalist pretension that universals are only "concepts" or "ideas" and that only individual things exist. Things are no longer understood within an overarching order or orientation, but only as discrete, monadic objects.

nings of the university of Paris. Her influence, however, was jeopardized when several students died after she sent in some knights to quell a riot that had broken out between drunken students and a local innkeeper. The masters shut down the university for two years (1229-30), and Blanche had to make concessions to have it reopen.

At the eve of the Protestant Reformation Catholic theologians had gener-ally failed to appropriate for themselves the wisdom and understanding op-erative in the differentiations of doctrine from Scripture, and of theology as systematic understanding from doctrine. Not understanding it, they could not pass those differentiations on. Little wonder, then, that the Protestant reformers tended to downplay or reject doctrinal and systematic differentia-tions in favor of a return to Scripture alone. As the unifying role of wisdom was lost in the universities, so the unifying function of ecclesial ministry was lost. Political powers exploited the religious differences and the wars of reli-gion ravaged Europe.

At the same time, however, there was a growing discovery of empirical scientific reason. The arid conceptualism that had dogged a decadent Scho-lasticism was challenged by the empirical orientations of the founders of modern science. It was a great irony, not lost on so illustrious a scientist as Werner Heisenberg, that the emergence of modern empirical science contin-ued orientations of classic Platonic and Aristotelian philosophy and yet was used to displace these, along with Scholasticism, in the academy. The empirical natural sciences have transformed the world of nature and of history profoundly.[11]

There is a transcultural dimension in the development of the natural sci-ences. There is not a European, American, Asian, or African physics, chemis-try, biology, zoology, neurology, or engineering. If, in the thirteenth century, the best and brightest students were studying philosophy and theology, in the twentieth they have pursued the natural sciences. Learning the sciences requires an intellectual asceticism, a training of the mind to move beyond the descriptive categories of sense impressions to the explanatory categories of the scientific and technological specializations.

If the first millennium of Christian higher education could be called the monastic millennium, the second is certainly the scientific university. This university millennium began by differentiating wisdom and science, theol-ogy and philosophy. It is now ending with both philosophy and theology relegated to the margins of the university, if there at all. As Nietzsche put it, they are the step-children of modernity. The eclipse of wisdom—Nietzsche's Zarathustra is "weary of wisdom"—leads to the fragmentation of unity and the loss of any sense of authority as genuine service of the truth. With the loss of wisdom traditions, modern cultures cultivate empirical sciences of the par-ticular. There is no heuristic attention to the intelligibility and pattern of the whole; instead there is attention only to the individual things, and any effort to pattern or order them are taken to be conventional. We have the Janus-crisis.

Adopting Alasdair MacIntyre's analysis of moral inquiry, one might say that the contemporary university finds whatever overarching pattern or or-

---

[11] Cf. Patrick Heelan, *Quantum Mechanics and Objectivity: A Study of the Physical Philosophy of Werner Heisenberg* (The Hague: Martinus Nijhoff, 1965).

der it has from either the encyclopedists or the genealogists. The encyclopedists attend carefully to the endless particularities open to human study, but lack any internal intelligent ordering of the whole. The alphabet provides the scholars, as it does also the administrative bureaucrats, with their impoverished substitute for order: the filing system. God is filed under "G" along with "gold" and "gorillas." The genealogists then come along to claim that any language is only a dialect with an army and a navy, so that all orders are only systems of dominative power. All order and pattern are merely conventional, so whatever pattern is operative is due to those in power deciding it is so. The genealogists have immanentized the arbitrary god of the nominalists. Truth becomes just another name for power.[12]

The achievements of the Enlightenment, while many and important, are not without their dark side. Properly scandalized by the wars of religion, the intellectuals of the day tended to rationalize their own flight from faith by criticizing religion, relegating it to the private sphere of individual conscience, and inscribing war into all of nature, including human nature. Thus they defined both religion and nature by their abuse rather than their proper activities. This was a fateful case of keeping the bath water (war) and throwing out the baby (religion). Little wonder, then, if the last two centuries would witness the most horrendous wars in human history, as modern science and technology were ever more devoted to inventing weapons of destruction.

In many ways the university millennium of higher education has developed enormously the practices and exercises of the mind attentive to particular and individual realities, what the ancients called the "ratio inferior." This scientific, empirical attentiveness is very demanding, as anyone who has specialized in a science knows. Nor is it surprising that the exercises and practices of the human mind that attend to mind itself and to the mind's spiritual and transcendent orientations are practically absent from the university.

This failure to cultivate the habits of philosophical and theological wisdom led thinkers to turn to mechanics for models to understand nature and society. The triumph of nominalism assured that discrete individual things, or "monads" in Leibniz's favorite term, were severed from any natural whole. Any order, whether natural or political or cultural, was only the result of force or power relating these individual things or monads to one another. Since all orders or patterns were deemed conventional, every thing was up for individual and collective choice. The post-Enlightenment orientation is one which fosters the development of scientific empirical habits of investigation, but cannot, because of its mechanistic and materialist reductionism, allow the empirical experience of intelligent and rational consciousness its own validity. Mind itself is not minded. At the end of the second millennium the only ordering principles in the university are those provided by the encyclopedist and administrator's alphabet or the genealogist's political power correctness.

---

[12] Alasdair MacIntyre, *Three Rival Versions of Moral Enquiry* (Notre Dame, Ind.: Notre Dame University Press, 1990).

The Intellectual Tradition and Theology:
Reintegrating Science and Wisdom

Can the intellectual tradition again be made the heart of higher education in America? Will Catholic universities recover their own Catholic identity in collaborating with others in this intellectual apostolate of beginning, as we approach the third millennium of Christian education, the enormous task of reintegrating science and wisdom? If the answer to these questions is going to be yes, it will require that more serious attention be paid to the graduate programs at Catholic universities. Graduate education is the future of higher education itself. Graduate programs, especially those at the doctoral level, are the matrix of the teachers and researchers who will hopefully pass on the intellectual skills and achievements they have learned to the next generation.

At the beginning of this essay, I mentioned that graduate theological education is in crisis. Generally, there is the secularization of Catholic higher education studied by Frank D. Schubert.[13] On the graduate level, there is Ray Hart's "Religious and Theological Studies in American Higher Education" which shows how there is a growing contradiction between theology, increasingly relegated to seminaries, and a religious studies in universities that is church-free, faith-free, and God-free.[14] Hart found more and more university administrators and faculty eschewing even the term "theology." David H. Kelsey's *Between Athens and Berlin* sketches the tensions between a more wisdom-oriented *paideia* inculcated in the Athens model, which he illustrates by reference to Cardinal Newman's *The Idea of the University*, and a more scientific and scholarly oriented *Wissenschaft* that he illustrates with reference to Schleiermacher and a professional, academic, and critical study of religion. He concludes the study by asserting that, while each approach corrects aspects of the other, at best only "an unstable truce" can be had between them since each is based upon different, and presumably contradictory, notions of reason and human nature.[15]

I disagree with Professor Kelsey. The historical review indicated how the quest for wisdom and the quest for scientific and scholarly objectivity are not based upon different notions of reason. Rather, they spring from different orientations of human intelligence. Wisdom relates to a differentiation of the "ratio superior," while the development of empirical sciences differentiates the "ratio inferior." Indeed, the pessimism regarding the possibility of integrating wisdom and science, as both contributing to an intellectual tradition

[13] Frank D. Schubert, *A Sociological Study of Secularization Trends in the American Catholic University: Decatholicizing the Catholic Religious Curriculum* (Lewiston, N.Y.: The Edwin Mellen Press, 1990).

[14] Cf. Ray Hart, "Religious and Theological Studies in North America: A Pilot Study," *Journal of the American Academy of Religion* 59 (winter 1991): 715-827.

[15] David H. Kelsey, *Between Athens and Berlin: The Theological Education Debate* (Grand Rapids: William B. Eerdmans, 1993). See also his *To Understand God Truly: What's Theological about a Theological School* (Louisville, Ky.: Westminster, 1992).

which should be at the heart of higher education, springs more from Protestant than Catholic scholars.

In a survey I did of doctoral theological education at Catholic universities in North America, I called attention to the disparity in hiring patterns between those Catholic programs, on the one hand, and the hiring patterns at the so-called nondenominational divinity schools and state university programs in religious studies, on the other hand. Prestige divinity schools (e.g., Harvard, Chicago, Yale) tend to hire their own graduates (almost 50 percent of their faculty) and from the other divinity schools (15 to 25 percent of their faculty). While they have many Catholic students, less than 5 percent of their faculty received doctorates from Catholic programs. Catholic departments of theology with doctoral programs, however, tend to hire those who received their doctorates in such divinity schools, or from other non-Catholic programs (35 to 70 percent of their faculty).[16] A problem facing Catholic graduate education is that fewer and fewer faculty themselves have extensively and deeply appropriated the intellectual, moral, and religious achievements of Catholicism. An irony is that many Catholic theologians claiming to be postmodern, while they laud difference and otherness, still cannot clearly account for differences between Catholicism and Protestantism, or post-Vatican II Catholicism and modernism.

Graduate theological education within the United States is at a crossroads. One path will lead such education into new and uncharted explorations of the great intellectual achievements of two millennial Catholic theological traditions. A recovery of Catholic intellectual memories will enlighten our postmodern world, offering new possibilities of creating cultures capable of properly relating wisdom and science, tradition and innovation, the university and the Church. Another path will lead such graduate theological education along more familiar vistas. They are the vistas we as moderns and postmoderns already take very much for granted. They are the vistas in which whatever graduate theological education does, it does not challenge the basic assumptions of modern and postmodern cultures about the relation between intelligence and faith, and how these are institutionalized in universities and churches. It is a path governed by a basic orientation that presumes there could be no great Catholic intellectual achievements capable of transforming empirical cultures.

On the first path, if we take it, we shall have to be very intelligent, for it is a path that we shall have to chart as we advance. The second path is well chartered. It is how in fact theology is being done in most so-called "inter" or "nondenominational" graduate programs now. It is a style of graduate education which fits in well with the privatization of religious faith in our post-Enlightenment culture.

World-class universities in the United States, those renown for their ex-

---

[16] Matthew L. Lamb, "Will There Be Catholic Theology in the United States?" *America* 162 (May 26, 1990): 523-34.

cellence in teaching and research, mirror the culture's dichotomy, often opposition, between intelligence and faith, between wisdom and science. Although some of the best were originally founded by Protestant churches, this religious identity, as George Marsden has so forcefully shown, could not hold off the secularism inherent in the Enlightenment ideals of empiricism and pragmatism.[17]

Indeed, as Marsden analyzes, the pervasive cultural influence of liberal Protestantism in American higher education tended to sacralize the Enlightenment ideals of freedom, democracy, and a public "nonsectarian" pluralism. This contributed to an intellectual stance in which the institutions of reason became increasingly secularized, while the institutions of faith became increasingly sectarianized. We either take our mind seriously, and bracket or privatize our faith; or we take our faith seriously and minimize our intelligence. This has been the dilemma left to the American academy from the very potent mixture of a Protestant emphasis upon the discontinuity between faith and reason, on the one hand, and of an Enlightenment privatization of faith and promotion of empirical science, on the other hand.

Catholic higher education in this country is at a *kairos*—a time of crisis and challenge. Graduate theological education shares in this crisis and challenge. Which path will Catholic colleges and universities take? Will we rededicate ourselves to forging a creative Catholic intellectual life, or will we follow the path charted by those eminent formerly Protestant sister institutions (e.g., Harvard, Yale, Princeton) in which theology and Church identity is now marginalized if not totally extinguished?

If one studies the great Catholic philosophers and theologians of this century, it is clear that they sought in various ways to integrate wisdom and science, intelligence and faith. Bernard Lonergan, Karl Rahner, and Hans Urs von Balthasar were fundamentally critical of any Kantian conceptualist approach to reason. Instead, their whole effort was to introduce their students and readers to a knowledge of intelligence attending to its own activities and orientations by initiating them into the systematic differentiations of Thomas Aquinas's cognitional theory and practice. The only proper reading of *Verbum: Word and Idea in Aquinas* and *Geist in Welt* is to engage in the intellectual exercise of exploring the intellectual and spiritual realities of one's own intelligence and imagination as the referents of the texts of Aquinas and of Lonergan and Rahner. The contemporary interest in von Balthasar springs in part from his own interweaving of his own explorations into his own appropriations of the many Catholic theological traditions.

To read Lonergan, Rahner, or von Balthasar in intellectual dialogue with Aquinas enables one to appreciate as well how Augustinian Thomas Aquinas was. For it is to just such an intellectual and spiritual exercise that Augustine invites the reader of his masterwork *De Trinitate*. Human intelligence is a

---

[17] George Marsden, *The Soul of the American University: From Protestant Establishment to Established Nonbelief* (New York: Oxford University Press, 1994).

created participation in divine infinite understanding and love; it is because of our minds that we are created in the image of God. This is not merely an abstract proposition or statement; the light of our intelligence, the conscious inquiring self-presence is a created participation in divine infinite intelligence. We have to undergo, as Augustine, Aquinas, and any serious student of the Catholic intellectual tradition, the intellectual conversion that opens us to the spiritual and dynamic reality of our own mind and its deepest desires.

Why, if the wisdom tradition is so open to being integrated with the scientific and scholarly, have Christian church authorities resisted so many of the modern scientific and scholarly developments? Lonergan offers two reasons:

> These changes have, in general, been resisted by churchmen for two reasons. The first reason commonly has been that churchmen had no real apprehension of the nature of these changes. The second reason has been that these changes commonly have been accompanied by a lack of intellectual conversion and so were hostile to Christianity.[18]

This is really quite a challenging statement regarding the entire problematic of Catholicism and the series of fundamental changes which have occurred over the last four centuries. The first reason, by the very Newman-like "no real apprehension of the nature of these changes," indicates how there has to be a practiced familiarity with the changes in human self-understanding, in modern science, in modern historical criticism, and in modern philosophy. For Catholicism to bring its millennial intellectual tradition to the heart of higher education, Catholic universities and colleges are going to have to excel in acquiring the habits of scientific, scholarly, and philosophical inquiry.

Indeed, their concern for intellectual development has to encourage an intellectual conversion that discovers the inner dynamism of human intelligence in act. Because the profound changes in modern self-understanding, modern science, modern historiography, and modern philosophy were accompanied by a "lack of intellectual conversion," that is, because those advancing these changes lacked the full self-knowledge fostered by the wisdom tradition, the changes they introduced were hostile to Christianity. How could one more drastically turn the tables on modern secularism and agnosticism? Intelligence in act is not hostile to Christianity. The diminishment of Christian faith, far from freeing human intelligence for an ever more full and wise use, is a diminishment of the light of intelligence and reason. So the Enlightenment was not as enlightened as it made itself out to be.

Such a challenging claim puts enormous responsibility upon theology. If modern changes were hostile to Christianity because they were accompanied by a lack of intellectual conversion, then it is understandable that such a con-

---

[18] Bernard Lonergan, *Method in Theology* (Toronto: University of Toronto Press, 1991), 317.

version is a *sine qua non* of doing theology up to the demands of our time. The issue, as with any real apprehension and assent, cannot simply be met by common sense strategies nor by the most coherent and comprehensive theories, though both of these are elements. The issue facing theology in our time is profoundly one with the task Robert Hutchins hoped Catholic universities would fulfill of restoring the intellectual tradition to the heart of higher education. Such an intellectual apostolate can cut no corners. We cannot ride cultural waves that do not measure up to the demands of intellectual conversion. Augustine, Aquinas, and the entire wisdom tradition teaches, from centuries of experience, that the deepening of intellectual conversion is "normally the fruit of both religious and moral conversion."[19] So attention to the intellectuality of both our moral and our religious transformations is integral to the task of making the intellectual tradition the heart of higher education.

Why are moral and religious conversions so integral to the intellectual tradition? Why is theology so important in the university's intellectual mission? Because we human beings cannot adequately understand the universe or our own nature and history if we ignore the moral, religious, and spiritual orientations of the universe and humanity.

Any realistic assessment of injustice and violence in human history will indicate a need to be open to the redemptive transformation of the kingdom of God revealed in the life, death, and resurrection of Jesus Christ. The openness of history posited by theologians who understand the fundamental importance of universal anamnestic solidarity with the victims of history insists upon redemption.

For faith in the eternal kingdom of God proclaimed by Christ is integral to keeping alive the thirst for justice. Victims of injustice can receive full justice within the limitations of neither life, as a biological span between birth and death, nor the limitations of a good life, as the life of excellent cognitive and moral self-constitution by human beings. For neither life nor the good life can raise the dead, bring back the murdered millions whose blood has drenched each page of history. No communities of life or the good life can resurrect the dead victims of the empires of violence, dominative power, and death. Only the eternal life present in the life, death, and resurrection of Jesus Christ can bring full justice to human life.[20]

The Enlightenment's rejection of theology has meant that the human sciences have studied men and women without the theological categories of sin and grace. Whatever evil humans do is then attributed to their natures. So violence and war and vice are taken as natural human attributes. And the good human beings do is likewise only attributed to them. Social policies and political regimes are built on such false premises, and so the violence,

---

[19] Ibid., 267-68.
[20] Matthew Lamb, "Christianity within the Political Dialectics of Community and Empire," in *Cities of Gods: Faith, Politics and Pluralism in Judaism, Christianity and Islam*, N. Biggar, J. Scott, W. Schweiker, eds. (New York: Greenwood, 1986), 73-100.

war, and evil are spread and compounded and intensified by all the modern means of communication and force. And, as the evils of injustice and violence spread, Pelagian admonitions are given to live virtuously and justly, usually to little avail.

Given sin and the massive injustices in human history, the importance of holiness and the theological virtues cannot be overestimated in the task of promoting a wisdom-oriented enlightenment. The fact that theology has disappeared from the cultural patrimony of our post-Enlightenment intellectual establishment has meant that empirical science is bereft of the wisdom it so desperately needs. For the empirical sciences are charting how human beings behave, how they act. They are ascribing that behavior—no matter how violent and sinful it is—to human nature behavioristically conceived. On the basis of such studies social policies are formulated, and so the violence and sin becomes structured into society and culture.

In such cycles of social and cultural decline the intellectually virtuous tend toward cynicism, while the morally virtuous tend toward stoicism. The intelligent quest for wisdom and science, as well as the moral quest for justice, cannot succumb to cynicism and indifference. Because as Catholics our kingdom is not of this world, we can dedicate ourselves to the creative and redemptive transformation of this world. Because through faith, hope and love we are in communion with the absolutely transcendent Triune God, we are members of one another in the historically immanent mediations of the missions of the Word and the Spirit to bring about the kingdom of God in our time and culture.

The intellectual dimensions of this place an enormous responsibility upon graduate theological education. Graduate students have to be thoroughly introduced to both the wisdom traditions of the first millennium of Christian education and to the scientific and scholarly traditions of the second millennium. Ideally, they would come with an undergraduate education that had begun the initiation into contemporary scientific and scholarly specializations. The masters level could then provide a broad and representative initiation into the wisdom traditions, while also further refining the scientific and scholarly specializations. Realistically, however, the students often lack the linguistic and philosophical skills required to begin a serious study of the primary sources in the wisdom tradition. Unfortunately, on the masters level the introductions tend to be too popular and reliant upon secondary literature.

Nor is this lack of linguistic and philosophical skills adequately addressed on the doctoral level. Too often the language requirements tend to be pro forma, and the student is not really proficient in, say, French or German, let alone Hebrew, Greek, and Latin. A survey of all the Ph.D.s in theology at Catholic universities completed over the past fifteen years indicates that 75 percent of them have been studies of twentieth-century figures or questions. If the nineteenth century is added, it will account for almost 90 percent of all the completed Ph.D.s. There is a dangerous lack of balance in terms of the expertise required to carry on the long Catholic intellectual tradition. The seriousness of this observation is strengthened when we observe that for the vast majority of Catholic theologians beginning to teach in seminaries and Catholic colleges and universities, given the scarce financial resources available for theological research, the longest period of sustained scholarly research in their entire lives will have been the years spent doing doctoral theses. To correct this situation will require a concerted and collaborative effort on the part of the theology departments and universities.

One would imagine that Catholic universities would be in the forefront of financing and promoting the scholarly appropriation of the many aspects of patristic, medieval, and Renaissance traditions of philosophical and theological wisdom and science. Unfortunately this is not the case. Nor is the situation going to ameliorate in the coming generation. When the majority of theology graduate students were religious and clerics, their religious communities provided a context and support for their learning as well as their moral and religious formations. Now that the majority of our students are lay people, they are often eager to acquire the linguistic and philosophical skills needed, but have to accept the fact that there is not the financial and academic support available. Hence we see the tendency to concentrate upon modern thinkers and questions.[21]

Without the linguistic and philosophical habits to learn from the primary texts, the students are not really equipped to be able to judge for themselves the adequacy of this or that translation, this or that recent interpretation. Without the intellectual, moral, and religious practices, and the virtues engendered by those practices, the students are not able to have a real apprehension and knowledge of the realities to which the texts are referring. Today we need Augustine's concern, expressed in the first three books of his *De doctrina Christiana*, for the appropriation of the theological virtues, along with the intellectual and moral, in order to discover and be in tune with the true realities revealed in Scripture and Christian teachings.

Otherwise our history will be left to historians who often know little theology. Insofar as historians are inculturated in contemporary secularist cultures, they will tend to make their histories intelligible to people living in contemporary secularist horizons. The process of critical history, of moving from historical experience to historical knowledge, should occur twice. As Lonergan has observed: "In the first instance one is coming to understand one's sources. In the second instance one is using one's understood sources intelligently to come to understand the object to which they are relevant."[22] The first phase of critical history is the very familiar one of identifying authors or historical agents, situating their actions and/or works in time and place, studying their historical contexts and sources. But then one should

---

[21] Walter Principe, "Catholic Theology and the Retrieval of Its Intellectual Tradition: Problems and Possibilities," *Proceedings of the Catholic Theological Society of America* 46 (June 1991): 75-94.

[22] *Method in Theology*, 189, 156-58, 161-62, 348-49.

move on to understand the objects, processes, events, and realities referred to in those critically established sources.

For example, take the works of an Augustine, Origen, Aquinas, or Teresa. A critical historian would set about establishing their very different historical, literary, cultural contexts, what sources they drew upon, what texts are more reliable, etc. This is fairly standard stuff in historical theology. One can read the results of such critical historical field work in the surveys and articles and books given to graduate students to introduce them to a subject. But can the critical historian make the move to the second phase or instance of critical history when what an Augustine, Origen, Aquinas, or Teresa are so obviously discussing is their friendship with the Triune God? What is moving forward in the historical communities of the faithful who down the ages continue to read and meditate upon these works in the contexts of their own deepening friendship with God? One cannot do justice to such a second phase of critical history without theology.

While a critical historian might not need to know faith, the spiritual life, or the mystery of the Trinity to do textual criticism, establish sources, compare one set of texts with another set of texts (after all, anyone who can read can begin to do that!), it is something else if he or she is going to engage in a history of faith, prayer, or theology as an *intellectus fidei*. If the critical historian has no knowledge of God, no familiarity with faith or prayer, then the critical historian is anything but "critical" in the full sense of that word. The so-called critical historian is in fact an ignorant historian when it comes to the realities discussed in the texts.

Then he or she is like a historian of mathematics who knows little about mathematics. Such a person might well be competent at comparing various mathematical texts, at dating and placing them more or less precisely, at working out certain social and/or cultural processes that were going on at the time the mathematical texts were being produced, at who used which text to get what advantage in this or that situation, how such a text was used in the production of weapons, what the weapons did, etc. Undoubtedly, such a history would be very readable for those who are not interested in knowing the history of mathematics so much as in knowing what else was going on when such and such a mathematics was being done. But no one would claim that such a history would merit the name of a genuinely critical history of mathematics.

How many genuinely critical histories of theology are being done now? No, theologians cannot leave our history to historians. The sad thing is that what passes for critical histories of religion and theology in modern secularist cultures are usually histories that are critical of (in the sense of negating) theology. They simply assume that what is really real is a secular horizon in which religion is at best a tribal prejudice or a private opinion, and at worst a neurotic delusion, or an ideology of oppression. In a secularist culture theology can become "public" only at the expense of negating its claim to be reflecting upon divine realities. So-called critical histories are histories ignorant of these realities which are transcendently immanent in human history.

Theologians must *know* the realities operative, the processes occurring, in morality, in religion, and in holiness.[23] If one is going to do a critical history of faith, prayer, or theology, one had best know something about the realities of faith, prayer, or theology. If critical history in theology is not advanced to this second phase, then theology as such ceases.[24] Instead we get what might be termed a comparative textology which only recognizes as real what is admissible into a secularist horizon. It is as if we had lost our knowledge of mathematics or science and were limited to doing empirical and literary comparisons of mathematical and scientific texts.

There is a need for us to concentrate upon building up serious historical theology that can go beyond the comparative textologies of the encyclopedists and the anachronistic projections of the genealogists. There are, moreover, doctrinal and systematic achievements of the past that are generally not acknowledged or appropriated sufficiently today. For example, there is a developing systematic account of eternity and time from Augustine, through Boethius, to Aquinas which not only requires intellectual conversion to be understood, but also is clearly and markedly different and more cogently intelligible than either what went before (e.g., the Platonists and Plotinus) or what has been developed in modern times. A meditative and wise listening to Augustine, on the one hand, and Plato or Plotinus, on the other, uncovers how the Eternal for Augustine creates and embraces time—an orientation the great philosophers did not comprehend. Another example would be the differentiation of systematic explanatory understandings of the sacred mysteries from the doctrinal affirmations of those same mysteries. Contemporary systematic theologians still have much to learn from an Aquinas or Bonaventure on the demands of intelligence questioning the inner intelligibility of the doctrines of the Christian faith.

Theology is not an infused habit, it has to be acquired. As with all our acquired virtues, the differentiations achieved in the past and present can too easily be lost and require relearning. Insofar as the Catholic Church has the longest intellectual tradition of any institution in the contemporary world, Catholic universities would fail in their mission if they did not cultivate those graduate programs which attend to such a rich and complex and long memory. Historical scholarship is the memory of the academic community; historical theology, with its research, interpretative, and historical-critical specializa-

[23] A central issue is how history requires judgment. From decadent Scholasticism on, there has been a tendency, carried over into modern post-Enlightenment cultures, to eclipse judgment into synthetic perceptions, ideas, or meanings, which require decision and power to be realized. Hence the equation of truth and knowledge with power as domination. On correctives to this, see Michael H. McCarthy, *The Crisis of Philosophy* (Albany: State University of New York Press, 1990). As Lonergan has indicated, we have to advert to the process of judgment correctly if we are going to resolve the issues raised by historical consciousness.

[24] On the development of modern secularism, see Michael J. Buckley, *At the Origins of Modern Atheism* (New Haven: Yale University Press, 1987) and James Turner, *Without God, Without Creed: The Origins of Unbelief in America* (Baltimore: John Hopkins University Press, 1985).

tions, needs to receive more attention in our graduate programs today. We need to recover, for ourselves and our students, the great intellectual traditions and achievements.

I would hope that by now it would be evident that such historical retrieval is not merely of archaic interest. The more daunting the challenges from the contemporary world of science and technology, the more daunting the innovations and new discoveries that are required to meet the demands of our age, the more we are going to need the wisdom and discernment provided by Catholic memory and traditions.

I have concentrated upon the importance of reversing the process in graduate theological education which leads to the overwhelming dominance of modern themes and figures, so that almost 90 percent of doctorates done in theology over the past decade and a half have concentrated upon these modern themes. There has been a definite *aggiornamento* in Catholic theology. What is needed now is that more attention be given to the *ressourcement* so that, two decades hence, there might be more Catholic theologians with degrees in those important resources for Catholic theology: patristic, monastic, and medieval philosophers and theologians. This, I have tried to show, is more than a merely historical task. It is a question of attuning the minds and hearts of Catholic theologians to the divine realities that would assure real, and not merely notional, apprehension and assent in theology. Past achievements of the Catholic theological tradition are important for those Catholic theologians engaged in contemporary theological issues. This applies also to those working in liberation theology, Afro-American theology, feminist theology, and environmental theology. The contemporary academy tends to distort these issues into either an encyclopedist praise of diversity or a genealogist quest for power.

Multiculturalism or encyclopedic diversity does not allow these theologies to challenge the lack of wholeness, and the pervasiveness of evil and violence, in post-Enlightenment cultures. The genealogists of power invite these theologians to instrumentalize the sufferings of the communities out of which they theologize, using such sufferings as trump cards in the struggles for power within the academy, the Church, and society. It is precisely these theologians who most need the wisdom orientations present in the great theological achievements of the past. For example, a great danger is to take class, race, sex, or environment in purely empirical terms defined by human senses. Contemporary sensate cultures promote this truncated empiricism. But then the categories of class, race, sex, and environment are not understood in an explanatory context. The roots of the alienation of racism, sexism, class, or environmental oppression are to be found in failures of intellectual and moral conversion. One judges someone only by skin pigmentation, sex, class status; the victims of this are then tempted to respond in like manner, so that they too judge only by skin color, sex, or class. All whites become supremacists, all males in authority become patriarchically biased, all wealthy become oppressors. This is not to go to the root of the alienation. The only way to understand race, sex, class, and nature properly is to transcend such sensate empiricism.

There is no way to heal the wounds of these alienations without the achievements of intellectual, moral, and religious conversion. Without this wisdom perspective, theologians are liable to follow the folly of Enlightenment intellectuals and reject this wisdom, ending up with impoverished encyclopedist or genealogist deformations. Instead of appropriating the healing wisdom in Catholic theological achievements of the past, these are not even recognized since the theologian is blinded by an ideologically distorted notion of race, sex, class, environment. So the violence and suffering increases as the missions of the Word and Spirit are ignored.[25]

Attention to the intellectual tradition of Catholicism would not be in any sense a withdrawal from the ecumenical orientation fostered by Vatican II. Quite the contrary. Those engaged in the ecumenical dialogues between the various Christian confessions identify a major need as educating the coming generation of theologians in their own traditions. Ecumenism has never thrived when the participants ignored their own traditions. The dialectical discernment in which each Christian confession has to engage in order to celebrate what is of the Word and Spirit in their tradition, and to repent of what is not of God, can only be done responsibly with a detailed knowledge of the tradition.

Conclusion

Theologically, just as the Triune God is more intimate to each individual than that individual is even to himself or herself, so also this incredible individual intimacy is universal. Each and every human being is loved by God. In God each instant of each human being's life is present. No human empires can redeem the sufferings, tears, and blood sinfully shed each day of human history. Only the eternal loving presence of God, as revealed in Jesus Christ and His proclamation of the kingdom of God, can redeem human suffering and heal human evil.

Catholic colleges and universities must discover the role of theology in an interdisciplinary collaboration with the natural and human sciences in the service of an architectonic wisdom—a wisdom that is open and integrative with all real advances in science and scholarship. Our graduate programs in theology need to be the matrix within which the reintegration of science and scholarship with wisdom will occur. If we are both faithful and creative, we may discover that the great intellectual tradition of which Hutchins spoke is,

---

[25] Gustavo Gutierrez spent many years of research on Bartolomé de Las Casas, thereby retrieving theological traditions important for a wisdom understanding of solidarity with the poor, see his *Las Casas* (Maryknoll, N.Y.: Orbis Books, 1993). The effort to appropriate the intellectual achievements of Catholic theologians of the past is fundamental to be able to understand and judge contemporary theologians. Our doctoral programs need to attend more directly to the doctrinal and systematic achievements of the patristic and medieval periods.

in fact, a vast and complex cathedral of the mind to which each generation of human beings is called to contribute—a cathedral of the mind far more enduring than those of stone, wherein we can cultivate attentive reverence for the goodness and holiness of every real question, of every act of correct understanding and discovery as ultimately a gift, a finite created participation in the wondrous, embracing the mystery of infinite understanding generating infinite wisdom spirating infinite love.

We need a cathedral of the mind in which each and every person's restless mind and heart feels at home, in which the real achievements of every age and every culture and every people will be celebrated. We need a cathedral of the mind in which we can repent of the blind stupidity that hangs like an ominous shadow over all of history, repressing unwanted insights into ourselves and oppressing countless minds and hearts by the blindness of racial, sexual, class, nationalist, and secularist biases.

Our minds are the very image of God in us, the God who enlightens every human being who ever has, is, and will come into this world. We are called to a cathedral of the mind wherein we can be forgiven by God and one another as we deepen our intellectual, moral, religious reorientation toward truth, goodness, holiness. We need such a cathedral of the mind in order to address the massive injustices of our times, not with mere moralisms that hurl invectives, but with intellectually sound alternatives that address the shortsighted stupidity which grounds the injustice. For justice to flourish practical wisdom is needed. To bind up the massive wounds of injustice requires both the compassion of the corporal works of mercy and the enlightenment of the spiritual works of mercy. All understanding involves a suffering, a *pati*, and when the lights of our minds are healed and intensified by the light of faith we can avoid the temptations to cynicism, skepticism, and despairing nihilism when, from all around us and deep within us, come the cries of the victims.

We need such a cathedral of the mind wherein we can experience how our own most intimately personal questions, insights, and orientations are intrinsically communal and interpersonal with both the concrete universality of the community of the entire human race and with the Three Persons who are more intimate to each of us than even we are to ourselves. On the eve of a new millennium the task of restoring the Catholic intellectual tradition to the heart of higher education might seem almost impossible, but the mission is as rock solid old and as refreshingly new as the gift and achievements of the mind itself enlightened by faith. We are not alone. The vast communion of saints and scholars beckons us into the Infinite Holiness, Intelligence, and Love who is blessed for ever and ever. Amen.

9

The Future of Graduate Education in Theology:
A Clear Sky with the Possibility of a Late Afternoon Thunderstorm

WILLIAM M. SHEA

Theology is doing quite well in the American Catholic university. Including the special case of The Catholic University of America, in thirty years we have built up nine theology facilities in the U.S. which grant a doctoral degree (Ph.D.). Those faculties employ over two hundred theologians and turn out over sixty new theologians a year.[1] The programs are filled with students and applications show no sign of dropping.[2] We publish at a decent pace—my colleagues at St. Louis University, a dozen doctoral teachers, put out nine books this year and ten professional and research journal articles, and the prognosis for the next two years is nine more books and more than two dozen journal articles. My faculty colleagues attend two professional conventions annually, and some of them attend a third. At these conventions there seem to be no lack of willing and able paper readers and general session speakers, and our several scholarly societies are flourishing.

---

[1] Programs are located at Boston College, Catholic University (two Ph.D. programs), Duquesne, Fordham, Loyola Chicago, Marquette, Notre Dame, and Saint Louis Universities. The following numbers have been culled from reports made to the annual gathering of chairpersons of theology doctoral departments, reports which are approximations and sometimes incomplete. Please view them with care and use them not at all! With Catholic University of America not reporting, the other doctoral faculty members number 243. In that number 56 percent are priests or religious; 44 percent are laity (including former priests and religious), 5.7 percent are Protestant clergy; 81 percent are male and 19 percent are female.

[2] See the caution in n. 1. Since 1990, 282 doctorates were granted. Fifty-seven percent of the graduates went into Catholic college and university teaching positions; 11 percent went into seminary teaching; 7 percent are pastors; 4 percent are in religious education programs; 3 percent are chaplains; 2 percent are in campus ministry; and 17 percent are "other." If one counts Protestants, then 70 percent go into the professorate. Over the next five years we will have put

In addition, when we step back from our day-to-day struggles and glance across the American educational scene, we can see that Catholic higher education, in its offering of a research doctorate in theology, is performing an irreplaceable service to American culture. As in the cases of Catholic hospitals and Catholic charities, Catholics in theology continue to display the broad cultural and social dedication characteristic of their tradition. In many respects American Catholic theology deserves a celebration of its past.

But there must be a dark lining to this silver cloud. The Marquette meeting was meant to pull out of us the problems which we may sense lying beneath the placid surface of contemporary Catholic theology and theological education. I will presume this is so in formulating this contribution which, rather than a paean of praise, is intended as an enumeration of problems. For the praise belongs to God alone; all we do on our own is sin.

I begin with a summary statement of the bad news. American Catholic theology has not, even in its own circle of Catholic graduate facilities, earned a special reputation for high academic quality, creativity, leadership, and any particular integrity. It may in fact measure up to its colleague disciplines in the humanities, but in few respects has it earned the special attention given it by administrations. It is only because of the unreviewed "fiction" that theology is decisive for the Catholic identity of our institutions that it had received a significant share of the meager resources of Catholic graduate schools. Theology departments are treading water, displaying many of the warts typical of the other academic departments in graduate schools and cannot be distinguished from or among them in terms of academic achievement. In the eyes of many it remains an academically "squishy" discipline in the humanities.

Theology, if it is to be properly judged, needs to be compared with America's humanities and social sciences research departments. We do not measure up in research to the best and even the better humanities and social sciences departments, and we do not come out ahead of or perhaps even with the Catholic graduate faculties in the humanities. My limited experience with national conferences of Catholic theologians, with conferences of intellectual and cultural historians and philosophers, and a decade working on a state

out 550 Ph.D.s since 1990 and 50 percent will go into Catholic higher education. We will need to have over 150 lines free for theologians in Catholic higher education in the U.S. Of the current 571 students in the doctoral programs, 66 percent are male and 34 percent female; 61 percent are Catholics and 39 percent Protestant. In our own historical theology doctoral program at St. Louis University we have thirty clergy/religious and forty-one lay students. To gather some data on areas of interest to doctoral students I correlated figures from four doctoral institutions for 1990-94: of 177 doctoral dissertation topics 82 were in historical theology, 78 were in systematic theology, and 15 were what appears from titles to be a mixture of the two. The important numbers seem to me to be the percentage of women, the percentage of Protestants, and the divided preference for systematic and historical topics. In our program in historical theology, in 1995-96, these percentages are: 64 percent male - 35 percent female; 42 percent clerical/religious - 57 percent lay; 50 percent Roman Catholic - 50 percent Protestant. The dissertations over the past fifteen years were written 45 percent in historical topics, 45 percent in systematic topics, and 8 percent mixed.

university campus leads me to think that we are a responsible enough group of academics, that we are reasonably well educated and articulate, that we are ethically committed to our work, but our scholarly output is modest and our reputation in academic circles is low. The overriding point of this essay, then, is that though the academic theologians can be proud of their past, they have but few academic laurels upon which to rest. In the academy, Catholic and otherwise, theology remains a marginal and ambiguous discipline.

Cold Front

We talk about the future of theology in a difficult stretch of time. First, the culture appears to be moving from the modern to a postmodern frame of reference at the very time when our ecclesiastical leaders decided that it was time we dealt with modernity. We now face a shift from the modern belief that the particular opens out on and finds its significance in the universal, that we can count on humanity being common, and that critical history provides us with the truth of our roots, to the belief that the universal is an illusion of a particular tradition, that there is no "human nature," and that we make up our history as we go, planting the seeds of a new historical narrative as the times change. To postmodernists the critical historical disciplines have become another form of folk storytelling and systematicians are caught in the countervailing forces of ideologies which render their every move suspect.[3]

My comfort is that we can find many outstanding American thinkers outside the field of theology who would counsel us to suspect the suspectors and to question whether postmodernism is a sharp turn in the road or a speed

---

[3] My own attempt to deal with one aspect of modernity, *The Naturalists and the Supernatural* (Macon, Ga.: Mercer University Press, 1984), is dated since its counterpoises archmodernist American naturalism and archThomist transcendental method, both of which are now commonly judged to be flawed and passé. A reading of Hans Küng and David Tracy, eds., *Paradigm Change in Theology: A Symposium for the Future* (New York: Crossroad, 1991), even if only the essays by the editors and the one by Matthew Lamb, will convince one of the extent and depth of the changes at work in theology, the numbers of methodological and ideological perspectives available to the theologian and the student of theology, and the difficulty of getting a unified grasp of the whole field. On suspecting the suspicious, see *Knowledge and Belief in America: The Enlightenment Traditions and Modern Religious Thought*, ed. William M. Shea and Peter A. Huff (New York: Cambridge University Press, 1995). The editors take the position that postmodernism is the skeptical Enlightenment born again to protest the naive and rationalist Enlightenment, a phase of the one intellectually and spiritually unstable break with all traditions which has now, ironically, become another tradition. Most of the contributors to the volume are critical of the position that the Enlightenment is over or that what is currently called postmodernist and post-Enlightenment thought represents anything particularly new or valuable. See especially the contributions of Jacob Neusner and Dennis Donoghue on the failures of the Enlightenment itself, and Richard Bernstein, Schubert Ogden, and David Tracy on the persistence and achievements of the Enlightenment. For comments on the reputation and performance of Catholics and theology from the point of view of national scholarship, see Michael J. Lacey, "The Conflicted Situation of American Higher Education and the Contribution of Catholics," *Current Issues in Catholic Higher Education* 16 (summer 1995): 16-25 and "The Backwardness of American Catholicism," *Proceedings of the Catholic Theological Society of America* 46 (1991): 1-15.

bump. While some see postmodernism as a profound development in Western thought, others regard it as another expected shift from a chastened but still rationalist phase of the Enlightenment (modernism) to reemergence of the Enlightenment's skeptical side, one more set in the dialectical unfolding of some basic mistakes of the Enlightenment itself. For more adequate categories perhaps we should distinguish with Lonergan between a First and Second Enlightenment, and anticipate an alternation between constructive and skeptical phases in each.[4] But, at any rate, the issue which postmodernism drops on our doorstep is the role of "theory" (i.e., postmodern criticism) in our doctoral programs. This remains on our agenda, largely unaddressed across our faculties, divided as they are by specialty and ideology.

The second movement of the time is the movement toward academic professionalization. Theology in my youth was a vocation riding on the back of the clerical vocation. Now, for some, theology is entirely a profession and not at all a vocation. For others it has become a profession and yet has remained a vocation. For some theology is still a religious/intellectual vocation, and the professional aspects are entirely secondary and epiphenomenal. These differences translate into serious disagreements among faculty over questions such as spiritual formation of theologians and the aims of undergraduate education.

Professionalization promotes academic standing by definition of the problems facing a discipline, imposition of common standards through professional associations, value placed upon field of specialization, and formalization and recognition of methods. In the case of philosophy, professionalization cut away all connection between the discipline and the problems of ordinary existence which the public philosophers of the American Golden Age thought they had to address, and confined the attention of philosophers to methods of logical analysis and to problems in the epistemological foundations of science.[5] Its influential practitioners, logical positivists, thought that their job was a scientific one—namely, to reflect upon scientific method and explain, in technical terms, how science works, and later, with the triumph of linguistic analysis, how ordinary language works.[6]

---

[4] See Bernard Lonergan, "Prolegomona to the Study of the Emerging Religious Consciousness of Our Time," *A Third Collection: Papers by Bernard J. F. Lonergan, S.J.*, ed. Frederick E. Crowe, S.J. (New York: Paulist Press, 1985), 55-99, esp. 63-65.

[5] See Bruce Kuklick, *The Rise of American Philosophy: Cambridge, Massachusetts, 1860-1930* (New Haven: Yale University Press, 1977), especially the section on the triumph of professionalism, 449-572. See also his tracing of the course of American theology and philosophy from Edwards through Dewey in *Churchmen and Philosophers* (New Haven: Yale University Press, 1985).

[6] Giovanna Borradori, *The American Philosopher: Conversations with Quine, Davidson, Putnam, Nozick, Danto, Rorty, Cavell, McIntyre, and Kuhn* (Chicago: University of Chicago Press, 1994) conveys a sharp sense of the restlessness of contemporary American philosophers with inherited formalism; John Patrick Diggins, *The Promise of Pragmatism: Modernism and the Crisis of Knowledge and Authority* (Chicago: University of Chicago Press, 1994) surveys critically the development of the American intellectual tradition in the nineteenth and twentieth century, revealing its struggle with method and hope.

The same process of professionalization with its trajectory toward the technical might engulf theology. Surely it is in full swing, and we treat it as an exigence of our work in research and training of students. The present strained ecclesiastical climate, the pull to more and more specialized research and publication, and absorption in methodological issues, could make withdrawal into technical and the avoidance of practical questions very attractive for many theologians. Professionalism has its perils (including replacing of loyalty from the educational locus to a suprainstitutional profession and the denial of the role of confessionalism in higher education), but the perils simply have to be met. Professionalization is irreversible as long as theology presents itself as an American academic discipline.

In the Church we see the third movement, from the Church as it existed before Vatican II to a Church still to be determined and in which considerable struggle goes on over alternative paths, each founded on a reading of the Council. On the surface it would seem that the pope will have the last word on directions. But still the Church, the most mysterious of entities at the best of times, now presents Catholic intellectuals with a spate of anomalies, tensions, conflicts, and more than apparent contradictions. Is the current state a passage, a cycle, a paradigm shift, a permanent state of conflict and confusion, or a brief nightmare brought on by acute historical and ideological indigestion? Are we now gradually pulling out of the tailspin of conciliar liberalism and leveling off or are we falling headlong into the grave of militant orthodoxy and doctrinal fundamentalism, a grave we left in the conciliar Pentecost? Or is there a "we" left? Has a set of Catholicisms in fact replaced the Tridentine Church? It all depends . . . . The point here is that disagreements on questions of Catholic identity are severe and deep, and as a consequence it is hard to answer questions of identity in Catholic higher education and theological education.[7]

The two processes, one from modernity to postmodernity, and the process called professionalization, create problems for theology and theological education. Both have arisen recently, and they are in our ken and are our disciplinary responsibilities. For these we have to answer, but the question about the Church will, I fear, not be answered by us in the main.[8]

---

[7] George M. Marsden, *The Soul of the American University: From Protestant Establishment to Established Non-Belief* (New York: Oxford University Press, 1994). See also the essays collected by Marsden and Bradley J. Longfield, *The Secularization of the Academy* (New York: Oxford University Press, 1992). Some press an analogy to Catholic higher education. See also Philip Gleason, *Contending With Modernity: Catholic Higher Education in the Twentieth Century* (New York: Oxford University Press, 1995).

[8] I have no indication that university theology, except for a theologian here or there who has earned the trust of bishops, will have any more effect on the decisions made by the Church leaders than will faculty members in English departments. The future of Catholic theological education will to a considerable extent be determined by two things over which theology has no control: (1) the negotiations between presidents and bishops over what will be called a Catholic institution and, within that context how much control bishops will have over university theology, and (2) the economic and social future of Catholic higher education.

Clouds

In the early twentieth century the long dominant evangelical theology lost its place in American culture as a whole, and now occupies no place at all in the modern research university.[9] Theology as a discipline is not taken seriously by the movers and shakers in the American university scene, and it has not been for a century. In this sense theology's position is far worse than that of philosophy. While it would be foolish of Catholics to worry about the standing of theology in the culture at large—genius, immense commitment, and special circumstances of the sort that led to the prominence of Reinhold Niebuhr can change that—we do have to worry about the place of theology in the academic culture and in graduate schools in particular. For us the issue is the intellectual respectability of theology in our own universities. In Catholic graduate education we face some critical internal difficulties:

(1) The academic level of our current faculties is at best competent even in financially favored departments, and surely not outstanding even within the limits of the Catholic graduate faculties. Outstanding faculty (as well as graduate students) continue to be attracted to non-Catholic universities and divinity schools for good and obvious reasons, chief among them that they maintain a reputation far beyond our own.

(2) The resources in Catholic institutions are limited and likely to stay so for some time to come. They have to be doled out carefully and I am not persuaded that theology should be at the head of the line. It certainly has not earned first place.

(3) The students who are attracted to work in our theology programs are at best competent even at the end of their training. In addition to the fact that our culture makes the practice of theology in the university as unlikely a prospect as it makes the celibate state, our students are not as generously supported by our institutions as they may be by others and they have limited prospects; they will not make a good living. In addition, they are often illtrained or undertrained for doctoral level work; they are without history, philosophy, and languages, and some are more intent upon theology as a ministerial service than as a life of scholarship. Moreover, many are headed for jobs in colleges in which they will teach four undergraduate courses a semester, introducing 160 students to religion and Christianity, and so find it a labor of Herculean proportions to publish even one decent research essay a year.

(4) Church leaders, who to a significant extent set the ethos within which

---

[9] This is not to say that there are no Evangelicals prominent in university research circles. See Mark Noll's *The Scandal of the Evangelical Mind* (Grand Rapids, Mich.: William B. Eerdmans, 1994). Evangelical thinkers and scholars such as Noll, George Marsden, Robert Wuthnow, and Nicholas Wolterstorff and several others are as prominent in the academy as David Tracy and Andrew Greeley. The problem is one for the profession/institution, and partial breakthroughs occur. See Van A. Harvey, "On the Intellectual Marginality of American Theology, " *Religion and Twentieth Century American Intellectual Life,* ed. Michael J. Lacey (New York: Woodrow Wilson International Center for Scholars and Cambridge University Press, 1989), 172-92. See also Michael J. Lacey, "Backwardness of American Catholicism."

we and many of our graduates must work, want cooperative theologians who know their ecclesiastical place and who do not behave in the public forum as the Western intellectual is wont to do, as a gadfly and a critic. The person who desires to be a serious scholar and also a public intellectual need not apply. Hans Küng, Andrew Greeley, and Charles Curran do not fit that patriarchal Roman style to which even U.S. Catholic theologians still give obeisance. Reinhold Niebuhr, for that very reason, would have been a disaster as a Catholic.

(5) The Church has a serious slump in religious and clerical vocations. The current younger generation of clerics and religious, male and female, have neither the leisure nor the inclination to take the life of scholarship seriously, and their superiors, especially their bishops, even when they might want to, are unable to let them live such a life.[10] Still, at this late date in the development of the American university, we Catholics do not get the point of a life of research, still we place nearly all the emphasis on teaching. As a result we have very little to say about the intellectual problems that preoccupy our academic colleagues.

(6) Ours is an isolated discipline in the college and university, caught by the demands of our own discipline and perhaps our own inclinations into conversations with ourselves about our own set of texts in our own turf cares. We love to see theology as the integrating discipline, but we do precious little integrating, not to say intercoursing.

(7) We are also rent by internal struggle over religious studies, regarded by some theologians as a different vocational, professional and bureaucratic entity from theology. Religious studies, in one view, lives by reason rather than faith, is anchored in the university rather than the Church, and strangles all commitment to religious practice.

(8) Finally, we all dance around mandate worries, hoping for a bureaucratic and political solution to that papal bomb beneath us.

In other words we have, and probably will have, at best competent theology pro-

---

[10] The Saint Louis University program has had no priest enter it since 1992. There are practical pressures upon bishops that prohibit them from supporting historical theologians or theological literary critics. It has not occurred to bishops yet to help educate theologians irrespective of clerical and religious status; as a result, lay persons, male and female, must assume that they are in business for themselves and not deemed to be pursuing an ecclesiastical vocation. These students get no help and no encouragement from the official spokesmen for the Church, and it is little wonder that their relationship to the Church may on occasion be less than ideal. So far as I know, no step has been taken by bishops or the Vatican to solicit the loyalty and professional talents of hundreds of Catholic theologians inside and outside Catholic universities. The irony here is that the Vatican has propelled the bishops into taking theological education seriously while it has confined that role to watchdog rather than patron. Among the Jesuits, and perhaps other religious communities who have the numbers to allow it, a high proportion of younger priests are sent to doctoral programs, including theology, but the numbers are small overall, given the large commitment the Jesuits have to institutions of higher education. In addition, some admit a hesitation to engage full time and for a lifetime in the academic enterprise. It is hard for them to see teaching as immediately related to the establishment of peace, faith, and justice, values predominant in current Jesuit self-understanding.

fessors in competent research faculties in competent graduate schools, attracting some-times competent students, but not much more.[11] We are not as a profession in as good shape as may appear, and one could easily understand why the best and the brightest might not want to join us.

Squalls

The foregoing is my perception of the difficulties in the world of Roman Catholic graduate theology in which my colleagues, students as well as faculty, now live. In what directions will (or must) theologians move in the near future? What are the questions and issues which press upon us?

One of the "Great Tasks" for Catholic theologians is to develop a clear and systematic answer to the question whether it is acceptable to be another kind of Christian or not a Christian at all and why. Flashy, celebratory, and pious ecumenism is all very well, but the theological bill for it has reached the table. The argument of the past decade over this matter seems to have terminated in a rejection by most Catholic theologians of the two extremes (christological exclusivism and relativism). In religious and theological politics, intersections of the religions will be at a higher order of occurrence. The relational question is unavoidable and no convincing theological answer is available. The official documents remain unclear. Yet we in our programs treat the question as settled: We hire Protestants and non-Christians (only a few) to teach in our programs and we make no formal distinctions between Catholic and non-Catholic students (40 to 50 percent is no token!), and we have not come to terms publicly and communally with either situation.

The inauguration of comparative theology is a start on this problem. Many have long realized that we cannot go on teaching Catholic theology in a religious and theological vacuum but, caught between the realization and our strong quarter of a century devotion to ecumenical attitudes, we have hesitated to face the fact that comparison is essential to our work. How can we apply comparison across the board without raising the question of adequacy and truth? How do we practice a comparative theology without compromising our ecumenism? Comparative theology gives us a good start but it doesn't supply the whole answer. Something in the order of Lonergan's dialectics will have to become a large part of our faculty practice and student experience. It is the best model we have for the practice of comparative theology.[12]

Second, problems are presented by "theory." Theory is a deliberate construction of knowledge and it is self-conscious criticism; it emerges when there is no consensus, when the classics are under fire, when things are in a quandary. Postmodernism emerges when the modernist world view or paradigm

---

[11] Would I want more? Yes. Some truly brilliant scholars and thinkers occasionally enjoying exceptional students from whom challenging and even publicly significant work might be hoped.

[12] Bernard Lonergan, *Method in Theology* (New York: Herder and Herder, 1972), 235-66. It is also published in the complete works from the University of Toronto Press.

breaks down. Before we take to postmodernism, with its "criticism" and "theory," to be the future, we have questions that should be asked about postmodernism itself and about its effects on theology. Is it a movement or a mood? Is it modernism turning on itself, or is it a radically new intellectual practice and attitude? Should theologians take it seriously? What can be salvaged from it? Can the hermeneutics of suspicion—the universal characteristic of theory—supply a constructive path for theology, or any other subject, and can the hermeneutics of reconstruction live after it? In the end, postmodernism seems in fact to be the widespread self-conception of the academy, and theology's immediate task as part of the academic culture is to at once absorb and transform it, as it has modernism.[13]

On the one hand, postmodernist theory may skew our efforts to understand the classics and our tradition (postmodernist suspicion could be poison rather than salt), and on the other it has already badly shaken that modernist confidence in the very reason and science which caused theology a century of lost self-confidence. Derrida and Rorty may not make a direct contribution to shaping our future, but they may have cleared away enough of the modernist self-satisfaction to make our work a bit easier (though it must be said that neither one shows any lack of Enlightenment self-confidence!). Above all, insofar as narrative is promoted we should be grateful, for Christianity and its theologians have a great narrative which no amount of effort on the part of theorists is going to replace or deeply condition. Our narrative makes sense historically, is morally transformative, retains its aesthetic appeal, promotes solidarity as none ever has, and it did not wait upon the suspicions of late twentieth-century theorists to undergo suspicion and thrive still. The Christian narrative will not wear out and will survive even the theorists.

Some think that all higher education, along with the theology, will have to work in theory; there will be no return to theological positivism. But theory must be developed within theology and not simply be imported from among the current range of postmodern theories. Theory should be understood as analysis of parameters and presuppositions of texts, contexts and interpretations, rather than an ideological critique of other ideologies, a narrow view which cannot support constructive scholarship.

Third, there is the question of Catholic identity. What ought to be the aims of our doctoral programs? Are we to produce Catholic theologians? We live with unresolved tension on this question. Doctoral-level theology and theology as a practice must be done in a world context and not be parochial. It must be specialized and rigorously theoretic, and yet in touch with the Church and with the culture. Faculty and students have to be involved in a set of conversations, across specializations in theology, across the divide between the university and the Church, across denominational lines and between traditions, across the bureaucratic lines in the university disciplines.

---

[13] David Tracy, *Plurality and Ambiguity: Hermeneutics, Religion, and Hope* (New York: Harper, 1987). See introductory essay of Shea and Haff in *Knowledge and Belief in America*.

Theology works a narrow slice of the academic field while proclaiming its unitive function. It is supposed to be decidedly Roman Catholic while it is openly and decidedly ecumenical and liberal.

The issue of the Catholic identity of the university is a university-wide problem and the solution is not theology, more theology, or better theology. The university will be Catholic as long as its administration and faculty and staff are largely Catholic in faith and practice. The energy which built the system is Catholic faith, and the drive to improve the system so evident over the past two decades stems from its Catholic convictions. Surely the system embraces a pluralism of religions and theological positions, but it does so as Catholic. The embrace is not eclecticism or liberalism (or conservatism!); it is *religious* and precisely *Catholic religious* when Catholic faith and practice provide the motive, the direction, and the aims of our research and teaching.

Protestant students tell me that they come to Catholic universities expecting an ecumenical theological education, but also expecting a strong Catholic identity, where the teachers teach from a religiously committed and explicit ecclesial stance. Perhaps the ecumenicity of the faculty is more a matter of attitude than of numbers, but the numbers display the attitude. No student I know wants the Catholic university to become a nondenominational university, but each hopes that in addition to a strong Catholic majority presence, there will also be a vital Protestant presence on the faculty. They expect that Protestant interests will be of interest to Catholic faculty members as well.

Judaism is vital to our theological and religious life. The intellectual, social, and political rupture with Judaism remains massive. The presence of Jewish experts on Judaism and Christianity is indispensable to our faculties of scriptural, historical, and systematic theology. "Never again" should Catholic theology present its next generation of theologians devoid of knowledge of and concern for Judaism and Jews. Never again should our Catholic theology be taught out of the hearing of these people. The threefold, dominant task of comparative and historical Catholic scholarship in the coming decades will be to develop an understanding of who these three are and how it is that they are God's: Judaism, non-Catholic Christianity, and the non-Christian religions.[14]

The overall aim of our programs should produce serious scholars. We should not compromise academic standards and program integrity for any reason. Research and publication practice must be built into the doctoral program itself and should not wait on the dissertation. A Ph.D. program is not a M.A. program with thirty more credits of the same, nor is it a Roman degree meant to prepare seminary professors who will teach but who will not become publishing scholars. The qualitative difference between B.A./M.A. and the Roman degrees on the one hand and the American doctoral degree on the other is embodied and exhibited in research and publication in the doctorate.

---

[14] See the essays in Francis W. Nichols, ed., *Christianity and the Stranger: Historical Essays* (Atlanta: Scholars Press, 1995), especially the introduction.

Catholic doctoral programs no longer aim mainly at producing competent undergraduate and seminary teachers. The primary aim is and should be to produce scholars. Students should be publishing before they complete their degrees. Students who are not interested primarily in research should be directed to theologates for their education.[15]

Lest this emphasis on research and publication be taken as a surrender to academic obscurantism brought on by a desire to imitate secularized American institutions of research, remember that we have tried alternate configurations of the Ph.D. and they do not work. The Ph.D. is not a license to reproduce the past, a teaching degree, or a gentleperson's finishing degree. It has been clear to American academics for one hundred years, and it is now agreed to by Catholic academic leaders, that the Ph.D. degree is a research degree. Now it should become clear that research as practiced must become collaborative. This is the heart of the educational future for theologians. The department seminar must imitate the annual professional meeting as an exchange between scholars all of whom, professor included in the case of the seminar, submit their work to criticism of colleagues.

Fourth, what of the theology-Church relationship? The university theologians' conflicts with Church authorities may get worse across the denominational band. Many students expect some tests of orthodoxy to be enforced. But this is taken stoically by them, as a tension that is permanent and endemic to the theological trade. They see it as an accompaniment of any attempt at reinterpretation. Church leadership should not be turned into an ogre by the theologians engaged in the tussle. We act as if we would be perfectly happy if "they" left us alone with our research and teaching. But they cannot and will not, for their stake in what we teach and publish is very large, and their every step in the area of doctrine and moral teaching is of concern to theologians. Both sides will have to work together when they can, and work through problems as quietly and professionally as possible. As the dream of American academic freedom, so, too, the dream of obedience of theologians to hierarchic control of teaching and publication: each is phantasmal. No one is going to get what he or she wants in this little tussal, but neither will lose its place or its mind (though I worry about theology's soul!). The issue will not be settled by deduction from orthodoxies, academic or ecclesiastical. The answer will emerge from the refiner's fire of experience and hard bargaining. In the case of Charles Curran (whose abandonment by his colleagues is a great blot on American Catholic theology's history and conscience), the bishops and the Vatican made it clear that theologians are not to contradict official

---

[15] With this we contradict the position taken over fifty years ago by George Bull, S.J.: "In sum, then, research cannot be the primary object of a Catholic graduate school because it is at war with the Catholic life of the mind ... The function of the Catholic graduate school is not specifically different from that of the Catholic college. The one differs from the other not in kind, but only in degree; in the degree of penetration into reality. (378-79)" George Bull, S.J., "Function of the Catholic Graduate School," *Thought* 13 (September 1938): 364-80, copy in my possession.

Church teaching; the theological societies and the university presidents have, in the face of *Ex corde Ecclesiae*, made it equally clear that Roman abstractions are going to have to bend to the actual conditions of American universities.[16] The opening positions are on the table, and we have a long and difficult time of discussion and argument before us.

Theology cannot function as an academic discipline alone. Religious practice and faith are both in some sense necessary. So a connection with the Church for both the university and the theologians is to be highly valued. Church sponsorship of the university is important. So also is Church use of and trust in academic theologians. In the future most theologians will come from the universities and reside there. Theologians may find themselves in the same ambiguous relation to the Church as intellectuals generally take up toward the culture. There is a word or two to be said about the value of such a relation, for the last thing the Church needs is what administrative and liturgical leaders seem to want theologians to be: an unexceptionably obedient and uncritical caste of catechists and consultants.[17]

An unpredictable contribution to this conversation will be made by the rising participation of laity. Lay theologians will make focusing on churchy issues more difficult. They are not likely to have the same interests and flashpoints as their clerical counterparts. They may more easily and rapidly develop the professional aspects of the discipline, with little admixture of the older, pervasive clerical corporatism. Theology has never in its history been professional—we face it for the first time. Lay people are often schooled outside seminaries, and have no "religious formation" and little of the general education in theology that seminaries afforded. They do not know and it is unlikely that they ever will know "the whole field" and they may not exhibit the fascination with ecclesiology that characterizes Roman Catholic clerics. In addition there is the related "collapse of the Catholic subculture"; the intellectual and spiritual implication of this for the next generation of Catholic theologians is far from clear.

Fifth, what are we to make of the submerged debate over religious studies and theology? It is difficult to know how to take this tension as it plays upon the relationship between the scholar and the Church and on graduate education in theology. If it means a scholarly interest in the religions of the world as well as Catholic Christianity, such an interest is a necessary mark of contemporary theological education and of higher education at large. Yet

[16] The lack of interest of American Catholic bishops in academic theologians is not a matter of the theologians' "liberalism," for they ignore conservative academics as well. See the comment by James Hitchcock in R. Scott Appleby and Mary Jo Weaver, *Being Right: Conservative Catholics in America* (Bloomington: Indiana University Press, 1995), 193.

[17] What it actually has, in this current and in the next generation of theologians is hard to make out. The story has it that on the three queues in heaven confronting the souls awaiting incarnation (brains, heart, backbone), theologians do quite well on the first two. If so, the bishops will get their good catechists but with bad consciences. Theologians may enact the famous silence of the American professorate on issues which pose danger (for example, in the case of Senator McCarthy) and the typical passivity of Catholics in the face of clerical authority (for instance, in the case of the attempted eradication of modernism).

some of our theology faculties have been rent by the tension between religious studies and theology. One way of approaching it is to say that religious studies is indirect discourse whereas theology becomes direct discourse, and this has very little to do with whether one has an academic expertise in religions. The theologians speak for and with and to the Church in the language of faith as well to the university, while the student of religions speaks *about* religions in the language of the academy only. Many of us already speak out of both sides of our mouth, and seem caught in the middle. In some faculties an ancient covenant seems to have been established allowing both to exist side by side. In others, periodic minor skirmishes and even wars are conducted.

Some few things seem clear on this issue: (a) the tension will not be resolved in the foreseeable future; (b) it would be very nice to have a "new paradigm" capable of embracing both sides of a single reflective enterprise; (c) the university itself is not equipped to solve it, and the Church has no business solving it; (d) unless it is carefully watched, it could mean the gradual elimination of direct discourse in theological research, writing, and instruction (a complete victory for professionalization) or a return to the ecclesiastical fideism and theological positivism which form so much of our heritage; (e) the tension may keep the theologians alert to the seriousness of methodological issues.

Finally, theology is theology and not religious studies, however important religious studies may be. Auburn Seminary in New York ran a colloquium in 1992 in order to bring together representatives of doctoral departments in theology and divinity schools to answer the questions why Catholic and other Christian schools hesitate to hire the graduates of the premier university departments and divinity schools (Harvard, Duke, Chicago, etc.) and why many moderate to conservative Protestants attend Catholic graduate schools rather than the premier universities. An answer was suggested by one of the Catholic participants in the concluding panel discussion: Catholic schools are still Christian and the others, including divinity schools, are not. So the Christian students come to places in which their faith will be respected and in which they can study the Christian tradition without intervening ideological prejudices.[18] Conceived this way, the issue is not so much religious studies versus theology, but rather whether research and reflection thrive easily in an atmosphere dominated by anti-Christian, anti-ecclesial ideologies (or,

[18] An excellent example of the pervasive anti-ecclesialism of a portion of the current academic population, see Robert Funk's introduction to his *The Five Gospels: The Search for the Authentic Words of Jesus* (New York: Macmillan, 1993). What theologian or exegete in full possession of their senses would send a graduate student to study with him? See the countervailing remark of Margaret Farley of Yale Divinity School and Religious Studies Department: "When I reflect on why Catholics have come to Yale to do doctoral work in religious studies, I draw the general conclusion that they came for the same reason other students do. That is, they are men and women who want to be scholars and teachers, and they perceive Yale as having a strong program in whatever specialty they have chosen. They also know that Yale has a faculty with which it is possible to study the Roman Catholic tradition (insofar as they wish) as well as other traditions of theology. They are drawn to religious studies (to theology or biblical studies or

the hermeneutics of suspicion).

Catholic and Protestants need to work in an ethos in which theology is conceived in faith, and not in ideological, anti-ecclesial "theory." A great deal of the future of Catholic university theology depends on the strengthening of that context for the study of Christianity, and we must continue our efforts to supply such an ethos while at the same time clarifying and strengthening our practice of a Catholic hermeneutic of that Christianity and strengthening our ties with the Church. As much as I think Rome's leadership is wrong-headed in conceiving theologians as catechists and casting the relationship in terms of authority and discipline, I have no doubt that our future lies in a solid and public relationship with the Church and with its leaders.

A full statement about the future of theological graduate education will need to deal with at least the following issues: the quality of our programs, students, and faculty compared with humanities units in American universities; the status of research specialization in student education and the extent and ambit of professionalization in the graduate theological faculties; the academic and political relations between theology and other university disciplines; the locus or social "home" of the theologians; the audiences to which we may speak; whether spiritual formation is any part of the responsibility of graduate faculties in theology; the steady rise in the numbers of lay men and women in current faculties and student bodies, and so the declericalization of current and future theology and of theological education; the ecumenical character of faculties, student bodies, programs, and theologies; the role of theory (=criticism) in graduate education and its relationship to religious practice; the historical emphasis in theological education; and graduate learning, teaching, and research as a collaborative enterprise. Some of these issues were raised here.

There are others not touched here: What is the subject matter of theology? Is there a canon for Catholic theology? Does one need to study under Catholics to be a Catholic theologian and to teach theology in Catholic institutions of higher education? Does one need to be a Catholic in order to be a Catholic theologian? Why do younger Catholics, and some say the best prospects, insist on attending non-Catholic graduate institutions? Does their attendance place a shadow on their Catholicity and, subsequently, on their attractiveness to Catholic colleges and universities as prospects for academic positions? Why is it that only 6 percent of our doctoral faculties are non-Catholic? (Forgive me if my figures are off here.) What role does Catholic practice and orthodoxy plan in our hiring, and why? What are all those Protestants doing in our student population [40 percent] and what are we doing for them? What about our Protestant students' theological future and what impact are they having on ours?

church history or ethics, etc.) to some extent because it is for them intellectually challenging and satisfying, but almost always also, I think, because of religious interests of varying kind and depth." See Henry J. Charles, "Roman Catholic Students and Graduates of Non-denominational University Related Divinity Schools," in *Partners in the Conversation: The Role of Ecumenical Divinity Schools in Catholic Education* (Yale Divinity School: Report of a Lilly Endowment, 1992).

10

Faculty Research and Catholic Identity

John C. Haughey, S.J.

As their institutions seek to become more distinguished and competitive in the world of higher education, faculty members are being increasingly pressed to produce quality research. This pressure is shaping the ethos of their colleges and universities as never before. But something more complicating is going on within Catholic and Jesuit institutions of higher learning, namely, the Catholic identity issue. I want to connect these two pressing matters in this essay because I despair of any resolution of the Catholic identity question unless it is connected with the faculty's perceptions of their research responsibilities and choices. These ideas about the research peculiar to faculty of Catholic colleges and universities do not presume to be descriptive of how faculty see their research at present, nor do they presume to have the force of the prescriptive behind them. They do not even presume that faculty members are Catholic. Rather, they are an envisioning of what is not yet. They look for a response to what might be.

The ideas herein contained are tied to several beliefs. First, a Catholic school is only as Catholic as its faculty think and teach catholically. (Needless to say this does not mean Roman Catholically, i.e., denominationally, but it does imply that faculty have some knowledge of, reverence for, and advertence to the story and tradition that has had their school come to be in the first place.) The second belief is that the faculty member's classroom effectiveness, in fact the quality of the education the school gives, will be in proportion to the depth and breadth of the faculty member's research. Third, the issue of Catholic identity will be endlessly vaporizing talk unless it gets down to the research choices of the faculty person and how these are rewarded by the institution. Fourth, although faculty spend much time inquiring into a limitless number of possible objects of their research, they spend little or no time on the spirituality that undergirds their research. This essay seeks to stimulate faculty reflection on their research choices. The fifth belief is that there is

145

virtually no Catholic college or university with a sufficiently compelling vision of what it is about to draw faculty attention beyond their own disciplines to choose their research topics in light of such a vision. This essay will have some suggestions about some of the ingredients of such a vision.

Should the research done by faculty in Catholic institutions have a different perspective, come from a different motivation, or inspiration, be done with a different finality in mind than research done in non-Catholic universities? I believe the faculty's operational answer is no while the institution's would be presumably yes. Should research in a Catholic university be evaluated by colleagues and the institution itself in the same way and with the same measures as research done in other universities? I believe the school's answer is that increasingly it is evaluated the same way but that it should not be.

The reaction of most faculty to these questions will be: "get real," or "let's face it" most research is chosen on the basis of what you can get funded for. They would contend that the state of the questions, the methods and developments within a given discipline should determine the research choices of a Catholic faculty member just as they determine the choices of faculty at other institutions. Further, they would contend that the mission of a Catholic university does not and should not affect the choices of its faculty with respect to their research. Since at all universities what is rewarded is research—to some extent, quality and more often, quantity—the fewer exogenous factors counted in, the better, faculty would be prone to insist. So, the idea of something like a university's understanding of its mission affecting a faculty member's research choices is financially, professionally and psychologically unreal, not to mention academically undesirable.

I reject these arguments, their spirit, and the understanding of research behind them and proceed here to supply some of the categories for what might develop into or be called a *spirituality of research*. These categories are submitted in the hopes that faculty will find them helpful in developing a clearer rationale for why they do what they do in their research.

(1) Call: Over the years I have been fascinated with how many faculty members I have spoken with informally who describe themselves as having undertaken their academic careers with the sense of having been called to do so. Opportunity beckoned, yes, but their deeper sense of themselves was not opportunistic. In the inventory of reflection prescribed here one would ask: What has explained my choice of discipline, my academic field of labor, from the beginning? Is it explained merely by my attraction to it, the right circumstances, and having the personal wherewithal to become credentialed in it? Or do I read my choice/attraction/ability in more vocational terms, like a call. If I have used this way of interpreting my choice of discipline, and maybe even my dissertation topic, would it not be consistent to see my ongoing research choices as needing to be a continuation of a unique call which was there from the start and had me choose the field in the first place?

If a faculty member's self-perception is one of operating out of a unique call, then his or her subsequent research choices and work will or, to some degree, should be original. These will not then be set by the pack. If this is true then conceivably one's research could be deemed "right" in the judgment of the discipline while "wrong" in light of the call, and vice versa. Further, the value of one's research will necessarily be measurable within the discipline but, by the same token, the discipline will not be able to take the measure of it.

(2) Interiority: There are rich categories in the thought of Bernard Lonergan that bear on our choices, in this case, research choices. These can come either from superficial or deeper layers of the self. The need for recognition or approval of those who can include me, advance me, or honor me is a strong one and certain to trivialize one's choice. Recall that Lonergan's four fonts of meaning are common sense, theory, transcendence, and interiority. Suffice it to say here that interiority is the font from which research is ideally chosen, and that any of the other three would give evidence of a lack of self-appropriation. While theory might appear to be the most promising font from which to choose and execute the research we do, it is interiority that takes all three fonts into account and radically internalizes them. Research chosen from the font of interiority takes seriously the measure of oneself, one's call, idiosyncracies, interests, talent, and experience. By contrast, theory is where the discipline in itself is at any given time. If theory *solo* dictates research choices one could be on the way to "gaining the whole world (of comprehension, inclusion, recognition, status) and suffering the loss" of oneself.

(3) The disciplines as sovereignties: Academic disciplines are "principalities," in the scriptural sense. They develop like little sovereignties internally constituted by their histories, findings, methods, conventions, giants, and particular boundaries. These cordon them off from the other disciplines. A discipline/principality cherishes its own autonomy, as it should. But for those scholars who ply their trade within it and whose horizon includes religious belief, it would have at best a penultimate autonomy. It certainly has an intramundane role and finality in and of itself but it also has, or should be open to, a transcendent finality which connects it to pursuing and attaining truth beyond itself, indeed beyond reason. Well-trained researchers who are also knowledgeable about their respective faiths would work in the light of a transcendent horizon. For Christians that horizon sees God as having subjected all things to Christ who, in turn, in the course of history is subjecting all things, their own principalities in particular, to God. Within this transcendent horizon one should be able to work less enmeshed in or limited by the foreshortened horizon of the principality. The *telos*, therefore, of one's discipline would be seen both in terms of itself and in light of the further horizon supplied by religious faith. One's self understanding, and the everyday particulars of teaching and research, will be affected accordingly.

(4) The common good: Faculty members, whatever their institutions of higher learning, inevitably must ask themselves what their research is for? Is it for itself? truth? career? tenure? recognition? institutional prestige? people?

societal change? simply to add to the store of human knowledge? Although the research need not be done to benefit people directly, it cannot, by the same token, be neighbor-numb. Research is an investment of personhood, time, and talent and can hardly be done blind to the inequities, the inequalities, the unevenness in the distribution of the good things of the earth, local and remote. Consequently, the issue of who is benefiting from one's research cannot be irrelevant and should become an object of explicit attention. If call (as suggested above) is part of the scholar's self-understanding, one would work for something larger than oneself, and one's discipline.

In this connection one could examine the category of pure research. There is undoubtedly justification for pure research, i.e., research that is simply concerned to know. But "pure" research can also be irresponsible, and claims about its purity used as a cover for not examining one's motivations more closely. Careerism, self-interest, and individualism take many forms in the academy but under the righteous rubric of pure research the actual motivations of one's research (e.g., like simply wanting to add to the store of human knowledge) can more easily go unexamined, undetected, and unsuspected.

(5) Stewards of the goods of information: Academics have a luxury enjoyed by few, namely, access to a trove of data that is increasingly astonishing, at least in its quantity. A steward in the raw biblical sense of the term is aware that the goods he or she has been commissioned to manage are not merely for their own interests, purposes, and uses. These goods were meant to benefit many, not the few. This slant on the meaning of steward again speaks to the issue of the beneficiaries of one's research. For whom are we doing it? Not unlike the more primal goods of the earth the goods of information are to be used for the sake of the many.

Since a research project is an effort to bring order to the goods of information out of the chaos in which we found them, a partial answer to the question of who is benefiting from them would be whether the medium one chooses to communicate one's findings is the best one for those who would most benefit from them. Academe's social responsibility is to more than one another; it is for the community who most need the information it masters.

(6) Discernment: Sorting out one's research choices presumes sensitivity to one's interior movements of attraction and disaffection. Research chosen and pursued on the basis of, or at least in the light of, these movements will be more discerningly chosen. These affective movements are best examined by stepping back from the drawing power of the subject matter to see what the attraction is to or, conversely, what the disaffection or indifference is to. Our motivations are complex and knowing their stripe or what is moving us is essential to developing a maturity about research choices by keeping a healthy distance from the internal draw of the field not to mention the politics of the place one plies one's trade. Discernment can assist both initial research choices and all the major choices called for in the execution of the project.

Taking stock of the effects of our research on our immediate relationships is one of the better ways of discerning it. What is it doing to one's relationship with self, spouse, family, neighbor, God? What advantage is it if it is contributing to disorder within these? It must be judged accordingly if I am advancing in my field while weakening or losing the relational base which has enabled me to come to this point of productivity.

Discernment is ever alert to the actual or foreseeable "fruits" of doing the research. There are affective signs that accompany one who is operating from one's call and signs when one is not. These are called the fruits of the Spirit in Paul's epistles. These signs or fruits are joy, peace, patience, mildness, patient endurance, etc. In general, I would say intellectual consolation and a growth in being membered to others, including those who will benefit most from the research, are two positive signs that the choice and manner of execution are well weighed. Conversely, the fruits of operating from an ethos that is self-generated (Paul's "flesh") are dissonance, agitation, ennui, blaming, complaining, division . . . in a word, dismembering (Gal. 5:19ff).

Developing and Awarding a Compelling Vision

What has been elaborated thus far needs another dimension, a second move, a further specificity, since so far it would appear that the faculty member is the only one on whom the onus rests for insuring the distinctiveness of the Catholic institution of higher learning. If simply left at that, this would be unfair. The best way of attracting faculty to act in the light of a horizon that includes but transcends their own interests and field of study is for the institution to develop a sufficiently specific vision of what it means to be Catholic so that faculty can identify with this and align themselves and their research to it. No mission statements that I know of draw or lure faculty to think and act in a horizon of Catholic identity. Rather, the generic, nice, pusillanimous pieties of such statements faculty easily live with but they evoke nothing other than the vaguest of assents or, more often, ennui.

Who or how a compelling vision will be articulated is difficult to say but two things about it I am sure. The first is it will not come from a committee. The second is the institution will have to act its way into the new way of thinking since it is most unlikely it will think its way into a new way of acting. The compelling vision is more likely to emerge if action is taken on the several things faculty and administration are likely to agree on from inventories and reflections done by faculty about their research which above I have called a spirituality of research. So rather than waiting for such visions to hatch, I will elaborate five of the characteristics that I anticipate could emerge from faculty reflection and from the simple logic of a Catholic institution of higher learning.

A good reason for spelling out these characteristics here is that research grants and research leaves could be awarded if faculty give evidence of wrestling with the horizon these characteristics hold out. As faculty choose their research subjects, it would seem right if their grants and leaves favored those who concern themselves with and can make a case for the relationship of their research to the institutional self-understanding and mission of the Catholic institution. These five are submitted in the spirit of a challenge to faculty to act their way into a new way of thinking rather than as strict criteria for qualifying for leaves or as a way of constraining faculty in the topics they choose.

(1) Before it means anything else, something has a Catholic characteristic if it lends itself to unity, to integration. In its root meaning, *Kata oλos* connotes "according to" or toward wholeness. If there is a native dynamism in the intellect toward the unitary and toward ultimacy, members of a university professing to be Catholic should not be content to leave their particular research's connection to these dynamisms unexamined or merely implicit. A faculty member should attempt to show how his or her research project assists in moving students toward a greater integration of understanding. Showing how one's partial contribution relates to the whole is probably more difficult as one gets to the hard sciences, of course, but faculty members of all departments including the hard sciences should not be without a sense of how their particular discipline relates to the overall educational mission. This criterion forces an articulation of how a discipline and one's research in it connects to the whole.

(2) Catholic universities exist because of the presumption that "nothing human is alien to the Church" and that knowledge which comes in discrete pieces ought to be part of a body of knowledge which, in turn, should be open to being seen in the light of revelation. Since most disciplines do not employ faith data directly in their research or methods, a dialogue between faith and reason should be part of what scholars at Catholic institutions are open to undertaking with their colleagues for the sake of the completeness of their own scholarship. Hence the question: What in your research might be a subject for further inquiry and dialogue with faith beyond what your research will focus on?

(3) "The cause of the human person will only be served if knowledge is joined to conscience."[1] First of all, how is your research serving the cause of the human person? And beyond this, are you taking into account the ethical implications of your discipline's methods and discoveries? Is your own research addressing these? One's research will seldom address these issues but by the same token the implications of what one is doing cannot be ignored.

(4) Does the subject matter you treat deal with the issues that the Church's tradition has addressed? If so, would it be appropriate to advert to this position? Would it be appropriate for you to take a position on its position?

(5) "The struggle against injustice and the pursuit of truth cannot be separated nor can one work for one independently of the other" (Fr. Ignacio Ellacuria, S.J.). How is the research you are proposing to do connected to the struggle against injustice? Has the inspiration to pursue it come from your own perceptions of social injustice or from relationships with poor people or those marginal to the privileges of higher education? Would there be any

[1] *Ex corde Ecclesiae* (Washington, D.C.: USCC, 1990), 18.

advantage to this population from your research?

Presumably most of us faculty would strike out on this last category because it presumes a consciousness of a preferential option for the poor that has not been a high priority in the academy. The preferential option for the poor has an uncertain future in theology and is finding a slow acceptance in Church circles. Further, it is probably the last thing on the minds of administrators as they seek to survive in the competitive world of higher learning. I believe the main reason there has been no compelling vision coming from Catholic institutions of higher learning is because this fifth category is the least explored. At best we mouth pieties about forming people "for others" or about educating for service while keeping the poor at a distance from us. But if the faith that is being promoted in Catholic schools is a faith that does justice to students it would seem justice is not being done to students by educational theories, programs, and institutions that believe they will think their way into acting differently than we who train them. Rather, they and we must act our way into new ways of thinking, acting with, learning from, and being more one with the portions of society that are, ironically, both needier and more learned in the very things about which we, the more privileged, need to learn. Can a person be catholically educated if he or she does not know existentially, experientially, that blessedness, indeed the kingdom of heaven, can be where the poor are?

So what is being envisioned here is a pincer's movement, a two-pronged strategy, one half of it moved by the faculty, the other by the institution itself. In the one pincer, faculty research (presumably no less competent than that done by colleagues in other institutions) would be done from a different horizon than their counterparts in non-Catholic institutions. The other pincer would come from the institution itself which came to a deeper comprehension of its connection with the poor and the Church and articulated this in a vision that faculty could identify with.

This thesis, this strategy, does not believe that the future of Catholicism in their colleges and universities is necessarily contingent on hiring or tenuring Catholics. It is contingent on faculty seeing what the institution stands for, if it stands for something along the lines mapped out here, and opting in or out of it on the basis of this compelling vision.

V

SEMINARY PROGRAMS

11

Theological Education in Seminaries

Msgr. Robert J. Wister

Introduction

The beginning of theological education in seminaries may be found in the Council of Trent's (1563) decree *Cum adolescentium aetas* which prescribed that seminaries for aspirants to the priesthood be established. This decree ordained that admission was restricted to young men who were "at least twelve years of age, were born of lawful wedlock, who know how to read and write competently, and whose character and inclination justify the hope that they will dedicate themselves forever to the ecclesiastical ministry." There they are to "study grammar, singing, ecclesiastical computation, and other useful arts; (they) shall be instructed in Sacred Scripture, ecclesiastical books, the homilies of the saints, the manner of administering the sacraments, . . . and the rites and ceremonies."[1]

In the United States the Third Plenary Council of Baltimore (1884) gave much attention to seminaries and their programs. The decrees outlined the levels of seminaries, their programs, conditions for admission and sources of support. There was concern for the intellectual and cultural preparation of clergy and a program of two years of philosophy and four years of theology was established as the norm.[2] Archbishop John Ireland of St. Paul opposed a proposal to require music, as Trent had wished, insisting that no amount of urging would drive men to sing.

Until comparatively recently Catholic theological education in the United States was almost exclusively within the domain of the seminaries. In the 1930s and 1940s seminary professors were major contributors to the founding of learned societies such as the Catholic Biblical Association, the American Catholic Historical Association, and the Catholic Theological Society of

---

[1]Henry J. Schroeder, ed., *Canons and Decrees of the Council of Trent* (St. Louis: Herder, 1941), 446-50.

[2]*Acta et decreta Concilii Plenarii Baltimorensis tertii. A.D. MDCCCLXXXIV* (Baltimore: John Murphy, 1886), 154-81, especially 167.

America. They formed the backbone of the membership that sustained and enhanced these associations for many decades.

If, a half century ago, a conference on "Theological Education in the Catholic Tradition" had been convened, it would have drawn an audience of seminary professors, with few exceptions. A presentation on "Theological Education in the Seminaries" would have practically exhausted the topic. Exactly fifty years ago, ninety-seven of the 104 founding members of the Catholic Theological Society of America were seminary professors.[3] In 1947 a woman and a seminarian bravely attempted to join the CTSA but were met with immediate rejection.[4] Currently, 19 percent of the CTSA membership is drawn from seminary faculties, an indicator of the smaller but still significant role seminaries play in theological education today.[5]

Thirty years ago, at the close of the Second Vatican Council, seminaries reached the peak of their enrollment and were riding high on the enthusiasm generated by the Council and the continuing growth of the Church in the United States. For some the seminary of the time was "a system no one questioned. A great amount of certitude prevailed. As in *Candide*, it was the best of all possible worlds."[6] There were 169 theologates enrolling 8,916 students. However, more than two-thirds of these institutions had fewer than fifty students.[7] This triumphal catalogue was not welcomed by all. John Tracy Ellis lamented that "the dismal procession of small and weak seminaries continued to appear in every part of the land."[8]

Throughout the 1950s and 1960s the self-critique of the seminaries focused on their physical and intellectual isolation and called for more involvement in pastoral training and greater efforts to achieve academic excellence.[9] They had begun to emerge from the period of the modernist crisis and the decree *Sacrorum Antistitum* (1910) which had applied the restrictions of *Lamentabili* (1907) and *Pascendi* (1907) to seminary formation. American and

[3] "The Charter Members of the Catholic Theological Society of America," *Proceedings of the Foundation Meeting*, The Catholic Theological Society of America (June 25, 26, 1946): 61-65.

[4] *Proceedings of the Catholic Theological Society of America*, 2 (1947): 12.

[5] *1992 Directory of the Catholic Theological Society of America*. The total active membership is 1,347, of whom 139 are associated with freestanding seminaries, ninety-five with theological unions and clusters, twenty-eight with university-related seminaries. The total seminary membership is 262 or 19 percent. The analysis of the *Directory* is by the author.

[6] Robert J. Wister, "The Effects of Institutional Change on the Office of Rector and President in the Catholic Theological Seminaries - 1965 to 1994," *Theological Education* 32, Supplement I (autumn 1995): 52.

[7] The statistics for seminaries in the academic year 1965-66 are drawn from "Catholic Seminaries in the United States - A Statistical Study and Directory prepared by the Seminary Department of the National Catholic Educational Association," *Seminary Newsletter* 7 (March 1966).

[8] John Tracy Ellis, "The Formation of the American Priest: An Historical Perspective," *The Catholic Priest in the United States: Historical Investigations* (Collegeville, Minn.: St. John's University Press, 1971), 79-80.

[9] See James Michael Lee and Louis J. Putz, *Seminary Education in a Time of Change*, (Notre Dame, Ind.: Fides, 1965); Stafford Poole, *Seminary in Crisis* (New York: Herder and Herder, 1966); and Joseph M. White, *The Diocesan Seminary in the United States - A History from the 1780's to the Present* (Notre Dame, Ind.: University of Notre Dame Press, 1989), 366-404.

European periodical literature was openly available; libraries were being developed with the assistance of the CTSA, aided by a grant from Cardinal Francis Spellman;[10] discussions, often rather heated, regarding academic excellence and theological methodology were taking place at the conventions of the National Catholic Educational Association and the CTSA.[11] The agenda of seminary reform was well under way; the 1960s and 1970s would bring about an official reform under the direction of the pastoral authority of the Church.

The Second Vatican Council called for a renewal of seminary studies in its *Decree on Priestly Training, Optatum totius.*[12] In 1969 the Congregation for Catholic Education published the *Basic Plan for Priestly Formation,* the *Ratio Fundamentalis.* The *Basic Plan* provided that each episcopal conference prepare a program of priestly formation attuned to the particular pastoral needs and times of the region. The *Program of Priestly Formation,* first approved in 1971, presents "principles according to which seminaries at every level should be conducted."[13] A single document governing the programs of both religious and diocesan seminaries was a new phenomenon. The impact of the *Program* was most strongly felt in the diocesan seminaries. However, since the religious accepted it, reserving their rights and privileges, it also effected them. Its most recent edition with revisions influenced by *Pastores Dabo Vobis,* Pope John Paul II's apostolic exhortation on priestly formation, was promulgated in 1993. While the *Program* is normative, it allows for the diversity in organization and programs that has always characterized American seminaries.

Institutional Realignment

Before the close of the Second Vatican Council, the religious seminaries had begun a process of consolidation that would give birth to the unions and various cooperative enterprises. "To a large extent the changes introduced between about 1966 and 1970 were a result of self-determination on the part of the orders and congregations, and were not imposed or proposed in any specific fashion by ecclesiastical agencies outside them."[14] Religious seminaries that "relocated generally did so in order to achieve proximity to a university, and sought some degree of formal relationship with it."[15]

[10]*Proceedings of the Catholic Theological Society of America* 6 (1951), 31.

[11]Edmond D. Benard, John Courtney Murray, and Eugene M. Burke, "The Thesis Form as an Instrument of Theological Instruction," (Panel Discussion), *Proceedings of the Catholic Theological Society of America* 11 (1956): 218-36. See also White, *The Diocesan Seminary,* 404.

[12]This document and other official documents relating to priestly training can be found in *Norms for Priestly Formation* (Washington, D.C.: USCC, 1994).

[13]*Program of Priestly Formation* (Washington, D.C.: NCCB, 1971), xii.

[14]John O'Malley, "The Houses of Study of Religious Orders and Congregations: A Historical Sketch," in Katarina Schuth, *Reason for the Hope: The Futures of Roman Catholic Theologates* (Wilmington, Del.: Michael Glazier, 1989), 29-45.

[15]O'Malley, "The Houses of Study," 40.

The Catholic Theological Union at Chicago, associated with the Chicago Cluster of Theological Schools and located near the University of Chicago, was established in 1968. In Washington, a similar institution was born in 1969 with the founding of the Washington Theological Coalition, now the Washington Theological Union. In California, the Franciscan, Dominican, and Jesuit theologates associated with the Graduate Theological Union at the University of California at Berkeley. Today, these schools together with the Weston Jesuit School of Theology enroll almost half of the religious order seminarians in the United States.[16]

Although the bishops officially encouraged consolidation,[17] their own seminaries would not follow this path. The few serious attempts to promote the consolidation of diocesan seminaries came to naught.[18] Although consolidation of diocesan seminaries did not occur, several formerly freestanding diocesan seminaries affiliated with Catholic universities. Today, diocesan seminarians study at thirty-four seminaries, freestanding and university-related.[19]

While the *Program of Priestly Formation* provides norms, it does not guarantee uniformity, even in structure. A seminary may be called a school of theology or a theologate, a house of studies or a divinity school, or even a department of theology. It may be "freestanding" in distinction to "university-related," religious rather than diocesan, not to mention something as simple as small, medium, or large. The range of seminarian enrollment runs from twelve to 164. It may be a regional seminary with a dual program in Spanish and English. Or it may be a religious order's school of theology in a federation with Protestant divinity schools and a public university. It may even be a diocesan seminary with fifty students in a rural setting.[20]

The Theological Program

"In accord with its ecclesial mission, the theologate also functions within the context of American higher education as a center of theological scholarship at the graduate level."[21] Theological education in seminaries is quite similar to but distinct from theological education in other settings. "Seminary theology" is not a separate species of theology with its own methodologies and subject matter. All theologies, I believe, irrespective of their publics, whether they are the academy, the Church, or society, are equally *fides quaerens*

---

[16]*CARA Seminary Directory 1995-1996* (Washington, D.C.: CARA - Center for Applied Research in the Apostolate, 1995), xvi-xvii.

[17]*Program* (1971), 248.

[18]*Memorandum of New York State Seminary Planning Board*, March 1972; *Memorandum*, Rev. William Coyle (Bishops' Committee for Priestly Formation) to the Advisory Committee on the New York State Seminary amalgamation Study, Washington, March 21, 1972, in Files, Seminary Department, National Catholic Educational Association, Washington, D.C.

[19]*CARA Seminary Directory 1995-1996*, xiv-xv. This number includes the North American College in Rome, the American College in Louvain and the Seminario Mayor in Puerto Rico.

[20]George Schner, "Pedagogy in the Theologate," *Seminaries in Dialogue* 22 (fall 1990): 29.

[21]*Program of Priestly Formation* (Washington, D.C.: USCC, 1993), 251.

intellectum, an ecclesial task to be performed with intellectual rigor, logical consistency, and critical mind.[22]

Seminary education must maintain a high level of excellence especially since "the higher level of education on the part of Catholics requires more than ever a thorough theological education on the part of the priest."[23] Pope John Paul II urges seminaries "to oppose firmly the tendency to play down the seriousness of studies and the commitment to them."[24] One measuring rod of this commitment is the membership in the CTSA of 262 seminary faculty. This represents about one-third of the faculty roster, theologians and non-theologians alike.[25]

What distinguishes seminary theologians from their university colleagues? It is not pastoral concern versus scholarship; it is not *obsequium* to the magisterium versus academic freedom; it is not *theologia cordis* versus *theologia mentis;* it is not christocentric focus versus theocentric focus; it is not emphasis on the good (*bonum*) versus emphasis on the true (*verum*). Any Catholic theology worthy of its name includes both sets of characteristics.

What sets seminary theologians apart from their colleagues is the immediate focus of their work, namely, the training of candidates for the priesthood. While a seminary may have a large number of lay students, its central purpose remains the preparation of priests who will "proclaim, expound, and guard the faith persuasively for the welfare of the faithful."[26] This focus shapes both the approach and content of the courses they teach, but it should modify neither their understanding of the nature of theology nor their theological method.

Contrary to the university where faith cannot be presumed and where diversity of faiths is the norm, in the seminary the unity of faith is already present, at least in inchoate form. In the seminary, "theological learning takes place within the life of faith," and "is essentially incomplete without a personal appropriation by seminarians."[27]

Furthermore, seminary education is structurally so organized that the three dimensions of priestly training, spiritual, intellectual, and pastoral, are intimately intertwined.[28] This goal of integration has not necessarily been achieved in all seminaries or at least to a satisfactory degree. But it is safe to say that serious attempts have been made and are being made to achieve integration.

The bishops' *Program* describes the curriculum as "comprehensive" and "extensive," including Scripture, dogmatic and moral theology, liturgy, Church

---

[22]This analysis is based on Peter Phan, "The Seminary Theologian in Service to a Multicultural Society," *Seminary News* 32 (fall 1993): 31-43.

[23]*Program* (1993), 338.

[24]*Pastores Dabo Vobis* (Washington, D.C.: USCC, 1992) 56; 152.

[25]*CARA Seminary Directory 1995-1996,* xxii-xxiii, and *1992 Directory of the Catholic Theological Society of America,* analysis of author. CARA reports 736 full-time faculty. Recent research by Katarina Schuth shows 881. One-third remains a fair percentage.

[26]*Program* (1993), 333.

[27]Ibid., 347.

[28]Ibid., 249.

history, patristics, spirituality, ecumenism, homiletics, canon law, and pastoral theology.[29] Because its fundamental goal is the training of pastors, this theological education must include the social teaching of the Church and be presented in such a way that it imparts an ecumenical and interfaith perspective.[30]

Just as there is a diversity of structure among the seminaries, there is a diversity of theological methodologies. While the academic program "should witness to the unity of the faith—according to tradition and the magisterium," it must also witness "its authentic diversity of theological expressions."[31]

Steven Bevans has offered five models of theological methodology or "contextual theology,"[32] which may be applied to seminaries. The first, the "translation" model, is the most conservative. It stresses fidelity to the Christian message. It presumes that all cultures possess the same basic structure and that divine revelation is primarily a communication of truths in propositional form. At the opposite end of the spectrum is the "anthropological" model. It emphasizes identification with culture and change. It views divine revelation not as a body of supracultural truths but as a process of God's self-manifestation taking place in each and every culture. The third, the "praxis" model, stresses social and cultural transformation in the light of the gospel message rather than fidelity to Christian identity or identification with local culture. The fourth, the "synthetic" model, combines the insights of the first three models; it recognizes the role of culture in the formulation of the Christian message and the necessity of fostering social transformation in light of the Christian message. It also stresses the need to maintain fidelity to the Christian tradition. The last, the "transcendental" model, starts from the *subject* doing theology. The theologian is one who is converted—intellectually, morally, and religiously—that is, a self-transcending subject. Though the emphasis is on the individual's personal conversion, the subject is not regarded as an isolated person but as a member of a community.

In seminary education one finds these models or various combinations of them. Seminaries of a more conservative bent obviously tend to favor the translation model. Its faculty are urged to expound accurately and defend the Christian faith, especially the teachings of the magisterium. More liberal and inculturation-minded seminaries, especially those designed to serve minority groups, would often tend to adopt the anthropological or the praxis model or some variant thereof. In all, the transcendental model is influential, emphasizing conversion and personal appropriation of one's traditions and Christian faith. In the words of the bishops' *Program*, "with such appropriation, as faith and knowledge penetrate interior understanding, intellectual conversion should follow."[33]

[29]Ibid., 340, 341.
[30]Ibid., 343, 345, 346.
[31]Ibid., 339.
[32]Steven Bevans, *Models of Contextual Theology* (Maryknoll, N.Y.: Orbis, 1992). This summary is adapted from Peter Phan, "The Seminary Theologian."
[33]*Program* (1993), 347.

The Faculty

The diversity of the schools and the theological methodologies employed in the seminaries are mirrored in their faculties. The faculty of a seminary traditionally had been drawn from the priests of the sponsoring diocese or religious order. Today about two out of three seminary faculty members are priests, one out of five is a woman, lay or religious, one out of ten is a layman.[34] This does not demonstrate all of the diversity. The ordained members of a faculty are often a mixture of religious and priests from a variety of dioceses.

Another sign of faculty diversity is educational background. In the past the ecclesiastical degree was almost exclusively the credential for seminary faculty. An indication of this is predominance of ecclesiastical degrees in the 1963 *Directory* of the CTSA. In that year more than 85 percent of the membership, chiefly seminary professors, listed an ecclesiastical degree as their terminal degree.[35] Today, in seminaries as elsewhere, the doctorate in philosophy, from Catholic and non-Catholic universities, is more and more common, although in most seminaries, it is not predominant.

At the same time as the faculties became more diverse, they became more "professional." Accreditation by regional associations and the Association of Theological Schools of the United States and Canada spurred those seminaries that were seeking academic excellence to adopt more of the procedures and criteria that characterize American higher education. This is not an unmixed blessing, bringing with it the inevitable bureaucracy of higher education.

Faculty roles are often, although not always, mixed. Their main task is teaching and research. As members of the theological community they have a responsibility to remain theologically vital by participating in the life of the academy of theologians. Since the seminarians will be relating to that academy through the theologians' writings, the professors' acquaintance with developments in the field of theology is essential. In many seminaries, particularly diocesan seminaries, faculty also participate in other aspects of the priestly formation program, serving as mentors, spiritual directors, and evaluators of readiness for ordination. Rising expectations in academic teaching and the increasing complexity of spiritual formation make this less workable and less common.

The growing diversity of the faculty has stimulated numerous questions. The proportion of priests on a faculty, the intersection of academic and spiritual formation roles, financial and professional support for faculty are but a

---

[34]*CARA Seminary Directory 1995-1996*, xxii-xxiii. Several years ago Eugene Hemrick and Robert Wister in *The Recruitment and Retention of Faculty in Roman Catholic Theological Seminaries* (Washington, D.C.: NCEA, 1992), 25, showed the proportion of priests as three out of four.

[35]*1963 Directory of the Catholic Theological Society of America*. Five hundred eighty of 679 members submitting resumes listed ecclesiastical degrees as their terminal degree. Analysis by author.

few. Some view diversity with alarm as damaging to a proper understanding of the priesthood and priestly training. Others view this diversity as a proper expression of a collaborative approach to ministry in ministerial training.[36]

The Students

The most obvious issue regarding students is their number. Since 1965 enrollment figures for seminarians in theological studies have dropped more than 60 percent.[37] Yet enrollment is neither the only student-related issue nor for many observers the most significant. The general academic and personal background of contemporary seminarians is increasingly far removed from what was considered the traditional background of candidates for the priesthood. Some students now come with little or no personal experience of Catholic culture or with only a very limited education in the Catholic faith. I venture to add that this phenomenon is not unique to the seminaries but presents them with very specific challenges.

Philosophy

Thirty years ago the majority of candidates who applied to theologates had attended a college seminary or had participated in a two-year philosophical program attached to a theologate. They had thereby experienced structured spiritual formation together with an academic program that emphasized the humanities, especially philosophical studies. As the years passed, more and more candidates applied with weak backgrounds in philosophy.[38]

Their readiness for traditional theological studies was further complicated by changes in the American educational system which moved further and further away from classical educational models. The popular understanding and appreciation of the study of the humanities had all but disintegrated. The teaching of theology did not draw as intensely on or relate as clearly to classical languages, philosophy, or the humanities. These shifts made it more difficult for the student to deal with the abstract nature of philosophical studies themselves and, in the opinion of many, had undermined the understanding of the relationship between philosophy and Catholic theology.[39] To assure a proper philosophical foundation for the study of theology, the 1993 *Program* raised the entrance requirement from eighteen to twenty-four credits in philosophy and specified the areas to be covered.[40]

---

[36]Hemrick and Wister, *Recruitment and Retention*, 55-59.

[37]*CARA Seminary Directory 1994*, v; "Catholic Seminaries in the United States," iii.

[38]See Eugene Hemrick and Robert Wister, *Readiness for Theological Studies: A Study of Faculty Perceptions on the Readiness of Seminarians* (Washington, D.C.: NCEA, 1993).

[39]David Denz, "Philosophy and Teaching Methodologies," *Seminary News (Special Edition: Report on Pre-Theology)* 31 (May 1993): 21-26.

[40]*Program* (1993), 170, 171, 515.

Religious Studies

Over the years the seminaries noticed that many of the applicants presented courses under the rubric of "religious studies," which clearly did not indicate a breadth or depth of knowledge of the Christian tradition. The fragility of religious education in the 1970s and 1980s, combined with a rather generalist and professedly neutral approach in many university departments of religious studies, resulted in applicants whose knowledge of Catholic traditions was much weaker than that expected of those about to begin graduate theological studies. A rector once lamented that an applicant had listed six credits in "Vedantic Studies 1 and 2" as fulfillment of the required studies in Catholic traditions.[41] To provide adequate basic knowledge of Catholic faith and traditions, the 1993 *Program* replaced the entrance requirement of twelve credits in "religious studies" with twelve credits in specified areas of "undergraduate theology."[42]

Culture

The power and diversity of American culture increasingly overshadowed every aspect of the seminary program. The character, the "qualities," the life experience of seminary students has changed and continues to change.

Generally, students had been well known in their parishes and had an active faith life, usually nurtured by supportive family structures. Most would have had a solid Catholic educational background. No small number would have been fortified with strong ethnic traditions that valued religious faith as part and parcel of their heritage. Today, the fragility of family life, the relativism of social mores and the mobility of American society effect seminary students as much as any of their contemporaries.

Seminary enrollment today draws from many cultural traditions. St. John's Seminary in Camarillo, California has a student body which is less than half Anglo and more than one-third Latino with the remainder of the students Vietnamese, Filipino, Korean, and Pacific Islander.[43] Last year at Seton Hall, where more than a third of the seminarians are noncitizens, my class of thirty-five seminarians studying American Christianity included eighteen students who had in recent years emigrated from Italy, Spain, Poland, Slovakia, Romania, Vietnam, The People's Republic of China, Mexico, the Philippines, Brazil, and Bangladesh.

The 1993 edition of the bishops' *Program* notes that "Because candidates for the priesthood are increasingly diverse in age, cultural background, religious heritage and personal experience, they often need additional prepara-

---

[41]Wister, "The Effects of Institutional Change on the Office of Rector and President," 137.
[42]*Program* (1993), 171, 235, 515.
[43]*CARA Seminary Directory 1995-1996*, xviii-xxi.

tion before beginning theological studies."[44] The bishops now require a one- or two-year "pre-theology" program to address "human and spiritual growth, intellectual and pastoral formation, and community living."[45]

The structure of the seminary has been altered, not simply by the promulgation of the 1993 *Program*, but by the changes of the past three decades. The program of priestly formation is now, for most seminarians, a five- or six-year program: one or two years of pre-theological studies and four years of theological studies. For some, it could conceivably be a seven-year program if they, as many do, engage in a year of pastoral activity away from the seminary between the second and third years of theological training. In a way the seminaries have returned to the six-year program of philosophical and theological studies of 1965 and earlier. However, there are major differences. The philosophical studies do not mesh as neatly with previous college studies nor with theological studies as they once did. Spiritual formation does not build as easily upon fragile personal backgrounds often devoid of a deep understanding of Catholic life and culture.

Lay Students

Diversity among the seminaries is also evident in their approach to programs for lay students. A number believe that, given the variety of ministries in parish and other pastoral settings, it is better to train a future priest in the context of wider ministries. Some institutions, particularly the unions, take great responsibility for educating lay women and men. They have simply opened registration for all qualified applicants. Most seminaries have established degree and nondegree programs for lay women and men. Freestanding seminaries either adopt an open registration policy or maintain a careful distinction between priestly formation and the preparation of lay ministers, operating separate and distinct degree programs.

As the number of seminarians continues to decline, the question arises whether the specificity of priestly training is being maintained. The 1993 *Program* emphasizes that "the mission of the theologate is the proximate preparation of candidates for the priesthood."[46] It recognizes that "many seminaries and study centers prepare not only candidates for the priesthood but also assist in the preparation for other ministries in the Church."[47] It warns that "If such programs are offered, the seminary must maintain the integrity and specialized nature of the program of priestly formation for both religious and diocesan candidates."[48]

With this caution in mind, seminaries, often encouraged by bishops, continue to offer a variety of such programs.

[44]*Program* (1993), 209.
[45]Ibid., 210.
[46]Ibid., 249.
[47]Ibid., 253.
[48]Ibid.

Challenges

The Seminaries

The declining number of candidates for the priesthood should, in the near future, impel small freestanding seminaries to enter into a serious discussion regarding their viability. At present, eleven[49] freestanding seminaries, some of which participate in "clusters," have fewer than fifty students. Whether the necessary "critical mass" for quality education exists in such small institutions is debatable. Whether or not there is a sufficient community for spiritual formation is also questionable. Declining numbers inevitably impact on morale when fifty or fewer seminarians live in a building erected for 200.

Declining enrollment exacerbates financial problems. Like most private educational institutions, seminaries face financial challenges. Precious few have a significant endowment. In fact, few have any endowment at all. Perhaps the time has come for diocesan seminaries to follow the example of religious orders and consolidate existing institutions. In a recent study,[50] a significant number of bishops agree, but the mechanism for initiating such action would be very cumbersome, and so far no serious action has taken place.

This should not be surprising. The maintenance of a seminary is a source of pride for a diocese. Quite often it is a center for the training of deacons, lay ministers, catechists, and others. Its faculty are often consulted by the bishop regarding theological questions. A diocese is hesitant to allow such a resource to disappear. At the very least, the seminaries should engage in serious planning for the future lest their future be determined for them by demographic changes and financial concerns.

Theological Programs

The maintenance of quality academic programs is ensured by accreditation and the seminaries have been described by Cardinal Baum as "generally satisfactory ... the majority are serving the Church well."[51] However, the Cardinal expressed concern regarding "a few cases of dissent from the Magisterium in the teaching of moral theology."[52] The rector of a diocesan seminary once told the story that he had asked three priests to pursue graduate studies in moral theology. All declined. One remarked, "Are you trying to get me into trouble?"[53]

[49]*CARA Seminary Directory 1995-1996*, xiv-xvii. This number includes the Seminario Mayor in Puerto Rico and the American College in Louvain. Currently, the Catholic University of America, thirty-three diocesan seminarians and fourteen religious order seminarians enrolled.

[50]Hemrick and Wister, *Recruitment and Retention*, 27.

[51]*Letter of Cardinal Baum to American Bishops on Visitation of Theologates*, September 14, 1986, *Origins* 16 (October 16, 1986): 315.

[52]Ibid., 315.

[53]Wister, "The Effects of Institutional Change on the Office of Rector and President," 129.

Tensions within the Church and between theologians and the pastoral authorities are felt in the seminaries. The seminaries' ecclesial and academic mission to educate the future pastors of the Church requires that the teaching of the ecclesiastical magisterium be presented faithfully and in its entirety. This does not mean that contrary theological opinions be avoided but that they be presented as such. The focus of the seminary on training public ministers of the Church necessarily affects its understanding of academic freedom but cannot lessen its commitment to clarity of expectations and due process. To maintain their ecclesial and academic integrity seminaries must honestly address these questions. The resultant discussion could assist in the further clarification of the role of theologians in the Church.

Faculty

The bishops' *Program* expresses the hope that "priest faculty members should teach significant portions of the course of studies in the major theological disciplines."[54] However, it does not specify any percentages. As much as seminaries seek to hire priests for their faculties, they continue to find it to be difficult, almost impossible to recruit a sufficient number of suitable priest professors. "The pool of priests who have advanced degrees in the sacred sciences is shrinking. No reversal of that trend is in sight. Uncomfortable alternatives loom: either the priest faculty is maintained with lower professional credentials, or the advanced degree becomes the determining factor, realizing that the presence of priests teaching in seminaries will dwindle accordingly."[55]

Seminaries are taking the second path, considering professional competence paramount, with an inevitable decline in the number of ordained faculty. In the last ten years the number of priests on seminary faculties declined almost 10 percent.[56] Almost all have been replaced by lay men and women. Of 142 seminary faculty searches over a two-year period, more than half did not require that applicants be ordained.[57] It is no longer unusual to see advertisements for seminary professors in *Openings*.

Keeping qualified priest faculty is as difficult as hiring them. For a variety of reasons, some priests find the university more attractive and leave seminary teaching for posts in colleges and universities. Others leave for pastorates. A commitment to assist graduate studies for qualified priests and a commitment to support faculty should be a first priority for the pastoral leadership if seminaries wish to maintain the "significant percentage" of priest faculty to which the *Program* alludes.

---

[54]*Program* (1993), 487.
[55]Howard Bleichner, "2001: A Seminary Odyssey," *Seminary News* 30, no. 2 (December 1991): 25.
[56]Katarina Schuth. Unpublished research provided to the author.
[57]Hemrick and Wister, *Recruitment and Retention*, 61.

Students

The continuing change in the qualities and background of students requires seminaries to adapt their programs and their teaching methodologies
to new generations whose skills and learning styles are quite different. In a
recent study, faculty cited "motivating students to read . . . responding to the
diversity of cultures . . . dealing with the students' lack of awareness of history and the Catholic tradition" as major challenges. They reported a major
difficulty to be "dealing with rigid, closed, defensive, theologically
fundamentalistic students who are convinced of their correctness."[58] These
challenges, together with the influence of secular culture and the variety of
cultures in the classroom, are not exclusively within the province or ability of
the seminary or even of the Church to correct. They simply reflect contemporary society. The intensity of these challenges will, in all probability, increase
as the years pass.

The Integration of the Program

The seminaries themselves, their theological programs, the faculties, the
students are each an aspect of the challenges which today's seminary must
address. The most important challenge is an integrated and effective program. The relationship among the spiritual, academic, and pastoral components of the program, although continually addressed, is the most difficult to
work out. It arises from a lack of resolution of the tension between *orthodoxis*
and *orthopraxis*. It continues and sharpens the discussion of questions theologians have been asking themselves for decades. How should theology be
taught? How can and ought it relate to the concrete situation of the students?
How much should be geared to formation for mission in the world? What
should be its starting point—lived experience, the tradition of the gospel? On
the practical level, do students find theology "usable" in their lives, pastoral
and spiritual? Have they the skills to translate it for their purposes? Do
students actually function in several worlds with distinct theologies, one for
teaching, one for spiritual direction, one for pastoral application? "Connections are not always made. At the worst there can be three parallel formation
programs with formation through academic courses being the least integrated
into the overall program, though contemporary theories of formation see integration as their primary goal . . . There are a host of questions which deserve to be addressed. Any Roman Catholic seminary could only benefit by
attempting to address them."[59]

---

[58]"Summary of Issues and Options in the Seminary Classroom," *Seminary Journal* (Special
Edition: Teaching a New Generation: Issues and Options in the Seminary Classroom) 1 (spring
1995): 9.

Reflection

As the seminaries, their programs, their faculties, their students, move toward the third millennium, they face these considerable challenges. Rooted in tradition, living in the present and looking to the future, their theological vitality and their very well-being will, in the short and the long term, impact on the spiritual lives of the many people their graduates will serve. Their response to these challenges will be determined by the fidelity and the stamina of the seminary leadership and professorate, on the backing and encouragement of the pastoral leadership of the Church, on the assistance of their colleagues in the theological academy, on the spiritual and material support of the Catholic people they serve, and on the help of Almighty God.

[59]Michael Putney, "Viability of Ministerial Formation: A Roman Catholic Response," *Ministerial Formation* (World Council of Churches) 66 (July 1994): 9-10.

12

Theological Faculty and Programs in Seminaries

KATARINA SCHUTH, O.S.F.

T he faculty of every school has a profound effect on the nature of the school and on the shape of its programs. In Roman Catholic seminaries,[1] the impact of the theological faculty is intensified because of the multiple roles they play in these institutions, providing not only academic instruction, but also human, spiritual, and pastoral formation. The context in which they do their work, the programs they have developed, and the students they teach all contribute to the quality of the Church's ministry. As seminary settings become more complex, faculty need to respond creatively to students who vary widely in age, academic background and ability, and ministerial direction. Being able to imagine how the Church can serve the people of God is essential to the work of seminary faculty, who carry major responsibility for generating the vision for the future.

Therefore, this essay provides background on the context in which faculty do their work—the types of institutions and the programs in them—and then focuses on the faculty themselves—who they are and how they view their work. Besides profiling the faculty, the essay analyzes the results of an extensive survey that measures overall faculty satisfaction and morale, their views of their institutions and leadership, working conditions, and opinions about teaching, students, and diversity. Comparisons between men and women faculty and between older and younger faculty are also made.

The Diverse Context: Varieties of Seminaries and Students

Structural Models. To understand the role and views of faculty more fully, we must recognize the wide diversity among the forty-five Roman Catho-

---

[1] In this essay, Roman Catholic seminaries include all institutions that enroll students who are studying theology in preparation for priesthood, and which may also enroll other students studying for a variety of ministries but who are not candidates for ordination. A more precise term for these schools would be "theologates," to distinguish them from high school and college seminaries, but since "seminary" is commonly used, it is employed here.

lic seminaries themselves. Several structural models are represented, including a majority that are freestanding institutions (twenty-five), others that are university-related (ten),[2] and a third group that combine their resources in several collaborative efforts (ten) (see Chart A).[3] By most standards, the enrollments are small, with at least ten schools enrolling fewer than seventy-five students, most enrolling around one hundred students, and only five or six having over two hundred students, including those who are part time. During the past ten years, five seminaries have closed and one has replaced another in the same state. Three have shifted from religious order to diocesan sponsorship, which means that more than half (twenty-four) are now diocesan-sponsored. Between 1985 and 1995, the enrollment of seminarians dropped from 4,058 to 3,292, including in 1995 some 511 in pre-theology, compared with 166 ten years ago. In effect, the number of seminarians enrolled in theology was 3,892 in 1985 and is 2,781 in 1995, a drop of over 1,000. The enrollment of lay students is not so well documented, but estimates put the numbers at about 2,200 in 1985 and about 2,700 in 1995.

During the past twenty-five years, the missions of more than three-fourths of these schools expanded from serving exclusively ordination candidates enrolled in a single program to serving a diverse student body enrolled in a variety of programs. Even more significant are evolving ecclesiological differences. Some schools have shifted to a model that is more representative and inclusive, operating with shared authority and a diverse student body, while others retain a more pre-Vatican II understanding of seminary, Church, and leadership. The attitudes and beliefs of faculty often reflect the dominant ecclesiology of each school, and consequently the ideological orientation of the courses and programs. The way faculty exercise their roles, therefore, varies considerably from one school to the other.

Student Profile. The results of several extensive surveys about seminarians are readily available.[4] Compared with about twenty years ago, students in all seminaries are on average about five years older. Also compared to twenty years ago, today's seminarians are more deeply affected by the secular values of our society, and they often lack a fundamental understanding of their faith. Contributing to changes in the backgrounds of seminarians is the present social fabric of this country, for example, greater mobility and the consequent lack of rootedness, emphasis on material goals and individualistic achievement, delayed vocational commitment, and the privatization of

[2] Three of these schools are located outside the United States, but are places where American seminarians study. They are The North American College in Rome, The American College at Louvain, and Centro de Estudios Dominicos in Puerto Rico.

[3] See Appendix at end of this chapter.

[4] For example, Ellis L. Larsen and James M. Shopshire published their findings about all North American seminarians, both Roman Catholic and Protestant, in "A Profile of Contemporary Seminarians," *Theological Education* 24 (spring 1988): 10-136. Eugene F. Hemrick and Dean R. Hoge surveyed Roman Catholic seminarians and published their findings in *Seminarians in Theology: A National Profile* (Washington, D.C.: United States Catholic Conference, 1986). Other NCEA studies have looked at views of seminarians and the newly ordained.

religion.   Theological education in seminaries is affected by these cultural trends, and faculty are searching for ways to respond to the changed circumstances.

Assessments of the quality of today's students vary from cautiously positive to negative. Many faculty assert that present-day students are as mature, intelligent, and well-intentioned as students have ever been. They describe them as stable, responsible, and highly motivated, as well as hardworking and sincere. A significant minority of seminary faculty, however, disagrees and has a decidedly low level of confidence in many students. These faculty also note a lack of academic and pastoral zeal, commenting that more students seem passive, dependent, and less able to deal with ambiguity than before. Few students, they assert, have a lived sense of the pre-Vatican II Church, a factor that may contribute to what is characterized as "neoconservatism" and a longing to return to a Church they have never known. Further, compared with twenty years ago, surveys show that fewer seminarians have studied at Catholic institutions at any level; thus, they may lack fundamental knowledge about their faith. Faculty are looking for ways to compensate for the composite Catholic culture that was previously learned and experienced through dogma, doctrine, ritual, and practice. They find that they need to adjust both the content and methodology of their courses to meet the needs of students, while at the same time challenging students to move beyond the stereotypes of their time and culture.

Lay students enrolled in theology share many of the traits of their seminarian counterparts, especially in their lack of knowledge of the faith, but they often exhibit fewer conservative tendencies. This difference can become a source of tension when the student body is mixed. Many faculty find the growth of both groups is enhanced by confronting these different understandings in the classroom setting. Faculty are becoming more cognizant of the views on issues that will touch future ministry held by students in their classes, both liberal and conservative, and they are actively addressing them.

Comprehensive information about the academic status of students in theology was lacking until recently. But in 1987, *An Academic Profile of Catholic Seminaries*, by Bernard Rosinski, S.C.J., was published, providing base data that will prove invaluable for future comparisons. Rosinski's findings reveal that 95 percent of students in seminaries are college graduates with a average grade point of 3.11 (B). The consensus of faculty is that the overall academic quality of students preparing for ordination is somewhat lower than previously, but they also point out that within a student body the range of talent is wide. Faculty portray the change in academic ability as "the top being cut off," meaning that the quality of most students remains about the same but the top 5 to 10 percent of the students of ten years ago is missing from the profile. Yet a significant minority believes that students have changed little over the past twenty years.

What are the implications of these various judgments about students? The societal and family context from which students come, their age and level of maturity, and their previous educational and religious backgrounds all affect their approach to theological education and to future ministry. Faculty need to be prepared to respond to a great diversity of students, since they are increasingly heterogeneous—by culture, age, family complexity, and academic and personal-relational competence. Multifaceted programs that offer these dissimilar students individual attention and some measure of stability are accomplishing an important mission.

Theological Education Programs: Formation for Ministry

Especially during the last decade, the faculties of seminaries have modified program and degree requirements to respond to the changing dynamics of parishes and the developing international mission of the Church. A greater number of lay ministers are serving side by side with priests, requiring transformation of established patterns of ministry. The international character of the Church is brought home by the realization that Western Europeans and North Americans are no longer dominant in number or influence, even in the United States. Parishes, once nearly homogeneous in race and class, are now highly diverse. All of these changes pose new challenges in preparing men and women for ministry that recognizes these shifts.

The Master of Divinity (M.Div.) continues as the basic professional degree in seminaries, but in the 1980s when lay students began enrolling in significant numbers, other masters-level degrees were added, for example, M.A.s in Theology, Religion, and Pastoral Studies, and Masters in Religious Education. All but one or two seminaries have several of these programs designed to respond to students of diverse backgrounds, ages, and ministerial aspirations. Since the M.Div. is representative, with other programs incorporating aspects of this program to a greater or lesser extent, what follows is a description of the M.Div.

Four separate but interrelated aspects of theological education—academic, human, spiritual, and pastoral—typically constitute programs designed for those who are preparing for ministry.[5] For the academic program, core courses include Scripture (on average eighteen semester hours are required), systematic theology (twenty-seven hours), moral theology or ethics (eleven hours), Church history (nine hours), pastoral studies (twenty-four hours), and electives (eight hours). In addition, credit is usually given for field education, averaging twelve semester hours.

Compared with the recent past, schools now require more pastoral and moral theology credits, reflecting changes in what congregations are expecting of their priests and lay ministers. In the 1990s, more attention is also being given to preparation for serving in multicultural congregations, already the typical parish type in many dioceses. For seminarians, the 1993 *Program*

[5] *The Program of Priestly Formation*, 4th ed. (Washington, D.C.: United States Catholic Conference, 1993), outlines the basic requirements for ministerial formation for priesthood.

of Priestly Formation emphasized anew the need for instruction about the meaning of priesthood, and many schools have added a course on this topic. These changes have reduced the already small number of elective credits to even fewer.

The question of precisely *what* should be taught is much debated. Faculty must consider both the kind of ministry priests will be called upon to exercise in the future and the role of professional lay ministers. Some believe that priests will continue to have heavy administrative duties, while others maintain that theirs will be an almost entirely sacramental ministry. All need to be prepared to engage in collaborative ministry, given the reduced number of priests projected for the near future. In addition to a general pastoral orientation of the curriculum, a number of special courses in pastoral studies dealing with canon law, homiletics, religious education, and pastoral leadership and counseling are part of theological education. Increased demands in parishes for professionally prepared priests and lay ministers, including the ability to preach and teach, to lead groups, and to counsel individuals, have given impetus to more emphasis on pastoral concerns.

How important and central a pastoral emphasis should be in the curriculum is an area of strong disagreement. A significant minority of faculty perceives that greater demands for spiritual and pastoral training since Vatican II have eroded the academic program. These faculty believe that the essential task of theological education is to prepare seminarians intellectually and not to train them in ministerial skills. These skills, they believe, can be learned on the job or during an internship. Other faculty assert that the academic program has been aided by the addition of pastoral studies, theological reflection, and field work. In their view, integration of traditional course material with these experiences helps students to apply theological principles in meaningful ways, thus increasing interest in, understanding of, and involvement with the academic subject matter. This debate continues to intensify as students come with ever-increasing varieties of background and experience.

Providing human and spiritual formation to help future ministers meet the demands of ministry is a widely accepted task in seminaries. Maturity, holiness, and an appropriate lifestyle for ministry require careful human and spiritual formation. Typical entering students are in their mid-twenties, an age at which transition to adulthood ordinarily comes to completion. During these years, individuals are expected to shift their focus from themselves to others, modify expectations of perfection in themselves and in others, and integrate personal idealism with the realism of the work world. On the level of faith, appropriate growth at this stage calls for a transition from uncertainty about, and lack of knowledge of, the faith to an attempt to understand and recognize God's revelation in one's own life and in the experiences of others. Within the context of ecclesial formation, adequate growth in community at this phase requires an increasing desire to be part of the public ministry of the Church. Programs to deal with these concerns exist in various stages of development and refinement, but the goals, content, and structures have many similarities.

Since Vatican II, pastoral field education has developed in response to the greater emphasis on pastoral concerns in the Church. The primary aim is to help students integrate the spiritual, human, and academic aspects of their formation and develop a habit of theological reflection on ministry. Other goals of pastoral field education are to provide a realistic test of what working in the Church will require, to teach students how to work within the structure of the Church, and to develop in them a sensitivity to people, their needs and aspirations, their circumstances of life, and their attitudes toward God and humankind.

Faculty Profile and Attitudes

Faculty Profile. The character and quality of faculty affect every aspect of seminary life, and ultimately alter the shape and substance of Church ministry. In recent years, seminary administrators have been directing considerable attention to recruiting and educating faculty. Among current teaching faculty, one-third have received their doctoral degrees from Catholic universities in the United States and Canada. Another one-third were educated in Roman Catholic European universities, the vast majority in Rome. Most of the remaining one-third were educated in private and state universities in the United States. About three-fourths of the current faculty hold doctoral degrees, but in individual seminaries the percent varies from about 50 to 100 percent. The average age of faculty is 50.6, fully a year younger than faculty in Protestant seminaries.[6]

The size, nature, and role of seminary faculties distinguish them from other faculties. The average number of full-time is small—about twenty per school; eleven have between ten and fourteen, ten have between fifteen and nineteen, fourteen between twenty and twenty-nine, and five have thirty or more. Priests constitute about two-thirds of all faculty, while women religious, lay men, and lay women comprise the other third. Some seminaries depend on dioceses to prepare and place priests, but as the shortage of priests makes itself felt, the supply for future faculty positions will diminish. The trend toward hiring women religious, lay men, and lay women was evident during the past decade when the proportion increased by almost 10 percent. However, given the specialized role of faculty, seminaries still endeavor to retain a majority of priests (see Chart B).[7]

The problem of finding time for research is especially acute for those who live in self-contained seminaries, where duties tend to be comprehensive and time-consuming, leaving faculty with little energy for scholarship. Highly

---

[6] These figures are based on data from the Project on the Future of Theological Faculty, which is being conducted at the Auburn Center for the Study of Theological Education by Barbara Wheeler and Katarina Schuth. The study, supported by grants from Lilly Endowment Inc., was begun in spring 1993.

[7] See Appendix at the end of this chapter.

qualified faculty who are also pastorally sensitive tend to devote their time to pastoral work. Motivation and incentive for publishing and research are often low: the tangible rewards are almost nonexistent, funding for sabbaticals is usually not available, and there is little expectation of publication at most schools.

If faculty are not focusing their energies on research and writing, what are they doing? On the whole, their roles have expanded in recent years. Many seminaries, particularly those educating diocesan candidates, expect faculty to function both in an academic role and in spiritual and ministerial formation. But it is difficult to combine these tasks, especially since professional training for work in formation is increasingly seen as necessary. Faculty are expected to assist with program and curriculum development and to do certain administrative tasks, including multiple committee assignments and program direction. Most faculty also are involved with service to parishes and religious communities.

The vocation of a seminary faculty member has an enhanced communal dimension when compared with other institutions. Community is intentional and encompasses an attitude of involvement and concern. Mark R. Schwehn speaks of this in "Religion and the Life of Learning." He says of community, "Like disciplined thought itself, community flourishes or perishes depending not only upon critical acumen of various voices that comprise it but also upon the extent to which and in the manner in which they respect and listen to one another."[8] A document published by the Congregation for Catholic Education in 1994, "Directives Concerning the Preparation of Seminary Educators,"[9] further reinforces this notion. Many of the seven qualities required of seminary faculty, as identified in the document, concern community, especially spirit of communion and capacity for communication. Most seminaries are so small that the whole corps of personnel needs to work cooperatively to achieve their goals. In fact, many seminary leaders believe that an indispensable dimension of belonging to a seminary faculty is the willingness to be involved in the unique process of ministerial formation, which consists of academic, pastoral, personal, and spiritual dimensions. A graduate degree in theology may ensure academic competence, but it cannot guarantee that the recipient is suited for the collaborative efforts required of a seminary faculty.

In the past, few seminaries had difficulty in hiring faculty for most disciplines. This situation is changing, however, and, even though it is easier to find faculty for some positions than for others, extensive searches are now needed to hire new faculty. The positions most readily filled are in Scripture and Church history, and in some branches of systematic theology. Many seminaries mention great difficulty in finding teachers of moral theology (ethics) and pastoral theology, including preaching but especially pastoral counsel-

[8] Mark R. Schwehn, "Religion and the Life of Learning," *First Things* 5 (August-September 1990): 34-43.

[9] Congregation for Catholic Education, "Directives Concerning the Preparation of Seminary Educators" (Washington, D.C.: USCC, 1994).

ing. Individuals with a knowledge of Hispanic ministry, particularly those of Hispanic background, are in very short supply. As the Hispanic population grows, faculty who understand how to teach others to minister in Hispanic parishes will be in great demand.

Faculty Attitudes and Views. To complement the faculty profile, part of the Auburn Seminary study of faculty included a survey of a random sample of faculty who teach at institutions that are members of the Association of Theological Schools. Among the 1,006 respondents, 216 (21 percent) were teaching at Roman Catholic theologates. This report focuses on the responses of those Catholic faculty, although comparisons are made with all respondents.[10] The survey furnishes information about faculty views on various topics related to theological education. It identifies the greatest sources of satisfaction and of discontent among faculty, as measured by sixty-three items. Moreover, the data allow us to see comparisons between men and women faculty and between older and younger faculty. The survey supplies data that enable us to confirm some popularly held views about theological faculty and to dispel others.

To begin with, the entire scope of the data is examined in order to assess which areas are considered by faculty most satisfactory and which are considered in some way unsatisfactory. Second, we look at several subsets of the data, including attitudes toward theological institutions and their leadership, measures of satisfaction with working conditions, and opinions about teaching, students, and diversity.

(1) *Overview of All Variables.* At the outset, we recognize that faculty in all theological schools are, generally speaking, highly satisfied. Considering responses to all sixty-three items that measure faculty attitudes and views, in only four instances does the average fall below the midpoint of 2.50 on a 4.00 scale.[11] Further evidence of high satisfaction is demonstrated by the percent (86.4) who would definitely or probably choose the same career again; only 5 percent would not, and 8.6 percent are not sure. For Roman Catholics, two items fall below 2.50 (see Chart C),[12] and only on thirteen of sixty-three items are average scores below 3.00. From the data, we can identify the main sources of faculty satisfaction and then look at those aspects of the job that are less favorably rated.

(2) *High Satisfaction Responses.* The top quartile, consisting of sixteen sur-

---

[10] The total number of faculty included in the Association of Theological Schools' (ATS) data base for 1991 was 3,475. Of these 789 (22.7 percent) were listed as full-time faculty in Roman Catholic theologates. A proportional number of respondents (21 percent) were from these schools, including rectors, presidents, deans, and others who are faculty members, though not necessarily teaching full time. In 1995, 881 faculty were counted in Roman Catholic theologates. The difference may be accounted for in that a few schools either did not report or are not members of the ATS.

[11] The four-point scale used was as follows: 4=Strongly agree; 3=Somewhat agree; 2=Somewhat disagree; 1=Strongly disagree; and 0=No opinion.

[12] See Appendix at the end of this chapter.

vey items that received the most positive responses, covers a range of topics.[13] These items can be grouped into four areas: teaching, students, working conditions (including relationships with faculty colleagues), and aspects of tolerance versus prejudice.

Teaching. Significantly, teaching is viewed as a major source of satisfaction for faculty. Not only do respondents regard themselves as effective teachers (3.62), but they also believe that the school values good teaching (3.62). Moreover, they maintain that institutional pressures to do research do not interfere with their effectiveness as teachers (3.49). They feel prepared to teach students of different ages (3.52), though some are less comfortable with teaching students from a variety of ethnic backgrounds (3.00) and religious backgrounds (2.97). When it comes to teaching students of different ages and with different religious backgrounds, women and older faculty feel significantly more prepared than do men and younger faculty. However, women and those under fifty feel more prepared to teach students from various ethnic backgrounds than do men and those over fifty (see table following).

Group	All	Men	Women	<50	>50
Different Ages	3.52	3.42	3.71	3.48	3.58
Different Religious Backgrounds	2.97	2.93	3.03	2.90	3.05
Different Ethnic Backgrounds	3.00	2.96	3.06	3.08	2.90

Some of the differences are self-explanatory—generally older faculty feel more secure as teachers than do younger faculty. They feel less prepared than younger faculty, however, when it comes to understanding students from a variety of ethnic backgrounds, perhaps because of lack of exposure to diversity in their own studies. The reasons for the stronger positive perceptions of older faculty about how much schools value teaching are not as evident. We might speculate that older faculty have seen good teaching rewarded and may use that experience as a gauge of how much it is appreciated. Even as we look at differences, it is important to note that all groups regard teaching as a highly satisfying dimension of their work.

Students. Closely associated with teaching is the regard that faculty have for students and the tasks associated with their development. One of the highly ranked items indicates that faculty believe they have excellent relationships with students (3.57). In the same category, faculty have strong views about their role with students. They believe that theological schools should

---

[13] From here on, the survey responses will refer only to those teaching in Roman Catholic theologates, unless otherwise specified.

help strengthen students' religious faith and moral character (3.77) and that faculty should play a role in judging the fitness of students for ministry (3.68). They also are interested in students' personal problems (3.53), an item that falls just below the top quartile. While the judgment about the quality of students is not as positive (3.11), faculty do value many aspects of working with them.

All subgroups of faculty, most strongly women, believe that they have excellent relationships with students, but some significant differences are found in the views of women and men regarding their work with students. Compared with the total sample of women, those women who teach in Roman Catholic settings agree more strongly that the school should help strengthen students' religious faith and moral character (3.73 vs. 3.55) and play a role in judging the fitness of students for ministry (3.64 vs. 3.24). Older faculty in Roman Catholic schools are more likely than younger faculty to say that they are interested in students' personal problems, but across all subgroups the averages are very high.

Faculty Colleagues and Work. Faculty have high regard for their colleagues, as indicated by several responses. Most feel that they have excellent relationships with other faculty (3.50) and that their colleagues are committed to the welfare of the institution (3.71). They are also satisfied with the competency of the faculty (3.57). In assessing their work environment, respondents are satisfied with the autonomy and independence they have in their job (3.52), and they believe they have sufficient academic freedom to do their work (3.43), an assessment that is virtually identical with faculty in all seminaries, and perhaps a surprising finding for some.

Relationship with the chief academic officer is also highly rated (3.39), but does not rank as high as it does for all faculty (21st vs. 15th). Unlike the situation when all faculty are considered, younger faculty in Roman Catholic schools view these three items more favorably than do their senior colleagues. Ranking just below the top quartile is a generic statement indicating overall satisfaction with the job (3.42), where both women and younger faculty are less satisfied than men and older faculty. Later, when we look at some of the factors that are seen as less positive aspects of the work environment, we will have a clear indication of reasons for these differences.

Aspects of Tolerance versus Prejudice. For the respondents as a whole, theological schools are places where tolerance is viewed as high and discrimination as minimal. The top ranked item of all sixty-three is that the school has not discriminated against the respondent on the basis of race (3.84). Since most faculty are non-Latino white, this finding is not surprising. For the larger sample, the African American score is significantly lower, but still at 3.52, suggesting that faculty are relatively tolerant and accepting of other faculty across the board. However, another item that ranks high overall, namely, that there is not a lot of racial conflict in theological schools (3.52), is ranked much lower by African Americans (2.97). For those in Roman Catholic schools, responses indicate that diversity and pluralism have not undermined the collegiality of the campus community (3.50), with women and younger faculty agreeing with that premise more strongly than men and older faculty. The fact that the overwhelming proportion of faculty are non-Latino white, especially on Roman Catholic campuses (95.7 percent), may distort, to a certain extent, the picture of racial harmony.

Another highly ranked item of similar character concerns gender discrimination. On the whole, faculty in Roman Catholic theologates have not felt discriminated against on the basis of gender (3.66, the same score as for the entire sample), and it ranks sixth of all items. Women differ significantly from men on this item and in Roman Catholic schools they rate it at 3.28 (compared with 3.19 for all women), which for them falls twenty-ninth of the sixty-three items. Looking at the situation in all theological schools, the environment is viewed much less favorably by African Americans and women, but, one would hope, more favorably than in many other work situations.

(3) *Lower Satisfaction Responses.* At the other end of the spectrum, the responses in the lowest quartile fall at or below 3.01 on a 4.00 point scale, but in Roman Catholic theologates only two are below the midpoint of 2.50, emphasizing again the generally positive views and attitudes of faculty. These lower sixteen items are somewhat more diverse than those in the highest quartile, with the exception of overwhelmingly more negative feelings about heavy workloads and lack of time. Other areas with low scores on two or more items are administration, salary and benefits, students, and aspects of curriculum. The content of the list is quite distinct from the areas that provide greatest satisfaction.

Workload and Lack of Time. The clearest finding about what causes faculty to be less content about working in theological schools is the sense of being overburdened with work and not having enough time to do their multiple tasks. The item ranking lowest of the sixty-three is that faculty believe their workload is increasing significantly (2.20). On a related item, they rate their satisfaction with workload at 3.03, just one above the bottom quartile. Because of a heavy workload, faculty feel they do not have sufficient time to keep current in their field (2.56) or produce research for publication (2.50). They also believe they spend too much time on governance and administrative activities (2.53), the fourth lowest item in the survey. The sense of being overwhelmed with work may contribute significantly to an otherwise rather puzzlingly low response about faculty morale (2.91). The ranking of this item (fifty-fourth) seems illogical given the positive response to so many other items. It may be that while faculty enjoy their work, colleagues, and students, they conclude there is simply so much to do that it affects overall faculty morale. One might also speculate that the perceived low morale comes not so much from within the institution—the subject of the survey—as it does from external factors, possibly the relationship to the larger Church or to the society as a whole.

On the six items discussed above, significant differences are found between younger and older faculty, especially in relation to workload and time demands. Older faculty are relatively less negative, though they still rate these items as the least desirable in their own situations. We might surmise that younger faculty are more burdened as they begin their careers—with teaching, writing, student advising, and other forms of service competing for their time. As experienced teachers know well, once having taught a course or written an article or worked with students, the second time is immeasurably easier.

The differences between men and women on these items are more varied. While only slight differences are found on perceptions about workload, time to produce research for publication, and time available for keeping current in the field, women are significantly less likely to feel that too much time is spent on governance and administrative activities (2.67 vs. 2.45). Yet men are more likely than women to evaluate faculty morale as high (2.95 vs. 2.81). Women in the larger sample are considerably less satisfied on all these issues than men, perhaps because at work they are always in the minority on faculties and so are called upon more often to be representatives on various committees and projects. They may also be advising more than their share of an increasing proportion of women students. Moreover, national studies show that women who work full time still do more work in the home than their male counterparts. Some of the variation between all women and women in Roman Catholic schools might be attributed to the fact that two-thirds of the women who teach in Roman Catholic theologates are women religious. In any case, in seemingly insignificant, but numerous ways, certain facets of the job contribute to a perceived disproportionate workload for women and younger faculty.

Administration. Given the attitudes summarized above, it is not surprising to find a few low items about administrators. One item in the bottom quartile concerns how effectively faculty and administrators cooperate in making decisions (3.01), and another states that administrative service is a respected professional choice at that particular institution (3.07). In both cases, all faculty rate these two items somewhat low. Other measures of relationship with administration tend to fall in the upper half of responses, suggesting that when asked about specific members of the administration, the responses are more positive than when thinking generically about administration. The response is similar to the rather low estimation of the morale of faculty; in general great satisfaction is registered in specific areas.

Salary and Benefits. Falling below the level of 3.00 are three items related to salary and benefits. Satisfaction with salary is sixth lowest (2.68), with younger faculty feeling significantly less pleased than older (2.53 vs. 2.85), and women less than men (2.55 vs. 2.75). Benefits are also rated rather low (2.93), with a similar pattern for women and younger faculty. Interestingly, for the total survey sample, satisfaction with overall benefits is somewhat higher (3.12). For those in Roman Catholic theologates, adequacy of faculty development also ranks rather low (2.94), with a similar distinction between younger and older faculty (2.80 vs. 3.09); however, women rate faculty development more positively than men (3.02 vs. 2.90). Since university salaries, benefits, and, in many cases, faculty development programs are generally better, it is not surprising that faculty identify this aspect of their jobs in theological schools less favorably.

Students. As mentioned under high satisfaction responses, students contribute an important positive dimension to working in theological schools. Nonetheless, faculty are somewhat likely to indicate that the quality of students is declining (2.90), with this response falling in the bottom quartile. A related item, ranking slightly higher, concerns satisfaction with the overall quality of students. The average is 3.11, but women are somewhat more satisfied than men (3.20 vs. 3.07). Also, opportunities for faculty to socialize with students are judged as less than optimal (3.04), with older faculty feeling least positive about this item (2.92). Another relatively low-ranked item relating to students, and also to diversity, is an evaluation of how well students of different racial/ethnic origins communicate with one another (3.06), and in this case women are least positive (2.96). In spite of these few relatively lower responses, relationships with students are generally considered very positive.

Aspects of Teaching and Curriculum. Other items in the lowest quartile are less easily categorized, but two concern curriculum. Rather low ratings are given to an evaluation of whether or not courses include minority group perspectives (2.48) and whether or not recent social movements such as feminism have made a difference in curricular offerings (2.91). These two items, combined with some uneasiness about teaching students from varied ethnic backgrounds, suggest a possible serious lacuna in faculty preparation. On another related topic, unlike the sample of faculty in all seminaries, those in Roman Catholic schools do not believe that the curriculum has suffered from faculty overspecialization (2.98 vs. 3.21). In part, this can be explained by the prescriptions of *The Program of Priestly Formation*, which requires a range of courses in the major theological disciplines.

Further analysis of the meaning of these responses is not so straightforward. For instance, women are less likely than men to say that many courses include minority group perspectives (2.37 vs. 2.54), but responses of women may be lower because of increased expectation that these perspectives should be included. In the larger sample, African American faculty rate this item somewhat, though not significantly, higher (2.85 vs. 2.65), probably because they incorporate minority group perspectives in their own teaching more often than not. Concerning the impact of social movements and feminism on the curriculum, women in Roman Catholic theologates rate the item somewhat lower than men (2.82 vs. 2.95), unlike the total population of women who rate the item somewhat higher than men (3.07 vs. 2.92), possibly because women in other seminaries have more opportunity to incorporate a wider variety of perspectives in their courses than do those in Roman Catholic seminaries.

What are some of the implications of these findings? Three areas deserve special attention. First, administrators and faculty leaders might explore the reasons for the different perceptions between their younger and older faculty members. Given the substantial number of older faculty who will be retiring in the next several years, it might be well to design ways to help younger faculty feel satisfied and more incorporated into their schools. The second area concerns the differences between women and men in the work place, a topic that has been examined from many points of view. As the number of women faculty and students continues to increase, it will be even more critical to establish good working relationships among those faculty who remain or come in as new faculty. Though the differences are not as sharp in Roman Catholic seminaries between women and men faculty and between older and younger faculty, it is still worthwhile to pay attention to potential areas of conflict. Finally, the predominant non-Latino white respondents clearly must become more attuned to the racial/ethnic climate that exists in their schools. Although the overall picture is positive, signs of some problems relating to diversity are emerging from just beneath the surface and can be addressed if recognized in a timely manner. Perhaps as much as anything, more education is needed about ethnic/racial concerns in Roman Catholic seminaries.

Conclusion

A central purpose of this essay was to examine the significance of the role of theological faculty in educating ministers for the Church. By examining the structures in which they work and the programs they have developed, we gain a clear sense of their positions. In reviewing the profile and attitudes of faculty, we come to understand who they are and how they function. As already suggested, the overall positive nature of the responses to the survey may be the most surprising finding of all. Faculty are satisfied with many aspects of their jobs, especially the nature of their work with students, their colleagues, and the overall environment in which they work. They are less satisfied with their workload and heavy time commitments, as well as with their salaries and benefits, but even these areas are not highly negatively perceived.

The ways in which these theological educators contribute to the development of seminary students and in that process affect the ministry of the Church are critical. In the final analysis, we want and need faculty who are aware of the Church's mission today—and what it should be tomorrow—and who can help form ministers to serve that Church well. We need people who can respond creatively to students who vary widely in age, academic background and ability, and ministerial direction. We need faculty who have vision and imagination about the Church in the future and can adapt programs accordingly. In sum, we want a faculty who understand their own role, the students they teach, the programs they provide, and the Church in which students will eventually minister.

Appendix

STRUCTURAL MODELS OF THEOLOGATES (CHART A)

I. Freestanding Schools

A. For Diocesan and/or Religious Priesthood Candidates

- Saint John's Seminary, CA Diocesan
- Saint Patrick's Seminary, CA (SS)
- Mount Saint Mary's Seminary, MD (Diocesan)*
- Saint John's Seminary, MA (Diocesan)
- Pope John XXIII National Seminary, MA (Diocesan)
- Kenrick-Glennon Seminary, MO (Diocesan)

B. Diocesan Candidates with Separate Programs for Others

- University of Saint Mary of the Lake Seminary, IL (Diocesan)
- Saint Mary's Seminary and University, MD (SS)
- Saint Joseph's Seminary, NY (Diocesan)
- Saint Charles Borromeo Seminary, PA (Diocesan)

C. Diocesan Candidates and Lay Students

- Sacred Heart Major Seminary, MI (Diocesan)
- SS. Cyril and Methodius Seminary, MI (Diocesan)
- Christ the King Seminary, NY (Diocesan)
- Athenaeum, Mount Saint Mary's of the West Seminary, OH (Diocesan)
- Saint Mary Seminary, OH (Diocesan)
- Saint Francis Seminary, WI (Diocesan)

D. Diocesan, Religious, and Lay Students

- Holy Apostles Seminary, CT (MSsA)
- Seminary of Saint Vincent DePaul, FL (Diocesan)
- Saint Meinrad School of Theology, IN   (OSB)
- Notre Dame Seminary, LA (Diocesan)
- Seminary of the Immaculate Conception, NY (Diocesan)
- Pontifical College of Josephinum, OH (Diocesan)
- Mount Angel Seminary, OR (OSB)
- Saint Vincent Seminary, PA (OSB)
- Sacred Heart School of Theology, WI (SCJ)

* Mt. St. Mary's Seminary, Emmitsburg, Maryland, is located on a college campus, but its programs make it freestanding.

II. University-Related

- The Catholic University of America, DC (Diocesan)
  (Diocesan priesthood students come mainly from Theological College.)
- Moreau Seminary, IN (CSC)
  (Students attend University of Notre Dame.)
- Immaculate Conception Seminary, NJ (Diocesan)
- Saint John's University, MN (OSB)
  (Priesthood students from St. Cloud Diocesan Seminary and from St. John's Abbey.)
- Saint Paul Seminary School of Divinity, MN (Diocesan)
  (School is part of the University of St. Thomas.)
- Aquinas Institute of Theology, MO (OP)
  (Students take some courses at St. Louis University.)
- Saint Mary's Seminary, TX (Diocesan)
  (Students attend University of St. Thomas School of Theology.)
- Centro de Estudios Dominicos (CEDOC), PR (OP)
  (Affiliated with Bayamon University.)
- The American College at Louvain, BEL (Diocesan)
  (Students attend Catholic University of Louvain.)
- The North American College, Rome (Diocesan)
  (Students attend several universities.)

III. Collaborative Schools

A. Union Model

- Catholic Theological Union, IL
- Washington Theological Union, MD

B. Federation Model

- Franciscan School of Theology, CA (OFM)
- Jesuit School of Theology at Berkeley, CA (SJ)
- Dominican School of Philosophy and Theology, CA (OP)
- Weston Jesuit School of Theology, MA (SJ)
- Oblate School of Theology, TX (OMI)
  (Residence for diocesan priesthood candidates is at Assumption Seminary.)

C. Consortium

- Dominican House of Studies, DC (OP)
- Oblate College, DC (OMI)
- DeSales School of Theology, DC (OSFS)

FACULTY COMPOSITION
COMPARISON OF 1985-87 WITH 1994-96 (CHART B)

	1985-87		1994-96		Change
	#	%	#	%	+/-
Diocesan Priests	292	32.5	272	30.8	-20
Men Religious (Incl. 5 Brothers)	392	43.7	315	35.8	-77
Women Religious	93	10.4	102	11.6	+9
Lay Men (Incl. 3 Ordained in Other Denominations)	88	9.8	138	15.7	+50
Lay Women	33	3.7	54	6.1	+21
Total*	**898**	**100.1**	**881**	**100.0**	**-17**
Women Religious, Lay Men and Women	214	23.8	294	33.4	+9.6
Diocesan Priests and Men Religious	684	76.2	587	66.6	-9.6
Men	772	86.0	725	82.3	-3.7
Women	126	14.0	156	17.7	+3.7

*Includes the same schools except omitting Mary Immaculate, Pennsylvania; Maryknoll, New York; and St. Anthony-on-the-Hudson, New York; and substituting Sacred Heart, Michigan for St. John's, Michigan.

HOW FACULTY IN ROMAN CATHOLIC THEOLOGATES VIEW THEIR WORK (Chart C)

Item #		All RC		Male RC		Female RC		50< RC		>50 RC	
Rank All	Survey Item	Rank	Mean	Rank	Mean	Rank	Mean	Rank	Mean	Rank	Mean
20.54* 1	The school in which I teach has discriminated against me on the basis of race.	1	(3.84)	1	(3.87)	1	(3.77)	1	(3.85)	1	(3.83)
20.24 2	A theological school like ours should help students to strengthen their religious faith and moral character.	2	3.77	3	3.79	2	3.73	3t	3.73	2	3.81
20.53* 3	The school in which I teach has discriminated against me on the basis of gender.	6	(3.66)	2	(3.86)	29t	(3.28)	3t	(3.73)	14t	(3.57)
20.6 4	Faculty are committed to the welfare of this institution.	3	3.71	5	3.72	5	3.68	6	3.70	3	3.73
24.5 5	I have excellent relationships with students here.	9t	3.57	10	3.53	8t	3.63	10	3.56	12t	3.58
20.48 6	The school in which I teach values good teaching.	7t	3.62	7	3.63	11	3.59	9	3.57	4	3.68
20.13* 7t	There is lot of racial conflict here.	4	(3.69)	4	(3.77)	14	(3.57)	2	(3.75)	7	(3.61)
23.3 7t	I am satisfied with my autonomy and independence at my job.	11t	3.54	11t	3.52	12t	3.58	13t	3.50	9t	3.59
20.31 7t	I regard myself as an effective teacher.	7t	3.62	8	3.58	4	3.70	7	3.64	9t	3.59
24.4 10	I have excellent relationships with my faculty colleagues.	15t	3.50	15	3.49	17	3.51	13t	3.50	18	3.49
23.2 11	I am satisfied with the competency of my colleagues at my job.	9t	3.57	9	3.57	12t	3.58	11	3.55	8	3.60
20.28 12	I feel prepared to teach students of different ages.	14	3.52	20t	3.42	3	3.71	15t	3.48	12t	3.58

HOW FACULTY IN ROMAN CATHOLIC THEOLOGATES
VIEW THEIR WORK (Chart C)
Page 2

Item #		All RC		Male RC		Female RC		50< RC		>50 RC	
Rank All	Survey Item	Rank	Mean	Rank	Mean	Rank	Mean	Rank	Mean	Rank	Mean
20.19* 13	Institutional pressures to do research interfere with my effectiveness as a teacher.	17	(3.49)	13t	(3.50)	18	(3.48)	17	(3.46)	16	(3.52)
20.52 14	The school in which I teach offers sufficient academic freedom for faculty members to do their work.	18	3.43	19	3.44	20t	3.41	18	3.42	21	3.44
24.2 15	I have a good relation-ship with my chief academic officer.	21t	3.39	27t	3.32	16	3.52	19	3.41	26	3.37
20.25 16	A theological school like ours should play a role in judging the fitness of students for ministry.	5	3.68	6	3.69	7	3.64	5	3.71	6	3.64
23.13 17	Overall, I am satisfied with my job.	19t	3.42	16	3.48	28	3.29	25	3.33	17	3.51
20.2 18	Faculty are interested in students' personal problems.	13	3.53	11t	3.52	15	3.56	15t	3.48	9t	3.59
20.12* 19	Diversity and pluralism have undermined the collegiality of our campus community.	15t	(3.50)	20t	(3.42)	6	(3.67)	8	(3.60)	24t	(3.39)
24.3 20	I have good relationships with other administrative staff.	27t	3.31	33t	3.25	20t	3.41	28t	3.28	28	3.34
20.20 21t	Library resources at our institution are adequate to support my teaching.	11t	3.54	13t	3.50	10	3.61	12	3.51	14t	3.57
23.8 21t	I am satisfied with the freedom I have to do outside consulting.	21t	3.39	23t	3.37	19	3.42	24	3.36	23	3.42
20.27 23	I know where to find resources to help me improve my teaching.	19t	3.42	30t	3.31	8t	3.63	21t	3.38	19	3.48
20.47 24t	The school in which I teach has been able to identify good candidates for faculty positions.	31t	3.28	33t	3.25	27	3.32	31	3.26	31t	3.29
23.5 24t	I am satisfied with my job security.	26	3.32	18	3.45	43t	3.06	34t	3.22	22	3.43

HOW FACULTY IN ROMAN CATHOLIC THEOLOGATES
VIEW THEIR WORK (Chart C)
Page 3

Item #		All RC		Male RC		Female RC		50< RC		>50 RC	
Rank All	Survey Item	Rank	Mean	Rank	Mean	Rank	Mean	Rank	Mean	Rank	Mean
23.12 26	I am satisfied with the employment opportunities that my spouse or partner has in this geographic area.	45t	3.04	57t	2.75	22	3.40	54	2.86	5	3.67
23.6 27	I am satisfied with the opportunity for advancement in rank at this institution.	31t	3.28	17	3.46	51	2.93	32t	3.24	29	3.32
20.3 28	Most faculty are sensitive to the issues of minorities.	34t	3.24	26	3.34	45t	3.05	32t	3.24	37t	3.23
20.49 29	The school in which I teach has hired the faculty it wants.	41t	3.10	41t	3.07	37t	3.16	44t	3.05	42	3.16
24.1 30	I have an excellent relationship with my chief executive officer.	36t	3.21	38	3.14	26	3.33	34t	3.22	39t	3.19
20.8 31t	Administrators consider student concerns when making policy.	23	3.38	23t	3.37	23	3.39	21t	3.38	24t	3.39
20.55* 31t	The school in which I teach has given me a much heavier work load than others in my institution.	27t	(3.31)	25	(3.36)	31t	(3.24)	37	(3.19)	20	(3.45)
20.50 31t	The school in which I teach faces a promising future.	48t	3.01	45	3.06	53	2.90	44t	3.05	50	2.97
20.9 34	Administrators consider faculty concerns when making policy.	24	3.34	27t	3.32	24	3.37	20	3.40	35	3.26
23.14 35	I am satisfied with the public reputation of my school.	39	3.15	39	3.11	33t	3.22	46t	3.04	33	3.28
20.5* 36t	Many students feel that they do not "fit in" on this campus.	27t	(3.31)	22	(3.41)	41	(3.10)	23	(3.37)	36	(3.24)
20.15 36t	Evaluation policies and procedures for faculty are fair and administered even-handedly.	25	3.33	30t	3.31	25	3.35	26t	3.29	26t	3.37
23.10 38	I am satisfied with my benefits, generally.	53	2.93	48	2.99	54	2.83	55	2.85	48	3.02

HOW FACULTY IN ROMAN CATHOLIC THEOLOGATES
VIEW THEIR WORK (Chart C)
Page 4

Item # Rank All	Survey Item	All RC		Male RC		Female RC		50< RC		>50 RC	
		Rank	Mean	Rank	Mean	Rank	Mean	Rank	Mean	Rank	Mean
20.42 39	The chief executive officer and the faculty generally agree about the mission and policies of this school.	33	3.26	32	3.28	33t	3.22	26t	3.29	37t	3.23
20.21 40	The library at my institution is a major resource for my research.	34t	3.24	36	3.23	29t	3.28	36	3.21	31t	3.29
23.1 41t	I am satisfied with the quality of students.	40	3.11	41t	3.07	35t	3.20	40	3.11	44	3.12
20.41 41t	The board and the faculty generally agree about the mission and policies of this school.	30	3.29	29	3.33	35t	3.20	28t	3.28	30	3.30
20.29 43	I feel prepared to teach students from a variety of ethnic backgrounds.	50	3.00	50	2.96	43t	3.06	42	3.08	54t	2.90
20.30 44t	I feel prepared to teach students from a variety of religious backgrounds.	51	2.97	53	2.93	47	3.03	51t	2.90	47	3.05
20.16 44t	Our institution is well administered.	36t	3.21	37	3.19	31t	3.24	38	3.17	34	3.27
23.11 46	I am satisfied with the quality of my research facilities and support.	41t	3.10	41t	3.07	37t	3.16	46t	3.04	41	3.18
20.4* 47t	The curriculum has suffered from faculty overspecialization.	36t	(3.21)	33t	(3.25)	40	(3.12)	30	(3.27)	43	(3.13)
20.40 47t	Administrative service is a respected professional choice at my institution.	43	3.07	47	3.04	39	3.13	48t	2.97	39t	3.19
20.11 49	Recent social movements such as feminism have made a difference in our curricular offerings.	54t	2.91	51t	2.95	55	2.82	50	2.96	56t	2.85
20.1* 50	The quality of students here has declined significantly in recent years.	56	(2.90)	55	(2.82)	42	(3.07)	51t	(2.90)	54t	(2.90)
23.4 51	I am satisfied with my work load.	47	3.03	41t	3.07	52	2.94	48t	2.97	45t	3.09

HOW FACULTY IN ROMAN CATHOLIC THEOLOGATES
VIEW THEIR WORK (Chart C)
Page 5

Item #		All RC		Male RC		Female RC		50< RC		>50 RC	
Rank All	Survey Item	Rank	Mean	Rank	Mean	Rank	Mean	Rank	Mean	Rank	Mean
20.18 52	Faculty and administrators cooperate effectively in making decisions.	48t	3.01	48t	2.99	45t	3.05	43	3.07	51t	2.94
20.10 53	Students of different racial/ethnic origins communicate well with one another.	44	3.06	40	3.09	50	2.96	41	3.10	49	3.01
20.51 54	The school in which I teach provides adequately for faculty development.	52	2.94	54	2.90	48	3.02	56	2.80	45t	3.09
23.9 55t	I am satisfied with my salary.	58	2.68	57t	2.75	59	2.55	58	2.53	56t	2.85
20.43 55t	Faculty morale is high.	54t	2.91	51t	2.95	56	2.81	53	2.88	51t	2.94
20.14 57	There are many opportunities for faculty and students to socialize with one another.	45t	3.04	46	3.05	49	3.00	39	3.14	53	2.92
20.26 58	Graduate study prepared me to be an effective teacher.	57	2.79	56	2.80	57	2.75	57	2.76	58	2.83
20.7 59	Many courses include minority group perspectives.	62	2.48	60	2.54	62	2.37	59	2.51	62	2.45
20.22 60	Faculty here are given sufficient time to produce research for publication.	61	2.50	61	2.51	61	2.47	61	2.42	61	2.59
23.7 61	I am satisfied with the time available for keeping current in my field.	59	2.56	59	2.60	60	2.50	60	2.49	60	2.65
20.17* 62	Too much faculty time is spent on governance and administrative activities.	60	(2.53)	62	(2.45)	58	(2.67)	62	(2.37)	59	(2.72)
20.23* 63	My work load is increasing significantly.	63	(2.20)	63	(2.23)	63	(2.16)	63	(2.00)	63	(2.45)

*Parentheses indicate inverted scores, i.e., faculty who disagree with these statements.

Scale: 4=Strongly agree; 3=Somewhat agree; 2=Somewhat disagree; 1=Strongly disagree; 0=No opinion.

VI

INSTITUTIONAL AND ECCLESIAL CONTEXTS FOR THEOLOGICAL EDUCATION

13

Theology's Place
in a Catholic University

JAMES L. HEFT, S.M.

I n order to address the question of what is needed for a theology department at a Catholic university to be what it should be, a larger question
should be answered first: What constitutes a Catholic university? After
addressing this larger question, I will describe a department of theology
within a Catholic university. Finally, I will point out some of the specific issues that need to be addressed and some of the decisions that need to be
made to ensure that not only the theology department but also other academic and support units within the university develop a distinctively Catholic ethos. What I have to say will not apply in the same way to all Catholic
colleges and universities given their great diversity; however, my main points
ought to be relevant to all Catholic institutions of higher education.

The Matter of Vision: What Constitutes a Catholic University?

I wish to address first the topic of what constitutes a Catholic university.
This topic has, of course, been addressed many times before, not only by
John Henry Newman's classic, *The Idea of a University*, but more recently in
our own country by many who care greatly about the distinctiveness of Catholic education.[1] And even though many leaders of Catholic institutions understand that the future of their institutions lie in their distinctiveness, few articulate well what is required of them and the faculty to distinguish themselves from comparable state and private secular institutions. Over twenty-
five years ago, Christopher Jencks and David Riesman observed that Catho-

---

[1] See, for example, *Issues in Academic Freedom*, ed. George S. Worgul, Jr. (Pittsburgh: Duquesne
University Press, 1992); *Catholic Universities in Church and Society: A Dialogue on Ex corde Ecclesiae*,
ed. John P. Langan, S.J. (Washington: Georgetown University Press, 1993); David O'Brien, *From
the Heart of the American Church* (Maryknoll, N.Y.: Orbis, 1994); *The Challenge and the Promise of a
Catholic University*, ed. Theodore M. Hesburgh, C.S.C. (Notre Dame, Ind.: University of Notre
Dame Press, 1994); and for official documents, *American Catholic Higher Education: Essential Documents, 1967-1990*, ed. Alice Gallin, O.S.U. (Notre Dame, Ind.: University of Notre Dame Press,
1992).

lic institutions should not try to emulate the research university, the "Harvard-Berkeley model." They went on to say that even if some few Catholic institutions were able to be a Harvard or a Berkeley, "there is as yet no American Catholic University that manages to fuse academic professionalism with concern for questions of ultimate social and moral importance."[2] This larger goal, the creation of an alternative to existing models, is what Jencks and Riesman encouraged Catholic universities to do. I think that Jencks and Riesman basically had it right. That is, I believe that Catholic universities need to make clearer than has been the case in the past how they embody a distinctive alternative to secular and even prestigious private but nonreligious universities.

David Burrell, the Notre Dame philosopher, recently brought out a similar point by posing a question in two distinct ways. Instead of asking "what makes a university Catholic," he asked "what makes for a Catholic university?"[3] If we ask the first question, he explained, we make the presumption that the meaning of a university is given. When, however, we ask the question in the second form, we sense that a Catholic university is more than just a generic university with a few religious elements added on to it, for example, a theology department or a strong campus ministry program.[4] It must be said that Catholic educators still have a lot to learn from the great universities and colleges of this country. Their sheer intellectual rigor, their support for research, their facilities and libraries that support learning are, for most Catholic institutions, areas in which we need to make considerable progress. Nonetheless, Catholic identity is something more than academic excellence with religious supplements.

The challenge of articulating a vision of a Catholic university is further complicated by our largely unconscious acceptance of models of excellence generated apart from the Catholic intellectual tradition. It takes a faculty and an administration with an intellectual vision of considerable depth, articulated well and persuasively, to sustain a process within an academic community that will lead to a truly distinctive model for teaching, research, and service. Those who lead this process must avoid the extremes of both trying to

---

[2] Christopher Jencks and David Riesman, *The Academic Revolution* (Garden City, N.Y.: Doubleday, 1968), 405.

[3] David Burrell, "A Catholic University," *The Challenge and Promise of a Catholic University*, 35.

[4] Some like to stress that in the words "Catholic university," the noun is "university," and the adjective is "Catholic," stressing thereby the importance first of being a university, respectable in the secular taken-for-granted meaning of the word. See Charles E. Curran, "The Elusive Idea of a Catholic University," *National Catholic Reporter* (7 October 1994): 13. Curran clarifies, "In other words, Catholic institutions of higher learning must first be colleges and universities in the American understanding of the term." In making this point, many educational leaders underscore the need for academic freedom and institutional autonomy, as well as for conditions that will support respectable academic work, especially publishable research. These factors are important, even though they need to be carefully articulated. Nonetheless, to speak of the noun-adjective distinction—or as a president of a Catholic university once put it to me, "the university part is the meat, the Catholic part is just the flavoring"—leads to the presumption Burrell warns us not to make.

force immediately a "total change" in an institution, a move that invariably rouses great opposition from many of the faculty, and resigning oneself to the status quo which pleases, in the long run, very few.[5] Moreover, such a process should not aim at recreating some alleged "golden age" of American Catholic intellectual life. Our situation today is different: largely dependent on lay leadership who live in a more pluralistic society and teach a more diverse student body.

In spite of the newness of our situation today, leaders in Catholic educa- tion have certain fundamental beliefs upon which they can and ought to draw to provide a distinctive model of higher education. *Ex corde Ecclesiae* (1990), the Pope's recent apostolic constitution on Catholic universities, articulates a number of those fundamental beliefs. Among them, I would here emphasize first that faith and reason relate dynamically, so that believing devoutly and thinking critically are both to be learned and lived. A second fundamental belief is that both knowledge and virtue are important and that, therefore, Catholic universities exist not only for intellectual but also for moral develop- ment—and not only of students, but also and even more importantly of fac- ulty, staff, and administrators. Third, the Catholic university, as a part of both the Church and of society, seeks as a community to reflect on the relationship between the gospel and human culture, and through this disciplined reflec- tion be an example to enable the gospel to inform, purify, and be enriched by culture. Fourth and finally, a Catholic university is based on the beliefs that teaching is not just a career but rather a calling, that learning without service atrophies the human heart, and that research ought to be worthwhile and beneficial to society.[6]

Instead of listing fundamental beliefs that ought to shape a Catholic uni- versity, we might emphasize what kind of experience students should have at a Catholic university. Many regional accrediting agencies are now requiring universities to demonstrate that what they assert in their mission statements they actually deliver to the students. Assessment presents an excellent op- portunity for a Catholic university to examine what kinds of students it wants to graduate. In a recent article, Richard McCormick, S.J., defines a great Catho- lic university precisely in terms of the kinds of graduates it produces. He lists eight qualities of such graduates: a Catholic vision (stressing the sacramental

---

[5] See the comments of Václav Havel, "The Responsibility of Intellectuals," *The New York Review of Books* (22 June 1995): 36, where he comments upon Karl Popper's criticism of "holistic social engineering," that is, "attempts to change the world for the better, completely and glo- bally, on the basis of some preconceived ideology that purported to understand all the laws of historical development." This approach, continued Havel, inevitably forced into a fixed box life's unfathomable diversity and predictability. Instead, Havel recommends to all who attempt to change institutions "a gradual approach" that remains "constantly in touch with experience and constantly enriching it." In other words, the process usually takes years and years.

[6] By stating that research should be worthwhile I do not mean to suggest that "pure re- search" is to be avoided, nor that all research must produce immediate practical applications. I do intend to suggest, however, that research should not be "neighbor-numb" to use the phrase John Haughey used in his paper published in this volume.

dimension); sensitivity to justice and injustice; appreciation of and thirst for knowledge; facility in the spoken and written word; open-mindedness; critical capacity; ability to listen; and willingness to serve. He considers a university great if a "significant number" (he suggests about the same number as are on the dean's list) of its graduates embody at least a recognizable number of these qualities. His way of approaching the topic is valuable, for it focuses attention on the educational goals for students instead of goals of the faculty, which too frequently are not the same.[7]

In summary, the distinctiveness of a Catholic university as a whole will draw upon fundamental beliefs about knowledge and character as integral and teaching, research, and service as vocations, all of which are aimed at empowering students to enter society with a valuable set of competencies and a commitment grounded in a Catholic vision of life.

The Department of Theology

I shall return to a further discussion of some dimensions of the Catholic university as a whole later in these remarks in order to illustrate how being a Catholic university requires more than a vital theology department. I wish now to turn to a discussion of the nature of a theology department within a Catholic university.

Rapid and extensive changes have affected theology departments over the last fifty years. The Jesuit John Haughey recently wrote that the objectives of these departments have changed "from moral and religious formation through catechetics and apologetics to religious education to preparation for the lay apostolate to developing a critical capacity to reflect on faith." As someone who has been teaching in such departments since 1963, he adds that "I can safely say that no other department has undergone so great a degree of change."[8]

Extensive changes have happened, not the least part of which has been the rise of religious studies as an approach to the study of religion.[9] Many

---

[7] See Richard McCormick, S.J., "What is a Great Catholic University?" *The Challenge and Promise*, 165-74.

[8] "Theology and the Mission of the Jesuit College and University," *Conversations* (spring 1994): 6. See also Lawrence S. Cunningham, "Gladly Wolde He Lerne and Gladly Teche: The Catholic Scholar in the New Millennium," *The Cresset* (June 1992): 4-16. As to great change in the focus and content of an academic department, veteran members of philosophy departments at Catholic universities might well think they have also witnessed great change.

[9] Helpful descriptions of the historical development of the study of religion in state universities and Protestant divinity schools can be found in Edward Farley, *Theologia* (Philadelphia: Fortress, 1983); and in *Shifting Boundaries: Contextual Approaches to the Structure of Theological Education*, ed. Barbara Wheller and Edward Farley (Louisville, Ky.: Westminster, 1991). For special emphasis on the various approaches to the study of religion in American society, see *Religion and Twentieth Century American Intellectual Life*, ed. Michael J. Lacey (New York: Woodrow Wilson International Center for Scholars and Cambridge University Press, 1989). No comparable book-length study of the development of the study of religion in Catholic colleges and universities exists.

have asked whether at a Catholic university there should be only a theology department or a department of religious studies or both a department of theology and of religious studies. Scholars involved in the academic study of religion at public universities disagree about how precisely to make the distinction between religious studies and theology. However, Schubert Ogden, commenting on a study done by Ray Hart, notes that many in secular institutions believe that the distinction should mean at least the following: (1) religious studies examines many religious traditions while theology studies only one; (2) religious studies presupposes no personal faith commitment on the part of the professor, while theology does; (3) religious studies exists appropriately in a university setting, while theology belongs in seminaries and divinity schools; and (4) religious studies may be appropriate for general education, while theology is appropriate only for committed members of the Church or synagogue or the relevant believing community.[10]

Should the distinction between theology and religious studies be drawn in this way? Such distinctions run the risk of creating a set of unnecessary dichotomies. For, given certain important qualifications, the two approaches can be made complementary. First of all, a theology department, while focusing its primary energy upon the Catholic traditions, for example, should study other religious traditions as well. How is it possible to understand humanity without understanding humanity's religious traditions?[11] Second, while theology presupposes a commitment of faith,[12] that commitment does not render the critical study of the religious traditions invariably prejudiced.[13] Third, a

---

[10] See Schubert M. Ogden, "Religious Studies and Theological Studies: What is Involved in the Distinction Between Them?" *Council of Societies for the Study of Religion Bulletin* 24 (February 1995): 3-4. Ogden is summarizing the findings of the survey by Ray L. Hart, "Religious and Theological Studies in American Higher Education: A Pilot Study," *Journal of the American Academy of Religion* 59 (winter 1991): 715-827. Ogden, incidentally, challenges making the distinction along these lines and points rather to the "constitutive questions" each discipline asks as the basis for their true distinction.

[11] It should be noted, however, that to study alone the very diverse, rich multicultural expressions of Catholicism that exist worldwide is not done, to my knowledge, by any Catholic university anywhere in the United States.

[12] This point is complicated, for it is possible to have a faith commitment that is ecclesial and one that is not; it is possible for a nonbeliever to have deep insights into a faith tradition, and for a person who believes he or she is orthodox to be otherwise; it is possible for an individual Lutheran theologian to be more Catholic in theological approaches than some who say they are Catholic. I have stated above that faith is needed for theology only in order to relate my assertion to the traditional Catholic description of theology as faith seeking understanding within an ecclesial community which recognizes the role of the magisterium.

[13] See for example Francis Schüssler Fiorenza, "Theology in the University," *Bulletin of the Council of Societies for the Study of Religion* (April 1993): 34, who underscores the importance of recent changes that include "the criticisms in epistemology of universalistic conceptions of rationality, the criticisms in pragmatism of foundationalism, the criticisms in hermeneutical theory of subjective certainty, the critique within post-empiricist philosophies of science of objectivism and the criticism within the post-modern social theory of progressive meta-narratives of history," changes which affect the self-understanding not only of the humanities, but of the social and natural sciences as well. Such change, Fiorenza continues, not only affects the nature of these disciplines, but also "weakens the contrast between theology and religious studies."

theology department in a Catholic university can combine critical and descriptive study of religious traditions characteristic of religious studies departments in state universities, even while it carries out the task of criticism from a committed stance. Fourth and finally, theology can and should form an integral part of a general education program at a Catholic university. Given these four qualifications, then, "theology," properly understood, should contain and presuppose all that is most excellent in "religious studies." Nevertheless, I still prefer for Catholic universities that the departmental designation be "theology," and not "religious studies," though more important than the title of the department is what the faculty actually do. Lawrence Cunningham, now the chair of the department of theology at Notre Dame, states his position in favor of theology even more strongly:

> Indeed, the temptation to turn theology into the more bland designation of "Religious Studies" is, in my estimation, a retreat for religiously sponsored schools. I would suggest that a theological faculty, dedicated to the Christian tradition in general and serious about its own denominational heritage in particular is an essential part of the self-identity of a denominational school. Religious Studies as an encompassing field may well be appropriate for a secular school, but theology is a discipline, and its absence from the curriculum of a religious school is, in my estimation, an abdication of responsibility.[14]

Catholic universities, then, ought to be "doing" theology, that is a study, as understood above, of religious traditions from a committed stance rooted in a living-faith community, the Church. At the very center of the study of religion in a Catholic university must therefore be the practice of theology. Catholic universities enjoy the distinctive possibility of putting theology at the center of and in the context of the study of religion more generally conceived.

The mistaken assumptions about the nature of theology typically held by those involved in the academic study of religion in state universities are also held by not a few other faculty in Catholic universities. If theology is viewed merely as opinion and not as real knowledge, if the discipline itself is seen as intellectually soft and its faculty as well-intentioned but credulous individuals, then theology departments invariably become marginalized within the university, much as religious studies departments are at state universities, and divinity schools are at private universities.[15] And it takes considerable

---

[14] Lawrence Cunningham, "Gladly Wolde He Lerne," 5.

[15] See Michael J. Lacey, "The Backwardness of American Catholicism," *Catholic Theological Society of America Proceedings* 46 (1991): 1-15; and Van A. Harvey, "On the Intellectual Marginality of American Theology," *Religion and Twentieth Century American Intellectual Life*, 172-92. Stanley Hauerwas, *Dispatches from the Front: Theological Engagements with the Secular* (Durham: Duke University Press, 1994), 156-57, can be counted upon to make this point sharply if even in a

vision and effective communication on the part of administrators to sustain, especially at times of budget constraints, a strong commitment to a well-supported theology department with university-wide requirements.[16] One wonders in times of restricted budgets and curricular redesign how many would vote to drop university-wide requirements in theology, and then how many students would still take theology courses if not required. (And would it be any different for courses in philosophy, physics, and mathematics?) Yet, as a discipline with its own tested methods and a body of knowledge, carefully elaborated over two millennia, Christian theology remains central to the curriculum and life of a Catholic university.

If theology is so important, what ought to be the vision that guides a theology department at a Catholic university? I shall concentrate here on the undergraduate level. I believe that in a Catholic university a theology department should focus on the Catholic tradition and introduce all students,

---

somewhat exaggerated form when he writes: "In our time it is not unusual for students in divinity school to say something like: 'I'm not into Christology this year. I really am into relating.' In response they are told: 'Well, then, you ought to take some more courses in Clinical Pastoral Education. After all, that is what the ministry is really about today [i.e., relating]. So take some courses that will teach you better how to relate.'

"It is interesting to contrast that kind of response to someone who might enter medical school thinking, 'I'm not really into anatomy this year. I'm really into relating. I'd like to take some more courses in psychology.' The response in medical schools is radically different from that in divinity schools. Such a student is usually told: 'We're not really interested in what you're interested in. You either take anatomy or you can simply ship out!'

"It is interesting to ask what accounts for these differences. I think they derive from the fact that no one anymore really believes that an incompetently trained priest might threaten his or her salvation, since no one really believes that anything is at stake in salvation; but people do think that an incompetently trained doctor might in fact do them serious harm. People no longer believe in a God that saves, but they do believe in death, and they know that they want to put it off as long as possible. They assume, wrongly, but no less dogmatically, that medical care can add significant years to their lives. Accordingly, the social power of medicine continues to increase in our society, and the power of religion diminishes.

"That medicine has such social power explains why medical education is so much more morally serious than the education of people going into the ministry. In medical education students are subjected to a rigorous discipline that trains them to attend to others in a way that gives them skills of attention and care. Thus, we continue to expect physicians to study and train themselves even after graduation in a manner that we do not expect of those in the ministry. What skills and knowledge do ministers have that anyone else does not already have?"

"The contrast between ministry and medicine is nicely exhibited in our respect for how each discipline structures its time. Physicians can be late for appointment, not show up at all, be curt in certain situations without the need for apology or explanation. It is simply assumed that such behavior is excused because they are attending to patients, studying to know how to better care for patients, or are under great stress. In contrast, those in the ministry have to be on time, always be available, and perpetually act pleasant."

[16] A recent article in the *Christian Century* (21 April 1993): 422-23, reports that religious studies faculties at state universities fear administrators who, in times of budgetary cuts and "downsizing," will see such departments as the least painful cuts, the most expendable of university programs. On the other hand, Claude Welch of the Graduate Theological Union in Berkeley, California, notes: "One of the underlying reasons why it seems so easy to cut back on religious studies, especially in public institutions, may be just the fact that many religious studies faculty have tried hard to distance themselves from the religious community and 'theology.'"

regardless of their own religious background, to the Catholic intellectual tradition and to the discipline of theology. At the same time, such a department can and must recognize and study other religious traditions, and address issues of interest not only to the faculty but also to the students.

A recent article by Thomas O'Meara on what a department of Catholic theology should emphasize in its curriculum illustrates well my position.[17] O'Meara states that a "contemporary Catholic" model must be both pluralistic and global. As to the subject focus of such a department, O'Meara writes: "Adequately ecumenical, it should not pursue the fundamentalisms of the Middle Ages or of today. It should offer the rich traditions (there is no such thing as *the* tradition in Catholicism) of western and eastern Christianity. The Catholic sacramental perspective should be recognized, and some courses (joining gospel and philosophy, theories and problems) should teach liturgy, church, spirituality, or ethics." O'Meara stresses the importance of good teaching. He states that "teachers in a theology department which wants to have a chance of interesting students cannot spend their entire time in transitory theories about epistemology, in historical denunciations of past cultures, or in fantastic revisions of the present, while in daily life religion is arousing new sects and igniting military conflicts, facing difficult issues of genetic research, and pondering the search for the mystical." Moreover, teachers of theology need to realize there is an affective as well as intellectual component to teaching theology: "A combination of experience and intellectual presentation marks the best teachers and creates a dynamic and personal atmosphere for the school."[18]

Finally, O'Meara advances a position that places squarely in front what he sees as the real needs of the students (all of whom, he seems to presume, will be Catholic): "College students should have the opportunity to learn something about their own faith at a mature level before being exposed to facts and theories about other religions. The dialogue between Christianity and the world religions is of the utmost importance but that would not be the excuse for a Catholic university to offer more courses in Iranian religion than in Christology."[19] In summary, according to O'Meara, at a Catholic university

[17] "The Department of Theology at a Catholic University," *The Challenge and Promise of a Catholic University*, 243-56. However, O'Meara's description of the second of his three models (first, department of religious studies at a state university; second, ecumenical; and third, contemporary Catholic) seems unfelicitously named, since by it he means several things, some good and some bad. On the negative side, he has in mind a department in which there are many courses that are a "melange of liberal Protestantism and modern philosophy," but "almost no courses on Christ, the Eucharist, spirituality, social ethics, the eastern churches" (pp. 251-52). He does recognize students' need to learn about other religious traditions, but criticizes a department that would try to be "essentially" ecumenical, without being mainly Catholic. Perhaps a better term for the second model would be "non-denominational," though that term, in reality, often is just another name for a fundamentalistically oriented Protestantism. Perhaps "pluralist" comes closer to describing his second model.

[18] O'Meara, "Department of Theology," 252-54.

[19] There may be in O'Meara's recommendation of focusing on Catholicism first a certain artificial chronology which presumes you learn your own tradition and then start talking

a department of theology should not try to be like a religious studies department in a state university. Rather, it should focus on the Catholic traditions while remaining global and pluralistic, and provide courses that will acquaint students with that tradition, and be staffed by professors who embody those traditions in both experience and understanding.[20]

It is easy to sense in O'Meara's treatment a genuine concern for the faith of Catholic students. I think this concern is neither patronizing nor misplaced. What should be done when students who are not Catholic, or who are Catholic but alienated from the Church, form an integral part of a particular class in Catholic theology? This is a complicated matter that O'Meara does not address. Here, I can say only that the subject matter should be treated in a sufficiently fair and intellectually stimulating way to interest students who are not Catholics, as well as even nonbelievers. Moreover, though the focus be on Catholicism, that focus cannot be exclusive. Discussions and even courses about other religions are also needed.

On some campuses, a sharp distinction has been drawn between the work of campus ministry and that of the department of theology, a distinction which taken to an extreme allows for faculty members, who may perhaps be preoccupied with achieving a sort of academic parity with other departments, to be concerned with only the intellectual aspects of religion, and campus ministry staff to be concerned with everything but the intellectual. To distinguish too sharply the pastoring function of campus ministry and the critical reflection of the theology department is wrong, writes John Haughey, for "teaching must retain a pastoral side to it—and all the more so if the subject matter is faith and reflection thereon."[21] I believe professors of theology should be aware of the very real practical and pastoral dimensions of theology, but avoid turning classrooms into forums for religious therapy. Theology is a disciplined way of thinking, a discipline into which too few are adequately initiated.

Besides a sensitivity to both the pastoral and intellectual need of students,

---

to"others out there"; very few American Catholics actually live like that any more.

[20] Though O'Meara does not say so, I presume that even on the undergraduate level, in a department of considerable size it would be good to have some theologians from other religious traditions. I shall leave aside the important question of what is best to do when even a significant minority of the student body is neither Catholic, nor eighteen to twenty-two years of age. Another important question is whether two or three required courses will be enough to cover the methods, concepts, and issues needed for a mature understanding of Catholic theology.

[21] "Theology and the Mission of the University," *Conversations* (spring 1994): 7. By pastoral, Haughey means "personalized guidance, caring for, leading the individuals in one's care beyond religious credulity into critical reflection on a faith that is not snuffed out by the teacher's rationalism or agnosticism or ignorance or bitterness, etc." (7). He adds that such concern is all the more necessary with undergraduates. For several years, I had the privilege of serving on the board of *Collegium*, a week long summer institute on "faith and the intellectual life" for students nearing completion of their doctoral degrees and for young faculty at Catholic universities. I was struck by the hunger that most of them—very sophisticated Ph.D.s—showed for spirituality, experiences of prayer and personal sharing of faith. I think that theology professors run the risk of underestimating the importance of this hunger, and of finding academically sound ways to inform and guide it.

I add one other concern. In recent years I have often heard it said by faculty of theology departments that they do not "do catechetics." By such a statement they intend, I suppose, to stress the necessary dimension of critical thinking which they assume to be absent in catechetics. But sometimes they are also alluding with dismay to the religious illiteracy of their students. In other words, they are asking how to teach students to reflect critically upon a faith of which they are ignorant. The first need of students, it seems to me, is to appropriate intellectually something integral to the tradition. If students lack that background, then the faculty should provide supplemental instruction just as history and language professors do to get students up to speed in the discipline. Once up to speed, students can be introduced into the rich theological work that has been produced by faculty who participate both in a believing community and in the academic community.

Catechesis, incidentally, is not just preparatory for theology, for theology always has a catechetical component, just as catechesis has a critical component. The department of theology at a Catholic university hands on the tradition (catechesis), reflects systematically and critically upon that tradition (theology), and recognizes the hierarchy of truths, as well as the importance both of official teaching and of being a part of the larger global reality of the Church (Catholicism).

Key Activities that Affect the Nature of a Catholic University

We have considered the distinction between theology and religious studies and the shape and emphases of the theological curriculum for undergraduates. Since faculty construct and sustain curricula, we must now consider the critically important matter of faculty selection.

Faculty Selection

In stating the implications of Notre Dame's Catholic mission, Father Malloy said in May of 1993 that "the Catholic identity of the University depends upon, and is nurtured by, the continuing presence of a predominant number of Catholic intellectuals."[22] Although Malloy might have found a less provocative word than "predominant," and might have also stated explicitly that anyone interested in the Catholic intellectual life and the mission of the university is welcome (a clarification he made subsequently), he is absolutely right in my view to have located the core of an educational institution's identity in the religious beliefs and research preoccupations of its faculty.[23]

I have stated that shaping a theology department at a Catholic university depends first on the shared vision of the department and the administration of

[22] Quoted in Wilson D. Miscamble, C.S.C., "Mission and Method in Constructing a Great Catholic University," *The Challenge and the Promise*, 214.

[23] Speaking of the Catholic university as a whole, David Burrell writes: "So long as the

what such a department should be and do. This is not to undervalue the critical importance of providing sufficient money for all needed faculty positions, efficient office support and capable research assistance, excellent teaching, office and library facilities, bright and interested students, and an administration that respects the faculty's work, guards the time for their reflection and research, and leaves them free to do it. Of course, most institutions do not have all of these resources. Many have only a few. But none of these resources of themselves or even taken together will insure that a university will have an excellent theology department. These optimal conditions are generic; that is, they would apply to any university. The real question then, is not about the kind of resources listed; the real question is about the vision that governs the expenditures of money, that guides the energies drawn upon, and graces the time it will take to build a theology department within a university.

Because the vision that guides a university is so important, I have spent some time describing what I believe are essential elements of a Catholic university and of a department of theology within such a university. Useful statements of vision are specific enough to provide orientation, general enough to empower administrators and faculty to make decisions to realize that vision, and open enough to accommodate the many different dimensions and departments of the university.

At no point does the instantiation of such a vision become as important as in the process of faculty selection. A good process for hiring will take considerable time, all of which is well invested, for, as Ray Schroth, S.J., once remarked, "hiring is the first step in a million-dollar relationship more permanent than most marriages, a forty-year opportunity to affect the beliefs of young people and the character of the institution."[24] In most universities, in contrast to the business world, hiring is a highly collegial process. To the extent that faculty governance is strong, guided by a common vision, as I have described it above, then hiring will strengthen the Catholic identity of the department. If it is not, then there will be some rough sailing for a while.

Federal laws have made certain personal questions about the faith of a candidate for a faculty position inappropriate. Yet, there are many ways to gauge whether a prospective faculty member will contribute to the overall

<hr />

quest for Catholic identity can be pursued in a sufficiently inclusive manner, calling upon all who see their life as a gift, their work as a call rather than a career, and our relation to the world as conservation rather than exploitation, we will find many people open to the invitation to join such a venture. They will be people of other faiths or of no recognizable faith at all, yet personally searching for something more than standard academe. If our Catholic heritage will allow us to become distinctive in that way, we can find willing and committed allies." This all-embracing vision of the faculty of the Catholic university as a whole needs to be more sharply focused when speaking of the faculty of a department of theology. On this see Burrell, "A Catholic University," 43. For an excellent discussion of the academic life as a vocation, see Mark R. Schwehn, *Exiles from Eden: Religion and the Academic Vocation in America* (New York: Oxford University Press, 1993).

[24] Ray Schroth, S.J., "Academic Freedom and the Catholic Identity" (paper presented at DePaul University, Chicago, Ill., April 30-May 1, 1987), 12.

mission of the university and the department in particular. If the position to be filled is at the senior or associate level, the task is less difficult. A careful reading of that person's publications usually indicates clearly the direction of his or her thinking. Candid conversations with the candidate's colleagues and perceptive personal conversations should provide a good sense of the person's "fit" with the vision.[25]

If the person to be hired is just beginning his or her academic career, the university must make known the importance of its mission and determine whether the prospective faculty member can contribute effectively to it. Such knowledge is especially important in the case of the department of theology. This process should begin in the position description itself, which in most instances ought to make clear the mission of the department and the university.[26] In addition, at different points along the hiring process, and not just at the end when the individual has an interview with the major academic administrator, the overall mission of the university and the role of the department should be explained. Obviously, members of the theology department and especially the chair should play key roles in communicating the distinct mission of the department.

We should not presume that being explicit about the mission of the university throughout the hiring process will deter good faculty candidates. Personally, I have heard many candidates fresh from their doctoral work say that they are looking for three things in a university: a place where both teaching and research are valued (often they add that this would be unlike the emphasis solely on research at the research institution from which they received their Ph.D.); second, a place where they can raise their family, by which I assume they mean a sense of community and family, the quality of colleagueship and, in general, the atmosphere of support; and third, though less frequently, a place where both excellence and religious inspiration are valued. If being explicit about the university's mission is appropriate in the hiring process for all faculty, it is, then, even more appropriate for the hiring of faculty for the department of theology. Effective faculty selection for the theology department depends on a shared vision grounded in an understanding of its mission, clear communication of that mission from the beginning of the selection process, and attention to the needs of the students and the role

[25] "Fit" does not mean that every person hired at a Catholic university is to be some sort of clone. We all know of too many Catholic faculty who contribute little to the mission of the university, while faculty from other faiths and sometimes from no particular faith effectively support the mission. Another topic that needs honest discussion is what to do with some Catholic faculty in theology departments who are disaffected from the Church and indifferent or even hostile to important dimensions of its intellectual heritage.

[26] I say in most cases, because it sometimes may happen that for certain other departments there are very few candidates who will be Catholic or who, at least at first, will resonate with the distinctive mission of the institution. Sometimes it is possible to find candidates who, while relatively ignorant of Catholicism, are genuinely interested in the educational ideals that flow from that tradition. Such candidates can, in time, make very valuable contributions to the mission of the university.

the department plays in the university.

For appointments to a department of theology, a university should not be put in a situation where it has to choose between a first-rate academic with no interest in the university's mission and a Catholic with little academic promise. At that point, the search should be reopened. The best departments and administrations do not advertise for a faculty position and then wait to see who will apply. Rather, they begin with a list of the most desirable candidates whom frequently they have already met at professional meetings or know about through colleagues and then proceed actively to recruit them. Search committees who take such a proactive stance rarely find themselves faced with choosing between a candidate with academic excellence and one with only a good fit with the university's mission.

Faculty Development

Faculty development, that is, investing in the strengthening of already existing faculty, can be as important as "hiring," and often is a key factor in creating an atmosphere that is attractive to individuals whom a department wishes to recruit. Faculty development is a very important way of bringing the best out of those faculty who are already committed to the university's mission, and those faculty who show the most promise in contributing to it. Faculty development works well when deans and chairs of departments devote as much time to developing the talents of the faculty as they do managing the efficient functioning of the various support systems integral to running an academic institution.

Ordinary means for faculty development are sabbatical programs, research leaves, and reduced teaching loads. University administrators should sustain a conversation among the faculty about research projects that not only interest faculty members, but also strengthen departmental offerings. Given a specific vision for the theology department, the research undertaken by the faculty should, on the whole, support that vision. Sabbaticals that contribute to the department or the university's mission, broadly understood, should have a competitive advantage over those that do not.

The administration plays a key role in articulating a vision of a Catholic university engaging enough that faculty are moved to shape their research agendas so that that vision receives intellectual embodiment in their academic work.

Curricular Development

Since the faculty develops the curriculum, faculty development has a direct impact upon the curriculum. Discussions about the curriculum, especially the required curriculum, often become contentious and protracted debates. Nonetheless, they can offer excellent opportunities to explore what the distinctive vision of the university really means, not only for the faculty, but also for the students, that is, what it means for a curriculum. Some discussions about the mission of a university produce only boredom. Most discussions about the core curriculum produce lightning and thunder. Yet, the key element in shaping the core curriculum should be the mission of the institution. When this curricular discussion is fruitful, when it is rooted in the distinctive mission of the institution, then the important role of the theology department should become more evident to the entire academic community.[27]

Interdisciplinary Initiatives

Another important area for faculty development is interdisciplinary initiatives. While individual faculty members sometimes attempt interdisciplinary efforts, they often find themselves swimming very much against the rules set by the larger academic world, which thinks of such faculty as likely to be incompetent in two disciplines, and lets them know this in the promotion and tenure process. It is precisely here that major academic administrators, including chairs of departments, need to support such efforts, precisely because they provide, when undertaken thoughtfully, connections and links between areas of knowledge that otherwise remain unconnected, for both faculty and students. The requirement of the research Ph.D. degree for admission to a university faculty, one of the causes of extensive specialization, has been with us only since the turn of the century. Yet, many departments have become "entrenched duchies,"[28] entities that need to be related to other departments so that the interconnectedness of knowledge becomes more apparent to both faculty and students. Sometimes administrators need to go beyond encouragement; they need to intervene to force departments to work more closely together or lose faculty positions or other resources. If Catholic universities are to be places of wisdom and not just of information and knowledge, then such connections need to be fostered both by faculty with real support from the administration. Interdisciplinary efforts often indicate what an institution really thinks is important for education. Unfortunately, truly interdisciplinary initiatives remain rare. If such interdisciplinary initiatives are not undertaken, the important contribution that a theology department can make in exploring the connections between various fields of knowledge will likely go unrealized.

One of the most significant interdisciplinary efforts at a Catholic university should be its general education, or core curriculum program. The theol-

---

[27] Unfortunately, very little is said today about the importance of philosophy departments in strengthening Catholic identity. While it is not desirable in my view to return to the Thomistic system that shaped the content of both philosophy and religion departments before Vatican II, there is a great need today to rediscover both the value of philosophy for a fuller Christian humanism and to find new ways for theologians and philosophers to engage each other in the process of thinking through issues that face the Church today. See David Burrell's essay, "A Catholic University," *The Challenge and the Promise*, 35-44, for a thoughtful description of the shape a philosophy department might have today at a Catholic university.

[28] Cunningham, "Gladly Wolde He Lerne," 6.

ogy faculty should be deeply involved in the conversation that creates that program. That conversation, which is a continuous one, helps create among the faculty a larger conversation about Catholic intellectual traditions. One can also bring faculty together for discussion, for example, about faith and their disciplines, or about the classics of Christianity and their own lives, or about the sciences and theology. In every instance, members of the theology faculty can make an important contribution to the distinctive intellectual concerns of the entire faculty.

Conclusion

One does not have to agree with John Henry Newman, or more recently, with Michael Buckley, S.J.,[29] who see theology as the ultimate point of the integration of knowledge in a Catholic university, to affirm that a theology department ought to play an important role within the university. If it remains understaffed, academically suspect, internally divided, or divided from the rest of the university, then an essential, if not the essential, dimension of a Catholic university remains missing. Immediately, the mission of a theology department rests on its faculty. In the long run, the department will achieve that mission if the administration of the university articulates continuously and persuasively the distinctive mission of a Catholic university and finds the resources necessary to support that mission.

---

[29] See his "The Catholic University and Its Inherent Promise," *America* 168 (29 May 1993): 14-16; see also his discussion with David O'Brien, "A Collegiate Conversation," *America* 169 (11 September 1993): 18-23.

14

Institutional Resources in the Seminary

Thomas R. Kopfensteiner

I n addressing the issue of institutional resources in the seminary, there is a need to further specify and limit further the context from which I speak. Kenrick-Glennon Seminary (St. Louis), where I teach, is a freestanding seminary, with cross registration available with a school of ministry, a university which has a graduate school of theology, and a variety of Protestant divinity schools in the metropolitan area. The reality, however, is that most seminarians do all of their course work at the seminary, and when students from other institutions attend classes at the seminary, it is because of sabbatical schedules at their home institution. So while preparation for ministry can take place in a variety of contexts, ours is a rather uniform one.

Our mission is simple: to prepare men for ordination to the priesthood in the Roman Catholic Church. The means to fulfill this mission is a five-year professional program of theological and pastoral education. All graduates receive the master of divinity; a few students each year elect to achieve a master of arts. If training men to be priests is the purpose or soul of the institution, then it is embodied and implemented through the resources at our disposal. Our resources are the same as any other school of theology: pedagogy, curriculum, and faculty development. Who are those teaching? What do they teach? And how do they teach? These three elements form an organic whole, interrelated in such a way that the discussion of one aspect requires a discussion of the others. When, for instance, we introduce a new program, we indirectly offer norms for the faculty; the way theology is to be presented effects the kind of faculty that is recruited, and conversely, the people who are recruited to teach will effect the program that is offered.

In our postmodern world, context is everything. We must continually evaluate the context of our teaching. Quite simply this means that we cannot transfer the teaching methods successful in one context into another. There must be a clear assessment of the background and talents of the students in order to adjust the course material accordingly. Though the students may all be seminarians preparing for ordination, what are their backgrounds? Is there a student profile which indicates their religious and educational background? What is the cultural ethos from which the students come? Where will they minister when they are ordained? Do those locations require unique personal or ministerial skills? In the same way, institutions need to be clear on the criteria by which potential faculty members will be assessed. A theologian may be looking for a job, but is he or she suited to the pedagogical and curricular needs of the seminary? What are the criteria of an effective or "good" teacher in this particular institution? Lacking a proper fit is a prescription for future problems. Concern for curriculum and pedagogy in a seminary also effects those not actually in a classroom. For instance, pedagogy and curriculum will effect the recruitment of potential candidates or sponsoring dioceses, the place of field education in the program, the spiritual formation of the students, the lay boards who evaluate and supervise pastoral interns, and even the financial expenditures to maintain an adequate library collection.

There are several metaphors that can help sculpt the discussion of pedagogy, faculty, and curriculum. Theoretically, metaphors set up cognitive topologies in which to identify, discuss, and solve certain problems. A change in metaphor has the power to disrupt traditional relationships within a cognitive field in a way that allows us to see and talk about the field in a new way. A first metaphor constructs theological education as the acquisition of skills and techniques. This metaphor relies on the language of cognitive psychology and underscores ministry as a practical science: a candidate needs certain skills to be an effective minister, though those skills can be minimally construed to mean "being able to administer the sacraments." As a moral theologian, however, I have initial hesitancy when talking about education in terms of skills. In our technological society it is easy to associate "skill" with the technological sciences where one can perform his or her duties by rote. Technological skills do not capture the commitment of our hearts that ministry requires. Schools of theology become little more than schools of technical expertise in which students fail to see the transformative power of theology. We encourage the situation described by Katarina Schuth when she writes: "At more progressive theologates where traditional students are in the minority and at more conservative theologates where liberal students are in the minority, such students acknowledged that they tend to keep their views to themselves until after ordination. The words of one seminarian speak for more than a few students: 'The message is to play the role until you are ordained, and then you can really express what you believe.'"[1] Or as one spiritual director has remarked, seminary training is like going through a car wash where one turns off the engine, pulls down the antenna, roles up the windows, and sits back and enjoys the ride without being touched in any way!

Another metaphor focuses on the rational character of education and ministry as a public profession built upon a certain body of knowledge. Priests

---

[1] Katarina Schuth, *Reason for the Hope: The Futures of Roman Catholic Theologates* (Wilmington, Del.: Michael Glazier, 1989), 119.

are to be intelligent and well versed in Scripture and Christian doctrine. George Schner labels this metaphor the "banking metaphor" of education.[2] Knowledge is stored up to be used later in a pastoral situation. Surely if the goal of education is to store up knowledge, the good teacher is the one who gives out an ample body of knowledge; a good curriculum is one that hoists a hefty number of hours on its students; and a good class will be one in which a student leaves with a good stack of notes with the confidence that he or she can apply it appropriately when needed. There is no doubt that education involves the gathering and retention of knowledge, but the gathering of information may be too secure a path for many of our candidates for ministry. There is a passivity to this metaphor. Theological education can lose its critical edge. Students are not challenged to explore the questions that will of necessity challenge and reshape the tradition. The promise for the truth is quickly reduced to the achievement of security.

A third metaphor constructs Christianity not in terms of skills or ideas, but experience. The metaphor of self-expression takes "experience" as its starting point but with a particular understanding of Christianity. When experience is the basis of education, good teaching emphasizes the appropriation of knowledge about faith. Good teaching is translating and applying the message of faith into new and varied contexts. If the banking metaphor emphasized the tradition at the expense of critical thought experiments, the metaphor of self-expression can lose any sense of the tradition in the name of relevancy. Certainly, we can recount the outrageous abuses of this metaphor in a variety of theological schools, but I would be surprised if any of our seminaries went so far as to completely discard the cognitive content of faith. In a legitimate way, the metaphor of self-expression is behind our asking if we are preparing ministers adequately for the twenty-first century. Are we preparing ministers aware of the pluralism in the Church? Are we preparing ministers sensitive to women? Are our candidates committed to fighting injustice or entering into solidarity with the weakest and most vulnerable members of our society? No doubt, these are legitimate questions. "Unlike the training or banking metaphors, the art of teaching according to the metaphor of self- expression does not consist in having the patience to insist on just the right exercises over and over again, nor having the assurance to insist upon the details of the matter, but rather being tolerant and encouraging of inventiveness."[3]

These three metaphors construct what is going forward when one is teaching. Each reflects the diversity of contexts in which theological education can take place. They illuminate the way in which one teaches, and what one teaches. Is teaching a matter of training, accumulation of ideas, or the encouragement of self-expression? Is the Christian faith a matter of skills, ideas,

---

[2] George Schner, *Education for Ministry: Reform and Renewal in Theological Education* (Kansas City: Sheed & Ward, 1993), 131-32.
[3] Ibid., 133.

or experiences?[4]

I would like to propose a fourth metaphor for theological education. It draws on recent work in virtue ethics, but is not entirely new to theological education. The metaphor of friendship can illuminate the task of teaching. In his wonderful treatment of the spirituality of education, Parker Palmer writes: "The teacher, who knows the subject well, must introduce it to students in the way one would introduce a friend. The student must know why the teacher values the subject, how the subject has transformed the teacher's life. By the same token the teacher must value the students as potential friends, be vulnerable to the ways students may transform the teacher's relationship with the subject as well as be transformed."[5] The metaphor of friendship subordinates the acquisition of skills, the attainment of knowledge, and cultivation of creativity to a larger reality.

Within the metaphor of friendship, there is the ability to be in conversation with the faith tradition. As teachers, we have been educated in a tradition. We do not merely possess the technique to teach well, we have been schooled in a tradition, a school of thought. We have acquired a certain vocabulary that allows us to identify certain problems, and to speak about them in a certain way. I think for instance of the schools of Louvain, Rome, Chicago, Yale, and Washington in the area of moral theology. Each school's graduates will be concerned with different issues, and if they share a common concern, they will speak and reason about it differently. Since faculties usually are not recruited from the same graduate programs, a faculty profile would identify the group of friends or community of scholars who have informed and shaped a faculty's teaching. Who are our educational ancestors? We carry with us the effective history of our education and educators and it is this effective history that we share with our students. Further, the friendship metaphor reminds us that education is a social affair. This is not only in the sense that ministry is the expression of a vocational commitment in the Church, but the theological enterprise has a communal character. None of us teaches alone. All of us are part of a larger curriculum to which we contribute and which determines, at least in part, what we teach. This corporate character of theology can be manifested in team taught courses, or by open classrooms in which other professors can lecture, or by overcoming the often lamented dichotomy between academics and field education.

Within the friendship metaphor there is also the ability to be enthusiastic for the tradition that we share. I do not mean a naive obedience to tradition or its authority, but the tradition that allows us to know anything at all. In doing so, we learn not only what we can ask, but the limits of the tradition itself. We know the questions and issues that challenge and have the power to reshape our tradition. A hermeneutic of tradition is complemented by a critique of ideology. We must have the courage to acknowledge the biases

---

[4] Ibid., 134.

[5] Parker J. Palmer, *To Know As We Are Known* (San Francisco: Harper and Row, 1983), 104.

and limits of our tradition in order to achieve more liberating possibilities. This goes far beyond the acquisition of skills or knowledge to a creative reimaging of the tradition when it encounters the other in dialogue. All friendships teach us something about ourselves, and we learn that not all friendships are virtuous. All contain an element of "dysfunction." We need to recognize what limitations or blind spots are inherent in our institutions. And here is a particular challenge to an institution such as a freestanding seminary. For instance, with such a homogenous situation, how do we train future ministers to deal with women or ecumenism? Why should we be surprised to hear negative feedback about our graduates in these areas when we exhibit systemic or institutional dysfunction in the same areas. How do we witness to toleration and diversity as an institution? Surely we do this within clear ecclesiastical boundaries, but nevertheless in ways that the seminary failed to do before the Second Vatican Council. Are there faculty from other faiths or denominations in our institutions? Is there a representation of the various vocations in the Church on our faculties—male and female, lay and ordained—to provide insight into the compatibility of both theological research and ministerial commitment?[6] Of particular sensitivity today is how this diversity contributes to a commonality of life, of which worship will be a significant part. Precisely here in a moment of unity, there is a counter-example of the mutuality and cooperation experienced elsewhere in the institution. As Schner reminds us, "the harmony of persons and activities which are ingredient in the corporate pedagogy of an institution risks losing an essential control over its own authenticity and credibility when worship becomes divisive, is experienced by any group as a hostile environment, or degenerates into being a forum for ideological concerns foreign to Christian belief's search for a radical integrity before God."[7]

While faculty excellence is in part measured by the institutions' relationship to the Church in providing adequate ministers, another concern of the seminary is the faculty's relationship to the academy. An institution's mission should not hinder the dialogue with the other disciplines that excellence in theological education requires. This touches a concern of many participants in this conference. Although theology in the academy is working to shed its modern ethos, the tradition-ing character of theological education (in the sense of incorporating students into a tradition of beliefs in order to minister) is often seen as a limit to the restructuring of theology. While theology in the seminary may seem a corrective to the modern ethos by protecting the authority of a tradition, failing to enter into dialogue with the other sciences leads to naive biblical scholarship, magisterial positivism, a suspicion of modern sciences, and an increasing tendency towards anti-intellectualism among ministerial candidates. Such an intellectually narrow audience puts an addi-

---

[6] Marjorie Suchocki, "Theological Foundations for Ethnic and Gender Diversity in Faculties or Excellence and the Motley Crew," *Theological Education* 26 (1990) 2:35-50.

[7] Schner, *Education for Ministry*, 160.

tional burden on faculty who feel isolated from the academy and who will often seek a more congenial atmosphere for their scholarship in other settings. Their loss further limits a seminary's credibility in the academy and the seminary's ability to recruit the requisite staff to meet its needs; it would limit the seminary to an ecclesial public. Seminaries are no longer able to depend upon religious congregations or local presbyterates to provide teachers and scholars. The problems have become exasperated, however, when new traditions of developing faculties emerge which of necessity begin to effect changes in the program that challenge the seminary to move beyond its traditional boundaries. Failure to reconfigure those borders—often in the name of ecclesiastical control—will move the very soul of ministerial preparation further and further away from the seminary. Seminaries that are isolated from the academy will do little more than train ideologues isolated from the faithful.

15

Bishops and Theologians

BISHOP FRANCIS E. GEORGE, O.M.I.

T he American philosopher Josiah Royce (1855-1916) devoted his life to constructing a normative philosophy, a metaethics, from the structures of human experience. His was an American response to the classic question of British empiricism: How does one derive "ought" from "is"? This essay seeks to uncover norms for the relationship between theologians and bishops from the Church's own self-understanding and from her current experience in this country. If the norms are pragmatically successful, harmony and mutual enrichment will characterize the exchange between bishops and theologians.

Because he was a philosophical idealist as well as a pragmatist, Royce presupposed that harmony was a richer and more normative experience than conflict. In the inadequate and painful experience of two opposing parties, Royce looked always for a third party, less a mediator than an interpreter, in order to move progressively toward more and more inclusivity in action, and in the world created by human action. In his epistemology, for example, Royce was helped by Charles Saunders Peirce to see that judgment is the interpreter which unites conception and perception. When he turned his mind to practical philosophy, Royce's preferred solution to social conflict was to turn each dyadic relationship into a triadic relationship which included the conflicted parties in a richer and more inclusive community. His models seem almost pedestrian, so intent was he to make philosophy practical. Royce spoke of insurance companies, for example, as interpreters between "adventurers" (the policy holders) and "beneficiaries." When adventurers take a risk, they put themselves in conflict with others who could lose by their failure. The insurer makes of these potential losers potential beneficiaries, thereby mediating the conflict between the two parties. What had been a dyadic relation is now triadic; a dangerous pair has become a new community.

I want to co-opt Royce's insight into the nature of community in order to justify bringing a third party into the relationship between theologians and bishops. The third party is the body of believers, Christ's faithful. John Henry Newman thought that theologians as well as bishops should consult the faithful on matters of doctrine, and Royce's theory of interpretation as a normative framework for intra-ecclesial relationships finds an analogue in Newman's lengthy Catholic introduction to his republished Anglican work, *The Via Media*. Newman made use of John Calvin's triple office of Christ the prophet, Christ the priest, and Christ the King or Shepherd to portray Church office in its fullness. Since Yves Congar made use of Newman to shape *Lumen Gentium*, the ecclesiology of Vatican II uses this same tripartite ministry to define the gifts of Christ that an ecclesial entity must possess and share in order to be called "Church" in the complete sense of the term. Newman, however, instantiates the three functions in a way different from *Lumen Gentium*. Christianity, he writes, "is at once a philosophy, a political power, and a religious rite: as a religion, it is Holy; as a philosophy, it is Apostolic; as a political power, it is imperial, that is, One and Catholic." Newman continues, "The instrument of theology is reasoning; of worship, our emotional nature; of rule, command and coercion. Further, in man as he is, reasoning tends to rationalism; devotion to superstition and enthusiasm; and power to ambition and tyranny."[1]

Paraphrasing and combining Royce and Newman, I would suggest that theologians develop doctrine; the laity develop devotion, in the sense of personal piety and popular religiosity; and bishops act as a kind of interpreter to unite the ecclesial community by judging devotional development in the light of doctrine and doctrinal development in the light of devotion. In fact, I believe this paradigm sets out the way most bishops actually think and work, whether self-consciously or not.

If an apparition is reported in the diocese, for example, the bishop's first question is: How is this message, if there is one, compatible with Scripture and Church teaching? Lay people, by contrast, will usually ask themselves if the apparition strengthens their devotion, their sense of closeness to God. The two reactions come together in the recognition that our closeness to God in Christ is attenuated when the faith of the Church is distorted. Without an ecclesially formed faith, the mind of Christ is, at best, only partially present to one searching for intimacy with God: "in faith, the believer seizes the faith of the Church and the *fides Christi* immediately, for it is hypostatically one with the *fides Dei* in Christ."[2]

When, on the other hand, a somewhat novel presentation of doctrine is published by a theologian, the bishop will, of course, ask if it seems consistent with divine revelation, but he must and will also ask whether this teaching will strengthen or weaken his devotion and that of the laity. Theologians, by contrast, once they have judged the evidence for the idea, will ask how the new thesis or novel methodological approach shifts the entire corpus of Church teaching in a way that clarifies and develops it or, perhaps, just makes it more intriguing.

---

[1] See John Henry Newman, *The Via Media*, xxxviii-xliii. Republished in the uniform edition of Newman's works; London: Longmans, Green, 1868-1881.

[2] Hans Urs von Balthasar, "Fides Christi: An Essay on the Consciousness of Christ," *Spouse of the Word* (San Francisco: Ignatius Press, 1991), 79.

Since we are here engaged in a conversation between bishops and theologians, permit me to make a case in point. How might a bishop respond in reading that the postmodern experience of God is panentheistic, especially when this assertion about religious experience is then used to support fundamental changes in trinitarian doctrine and ecclesial polity?[3] The bishop's first reaction is probably to recall that panentheism was condemned by the First Vatican Council: "Si quis dixerit . . . Deum esse ens universale seu indefinitum quod sese determinando constituat rerum universitatem in genera, species et individua distinctam: A.S."[4] The bishop's probable second reaction is to ask himself if he has lost his chance to be postmodern since, in his spiritual life, the classic doctrine of the indwelling of the Trinity expresses very well his sense of intimacy with God, and this doctrine precludes panentheism. His third reaction is therefore to judge the statement theologically wrong-headed and spiritually pernicious, while his fourth reaction is to ask how he can say that without sounding mean-spirited or closed-minded. His fifth reaction is relief at not having to say anything at all because, among the Mexican farm workers, the Anglo orchardists, the Filipino vegetable growers, and even the native peoples of the diocese, there seems to be not a single panentheist. The theological assertion seems out of touch with the faith of the people he serves, as evidenced in their devotion.

In fact, even as a working hypothesis for sorting out intra-ecclesial roles, this ideal ecclesial triad of theologians-bishops-people, like Royce's ideal absolute community itself, finds concrete expression only with difficulty. It presupposes effective contact and communication among all parties in the Church. Major obstacles to such communication are the nonecclesial filters through which both lay devotion and theological doctrine pass today. Bishops can, if they care to, create and somewhat control an ecclesial theater of expression for their judgments in the form of sermons and pastoral letters, even if these have only limited influence. Laity and theologians must find other means.

When Newman spoke of "devotion" he meant the expression of what theologians and bishops call the *sensus fidei* among the faithful. Where and how is this sense of the faith expressed in the United States? One locus for such expression used to be popular devotions such as novenas. Because popular religiosity is often crowded out by official liturgy in the U.S. Church today, the faithful sometimes turn to movements of various sorts or to the mass media to express their faith publicly. A bishop trying to interpret what he reads or hears from laity often finds himself questioning whether a request from a movement or a declaration in the press is evidence of popular religiosity, which is more surely normative for the faith, or simply an expression of popular opinion, which may or may not be normative for the faith. Mass movements

---

[3] See, among others, Elizabeth Johnson, *She Who Is: The Mystery of God in Feminist Theological Discourse* (New York: Crossroad, 1992).

[4] DS, 1804.

and mass media can be manipulative, even when their users are sincere. The media are often poor vehicles for authentic expression of religious faith. How is the bishop to gauge devotion in order to interpret it to those theologians open to its correction?

Academic theologians, for their part, can express themselves in their classroom, in professional associations, or in the specialized journals of their profession. But the subculture of modern academic institutions is often no more ecclesial or apt for the expression of doctrines of the faith than are the mass media. The dominant feature of the contemporary university's organization is the department devoted to a particular discipline. It makes specialization possible and controls the reward system for professors and students. Requirements for courses and degrees are the moats defending the departmental castle, the forts protecting the discipline's turf. To allow interlopers, even episcopal interlopers explaining the faithful's devotion, into a department brings with it the risk of not being taken seriously in the academy.

Further, the social structure of the university not only defends interests; it also canonizes values. It insists that dogmatism stifles truth, but it will not acknowledge that pluralism can obscure truth. Its primary value, since the Age of Enlightenment, is Cartesian doubt too often masquerading as critical intelligence. Its founding myth is that of the solitary and courageous intellectual taking on obscurantist and authoritarian systems of all sorts, especially ecclesiastical. In this kind of academic milieu, there is silence about ultimates, unless they can be treated as the foundations of academic disciplines or traced to private choices. Pluralism as an ideal makes even theologians who are professional academics hesitate to speak in ways that could be labeled contrary to the spirit of completely open-ended discourse. Faith then is no longer the basis of life but something added to it. Catholicism becomes "our tradition" rather than the vehicle for the Tradition that unites us to Christ.

If dialogue with the faith remains something to be pursued because a university is Catholic in its foundation and heritage, the modern university, by its inner logic, engages in this dialogue with and through the department of theology. The professional theologians who staff this department might very well admit that theology draws on the faith community for theology's primary data and that the intellectual content of faith needs to show its compatibility with the popular expression of faith, but specifically as academics they have difficulty maintaining their status in the university while entering into normative dialogue with either Church authority or lay devotion. Without welcome entry into theological circles, however, how can bishops evaluate theological work-in-process so as to shape lay devotion?

If our current experience as Church fosters isolation, future ecclesiastical harmony will seem almost impossible. The situation, somewhat overdrawn for the sake of discussion, harms theology. We are all familiar with Newman's judgment that the Spanish Inquisition, despite its use of the best theologians of its day, went terribly wrong because it was divorced from the bishops' pastoral governance.[5] Newman justifies pastoral authority by appeal to the history of heresy: "In reading ecclesiastical history, when I was an Anglican," he wrote in his autobiography,

> it used to be forcibly brought home to me, how the initial error of what afterwards became heresy was the urging forward of some truth against the prohibition of authority at an unseasonable time. There is a time for every thing, and many a man desires a reformation of an abuse, or the fuller development of a doctrine, or the adoption of a particular policy, but forgets to ask himself whether the right time for it is come; and knowing that there is no one who will be doing any thing towards its accomplishment in his own lifetime unless he does it himself, he will not listen to the voice of authority, and he spoils a good work in his own century, in order that another man, as yet un-born, may not have the opportunity of bringing it happily to perfec-tion in the next. He may seem to the world to be nothing else than a bold champion for the truth and a martyr to free opinion, when he is just one of those persons whom the competent authority ought to silence; and, though the case may not fall within that subject-matter in which that authority is infallible, or the formal condition of the exercise of that gift may be wanting, it is clearly the duty of authority to act vigorously in the case.[6]

My purpose in quoting so lengthily from Newman's *Apologia* is less to defend the record of hierarchical intervention in the theological community than to insist upon the harm to all because of the structured isolation of bish-ops, theologians, and laity from one another. For the sake of more vigorous discussion here, I would like to state that, of the three groups, academic theo-logians most risk isolation in the ecclesial community. In the normal course of the Church's life, laity and bishops must speak to each other; and bishops who have pastoral responsibilities must come to terms with the opinions and desires of the people they serve, if only, finally, to disagree with them. Theo-logians, however, need not be party to intra-ecclesial discussion at all. In the end, however, it is not just theology that is harmed; it is the Church that suf-fers.

How might a healthy triadic relationship of laity-bishop-theologian be established and strengthened? The bishop's role in the Church has been greatly clarified in the ecclesiology of the Second Vatican Council, but the exercise of pastoral oversight often leaves him little time to listen carefully to theolo-gians. The laity need a place to express their faith more publicly, and theolo-gians have to find ways to hear the faith of the people and to share their own expertise beyond university settings. Ideally, the next several years might

---

[5] See Newman, *The Idea of a University* (London: Longmans, Green, 1898), 215-16.
[6] See Newman, *Apologia pro Vita Sua* (London: Longmans, Green, 1918), 259.

witness the development of ecclesiastical fora where all three groups can interact in mutual respect. Such places and events would have to be planned so as to foster love rather than distrust. Too often do we seem to come together in suspicion or even anger. Royce's ideal community was beloved; and faith tells us that we cannot change what we do not love.

The love shared in the Church, finally, is Christ's. Institutional planning can create fora in which the laity can come to respect the honesty and seriousness of theologians' work, where theologians can develop an ever-deeper understanding of the laity's faith, and where bishops can become more attentive to what both theologians and laity are really saying. But Christ sends the Spirit who transforms these relationships into Church by giving us faith to interpret what our hearts know to be true.

16

Theologians and Bishops

ROBERT P. IMBELLI

I n his masterful study, *Magisterium*, Francis Sullivan remarks with wry humor:

It seems inevitable that on the question which I propose to treat in this final chapter, statements by members of the hierarchy will tend to stress the authority of the magisterium and the obligation on the part of theologians to follow its directives, while statements by theologians will tend to stress the freedom of theological research and publication, and the critical role of theology even with regard to documents of the magisterium. It is not easy to handle this question in such a way as to satisfy the legitimate preoccupations of both sides.[1]

Sullivan himself, in the chapter to which he refers, does a fine job of satisfying those "legitimate preoccupations" by providing a balanced and insightful commentary on the "Theses on the relationship between the ecclesiastical magisterium and theology," published by the International Theological Commission in 1976.[2]

In the following, though I write as a member of the "guild of theologians," I hope to display that equilibrium that acknowledges the legitimate concerns of both theologians and bishops as they pursue their indispensable, inseparable, yet distinct ministries within the Church.

Let me begin, then, with three general observations which govern all the remarks that follow. First, serious theological discussion of the relations be-

---

[1] Francis A. Sullivan, S.J., *Magisterium: Teaching Authority in the Catholic Church* (New York: Paulist, 1983), 174.

[2] Sullivan in *Magisterium*, 175-76, gives a brief history of the Commission. In Sullivan's article, "The Theologian's Ecclesial Vocation and the 1990 CDF Institution," *Theological Studies* 52 (March 1991): 51-68, he regrets the CDF's "failure to make use of the work done by the International Commission" with the result that the Instruction lacks a certain "equilibrium" (p. 51). Significantly the theses *are* drawn upon in the important guidelines approved by the United States Bishops entitled "Doctrinal Responsibilities: Approaches to Promoting Cooperation and Resolving Misunderstandings between Bishops and Theologians," *Origins* 19 (June 29, 1989): 97-110.

tween bishops and theologians must be situated in the generative and vivifying context of the Christian community itself. Bishops and theologians do not exist *in abstracto*, but *in concreto*: *in medio ecclesiae*. Though this observation may seem a mere commonplace, it immediately situates the discussion in its properly spiritual and ecclesial framework, where the ultimate authority, to which both bishops and theologians are subject, is the authority of the Holy Spirit. It thereby shows the inadequacy of Enlightenment thought forms that move in the direction of "power" and "rights" (a trend that Roman Catholicism, from the French Revolution up to the preparatory work for Vatican II, did not always successfully avoid) and their replacement by the more scriptural and patristic categories of "charisms" and "responsibilities."

Cardinal Ratzinger's presentation of the CDF's "Instruction" noted: "the document treats the ecclesial mission of the theologian, not in the context of the *dualism* Magisterium-theology, but rather in the framework of the *triangular* relationship defined by the people of God, understood as the bearer of the *sensus fidei* and the common locus of all faith, the Magisterium and theology."[3] This insertion of any discussion of the relations between bishops and theologians within the context of the mystery of the Church is the *conditio sine qua non* of its faithfulness and fruitfulness.

A second preliminary observation concerns the danger against which the Catholic University theologian, Joseph Komonchak, warns, with admirable empirical sensitivity:

> so to hypostatize "faith," "truth," "magisterium," "theology," "dissent," that these abstract nouns appear almost to be personal agents themselves. But "theology" does not do anything—theologians do; similarly, the "magisterium" at any particular moment means the pope and the bishops, quite specific agents. The whole discussion would be helped greatly if we were to get down to concrete cases and instances, historical or imagined.[4]

And Cardinal Ratzinger concurs: "the problems lie in the concrete."[5]

A final preliminary observation extends this insistence upon the concrete from persons to history. The concrete relationship between quite specific bishops and theologians exists, not *sub specie aeternitatis*, but in quite concrete historical circumstances and situations, themselves the product, in part, of specific historical developments and inheritances. Thus the relation between bishops and theologians has been different in different historical settings and to-

---

[3] Joseph Cardinal Ratzinger, *The Nature and Mission of Theology* (San Francisco: Ignatius Press, 1995), 104-5; italics mine. From the point of view of the North American cultural context, the American philosopher Josiah Royce, influenced by Charles Peirce, often warned against the danger of "dyadic" relations and the benefit of "triadic" relations.

[4] Joseph A. Komonchak, "The Magisterium and Theologians," *Chicago Studies* 29 (1990): 325.

[5] Ratzinger, *Nature and Mission*, 61.

day it will be lived out in the particular constellation of meanings and values, sensibilities and challenges that comprise what many deem to be a "postmodern" world.[6]

These observations suggest, then, the following order of presentation. I will first recall the present ecclesial context. Second, I will indicate my understanding of the theological challenge it poses. Third, I shall sketch some characteristics of a theological model, along the lines indicated by Avery Dulles when he speaks of an "ecclesial-transformative" approach to theology.[7] Fourth, in light of the preceding, I shall consider bishops and theologians within the Church, reflecting on common commitments and concerns, distinctive charisms and responsibilities, and inevitable tensions. Fifth and finally, I shall offer some suggestions concerning ongoing dialogue and discernment.

Ecclesial Context

There is little doubt that the Second Vatican Council constitutes the decisive ecclesial event of the twentieth century. Whether we speak of the "Copernican Revolution in Ecclesiology" effected by its two constitutions on the Church or, with Karl Rahner, of the new epoch of the multicultural world Church which it inaugurated,[8] the Council has clearly set the agenda for the next decades of ecclesial life and theological reflection.

In saying this I am also suggesting that the Council itself is still being "received" by the Church. Much of its accomplishment remains in the form of "blueprints" yet to be actualized. As Walter Kasper remarks trenchantly: "Whether this council will count in the end as one of the highlights of church history will depend on the people who translate its words into terms of real life."[9]

Thirty years after the close of the Council one is humbled in considering the labors and generosity of so many who have sought and are seeking to implement the Council. One thinks of the products of their labors: the new lectionary and sacramentary, new rites and music, new catechisms and social-justice initiatives. Undoubtedly, not all will stand the test of time; some are already being revised. Yet they are stages on the way to the realization of the Council's dual dynamic: a return to the sources (*ressourcement*) so as to

[6] For a brief treatment of the different historical forms of the relation between magisterium and theology, see Sullivan, *Magisterium*, 181-84; also Avery Dulles, "The Magisterium in History: A Theological Reflection," *Chicago Studies* 17 (summer 1978): 264-81. For a development of the notion of "postmodernity" and its implications for theology, see Hans Küng, *Christianity: Essence, History, Future* (New York: Continuum, 1995), esp. 764-97.

[7] See Avery Dulles, *The Craft of Theology: From Symbol to System* (New York: Crossroad, 1992), esp. chap. 1, "Toward a Postcritical Theology" and chap. 2, "Theology and Symbolic Communication."

[8] See Rahner's now classic article, "Basic Theological Interpretation of the Second Vatican Council," *Theological Investigations* 20 (New York: Crossroad, 1981), 77-89.

[9] Walter Kasper, "The Continuing Challenge of the Second Vatican Council," *Theology and Church* (New York: Crossroad, 1989), 166-76, at 168.

orient and empower a discriminating engagement with the cultures in which the Church is to be sign and witness (*aggiornamento*).[10]

Underlying all the concrete initiatives and projects inspired by Vatican II is the sense, voiced by Ratzinger, that the Council outlined a "new mode of seeing and expressing the faith."[11] And another theologian affirms: "Vatican II, in taking four centuries of religious and cultural developments seriously in a novel fashion, and in facing up to an unprecedented global challenge, must be understood to have *inaugurated a significant rearrangement of the themes and emphases of the Catholic faith and identity experience*."[12]

What we are working out at this level of depth is nothing less than the sense of our own identity as Catholic Christians and of the mission that is thus incumbent upon us in the world of the late twentieth century and the coming new millennium. No wonder that thirty years after the Council (long in the lifespan of any individual; still relatively brief in the life of the Church) we have only barely begun. No wonder the disorientation produced by the collapse of a clear, if too constricted, sense of identity and mission. No wonder that polarization often ensues from diverse views of what constitutes Catholic identity and how it is to be embodied—for so much is at stake. No wonder the vertigo produced by so rapid a transition from rigid uniformity to a sometimes promiscuous pluralism.

For thirty years now, amidst the "booming, buzzing confusion," I have found sustenance in the spiritual wisdom of one who longed for and anticipated the *aggiornamento* of Vatican II: Friedrich von Hügel. Forty years before the Council, he urged the need for "ample patience and delicate discrimination";[13] a need, no less urgent thirty years after the Council, and incumbent upon all the people of God, not least bishops and theologians.

Theological Challenge

Having "situated" the concrete individuals who are bishops and theologians within the context of the Church as the *congregatio fidelium* existing in a particular historical situation, one must also situate the theological task both among the various activities of believers and within the particular setting of a post-Vatican II and, indeed, postmodern age.

[10] I have spoken of Vatican II's dual dynamic as its "recovery of tradition" as both *tradita* (what has been handed down) and *traditio* (the ongoing process of handing down and interpreting). See Robert Imbelli, "Vatican II: Twenty Years Later," *Commonweal* 109 (Oct. 8, 1982): 522-26. This view has been favorably taken up by Avery Dulles, "Vatican II and the Recovery of Tradition," *The Reshaping of Catholicism* (San Francisco: Harper and Row, 1988), 75-92; and Timothy G. McCarthy, "Vatican Council II" in *The Catholic Tradition: Before and After Vatican II* (Chicago: Loyola University Press, 1994), 61-82.

[11] Ratzinger, *Nature and Mission*, 101.

[12] Frans Jozef van Beeck, *Catholic Identity After Vatican II* (Chicago: Loyola University Press, 1985), 4; italics in the original.

[13] Friedrich von Hügel, *Essays and Addresses on the Philosophy of Religion*, Second Series (London: Dent, 1963), 250.

On the one hand, faith certainly transcends theological articulation; and the overturning of theological positions or even the demise of theological schools need not impugn the substance of the faith. One might even imagine a genuine and flourishing Christian community in which the species "theologian" was unknown. On the other hand, accepting Anselm's view of theology as "faith seeking understanding," leads one to acknowledge incipient theologizing in all adult Christian faith, seeking to understand and to give an account of its hope.

Von Hügel, inspired by Newman, speaks of the three constitutive elements of religion: the institutional, the intellectual, and the mystical; and sees their fruitful, if ever tensive relation to be necessary for religion's well-being.[14] Here, of course, theology, as the systematic articulation and elaboration of the intellectual element, moves beyond the incipient "seeking of understanding" by the adult believer; but it always remains rooted in this activity of a faith that is instinct with logos.

Like the ecclesial magisterium, systematic theology, as the product of concrete believers, has assumed many forms and embodiments in the course of history. Germane to our present purpose is the remark with which Walter Kasper introduces his volume of essays, collected under the title *Theology and Church*. "There is no doubt that the outstanding event in the Catholic theology of our century is the surmounting of Neoscholasticism."[15]

For half a century Neo-Scholasticism had provided a coherent and attractive intellectual articulation of the Catholic sense of identity and mission; but of a sort and on a scale that has proved insufficient to the expanded vistas inaugurated by Vatican II. Even in the hands of its best proponents it was insufficiently scriptural and historical in its sensitivities. In addition it often exuded a marked antipathy to modern thought and culture. In the hands of its rote practitioners, it became the intramural tinkerings of what Henri de Lubac decried as a "separated theology" and Hans Urs von Balthasar dismissed as "sawdust Thomism."[16]

But, its demise and the failure as yet to achieve a comprehensive theological synthesis leaves Catholic theology in a situation that has been described

---

[14] Friedrich von Hügel, *The Mystical Element of Religion*, two volumes (London: Dent, 1923). For Newman's notion of theology as "regulating principle" of Church life and for Newman's influence upon von Hügel, see John Coulson, "The Regulating Principle," chap. 10, *Newman and the Common Tradition* (Oxford: Clarendon Press, 1970).

[15] Kasper, *Theology and Church*, 1. For a typically balanced treatment of the strengths and weaknesses of Neo-Scholasticism, see Dulles, *The Craft of Theology*, chap. 3, "The Problem of Method: From Scholasticism to Models." A cogent statement of Neo-Scholastic philosophy's role as the integrating discipline for Catholic higher education and the void left by its collapse may be found in Philip Gleason's essay in this volume.

[16] For de Lubac, see Joseph A. Komonchak, "Theology and Culture at Mid-Century: The Example of Henri de Lubac," *Theological Studies* 51 (December 1990): 579-602; for von Balthasar, Edward Oakes, *Pattern of Redemption: The Theology of Hans Urs von Balthasar* (New York: Continuum, 1994), 2.

as "a time of paradigm shift."[17] Analogous to the situation in science when one overarching model has proved deficient, yet no generally accepted alternative has arisen that can both order the data and suggest fruitful orientations for further research, so the present state of theology in the Catholic tradition seems sometimes marked by a confusion bordering on anomie. So experienced and sober a commentator as Avery Dulles has written of the present situation in Catholic theology: "Theologians lack a common language, common goals, and common norms."[18] If he is correct in his assessment, then this has obvious implications for any discussion of the topic of theologians and bishops, lest we fall prey to disincarnate abstractions.

One could argue the case that the present situation in theology resembles that of the second century with its variety of gnostic movements appealing to "gospels" that were not ultimately received into the canon. Just as the great theological figures of that century, Irenaeus in particular, helped establish the canon of Scripture and to articulate the *regula fidei* of the Church united in the apostolic tradition, so today we face a like challenge of theological discernment and synthesis. It will require a unique blend of radical fidelity and courageous creativity.[19]

Part of what is entailed is to recover the integrity of Christian language whose coinage has often been debased by promiscuous usage. This is, of course, the ongoing challenge of *ressourcement* that the Council has set us. But authentic Christian language also needs to be reinvigorated so that a vital connection to the often inarticulate yearnings and half-formed hopes of our contemporaries is manifest—Vatican II's ongoing challenge to *aggiornamento*. The challenge, then, is that of elaborating a new theological synthesis that offers a *via media* between a nostalgic and paralyzed integralism and a mindless and protean modernism. It will seek to promote identity and openness, content and relevance.[20] Avery Dulles provides a sketch of such a *via media* by suggesting an approach to theology that he terms "ecclesial-transformative."[21]

---

[17] To my knowledge the Lutheran theologian George Lindbeck of Yale University first applied Thomas Kuhn's "paradigm analysis" to the field of theology. I used the concept in an article, "A New Paradigm for Theology," *The Ecumenist* 14 (Sept.-Oct., 1976): 81-85. It has recently been extensively employed by Küng in his book, *Christianity*, though in too indiscriminate a fashion.

[18] Dulles, *Craft*, viii. An effort to address the situation was made at the 50th anniversary convention of the Catholic Theological Society of America. A pre-convention seminar was organized on "Criteria of Catholic Theology," with a presentation by Avery Dulles, that has now been published in *Communio* 22 (summer 1995): 301-15.

[19] For a good summary of ancient gnosticism, see Küng, *Christianity*, 136-49. An excellent exposition of Irenaeus, with an application to our present situation, is given by Douglas Farrow, "St. Irenaeus of Lyons," *Pro Ecclesia* 4 (summer 1995): 333-55.

[20] I have found Frans Jozef van Beeck's work exemplary in this regard. His systematics in process, under the title *God Encountered*, is one of the real signs of hope in contemporary Catholic theology. See my review article, "Catholic Identity After Vatican II: On the Theology of Frans Jozef van Beeck," *Commonweal* 121 (March 11, 1994): 12-16. For van Beeck's discussion of integralism and modernism, see *God Encountered*, vol. 1, *Understanding the Christian Faith* (San Francisco: Harper and Row, 1988), chap. 3, "The Loss of Catholicity."

[21] See note 7 above.

Catholic Theology as Ecclesial-Transformative

Invoking von Hügel, we affirmed the need to honor the three constitutive elements of religion and acknowledged the inevitable tension among them. Moreover, each manifests totalitarian impulses and seeks to dominate the other legitimate elements. What is clearly required is a comprehensive vision that can integrate the three, allowing each its due contribution to the well-being of the whole body. Applying the analysis to his own day (in the midst of the antimodernist suspicion), von Hügel identified the weakness of early twentieth-century Roman Catholicism as the underdeveloped state of the intellectual-critical element and the overwhelming dominance of the institutional-hierarchical element.

The one-sided emphasis upon this element in Roman Catholic ecclesiology was overcome in the great "Copernican Revolution" of *Lumen Gentium*, whereby the chapter on the hierarchical constitution of the Church was inserted into the more comprehensive and vivifying context represented by chapter two on "The People of God."

Yet, subsequent to the Council, one often encounters a polarization between advocates of chapter three and advocates of chapter two of *Lumen Gentium*, with those supporting the latter, in effect, promoting the intellectual-critical element. It is in this polemical context that one can situate Cardinal Ratzinger's lament that after the Council "theologians increasingly felt themselves to be the true teachers of the Church and even of the bishops . . . The Magisterium of the Holy See now appeared in the public eye to be the last holdover of a failed authoritarianism."[22] Such an assessment led to the CDF's attempt in its Instruction of 1990 to clarify the ecclesial vocation of theologians and their relation to the magisterium.

But one might also develop von Hügel's analysis further and suggest that, contributing to our present malaise in theology and Church, is the atrophy of the "mystical" element in this conflict between the institutional and the intellectual; and to ask whether the way "forward" is not the way "down": the "descent" to the mystical. In effect, I maintain that the only way to do full justice to *Lumen Gentium* 3 and *Lumen Gentium* 2 is to root them in the mystical soil that is their engendering context, namely, chapter 1, "The Mystery of the Church."

In this regard Cardinal Ratzinger makes an interesting appeal to an article by the well-known Italian historian of theology, Giuseppe Alberigo. In a discussion of the rise of a "scientific" scholastic theology in the thirteenth century, Alberigo writes:

> an ever more pronounced "hiatus develops between the Christian community and the institutional Church, on the one hand, and the guild of theologians, on the other. The fact that the university be-

---

[22] Ratzinger, *Nature and Mission*, 102.

came the new seat of research and of the teaching of theology without a doubt enervated its ecclesial dynamism and furthermore severed theology from vital contact with spiritual experiences." (And
Ratzinger draws his contemporary moral:) A theology wholly bent
on being academic and "scientific" according to the standards of the
modern university, cuts itself off from its great historical matrices and
renders itself sterile for the Church.[23]

The "descent to the mystical" that, following von Hügel, I think required,
is congruent with one of the most promising developments in postconciliar
Catholic theology. I refer to the overcoming of the separation between
theology and spirituality made possible by such seminal theologians as
Karl Rahner and Bernard Lonergan. Rahner's recovery of an authentic
Catholic understanding of "Mystery" and of the "mystagogic" function
of dogmatic statements moves beyond the conceptualism of the Neo-Scholastics and, through an appreciation of the role of symbol, engages the whole
person, affect as well as intellect.

Lonergan, as is well known, places reflection upon conversion at the foundations of the theological task, thereby committing the theologian to an
ongoing quest for authenticity of both thought and life. Both Rahner and
Lonergan thus provide important resources for an ecclesial transformative approach to theology. The pressing challenge to Catholic theology is
to develop these resources systematically so that they might form the
guiding principles of a new theological approach and, ultimately, synthesis.
For, as Walter Kasper justly laments:

> theology is not supposed merely to communicate theoretical, specu-
> lative insights. It aims at the actual, specific practice of faith, hope,
> and love. Seen under this aspect, what a poor figure is cut by many a
> fat and learned tome! And how rightly many students, and many
> "ordinary" Christians, cry out at the present time for this spiritual
> and mystical dimension, which is so inexcusably neglected in the con-
> duct of our average academic theology.[24]

If a renewed theology is to serve its integrating function in Church and
academy, it must be clear about its common ground, its principles, and criteria. Let me offer, then, a number of characteristics of such an ecclesial-transformative approach to theology.[25]

---

[23] Ibid., 116, including citation from Alberigo. See also the essay by Keith Egan in the present volume.

[24] Kasper, *Theology and Church*, 12.

[25] As Dulles has indicated in *Craft of Theology*, 20, such an approach "leaves room for more than one concept of theology, more than one mode in which faith may be understood." Thus he speaks of a more "contemplative" or a more "academic" mode; united, I presume, by a certain family resemblance, a common commitment to certain governing principles and persuasions.

(1) The presupposition of theology, thus understood, is the historical faith and witness of the Church. Theology does not independently generate its own data, but proceeds from the revelation given to the community of believers, articulated in its Scriptures, and carried by its tradition. The fulfillment of this revelation is given in Jesus Christ, as Vatican II's constitution, *Dei Verbum*, teaches; and all grace is Christic in its filial pattern.

Moreover, the theologian is not a detached observer or a dispassionate reporter upon the activities of others, in the manner of a practitioner of phenomenology or philosophy of religion; but personally participates in the faith being reflected upon. As Lonergan suggests, foundational to the doing of theology is reflection upon conversion, not only upon the witness of the conversions of others in the community of the Church, but upon one's own as well.

(2) The privileged locus of this participation in the life of the Church and hence a privileged source of theological reflection is the Church's liturgy. As Dulles says, "If theology is not to regress, it must retain its close bonds with prayer and worship."[26] Van Beeck's theology is so appealing precisely because of its stress upon the centrality of worship to the life of the Christian community and its theological reflection.[27]

In the liturgical celebration the Real Presence of Christ achieves sacramental fullness; and in the community's encounter with its Risen Lord it receives both its distinctive identity and its mandate for mission (cf. Matt. 28:16-20). No liturgical celebration expresses the "logic" of Christian liturgy more fully than the Easter Vigil in the course of which the initiation of new Christians takes place. Nowhere else is there such a comprehensive symbolic and sacramental enactment of what *Ex corde Ecclesiae* affirms conceptually: "a vision of the human person and the world that is enlightened by the Gospel and therefore by a faith in Christ, the Logos, as the center of creation and of human history."[28]

(3) Implicit in the first two points with their accent on the revelational given that is the matrix of Christian theology and the liturgical celebration that is its privileged locus is the third characteristic of an ecclesial-transformative approach to theology: its trinitarian structure. Christians are baptized "in the Name of the Father and of the Son and of the Holy Spirit"; and their liturgical prayer is addressed to the Father, through Jesus Christ, God's Son and our Lord, in the power and communion of the Holy Spirit.

This insistence on the trinitarian content of Christian faith would be otiose were it not for a disquieting trend toward a "unitarian reduction" of trinitarian fullness. Whether from a sense that the doctrine of the Trinity rep-

---

For another articulation of these principles and persuasions, see Robert Imbelli and Thomas Groome, "Signposts Towards a Pastoral Theology," *Theological Studies* 53 (March 1992): 127-37.

[26] Dulles, *Craft*, 9.

[27] Van Beeck, *God Encountered*, vol. 1, chap. 7: "Doxology: The Mystery of Intimacy and Awe."

[28] *Ex corde Ecclesiae*, 16.

resents an intrusion of Greek metaphysics into Christian faith, or from a laudable concern for ecumenical dialogue among the monotheistic faiths, several influential contemporary theologians seem to verge on a unitarian understanding of the Christian God. The consequence, of course, is to reduce Christ's status from what orthodox Christian faith has confessed him to be.[29]

An ecclesial-transformative approach to theology will restore, in the accents of our own day, the wonderful image of St. Irenaeus that Christ and the Spirit are the "two hands" of God with whom God accomplishes all the work of creation and redemption. Even as the beginning and focus of a renewed Catholic theology is this trinitarian "economy of salvation," God for us through Christ in the Spirit, it will culminate in the doxological affirmation of God's own inner life as the mystery of trinitarian communion.[30]

(4) From God's trinitarian life and economy follows an understanding of the Church whose distinctive mark is that of "communion" or *koinonia*. The ultimate identity of the Church is to make visible in the world, to sacramentalize, that mystery of communion that is the very life of the Trinity. Under the conditions of finitude and fallenness such communion is realized only through the paschal mystery of Christ. Hence the sacramental celebration of the paschal mystery in the Eucharist is the very life-blood of the Church. As the ancient adage holds: "the Church makes the eucharist; the eucharist makes the Church." And the very heart of the matter, the *res sacramenti*, is communion, with God and, inseparably, with the brothers and sisters through Christ and in the Spirit.[31]

This emphasis on Church as communion counters the tendency in some quarters to insist upon particularity and inculturation to the point of jeopardizing the Catholic identity and mission of the whole Church. Thus the one-sided centralization and abstract universality of pre-Vatican II ecclesiology risks being replaced by an equally one-sided and implicitly congregationalist pluralism. The challenge of communion ecclesiology is to elaborate the vision and requirements of a concrete universality that holds unity and plurality in life-giving tension. In so doing it will draw upon the teaching of Vatican II regarding the collegiality of the bishops under the Petrine ministry of the pope. But it will also insist, with Vatican II, on the *actuosa participatio* of all the baptized in the Church's liturgy, life, and mission.

(5) An ecclesial-transformative approach, as its very name indicates,

---

[29] See my review article, "Who Is Jesus?" *Church* 6 (spring 1990): 62-65. In my view Hans Küng's challenging and provocative book, *Christianity*, tends in this direction.

[30] Wolfhart Pannenberg draws upon this image of Irenaeus in presenting a trinitarian account of creation in *Systematic Theology*, II (Grand Rapids: Eerdmans, 1994), 109-15. For the influence of Irenaeus on the new *Catechism of the Catholic Church*, see Brian E. Daley, "A Mystery to Share In: The trinitarian perspective of the new Catechism," *Communio* 21 (fall 1994): 409-36. Among Catholic theologians Walter Kasper has most advanced the project of a renewed fully trinitarian theology: see *The God of Jesus Christ* (New York: Crossroad, 1984). For the important task of elaborating a "Spirit-Christology," but within a comprehensive trinitarian perspective see Ralph Del Colle, *Christ and the Spirit* (New York: Oxford University Press, 1994).

[31] One of the richest treatments is that of Kasper, "The Church as Communion: Reflections

stresses the ongoing transformation that is intrinsic to Christian life and hence to the identity and mission of Church. Conversion to God, through Jesus Christ, in the Spirit initiates a journey of personal and communal discipleship whose ultimate goal is the transfiguration of all created reality. This transformative process, as Romans 8 emphasizes, is the special province of the Holy Spirit, who mediates what has been realized in Christ to all those called to be incorporated into the one body of Christ.

This suggests a dynamic understanding of ecclesial existence as an ongoing ecclesiogenesis in the Spirit. In the words of the Venerable Bede: "Everyday the Church gives birth to the Church." This theme of the Church's ongoing self-realization is prominent in the ecclesiological reflection of Joseph Komonchak. In developing it he seeks to correlate systematically the data of Christian tradition with contemporary sociological insights.[32]

(6) The self-realization of the Church's identity is, inseparably, a self-realization of the Church's mission; for ecclesiogenesis occurs in the world and embodies both an invitation and challenge to the world. Christ himself came "for the life of the world"; and the mission of his Church is to witness to and communicate that life "to all nations." The salvation achieved through Christ is comprehensive; and the Church's catholicity must image that of Christ himself, recapitulating all things in Christ.[33] Hence ecclesial identity and mission are two sides of one coin; they cannot be sundered.

To fulfill its mission the Church must engage in a discriminating dialogue with the cultures in which it finds itself, as Paul VI so powerfully taught in *Evangelii Nuntiandi*. And the Catholic university is a rich vehicle for fostering such dialogue, as John Paul II acknowledges in *Ex corde Ecclesiae*, and for promoting what *Evangelium Vitae* calls "a culture of life." A signal responsibility of theologians is to undertake a critical mediation between the ecclesial tradition and the particular culture in which the theologians live. To do so they must engage in a profound examination of the *paideia* of their given culture to discern its openness, its resources, and obstacles to the preaching of the gospel. In this task they require all the discrimination and courage that characterized an Augustine and an Aquinas, perennial models of Catholic theological wisdom.[34]

This mediating function of theology is intrinsic to a faith that is instinct with logos and that, consequently, is ever ready to give an account of the hope that it embodies.

---

on the Guiding Ecclesiological Idea of the Second Vatican Council," *Theology and Church*, chap. 8 (New York: Crossroad, 1989), 148-65.

[32] See, for example, Joseph A. Komonchak, "Theologians in the Church," ed. Peter Phan, *Church and Theology* (Washington: Catholic University of America Press, 1995), 63-87; also Komonchak's essay in this volume.

[33] The classic statement remains that of Henri de Lubac, *Catholicism* (San Francisco: Ignatius Press, 1988). See also Avery Dulles, *The Catholicity of the Church* (New York: Oxford, 1985).

[34] For a good presentation see, van Beeck, *God Encountered*, vol. 1, chap. 2: "Systematic Theology and its Tasks."

In summary, an ecclesial-transformative approach offers a truly comprehensive structure for a renewed Catholic theology and supports a renewed appreciation of the reciprocal and indispensable roles of theologians and bishops.

Theologians and Bishops within the Church

Discussions of the relationship between theologians and bishops ordinarily begin by stressing the *commonalities* that bind them in the one people of God.[35] It will pay to underline them again. Bishops and theologians are bound to a common hearing and submission to the Word of God as it is conveyed in the sacred Scriptures, in tradition, and in the *sensus fidei* of the whole redeemed people. Their function is not to supersede the Word, but to live by it, to proclaim it, and to interpret it in the ever new situations of history. Their task, in the suggestive phrases of the biblical scholar Walter Brueggemann, is one of "obedient interpretation" and "interpretive obedience."[36]

Second, this common hearing of the Word entails a common call to ongoing conversion. Psalm 95's invitatory, "If today you hear God's voice, harden not your hearts," applies to all God's people, but especially to those who bear teaching responsibilities in the Church.

A third unitive factor is the common celebration of the Eucharist: the gathering of the whole people in ecclesial communion to rejoice in and be nourished by the Real Presence of the Lord. This "participatory knowledge," mediated by sacramental symbols, precedes and sustains all conceptual articulation of the saving mystery of the faith by either bishops or theologians.

Finally, a common concern and responsibility for the Church's identity and mission unite the respective charisms of bishops and theologians. When one considers the crucial and complex nature of ecclesiogenesis, especially under the conditions of the communications revolution of postmodernity, the necessity of respectful collaboration between the episcopal chair and the professorial chair is patent and urgent.

Distinct Charisms and Responsibilities

In this section I do not intend to suggest a simplistic reduction of roles. In concrete practice there is much mutual enrichment and participation. As the CDF writes: "To be sure, theology and the magisterium are of diverse natures and missions and cannot be confused. Nonetheless, they fulfill two vital roles in the Church which must interpenetrate and enrich each other for the service of the people of God."[37] Indeed, such "interpenetration" and "enrichment"

---

[35] So the International Theological Commission's "Theses on the relationship between the ecclesiastical magisterium and theology," theses two and three, in Sullivan, *Magisterium*, p. 174f. Also United States Bishops' "Doctrinal Responsibilities," *Origins* 19 (June 29, 1989), 99-100.

[36] Walter Brueggemann, *Interpretation and Obedience* (Minneapolis: Fortress Press, 1991), 1.

[37] "Instruction on the Ecclesial Vocation of the Theologian," *Origins* 20 (5 July 1990): par 40, 125.

marked the actual unfolding of the Second Vatican Council and, more recently, the compiling of the *Catechism of the Catholic Church*. Let me hazard, then, the following delineation.

Bishops, by virtue of their charism and office, bear particular responsibility for the authoritative proclamation and preaching of the faith handed down from the apostles. Through the anointing of the Holy Spirit, they continue in this apostolic succession of witnesses to the mystery of God made manifest in Christ. Theologians, by virtue of their charism and training, seek a systematic understanding of that faith. They seek to sound the depths of the revealed mystery and to relate it to understandings gleaned from the efforts of human intelligence in the arts and sciences.

Hence a focal concern for the holders of the episcopal office is the specific identity of the community of faith, its distinguishing way of life and belief. Though this concern receives thematic expression in the Pastoral Epistles of the New Testament, it clearly permeates the letters of Paul from First Thessalonians on. Connected with this is the apostolic and episcopal concern for the integrity of the language of faith: a concern not to adulterate sound teaching with merely human fantasies and fables. This concern to safeguard the authentic *tradita* is crucial to the identity of the community over time, its union with the great Church Catholic through the ages.

Theologians join to this concern for distinctive identity a special concern for the openness of the faith, its vital capacity to assimilate to itself new dimensions of human experience and knowledge. They seek through their intellectual and critical explorations to discern the relevance of the faith to new social and cultural contexts. The questions posed in systematic fashion by generations of theologians have served to promote the *traditio*, the ongoing appropriation of faith's understanding that can lead the whole Church to authentic doctrinal development.

On the basis of the foregoing delineation of concerns and competencies, one might suggest that, *in this sense*, bishops embody a more conservative interest and theologians a more progressive one. The thrust of episcopal concern is the maintaining of continuity, the ongoing fidelity to the gospel of Jesus Christ. The thrust of theological concern lies in the direction of fuller appropriation, the ongoing fruitfulness of the gospel of Jesus Christ. To reiterate: such "functional specialization" is generic and admits of considerable overlap.

On its basis, however, we can acknowledge two points that are crucial for this discussion and for Catholic ecclesiology in general. First, the bishops' ecclesial magisterium entails a crucial service of *episcope* within the community. Bishops are charged with the responsibility of discerning and judging the fidelity of teaching to the Church's proclamation. As the document *Doctrinal Responsibilities* (itself the product of collaboration between bishops and theologians) states: "Theologians . . . acknowledge that it is the role of bishops as authoritative teachers in the church to make pastoral judgments about the soundness of theological teaching so that the integrity of Catholic doctrine and the unity of the faith community may be preserved."[38]

Second, within the commitment to the faith of the Church and the structures of Catholicism, a certain "relative independence" of the theological task needs also to be acknowledged. In line with his espousal of an ecclesial-transformative approach to the theological enterprise, Avery Dulles affirms "the relative autonomy of the hierarchical magisterium and the theologians in the performance of their specific tasks"; and he goes on to assert: "Theology, therefore, possesses a certain freedom over against even the hierarchical magisterium. Without that freedom it could not be theology, and hence it could not be of service to the Church."[39]

Historically, this view challenges the model of the relationship between magisterium and theology, first advocated by Pius IX and seconded by Pius XII in *Humani Generis*, which seemed to restrict theologians' task to that of a mere *ancilla* to the hierarchical magisterium. Quite in contrast to this position is Cardinal Ratzinger's striking assertion. He writes:

> Theology is not simply and exclusively an ancillary function of the magisterium: it is not limited to gathering arguments for a priori magisterial decisions. If that were so, the Magisterium and theology would draw perilously close to an ideology whose sole interest is the acquisition and preservation of power.[40]

The ultimate basis for this "relative autonomy" of the theological ministry in the Church is that it derives from the Spirit's distribution of charisms as he wills. And one of these charism-based ecclesial ministries is the doing of theology. After a careful and nuanced discussion, Francis Sullivan concludes: "I believe that there is an ecclesial ministry of teaching theology which is distinct from and not derived from the teaching authority of the hierarchy, even if it is necessarily subordinate to this and must accept its 'vigilance' over what it teaches and publishes."[41]

Acknowledging these two points, the oversight responsibility that pertains to the bishops and the relative independence due to theologians, seems to me to be the condition for the possibility of genuine collaboration, mutual enrichment, and fruitful service in the building up of the body of Christ.

Inevitable Tensions

Having presented the normative basis for and the urgent need of collaboration, one must admit the practical inevitability of tensions between the bear-

---

[38] *Doctrinal Responsibilities*, 102. See also Dulles, *Craft*, 12-13.

[39] Ibid., 107 and 169.

[40] Ratzinger, *Nature and Mission*, 104. For the position of Pius IX and Pius XII, see Sullivan, *Magisterium*, 183.

[41] Sullivan, *Magisterium*, 203.

ers of the diverse ministerial functions within the Church. Adverting to von Hügel's analysis of the three elements of religion already alerted us to this inevitability and, paradoxical as it may seem, desirability. Such tension is not a negation of the Spirit's presence, but often a sign of it.[42] The challenge, therefore, is not to eliminate the tension, by denying or reducing one of its components, but to render the tension fruitful and not enervating. As Cardinal Ratzinger writes:

> The document [on the Ecclesial Vocation of the Theologian] does not conceal the fact that there can be tensions even under the most favorable circumstances. These tensions, however, can be productive, provided that each side sustains them in the recognition that its function is *intrinsically ordered* to that of the other.[43]

I think cultivating several intellectual attitudes and dispositions can help promote the fruitfulness of the tension. First, both bishops and theologians need to be cognizant of the abuses and polemics of the still recent past. The condemnation of Modernism early in this century and the fierce anti-Modernist measures it spawned created a climate that was not favorable to free theological research and teaching. The familiar litany of names, including de Lubac, Congar, Rahner, and Murray, who labored under such a cloud of suspicion and condemnation, only to be finally vindicated by Vatican II, should serve as a cautionary tale to us all. As Cardinal Ratzinger himself admits (though with fitting nuance): "The danger of a narrow-minded and petty surveillance is no figment of the imagination, as the history of the Modernist controversy demonstrates—even though the summary judgments which are so widespread today are too unilateral to do justice to the seriousness of the issue."[44] What is often not sufficiently appreciated is the immense *pastoral* toll such measures took, leaving the Church as a whole less prepared for the reforms of Vatican II and thus contributing to the postconciliar polarization and lack of depth.

A second intellectual disposition required can be summed up in the truism that the effects of original sin continue to impact both bishops and theologians. But this truism needs to be translated into a renewed recognition of the presence in us all of what Augustine calls the *libido dominandi*. Certainly our century provides us with ample evidence of the pathology of power and the propensity for self-inflation that characterizes, in perfectly inclusive fashion, the sons and daughters of Adam and Eve. Joseph Komonchak's blunt words

---

[42] For suggestive remarks about the tension that characterizes life in the Spirit, see James Dunn, *Jesus and the Spirit* (Philadelphia: Westminster, 1975), 338-39. To my mind, Gnosticism, as perennial spiritual temptation, is marked, among other traits, by a desire to eliminate the complexities and tensions of historical existence.

[43] Ratzinger, *Nature and Mission*, 106: italics mine. See also thesis nine of the International Theological Commission in Sullivan, *Magisterium*, 212-13.

[44] Ratzinger, *Nature and Mission*, 66.

regarding the "Instruction on the Ecclesial Vocation of the Theologian" are apposite:

> What is striking about the Instruction's treatment is that the whole burden of virtue appears to fall upon theologians. There is not a word about the responsibilities of the Magisterium, about the possibility of its over-reaching, about the temptations to which it is subject, despite the assistance of the Spirit.[45]

And, of course, the same caution, in other circumstances, needs to be addressed to theologians as well.

A third intellectual attitude required is the absolute conviction of the inexhaustibility of the mystery of the faith and the ensuing need for multiple probings and models of the mystery. Thus plurality is not a concession to human weakness, but a testimony to the infinite richness of God's mystery in Christ. As the CDF's Instruction states: "The ultimate reason for plurality is found in the unfathomable mystery of Christ, who transcends every objective systematization."[46] This attitude is not that of a lazy relativism that traffics in a promiscuous pluralism, but an intellectually serious and discriminating pluralism which is correlative to a robust and rich unity.

A final intellectual disposition required is the ability to discriminate the relative authority of magisterial pronouncements and hence the range of responses they call forth. A dogmatic definition solemnly proclaimed in ecumenical council obviously differs in authoritative weight from the teaching of a papal encyclical, which, in turn, makes greater claim than a disciplinary finding of a Roman Congregation. In his commentary on the Instruction of the CDF, Cardinal Ratzinger writes:

> The text also presents the various forms of binding authority which correspond to the grades of the Magisterium. It states—perhaps for the first time with such candor—that there are magisterial decisions which cannot be the final word on a given matter as such but, despite the permanent value of their principles, are chiefly also a signal for pastoral prudence, a sort of provisional policy.[47]

A careful and discerning hermeneutic of magisterial statements on the part of both bishops and theologians can contribute to making inevitable tensions productive and situate the discussion within the common faith of the Church and the hierarchy of truths it structures.

Now I think it probable that the majority of bishops and theologians would give notional assent to the points just made. However, the present situation

---

[45] Joseph Komonchak, "The Magisterium and Theologians," 325.

[46] "Ecclesial Vocation of the Theologian," 34.

[47] Ratzinger, *Nature and Mission*, 106. For a discussion of the different types of pronouncements, see Dulles, *Craft*, 108-11.

of polarization and even mistrust seems to demand more than merely notional assent. Therefore, I would like to devote a last series of reflections to what might be called a "spirituality of communion." My hope here is to move, with von Hügel, from the institutional and critical elements of religion (indispensable as these are) to the mystical. In terms of *Lumen Gentium*: to root the entire people of God in the soil of the Church's mystery.

Toward a Spirituality of Communion

In discussing the characteristics of an ecclesial-transformative approach to theology, I have already highlighted *koinonia* or communion as the distinctive mark of a Catholic ecclesiology. I think there is a pressing need to cultivate, collegially and singly, a spirituality of communion. Such a spirituality appreciates affectively that communion is the *novum* of the New Testament, the new life of the Spirit.[48] Being convinced that communion is the Spirit's desire and fruit, we are required to be proactive in its regard. Let me offer some "markings" on the way to such a spirituality.

First, while not dismissive of the juridical, a spirituality of communion does not countenance a reduction to the juridical, for communion is the summit of personal existence and flourishes in interpersonal exchange.[49] Thus it will eagerly promote personal relations among bishops and theologians, seeking opportunities for dialogue, consultation, and collaboration. There have been ample examples of such exchange in the North American context and these should be a source of pride and stimulus.

A second aspect of a spirituality of communion is that it is both comfortable with and desirous of *parresia*, that bold and open speech that is so crucial a New Testament virtue. There can be no greater ecclesial service than such "speaking the truth in love" (Eph. 4:15), for it promotes the integration of all things in Christ. Yet, if such a virtue is quintessentially ecclesial, we know that it can be as rare in Church circles as it is in the wider society.[50] But communion is not conformity; and authoritative discernment requires the wisest and most forthright counsel available. Surely, those radiant doctors of the Church, Catherine of Siena and Teresa of Ávila, provide exemplary models of *parresia*!

Third, the discernment necessary to promote and safeguard communion is itself a spiritual attainment, a gift of the Spirit. And both theologians and bishops need to pray earnestly to receive it as did Solomon. It is certainly closely related to a generosity of spirit that seeks to "save" everything pos-

---

[48] Difficult but extremely rewarding reflections in John Zizioulas, *Being as Communion* (Crestwood, N.Y.: St. Vladimir's Seminary Press, 1985).

[49] For a rich probing of the mystical element of Catholic faith and the development of a spirituality of "exchange," see Rosemary Haughton, *The Passionate God* (New York: Paulist Press, 1981).

[50] For precious contributions to this aspect of communion spirituality from a secular standpoint, see Václav Havel, *Open Letters* (New York: Knopf, 1991).

sible for the sake of communion. What Ignatius of Loyola (who had had some experience with the Inquisition) placed as the "Presupposition" to the *Spiritual Exercises* should be the presupposition of all dealings between bishops and theologians:

> That both . . . may be of greater help and benefit to each other, it should be presupposed that every good Christian ought to be more eager to put a good interpretation on a neighbor's statement than to condemn it. Further, if one cannot interpret it favorably, one should ask how the other means it. If that meaning is wrong, one should correct the person with love; and if this is not enough, one should search out every appropriate means through which, by understanding the statement in a good way, it may be saved.[51]

A discerning generosity and a generous discernment must mark our ecclesial exchanges.

This becomes particularly important on those (presumably rare) occasions when episcopal responsibility may require inquiry and judgment concerning specific theological views and positions. Theses eleven and twelve of the International Theological Commission's 1976 document on the relation between the ecclesiastical magisterium and theology offer sage general counsel, and the American Bishops' 1989 guidelines on *Doctrinal Responsibilities* suggest some specific approaches and procedures, from the more informal to the formal, with the aim of resolving misunderstanding and safeguarding responsibility. The relevance of both documents is undiminished. Their inspiration is not primarily the liberal society's sense of individual rights, but the ecclesial community's sense of the common good, its responsibility to the common life in the Spirit. I would simply underscore the importance of due process and procedure as a requirement of intellectual integrity, moral justice, and religious charity. Especially repugnant to a spirituality of communion is anonymous and faceless accusation.

A spirituality of communion recognizes that commitment to communion requires an ongoing conversion in the today of faith. The eyes of faith see bishops and theologians not as competitors, much less adversaries, but as collaborators: fellow-workers in recapitulating all things in Christ (Eph. 1:10), together being built into "a dwelling place of God in the Spirit" (Eph. 2:22).

---

[51] *Ignatius of Loyola* (New York: Paulist, 1990), 129.

17

Faith: Normative for Bishops and Theologians

Archbishop Oscar H. Lipscomb

Fr. Earl Muller, inviting me to share in this panel, offered one general rubric: "Be bishops." With that basic qualification somewhat authenticated by the past fifteen years in my case, let me offer an overarching perspective for consideration of theological education in the Church which is common to both bishops and theologians: our Catholic faith as proclaimed, refined, and appropriated over the centuries. It is a reality that corresponds to God's freely given love in revelation, intimately bound to the life of the Church, and intimately binding those who receive it to Christ, to the Church, and to each other. Such is the reality of faith.

In service to this faith bishops need theologians and theologians need bishops. Neither can lose sight of faith in their quest to serve it through the development and sharing of the theological enterprise. In the tasks specific to each there is a fundamental compatibility for theologians and bishops. This compatibility finds concrete expression for those engaged in theological education: the end result in learners should not only be a more personal appropriation of God's truth, but also a concomitant grasp of the channels that mediate such truth, and a like appropriation of them. Recognition of the ways in which bishops and theologians are true collaborators enhances such an appropriation and contributes to an enrichment of faith life in individuals and in the life of the Church. It should also be noted that where the respective roles of theologians and bishops are misunderstood, faith life suffers, whether of individuals or of the wider Church.

A theologian cannot help but be influenced by the academic context within which she, or he, does theology, and within which the discipline of theology itself has a rightful place. In the Enlightenment and post-Enlightenment milieu, higher education has grudgingly afforded such a place to theology, if indeed it recognizes it at all. Hard pressed, theologians have nevertheless maintained their discipline with greater or lesser success depending upon the institution and the cultural background of the society that, in the end, influences the identity, mission, and goals of such institutions. The fact that theology has survived at all is an affirmation that our basic relationship to God, however denied or disguised, cannot be escaped as a fact of human existence and experience. Our own society, whether as a residue of past conviction or a felt need with respect to psychological or behavioral inadequacies, is confronted with "the problem of God." Whether by its proper name, or by some other name, it theologizes about such a problem.

The reality and context within which Roman Catholic theology finds itself is vastly different. Called the *regina scientiarum*, theology in the past truly crowned all other intellectual endeavors, somehow formed a unifying factor, and, indeed, surpassed in its ultimate understanding *scientia rerum per causas*—and this because of faith. From a bishop's perspective, such an end result as a consequence of the study of theology is still very much a desired goal and outcome. It means that theology must somehow hold fast to its rightful place, not compromising either its foundation or its methodology, and I do not need to tell you who are theologians how difficult that is today, and still enjoy the respect of academic peers. One difficulty might lie in the fact that the word "peers" is extended without justifiable warrant to include the wider academic community. While there is a certain likeness of interest and universe of concern among the faculty of a given college or institution, only those within a like discipline have the understanding and competence to exercise peer judgment when determining not only such matters as academic adequacy or excellence, but even in more global issues such as that of academic freedom. Nevertheless, the serious scholar, the serious theologian, if he or she is to be taken seriously, cannot operate outside academe or independently of its pressures and presuppositions. That is not to say such an individual must buy into such pressures and presuppositions universally and uncritically.

A bishop's concern in service to the faith will be broader. It will extend to those who have the faith and the concomitant opportunity and responsibility to grow in it, to those who do not have faith and nevertheless seek it with open hearts and minds, and finally to those who have no interest in faith but nevertheless encounter it as a fact of human existence in others. In the first group, a bishop will hope to foster growth, in the second, invitation, and in the third a certain witness that, in God's own time and by God's own grace, may turn to invitation. Each of these tasks has a pastoral dimension that, while necessarily allied with intellectual and educational needs and responses, is by no means confined to them. In fact, the bishop, as is true of every other minister as well, will begin the process of serving the faith, more often with a movement of the heart rather than of the head. Theological education must encompass this pastoral dimension as a necessary part of its agenda. Obviously, in wide areas of its research and teaching, parts of theology will not be primarily concerned with the pastoral dimension. On the other hand it must always be mindful of it and leave a solid groundwork for pastoral formation in those who study theology systematically.

At the heart of our enterprise of being either bishops or theologians, or sometimes both, lies the fact and virtue of faith, God's free gift, freely accepted by the believer. It, in the last analysis, is the foundation for certitude.

While the gifts of the intellect and the powers of the mind in reasoning are not excluded from the process of faith, neither do they contribute to it so essentially as to be determinative of the final outcome: certitude. Nor can the supernatural dimension of the virtue of faith be excluded from its reality, or our consideration of it, in its salvific effect on the life, and the certitude, of the believer. While the intellectual components, and propositions, that result from a profession of faith may be distinct from its lived experience, they are, in fact, never apart in the life of the believer. This faith is an essential component of Catholic identity, it forms not only the background for both bishops and theologians, it is normative of the truth which both seek to mediate in the task of fulfilling their respective roles and responsibilities.

Outside the Catholic context, and indeed for much of academe, such faith is little understood and often rejected. Such a reality places strains and tensions upon the theologian- bishop relationship. On the one hand, the theologian is measured by academic peers in ways that are often unrealistic with respect to the truth and methodology of the discipline of theology. On the other hand, the bishop often finds himself at variance with a theologian who appeals to that same academic authentication to vindicate a point at issue or in controversy. And, invariably, there is an appeal to academic freedom when the issue or controversy cannot be satisfactorily resolved.

Elsewhere[1] I have written on the issue of academic freedom which ultimately is in service to truth and put forth the proposition that in keeping with the various disciplines which it seeks to serve, academic freedom is not an unequivocal but an analogous concept. I find such a distinction appropriate, by reason of the normative truths and methodologies of the different disciplines which appeal to academic freedom. The judgment of peers in science has as its norm the objective reality of objective evidence constantly explored and tested by those who seek to know the truth about it. The judgment of peers in theology, and specifically in Roman Catholic theology, has as its norm the truth of faith which is of quite a different order, though certainly no less true. Its norm is revelation, certainly subject to inquiry and development in keeping with our human situation, but ultimately authenticated by the teaching authority of the Church. Such authentication is no more extraneous to the discovery of truth for theology than the discovery of factual data for the scientist—though quite distinct in the order of its knowability. If the methodology by which science and theology arrive at a determination of truth is thus distinct, and diverse, certainly the criterion of academic freedom which is applied to that methodology ought to be distinct, and diverse, hence my contention that it is an analogous concept.

The often cited teaching of *Gaudium et Spes* in Vatican II in support of academic freedom specifically rests on the "two orders of knowledge" that I have just cited. The Council notes specifically the distinction between knowl-

---

[1] Oscar H. Lipscomb, "Faith and Academic Freedom," *America* (3-10 September 1988): 124-25, 151.

edge arrived at by faith and knowledge arrived at by reason. It asserts a long-standing tradition that "when the human arts and sciences are practiced they use their own principles and their proper method, each in its own domain."[2] It is precisely in the areas of principles and proper method that the other sciences and theology are markedly different.

It is from a pastoral perspective that the bishop will also view efforts at significant change in theological education, not so much with regard to methodology, as with a view toward the bottom line of such education: fidelity to the Catholic tradition. Hence it is that often new theories or initiatives in the enterprise of doing theology will come under close scrutiny and not be accepted unless and until the new can be proven to be a benefit in living the faith. There is no doubt but that we are moved, and in some ways conditioned by our own experience. Let me cite for you one such experience that I received this month in the form of a letter from a mother whose child I confirmed within the Archdiocese of Mobile. She wrote after having come back to the Church during an absence that was certainly in part engendered by the changes that somewhat indiscriminately followed Vatican II in the late 1960s and throughout the 1970s. Here is the way she described the situation in those days at least as it appeared to one of the then young people in the pews.

> People had lost reverence and respect for the Holy Father and started to think of him as an old stooge (God forgive them) and the numbers of those have increased through the years worldwide. I was a teenager during these times and I turned away from a confusing church of changes and turned to the pleasures of the world. Everyone was partying, smoking pot, drinking, doing drugs. Religion seemed to be lost in the abyss and feeling good was what seemed important. Why should we believe when the Church seemed broken and changing to fit our "feel good" times. Everyone was doing their own thing even priests and religious. Many scandals plagued our churches and we, the young of America, loved it because it helped support our immorality and hedonistic behavior. Many of our parents "evolved" with the times. Their principles became lax following in the footsteps of a more lax and "evolving" Church. And we, the youth of the world, ran wild with it and the world has paid dearly for it.

This mother's concerns are by no means isolated or rare. Such concerns do not form the whole picture of being a bishop; they do constitute an important part of our experience in trying to be shepherds to the flock and responsible stewards of the mysteries of God. This is not to say that we are alone in such responsibility; it is shared in the first place by those in theology whose task it is to make the truth of those same mysteries accessible and inviting

[2] *Gaudium et Spes*, n. 59.

without in any way changing their content.

The tasks of bishops and theologians, and especially in their roles as teachers, are played out within a society that in the use of its most widespread and effective means of communication is not only skeptical of faith and faith values, but inimical to them. I refer not only to the entertainment media, but specifically to those areas of mass communication whether by print or electronic images, that seek to keep people informed and current in today's world. Presentations are by no means disinterested or objective. Their genre is often sensationalism and controversy. Bishops and theologians are routinely cast as adversaries and, not infrequently, we ourselves contribute to such characterizations. The end result is a sense of confusion with regard to what is, or is not, authentic Catholic teaching. Those who are learners in theology cannot be expected to be unmoved or uninfluenced by such information. It not infrequently breeds extremism on either side. An extreme position is not one from which its occupant can consider dispassionately the objective merits of truth. This is by no means an indictment of those legitimate initiatives in theological research that necessarily require testing and peer review as a part of their authentication. But the process that was once confined to learned journals and scholarly symposia is today, however, circumscribed, and often preempted by more popular, widespread, and uncritical presentation and value judgment. The result can be, pastorally, disastrous.

A bishop, therefore, will look to theological education to pass on with integrity our Catholic tradition in the fullness of its essential truth with the obvious openness to pastoral outcomes that so deeply affect the whole Church. In such a task, and for the sake of such an outcome, bishops and theologians are both cooperators and collaborators. It is important that we recognize our respective roles with their legitimate limitations. Bishops, for example, are bound by that same Catholic tradition, and not by personal preference or emphasis, in evaluating the outcomes of theological education. Theologians in their quest for truth and in their role of imparting it to others are similarly bound to respect the Catholic tradition as they seek to give it a new voice, not a new identity, in changing circumstances so that it may be appropriated by large numbers of individuals. It is that tradition, an expression of faith, that is normative for both bishops and theologians. To the extent that either departs from it in the exercise of concrete roles, it then becomes the responsibility of the Church, under the guidance of the Holy Spirit, to offer the appropriate corrective.

Let my final word be one of recognition and affirmation of the indispensable role and work of theologians within the Church. It has been my good fortune to enjoy a close association with many whom I consider to be the brightest and the best. I am convinced that the personal relationships thereby formed, the mutual respect engendered by our collaboration, and, I do not hesitate to say, the esteem and affection that has accompanied this process I found to be among the richest of my experiences as a bishop. And it has served as a salutary reminder that a bishop is by no means alone in his concern for the integrity of the faith and in the challenge of proclaiming it to a contemporary world.

At one point in the long process of developing the many drafts that finally emerged as *Doctrinal Responsibilities* the several theological colleagues at the subcommittee level included John Boyle, Michael Buckley, and Leo O'Donovan. During one particularly intense discussion about matters that caused me some concern and reservation, I remember expressing an opinion that the office of bishop would not permit those who exercised it to approve of a certain line of reasoning that I felt led to a diminishment of the lived experience of the Catholic faith. To the best of my recollection, it was Leo O'Donovan who responded with a simple but powerful statement: "For you it may be a role of office, for us it is our whole life!" It was a lesson I have never forgotten, and pray that I never shall.

18

Theologians and Bishops: With Each Other

BISHOP JOHN J. LEIBRECHT

My conviction is that theologians and bishops are called to be in a relationship which is cooperative and respectful of one another's roles. Part of the pastoral responsibilities of bishops is to support theologians. In their research and teaching, theologians share in the Church's and bishop's pastoral ministry.

Application of these convictions in practice, bishops among bishops, theologians among theologians, and theologians and bishops with each other will, at times, be different—even contradictory. But, it seems to me, all theologians and bishops need shared commitments to mutual support within their differing roles.

Today, I want to express gratitude to theologians of two Catholic universities which have directly assisted the life of the Church in my missionary diocese of Springfield-Cape Girardeau in southern Missouri. The diocese has no Catholic institutions of higher education. Catholics are 6 percent of the total population in a 26,000 square mile area.

Last year, twelve of our faithful in the diocese attained their master's degree in religious studies from Loyola University in New Orleans. Next year, nine more will complete requirements for their degree and a new class will begin its work the following year. The Loyola Institute for Ministry created a way, through correspondence between professors and students all over this country, of working with bishops to advance sound religious education resources of the local church.

Several years ago, almost 200 of our faithful completed a two-year course sponsored by Creighton University. Creighton flew in professors each Saturday for day-long sessions, once a month, for a period of two years. Of the 220 people who started the course, 187 completed it. Most graduates are helping, in various capacities, in parishes across southern Missouri. Creighton University's effort to help a diocese like ours significantly improved the religious literacy and ministry within parishes across southern Missouri.

This October, our annual Priests' Institute will be held. From Monday through Friday, for the twenty-eighth successive year, priests of the diocese will gather for theological reflection with professors from Catholic colleges, universities, and seminaries. The result of these many annual institutes is a more informed and graced leadership for our local church.

As is clear by these three examples, I have personally experienced cooperation between theologians and bishops for the good of the Church.

Looking to the future, as a bishop, I would like to make two comments. First, the Church needs theologians whose identifying characteristic is that of the investigative scholar. Such theologians also teach, of course, but their personal gifts and interests are in theological investigation and scholarship of the highest quality. Religious, laity, and clergy will make up this cadre of theologians. The intellectual prowess and skills in languages of such theologians, networked nationally and internationally with other theologians whose work is also characteristically investigative, places them on the cutting edge of theological development.

Second, the Church needs teachers who are truly scholars, but whose identifying characteristic is that of teacher. They do research and report it, but their first commitment is to teaching. Such professors help form the Catholic faith community by informing it. They continually provide clarity about discipleship within the Catholic tradition. They are the seventy-two disciples sent out by the Lord, in our times, into various environments of leadership and influence.

Each group of theologians, those focused on research though teaching, and those focused on teaching based on solid scholarship, needs the other. The Church needs both as does the bishop.

Speaking as an individual bishop, for what kind of theology do I hope in the future? First, I hope for a theology which addresses the inner life of the Church. Catholics need to understand themselves and their Church more clearly and more fully. Holiness, discipleship, interrelationships between members of the Church, sacramental living, mission—these are some of the vital content areas helpful to the life of the faithful.

Second, I hope for a theology of apologetics. Atheism, secularism, and relativism, in my opinion, call for a renewed interest in scholarly supported apologetics. Better ways must be found to challenge these issues, if the gospel is to meet its contemporary challenges. Courses in apologetics, an appropriate apologetic sensitivity within other courses, or both, can be highly beneficial. The times are right, once again, for apologetics to be an important part of the life of the Church.

Next, I would like to see theology which addresses the assumptions and values which influence the daily living of a citizenry. The pastoral letters of U.S. bishops on the economy and world peace, to which theologians contributed so significantly, serve as an example of life issues needing theological reflection. Many social teachings of the Church need further development so that they can be brought to the public forum, to help frame and influence public debate and policy.

Lastly, I would like to see further development of theology which is ecumenically engaged. Several dialogues between our Roman Catholic tradition and other Christian churches offer hope for the future. Divisions within Christianity have been too long-standing. The Holy Father's recent call for further ecumenical attention to the Petrine office is a significant development. We Christians, possibly too settled in our divisions, need theologians to help us see how those divisions might be eased toward reconciliation. Progress in ecumenical dialogues can enhance our inter-faith dialogues.

I return to the place from which I began. I have experienced cooperation between bishop and theologian for the good of the faithful. What I hope for in the future can be more fully realized, through God's grace and power, when bishops and theologians see themselves in a relationship which respects, supports, and encourages their distinctive roles in the Church.

19

Inculturation and Acculturation for an American Bishop and Theologian

Bishop Donald E. Pelotte, S.S.S.

Introduction

In 1974, when I completed my Ph.D. in Theology with a focus on American ecclesiology at Fordham University in New York, I expected to be spending the rest of my life teaching theology at a university or in some seminary. I was excited about this possibility. However, totally beyond my control, just after my graduation in June of 1975, I was appointed Formation Director of my province and moved to Chicago to live with our seminarians who were studying at the Jesuit School of Theology. This school of theology worked in collaboration with its neighbors: the University of Chicago and the Lutheran School of Theology. This was a mind-expanding experience for me. Because, while I was there as a recently graduated, professional theologian I had the privilege of interacting with the world's greatest theologians like Karl Rahner, Bernard Lonergan, Carl Braaten, David Tracy, Wolfhart Pannenberg, and many others. This situation provided both an ecumenical and theological challenge.

After two years there and after another brief two years as rector/superior of our seminary/parish community in Cleveland, Ohio, I was elected provincial superior of our American province of the Congregation of the Blessed Sacrament. This province included all of the United States, England, Ireland, the Philippines, East Africa, and Vietnam. My first visits to these countries, especially East Africa and the Philippines, were mind-boggling. Immediately the whole issue of the relationship between faith and culture was there before me. I was forced to reflect on the true meaning of inculturation, i.e., the process by which the gospel is adapted to a particular culture. The Second Vatican Council made the first detailed statement about the relationship of the Church to diverse cultures in the *Pastoral Constitution on the Church in the*

Modern World.[1] In order to evangelize, pastoral initiatives need to be carried on from *within* the cultures of humankind.[2] Through inculturation the Church endeavors to reformulate Christian life and doctrine within the thought-patterns of each people. Efforts to achieve such integration have not been easy and continue today to be difficult and pastorally delicate.

Within this context and with nine years experience as provincial superior dealing with this issue of inculturation/acculturation, I was appointed Coadjutor bishop of the Diocese of Gallup, New Mexico in February of 1986. I fully succeeded the retiring bishop in 1990. The Diocese of Gallup is in the southwestern part of the United States and was established by Pope Pius XII in 1939 as the "American Indian" diocese. While the boundaries of this 55,000 square mile diocese were partly established based on the geographical boundaries of the Navajo Nation, which is 25,000 square miles with a population of 200,000—the largest tribe in the United States—the diocese also includes six other tribes: the Laguna, the Acoma, the Hopi, the Zuni, and two tribes of Apache. Of the approximately 50,000 Catholics in the diocese, 51 percent are Native American; they are followed by the Hispanics as the second largest population. Thirty other ethnic groups are represented in addition. Thus, the diocese begins just on the west side of the city of Albuquerque and goes all the way west into Arizona up to the northern rim of the Grand Canyon.

Because of the large Native American population, who are predominantly very poor, the diocese is considered the poorest in the United States and counts almost completely on outside support for survival. Many parts of the Navajo reservation have no running water or electricity and with a population of 200,000, whose average age is twenty-nine, the unemployment can be as high as 65 percent. This makes this whole mission diocese as Third World as anything I ever experienced among the primitive, nomadic Masai people in East Africa or as poor as some of the slums of downtown Manila in the Philippines.

Within this unique pastoral context I serve as bishop and theologian. My challenge at this "Conference on Theological Education in the Catholic Tradition" is to describe how in very concrete ways we have responded to the theological, educational, and formational needs in a diocese where there are no Catholic colleges or universities or seminaries. For example, how do we theologically prepare our seminarians for ministry as priests within this unique Third World setting? What about the theological preparation of permanent, married deacons and lay catechists, especially from the indigenous peoples? What is being done to strengthen the ministry of the 100 priests and 220 sisters with continuing theological education? And most importantly, how is this being done in view of the sensitivity needed around the area of inculturation and acculturation mentioned above?

[1] #258.
[2] Pope Paul VI, "On Evangelization in the Modern World," [*Evangelii Nuntiandi*] (Washington, D.C.: USCC, 1976).

There are other important questions to be looked at: Is this theological/ educational formation collaborative and ecumenical in approach? How are limited resources being shared with the other Christian churches who find themselves in the same unique situation? Finally, how can Catholic universities and colleges like Marquette or seminaries nationally support and be of service to these pastoral efforts?

Theological Formation of Seminarians

When I began my work here in 1986, my predecessor had his own local seminary in Gallup where he personally worked at preparing the candidates for theology. The focus was on getting to know the area well, the various cultures present in the diocese and more especially the Native American cultures. In addition to having them work in the local soup kitchen which caters to poor Navajo people, they were required to take courses at the local branch of the University of New Mexico here in Gallup which provides courses in Native American history and culture. Courses were also available for those wanting to learn the Navajo language. Once they had completed what he called their "acculturation" into the diocese, they were assigned to a seminary in the Northeast to begin their theological formation. My own personal opinion is that while the theological preparation for priesthood was adequate it did not sufficiently prepare them with the principles needed to reflect theologically on the unique situation in which they would be ministering.

Nonetheless, during the summers, a program of "acculturation" was held for the seminarians in an attempt to deal with the specific, local, pastoral issues and the ministerial style required here in the Southwest. Presently we have just a few seminarians who study at St. Benedict's, in Mount Angel, Oregon. I believe this seminary is better prepared to deal with theological and formational issues relating to a missionary diocese. St. Benedict's trains mostly seminarians from California, from here in the Southwest, and the northwestern states in addition to students from Columbia, South America, and Samoa. Our seminarians always return here for the summer where they are normally assigned to a "reservation pastor" who has a lot of experience and who can help them reflect theologically on their ministry with the Native people.

For the future, I do not ever expect to see a "Native American" seminary established. Nonetheless, I believe it is extremely critical for seminaries to provide some solid input for the candidates on the relationship between faith and culture and help make concrete in their theological and spiritual formation the principles of inculturation/acculturation.

Theological Formation
of Permanent Deacons and Lay Leaders/Catechists

When I arrived here, I came to see very quickly that my predecessor was not very keen on lay leadership formation. In a diocesan survey I initiated a year or so after I arrived, the need for the ongoing theological formation of our lay people was strongly affirmed. The permanent diaconate program had been well established and I believe continues to be one of the best in the country. My predecessor was one of the first bishops in the United States to implement the diaconate program after the Council. It has proven very successful. The faculty is made up of highly qualified teachers from among the priests, sisters, permanent deacons, and lay people. Nonetheless, the program had only attracted two Native Americans to the diaconate—a Navajo and a Kiowa Indian. My sense is that they always felt like second-class citizens and not fully a part of the program.

From their Native American perspective the program was perhaps too academic and not experiential and practical enough nor very sensitive to their indigenous cultures. Accordingly, when I assumed leadership of the diocese in 1990, I established a Native American Lay Ministry and Diaconate Formation Program using the Jesuits John Hatcher's and Patrick McCorkell's *Builders of the New Earth* as our format.[3] It has been extremely successful. Initially, Father Hatcher came to Gallup to train the faculty. Presently there are approximately fifty candidates on the Navajo reservation and another thirty or so candidates among the Acoma/Laguna. The priests and sisters working with the White Mountain Apache in southwestern Arizona hope to establish the program very soon.

In May of this year I ordained two Navajo men to the permanent diaconate and commissioned their wives as lay leaders/catechists. Now these deacons teach as members of the hierarchy of the Catholic Church and give a Navajo direction to their Church. Only now do they preach Christ from a Navajo world view. Only now are there Navajo answers to the Navajo questions about Christ.

Navajo men and women rooted in the tradition of their culture, living in modern America and aware of Jesus Christ's readiness to share with them, are forming their local church within the universal Church. The beatification of Kateri Tekakwitha on June 22, 1980, by Pope John Paul II in the presence of many American Indian people gave them even greater encouragement and support. So too did his strong address of affirmation on the occasion of his visit with the Native American community in Phoenix, Arizona, in September, 1987. Our Native people no longer function with fear and uncertainty before an unknown cultural tradition. They do not hesitate before cultural patterns and practices which differ from those of their own cultural tradition.

---

[3] John E. Hatcher and Patrick M. McCorkell, *Builders of the New Earth*, 3 vols. (Rapid City, S.D.: Diocese of Rapid City, 1975; 1986).

They know themselves. They know their people. They know Jesus Christ. Jesus Christ acts and speaks through them.

Hatcher's and McCorkell's program of theological and spiritual formation is based upon their three volume *Builders of the New Earth*. The three volumes have six books with eighteen lessons to each book. The material covered is Scripture, canon law (especially of marriage), and moral theology. The class meets once a week from September until May for four years and is meant to prepare people for lay ministry as well as the diaconate. There are normally ten to fifteen people in the class made up of both men and women. The material in the textbooks is supplemented by a day of recollection/education in the spring and the fall. These days are devoted to some prayer and some education.

There are important underlying principles to this program. (1) The model stresses formation rather than merely information. It is seen as critical that the candidates have a strong foundation in order to be able to minister effectively. (2) The spirituality of each person needs to be respected. Each person is a gift of the Holy Spirit to every other member of the group. (3) People are asked to pray over the ideas. During the week, before the class, each person is asked to read the material and pray over it for a time each day. They are asked to write their insights in the text so that they can bring them to the other members of the class. The method does not ask people simply to repeat back what is in the text. The method tries to get people to filter the lessons through their lived experience of the faith and then in a reflective manner comment on the text. (4) People are asked to share their experience of God. Each person must be committed to talk on a very personal level about their experience of God. (5) The spiritual heritage of the Indian peoples must be respected. The method tries to get people to reflect on the ideas and Scriptures and filter them through their cultural experience. It is here that the important work of inculturation takes place. The method expects that people will form a Lakota, Navajo, Acoma, etc., Catholic theology.

Continuing Theological Education for Missionaries Among Native People

The Sioux Spiritual Center in Plainview, South Dakota, founded and directed by Hatcher and his staff, provides an annual program called "Basic Directions in Native Ministry." This is a ten-day institute for personnel beginning work in Native American ministry and is sponsored by the National Tekakwitha Conference and the National Conference of Bishops' Ad Hoc Committee on Native American Catholics. There are fifty hours of class work associated with the workshop. Topics include missiology, anthropology, liturgy, catechetics, collaborative ministry, native culture, and religion and principles of recovery using Alcoholics Anonymous. Native people involved in catechetics, parish administration, and youth ministry discuss their work with the participants. Although the institute takes place in a Lakota setting, it aims to develop basic principles of inculturation that can be used in approaching any culture.

This program has proven very positive and my diocese sends three to four individuals each summer, especially newly arrived missionary priests or sisters. In addition to this "Basic Directions in Native Ministry Institute" the Sioux Spiritual Center directs a five-day "Native Catechists Workshop" each year. This program is also sponsored by the National Tekakwitha Conference and is meant as an "enrichment" for catechists, i.e., Native people doing catechetical work and who have already completed or are in the process of completing the three-volume *Builders of the New Earth*. The last session was held recently, July 17-21, 1995, and was extremely successful in the ongoing theological, catechetical, and spiritual formation of our Native catechists.

Continuing Education of Priests, Sisters, Deacons, and Laity

In addition to the programs mentioned above, in which many of our priests and sisters have participated, the diocesan office of education after consultation with the priestly life and ministry committee is responsible for organizing four continuing education days during the year. Most often experts are brought in from the outside to address the groups on issues relating to their ministry. Recently, a day was spent on the topic of Mormonism, which presents serious pastoral problems in many parts of our diocese. Next spring an expert on the theology of Eucharist will give a day on that subject. Very often these "guest speakers" who recognize the poverty of the diocese only ask us to cover their traveling expenses. Marquette University or any other Catholic college could be of help to us here by freeing up some of their theological experts to come to Gallup to assist in our ongoing theological formation.

Beyond the priests' continuing education program provided by the diocese, some of our priests have participated in the Seton Hall Institute for Priests, the "Beginning as Pastors" program in California, as well as the continuing education programs in Louvain and Rome. But, in general, these are too expensive for a poor diocese like Gallup.

The "Beginning as Pastor" program is designed for first-time pastors and parish administrators. Created as a year-long process, the program involves an integrated two-week experience and draws upon participants' actual practice of ministry over the entire year as one of its main resources. "Beginning as Pastor" focuses on the pastor's personal understanding of his ministry and the skills needed to implement it. The topics included in this workshop are the transition to a new parish, the role as pastor, pastoral planning, personality type and pastoral style, the development of staff into effective teams, time management, personnel from creating a job description to termination, conflict management, financial management/stewardship, models of parish organization, and spirituality for pastors.

Besides what I have described above, a number of our teachers in our Catholic schools participate in the *Catholic Home Study Institute* (CHSI). Approximately 20 percent of CHSI's worldwide student body enroll in courses to earn college credit. Institutions such as the Franciscan University of Steubenville, Regis University, the University of Dallas, Regents College, Cardinal Stritch College, Saint Mary's University (San Antonio), Thomas Edison State College, Liberty University, and Holy Apostles Seminary awarded credit to CHSI students. Also some of our lay catechists have participated in the University of Dayton *Catechists Formation Program* and Loyola University's (New Orleans) "Institute for Ministry." For me it is absolutely critical that all of the above programs be sensitive to the principles of inculturation and help its participants to reflect theologically on the relationship of faith and culture.

Ecumenical/Theological Collaboration

Finally, the Diocese of Gallup along with the other two Catholic dioceses of New Mexico are collaborating with the New Mexico Council of Churches in establishing a "Theological Education Consortium." This consortium, in which all participating dioceses/judicatories would make some contribution, is hoping to provide at least undergraduate credit courses at various locations throughout the state. The mission of the Consortium is the lifelong education for ministry for laity and clergy of the faith communities in New Mexico. Initial course offerings will be in the core disciplines of Christian theological education: biblical studies, the history of the Christian tradition, and systematic theology. Courses are intended to train students to become effective leaders in their own faith communities, to provide a favorable and respectful climate for ecumenical interaction, and to serve the spiritual, emotional, and intellectual growth of students. Later plans include offering a variety of practical courses for specific lay training, and providing an accredited master's degree program locally for those holding or seeking professional lay leadership roles in the churches. In its degree programs especially, the Consortium will be guided by the standards of the American Association of Theological Schools, with a view to eventual accreditation. The exact details are still being worked out but this is an extremely challenging, exciting, ecumenical endeavor in response to our unique situation in the Southwest.

Conclusion

What I have shared above demonstrates that there are creative ways to respond to unique needs. In the absence of a Catholic college or seminary in the local area, the Diocese of Gallup tries nonetheless to provide the appropriate theological education and formation of its members.

Within this presentation I have made a few suggestions as to how the seminary, the college, or the university might be of help in addressing a situation similar to that in this local church. Just as Fathers Hatcher's and McCorkell's *Builders of the New Earth* program in Rapid City was developed under the tutelage of the faculty while these priests were at Regis College in

Toronto, so, similarly, Catholic universities and colleges should be exhorted to extend beyond the university community and become more active in the life of the culture because many bishops need help in meeting new and serious problems that are rapidly emerging and for which those responsible for them are at times unprepared.

Just as importantly, what I have said about inculturation applies to the university, the college, and the seminary, particularly as we reflect together on *Ex corde Ecclesiae*. *Ex corde Ecclesiae* asks that the university help the Church understand the positive and negative aspects of various cultures.[4] The Church looks to the college and university to lead the dialogue between Christian thought and the sciences.[5] Religion offers insights for reflection on human life, justice, family life, the environment and nature, peace and political stability.[6] Also, *Ex corde Ecclesiae* asks the Catholic colleges and universities to promote ecumenical dialogue.

In view of what we have heard from some of the speakers at the Conference on theological education in the Catholic tradition, assisting students to relate faith to culture has become difficult because of religious illiteracy among many students. Accordingly, I simply want to pose the questions: How might that situation be addressed? How might a relationship between faith and culture be addressed in the case of students who are not Catholic? These are challenging questions for me and for you for years to come.

Because of our unique Native American character the greatest challenge that faces those ministering in the Diocese of Gallup is that of inculturation. Although the Second Vatican Council initiated serious efforts toward inculturation, much work remains to be done to achieve what is implied in Acts 10:34-36: "Then Peter began to speak to them: 'I truly understand that God shows no partiality, but in every nation anyone who fears him and does what is right is acceptable to him.'"

---

[4] *Ex corde Ecclesiae*, 44.
[5] Ibid., 46.
[6] Ibid., 32.

VII

INTEGRATION AND INCULTURATION IN THE THEOLOGICAL CURRICULUM

20

Biblical Studies in University and Seminary Theology

LAWRENCE E. BOADT, C.S.P.

The Importance of Scripture for Theology

Contemporary Catholic theological studies do not limit themselves to the narrow definition of doing theology as "theological investigation of one particular religion by a critical observer committed to that religion and from within the context of the living religious community today."[1] Theology can and indeed always has gone on outside of the academic critical canons derived from the rationalism of the Enlightenment. There is a natural dialogue that develops between the Church's search for the inner dynamics of intelligibility and coherence belonging to its faith, which is a proper internal search for meaning, and the university's critical inquiry into the religious belief of this or that faith system from an outside perspective. They both at least share a common goal together: to relate the particular beliefs of this faith to the whole range of human experience.

So, too, the field of biblical studies does not limit itself simply to the positive task of a delineation of doctrinal beliefs as they are rooted in the Scriptures nor to the explanation of ancient ways of expression in order to discover how those beliefs were articulated. As a result of years of interest in pursuing the historical-critical method, biblical scholarship has focused on understanding all biblical texts against the culture and thought frame of the Ancient Near Eastern and Greco-Roman worlds, with an eye to the development of, and changes in, the religious tradition(s) throughout the Bible's long history. In recent years there has been growing attention to both the Bible's literary art as a bearer of communication and the situation of the contemporary reader as a controlling element for the act of interpretation. This has led to a substantial interest by biblical studies in hermeneutical questions and the philosophy of

---

[1] This is the majority opinion of professionals in the field today, according to Ray L. Hart, "Religious and Theological Studies in American Higher Education: A Pilot Study," *Journal of the American Academy of Religion* 59 (1991): 715-827.

language, a concern shared equally today by systematic theology in both university and seminary programs. Where systematics struggles to abstract and formulate larger and more universal articulations of faith, biblical studies wrestles with the particularity of texts in their very concreteness as expressions of human experience.

As a result, biblical studies as it is done by either university theology or seminary theology has to deal with this specificity that is reflected in the text itself, even as it relates the text to contemporary hermeneutical understanding. Granted that all biblical studies today seem to have these same interests, are there still significant differences between the university study of Scripture and the seminary programs? A brief examination of the contemporary seminary approach to biblical studies may highlight effectively any similarities and differences between the two educational systems in their goals and consequent teaching approaches.

The Role of Scripture in the Seminary Program

The initial premise of a master's level seminary program is that our students are already well versed in Catholic beliefs derived from the Scriptures, the liturgical readings from the Bible, and the general sacred character of the biblical text as revelation. It is also usually understood that they have some firsthand knowledge of the Bible as a book. But this is often not the case. This means all that follows about the goals of the course of biblical studies in the seminary is burdened by the further constant need to provide basic background information while using that information to get students to think critically.

Before the Second Vatican Council, seminary level Scripture usually concentrated on familiarizing priest candidates with the overall contents of the biblical canon and then dealt in depth with the significant individual texts that pertained to the development of specific doctrines or common practices of the Church. Critical questions mostly dealt with revelation and inspiration or with certain general biblical literary forms such as parables and miracle stories in the Gospels.[2] Attention was also given to biblical theology, mostly in blocs: Old Testament theology, Pauline theology, the theology of the gospels (as a whole), etc.

In the wake of the call to critical study of the sacred texts based on historical investigation and the use of modern methods, a new paradigm emerged.[3]

---

[2] For a typical Roman Catholic seminary textbook on Scripture, see John Steinmueller, *A Companion to Scripture Studies* (New York: Wagner). It was originally published in 1944 and updated through 1962. Note, however, that even in the last revision, volume 1 contained 614 pages on inspiration, canonicity, and related propaedeutic questions; volume 2 dealt with the entire Old Testament in only 325 pages, with no discussion of methods of interpretation; and volume 3 treated the New Testament in 372 pages, with only a section on method titled "Against Rationalist Methods" of twenty-three pages.

[3] For typical examples of this in Catholic settings, see Pheme Perkins, *Reading the New Testament: An Introduction* (Mahwah, N.J.: Paulist Press, 1982, 1991) and Lawrence Boadt, *Read-

Most seminary professors that I know present a model of interpreting Scripture that attempts the following:

(1) The course is designed to show that individual books and traditions are the product of long historical development, and that the literary claims of the text do not always reflect their real age, stages of growth, or authorship. The presentations help the student discover an "Israel" or a "New Testament community" that had cohesive and intelligible growth in its own religious understanding which are reflected in the final shape of each biblical book.

(2) The first corollary of this approach is about historical knowledge of the past. Ancient documents and social customs are presented in order to context biblical books; and methods are explained by which historians, anthropologists, archaeologists, and literary analysis attempt to recover the past, often by hypothetical reconstruction. At the same time, emphasis is placed on the cultural similarities and differences among ancient peoples or within Greco-Roman society in order to help students appreciate the clash of values and the inculturation of the Scriptures.[4]

(3) A second corollary of this historical-critical approach is to deal with discrepancies in the ethical and moral teachings of different parts of Scripture, or between the Scriptures and contemporary ethical convictions. This applies equally to various biblical formulations about the nature of God, or human ideas of worship and sacrifice, and slavery, etc. Tradition-critical methods highlight how older values and ethical understandings are often absorbed, repackaged, or treated as historical reminiscences only as the canonical shape of the Scriptures developed.

(4) There is a major shift toward combining historical questions about the growth of the text with appreciating the individual books as literary wholes. Students are taught to see the ways that authors structure literary genres and plots to achieve a literary effect or to communicate their message in the end product. This concern leads courses also to survey the breadth of the Scriptures from Genesis to Revelation.

(5) Some perennial theological topics still get individual treatment across biblical traditions: messianism, covenant, sin (especially original sin), the role of prophecy, the historical Jesus, apocalyptic developments, and Hellenism (especially in Paul's thought). Perhaps less consistently but still often, teachers address directly the problem of anti-Semitism in the New Testament and the relationship of Christianity and Judaism as sister faiths across the two testaments.

(6) In order to organize this as part of the biblical preparation of the student, most programs insist on at least one introductory Old Testament course and one on the prophets or other major bloc of Old Testament tradition, as well as three in the New Testament: some kind of introduction, perhaps in-

---

ing the Old Testament: An Introduction (Mahwah, N.J.: Paulist Press, 1985).

[4] This goal also fulfills the mandate of *Gaudium et Spes*, Vatican II's document on *The Church in the Modern World* #58, that "the church must enter into communion with different forms of culture, thereby enriching both itself and the cultures themselves."

cluding the Gospels, Paul, and Johannine literature. Substantive time is given to methodological questions: particularly historical-critical method, literary methods, and contextual methods such as feminist or liberationist or sociological approaches.

If the current model of interpreting Scripture is done well, the seminary student develops a familiarity with the Bible as a whole, a good sense of how it was composed and when the parts originated and came together, and what the final form of each book intended to teach. Students will also understand revelation as an ongoing process of Israel's and the early Church's encounter with God that gradually took shape in sacred writings, which were gradually recognized as normative by the Synagogue and the Church. The entire process was guided by the Holy Spirit, both as the books were written and as they were recognized as sacred. Students will also have a rich appreciation of the continuity between Old and New Testaments as the source of their Christian faith.

Current professors of Scripture have a tendency to neglect some of the following items in their teaching:

(1) the role of the Old Testament as Torah and its halakhic function for the Jewish community of both Israel and today;

(2) the in-depth treatment of the meaning of inspiration, revelation, inerrancy, canonicity, and so forth, which used to dominate introductory biblical studies;

(3) serious attempts to develop a coherent integration of the theology or theologies implicit in the biblical books themselves;

(4) the role that biblical texts have played among believing communities for liturgy, spirituality, or popular piety as distinct from its study in the academy;

(5) discussions of the students' own reactions to these texts as sacred and central to their Church ministry, including how they relate the claims of the text to their personal faith;

(6) what usefulness the students see in biblical texts for their ministries in the Church, including preaching and teaching them;

(7) biblical spirituality in any form;

(8) familiarity with how Jews read the Old Testament within their interpretive tradition as the Hebrew Scriptures;

(9) attempts to relate academic historical-critical, literary, or other hermeneutical *methods* with the personal methods of appropriation of Scripture as (a) truth to be believed, (b) a relationship with God to be cultivated, (c) a guide for life decisions, and (d) a source of prayer;

(10) critiques of the critical methods we personally teach. (We always point out the shortcomings of the methods we do not agree with, but do we also admit the shortcomings and limits of the methods we do use, or do we come across as narrow idealogues?)

If too many of the goods listed above are missing, students experience a sense of disconnectedness to the vital role the Scriptures play in the daily life of the Church for liturgy, personal prayer, catechetics, and even for theology.[5] They also lose the sense of growth and diversity in history and the values in cultures. The future ministers of the Word and teachers of the Church know all about the original message of the Scriptures and yet remain very fuzzy about its application and relevance for Christian living in the contemporary world.

Beyond "Historical-Critical" Teaching of the Bible

If seminarians are generally deficient in the mature knowledge of their Catholic faith and in lifelong familiarity with its liturgical and spiritual traditions, then an overemphasis on the historical-critical method alone can seem to bring into question even the few basic stories and certitudes about Jesus and the Old Testament that they had relied on. Suddenly their scholarly studies are presenting them with a version of God's actions in revelation far different from the one they learned as children and that their parents (or their congregations) believed in.[6] Some seem to reject their academic study as a result.

It is crucial that education in the Scriptures today for a believing community combine both critical reflection and an introduction to the ecclesial use of Scripture. The critical side will raise the questions, seek the sources, explain the development, and explore new challenges to our traditional understandings of the text; and the ecclesial context will examine the role of Scripture for the Church both in its uses in catechetics, liturgy, prayer, and doctrines today and in its rich history of interpretation through the centuries past. Luke Timothy Johnson tells of his "experience/interpretation" model. He first invites students to reflect on their own social context and the Bible: as university-level students what questions should they bring to the study of the text? As individuals, what role do they see the Bible playing for themselves, their contemporaries, and the Church.[7] When he actually has them study texts, he asks them to read them on a four dimensional scale: the *anthropological*, in which they take seriously how they give expression to real human experience; the *historical*, in which they try to understand the original setting of the message in its ancient context; the *literary*, in which they look closely at the art and literary purpose of the texts; and the *religious*, in which they first examine the religious experience that shaped the text before they examine its theology.

This is an important first start in bringing together the goals of critical study of the Bible and the actual world of the student of the text and their concerns and goals for examining the Scriptures. But it is still short of the ideal knowledge of the role of the Bible in the Church that must accompany any critical knowledge of its origins and original meaning. Beyond what Johnson proposes, seminary education needs to address several other issues

---

[5] The Vatican Council's Decree, *Dei Verbum*, par. 24, calls Scripture "The Soul of Theology."

[6] Luke Timothy Johnson, "The New Testament and the Examined Life: Thoughts on Teaching," *The Christian Century* (February 1-8, 1995): 108-11.

[7] Johnson, "The New Testament," 110-11.

in biblical courses.

(1) How were the Scriptures interpreted in the earliest Church? How did the New Testament read the Old? How did the Talmud use biblical texts? Can we teach students to put aside modern conceptualizations and unlock the metaphors and images of these early interpreters?[8]

(2) Where is the history of the great reflective thinkers of the Church who theologized from the Scriptures: e.g., Origen, Augustine, Aquinas? Do our commentaries include any interpretations of biblical texts by classical Christian thinkers or have they become simply source books for historical-critical study of the text?[9] How much do we expose students to typological or allegorical readings of the text that prevailed for fifteen hundred years? Or to *lectio divina*? Or to the *Biblia Pauperum*?

(3) Do we really teach the function of the Bible as the book of a structured religious community that grounded its rules, its basic doctrinal demands and its most important institutions? Do we relate these to the structure, the rules, and doctrinal formulations of the living Church? Or does the Bible always remain a normative book of the past in our teaching, one that was then used in many diverse ways almost at the whim of different ages and religious thinkers or even ecclesiastical authorities?

(4) Hans Frei locates the meaning of the text in the living relationship between the text read in an "intrabiblical" context (i.e., understanding how it reuses its own traditions for the later life of the community), and the community of authoritative interpreters (the ecclesiastical authoritative interpreters and the scholars who are part of the Church as a community of believers).[10] Moshe Greenberg, a Jewish scholar, proposes "holistic interpretation," in which exegetes come to the text convinced that it is designed to convey a message; this is the exegete's analogue to the Church's proclamation to the faithful to be open to hearing God's Word in the text.[11] Both of these suggestions challenge the teacher to keep critical and ecclesial dimensions of interpretation together in their classes.[12]

(5) The seminary above all must keep in mind that it teaches the Scriptures as a sacred book for the faith of the students, as a text for believers. If we

---

[8] See the call for such education in Emmanuel Levinas, "The Jewish Understanding of Scripture," *Cross Currents* (winter 1994-95): 488-504.

[9] This issue has not been entirely neglected. William Farmer is editing a new one- volume Catholic Commentary on Scripture, due in 1998, that will feature the history of the interpretation of the text in Church life and writing as well as direct exegetical commentary.

[10] Hans Frei, *The Eclipse of Biblical Narrative. A Study in Eighteenth and Nineteenth Century Hermeneutics* (New Haven: Yale University, 1974), 60-62.

[11] Moshe Greenberg, "The Vision of Jerusalem in Ezekiel 8-11: A Holistic Interpretation," in *The Divine Helmsman: Lou H. Silberman Festschrift*, ed. James Crenshaw and Samuel Sandmel (New York: Ktav, 1980), 143-54.

[12] Robert Bellah has proposed a *via media* between the religious orthodoxy characteristic of seminaries, and the "enlightenment orthodoxy" characteristic of the secular university which he envisions as the study of religion through the "second naivete" of Ricouer which insists upon an explicit religious consciousness. He criticizes the university study of religion today as inevitably promoting a relativism about religion, and more importantly, the functional and conceptual categories of the scholar assume a priority over the object of study. See "Religion in the

are constantly attentive to the "inner-biblical exegesis" of the Scriptures themselves (e.g., as the Exodus is reapplied to the exilic situation of Judaism, and
reapplied again to the death and resurrection of Jesus), we can invite the students of the text to see how this same dynamic applies to their application
and new reading of the text in preaching and teaching. Historical examples
of this application in the Church can also be brought out. We might, for example, relate the exodus motif to the development of the motifs of deliver-
ance by water in the sacrament of baptism or the Eucharist as the manna for
the desert journey of life.[13]

(6) Pheme Perkins argues that we need to shift our teaching of academic
biblical studies from a primarily historical-critical method to one with a theological viewpoint. She laments the "academic positivism" that does not "adequately engage the dynamic challenge of the Bible as the founding vision of
Western culture."[14] Genuine engagement with the experiences represented in
the biblical tradition requires more awareness of the place of community for
human religious expression. To approach the Bible from a theological vision
offers a perspective for both seeing the importance of the biblical message for
a living faith community, but also for seeing its contribution to the good of the
entire human community.

(7) A final observation is in order on this topic. The foregoing reflections
have dealt largely with the role of Scripture as a theological subject for critical
analysis and not with its pastoral applications in liturgy or preaching or counseling courses. But I have tried to show all the way through that for both the
university and the seminary the same basic rules may apply—no serious study
of the biblical text can be divorced from its existence and active role in the
believing community from which it arose and for and to which it speaks. This
should not be seen simply as a capitulation to pastoral goals. It is the theme
of what we can best term "postcritical interpretation," and which is finding
strong support among exegetes. A leading proponent of this approach, Peter
Ochs, puts it this way:

> The postcritical scholar's return "to the text itself" is *not merely to that
> composition of letters you could see with your eyes on those parchments.* It
> is more helpful to say that the scholar has returned to participate in
> some relationship that is already ongoing among that composition
> *and* community/tradition of interpreter/practitioners *and* the Author
> of that composition as a whole. According to the composition as a

University: Changing Consciousness, Changing Structures," in Claude Welch, *Religion in the
Undergraduate Curriculum: An Analysis and Interpretation* (Washington, D.C.: Association of American Colleges, 1972), 13-18.
    [13] Michael Fishbane, *Biblical Interpretation in Ancient Israel* (Oxford: Oxford University Press,
1985) offers many illustrations of how inner-biblical exegesis not only affected later biblical
texts but provided the basis for rabbinic exegesis and application.
    [14] Pheme Perkins, "Revisioning the Teaching of Scripture," *Current Issues in Catholic Higher
Education* 7 (winter 1987): 29-32.
    [15] Peter Ochs, "Returning to Scripture: Trends in Postcritical Interpretation," *Cross Currents*

whole, this author is "the Lord God," who speaks to the community/ tradition of Israel by way of the words of this composition. The return to the text is, in this sense, a means of participating once again in a tripartite relation among God, word and community of interpretation.[15]

University scholarship may limit its task to the examination of how this relationship works itself out in the actual composition of the biblical texts and its history of interpretation, but seminary biblical studies must also communicate to its students how to translate this into the lives of a believing community.[16] That is a major difference in purpose, but it does not invalidate the insight of postcritical scholarship that there are probably no readers of the text who do not need to understand a user's ecclesial context.

Integration of Biblical Studies in Seminary Curricula

In order to achieve the integration of the scholarly and the personal dimensions of Scripture within the goals of the seminary education of priests and ministerial personnel, the study of the Bible cannot stand alone. It is commonly understood to be necessary preparation for doing systematic theology, Christology, moral theology, preaching, and liturgy and so often stands early in the seminary program at the master's degree level. But this view relegates Scripture to a positive body of literature, and a positive theology of the past that must be mastered before the student moves on *past* this level to further developments in theology, ethics, and other ecclesial studies. Scripture runs the risk of becoming irrelevant as a living partner in the doing of theology. This may be a legacy of the strong philosophical context for systematics and a loosening of the bonds that kept theology close to the Scriptures in the early Church and medieval system of theological education. However, it needs to be addressed more fully once again.

In November 1993, the Pontifical Biblical Commission issued a comprehensive guideline on exegesis directed to Catholic scholars. Joseph Cardinal Ratzinger wrote the preface, quoting *Dei Verbum* (24) in the opening sentence: "The study of the Bible is, as it were, the soul of theology."[17] To speak of the

---

(winter 1994-95): 437-52, esp. 449; and also Peter Ochs, ed., *The Return to Scripture in Judaism and Christianity: Essays in Postcritical Scriptural Interpretation* (Mahwah, N.J.: Paulist, 1993) for a wide range of articles on this topic of postcritical interpretation.

[16] Note for example the formulation of this goal in the "Mission Statement" of the 1995 *Catalog* of the Washington Theological Union: "The WTU believes that effective ministry requires excellent instruction and sound material. It calls for ministers imbued with a broad theological understanding, spiritual depth and personal good character as well. The Roman Catholic educational tradition is one of *scholarly and systematic reflection* on the revealing Word of God. The Union's programs for ministry embody this *serious academic heritage wherein theological knowledge is valued* for the enrichment of the person—the person who is witnessing Christ in the world—and *not simply for application in practice* [emphases added]."

[17] "The Interpretation of the Bible in the Church," *Origins* 23 (January 6, 1994): 519.

study of Scripture as the "soul" suggests the animating principle by which theology is to derive its power and its sources. Indeed, after examining at length various exegetical methods in relation to the ecclesial use of the Bible, the document adds a section on "The Relationship with Other Theological Disciplines" in which it treats particularly the relationship of presuppositions of theology and exegesis that interface with one another, the link between Scripture and tradition as theological sources, the objects of systematic theology that are often neglected in the texts by exegetes, the risks of a separation between theological formulations and their linguistic expression in Scripture, and the importance of exegetical background for ethical claims.

In general, little has yet developed to follow up these guidelines in the scholarly literature or in discussions of the seminary faculties with which I am familiar.[18] Some such discussion is badly needed in the following areas, however.

(1) Systematics and biblical faculties need to share some strategies and common approaches to dealing with basic questions such as the role of the Scriptures as normative documents of the Church, especially in relation to revelation, inspiration, and canonical authority.

(2) Scripture relies on narrative, legal, and persuasive literary genres to communicate its message, and exegetes have shown strong interest in contextual methods of interpretation (such as reader-response, narratology, deconstructionism, sociological, and social history readings), while there is equally a growing interest among contemporary theologians in narrative theology and social contexts for the theological use of texts. But this needs to be better discussed between the two disciplines.

(3) There are few efforts to coordinate the presentation of important theological topics such as the Trinity as they appear in the liturgical readings for Sundays with their scriptural exegesis. Systematicians and biblical scholars could work on some of these to fashion a common or basic set of themes for preaching and teaching on these Sundays.

(4) Since many points in the sections above call for an expanded knowledge of the history of interpretation of biblical texts in the Church, scriptural departments need to coordinate more closely some program of education in the area of patristic and medieval Church history which includes biblical interpretation in these historical periods.

(5) The persistent and nagging question of whether there can be a positive biblical ethics or a distinctive New Testament ethics does not go away. Moral theologians and scriptural departments need to develop nuanced ways of presenting the two sides of the debate in the seminary curriculum.

(6) Although not strictly a matter of integrating theological approaches or methods in the seminary curriculum, the interface between Scripture, preaching, and liturgy is so close and so significant to any long-range hope of having a personal and ecclesial as well as critical knowledge of the Bible in the master's level graduate that mutual planning between these pastoral and

---

[18] One such is Joseph Fitzmyer, *Scripture: The Soul of Theology* (Mahwah, N.J.: Paulist, 1994), 497-524.

academic departments should be encouraged. Cooperation between these departments in the teaching of courses might also be profitably explored.

(7) Ultimately, all of the preceding suggestions are based on the conviction that systematics, moral, Bible, homiletics, and liturgy have too often been compartmentalized, and there needs to be an ongoing dialogue within seminary faculties on how all work together. The emphasis in this essay on the inseparable connection between the critical study of biblical texts and the function they play in a believing community can only be truly grasped by a student when the entire theological training recognizes it as a goal in which each department or area of theology contributes as part of a single vision. Practically speaking, it seems to me that the easiest way to begin to work towards a closer cooperation between different branches of theology is for joint departmental meetings at which the faculty members share together key articles and books that best articulate for each department the issues within their field that touch on their integration with other aspects of theology.

Conclusion

The bottom line is that any study of academic theology, which includes biblical studies, must be both critical and practically relevant. We are moving towards teaching biblical studies as an academic discipline that respects the nature and purpose of a text directed to making sense of life. But this is just as true of other theological disciplines such as moral theology/ethics or systematics. A professor from the University of London, Francis Watson, proposed a new "ecclesial hermeneutic" for biblical studies which must take seriously the various currents of society that put demands on the university and the practitioners of the academy while respecting the role of the text in living-faith traditions. He articulates a threefold task that might apply as well from a Catholic perspective: (1) keep interpretation focused on the biblical text (or on the doctrinal tradition, if it is systematics); (2) be open to critical evaluation; (3) be sensitive to currents from outside the theological community.[19] This is a mutual task of the theological enterprise as a whole in dialogue. It needs to be put into practice by seminary faculties among themselves, university religion departments among themselves, and both together.

Good integration of a seminary theological program will require hard work to develop a core curriculum and a faculty that dialogues with one another and with the university. But it will not demand that academic requirements be lessened nor that the desirability of commitment to critical evaluation which is shared with university theology be attenuated. The end result of this effort will be a student body that understands both sides of the educational process as applied to their theological education—the best of critical scholarship in theology today and the ability to interpret it to those to whom they minister through their own appropriation as well as through the life and practice of the believing Christian community.

[19] Francis Watson, *Text, Church, and World: Biblical Interpretation in Theological Perspective* (Grand Rapids: Eerdmans, 1994).

21

Historical Theology in the Curriculum

JOSEPH T. LIENHARD, S.J.

The goal of this essay may be too ambitious. The essay attempts to say something about several topics, instead of treating one topic thoroughly. As the preparation of the essay was under way, it became clear that while historical theology obviously exists in practice, it has been the subject of relatively little theoretical reflection. Hence it seemed worthwhile to set several goals: to sketch the rise of historical theology in Catholic curricula; to make some attempt to define historical theology and its subject, object, and approach; to sketch the history of its precedents in the Church; and, finally, to make some comments about present practice and future prospects. Perhaps the result will not be entirely useless.

"Historical Theology" in Catholic Theological Education

The designation "historical theology" for one major part of the theological curriculum is now common in Catholic universities in the United States. But the use of this term in Catholic theological curricula is fairly recent, and students and faculty still often call it "Church History." The historical approach to theology began in Germany as a Protestant discipline. Both Johann Salomo Semler (1725-91) and Ferdinand Christian Baur (1792-1860) have been called the founders of historical theology, although their own term for this discipline was "historical-critical theology." Jean Leclercq dates the beginnings of historical theology in Catholic theological curricula to the 1920s, when the disciplines of history and theology entered upon a new synthesis.[1] German writers on Catholic theological curriculum began to use the term in the 1930s; one such curriculum divided theology into apologetics, historical theology, doctrinal theology, and practical theology, in which historical theol-

---

[1] Jean Leclercq, "Un demi-siècle de synthèse entre histoire et théologie," *Seminarium* 29 (1977): 21-35.

ogy comprised biblical history and the history of the Church.[2] In 1965 the Jesuit seminaries of the United States and Canada adopted the name for one part of their curriculum, which was to comprise sacred Scripture or biblical theology (the authors used both terms without distinguishing their meaning), historical theology, systematic theology, and theologico-pastoral theology. Historical theology and systematic theology were to be the two divisions of the former dogmatic theology.[3] The doctoral program at Fordham, begun in 1964, first used the odd term "systemic religions," then varied between "historical studies" and "history of Christianity" until "historical theology" was adopted in 1985.

The Jesuit seminary curriculum proposed in 1965 (and known as the Rockhurst Plan) is clearly documented, and can serve as an example of the changes that took place in the mid-1960s in Catholic theological education. The turmoil, the drive for change, and the naive optimism typical of the mid-1960s can easily be sensed from the document.

The Second Vatican Council met from 1962 to 1965. In the Jesuit order, the long-lived Father General John Baptist Janssens died in 1964, and the Jesuits held a general congregation in two sessions in 1965 and 1966. Vatican II appeared to put an end to Neo-Scholastic theology and to give more than a nod of approval to the *nouvelle théologie*, as well as to continued biblical research, historical studies, liturgical reform, ecumenism, and interreligious dialogue. In the spirit of these movements, representatives from seven Jesuit theologates met at Rockhurst College in Kansas City in November of 1965, and passed twenty-seven resolutions. Rockhurst dismantled the Roman-style way of teaching, and proposed both a new curriculum and a new pedagogy. Courses were not to be taught in cycles; civil degrees were to be granted; a high proportion of electives was to be incorporated into the program.[4] The theology curriculum was to be divided into four areas: biblical, historical, systematic, and theologico-pastoral.[5]

Nothing more was said in the resolutions about these four areas. But an "Informal Memorandum," added as an appendix to the resolutions, contained a sample curriculum to indicate the type of program the group had in mind. In this curriculum the first area is "Sacred Scripture" (and not "Biblical Theology," as the resolution had it). The second is "Historical Theology," divided into two parts: "General Church History" and "Special History of Christian Ideas." The third is "Systematic Theology," divided into "Fundamental The-

---

[2] See M.-J. Congar, "Théologie," *Dictionnaire de théologie catholique* 15 (1946): 341-502; the section on the divisions or parts of theology is found on cols. 492-96. The curriculum described was proposed by Jacob Bilz under the influence of Johann Sebastian von Drey, in *Einführung in die Theologie: Theologische Enzyklopädie* (Freiburg: Herder, 1935), and in an article in the *Lexikon für Theologie und Kirche* in 1938. The schema was not much more than a rearrangement of the standard seminary courses.

[3] See "Inter-Faculty Program Inquiry Report," *Woodstock Letters* 95 (1966): 335-56; and Justin S. Kelly, "Toward a New Theology: The Implications of Rockhurst," ibid., 357-71.

[4] "Inter-Faculty Program," 339. Resolutions 13, 11, 10.

[5] Ibid., Resolution 16.

ology" and "Special Systematics." Finally, "Theologico-Pastoral Theology" is divided into "Moral-Canonical" and "Pastoral."

Only "Historical Theology" is preceded by a note, which suggests that the category was unfamiliar. The note reads: "The explanation is added with regard to this area (historical theology) that it is understood to include not only what is now generally known as Church history, but also patristics, and the history of theology, heresies, and dogma; the intention is that these subjects should be treated from a more historical perspective and with the measure of autonomy proper to history."[6] At the end of the section on "Special History of Christian Ideas," a minority report appears that suggests, as well as anything in the whole report, the tone and tensions of the meeting. It reads: "The topics of SPECIAL HISTORY represent the majority opinions at the caucus, but it [sic] does not seem to be the best expression of the principles operative in setting up the area of historical theology, the emphasis being taken away somewhat from the dialectic of creative ideas and put rather on the judgmental decision of the Church."[7]

In an analysis of Rockhurst, Justin S. Kelly sees the key step taken there as the division of dogmatic theology into two areas: historical and systematic.[8] Historical theology, Kelly writes, is "to treat certain past ideas *as historical*, that is, as past, no longer current." "A historical theology," he continues, ". . . depends on the correlative possibility of a theology which would *not* be historical—or not primarily. Its existence as a distinct area of dogmatic theology makes sense if, and only if, there also exists a *contemporary* theological problematic." In summary, "historical theology, then, discusses the theological questions and answers of the past; systematic theology explores *our* questions."[9]

Kelly has high hopes for historical theology. He writes:

> But the Rockhurst delegates affirm the possibility and even necessity of a distinct area of historical theology. It is to be a history of Christian ideas, uniting dogmatic definitions, theological thought, and history (secular and ecclesiastical). Its aim will be to replace [sic] both dogma and theology in their historical setting. This will involve more extensive use of political, social and cultural history than is possible under the "tract" system, yet the focus will ultimately be theological. Institutional history will be subsumed into the history of Christian thought, with special (but not exclusive) emphasis on the Church's official pronouncements.[10]

The documents show that the committee used "historical theology" at a time when it was obviously not a familiar term, and its meaning needed ex-

---

[6] Ibid., 349.
[7] Ibid., 351.
[8] Kelly, "New Theology," 362.
[9] Ibid.
[10] Ibid., 363.

planation. Two currents run in different directions. One would simply gather familiar historical tracts under a new title. The other wants to study the "dialectic of creative ideas" from the past, a rather romantic description of the history of doctrine and theology.

Kelly's desire to divide ideas "as past, no longer current" from a contemporary theological problematic that explores "our" questions is itself seriously problematic, since it cuts off the Church's tradition, as past, from theologians' questions, as present. But theology cannot work that way. Kelly's phrases do, however, illustrate the ongoing problem of distinguishing historical from systematic theology, if they should be distinguished.

The Meaning of "Historical Theology"

The origins of the term "historical theology" are not obvious, and its meaning is not often discussed. The term appears only infrequently in encyclopedias and library catalogues. The *New Catholic Encyclopedia* has no entry under it; neither does the *Dictionnaire de théologie catholique*, the *Theologische Realenzyklopädie*, or the Protestant encyclopedia *Religion in Geschichte und Gegenwart*. The third edition of the Catholic *Lexikon für Theologie und Kirche* has an entry, but no article, under "Historische Theologie," and refers the reader to five other articles: "History of Dogma," "History of Heresy," "Church History," "Patrology," and "History of Theology."

A few books in English also have the title "Historical Theology."

In 1863, the executors of William Cunningham published a two-volume work of his entitled *Historical Theology: A Review of the Principal Doctrinal Discussions in the Christian Church since the Apostolic Age*.[11] It is a long-forgotten textbook. More recently, the second volume in the Penguin Guide to Modern Theology, published in 1969, was entitled *Historical Theology*.[12] The book contains three disparate essays—on patristic literature, liturgy, and modern ecclesiastical history—by three authors.[13] In 1978, Geoffrey W. Bromiley published a book entitled *Historical Theology: An Introduction*.[14] It is a history of theology, presenting the thought of Christian writers and theologians. The fourth book is by far the most helpful and interesting for the present project. It is entitled *Historical Theology: Continuity and Change in Christian Doctrine*, written by that tireless practitioner of the discipline, Jaroslav Pelikan, and published in 1971.[15] It is the one book that deals, albeit with lapses into the history of doctrine, with the nature and purpose of historical theology as a theological discipline.

---

[11] Edinburgh: Clark, 1863. The book reached a third edition in 1870.

[12] J. Daniélou, et al., *Historical Theology, Penguin Guide to Modern Theology*, vol. 2 (Harmondsworth, England: Penguin, 1969).

[13] Jean Daniélou writes on "Patristic Literature" up to Augustine. A. H. Couratin writes on "Liturgy," and provides a history of the liturgy from its origins to the liturgical movement in 100 pages. And finally, John Kent writes on the "Study of Modern Ecclesiastical History since 1930."

[14] Grand Rapids: Eerdmans, 1978.

[15] Jaroslav Pelikan, *Historical Theology: Continuity and Change in Christian Doctrine, Theological Resources*, vol. 23 (New York: Corpus, 1971).

"Historical theology" has been used in several different senses. It has designated, Pelikan writes, "not only the genetic study of Christian faith and doctrine but the entire study of the history of the Church and even, occasionally, all those theological and paratheological disciplines whose methodology is historical."[16] "More often," though, he continues, "historical theology was used as a loose synonym for church history. Theological studies were divided into four basic categories: biblical theology, systematic theology, historical theology, and practical theology. Within this structure, historical theology was the term for the history of Christianity, which usually was equivalent to church history."[17]

To put the matter a little more schematically: when the meaning of the term "historical theology" is sought, two general approaches are found in recent authors. One approach is to make "historical theology" an umbrella term for a group of other, more familiar disciplines. The *Lexikon für Theologie und Kirche*, as noted, refers its readers from "Historical Theology" to "History of Dogma," "History of Heresy," "Church History," "Patrology," and "History of Theology." When Pelikan discusses the meaning of historical theology, he measures it against history of dogma, history of theology, history of Christian thought, and history of doctrine. The curriculum proposed at Rockhurst meant to include under historical theology not only what is generally known as Church history, but also patristics, and the history of theology, heresies, and dogma.

The other approach is recognizing historical theology as a theological discipline in its own right. As such, Pelikan defines it as "the genetic study of Christian faith and doctrine."[18] Yet he ends up preferring to call his undertaking "history of Christian doctrine." In his well-known five-volume work entitled *The Christian Tradition*, Pelikan defines doctrine as "what the church of Jesus Christ believes, teaches and confesses on the basis of the word of God."[19] The most important point of his definition is probably his effort to distinguish doctrine, as the collective belief, teaching, and confession of the Church, from theology, the thought or ideas of one person—by expectation, a learned one—on the way to understand and synthesize the Church's teaching and relate it to other, usually contemporary, questions and concerns. But Pelikan's definition is a useful one. To suit historical theology it might be expanded to "the genetic study of Christian faith, doctrine, and theology."

Once this definition is accepted, one can ask how the historical theologian perceives himself, what the object of his study is, and what approach he takes to that object. The historical theologian can see himself primarily as a historian, or primarily as a theologian.[20] If he sees himself as a historian, his

[16] Ibid., xiv.
[17] Ibid., xv.
[18] Ibid., xiii.
[19] *The Christian Tradition*, vol. 1: *The Emergence of the Catholic Tradition (100-600)* (Chicago and London: University of Chicago, 1971), 1.
[20] See Bromiley, *Historical Theology*, xxiii-xxix.

subject matter is the history of Christian thought, ideas, and perhaps institutions, and he uses the ordinary methods of historical science. He will often assert his objectivity, and assure his readers that faith does not interfere with his scholarly pursuits. If he sees himself primarily as a theologian, then his task is more delicate. He lives with the ambiguity of joining the terms "history" and "theology," the one dealing with the singular in space and time, the other with the Absolute beyond space and time, and seeks to balance the scholarly norms of historical science with the commitment of a believing theologian. If theology is faith seeking understanding, then historical theology must be that, too, seeking that understanding from the past, even if that past extends to yesterday. "Historical" is the adjective, "theology" the noun, and the noun defines the discipline.

The object of historical theology includes not only the public expressions of Christian faith (for example, baptismal creeds and the liturgy) and of the Church's doctrine (for example, conciliar creeds and the dogmatic decrees of the councils), but also the writings of theologians—that is, the thought and ideas of learned Christians (taken in a sense broad enough to include writings on exegesis, morality, spirituality, and similar areas) on how to understand and synthesize the Church's teaching and relate it to other questions and concerns.

The approach that historical theology takes to its object is decisive. It does not mine the past out of antiquarian curiosity or to confirm a modern thesis, but attempts, first of all, to read and understand the Christian writings of the past in their own context, for all they have to offer; and then to discern the growth in understanding of God's definitive self-revelation in Christ across the centuries, as it is worked out in the interpretation of Scripture, in the Church's teaching, in the liturgy, and in theology. Historical theology, as theology, studies the past as past in such a way that the present could not exist without it. T. S. Eliot dramatically depicts the result of losing this sense of the living past in *Murder in the Cathedral*, where the Tempter says to Thomas Becket:

> And later is worse, when men will not hate you
> Enough to defame or to execrate you,
> But pondering the qualities that you lacked
> Will only try to find the historical fact.
> When men shall declare that there was no mystery
> About this man who played a certain part in history.

Historical theology rather follows what G. L. Prestige wrote, that tradition is the living faith of the dead, not the dead faith of the living, for the doctrine of the communion of saints is crucial to its self-understanding.

Historical theology can be distinguished from other, similar disciplines. Church history studies the history of an institution, and uses the methods of historical science. History of dogma, in the strict sense, studies the publicly defined teachings of the Church. History of theology deals with the ideas and opinions of theologians. History of Christian thought embraces an object broader than history of theology, to include Christian ethics and piety, and other such areas.

Historical Consciousness, Historicism, and Historical Theology

No discussion of historical theology can take place without considering its relation to historicism. As noted, historical-critical theology arose in the eighteenth and nineteenth centuries, with Semler[21] and Baur,[22] among others. The term "historicism" was coined in the late nineteenth century to criticize the theology they had begun.[23] Philosophically, historicism has been superseded; but in practice the historical method continues in vigorous use. Historicism locates the meaning of ideas and events so firmly in their historical context that history, rather than philosophy or nature, becomes the norm of truth.[24] The method seeks out and highlights differences, and finds consensus either uninteresting or suspect.

The rise of historicism in the nineteenth century is usually perceived as the great dividing line in the methods of exegesis and theology. But to say that before this point the main interpretative category in theology was being, and after it, history, is too simplistic. The actual pattern, I would suggest, was closer to a three-step, one almost Hegelian in its outline. A sort of historical consciousness, albeit mostly uncritical, existed in the Church from its earliest centuries. Beginning in the eleventh century, history began to take on a critical function: the history of the Church was used to criticize the Church. This movement reached its high-water mark in nineteenth-century history of dogma. Historical theology, as known in Catholic theological curricula for the past seventy-five years or so, is a positive new effort to synthesize the disciplines of history and theology without yielding to the relativism implied in historicism.

One of the earliest forms of historical consciousness in the Church was the history of heresy.[25] It began at the end of the second century with Irenaeus, who catalogued the various forms of Gnosticism, beginning with the archheretic Simon Magus. In the third century, Hippolytus of Rome wrote the *Refutation of All Heresies* in ten books, and traced heresy back to Christians

---

[21] See Gottfried Hornig, *Die Anfänge der historisch-kritischen Theologie. Johann Salomo Semlers Schriftverständnis und seine Stellung zu Luther* (Göttingen: Vandenhoeck & Ruprecht, 1961).

[22] See Peter C. Hodgson, *The Formation of Historical Theology: A Study of Ferdinand Christian Baur* (New York: Harper & Row, 1966). Hodgson wrote his book at Yale as a dissertation under the direction of Hans W. Frei. It was published in the series Makers of Modern Theology, edited by Jaroslav Pelikan, and Pelikan wrote the preface to the book.

[23] See A. Mirgeler, "Historismus," *Lexikon für Theologie und Kirche* 5 (1960): 393-94.

[24] See Gertrude Himmelfarb, "Tradition and Creativity in the Writing of History," *First Things* 27 (November 1992): 28.

[25] See Karl Rahner, "Häresiengeschichte," *Lexikon für Theologie und Kirche* 5 (1960): 8-11.

who drew on pagan philosophy, astrology, and magic rather than Christian revelation. Towards the end of the fourth century Epiphanius of Salamis composed his *Panarion* or "Medicine Chest," offering cures for the eighty heresies he listed. Theodoret of Cyrus, in the earlier part of the fifth century, composed his *Haereticarum fabularum compendium*, or "Compendium of the Heretical Fables," a description of heresies, up to Eutyches, in five books. In the West, Filastrius of Brescia, at the end of the fourth century, was able to collect 156 heresies for his *Diversarum haereseon liber*. Augustine drew on it for his own *De haeresibus*, written towards the end of his life, in which he enumerates eighty-eight heresies, from Simon Magus to Pelagius and Celestius. Writing the history of heresy more or less died out at the end of the patristic era or the beginning of the early Byzantine period. It was revived vigorously in the Reformation. And in the eighteenth century histories of heresy, as well as dictionaries and lexica of heresies, began to appear. To give one well-known example, Gottfried Arnold (1666-1714) published his pioneering *Unparteyische Kirchen- und Ketzer-Historie* in 1700. Nevertheless, and probably rightly, as Karl Rahner writes, "history of heresy" never became a tract within theological education.[26]

Another sign of historical consciousness in early Christianity is the writing of the history of the Church.[27] While there were some earlier attempts at doing so, Eusebius of Caesarea deserves the title "Father of Church History," if only because he inspired so many translators and continuators. Eusebius first published his *Ecclesiastical History* in seven books in 303; the final edition, completed after the fall of Licinius in 324, comprised ten books. Eusebius's work is unabashedly apologetic: the triumph of Christianity is the best proof of its divine origins. He is a good enough Roman citizen, however, to divide the books by the reigns of the emperors, good or bad. The best of Eusebius's continuators was Socrates Scholasticus, who treated the period from 305 to 439 in seven books, and thus the fourth century, so crucial for the development of the doctrine of the Trinity. Sozomen, who treated the period from 324 to 425 in nine books, used Socrates's work extensively, but added new documents. In 449/50 Theodoret of Cyrus wrote a Church history that covered the period from 325 to 428. The industrious translator Rufinus of Aquileia prepared a Latin translation of Eusebius's work and continued the narrative up to 395. The equally industrious Cassiodorus, in the later sixth century, continued Rufinus's version of Eusebius, and also had the histories of Socrates, Sozomen, and Theodoret translated and worked together into the *Historia tripartita*, which became in the Middle Ages one of the most important reference works for the history of the Church.

A third sort of historical work was chronicles. Again, Eusebius was a pioneer. Around 303 he published a fascinating work, an attempt to coordinate in synchronic tables (beginning with the year of Abraham's birth) the

---

[26] Ibid., 11.
[27] See Hubert Jedin, "Kirchengeschichte," *Lexikon für Theologie und Kirche* 6 (1961): 209-18.

events of profane and sacred history. Such chronicles had precedents among the Apologists, who tried to coordinate biblical and secular history to show that the biblical truth was older than, and therefore superior to, Greek philosophy. Jerome translated the latter part of Eusebius's chronicle, and the work became a standard reference tool in the Middle Ages. Sulpicius Severus also published a chronicle, from the creation of the world to A.D. 400. Cassiodorus, among several others, continued the tradition. In the Middle Ages, countless chronicles and annals of dioceses, abbeys, and other institutions were produced.

The history of theologians or Christian writers also has ancient roots. Jerome wrote his *De viris illustribus* in 393, to prove that Christians had as many distinguished writers as the pagans did. He listed 135 writers, beginning with St. Peter and ending with himself. His work was continued by Gennadius of Marseille and Isidore of Seville. In the ninth century in the East Photius produced his *Bibliotheca*.

History of dogma is clearly a modern discipline. Nevertheless, a few works appeared in the early Church that might be considered forerunners of history of dogma: for example the dogmatic summaries of John of Damascus and Isidore of Seville, or the *Panoplia dogmatica* of Euthymius Zigabenus in the early-twelfth century. Moreover, the fact that some authors attempted to show that the Church's doctrines were unchanging meant that the opposite was at least conceivable. Such a principle lurks behind Vincent of Lérins's famous canon.[28] In the later Middle Ages, historical approaches to dogma also began to appear in commentaries on the *Sentences* of Peter Lombard, for example in William of Ware's commentary.

Historical studies received significant impetus in the fifteenth and sixteenth centuries. Printing made countless ancient and medieval writings readily available, in editions that grew more and more trustworthy. The revival of Greek learning, and Greek manuscripts brought from the East and translated into Latin, introduced the West to many hitherto unfamiliar writings, such as those of Athanasius.

The seventeenth century saw the first great works of gathering and editing, most of them carried out by Catholics. Early in that century, Heribert Rosweyde (1569-1629) and John van Bolland (1596-1665) began the *Acta Sanctorum*, a critical edition of the lives of the saints based on authentic sources, sometimes called the most scholarly project the Society of Jesus has ever undertaken. The Benedictine congregation of St.-Maur, founded in 1621, began in 1672 to devote itself to great historical and literary works. Jean Mabillon (1632-1707) established the science of Latin paleography and edited the works of St. Bernard. Bernard de Montfaucon (1655-1741), also a Maurist, edited the works of Athanasius and John Chrysostom, and made Greek paleography a science. Other Maurists had equally remarkable achievements. In Italy, Giovanni Domenico Mansi (1692-1769) supervised the publication, in thirty-

---

[28] *Commonitorium*, I, 23.

one volumes, of the documents of the councils and synods of the Church; this *Sacrorum Conciliorum Nova et Amplissima Collectio* was published from 1758 to 1798.

Beginning with the reform movements of the eleventh century, a second element accompanied historical consciousness: history as a motive for reform. The Gregorian reformers' appeal to the *ecclesia primitiva* proposed a pattern of ideal beginning, decline, and the possibility of restoration. The same pattern is also found in early Protestantism, where historical studies took a clearly apologetic turn: historians set out to find the Deformation that justified the Reformation. The most famous work produced in this spirit was the *Historia Ecclesiae Christi*, or *Centuries*, of Matthias Flacius Illyricus (1520-75) and the so-called Centuriators of Magdeburg (published at Basle, 1559-74). The Catholic Cesare Baronius (1538-1607) responded to the Centuriators of Magdeburg with his own apologetic history, the *Annales ecclesiastici*, published from 1558 to 1607. In the same spirit, but centuries later, Newman was to respond to Gibbon.

In the twelfth century Joachim of Fiore (c. 1132-1202) introduced a different scheme, one that was progressive, evolutionary, and trinitarian. The Church had already passed through two ages, and Joachim believed that the third age, the age of the Holy Spirit, was to begin around 1260. But the theory of decline and reform was to dominate the spirit of Protestant Church history and historical studies for several centuries.

Thus the rise of historicism represented, not a radically new element in theology, but an intensification of a critical spirit that had long been present and its elevation to a metaphysical (or rather anti-metaphysical) principle. Its most typical form was the history of dogma.[29] True history of dogma begins only at the end of the eighteenth century, and presupposes the historical consciousness of Hegel and the Romantics.[30] The rise of the history of dogma in Protestant theological faculties parallels the rise of historical-critical exegesis. "Dogmengeschichte" was founded by Johann Salomo Semler, and refounded by Ferdinand Christian Baur out of idealism. The history of dogma, in the classical period of the nineteenth century, was also the criticism of dogma. The critical edge of classical German *Dogmengeschichte* was best expressed by David Friedrich Strauss, who wrote that "the true criticism of dogma is its history."[31] Most Protestant histories of dogma postulated some sort of theory of decline, or "Abfallstheorie." Adolf von Harnack's justly famous *History of Dogma* is a history of the corrupting Hellenization of true Christianity. Friedrich Loofs followed Harnack. Martin Werner, writing in the 1930s, stressed the deëschatologization of Christianity. When historicism was applied to theol-

---

[29] See J. Auer, "Dogmengeschichte," *Lexikon für Theologie und Kirche* 3 (1959): 463-70, and Wolf-Dieter Hauschild, "Dogmengeschichtsschreibung," *Theologische Realenzyklopädie* 9 (1982): 116-25.

[30] Auer, "Dogmengeschichte," 467.

[31] *Die christliche Glaubenslehre in ihrer geschichtlichen Entwicklung und im Kampfe mit der modernen Wissenschaft*, 2 vols. (Frankfurt: Minerva, 1984), 1:71.

ogy, it added, most of all, the criticism that arises from relativism.[32]

Historical theology, as known in Catholic theological curricula for the past seventy-five years or so, represents a third stage, a positive new effort to synthesize the disciplines of history and theology without yielding to the relativism implied in historicism. It arose both as a posthistoricist attempt to deal with the problem of faith and history, and out of dissatisfaction with the methods of Neo-Scholasticism, as well as to rectify the imbalances and prejudices implicit in Protestant historiography and histories of dogma. Thomas Aquinas and the Neo-Scholastics had sought necessary reasons. Historical theology was to seek free reasons. Unlike historicism, it did not deny the possibility of reaching transcendent truth, but affirmed that such truth was to be found in God's free self-giving and not in a necessary order. Jean Leclercq has described the growth of historical theology among Catholics in the half-century from 1920 to 1970.[33] Following him, I would like to mention just a few great theologians, and great projects, from that period.

Leclercq notes that some nineteenth-century theologians anticipated this beginning; such names as Johann Adam Möhler, Matthias Scheeben, John Henry Newman, and Johann Baptist Franzelin come to mind. But their influence never reached as far as the ordinary theological curriculum. As the 1920s began, history and theology were not only distinct disciplines, but parallel, and habitually separated. The Thomistic revival had brought about a thorough knowledge of Thomas's writings and thought. But it was still ahistorical, and anything that preceded Thomas—the writings of the Fathers, for example—was usually classed with Christian archaeology. The very title of the *Dictionnaire d'archéologie chrétienne et de liturgie*, begun in 1907, was telling: liturgy and archaeology were paired. From 1920 to 1970, Catholic theology changed from a theology of conclusions to a theology of sources. Until this period, seminary theology had been deductive: principles were established and conclusions drawn from them, and these conclusions were then proved from the tradition. Historical work was mostly "Quellenforschung," the search for a writer's sources; it explained a writing by earlier writings, and all but eliminated or ignored originality.

Then, in the 1920s, the Dominicans at Saulchoir began to study St. Thomas's "authorities"—that is, the authors he read and quoted, and thus to see him in his historical context. Yves Congar and Marie-Dominique Chenu were educated in this way. At the same time Étienne Gilson, searching for Descartes's sources, reached back to the thirteenth century, and then discov-

---

[32] Classical history of dogma was not properly a Catholic discipline, but Catholics did begin to write histories of dogma in the nineteenth century. The first real texts appeared around 1860. Among the best was the three volumes by Joseph Tixeront. Histories of the doctrine of the Trinity were written by Théodore de Régnon, Jules Lebreton, and Michael Schmaus; of the doctrine of redemption by Jean Rivière; of the doctrine of grace by Henri Rondet, Johann Auer, and Henri de Lubac; and of moral theology by Odon Lottin. The great French encyclopedia *Dictionnaire de théologie catholique* was structured on historical principles. Since 1951 Catholics have also been producing fascicles of the *Handbuch der Dogmengeschichte*.

[33] See "Un demi-siècle de synthèse."

ered that one could not understand the thirteenth century without understanding the twelfth—a surprising assertion for its time. In Germany, Martin Grabmann distinguished four successive stages in medieval scholasticism, and thus explained the context in which Thomas had lived and written.

In the 1930s, study of the Fathers began to be undertaken not to bolster scholastic theses but for itself, and first by liturgists: Ildefons Herwegen and Odo Casel at Maria Laach were leaders. Anton Baumstark founded the science of comparative liturgy. In the same decade, Gilson published books on Anselm and Bernard, and Georges Florovsky wrote an important book on the Byzantine fathers of the fifth to the eighth centuries.

Leclercq describes the two decades from 1940 to 1960 as the high-water mark of Catholic historical theology. Historical research moved beyond liturgy to theology itself. A litany of names is easily composed: Louis Bouyer, Lucien Cerfaux, Jean Daniélou, Bernard Häring, Josef Jungmann, Jean Mouroux, Pius Parsch, Hugo Rahner, Eduard Schillebeeckx. Authors began to interrogate the sources and to let them speak for themselves. Theologians read the Fathers' works whole, and assembled anthologies: Erich Przywara's *Augustine Synthesis* was published in 1934, Hans Urs von Balthasar's selections from Augustine's *Enarrationes in psalmos* in 1936, and his *Geist und Feuer*, a beautiful anthology of Origen's writings, in 1938. In 1938, too, de Lubac published his *Catholicisme*, which Leclercq calls "a charter, program, and model of erudite, penetrating, contemplative integration of the whole of patristics into the whole of theology."[34] Despite the disruption brought on by World War II, remarkable new projects were undertaken. The first volume of the series *Sources chrétiennes* was published in 1942; it has just passed its 400th volume. In 1946, de Lubac's *Surnaturel* appeared. The eighth centenary of St. Bernard's death in 1953 was the occasion for several important conferences; the papers were published, and they in turn spurred an intensified study of monastic theology. In 1959, the first volume of de Lubac's *Exégèse médiévale* appeared. Von Balthasar began to publish *Herrlichkeit* in 1961. The famous series *Théologie historique* was founded in 1962.

The turn from the theology of conclusions to the theology of sources was nowhere more evident than at Vatican II. In what was nothing short of a revolution, Neo-Scholastic schemata were regularly rejected and replaced with earnest readings of the sources. Leclercq writes of "documents elaborated in a liturgical atmosphere, based on the gospel, and prepared by experts imbued with the doctrine of the Fathers and of the theologians of the Middle Ages, but who were not ignorant of the currents of contemporary thought."[35]

Vatican II set the task of historical theology in *Dei Verbum* when it wrote:

This tradition, which comes from the apostles, develops in the Church with the help of the Holy Spirit. For the understanding both of the

[34] Ibid., 25.
[35] Ibid., 29.

realities and of the words handed down grows. This happens both through the contemplation and study of believers, who treasure these things in their hearts, and through the intimate understanding of spiritual things that they experience, as well as through the preaching of those who have received the sure charism of truth along with episcopal succession. For, as the centuries pass, the Church steadily moves forward toward the fullness of divine truth until the words of God shall be fulfilled in her.[36]

The Present and the Future

Gigantes erant super terram in diebus illis. In the quarter-century since 1970 historical theology has continued to flourish, although in a somewhat chastened state. The excitement of rediscovering the past has waned, and other movements in theology draw more attention. The practitioners of historical theology grow more cautious, often in the name of professionalism. There are risks and dangers, but also new opportunities.

Retreat into the trivial is always a danger. Not every topic in every author is worth a dissertation; timid students and timid directors can turn out dissertations that are intellectual cul-de-sacs. Diminishing skill in Greek, Latin, and other languages poses another danger. Dissertations based on English translations and using only English-language literature should not be encouraged. Historical theology also risks being pushed aside by social history. The latter has its place; but the ground won by historical theologians precisely as theologians should not be yielded. Nor should historical theology isolate itself from systematic theology with a defensive claim to objectivity. The move of theology from seminaries to universities has increased the risk of theology's anxiously claiming a false objectivity that it does not and should not have. Erudition alone does not make a theologian; historical theologians should not forget that they are theologians.

On the positive side, one opportunity stands out, which scholars could not even have imagined twenty-five years ago: the availability of patristic and medieval texts in electronic form. The corpus of Augustine's works can now be searched in two or three minutes. Or as one scholar said, "Years ago I wrote that Chrysostom never used a particular word. Now I can know that I was right."

In the United States, interest in patristic exegesis has taken a highly concrete form. As dissatisfaction with the current state of exegesis grows, two projects to publish great commentaries on the whole Bible drawn from the Fathers of the Church have been undertaken. Both are in the planning stages.

The relation of historical theology to biblical theology, or sacred Scripture, or biblical studies, depends to a significant extent on how exegetes un-

---

[36] *Dei Verbum* 8, translated in *The Documents of Vatican II*, ed. Walter M. Abbott (New York and Cleveland: Corpus, 1966), 116 (altered).

derstand their task: as philologists, as historians of religion, or as theologians. As an outside observer, it seems to me that the biblical section risks isolating itself from the rest of the department of theology, to the detriment of all sections.

The relation of historical theology to systematic theology is a much closer one; in this case, the problem is making a proper distinction. Many dissertations in systematic theology appear to be historical in method: to say that Augustine on grace is historical theology, but Rahner on grace is systematic theology, leaves the question unanswered. It may become clear, someday, that the current division of historical from systematic theology was not the right one.

Despite some difficulties, the future of historical theology is hopeful. At its best, it represents a distinctive new approach to theology. Historical theologians should not lose their courage, their skills, or their vision. We need, for example, several one-volume surveys of doctrine in English written by Catholics from a Catholic perspective, books that are suitable for advanced undergraduates or for graduate students. In one sense historical theology is still an "auxiliary discipline," compared with systematic theology. But it also serves as a norm for systematic theology, which must be consonant with the Church's tradition. So long as historical theologians remain faithful to their call, they will have much to contribute.

22

Liturgy: The Integrative Center of the Theological Disciplines

Susan K. Wood, S.C.L.

y assigned task is to address the integration of program components within Catholic theological education from the perspective of systematic theology. I do this by proposing that the liturgy of the Church constitutes the integrative center of the theological disciplines. This derives from the premise that the ultimate purpose of all theology is doxology, the praise of and right relationship with God. The proposal that the purpose of theology is doxological is certainly not a new one,[1] but I suggest that our theological disciplines will be integrated when we understand and pursue them as related to this end in terms of the communal worship of the Church in the liturgy.[2]

From the beginning it is essential to avoid certain misunderstandings. First of all, this does not mean that theological discourse is to lose its intellectual rigor or that the practice of prayer becomes theology. Praying to God does not take the place of thinking about God. This would misrepresent the dictum of Evagrius Ponticus (d. 399) that "the theologian is one who prays in truth, and the one who prays in truth is a theologian." It is equally important,

---

[1] See for example, Aidan Kavanagh, *On Liturgical Theology* (Collegeville, Minn.: The Liturgical Press, 1992); Catherine Mowry LaCugna, "Can Liturgy Ever Again Become a Source for Theology?" *Studia Liturgica* 19:1 (1989): 1-16; Henri Nouwen, "Theology as Doxology: Reflections on Theological Education," in *Caring for the Commonweal: Education for Religious and Public Life*, ed. Parker J. Palmer, Barbara G. Wheeler, and James Fowler (Macon, Ga.: Mercer University Press, 1990); Dietrich Ritschl, *The Logic of Theology* (Philadelphia: Fortress, 1987); Geoffrey Wainwright, *Doxology: The Praise of God in Worship, Doctrine, and Life* (New York: Oxford University Press, 1980).

[2] Note Paragraph 16 of *The Constitution on the Sacred Liturgy*: "The study of sacred liturgy is to be ranked among the compulsory and major courses in seminaries and religious houses of studies. In theological faculties it is to rank among the principal courses. It is to be taught under its theological, historical, spiritual, pastoral, and juridical aspects. In addition, those who teach other subjects, especially dogmatic theology, sacred Scripture, spiritual and pastoral theology, should—each of them submitting to the exigencies of his own discipline—expound the mystery of Christ and the history of salvation in a manner that will clearly set forth the connection between their subjects and the liturgy, and the unity which underlies all priestly training."

however, not to conceive of the liturgy too narrowly as participation in a communal prayer form limited to a specific place and time. Liturgy is not reducible to rite or liturgical celebration; it is not simply cult. Furthermore, to say that the liturgy is the integrative center of the theological disciplines does not mean that these disciplines must be uniquely oriented to liturgical studies. Liturgy and liturgical studies, though related, are distinct. Liturgical studies can themselves be alienated from their proper object. Finally, liturgy is not prayed dogma nor is liturgy primarily an authority or a source to be mined by systematic theology.

What is meant is an envisioning of the liturgy in all its depth as the symbolic recapitulation of the Christian life in the return to the Father through Christ in the Spirit. Liturgy is worship, doxology, proclamation. Liturgy is the "ontological condition of theology . . . because it is in the Church, of which the *leitourgia* is the expression and the life, that the sources of theology are functioning precisely as sources."[3] It is communal rather than individual. It is not divorced from the world, but the focal point and summit that encapsulizes and expresses the relationship of the created order to the Father, Son, and Spirit. Liturgy does not only contain doxological prayers, is not only trinitarian in its structures, but realizes in the full sense of that word the economy of the Christian life in its orientation to God. Liturgy is the sacramental realization of what is already being lived in other dimensions of the Christian life in terms of the mutual relationship between God as Father, Son, and Spirit and the Christian. In sum, liturgy incarnates, represents, and makes present under symbol the economy of trinitarian life with us which is our salvation. Insofar as doctrine explicates this economy, and Scripture is an account of that economy and the Church's response to it, the liturgy becomes the interpretative center of doctrine and Scripture. In other words, what we profess by right doctrine, orthodoxy, is professed as worship in the context of the liturgy. Orthopraxis, right conduct, is the living out of liturgical relationships, particularly those created within baptism and the Eucharist. It is in this sense that the liturgy is "the summit toward which the activity of the Church is directed" and the "fount from which all her power flows."[4]

Dietrich Ritschl, even though he does not expressly identify worship as liturgical, expresses the relationship between theology and worship well when he identifies worship as "the sphere of the primary verification of all statements which is ultimately the subject-matter of theology."[5] He notes that worship is "the place of speaking about and to God," where the overarching Christian story is contained, where theology discovers its tasks and problems, where theology proves itself "in preparatory clarification and in subsequent criticism and self-reflection." Worship is the locus of the reciprocal legitima-

---

[3] Alexander Schmemann, "Theology and Liturgical Tradition," in *Worship in Scripture and Tradition*, ed. Massey Shepherd (London: Oxford University Press, 1963), 175; cited in Aidan Kavanagh, *On Liturgical Theology* (Collegeville, Minn.: The Liturgical Press, 1992), 75.

[4] *The Constitution on the Sacred Liturgy*, 10.

[5] Dietrich Ritschl, *The Logic of Theology* (Philadelphia: Fortress Press, 1987), 98.

tion of doxological and descriptive language. That is, we claim that the God we worship is the God described in theological language. Conversely, the God we write about theologically is the living God we meet in worship. If this reciprocal legitimation is not present, we have false worship or false theology. Ritschl cautions that doxology is not a definition of the nature or function of theology, but is rather a demarcation of its limits.[6] He sees doxology as the open end of theology rather than its starting point. I understand this as not limiting theological reflection to the content or forms of the liturgy, but as setting worship as the ultimate test of theological affirmations.

Corollaries

Two corollaries follow from this thesis that the liturgy is the integrative center of the theological disciplines.

(1) *Theology is primarily practical rather than speculative.*

The first corollary to this thesis is that theology is inherently practical rather than speculative.[7] For instance, Rebecca Chopp comments that "Christian doctrine has to do with guiding the instruction and practices of Christian community."[8] She reminds us that texts such as Augustine's *On Christian Doctrine*, Thomas Aquinas's *Summa Theologia*, Calvin's *Institutes of Christian Religion*, and, more recently, Karl Rahner's *Foundations of Christian Faith* were written as teaching manuals. Chopp asserts, "taken with a broad historical lens, what is systematic about systematic theology is the organic relatedness of the doctrines for creating spaces for communal belief and practice. The *system* in systematic theology is thus the fluid relatedness of symbolic aesthetics rather than the tight deductive logic of analytical proofs. As a historical discipline, systematic theology continually refashions Christian teachings in relation to the needs of Christian praxis."[9] I would argue that systematic theology rearticulates rather than "refashions" Christian teachings in the language and thought structures of a particular age. The expression of doctrine is reformulated; we do not have new doctrines. Nevertheless, I believe that Chopp correctly identifies both the purpose of theology, "guiding the instruction and practices of the Christian community," and its method, "the fluid relatedness of symbolic aesthetics rather than the tight deductive logic of analytical proofs." I extend her definition by identifying the "spaces for communal belief and practice" as liturgical space. The organic relatedness of doctrines thus serves Christian worship. This is what is practical about Chris-

---

[6] Ibid., 285.

[7] This is an underlying principle articulated by Catherine LaCugna in *God For Us: The Trinity and Christian Life* (New York: Harper Collins, 1991) and "Can Liturgy."

[8] Rebecca Chopp, "Recent Works in Christian Systematic Theology," *Religious Studies Review* 30:1 (1994): 3.

[9] Ibid.

tian doctrine—and thus systematic theology. It is not thought for thought's sake. Theological truths make a difference because they impact on how we pray to God and relate to one another.

(2) *Prayer, specifically liturgical prayer, is the context for theological work and the utterance of theological truths.*[10]

In the first instance, this means that creedal statements are doxological before they are propositional. This profession of faith takes place in the liturgy. The theological work in the first centuries that resulted in creedal statements and the theological work in our own time that attempts to rearticulate the content of these statements of faith in language and thought forms for our cultures represent an account of the faith of the Christian community. As Anselm said, theology is faith seeking understanding, *fides quaerens intellectum*.

Second, it is primarily this context of prayer and orientation to the liturgy that distinguishes theology from religious studies. This is different from the more common practice of distinguishing theological from religious studies with respect to what is being studied, generally a single religious tradition as opposed to multiple religious traditions; who is doing the studying, i.e., a committed rather than a noncommitted person; where it is being studied, a theological school or seminary as opposed to a department within a university; and the audience of the study, living religious communities rather than members of a primarily secular culture.[11]

If the public worship of the Church constitutes the distinguishing characteristic of theology, the proper characteristic of this study is that we dwell within the reality which we study; it is not a confessionally value-free endeavor. Theology cannot make objective assessments of claims to validity apart from judgments about the coherence or lack of coherence of truth claims with each other and the data of revelation and human experience upon which they are based. In other words, theology cannot prove the validity of truth claims although negatively it may be able to demonstrate invalidity. Furthermore, the knowledge of theology involves a participatory knowledge similar to what Michael Polanyi calls "tacit knowledge." It is not by looking at things, but by dwelling in them that we understand them.[12] Polanyi describes religious ritual as "the highest degree of indwelling that is conceivable."[13] We act

---

[10] This principle is also articulated by Catherine LaCugna, "Can Liturgy," 2, and by Don E. Saliers, *The Soul in Paraphrase* (New York: Crossroad, 1980), 82-83.

[11] Ray L. Hart, "Religious and Theological Studies in American Higher Education: A Pilot Study," *Journal of the American Academy of Religion* 59 (winter 1991): 715-827; Schubert M. Ogden, *On Theology*, 2nd ed. (Dallas, Tex.: SMU Press, 1973); Schubert M. Ogden, "Religious Studies and Theological Studies: What Is Involved in the Distinction Between Them?" *The Council of Societies for the Study of Religion Bulletin* 24 (February 1995): 3-4.

[12] Michael Polanyi, *The Tacit Dimension* (Garden City, N.Y.: Anchor Books, 1967), 18;. *Knowing and Being* (Chicago: The University of Chicago Press, 1969), 148.

[13] Michael Polanyi, *Personal Knowledge* (Chicago: University of Chicago Press, 1958), 198.

our way into knowing, and liturgy becomes the ritual action by which we live and enact the faith. Faith, then, is performative before it is intellectual assent. The consequences for theological study are found in the fact that worship provides the parameters for thinking about Scripture and theology by keeping these reflections oriented toward their proper object, God, and within their proper context, the Christian community. It is in liturgy that we encounter the reality and mystery of God, the object of our study. This encounter grounds our study in the primary narratives, symbols, and concepts of the faith we seek to understand.

This raises the question whether a theologian needs faith in order to practice the craft of theology. One does not need faith to be a historian, a literary critic, or a linguist. A certain connaturality with the object of study, however, is necessary for participatory knowledge although this does not replace formal training and hard intellectual work. Here, we need to distinguish between knowledgeability and spiritual discernment.[14] Knowledgeability may concern doctrines, individual theologians, religious history, while spiritual discernment deals with assertions about God and God's ways with human beings. Insofar as the latter are part of theological inquiry within systematics or spirituality, discernment and participatory knowledge within the Christian community are important. In other words, the closer theological study is to its object, the more is required of the theologian. Although foreign to the twentieth century academy, this was in fact the context of theology in the patristic period and purdured up to the Enlightenment when faith and reason became divorced.

Historical Precedents

The very call for reflection on the integration of program components within Catholic theological education implies a certain lack of integration, a certain fragmentation, if not alienation, among the theological disciplines due to the specializations becoming more and more technical, each with its own methodologies. A service Catholic theological education can bring is to render theology once again catholic, that is, all-embracing, inclusive, holistic. Three historical precedents within the tradition speak to this unity: the patristic tradition, the monastic tradition, and the movement in France in the 1940s known as *la nouvelle théologie*. These traditions are not really separate since the monastic tradition strongly incorporated the patristic heritage. Likewise, the French movement called for a return to the patristic sources.

Polanyi contrasts this indwelling, however, with that of other kinds of knowledge in that it is never enjoyed, never consummated; we never achieve complete understanding. He notes that the ritual of worship is expressly designed to induce and sustain a state of "anguish, surrender and hope." Christianity fosters mental dissatisfaction by offering us the comfort of a crucified God.

[14] Saliers, *Soul in Paraphrase*, 83.

(1) *Patristic Theology*

Patristic theology can be divided into several phases: the beginning period before the accession of the emperor Constantine (second to third centuries), the Golden Age of patristic thought (fourth to fifth centuries), and the later patristic period (sixth to seventh centuries).[15] It is also possible to distinguish them geographically and linguistically: Latin West, Greek East, Egyptians, Asiatics, Syrians, and Palestinians.[16] The patristic writers are not a homogeneous group, so one generalizes about this group only with great caution. Nevertheless, we might identify antiquity, holiness of life, and what was recognized as orthodox teaching for that time as the general criteria for determining who a Father is.[17] The point here is that holiness of life and orthodox teaching are not just two separate criteria, but are interrelated. Patristic ways of reading the Scriptures and thinking about God represent a unity of worship, life, and theological reflection. Christian life and worship rather than doctrine was the principal concern of patristic theology.[18] Or, more exactly, doctrine was of interest because it affected Christian life and worship. The deep concern in patristic literature about salvation, for example, lay behind much of the discussion of Christology. If Christ was not divine, he could not save.

One consequence of the interrelation between holiness of life and teaching was that knowledge was influenced by participation in what was known. Christian life and worship developed a character in which there was the likeness of God. Roberta Bondi reports that real knowledge was based on an affinity between the knower and the thing known.[19] One was able to understand doctrine because of how one lived and because of the prayer within which one was rooted. Christian life and prayer conformed one into the image and likeness of God thus forming the connaturality by which one was able to know and understand the affirmations made about God. As an illustration Bondi cites Gregory of Nyssa's *Address on Religious Instruction* where Gregory argues that if humanity came into being to participate in the divine goodness, it had to be fashioned in such a way to share in this good, that is, had to have something of the divine mingled in it—as the eye, to share in the light, had by nature inherent brightness in it.[20] This is very reminiscent of Michael Polanyi's postmodern epistemology of knowledge by participation.

[15] David G. Hunter, "Patristic Spirituality" in *The New Dictionary of Catholic Spirituality*, ed. Michael Downey (Collegeville, Minn.: The Liturgical Press, 1993), 724.

[16] Boniface Ramsey, "Fathers of the Church" in *The New Dictionary of Theology*, ed. Joseph A. Komonchak, et al. (Collegeville, Minn.: The Liturgical Press, 1987), 388.

[17] Boniface Ramsey, *Beginning to Read the Fathers* (New York: Paulist Press, 1985), 4-5.

[18] Roberta Bondi, "The Fourth-Century Church: The Monastic Contribution," *Faith to Creed: Ecumenical Perspectives on the Affirmation of the Apostolic Faith in the Fourth Century*, ed. S. Mark Heim (Grand Rapids, Mich.: Wm. B. Eerdmans, 1991), 64.

[19] Ibid., 63.

[20] "Address on Religious Instruction," 276; cited by Bondi, "Fourth-Century Church," 63.

Conversely, "the capacity to be formed in that character also depended on a faithful and real understanding of doctrine."[21] In this same oration Gregory of Nyssa writes that what happens to a person in baptism depends on what that person confesses concerning the nature of the Trinity. A person who confesses the uncreated nature of the Trinity enters into a life which is unchanging while the one who confesses a created Trinity enters into a life subject to change.[22] Even though this may seem overly subjective to us today, it represents an interesting understanding of a relationship between doctrine and sacramental efficacy.

Patristic literature is further characterized as having a deep respect for tradition and employing symbolism and imagery extensively.[23] This is especially evident in the typological reading of Scripture.[24] This last was a method of interpretation which allowed scriptural texts to illuminate one another according to the various senses of Scripture: the literal sense, the typological sense which applied the passage to the life of an individual, the allegorical which interpreted the text according to Christ or the Church, and the analogical or eschatological sense which envisioned the final completion of all in Christ. The Scripture was approached as a whole with the Old Testament seen as including the New and the New as encompassing the Old.

(2) *Monastic Theology*

Monastic theology is in many respects a prolongation of patristic theology. Jean Leclercq writes that there are three principal literary sources of monastic culture: Holy Scripture, the patristic tradition, and classical literature. Furthermore, the liturgy is "the medium through which the Bible and the patristic tradition are received, and it is the liturgy that gives unity to all the manifestations of monastic culture."[25] The liturgy was not only a vehicle through which the monks made contact with Scripture and the Fathers in the readings, but it was also the liturgy itself which formed the commentary on these texts.[26] As one example, Leclercq notes that the liturgy supplied themes for sermons even when these were interpretations of Scripture. Beyond this,

---

[21] Ibid.

[22] Gregory of Nyssa, "Address on Religious Instruction," 322; cited by Bondi, "Fourth-Century Church," 63-64.

[23] Ramsey, *Beginning to Read the Fathers*, 12-14.

[24] See Walter Burghardt, "On Early Christian Exegesis," *Theological Studies* 11 (1950): 78-116; Henri de Lubac, "'Typologie' et 'Allégorisme'," *Recherches de science réligieuse* 34 (1947): 180-226; R. B. Tollinton, *Selections From the Commentaries and Homilies of Origen*, Part III: The Holy Scriptures—Principles and Examples of Exegesis, (New York: Macmillan, 1929): 47-69. For an early monastic example see John Cassian, Conference Fourteen: "On Spiritual Knowledge," *John Cassian Conferences, The Classics of Western Spirituality* (New York: Paulist, 1985), 155-74.

[25] Jean Leclercq, O.S.B., *The Love of Learning and the Desire for God* (New York: Fordham University Press, 1982), 71.

[26] Ibid., 237.

the rites themselves symbolized the highest mysteries of the incarnation, passion, death, resurrection, and ascension of Jesus Christ. Monastic theology was an effort to understand what was said in prayer and in psalmody.[27] Leclercq comments that "monastic speculation is the outgrowth of the practice of monastic life, the living of the spiritual life which is the meditation on Holy Scripture. It is a biblical experience inseparable from liturgical experience."[28] Finally, the monastic way of life itself was viewed as a living out of the sacramental life. This was true above all for baptism, but there were parallels with other sacraments as well, whether this profession was seen as a spiritual marriage or monastic discipline as a form of public penance.[29]

Leclercq describes monastic theology in the Middle Ages as having a different orientation and procedure from the theology in the schools. In the monastery a life of faith and the quest for truth were joined. He notes that although for St. Jerome as for St. Benedict *lectio divina* was the text itself, in the Middle Ages the expression referred more to the act of reading. In the cloister it was the reader and the benefit derived from reading that was given attention while in the schools *lectio divina* referred to the text under study and Scripture was studied for its own sake. The scholastic *lectio* was oriented to the *quaestio* and the *disputata* while the monastic *lectio* was oriented to *meditatio* and *oratio*. Leclercq identifies the object of the Scholastic as science and knowledge, that of the monastic as wisdom and appreciation.[30] The monk was oriented to tradition while the Scholastic turned toward the pursuit of problems and new solutions.[31] Leclercq comments that Scholastic theology had recourse more frequently to the philosophers while monastic theology refers to the authority of Scripture and the Fathers.[32] For the monastic the goal of theology was the experience of God, while for the Scholastic it was understanding.[33]

We may well ask today whether this monastic activity is theology. Leclercq adopts Yves Congar's definition of theology: "the discipline in which the truths of the Christian religion, based on and illuminated by revelation, are interpreted, developed, and ordered into a body of doctrine."[34] It is Leclercq's judgment that monastic theology complies with the terms of this definition even though it differs from the theology of the universities. He notes that the monastics were able to engage in speculation and disputation as much as the

---

[27] See Rupert of Deutz' prologue of *On the Divine Offices* cited in Leclercq, *Love of Learning,* 238.

[28] Ibid., 213.

[29] Jean Leclercq, *Aspects du monachisme hier et aujourdh'hui* (Paris: Editions de la Source, 1968), 69-97.

[30] Ibid., 72. See also Michael W. Strasser, "Anselm and Aquinas: Center and Epicenters," in *From Cloister to Classroom: Monastic and Scholastic Approaches to Truth,* ed. E. Rozanne Elder (Kalamazoo, Mich.: Cistercian Publications, 1986), 130-47.

[31] Leclercq, *Aspects du Monachisme,* 201.

[32] Ibid., 213.

[33] Ibid., 212.

[34] Yves Congar, "Théologie," DTC, 15: 341-502; cited by Leclercq, *Love of Learning,* 192.

others, but that it was both the context, an attitude of prayer and humility, the goal or end of theology, wisdom and the experience of God, which distinguished them.

While Leclercq's broad outlines of the characteristics of monastic theology and its distinctiveness from Scholastic theology may be generally accurate, I question whether he is altogether fair to the Scholastics. While Thomas Aquinas does incorporate the thought of the philosophers, namely, the Neoplatonists and Aristotle, the *Summa* is replete with references to Scripture and the Fathers. Nor is prayer or humility absent from his work. His criticism may be more applicable to the Neo-Scholastics than to the Scholastics themselves. When we contrast the two models of theology, monastic and Scholastic, the real difference is that the first is symbolic, experiential, particular, and inductive, while the Scholastic does tend to be deductive, speculative, metaphysical, and universal. The first seeks wisdom; the second, knowledge.[35] Jean Leclercq summarizes the history of the monastic/Scholastic distinction thus:

> We could say that in the twelfth century the situation was neatly summed up in three words: "monastic *and* scholastic"; far from there being an opposition between them, at that time they profited one another and yet remained distinct. In the thirteenth century, it seems that, when faced with a choice between "monastic *or* scholastic," the greatest minds chose the latter. But because of the way things developed, there arose in the fourteenth and fifteenth centuries a clash, "monastic *versus* scholastic." Still later, one often gets the impression of a "scholastic *without* monastic" theology. Perhaps the real problem is how to fit "monastic *within* scholastic" and "scholastic *within* monastic."[36]

Leclercq cites Michel Corbin, S.J., who suggests an integration by re-establishing theology as a *wisdom*, not under, but above science which is always abstract, partial and positive.[37]

To some extent this distinction represented by monastic and Scholastic theology has purdured in theological education as a distinction between *paideia*, spiritual formation, and *Wissenschaft*, critical inquiry,[38] as well as in the distinction between practical knowledge—known for the sake of something else—

---

[35] Both were susceptible to extremes. Jean Leclercq comments that in the thirteenth century the distinction between monastic and Scholastic theology was more marked to the point that "monastic circles were menaced with slipping into ignorance and the schools with excessive reasoning." Benedict XII imposed a *ratio studiorum*, a program of studies for monks. "Monastic and Scholastic Theology in the Reformers of the Fourteenth to Sixteenth Century," *From Cloister to Classroom*, 182.

[36] Ibid., 194.

[37] Ibid., 201.

[38] David H. Kelsey, *To Understand God Truly* (Louisville, Ky.: Westminster/John Knox Press, 1992).

and speculative knowledge—known for its own sake.[39] *Paideia* is frequently associated with seminary education and formation; critical inquiry with academic theology as done in the universities. We need to ask, however, whether this is a necessary dichotomy, whether we need to separate wisdom and knowledge, and whether these two methods of practicing theology are so incompatible as to be oriented to different theological disciplines. If they are not incompatible, there must be a unifying integrative principle which unites them.

(3) *La nouvelle théologie*

An article by Jean Daniélou, "Les Orientations Présentes de la Pensée Religieuse," outlined the interests of a theological movement of the 1940s in France known as *la nouvelle théologie*. It noted the distance which had developed between theology and the pressing concerns of the day, a progressive rupture between exegesis and systematic theology with each discipline developing according to its own method, and a consequent progressive aridity with systematic theology.[40] Although Daniélou's dialogue partner in 1946 was Neo-Scholastic theology, this criticism of the theological scene rings true today. Daniélou called for a new orientation aimed at a reunification of theology, including a return to Scripture, a return to the Fathers, and a liturgical revival. He envisioned a biblical renewal which restored an interpretation of the Old Testament as prophecy and figure and which restored its relation to the New Testament. Patristic studies incorporated just such a figurative interpretation of the Old Testament and was largely a vast commentary on Scripture. The liturgical renewal associated with this movement affirmed the mystery of a personal God and sought to use liturgy as a theological source. As a balance to a notion of liturgy emphasizing the efficacy of liturgical action, the liturgical renewal reaffirmed the sign value of liturgy and sought better to understand the symbolic elements of liturgical worship. Daniélou also saw this new approach as retrieving a number of categories within contemporary thought which scholastic theology had lost, namely, what we would call today historical consciousness and a concept of salvation envisioned collectively rather than individually.

Louis Bouyer, also associated with this movement, notes the contribution of patristic study to a more existential theology.[41] As Bouyer expressed it, the Fathers were "Fathers" not only of a Christian civilization, but were "fathers" who engendered the faith since their sanctity, for the most part, influenced their intellectual work in the Church. According to Bouyer, one of the most distinctive characteristics of the Fathers was their integrative vision. Scrip-

---

[39] For a discussion of the problem of the dichotomy between theory and practice and the role of systematic theology in integrating them see Charles M. Wood, *Vision and Discernment* (Atlanta: Scholars Press, 1985).

[40] Jean Daniélou, "Les Orientations Présentes de la Pensée Religieuse," *Etudes* 249 (1946): 5-21.

[41] Louis Bouyer, "Le Renouveau des études patristiques," *La vie intellectuelle* (February 1947): 6-25.

tural commentary, spirituality, liturgical tradition were all integrated in a view of the unity of the whole. Since their theology was situated within a context of faith, their witness to the faith provided the existential dimension of their theology.

Although the controversy surrounding the "new theology" tended to set the proponents of Scholasticism over against those wishing to return to patristic sources, Bouyer notes that the origins of Scholasticism were in close and extensive contact with patristic thought, a fact eminently clear in the work of Thomas Aquinas. Moreover, the Scholastic tradition was but one intellectual tradition in the Middle Ages. The monasteries, particularly, used the Fathers not only as authorities, but as the inspiration for the form and orientation of monastic theological questions. Bouyer noted that the real rupture with patristic thought occurred only on the eve of the Renaissance and the Reformation. The Counter Reformation, the silver age of Scholasticism, witnessed "an arbitrarily simplified Thomism cut from its roots." This resulted in a disproportion between the perceived importance of the dialectic apparatus of Scholastic argument and of the scriptural and patristic base on which this dialectic rested. The first result of a retrieval of patristic theology would thus be a theology renewed at its foundation. Second, this renewed theology would unify knowledge and wisdom because purely speculative knowledge would be complemented by a kerygmatic theology that announced the Word of God. Third, the rationality of speculative knowledge would be balanced by a renewal of an appreciation of mystery within dogma.

Most of the public discussion of *la nouvelle théologie* came to a halt in 1950 with the publication of *Humani Generis* on August 12, 1950, by Pope Pius XII. In addition to its condemnation of certain interpretations of Thomas Aquinas on the orientation of human beings to the beatific vision and condemnation of the concept of progressive evolution, this encyclical reiterated the importance of Scholasticism and cited the dangers of existentialism. No theologians were mentioned by name in the encyclical, but those associated with the "new theology" were clearly implicated.

Commonalities Within These Historical Precedents

Several characteristics recur throughout these historical precedents for an integrative theology: the concept of history as an account of the saving actions of God, the use of Scripture in a typological sense that linked the Old Testament with the New, the strong symbolic character of this theology, and the liturgical context which shaped the theology. These characteristics are mutually interdependent. What drove the efforts of the *nouvelle théologie* to retrieve patristic thought and categories was an attempt to heal a perceived rift between Christian thought and Christian life, between theology and spirituality. The very effort to revivify the relationship between theology and the Christian life implied a certain theology of history and hermeneutics.

There is a close association between the interest in the spiritual interpretation of Scripture and liturgy which in turn presupposes a relationship between the Old and New Testaments. The liturgy is a perpetual commentary on the mysteries of Christ by Old Testament texts. Jean Daniélou, in an article on the symbolism of the baptismal rites, describes this interrelationship as a symbolism of several dimensions:

> The Christian faith has but one object: the mystery of Christ dead and risen. But this one only mystery subsists under different modes. It is prefigured in the Old Testament; it is realized historically in the life of Christ on earth; it is contained by way of mystery in the sacraments; it is lived mystically in souls; it is accomplished socially in the Church; it is consummated eschatologically in the kingdom of heaven. Thus the Christian has at his disposal, for the expression of that single reality, several registers, a symbolism of several dimensions. All Christian culture consists in grasping the bonds of union that exist between the Bible and liturgy, between the Gospel and eschatology, between the mystical life and the liturgy. The application of this method to Scripture is called spiritual exegesis. Applied to the liturgy, it is called mystagogy; this latter consists in reading in the rites the mystery of Christ and contemplating beneath the symbols the invisible reality.[42]

The integrative vision of theology as articulated by Jean Daniélou falls on hard times when the approach to history and Scripture is exclusively historical-critical. The typological approach to Scripture seems to be precritical and unfaithful to the intentions of the biblical author at the same time the *Heilsgeschichte* approach to historical events seems to ignore discrepancies and disjunctures in the biblical record, to mask divergent theological viewpoints, to confuse event with interpretation, and to dichotomize between secular history and salvation history. Given the interdependence between liturgy and spiritual exegesis, the discrediting of such a precritical exegesis isolates the liturgy from the rest of theology.

Even though the French and Belgian effort to revivify theology came to a halt in 1950, the Second Vatican Council benefited from the biblical, patristic, and liturgical studies that preceded it. The conciliar texts liberally cite patristic sources. The *Constitution on the Sacred Liturgy* was the first document promulgated by the Council. The twentieth century has witnessed a massive effort by Roman Catholic exegetes in the area of historical-critical biblical exegesis. Within the Church, generally, there has been a broad interest in spirituality. Nevertheless, problems remain. The theological disciplines seems more and more isolated and fragmented as they become more highly specialized. It certainly cannot be said that the disciplines are intentionally oriented to the liturgy.

---

[42] "Le symbolisme des rites baptismaux," *Dieu vivant* I (1945): 14, trans. Robert Taft, *Beyond East and West: Problems in Liturgical Understanding* (Washington, D.C.: The Pastoral Press, 1984), 11.

Contemporary Appropriations

We cannot uncritically return to a "golden age" of typological interpretation of Scripture or a naïve reading of the prophetic witness of the Old Testament as explicitly and intentionally oriented to Jesus.[43] Such an endeavor would correspond to Ricœur's first naïveté. However, a second naïveté may be possible which critically appropriates the biblical text as symbol vis-à-vis the liturgy. As Wainwright notes, "The liturgy was, and *mutatis mutandis* remains for us, the locus in which the story of the constitutive events is retold in order to elicit an appropriate response in worship and ethics to the God who remains faithful to the purposes which his earlier acts declared. As the book in which the original stories have been deposited, developed, and classically defined, the scriptures subserve that continuing function of the liturgy."[44] Thus the event that the liturgy celebrates, the paschal mystery of Christ's passage from death to life, appropriates the symbolism of the Jewish passage from the bondage of Egypt. In other words, the interpretive lens for the biblical text is the liturgy.

This is, after all, part of what makes the canon the canon. First, much of the material of the Old and New Testaments originated in the context of worship.[45] Then, in part, liturgical use of texts contributed to their being included in the canon. The Muratorian fragment (second century) containing the earliest listing of New Testament books indicates that use in the Church was a criteria for canonicity. The gospels were read in worship by the time of Justin Martyr.[46] Admittedly, the liturgy draws on some texts more heavily than others. Nevertheless, we can claim that scriptural texts are of theological interest in addition to their historical and literary interest precisely because they are the interpretive texts in Christian belief and worship. Thus in origin and use the Bible is a liturgical book.[47]

Even with this assertion we have not exhausted the importance of the liturgy for the scriptural text. With Louis-Marie Chauvet we can assert that "in a completely literal sense the liturgical assembly (the ecclesia in its primary sense) is the place where the Bible becomes the Bible."[48] Chauvet

[43] For an attempt to situate an allegorical interpretation within modern biblical scholarship, see James Barr, "The Literal, the Allegorical, and Modern Biblical Scholarship," *Journal For the Study of the Old Testament* 44 (1989): 3-17 and Brevard S. Childs' response, "Critical Reflections on James Barr's Understanding of the Literal and the Allegorical," *Journal for the Study of the Old Testament* 46 (1990): 3-9.

[44] Geoffrey Wainwright, *Doxology* (New York: Oxford University Press, 1980), 153.

[45] To name but a few examples, one can cite the psalms, canticles such as the songs of Moses (Exod. 15), of Deborah (Judg. 5), Hannah (1 Sam. 2), as well as those of Zechariah, Mary, and Simeon in the New Testament. There are also prayers such as the Lord's Prayer and confessional statements such as Phil. 2:2-11. A large part of Exodus was written as a Passover liturgy.

[46] Justin, *Apol.* I, 67.3, cited by Wainwright, *Doxology*, 164.

[47] E. H. Van Olst, *The Bible and the Liturgy* (Grand Rapids, Mich.: Wm. B. Eerdmans, 1991), x.

[48] Louis-Marie Chauvet, *Symbol and Sacrament: A Sacramental Reinterpretation of Christian Existence*, trans. Patrick Madigan and Madeleine Beaumont (Collegeville, Minn.: The Liturgical Press, 1995), 212.

explains this thus: "In the Liturgy of the Word texts are read from the canonically received Bible. These texts which relate a past experience of the people of God are proclaimed as the living Word of God for today to an assembly which recognizes them as an exemplar of its identity. Finally, the assembly is under the leadership of an ordained minister who exercises the symbolic function of guarantor of this exemplarity and the apostolicity of what is read."[49] Chauvet points out that these four constitutive elements of the Liturgy of the Word parallel the four constitutive elements of the biblical text as the Word of God. First there are the instituted traditions of the community gathered in the oral and later written forms and finally into the biblical corpus as such. Then the hermeneutical process interprets this in relation to the present thus rewriting the text in relation to the present. As an example of this one can cite Israel's interpretation of the Exodus in the light of the Babylonian captivity. The community becomes the agent in this process as it writes itself into the book it is reading. Finally there is the canonical sanction of this reading by legitimate authority.[50]

In both instances we have event and interpretation. The Christian Scriptures join both Testaments in the light of the death and resurrection of Jesus Christ. The event which is interpreted is historical in two senses: first, it recounts a past event; second, that event is transposed into the present life of the ecclesial community in its remembrance. As such it is also historical or historical at two different points in time, past and present. It is precisely the proclamatory nature of the word within the liturgy that moves the text from its identity as a literary narrative to an interpretation of a past event as now present in the life of the community. The fact that it is a proclaimed word and not merely a collection of venerable and sacred texts is crucial. The historicity of the liturgical moment grounds the aesthetic interplay of symbols within a historical and sacramental realism whereby the narrative is no longer a literary story, but the very life of the community. In short, the very word becomes sacramental, making present under symbol the event it recounts. As a proclamatory speech-act, liturgical proclamation is performative; it accomplishes what it proclaims.

The question arises as to whether approaching the text in the context of liturgy dispenses with the historical-critical method, whether it represents a retreat from history to flights of allegorical fancy, and whether it is exegesis in its worst form. A critical problem facing any typological reading of the text is the text's historicity. Jean Daniélou identifies a typological reading of the biblical text as a historical symbolism which notes the correspondences between different moments of sacred history such as identifying Adam as the "figure" of Christ (Rom. 5:14) or the Flood as a type of baptism (1 Pet. 3:21).[51]

---

[49] Ibid., 210.

[50] Ibid., 212.

[51] Jean Daniélou, "Symbolisme et théologie," *Interpretation der Welt: Festschrift für Romano Guardini zum Achzigsten Geburtstag* (Wüzberg: Echter, 1965), 670.

Daniélou, citing Thomas Aquinas before him, emphasizes that a typological reading of Scripture is not a sense of the Scripture, that is, a sense of the text, but is a sense of the events themselves. Most specifically, it is an interpretation of the events from an eschatological perspective. Daniélou identifies the source of typology as the plan of salvation. In other words, the events in the history of Israel prefigure the events at the end of time which appear to us in Christ. A typological reading is thus necessarily eschatological. This prevents a typological reading from being an arbitrary and rather superficial imposition of the New Testament on the Old or from being an allegorical reading not rooted in history, although in the hands of some practitioners it may have approached this, especially when they became too engrossed in minute detail rather than limiting themselves to the larger scheme of things.

This emphasis on event rather than text may represent a significant difference between a typological reading and the historical-critical method. What is primary are the events of salvation. The Scriptures bear witness to those events. The liturgy interprets them eschatologically with the use of typology. Typology is not merely a relic of past methodology, but retains an important function today. Geoffrey Wainwright concurs: "In my view, typology—precisely in that it respects the concrete history of salvation to which the scriptures bear literary witness—provides an appropriate, and even indispensable, though perhaps not the only, way of relating the Old Testament and the New. And renewed attention to Daniélou's work can help us recover a generous, though by no means wild or uncontrolled, use of it."[52] This raises, however, further questions about a theology of history, questions beyond the scope of this essay.[53] The historical grounding inherent to typology is essential for the truth claims of Christianity to be more than a subjective interpretation. Texts, even events, are multivalent, but there are limits of verification.

Chauvet contributes helpfully to the attempt to distinguish between the historical-critical method and the use of biblical texts within a liturgical assembly. He distinguishes between decoding a text and reading it, identifying the historical-critical method with decoding, and a semiotics of the text and the active participation of the reader in its interpretation as reading the text.[54] No reading can dispense with the prior task of decoding. To return to Rebecca Chopp's definition of systematic theology as "the fluid relatedness of aesthetic symbols," the task of theology is to approach the text with full awareness of the intent of the author and its own task of reappropriation of the symbols. By doing so it will not in a first naïveté presuppose that the intent of the biblical author of the Old Testament was to foreshadow events in the Christian dispensation thereby distorting the text in its historical-critical location. In a second naïveté, however, we appropriate the text as sacramental symbol

---

[52] Geoffrey Wainwright, "'Bible et Liturgie': Daniélou's Work Revisited," *Studia Liturgica* 22 (1992): 154.

[53] See Jean Daniélou, *Lord of History: Reflections on the Inner Meaning of History*, trans. Nigel Abercrombie (Chicago: Henry Regnery, 1958).

[54] Ibid., 205.

historically grounded in the event of the life, death, and resurrection of Jesus Christ. The historical grounding of a liturgical reading of the text is primarily christological. This means that the texts are used liturgically to interpret the Christ event by way of the historical events to which the texts bear witness. The events of the testaments are interpreted through this lens. The historical event represented in Jesus is the eschatological completion of the events which prefigure him. Perhaps one of the mistakes we have made in the past is to attempt to read Christ into the Exodus, or some of the messianic prophecies, for example, instead of reading the Exodus and the prophecies into Christ. The first would be a form of Christian exegesis. The latter respects the historical-critical location of the text at the same time it treats the two testaments as a unity and explicates the Christ event in continuity with the Jewish tradition. Arguably this is also how Paul read the Scriptures in relationship to Christ, and the Jews in exile read the Exodus before him.

This essay has largely dealt with the liturgy as the integrative center of the theological disciplines by addressing the significant problem raised by its use of biblical texts, a use not sanctioned by the historical-critical method of biblical interpretation. This was necessary not only because the typological reading of Scripture figured significantly in the three historical precedents of a unitative view of theology, but also because it is presupposed within the liturgy. Systematic theology—as the articulation of the interrelatedness of the scriptural and doctrinal symbols which coalesce within the liturgy—integrates historical and practical theology and evidences a concern for the wholeness of the Christian witness by showing its consistency and integrity. For example, systematic theology as the explication of the coherence within doctrines serves right worship in that the critical thinking and study integral to this discipline aim to assure that we worship the true God and not a false God. Salvation, interpreted within systematic theology as communion in God through Christ in the Spirit, is doxological in structure. Christian ethical life is the living out of sacramental relationships. It is a liturgy continued in the world, as the Orthodox tradition would maintain. Thus liturgy is arguably the integrative center of our theological disciplines since it is the place and the moment within history in which the economy of the Christian life is sacramentally realized, that is, made present under symbol. This includes the sacramentality of the word which represents this economy in its eschatological fullness. With this awareness of our liturgical center, many of our current practices in current theological education may remain the same. There will always be a need to situate a biblical text in its historical location, for example. Nevertheless, situating our tasks in the context of the liturgy may provide the focus and integration we seek.

23

The Divorce of Spirituality from Theology

Keith J. Egan

his essay explores some moments in the long separation of spirituality from theology. Historical investigations like this promote, it is hoped, the integration of spirituality and theology so widely sought in our time. Freud taught the modern world that disintegration precedes integration. Perhaps attention to the disintegration of spirituality from theology may aid in the search for the integration of these two disciplines both of which have suffered because of their long estrangement.

In recent years scholars have sought to identify spirituality's proper place among academic disciplines and to identify methods for the study of spirituality which is a newcomer to the academy as an independent discipline.[1] This essay has profited from these discussions, but it is not here concerned directly with this process of identification of a discipline and its methods. Rather, as called for by the theme of the conference, this paper attends to the relationship between spirituality and theology as part of the theological enterprise at Catholic institutions of higher learning. It proceeds by exploring, albeit limitedly, the long-standing divorce between spirituality and theology.

My introduction to this theme occurred some years ago at Marquette University when, as a teacher of graduate and undergraduate courses, I struggled to understand for myself and students how courses on Christian spirituality, monastic theology, Western mysticism, Teresa of Ávila, John of the Cross, etc., fit under the rubric of historical theology. I am grateful to Marquette University for that experience and for the opportunity now to share the fruits of my reflections on this unseemly divorce.

For this essay I use Anselm of Canterbury's simple description of theology as faith seeking understanding but with the addition of Avery Dulles's

---

[1] See Bernard McGinn, "The Letter and the Spirit: Spirituality as an Academic Discipline," *Christian Spirituality Bulletin* 1 (fall 1993): 3-10; Sandra M. Schneiders, "Spirituality as an Academic Discipline: Reflections from Experience," *Christian Spirituality Bulletin* 1 (fall 1993): 10-15; idem, "A Hermeneutical Approach to the Study of Christian Spirituality," *Christian Spirituality Bulletin* 2 (spring 1994): 9-14.

definition of modern theology as "scholarly reflection upon the faith."[2] The definition of the spirituality that I follow is that of Walter Principe: "life in the Holy Spirit as brothers and sisters of Jesus Christ and as daughters and sons of the Father,"[3] a spirituality rooted in trinitarian and christological faith.

I shall use the word spirituality with what Principe calls its third level of meaning, that is, the *"study* by contemporary scholars of the lived reality [of the spiritual life] and [of] the teachings that have been formulated."[4] Principe's preferred term for the study of spirituality in a theological perspective is theological spirituality, a term that fits well the aims of this essay: (1) to explore some moments in the separation of spirituality from theology, (2) to make some recommendations for the healing of that divorce.

In this essay spirituality and theological spirituality include the disciplines once referred to as ascetical theology, mystical theology, and spiritual theology. Then as now the danger is that praxis is too often divorced from theory. Thus Christian mysticism is rooted in sacramental experience or praxis, and suffers when this praxis is ignored. Moreover, keep in mind the venerable usage derived from Pseudo-Dionysius in which mystical theology is not study or research but a description of an intensified experience of the divine, that is, contemplation. John of the Cross in the sixteenth century still used mystical theology in its primitive sense. The Spanish mystic wrote: "... contemplation is also termed mystical theology, meaning the secret or hidden knowledge of God."[5] While I shall speak of spirituality as an academic discipline, I do so fully aware that the study of spirituality should never be separated from experience, mystical and otherwise.

The Roots of the Divorce

In 1950 the Benedictine François Vandenbroucke published a study of the origins of the divorce between theology and mysticism.[6] Vandenbroucke's "mystique" is a broad term that includes what we would call spirituality. He concluded that mysticism and theology went separate ways in the late fourteenth century because of a degenerative speculative mysticism on one hand and the character of *Devotio moderna* on the other.[7] Mysticism, according to Vandenbroucke, had become subjective and psychological, a far cry from what he saw as the objective and metaphysical mysticism of Thomas Aquinas and

---

[2] Avery Dulles, *The Craft of Theology: From Symbol to System* (New York: Crossroad, 1992), 167.

[3] Walter Principe, *Thomas Aquinas' Spirituality* (Toronto: Pontifical Institute of Mediaeval Studies, 1984), 3; idem, "Aquinas's Spirituality for Christ's Faithful Living in the World," *Spirituality Today* 44 (1992): 112.

[4] Principe, *Thomas Aquinas' Spirituality*, 4.

[5] *The Spiritual Canticle* (B) 39.12, *The Collected Works of St. John of the Cross*, rev. ed.; trans. Kieran Kavanaugh and Otilio Rodriquez (Washington, D.C.: Institute of Carmelite Studies, 1991), 626.

[6] F. Vandenbroucke, "Le Divorce entre Théologie et Mystique: Ses Origines," *Nouvelle Revue Théologique* 72 (1950): 372-89.

[7] Ibid., 389.

others in the thirteenth century and even the similarly grounded mysticism of the Rhenish mystical writers in the fourteenth century, namely, Meister Eckhart, Johann Tauler, Henry Suso, and Jan von Ruysbroeck.

After these Rhenish authors, mystical and spiritual writers wrote separate treatises that were no longer directly grounded in the great mysteries of the Christian faith. Vandenbroucke found that there was an unfortunate turn from a mysticism of the intellect and truth to a mysticism of the will and the good. Vandenbroucke's critique, however, did not give sufficient weight to the rigors and the depth of the mystical writings of Franciscan authors like St. Bonaventure whose classical study *Intinerarium Mentis in Deum* unites rich symbolism with a metaphysical grounding as well as an emphasis on the will and the good. To the detriment of his argument Vandenbroucke espoused an exclusively Thomistic theological perspective.

Vandenbroucke's research focused on the late fourteenth century as the time of the inception of this divorce. At this time, said Vandenbroucke, theologians and mystical authors began to engage in separate enterprises. Theology done in the schools and much later at the seminaries went the way of speculation, often ignoring spiritual experience while spiritual and mystical writers no longer submitted their writings to theological reflection.

Vandenbroucke's criticism of the spirituality of the *Devotio moderna* also requires some updating. There are many more positive aspects to this movement than he perceived.[8] This Benedictine scholar found the spirituality of this movement moralistic, psychological, voluntaristic, anthropocentric, and pessimistic. He demonstrated that the spiritual texts of the time were not articulated under the influence of major theological themes. Moreover, these characteristics of the age occurred partially because of the anti-intellectualism discernible in works like the classic of this movement *The Imitation of Christ*. Theology became abstract while spirituality tended to be preoccupied with practices and methods of prayer, losing its biblical, patristic, liturgical, and theological grounding. Vandenbroucke has, indeed, discerned important moments in the gradual separation of theology and spirituality even though his analysis of causes requires some serious revisions like those indicated above. This separation of spirituality and theology, detected by Vandenbroucke, continued well into the twentieth century and was exacerbated as time went on.

In 1939, before he left to accompany French forces in the war against Germany, Yves Congar submitted his study of the history of theology to the *Dictionnaire de Théologie Catholique*. There he succinctly commented on the divorce between "Scholastic Theology and Mystical Theology":

> With a Thomas or a Bonaventure mysticism is integrated into theology, so that theology can fulfill all the obligations of its function of wisdom. From this plenary viewpoint, a separate mystical or spiri-

---

[8] See John Van Engen's Introduction to *Devotio Moderna: Basic Writings* (New York: Paulist Press, 1988), 24-25 and passim.

tual theology had no purpose. Nevertheless in the fifteenth century a separation starts taking place. Toward the end [sic] of the sixteenth century, the *Exercises* of St. Ignatius will appear, then a little later, the writings of the reformed Carmel, then those of St. Francis de Sales. These spiritual works are masterpieces, but they do not stem from the classical speculative theology.[9]

Cardinal Congar noted that some voices lamented this divorce between theology and spirituality. Quite early in the separation Jean Gerson who died in 1429 regretted the divorce and wrote: "since up to now our study was to blend this mystical theology with our Scholastic theology."[10] Here Gerson was describing mystical theology not as a discipline but as the experience of God. In the seventeenth century two French Dominicans, Louis Chardon (1596-1651) with his *Theologia Mentis et Cordis* and William Vincent Contenson (1641-74) in his *The Cross of Jesus* championed an integration of speculative theology and spiritual experience.[11] If not as productive as Chardon and Contenson, there have been since their time those who have decried the separation of theology and spirituality, but these expressions of regret did little to heal this broken relationship.

Deeper Roots of this Divorce

The roots for this divorce of spirituality from theology lay, I believe, much earlier than the fourteenth century and, in fact, are, to some extent, congenital to the human effort to understand the divine. Already the Hebrew and Christian Scriptures strove here and there to name and to understand God's action in human history. The human capacity to understand the divine was then and always will be restricted by the otherness and utter transcendence of the divine mystery and the limitations of human rationality. Thinking about God and about religious experience is what the French call a *cas limit*. The ability to achieve the kind of depth and integration found in Thomas Aquinas and Bonaventure is rare and limited even in their exceptional hands.

The stories and the symbolism of the Hebrew and Christian Scriptures attempted to reveal divine reality, but this narrative theology was never able to impart a full understanding of the divine. Early on, authors like Origen found that the spiritual interpretation of the Scriptures was a way of delving into the divine mysteries and finding there guidance for believers. The spiritual or mystical interpretations of the Scriptures kept theology and spirituality in tandem as well as could be expected well into the twelfth century and to some extent into the thirteenth especially in the hands of great theological

---

[9] The quotation is from the revised article in the DTC (vol. 15) published in translation as *A History of Theology* (Garden City, N.Y.: Doubleday, 1968), 166.

[10] Ibid.

[11] Ibid., 166-67; C. Hahn, "Chardon, Louis," NCE 3 (1967): 459-60 and C. Lozier, "Contenson, Guillaume Vincent de," NCE 4: 264.

interpreters of Scripture like Origen, Gregory of Nyssa, Augustine, Gregory the Great, Bede, and Bernard of Clairvaux. Theology and spirituality were done simultaneously in those centuries in great measure because theology was integrated into the process of the interpretation of Scripture. A common object of study and prayer, the Scriptures kept theology and spirituality together especially as this theological exegesis was practiced in what has been called monastic theology.

The patristic era was especially adept at keeping spiritual and theological inquiry connected to each other. As Andrew Louth has written:

> This formative period for mystical theology was, of course, the formative period for dogmatic theology, and that the same period was determinative for both mystical and dogmatic theology is no accident since these two aspects of theology are fundamentally bound up with one another. The basic doctrines of the Trinity and Incarnation, worked out in these centuries, are mystical doctrines formulated dogmatically.[12]

The patristic era of integration gave way to medieval Scholasticism when division and separation of subject matter became the accepted way of doing theology. Yet, despite the impact of dialectics and especially Aristotelean logic, metaphysics, and epistemology on his theology, Thomas Aquinas kept intact the relationship between intellectual understanding and biblical narrative. Thomas's biblical commentaries were the basis of his theology, a theology much influenced by the biblical commentaries of the patristic and earlier Middle Ages. Both spirituality and theology would in our day gain much by greater attention to Thomas's biblical commentaries and their relationship to his theology. Thomas the *magister in theologia* ever remained the *magister in sacra pagina*.[13]

The specific division in the late fourteenth century between theology and mystical writings that Vandenbroucke noted in 1950 had roots in an even earlier Scholasticism, at least as far back as the twelfth century. The early Scholasticism of the twelfth century, through the use of dialectics and the divisions and categories inherited from an earlier age and expanded upon with the help of the re-emerging Aristotle, were laying the groundwork for the separation of theology and spirituality. Extreme rational distinctions were reached by the Latin Averoists, and the separation of philosophical and theological inquiry in the fourteenth century resulted in a fideism that kept the intellect and the will in separated spheres. It is not surprising that in this climate theological and spiritual texts went separate ways.

So far we have explored the origins and roots of spirituality's separation

---

[12] Andrew Louth, *The Origins of the Christian Mystical Tradition* (Oxford: Clarendon, 1981), xi.

[13] M.-D. Chenu, *Toward Understanding Saint Thomas*, trans. A-M. Landry and D. Hughes (Chicago: Henry Regnery, 1964), 243.

from the discipline of theology. There were other, perhaps more subtle, developments in the tradition that have contributed to the divorce of spirituality from theology. I now turn to one of them.

A Lesson from the Tradition of Moral Theology

The Jesuit moral theologian John Mahoney has studied the historical development of Catholic moral theology.[14] Mahoney's study of this tradition has instructive intimations for the way that spiritual doctrine became separated from theology. Moral theology did not become a distinct discipline until the late sixteenth and the early seventeenth century.[15] Yet, there were earlier developments that led to both the separateness and the distinctive character of Catholic moral theology.

Mahoney found that from the time of the early Church's wrestling with the readmission of public sinners, through the Celtic penitential movement and its consequent fostering of auricular confession, to the manuals for confessors in the late Middle Ages there was a preoccupation with sinfulness, if not on the part of all Christians,[16] certainly with many practitioners of pastoral care and authors of pastoral texts. Mahoney put special emphasis on auricular confession and its role in Catholic life as a source for this focus on sin and guilt.[17]

Mahoney also found that St. Augustine's pessimism about the power of the human person to resist evil, and I might add the pessimism of his times, have left a large and long shadow over Christian moral teaching. Mahoney attributes a pessimistic viewpoint to Augustine; I would say that Augustine's pessimism has at times been intensified by the lens through which he has been read, e.g., the Jansenist prism from the seventeenth century onwards. This pessimism about the enfeebled human condition is being challenged in Catholic circles only in this post-Vatican II era. Note the startling impact of the optimism of Pierre Teilhard de Chardin when it broke upon religious consciousness some forty years ago.

Mahoney's study has led me to reflect on the effect of a confession-oriented pastoral ministry and pessimistic moral theology as contributors to the isolation of spirituality in the theological endeavor. Once again Thomas Aquinas can be cited as one who integrated into his overall schema of theology (or sacred doctrine as he called theology) his teaching on the spiritual life and morality. Indeed, Thomas's teaching in both of these areas is upbeat and optimistic about the human ability to cooperate generously with God's grace and about the human capacity to know something about the great divine

[14] John Mahoney, *The Making of Moral Theology* (Oxford: Clarendon, 1987).

[15] Charles E. Curran, "Moral Theology," *The HarperCollins Encyclopedia of Catholicism*, ed. Richard P. McBrien (San Francisco: HarperCollins, 1995), 892.

[16] Professor John R. Shinners, an expert in the manuals for confessors, has cautioned me that the manuals for confessors were not as widely dispersed as one might suppose.

[17] See Mahoney, *The Making of Moral Theology* (Oxford: Clarendon, 1987), chap. 1.

mysteries. Thomas had profound trust in the human capacity to know and to love God.[18] But, Aquinas's magnanimous appreciation of the human spirit did not prevail.

The moral theology that became a separate discipline after the Council of Trent possessed the characteristics mentioned by Mahoney. Moreover, Catholic theology and especially Catholic moral theology following Trent became, until this century, largely a science studied in the seminaries that Trent devised. At Trent when various areas of study were advocated, the seminarians were charged to be versed ". . . particularly [in] all that seems appropriate to hearing confessions."[19] This centrality of confession in Catholic piety caused confessors and their professors to be preoccupied with moral matters that were too often studied apart from reference to the Bible and to the great mysteries of Trinity, Christology, and grace.

Focused on sin and weakness in the human person, students of moral theology in the centuries after Trent had too little exposure to the study of holiness and not much incentive to engage the holiness tradition from a theological perspective. The presumption at least in practice, if not in theory, was that holiness was the concern of the few, namely, religious and even more restrictively, cloistered religious. The theology of divinization that is so much part of Eastern Christianity would have been a corrective to this overemphasis in the West on sin, guilt, and confession. But, late medieval efforts at healing ties between East and West were futile and the cross-fertilization between Eastern and Western theology and spirituality had to wait for the renewed interest in that dialogue during this century. Now it is time for Eastern Christian theological and spiritual traditions to be fully explored in the West.

In the nineteenth and first half of the twentieth century separate courses in ascetical, mystical, or spiritual theology were introduced into the seminaries. However, these courses were not given near the attention that moral theology received. Indeed, ascetical and mystical tracts were often taught quickly at the end of the rotation of courses or even omitted as unimportant for the seminarian nearing ordination. The prospective confessor was expected to prepare diligently for the examinations that could qualify him to receive faculties to hear confessions. Seminarians got the message that the study of holiness was not nearly so crucial to their ministry as was adequacy in the administration of the sacrament of penance. This was a worthy goal but should not have been the exclusive goal of the Church's spiritual guides.

Some seminarians and many religious in North America were exposed from 1930 until the early 1960s to a quite detailed textbook on holiness. This book was Adolphe Tanquerey's *The Spiritual Life: A Treatise on Ascetical and Mystical Theology*.[20] This widely disseminated book had the same handicaps

[18] See Principe, *Thomas Aquinas' Spirituality*, 22ff.

[19] Council of Trent, Session 22, Decree on Reform, Canon 18, *Decrees of Ecumenical Councils*, vol. 2, ed. N. Tanner (London, Washington, D.C.: Sheed & Ward, Georgetown University Press, 1990), 751.

[20] 2d ed. rev.; trans. H. Branderis (Tournai, Belgium: Society of St. John the Evangelist and Desclee, 1930).

as the manuals of dogmatic and moral theology. These manuals were categorical; mystery and creativity were sacrificed to clarity; and speculation gave way to pragmatic application.[21] Moreover, inspiration never made it into these texts.

Ever since the Quietist crisis of the seventeenth century, Catholicism was shy about its mystical tradition. Tanquerey's manual was no exception. Its emphasis was on the ascetical rather than the mystical, on the practical more than the theoretical and, as with the above texts, inspiration was almost nowhere to be found in this widely used text.[22] In fact, this text was forbidding and tedious with its endless classifications.

Catholic theological training in North America took place almost exclusively in the seminaries until the Second Vatican Council. Note the exception of the Graduate School of Sacred Theology at St. Mary's College in Notre Dame, Indiana, where seventy-nine doctorates in theology and about 325 masters degrees in theology were awarded to women between 1943 and 1970.[23]

Seminaries emphasized the study of moral theology and left little opportunity for the study of the spiritual tradition beyond the prescribed periods of spiritual reading when seminarians were free to choose from the seminary library's devotional books that consisted largely of traditional hagiographies. The administration of the sacrament of penance would have benefited from dialogue with the ideals of the spiritual tradition just as the spirituality of the time would have gained much from theological reflection.

So strong a proponent of the unity of the theological enterprise as the late Yves Congar pointed out the pedagogical necessity for the divisions of material that occur in theology.[24] The medieval scholastics faced the task of turning a theology done through biblical commentaries into an "organized science."[25] However, the subdividing of theology into separate disciplines, in the hands of those with narrow perspectives and with poor dialogical skills, led to the neglect of themes like holiness, ordinary religious experience, the experience of the Holy Spirit, and mysticism. But, it is interesting that some modern ecclesiastical documents, like Pius XI's *Deus scientiarum dominus*,[26] spoke of ascetical and mystical theology as complements of moral theology.[27] In practice these complementary disciplines received far too little attention. One may well ask: to what extent was moral theology impaired by this neglect of the mysteries of faith and religious experience?

---

[21] Richard Gaillardetz, "Manualists," *Encyclopedia of Catholicism* 892; see also P. Ikechukwu Odozor, *Richard A. McCormick and the Renewal of Moral Theology* (Notre Dame, Ind. and London: University of Notre Dame Press, 1995), 7ff.

[22] Keith J. Egan, "The Prospects of the Contemporary Mystical Movement: A Critique of Mystical Theology," *Review for Religious* 34 (1975): 901-10.

[23] Sandra Yocum Mize of Dayton University is conducting research on this Graduate Program in Theology.

[24] Congar, *History of Theology*, 275ff.

[25] Chenu, *Toward Understanding St. Thomas*, 301-2.

[26] *Acta Apostolicae Sedis* 23 (1931): 241-62.

[27] Congar, *History of Theology*, 276.

Though specialization requires the division of disciplines and labor, theology and spirituality will remain disassociated if steps are not taken to keep these two areas of theological concern related through the creative tension that keeps one discipline listening to another. The collaboration of those who do theological research and those who study the spiritual tradition is imperative. What Bernard Lonergan wrote in his usual directness about method is true of this task of Christian scholars who seek a reunion of spirituality and theology. Lonergan wrote: "Method is not a set of rules to be followed meticulously by a dolt. It is a framework for collaborative creativity."[28] Overcoming polarizations that have been in place for a very long time demands common conversations, collaboration, creativity, and courage.

Collaboration calls for the common study by the two disciplines of the classics where theology and spirituality have been well integrated, e.g., texts by Origen, Gregory of Nyssa, Augustine, Gregory the Great, Pseudo-Dionysius, John Scottus Eriugena, Bernard of Clairvaux, William of St. Thierry, Thomas Aquinas, and Bonaventure to name the best known of these authors. There are, in addition, spiritual classics so shaped by theological wisdom that they also deserve collaborative study. Hugo Rahner pointed out the theological wisdom of Ignatius,[29] and the theological insights of John of the Cross are well established.[30]

Recommendations

What follow are some recommendations for healing the divorce between theology and spirituality. These recommendations have emerged not only from this brief exploration of a few historical moments in the separation of two "disciplines" which need each other for mutual growth but also from the personal struggle to keep spirituality and theology as conversation partners in my own teaching and research.

(1) Theology and theological spirituality must be done by women and men in whom there has occurred some integration of intellectual and spiritual experience. The practitioners of these disciplines must be in touch with traditions where intellectual and religious transcendence has occurred. Whoever would go beyond the mere rearranging of categories and curricula must be touched by that wisdom of which Augustine was so fond. Thomas Aquinas commenting on Colossians wrote: "Wisdom is knowledge of divine things; whatever can be known about God pertains to wisdom."[31] Whoever will bring integration to the study of theology and spirituality, must in the phrase of

---

[28] Bernard Lonergan, *Method in Theology* (New York: Herder and Herder, 1972), xi.

[29] Hugo Rahner, *Ignatius the Theologian*, trans. Michael Barry (New York: Herder and Herder, 1968).

[30] See Louis Dupré, *The Other Dimension: A Search for the Meaning of Religious Attitudes* (Garden City, N.Y.: Doubleday, 1972), 524-45.

[31] Thomas Aquinas, *In Omnes S. Pauli Apostoli Epistolas Commentaria* 7th ed. (Turin: Marietti, 1929), 2:127.

Philip Sheldrake be a "theological person,"[32] and, I would add, a theological person transformed by the spiritual wisdom of the tradition. Bernard Lonergan spoke of intellectual, moral, and religious conversion in this regard.[33] The training of theologians and of those who aspire to teach spirituality must include the whole tradition with the various currents that have, too often in the past, been divorced from each other.

(2) In particular, theology and spirituality are called to explore mystery. These two disciplines will be drawn closer together if they keep a common and central focus on mystery. These disciplines must never stray far from reflection upon the mystery who is God and the mystery of the human person and all creation. I recall the powerful impact made upon me on the occasion of the 750th anniversary of the deaths of SS. Thomas Aquinas and Bonaventure in 1974. In Rockefeller Chapel at the University of Chicago, Karl Rahner addressed in a single lecture the mystery of God and the mystery of the human person.[34] Rahner said: "How simple Christianity is then: the intention to surrender oneself in capitulating love to the incomprehensible God."[35] I suggest that theology and spirituality will again be companions if both search continually for a deeper understanding of divine and human mystery. Christian theology and Christian spirituality have at the heart of their agenda one in whom this twin mystery is located, the Incarnate Christ[36] who must always be the central focus of all Christian inquiry. As Avery Dulles has said, "Christian theology must always keep its primary focus on God and on Jesus Christ as the great revelation of God."[37]

(3) Christian theology and spirituality will also be kept in tandem if they remain ever refined by the core characteristics of Christian experience. That is, if they are continually shaped by the Scriptures, if they are rooted in the mystery of Christ, as mentioned above, if they are sacramentally celebrated, especially in baptism and Eucharist, and finally if theology and spirituality are lived ecclesially.[38] If theology and spirituality constantly return to these characteristics, they will be doing what patristic authors did: they explored Scripture and liturgy as resources for articulating the identity of the Triune God, Christ, and the Church. Neglect of these primary resources will surely be a barrier to the reunion of spirituality and theology. These core character-

---

[32] Philip F. Sheldrake, "Some Continuing Questions: The Relationship Between Spirituality and Theology," *Christian Spirituality Bulletin* 2 (spring 1994): 16. See also Illtyd Trethowen, *Mysticism and Theology* (London: Chapman, 1975).

[33] Lonergan, *Method in Theology*, 237ff.

[34] Karl Rahner, "Thomas Aquinas on the Incomprehensibility of God," *Celebrating the Medieval Heritage: A Colloquy on the Thought of Aquinas and Bonaventure, Journal of Religion* 58, Supplement (1978): S107-25.

[35] Ibid., S125.

[36] See Rowan Williams, "Mysticism and Incarnation," in *Teresa of Ávila* (Wilton, Conn.: Morehouse, 1991), 143-73.

[37] Dulles, *Craft*, 195.

[38] See Jean Leclercq, "L'idéal du théologien au Moyen âge: Textes inédits," *Revue des Sciences religieuses* 21 (1947): 121-48.

istics of Christian experience lead to the next two recommendations.

(4) Spirituality and theology will benefit from a turn to the liturgical tradition. Attention ought to be paid to the implications of the *lex orandi, lex credendi* tradition, that is, the way of praying as the way of believing. The implications of this aphorism have much to say about the complementarity that would accrue to theology and spirituality by attending to this living resource. Authentic worship must be a common source for the enrichment of both spirituality and theology.[39]

(5) Greater attention should also be given to the sacramental character of Christian mysticism. Is not the mystical life a growth of the Christ life birthed in every Christian at baptism/confirmation and nourished in the Eucharist. Here is a meeting ground for theology and mysticism; in fact, mysticism can then be perceived as a *locus theologicus*, a place for theological inquiry.[40] Reflection on the sacramental foundations of Christian spirituality is an illustration of a specific application of recommendations made by Karl Rahner,[41] Andrew Louth,[42] and others that mysticism should be seen as a locus for theological reflection.

(6) Just as theology in the West has a tendency to abstraction so spirituality has a recurring penchant for elitism and esotericism. To avoid these extremes, spirituality and theology must be in touch with human experience. Is not theology an examination of the divine reality as it is reflected in the universe and in human experience? Are not the spiritual life and mysticism a divine intensification of human experience? In this experience the human and the divine intersect. Augustine would have its culmination occur in the *apex mentis*, and Teresa of Ávila discovered this intersection in the seventh mansions of the *Interior Castle*. In both instances the crowning encounter with the divine occurs in human, albeit much graced, human experience. Theology and spirituality must never relinquish a collaborative quest of the divine in this valley of sorrows where human existence struggles to seek God, assured by John of the Cross that God always seeks the searcher much more than the searcher seeks God.[43]

(7) Women's experience and the wisdom which women draw from this experience have a crucial role in bringing theology and spirituality back into a mutually enriching relationship. Deeply spiritual and highly literary women mystics there have been aplenty as recent publications and numerous dissertations from the Divinity School at the University of Chicago attest. However, professional women theologians are largely a modern phenomenon.

[39] See G. Wainwright, *Doxology*.

[40] M.-L. Gondal, "La Mystique est-elle un lieu théologique?" *Nouvelle Revue Théologique* 108 (1986): 666-714.

[41] Harvey Egan, "The Devout Christian of the Future Will . . . be a 'Mystic'. Mysticism and Karl Rahner's Theology," *Theology and Discovery: Essays in Honor of Karl Rahner, S.J.*, ed. William J. Kelly (Milwaukee: Marquette University Press, 1980), 139.

[42] Louth, *Origins*, xi-xii.

[43] *The Living Flame of Love* 3.28, *The Collected Works of St. John of the Cross*, p. 620.

Women theologians and women teachers of spirituality have integrative skills not so well exercised by men in the past. Note in this regard the roles of the only two women who have been declared doctors of the church, Teresa of Ávila and Catherine of Siena.[44]

(8) Readers have, I am sure, anticipated the following recommendation: that the disciplines of theology and spirituality study closely the volumes of Bernard McGinn's *The Presence of God: A History of Western Christian Mysticism*,[45] which are an exemplar of the task of historical theology. The two volumes published thus far have already revealed how the study of Christian mysticism, by extension spirituality, is a theological enterprise. McGinn's work illustrates the current need for the historical and theological recovery of this mystical tradition. Moreover, McGinn has taught us not to get caught up in some of the minutiae and nonquestions that in the past so preoccupied investigators of the spiritual and the mystical tradition, e.g., the impossible quest of who is and who is not a mystic. Theology and spirituality have questions for each other but they must be questions that penetrate to the Mystery which is their common concern.

Conclusion

There is much more to be said about the divorce of spirituality from theology. The dialogue about this divorce has only begun.[46] And recommendations, here and elsewhere, need to be tested. But, if Karl Rahner's prognostication was valid—that "the devout Christian of the future will either be a 'mystic', one who has 'experienced' something, or he will cease to be anything at all,"[47] then theology and spirituality have a telling mandate from a theologian who knew well the riches of the spiritual tradition.

Perhaps Thomas Merton's conviction about the unity of monasticism, spoken at Calcutta in 1968, has wisdom for theology and spirituality as they struggle to become better conversation partners: "My dear brothers, we are already one. But we imagine that we are not. And what we have to recover is our original unity. What we have to be is what we are."[48]

[44] Keith J. Egan, "Catherine and Teresa: Doctors of the Church," *Commonweal* 122 (November 22, 1995): 10.

[45] Bernard McGinn, *The Presence of God: a History of Western Christian mysticism* , 4 vols. (New York: Crossroad, 1991-).

[46] See Philip Endear, "Theology out of Spirituality: The Approach of Karl Rahner," *Christian Spirituality Bulletin* 3 (fall 1995): 6-8; Mark McIntosh, "Lover Without a Name: Spirituality and Constructive Christology Today," *Christian Spirituality Bulletin* 3 (fall 1995): 9-12; J. Matthew Ashley, "The Turn to Spirituality? The Relationship Between Theology and Spirituality," *Christian Spirituality Bulletin* 3 (fall 1995): 13-18.

[47] Karl Rahner, *Theological Investigations*, vol. 7, trans. David Bourke (New York: Herder and Herder, 1971), 15.

[48] *The Asian Journal of Thomas Merton*, ed. Naomi Burton, Patrick Hart, and James Loughlin (New York: New Directions, 1973), 308.

24

The Integration of Theology and Spirituality: a View from the Seminary

Austin C. Doran

T his essay notes some of the challenges and possibilities for the integration of spiritual growth with theological study in the context of priestly formation. These reflections are of a practical and pastoral nature, centering on some observations about the way in which the integration of theology and spirituality comes about in a freestanding Roman Catholic seminary theologate.

The Seminary Setting

Fr. Avery Dulles has noted that while no sharp opposition can be drawn between theology done at the university and that done in a forum such as the seminary, "theology does tend to take on different hues depending on the environment in which it is practiced."[1] In a brief description of theology in the seminary setting Father Dulles mentions its orientation toward the formation of future clergy, its emphasis on teaching rather than on research, its relative intellectual isolation, as well as its intent to transmit safe and established doctrine. These factors distinguish the tone of the theology taught in a seminary compared with that taught in a university where theology may be in close contact with other disciplines, addresses a widely diversified audience, and concentrates on open and unsolved questions.[2]

Certainly it is distinctive of the seminary setting that the teaching of theology forms part of a larger formational program. This creates both a tension and an opportunity. The tension arises from the fact that so much of the time and energy of both students and faculty is claimed by nonacademic programs

[1] Avery Dulles, *The Craft of Theology: From Symbol to System* (New York: Crossroad, 1992), 150.
[2] Ibid., 154-55.

308

and activities. The seminary is a graduate school in which the frequent complaint is not having enough time to study. On the other hand, to the extent that students and faculty in the seminary relate to one another on a daily basis as part of a worshiping community committed to justice and charity, the study of theology will find vibrant spiritual context, motivation, and energy.

In the seminary setting the integration of theology and spirituality has special prominence in that it takes the form of an explicit and inescapable foundational mandate. All of the charter documents for seminaries speak as one in their insistence on the integration of theology and spirituality as an essential dimension of priestly formation. The Second Vatican Council's *Decree on the Training of Priests* insists that theological disciplines should be taught in the light of faith, so that seminary students may accurately receive Catholic doctrine, and also profoundly enter into it, "making it the food of their own spiritual life."[3] Pope John Paul II notes that theological and spiritual formation, in particular the life of prayer, "meet and strengthen each other, without detracting in any way from the soundness of research or from the spiritual tenor of prayer."[4] Our current national *Program of Priestly Formation* identifies the goal of intellectual formation as the "conversion of mind and heart, which is the only sure foundation for a lifetime of teaching and preaching."[5]

Because of this insistence, the integration of intellectual and spiritual formation in seminaries constitutes an explicit institutional priority demanding the energy and time of all faculty members, whether their particular work in the seminary is primarily academic or primarily formational. Those of us who work in seminaries find ourselves regularly confronted with this issue of the integration of theology and spirituality. The goal of integration serves as a major criterion by which we can assess the appropriateness and effectiveness of our academic curriculum, methodology, policies, and procedures, as well as the aptness of our spiritual formation program. At the same time, very frankly, this issue can be taken up as a weapon of attack by any interested party with a complaint about what we teach or how we teach in the seminary. Cries for a more "spiritual" approach in a theology school can be a healthy challenge to Catholic educators, but in the mouths of some critics such appeals may reflect a fear of scientific rigor, a lack of imagination, or a narrow theological horizon.

Three Responses

With that as background, let me tell you what happens when I ask seminarians, "What impact is your study of theology having on your spiritual

---

[3] *Decree on Priestly Formation*, art. 16, *Decrees of the Ecumenical Councils*, vol. 2, ed. Norman P. Tanner (London: Sheed & Ward, 1990), 955.

[4] John Paul II, *Pastores Dabo Vobis*, Origins 21 (April 16, 1992): 744, art. 53.

[5] *Program of Priestly Formation*, 4th ed. (Washington, D.C.: United States Catholic Conference, 1993), art. 355, 64.

life?" Responses to this question tend to fall into three categories. Some students view their study of theology as just hard work—reading, exams, and papers—a set of tasks unconnected to those warm and pious feelings they spontaneously identify as their spirituality. They approach theology as a competence they must acquire, a hard discipline, a daunting collection of new words, concepts and methodologies. A second category of response encompasses those who are finding theology very useful pastorally. They readily associate their spirituality with their service to others, and find in theology a way to help people find answers to their religious questions. In a third category are those who claim that the study on theology has had a deep impact on their spirituality because it has occasioned a transformation in their own understanding and appreciation of themselves, their lives, and the world and people around them. The study of theology has become more important for them because of its impact on their spirituality.

While this third category of response suggests significant progress toward the ideal of theology and spirituality giving life to each other, each of the three categories I mentioned raises its own issues and carries its own implications, which I wish to draw out.

Theology Separate From Spirituality

Let us begin with the seminary students whose spirituality seems separate from the hard work, technical jargon, and puzzling methodology that confronts them in the theology classroom. Some students keep theology and spirituality separate because they never penetrate the technicalities of theology so as to grasp and be grasped by its meaning. The inherent difficulty of the subject matter may sometimes be compounded by the deficient educational backgrounds of some students. Others have English as a second or third language and for some of these the subtleties remain elusive. In some cases it becomes clear that a student is unable to enter deeply enough into the study of theology to complete the seminary program. But there are situations in which a seminarian may, in fact, complete the seminary program with only a marginal grasp of theology. To some seminary students, the world of academic theology may remain largely unknown, yet they pass their courses by dint of sincere, brute effort and everyone's massive goodwill. Obviously if theology is not being learned, it cannot be integrated with one's spirituality.

For many other students there is at least an initial and painful difficulty in moving from the common-sense realm of faith and religion, so laden with affective power, to the theoretical realm of academic theology. Bernard Lonergan speaks of the "strange contrast and tension between the old common-sense apprehension instinct with feeling and the new theoretical apprehension devoid of feeling and bristling with theorems."[6]

---

[6] Bernard Lonergan, *Method in Theology* (New York: Herder and Herder, 1972), 114-15.

Even when a student has negotiated the transition to the theoretical realm, there still remains the quite distinct task of integrating the common sense and theoretical realms. It is no easy task to come to appreciate the value as well as the limits of familiar religious symbols, creedal statements, and theological affirmations. The two realms cannot themselves integrate each other, but must be reconciled in yet a third realm: that of interiority. This happens through a form of self-knowledge, self-appropriation, a heightening of intentional consciousness through "the long and confused twilight of philosophic initiation."[7] It requires an even further step to open oneself in faith and wonder to the realities behind and beyond the words. Some quite competent theology students resist the invasion of critical reflection into their "spiritual space." They are at home in the realm of the common sense and are growing competent in the realm of theory, but the two realms seems to have no vital point of contact.

I believe that, in this case, what may be at issue is not only understanding but also desire. Longing and yearning are always operative in the learning process. Pope John Paul II has stressed that human formation gives the necessary foundation for all formation, including intellectual formation.[8] This human formation surely includes the education of the heart. So where are our human hearts in the process of studying and teaching theology? What moves us? What do we seek? What desires summon and marshal our energy as we take up the project of learning and teaching?

Study and the Desire of our Hearts

Though it is dangerous to generalize about so diverse a group as today's seminarians, for many I meet, the study of theology seems to answer a profound hunger and thirst for personal meaning, social stability, and intellectual comfort. Many seminarians could be called refugees. Some are literal refugees coming to us from countries plagued by warfare, oppression, or economic distress. Others might be figuratively called refugees, having escaped from dysfunctional and morally confused family backgrounds, from an alienated and self-indulgent young adulthood, or from an ultimately unsatisfying first career in business or industry. Many of these students come to the classroom seeking intellectual security, clear boundaries for truth and falsehood, verification and clarification of what they already believe and know. Through the study of theology they want to find a religious and intellectual home, not to go exploring.

This yearning on the part of students can be at odds with the taste for exploration, inquiry, and critical thought which their professors would impart. To risk some further generalization, many of us teaching Catholic theology today were educated in highly conservative institutions, but in a crucial era, the 1960s and 1970s, years during which those very institutions were

---

[7] Ibid., 85.
[8] *Pastores Dabo Vobis*, art. 43, 738.

acknowledging in unprecedented ways that Catholic theology was in need of drastic updating and rethinking. One of the most important things we learned in theology school was that yesterday's theological syntheses often could not meet the needs of people of our times. By the time I first studied theology in the seminary the old manuals and treatises had just been set aside, replaced often enough by xeroxed articles from current journals. The excitement, the thrill, the passion of the theology I learned was in delving deeply into the Catholic theological tradition, but then allowing that tradition to feel the impact of vital contact with contemporary intellectual and cultural trends, with diverse religious traditions, and with reflection upon common human experience.

Intent as we are on transmitting Catholic tradition, many of us teaching Catholic theology today have also acquired a passion for looking outward from our Catholic perspective to other ways of thinking, other ways of believing, and other ways of life. If at one time Catholic theology looked toward other ways in order to answer them, refute them, solve them, or convert them, more recently many theology teachers in my generation seem to harbor at least an equal expectation that our Catholic perspective will be enriched, contextualized, and even corrected by contact with diverse, contemporary reflection and experience.

The result of this can be tension and resistance, even a war of wills, as professors seek to impart a methodology for faithfully asking difficult intellectual questions, while their students long for the reliable answers to keep those same questions at a safe distance. Sometimes teachers want to take their students exploring, while the students are longing to find a home. Teacher and student may meet each other in the doorway of Catholic tradition, but may find themselves faced in opposite directions, looking longingly over one another's shoulder. Are our students being asked to welcome the spiritual impact of a project the whole direction of which does not resonate with their own heart's desire? We would do well to take this possible tension into account both in our teaching and in our programs of spiritual formation.

At the same time it would be wrong to speak of our desires as if these were static, fixed, and predictable. The transformation of desire is a key issue in spiritual growth. While we bring the particular desires of our hearts to our teaching or study, there is at work in theology another and far greater desire, and that is God's desiring. Jürgen Moltmann has stated recently that "theology is for me a suffering from God and a passion for God's kingdom."[9] Moltmann insists that theology springs from a divine passion or pain, as well as from God's love for life, and from the tension between these is born hope for the Kingdom. His words are a reminder that, while each of us may find the particular desires of our hearts fulfilled or frustrated in the study of theology, the divine desiring, at the same time, draws us into itself and gives us a share in its own pain and in its own life.

---

[9] Jürgen Moltmann, "Theology and the Future of the Modern World" (Pittsburgh: The Association of Theological Schools, 1995), 1.

The Pastoral Motive as an Integrating Factor

Harkening back to the second of my three original categories, I said that some seminary students find their study of theology spiritually enriching insofar as it allows them to be pastorally useful. Theology offers a gift of knowledge which can be used to help others address the questions and issues in their lives. The study of theology prepares and empowers one for this spiritual work. Whether this pastoral motive engenders a narrow, utilitarian approach to theology, or constitutes a solid place of departure for spiritual integration will depend greatly on one's conception of pastoral ministry. If Christian ministry is simply what I do for people, then the theology I need may be a storehouse of useful information, practical wisdom, and helpful guidelines. But a more profound understanding of Christian ministry carries us into the paschal mystery, at which point we have arrived at the very core of both Catholic theology and Catholic spirituality. The aspirant to priesthood, drawn to ministry as one among the many beneficent professions, may learn through the experiencing of his own weakness and distress, as well as through compassion for the sufferings of others, that the heart of Christian ministry beats with the pulse of death and resurrection. Ministry is not only a power to do good, but leads the minister to compassionate powerlessness and faithful surrender. This progressive deepening of the pastoral sense was ably described nearly twenty years ago by a distinguished predecessor of mine at St. John's Seminary in Camarillo, the late Monsignor James O'Reilly.

Anxious as he is to take his place in the world of today, the student may nurture the ambition to become a "power for the good in the world." Just as a physician exists to solve health problems for his patients and the lawyer to solve legal problems for his clients and the city administrator to solve urban problems for the citizens, so the student for ministry might easily conceive his vocation as that of being yet another problem-solver but at the high level of religious or moral life. Armed with counseling techniques and enriched with theological insights he could then take his place in the world of useful specialists.

Not the least function of a program of spiritual formation would be to help the student to recognize and deal with this fascination with ministry as power in a world of power. Part of the task of the student's (spiritual) director would be to lead him through prayerful reflection to a gospel perspective of his ministry. Through wise (spiritual) direction the student would be brought to see that, while there are indeed problems in this life for the solution of which people might well consult a minister of religion, that is the least of his "uses" to his flock. More truly the minister is one to whom his people can come at those junctures of life when they have come face to face with the unsolvable, those moments when they meet with the limits of creaturely power, when they experience darkness or have intimations of mortality. At such moments, people have need to draw near to one who, while able like other men to swim in the waters of life and stay afloat in them, is not averse to drowning graciously in them, able to be overcome. People need one who has entered deeply into the paschal mystery of Jesus, rejoicing in life but at ease with death.

Mastering the negative is the acid-test which distinguished the disciple of Christ from the purveyors of non-Christian humanisms. Clearly it is of paramount importance that the positive thrust of academic studies in theology . . ., the positive drive behind pastoral training . . ., and the positive accomplishments of life in the student-faculty community . . .—that all these positive elements in seminary life operate in such a way as not to hinder the student from keeping a place in his heart for the sweet powerlessness by which we are to be carried into the hands of the living God.[10]

O'Reilly's aim in these reflections is to highlight the role proper to spiritual formation in the training of priests, but I believe his observations also suggest something about the teaching of theology. A spiritually mature, gospel-oriented sense of pastoral ministry relieves the seminary student of a superficial view of theology as merely a body of useful information supplying the answers to people's questions. That same maturity will grow impatient if it finds in the academic study of theology a useful set of tools, skills, and criteria for doing intellectually acceptable research and reflection, but no more than that. While it would be tiresome and inhibiting to demand that every work of theological scholarship display its spiritual and pastoral credentials, all of Catholic theology, even at its most technical or esoteric, will be asked to contribute consciously to a larger synthesis, a faith-inspired vision of life which relates itself to its christological center and remains cognizant of its ecclesial orientation. Those striving to receive, understand, live, and share the Good News of Jesus Christ look to theology for perspective and insight.

Precisely this hope and expectation on the part of students allows the teacher of theology to contribute mightily to the student's process of spiritual growth and integration. My work with seminarians, immersed as they are both in the academic study of theology and in an intentional process of spiritual formation, confirms for me the necessity of rigorous theological study to purify and complete a seminarian's personal faith perspective and to serve as a point of departure for a healthy and holistic spirituality.

[10] James O'Reilly, "Spiritual Formation in Relation to Seminary Life," a paper prepared for the consultation on spiritual formation held at St. Andrew's Priory, Valyermo California, July 1977. Privately published. Copies available from Paul Ford, Ph.D., St. John's Seminary, Camarillo, California.

Theological Formation and Personal Discernment

For example, as a spiritual director for seminarians I note time and again the vital interplay between their study of theology and the discernment of their vocations. The discernment of the vocation to priesthood tends to be the major issue in seminary spiritual direction at the theologate level. In the discernment process ongoing and consistent prayer yields a knowledge of one's own motives and desires and sets the stage for the mature and loving commitment of one's life in response to the Lord's perceived invitation. Discernment is both a work of self-knowledge and the realization of a creative, intimate partnership with God. While discernment is not an academic exercise, the process will have increasing validity for Christian living as the seminarian develops his own solid theological synthesis. Far more than a set of instructions for good decision-making, Christian discernment is a way of setting in motion a personal and concrete response to Jesus Christ and his gospel. Discernment assumes a solid moral education; it also demands and rests upon the personal appropriation of a sound theological anthropology and a Christology.

Ignatius of Loyola's rules for discernment build upon the theological anthropology of which his principle and foundation[11] is the summary statement. The ultimate norm for Christian discernment is Jesus Christ; thus the crucial significance of Ignatius's Christology, depicted in symbolic language such as that of his meditation on the two standards.[12] These expressions of Ignatius's synthesis, so apt for his time and richly expressive of his own life experience, challenge and inspire us today. Yet one cannot simply borrow Ignatius of Loyola's theological synthesis. Not only is the theology of Ignatius very much that of his own era and not ours, but it also seems part of the genius of his *Spiritual Exercises* that his theological synthesis is made present without being fully elaborated. One must enter for oneself into the gospel, desiring and asking for the grace to make one's own personal appropriation in the context of one's own milieu and life experience. Only then does one begin to find oneself in God and to find God in Jesus Christ and then to value or disvalue all things in light of Christ.

As often as the seminarian, in the course of his study of theology, glimpses with fresh excitement and wonder the face of God in Christ he acquires a spiritual sensitivity and fervor which enable Christian discernment. As often as he is personally challenged, even left breathless, by the paradoxes of God's Kingdom, he sharpens his spiritual vision. The personal discernment process can be fueled and moved forward by the study of theology. The purification of the student's image of God and the clarification of his understanding of the gospel message resulting, for example, from the study of Scripture or the so-

---

[11] *The Spiritual Exercises of Saint Ignatius* [23], trans. George E. Ganss, S.J. (Chicago: Loyola University Press, 1992), 32.
[12] Ibid., [135-46], 65-67.

cial teaching of the Church, can and do occasion breakthroughs into a more profound self-understanding, and a keener focus concerning his personal and ecclesial mission.

Theology Needs Spirituality

If, for seminarians, the study of theology provides a crucial point of departure for a healthy spirituality, it is also a truism that theology, if divorced from that broader sphere of human experience embraced by the term spirituality, tends toward idle chatter. This century has seen what Dermot Lane calls "the recovery of experience as an integral element in the exercise of theology."[13] This is so much the case that Lane cites the warnings of theologians that this relationship between theology and experience does not imply a reduction of theology to experience.[14] Yet, it seems to me that a theology that has learned to speak much about experience is especially in danger of substituting speech for experience. The verbal-conceptual needs a nonverbal context, for theology can describe and evaluate much, but can replace nothing of the reality of life in the human body, social interaction, the power of religious symbols, and apophatic experience, however inchoate.

Gregory the Great, speaking of that wisdom which comes only through experience, reminds us that "it is one thing to hear food named and quite another thing to taste it."[15] Students need to hear the words of teachers who have themselves tasted through experience the realities of which they speak. We all need teachers whose theology obviously draws life from the often unseen roots of their own prayer, love, suffering, and hope. Such teachers speak, not so as to satisfy us, but to stimulate our appetite, to make us hungry to taste and see for ourselves.

Many of us hear the voice of such a teacher in Karl Rahner who, faced with the conundrum of saying something about the incomprehensibility of God, is neither mute not glib, but writes:

> As long as we measure the loftiness of knowledge by its perspicuity, and think that we know what clarity and insight are, though we do not really know them as they truly are; as long as we imagine that analytical, co-ordinating, deductive and masterful reason is more and not less than experience of the divine incomprehensibility; as long as we think that comprehension is greater than being overwhelmed by light inaccessible, which shows itself inaccessible in the very moment of giving itself: we have understood nothing of the mystery and of the true nature of grace and glory.[16]

[13] Dermot A. Lane, *The Experience of God: An Invitation to Do Theology* (New York: Paulist Press, 1981), 1.

[14] Ibid., 3.

[15] Gregory the Great, *Moralia in Iob* 11.6.9, CCSL, vol. 143A (Turnholt: Brepols, 1979), 590.

[16] Karl Rahner, *Theological Investigations*, vol. 4, trans. Kevin Smyth (Baltimore: Helicon Press, 1966), 56.

Rahner's words about the Christian mystery, far from confronting us with an intellectual dead end, constitute an exciting invitation to Christian experience, as well as to continuing effort to understand that experience. The process of critical reflection which has progressed to the point that it may surrender in worship and love, is continually revitalized, stimulated afresh. It is a reasonable expectation that in the course of studying and teaching theology we and our students will encounter a Truth, attractive and inexhaustible, in which we find ourselves personally implicated. Our faith is that we ourselves are sought by that Truth, in whom we find the fullness of life.

Some Factors Favoring Integration

Some factors would seem to favor the successful integration of spiritual growth with theological study in the seminary.

The student's transition from the common-sense realm of faith and religion to the theoretical realm of academic theology will be aided by those crucial courses which introduce them to theological method. Such instruction, whether at the level of the seminary college, the pre-theology program or the theologate, must be sensitive and responsive to the varied educational backgrounds and personal motivations with which students approach the study of theology.

Seminary spiritual formation needs to give explicit attention to the challenge of intellectual conversion, along with moral conversion and spiritual conversion. Individual spiritual direction, spiritual conferences, retreats, and intensive periods of spiritual formation are all occasions for students to grasp more deeply the spiritual dimension of their theological studies, both as a factor in their own relationship with God and as an invitation to a sharing in the pastoral charity of Christ.

Of course, there is no substitute for excellence in teaching. Integration is favored by instruction in which scholarly integrity and accomplishment is matched by able pedagogy, spiritual depth, and pastoral sensitivity.

At the same time, no single professor or spiritual director can be as influential as the seminary ambiance, which teaches its own lessons. Integration is favored by a seminary atmosphere in which study is taken seriously and linked to vibrant liturgical life, healthy community interaction, and a general spirit of servanthood.

25

Theological Education of African American Catholics

M. SHAWN COPELAND

For the first time in the history of the Catholic Church in the United States, there is a group of formally educated theological scholars, women and men of African American descent—canon lawyers, ethicists, historians, religious educators, sociologists and anthropologists of religion, and systematic theologians.[1] The roots of advocacy for such a group lie deep in the nineteenth-century struggle of black Catholics to enjoy and exercise full membership in their Church. The contemporary efforts of African American Catholics for evangelization, catechesis, and theological education echo those of members of the Afro-American Catholic Congress Movement. Proceedings of the first Congress record their eagerness "to cooperate with the clergy in the conversion and education of our race."[2] Al-

---

[1] Augustus Tolton is generally recognized as the first African American Catholic priest but, prior to his ordination, there were three others: the Healy brothers—James Augustine, Sherwood, and Patrick. Sons of an enslaved black woman and an Irish Catholic planter, they had been isolated by their father's money and social association from the vicious brunt of racism. But, this left them with little explicit race identification and consciousness. Sherwood Healy was, more than likely, the first Catholic theologian of African descent. A canon lawyer and theologian, he served as a theological *peritus* or expert to Boston's Bishop John Joseph Williams. Healy is reported to have traveled with Bishop Williams to the Second Plenary Council of Baltimore in 1866 and to the First Vatican Council in Rome in 1870. Albert S. Foley, S.J., "U. S. Colored Priests: Hundred-Year Survey," *America* 89 (13 June 1953): 295-97.

[2] From 1889 until 1894, African American Catholic laity conducted an increasingly vigorous congress movement to importune their Church to "take an active interest in what concerns, not only the spiritual but also the temporal welfare of all the people entrusted to your [its] care." See *Three Catholic Afro-American Congresses* (Cincinnati: The American Catholic Tribune, 1893; repr. New York: Arno, 1978), 14. The call for a meeting of "Colored Catholics . . . for the purpose of taking the status of the race in their relation to the church" was the inspiration of Daniel Rudd, the publisher and editor of the *American Catholic Tribune*, the only national newspaper published by and aimed at Catholics of African descent in the United States in the nineteenth century. For discussions of the Congress Movement, see David Spalding, C.F.X., "The Negro Catholic Congresses, 1889-1894," *The Catholic Historical Review* 55 (October 1969): 337-57; Cyprian Davis, O.S.B., "Black Catholics in America: A Historical Note," *America* 142 (3 May 1980): 378; idem, *The History of Black Catholics in the United States* (New York: Crossroad, 1990).

though numbering less than twenty, today's seminary and university teachers, researchers, and writers are determined to develop theological, pastoral, and religio-cultural formulations accountable to the experience of *being black and Catholic.*[3]

Yet, the very existence of a group of African American Catholics prepared in the ecclesial disciplines is a sign of ambiguity and contradiction, of differentiation and creativity, of struggle and transcendence. For although Catholics form a culturally, ethnically, racially diverse, yet united community of faith, neither they, nor their institutions reside in a vacuum. Catholics along with their schools, colleges, seminaries, and universities are fully inserted in historical, social, and cultural realities of local, national, international, and global scale. If the development of an authentic African American Catholic theological perspective and if the theological education of African American Catholics are not to be jeopardized, then there are several issues to be identified and addressed.

First, racism remains an inescapable and lived reality in the United States, even an inescapable and lived reality of Catholic life. Racism does not merely concern attitudes, feelings, or preferences. It denotes intentional protracted structured, institutionalized oppression of one race by another. In the United States, either directly or indirectly, racism permeates and governs every social (i.e., political, economic, technological), cultural, personal, even, religious encounter or exchange between the racialized human subjects.

Second, African American Catholic women and men enter the field at a time when theology is undergoing large-scale or paradigm change. Under the press of certain powerful historical, cultural, and social shifts (e.g., the Shoah, the emergence of postmodernity, the bold resurfacing of Christianity in Eastern Europe), the ways in which theology has understood its presuppositions, tasks, sources, and methods are shifting quite fundamentally.[4]

Third, one consequence of shifts in theology is focus on the notion and meaning of experience. What is meant by experience? What does it mean to theologize about experience? to theologize about the black experience? women's experience? the experience of the mestizaje? Indeed, *whose* experience counts in theological reflection?[5] This line of questioning uncovers the insinuation of normative and universalistic concerns in theology's hermeneutical task.

---

[3] Twenty years ago, black Catholic priest and scripture scholar Joseph Nearon, in a report to the annual assembly of the Catholic Theological Society of America (CTSA), pressed for the "absolute necessity [of] a corps of competent black Catholic theologians." See "A Challenge to Theology: The Situation of American Blacks," *CTSA Proceedings* 30 (1975): 177-202, esp., 201; idem, "Preliminary Report: Research Committee for Black Theology," *CTSA Proceedings* 29 (1974): 413-17; also see Preston N. Williams, "Religious and Social Aspects of Roman Catholic and Black American Relationships," *CTSA Proceedings* 28 (1973): 15-30.

[4] See Hans Küng and David Tracy, eds., *Paradigm Change in Theology* (New York: Crossroad, 1989).

[5] Monika Hellwig, *Whose Experience Counts in Theological Reflection?* (Milwaukee, Wis.: Marquette University Press, 1982).

Fourth, inasmuch as ways of apprehending theology and its tasks are shifting, so too ways of grasping the purpose and nature of theological education are shifting. The range of concerns is wide: What is the relation of theology to religious studies? How are we to understand and incorporate varying feminist and/or womanist and/or *mujerista* critiques in theological education? How are other religions to be encountered in Christian theological education? Can Christian theological education absorb cultural diversity? What factors determine and ensure the adequacy, scope, depth, and quality of theological education? In the past decade in North America, these issues have been debated, for the most part, by mainline Protestant theologians and theological educators.[6] But Roman Catholics are not exempt from these concerns. The very migrations of theology within our Roman Catholic context—from the monastery to the university, from the domain of the clergy to the laity, from the province of men to that of women—may present fresh *inspirited* imperatives.

Fifth, Peter Paris has observed that with the irruption of black theology, "for the first time in the history of religious academe, African Americans [have] a subject matter and a methodological perspective . . . peculiarly their own and capable of rigorous academic defense."[7] Yet, that subject matter, heretofore, has been accorded little if any attention in Catholic seminaries or college and university departments of theology.

Sixth, the exclusion or marginalization of Black Studies in the theological curriculum of most European or American Catholic educational institutions where most African American theologians and scholars are trained often alienates students from the potential of Black Studies and/or from the very educational ethos of those institutions. This provokes and feeds identity frustration among black Catholics.[8]

Seventh, nearly all African American Catholic theologians and scholars of

---

[6] This literature is quite extensive. For a bibliography of works on theological education since 1983, see W. Clark Gilpin, "Basic Issues in Theological Education: A Selected Bibliography, 1980-1988," *Theological Education* 25 (spring 1989): 115-21. The following authors are representative of some of the tensions in the current debate: Edward Farley, *Theologia: The Fragmentation and Unity of Theological Education* (Philadelphia: Fortress, 1983); idem, *The Fragility of Knowledge: Theological Education in the Church and the University* (Philadelphia: Fortress, 1988); The Mud Flower Collective, *God's Fierce Whimsey* (New York: Pilgrim Press, 1985); Joseph C. Hough, Jr., and John B. Cobb, Jr., *Christian Identity and Theological Education* (Chico, Calif.: Scholars Press, 1985); Charles M. Wood, *Vision and Discernment* (Atlanta: Scholars Press, 1985); Max L. Stackhouse, *Apologia: Contextualization, Globalization, and Mission in Theological Education* (Grand Rapids, Mich.: Wm. B. Eerdmans, 1988); Barbara G. Wheeler and Edward Farley, eds., *Shifting Boundaries: Contextual Approaches to the Structure of Theological Education* (Louisville: Westminster/John Knox Press, 1991); David H. Kelsey, *To Understand God Truly: What's Theological about a Theological School* (Louisville: Westminster/John Knox Press, 1992). In his *Between Athens and Berlin: The Theological Education Debate* (Grand Rapids, Mich.: Wm. B. Eerdmans, 1993), Kelsey provides a provocative typology through which to grasp the contrasting positions of Farley, Hough and Cobb, the Mud Flower Collective, Stackhouse, and Wood.

[7] Peter J. Paris, "Overcoming Alienation in Theological Education," *Shifting Boundaries,* 183.

[8] Ibid., 186.

religion teach in predominantly white Catholic institutions. While these women and men cannot escape those slices of social location that they share with other black women and men, they risk alienation from the perspective of blacks in favor of an "academicized" Black Theology. At the same time, these African American Catholics meet tokenization and trivialization from their Celtic, Anglo, European American Catholic colleagues. So, African American Catholic women and men trained as historians, moralists and ethicists, doctrinal and systematic theologians are reduced to that slice of social location. Their disciplinary expertise is either diminished, ignored, or subordinated to racial incidents; they become experts on the black situation for their Celtic, Anglo, European American colleagues. Yet, if we African American Catholic historians, moralists and ethicists, doctrinal and systematic theologians do not take responsibility for sustained theological research and reflection on the black experience, we shall deprive our Church and our people of riches.[9]

Eighth, while "the academy" increasingly has become a site of competition for status and prestige, scholars trained in the humanities are losing this competition to those trained in science and technology.[10] This is as disastrous for science and technology as it is for the humanities, for theology itself. Human persons are not reducible to atoms or theorems, to statistics or social problems; nor are they reducible to metaphors or attributes, to descriptions or categories. Women and men are instances of the intelligible in the world and instances of incarnate moral choice in a world under the influence of sin, yet in relation to a field of supernatural grace.[11]

Ninth, a theology is not only the product of faith but also of a culture. Catholic theologians are challenged, not only to acquire knowledge of the culture(s) in which they are living and studying, writing and teaching, but

[9] For some discussions of the dilemmas, failures, paradoxes, vocation, and struggle of living a black intellectual life in the United States, see E. Franklin Frazier, "The Failure of the Negro Intellectual," *Negro Digest* (February 1962): 26-36; John Hope Franklin, "The Dilemma of the American Negro Scholar," *Soon, One Morning, New Writing by American Negroes, 1940-1962,* ed. Herbert Hill (New York: Knopf, 1963), 62-76; Harold Cruse, *The Crisis of the Negro Intellectual: From Its Origins to the Present* (New York: William Morrow, 1967); Ralph Ellison, "The World and the Jug," *Shadow and Act* (New York: Random House, 1964), 107-43; Vincent Harding, "The Vocation of the Black Scholar and the Struggles of the Black Community," *Education and Black Struggle: Notes from the Colonized World* (Cambridge, Mass.: Harvard Educational Review, 1974), 3-39; Martin Kilson, "Paradoxes of Blackness: Notes on the Crisis of Black Intellectuals," *Dissent* (1986): 70-78; Michele Wallace, *Invisibility Blues: From Pop to Theory* (New York and London: Verso, 1990); Bell Hooks and Cornel West, *Breaking Bread: Insurgent Black Intellectual Life* (Boston: South End Press, 1991); Jerry Gafio Watts, *Heroism and Black Intellectual Life* (Chapel Hill: University of North Carolina Press, 1994); Cornel West, "The Dilemma of Black Intellectual," *Cultural Critique* 1 (fall 1985): 132-46; idem, *Race Matters* (Boston: Beacon, 1994).

[10] C. West, "The Postmodern Crisis of Black Intellectuals," *Beyond Eurocentrism and Multiculturalism: Prophetic Thought in Postmodern Times* (Monroe, Me.: Common Courage, 1993), 92-93.

[11] See Bernard Lonergan, *Insight, A Study of Human Understanding* (New York: Philosophical Library, 1970), 422; idem, "Finality, Love, Marriage," *Collection: Papers by Bernard Lonergan, S.J.,* ed. Frederick E. Crowe (Montreal: Palm, 1967), 16-53.

also to grasp that there must be a "multiplicity of theologies" that expresses the one faith.[12] Diversity and pluralism are obvious, if testy, dimensions of life in the United States. They are also characteristic (whether we like it or not, whether we acknowledge it or not) of a global, a world Church.[13]

This list is not exhaustive. Certainly there are other issues that confront the theological education of African American Catholics (e.g., evangelization, how to finance theological studies for black Catholic lay women and men, the flight of the Church from the country's "chocolate cities," and so on). This essay explores three issues—racism, African American culture, and the irruption of black theology—and their affect on Catholic theological education. These issues present a point of departure from which to consider just how we might recruit, educate, train, cultivate, and support the next generation of African American Catholic theologians and scholars in the Church.

Racist Culture and Catholic Theological Education

There are so many repugnant aspects of racism, but none more daunting, more infuriating, more dispiriting than its pervasive ordinariness. In the United States, living flesh and blood children, women, and men live out their daily lives within a context structured by racism. The most mundane activities—grocery shopping, banking, registering for school, inquiring about church membership, riding public transportation, hailing a taxicab—pulse with negative charges. This pervasive ordinariness can twist and distort the very meaning of generous and compassionate human living. Indeed, racism (and sexism) is not a mere problem to be solved, rather it is a way in which we in the United States define our reality, live the most intimate moments of our lives. Racism (and sexism) is not something *out-there* for us to solve or fix, rather it is *in us*, sedimented in our consciousness. Thus, Frantz Fanon's chilling indictment: "The racist in a culture with racism is . . . normal."[14] Catholic theology is practiced in this racist culture and Catholic theological education takes place within it. What does it mean to speak about *culture as racist* or *racist culture*? How are we to account for the emergence, transformation, extension of culture as racist?

[12] B. Lonergan, *Doctrinal Pluralism* (Milwaukee: Marquette University Press, 1971); idem, *Method in Theology* (New York: Herder and Herder, 1972), 363, 271.

[13] When Pope Paul VI presided over the final session of the Second Vatican Council in 1965, the assembled cardinals and bishops represented and presented, for, perhaps, the first time, a world Church. In 1919, the Roman Catholic Church had no bishops of non-European origin, except for the four men belonging to the Indian hierarchy created by Leo XIII in 1896. Both Pius XI and Pius XII were instrumental in widening the racial and cultural diversity of the hierarchy in the twentieth century. Development of the theological notion of "world church" has been the work of Jesuit theologian Karl Rahner. See his *Foundations of Christian Faith: An Introduction to the Idea of Christianity* (New York: Seabury, 1978), esp. 322-401.

[14] Frantz Fanon, "Racism and Culture," in *Toward the African Revolution, Political Essays,* trans. Haakon Chevalier (New York: Grove, 1969), 40; idem, *Black Skins, White Masks* (New York: Grove, 1967).

Culture is a dynamic activity of critical imagination, understanding, judgment, and mediation. Culture is a set of meanings and values that inform a way of life. These meanings and values are expressed in art, language, symbols, ideas, attitudes, and orientations. Concretely presented in the institutions, roles, tasks, operations, and cooperations of the social order, these meanings have cognitive, effective, constitutive, and communicative functions. Thus, racist culture includes:

> ideas, attitudes, and dispositions, norms and rules, linguistic, literary, and artistic expressions, architectural forms and media representations, practices and institutions. These cultural expressions and objects embed meanings and values that frame articulations, undertakings, and projects, that constitute a way of life. In this sense, a culture is both, and interrelatedly, a signifying system and system of material production.[15]

In a racist culture, definition and displacement, control and mastery, order and rule, violence and power obtain. To state that a racist culture "consists in knowing and doing" is to insinuate the thorough-going ideological character of that culture.[16]

In a racist culture, each and every human person is racially apprehended, conceived, judged, and manipulated. Each and every human person is reduced to biological physiognomy. The implications of innocuous physical traits—skin color, hair texture, shape of body, head, facial features, blood traits—are identified, exaggerated, ordered, and evaluated. On this basis, each woman and man is assigned a racial designation that structures her or his relations to other women and men of the same and of different races. In this set up, one racial group is contrived as "the measure of human being," one racial group is deemed normative. For, meanings and values have been embedded in those differences so as to favor or advantage that group which has been conceived as "the measure of human being." So, virtue, morality, and goodness are assigned to that racial group, while vice, immorality, and evil are assigned to others. Entitlement, power, and privilege are accorded that racial group, while dispossession, powerlessness, and disadvantage define others. Finally, in a racist culture or a culture based on racial privilege and preference, racial differences are rendered absolute "by generalizing from them and claiming that they are final."[17] If the difference is totalized, if it "penetrates the flesh, the blood and the genes of the victim. . . . it is transformed into fate, destiny, heredity."[18] And once the difference is transformed

---

[15] David Theo Goldberg, *Racist Culture: Philosophy and the Politics of Meaning* (Oxford: Blackwell, 1993), 8; also see Thomas F. Gossett, *Race: The History of an Idea in America* (New York: Schocken, 1965).

[16] Ibid.

[17] Albert Memi, *Dominated Man* (Boston: Beacon, 1968), 185; see also idem, *Colonizer and the Colonized* (Boston: Beacon, 1967).

[18] Ibid., 189.

into fate or destiny or heredity, then that absolutized difference is *naturalized*. Now it encompasses not merely each individual person, each lone human subject, but all persons like her or him. Whatever the difference, it is made to penetrate profoundly and collectively; it is final, complete, inescapable.

Racist culture or culture founded on racial privilege is *biased* culture. Certainly, Bernard Lonergan captured the pathos and the poignancy of our enmeshment in a culture deformed by racist practices and privilege when he posed these questions:

> How . . . is a mind to become conscious of its own bias when that bias springs from a communal flight from understanding and is supported by the whole texture of a civilization? How can new strength and vigour be imparted to the detached and disinterested desire to understand without the reinforcement acting as an added bias?[19]

Lonergan gives the term bias a very technical and specific denotation. In this way, he distinguishes it from a common sense notion of bias as attachment to a particular preference or an inclination of temperament. In Lonergan's account, bias is the more or less conscious and deliberate choice, in the face of what we perceive to be a potential threat to our well-being, to exclude further information or data from consideration in our understanding, judgment, reflection, and decision. All human beings are susceptible to bias which distorts and inhibits our conscious performance in everyday living by blinding our understanding. Lonergan distinguishes four principal manners in which this distortion may occur—*dramatic, individual, group*, and *general bias*.

Dramatic bias takes the form of the denial of affect in the day-to-day living out of our lives. It reveals itself not only in a refusal to understand, but in a refusal to behave and grow emotionally in healthy and life-giving ways. Dramatic bias projects into our imaginations an idealized picture of ourselves. When we come to make decisions, we are enticed to eliminate from consideration any affect that is at odds with that idealized picture. But attentiveness to our feelings is important. If we deny that we feel resentment or anger or fear, that we feel used or exploited, that we feel disappointed in a parent or spouse or child or friend, we are repressing feelings that we feel. For most of us this has a most threatening quality. To deny them is to "make our story more of a lie than a symbol of the ongoing negotiation of our lives."[20] Dramatic bias thrives in a racist culture. Members of the dominant or privileged racial group are given permission to project their personal inadequacies on members of the dominated or non-privileged racial group(s). These women and men harm not only themselves by blunting the invitation to self-transcendence, but they cause incalculable suffering to those whom they domi-

---

[19] B. Lonergan, *Insight*, xiv. For a fuller discussion of bias, its settings, and consequences, see chaps. 6 and 7.

[20] Nancy C. Ring, "Sin and Transformation From a Systematic Perspective," *Chicago Studies* 23 (1984): 303-19.

nate. The oppressed too are unable to face and incorporate personal inadequacies into their daily living; they are beset with internalized self-doubt and self-hatred.

Individual bias is conscious distortion in development not only of the individual's intelligence, but of her or his affective and experiential orientation as well. In a racist society, individual bias manifests itself in selfish pursuit of personal desires at the expense of human relationships and social co-operations, at the expense of the common human good of culture and society. When we yield to the temptation of individual bias, we refuse opportunities to meet others who are "different" from us, to engage with them, and to open ourselves to them. When we yield to the temptation of individual bias, we repudiate the intersubjectivity that is a basic component of our humanity, for affective and cognitive development occurs only within an intersubjectivity.[21] When we yield to the temptation of individual bias, we wind up with a set of distorted experiences which become the foundation for distorted understandings of other women and men and their cultures.

Although individual bias is potentially operative in any society, the distortions that result in political, economic, and technological patterns or configurations in that society cannot be attributed to individual bias alone. In a racist culture *group bias* finds particular expression in ethnocentrism and racial conflict. Group bias sacrifices intelligent, responsible discernment, and action to the vicious pursuit of the interests of the dominant racial group and stifles and represses the insights that include the experiences of other racial groups. Members of the dominant group reject authentic forms of solidarity with the pain and suffering of marginalized peoples. Thus, they withdraw from sensitive and experiential contact with the dominated or nonprivileged members of society. Their biased decisions and actions are enforced not only through legislation and custom, but also through police control. In this situation, marginalized racial groups irrupt in bitterness, in frustration, in civil disobedience, and in rebellion. In this situation, the course of authentic human and social development is derailed. The conditions for generating new intelligent insights and taking practical, responsible, healing, and creating action to meet and reverse the deteriorating decline in society are precluded.

Finally, there is the *general bias of common sense* by which common sense considers itself omnicompetent or sufficiently adequate in all situations. Because through self-correction common sense masters several situations, it assumes that it can pass judgment on all matters, whether theoretical or philosophical or scientific. This form of bias plays a distinctive role in constricting and distorting insights in a racist culture for the practical, intelligent, and imaginative ordering of the good in that culture. The general bias of common sense restricts intelligence to the immediate and the short-term, while ignoring the long-term consequences of such patchwork or ad hoc measures. The general bias of common sense focuses on short-term practicality; its preoccu-

[21] Ibid., 311.

pation is whatever is immediately realizable with whatever means are immediately at hand. When the general bias of common sense conspires with group bias, it accounts for the tendencies of dominant or privileged groups to exclude from their consideration any fresh and fruitful ideas that come from so-called less influential or nonprivileged groups and to distort the good ideas of these groups by selfish and expedient compromise.

What is the stance and practice of theological education when the very task of education is situated within a racist culture? In a racist culture, Catholic theological education must take on, at least, the *responsibilities of resistance and engagement*. To resist racist culture, Catholic theological education must vigorously contest and dispute any and all exclusionary values, criteria, and practices.[22] At the same time, Catholic theological education is challenged to engagement, to articulate new values, new criteria, new practices.

To resist the powerful racism that has shaped our concrete vital living and our notion of culture in the United States, we Catholic theological educators must take race and racism seriously. To take race and racism seriously is to reject liberal modernity's reduction of race to a morally irrelevant category and of racism to the personal prejudices of individuals. This entails a repudiation of liberal modernity's consideration of the use of racist epithets and racist discourse merely "as irrational appeals to irrelevant categories, to distinctions that delimit universal liberal ideals" or rights. Taking race and racism seriously means to expose liberal modernity's racialized history and its accompanying histories of racist exclusions and brutalities which are concealed beneath self-promoting new master narratives.[23]

To resist racism, we Catholic theological educators must provide a critical account of the Western notion of culture and its hegemonic collusion with racism. This suggests careful, thoughtful attention to an understanding of culture and the relation of theology to it. Bernard Lonergan's discussion of the transition from a classicist world view to historical-mindedness can serve as a heuristic.[24] From the classicist world view, there is only one culture, and it is both universal and permanent. Culture is apprehended as something static and ahistorical to be encapsulated in the ideal, and the immutable. This understanding of culture is rooted in appropriation and mediation of the culture of ancient Greece. Yet, it is one thing to emulate Greek excellences and another thing to set up culture on classicist terms. A classicist notion of culture fails to emulate the Greeks truly insofar as it stops up the very source of wonder and creativity by which the Greeks had founded and nourished philosophy, science, and the arts. Wittingly or unwittingly, the classicist notion of culture simultaneously exalts and truncates the Greek mediation of mean-

---

[22] Goldberg, *Racist Culture*, 224-37.

[23] Ibid., see also Cornel West, *The American Evasion of Philosophy: A Genealogy of Pragmatism* (Madison: University of Wisconsin Press, 1989), esp. 92-93.

[24] B. Lonergan, "The Transition from a Classicist World-View to Historical-Mindedness," *A Second Collection: Papers by Bernard J. F. Lonergan*, ed. William F. J. Ryan and Bernard J. Tyrrell (Philadelphia: Westminster, 1974), 1-9; and *Method in Theology*, xi, 124, 301.

ing by failing to get beyond the logical ideal of science and by *canonizing* what is only relatively good and true in a kind of ahistorical orthodoxy or dogmatism.

To resist the powerful racism that has shaped our notion of culture in the United States, we Catholic theological educators must open ourselves to other cultures, to different cultures within the United States.[25] Certainly, in a historical and social matrix dominated by racism, genuine openness to other and different cultures is never easy. On the one hand, we need to be wary of superficial approaches to those cultures. For, we can find ourselves enthralled with the new, the different, the exotic—simply because it is new, different, and exotic. Then it is easy to slip into a relativism that shifts position, not to gain perspective, but to gain powerful and relative distance. From that distance, we can move on to seek out the next novelty, the next people, and the next culture. We find that our attention is easily distracted, our understandings cursory, our judgments perfunctory, and our criticisms facile. Too often, with little or no historical understanding, we simply *imitate* values, norms, institutions, and practices that are constitutive and communicative of a particular culture (e.g., inauthentically appropriating Native American sweat lodges or drums or the sacred pipe). Lacking critical authentic understanding, we fail to recognize that such inclusion, often, is sheer tokenism and arrogance. Lacking authentic judgment, we omit criteria crucial in grasping the internal coherence and relation of practices or values one to another. Lacking authentic commitment to the "hard" habitual work of the daily living and of incarnating a culture, we have little appreciation for the particular demands of sustaining those meanings, values, norms, institutions, and practices.

On the other hand, we cannot simply retreat from the challenges of engaging other and different cultures, simply because such engagement is difficult and fraught with negative possibilities. Rather, we must risk, not only that engagement, but the change and the conversion which it may bring about. Resisting racism will bring about change in us: change in our attentiveness, in our questions, in our reflection, in our judgments, in our decisions, in our choices, in our living, and in our loving.

African American Culture and Catholic Theological Education

If Catholic theology is to continue to root itself in African American culture, we Catholic theological educators must teach differently. If we are to teach African American women and men, we must learn something of African American culture and the persons who embody it. We must learn something of African American familial, relational, aesthetic, and intellectual traditions; something of African American ideas and beliefs, expressive symbols, and value patterns; something of African American cultural practices and institutions. But, our learning is made difficult by the racism that so

[25] See William Cenkner, ed., *The Multicultural Church: A New Landscape in U.S. Theologies* (Mahwah, N.J.: Paulist, 1996).

enervates our perceptions, our understanding, our judgment, our decisions, and our living.

Indeed, African American culture is a disputed and contested notion.[26] African Americans and non-African Americans have internalized four basic judgments regarding the very notion of African American culture: (1) that African American culture does not exist; (2) that if African American culture does exist, it is pathological; (3) that African American culture does exist, but it is a deprived or aberrant culture; and (4) that African American culture does exist and is different.[27] The first three judgments stem from biased intelligence and a classicist world view. The fourth judgment opens us to cultural diversity and its possibilities. For nearly two decades now, African American Catholic psychologist Dr. Edwin C. Nichols has been conducting research exploring differences in value, cognition, and behavior generated by cultural differences. His work provides a heuristic with which we may approach an analysis of cultural difference.

Nichols's research contends that human persons of different cultures determine, assign, and affirm or disaffirm values differently (axiology); accord different weights to discrete moments in the cognitional process (epistemology and logic); and utilize, implement, and construct what they learn and know differently (process). Nichols works out an "ideal typology" (see Figure 1 below) that locates differences in group tendencies and orientations between European and Celtic, Anglo, European Americans (C/A/E Americans) and African and African Americans (Afr-Americans).[28] Of course, Nichols

---

[26] The notion that the enslaved Africans had "no culture" dominated Western culture from the late sixteenth century through the aftermath of the Civil War, while the notion that African Americans had a "pathological culture" held sway from the American Reconstruction through most of the early twentieth century. Along with Carter G. Woodson, anthropologist Melville J. Herskovits was one of the foremost proponents of the notion that African cultures, indeed, did exist and that remnants of those cultures were retained by the enslaved peoples in the creation of African-American culture. Herskovits's *The Myth of the Negro Past* (Boston: Beacon Press, 1958) ignited a controversy that continues. The foremost opponent of Herskovits's was sociologist E. Franklin Frazier, *The Negro Church in America* (New York: Schocken, 1964). See Carter G. Woodson, *The African Background Outlined* (New York: Negro University Press, 1968); Joseph E. Holloway, ed., *Africanisms in American Culture* (Bloomington and Indianapolis, Ind.: Indiana University Press, 1990); Sterling Stuckey, *Slave Culture: Nationalist Theory and the Foundations of Black America* (New York: Oxford University Press, 1987), esp., 3-97; and Sidney W. Mintz and Richard Price, *The Birth of African American Culture: An Anthropological Perspective* (Boston: Beacon, 1992).

[27] For an excellent discussion of African American culture as a source for black Catholic theology, see Jamie T. Phelps, O.P., "African American Culture: Source and Context of Black Catholic Theology and Mission," *Journal of Hispanic/Latino Theology* 3 (February 1996):43-58. I am grateful for the many telephone conversations Dr. Phelps and I have had about issues of race and culture over the past several years. Her insights and challenges have, on more than one occasion, provoked me to further reading, study, and questions. See also Yehudi O. Webster, *The Racialization of America* (New York: St. Martin's, 1992).

[28] Edwin Nichols, "The Philosophical Aspects of Cultural Difference," paper given at meeting of the World Psychiatric Association and Association of Psychiatrists, University of Ibadan, Nigeria, 10 November 1976, typescript. This outline compares Europeans and European Americans, Africans and African Americans, and Asians and Asian Americans. For the purposes here, I focus only on the differences between Celtic, Anglo European Americans and African Ameri-

makes clear that although these are group tendencies and orientations, individual flesh and blood children, women, and men within the same cultural group may exhibit differing behaviors.

Figure 1

The Philosophical Aspects of Cultural Difference				
Ethnic Groups	Axiology	Epistemology	Logic	Process
C/A/E Americans	Man-Object	Cognitive	Dichotomous	Technology
Afr-Americans	Man-Man	Affective	Diunital	Ntuology

As a first cultural difference, Nichols suggests that Celtic, Anglo, European Americans accord the highest *value* to objects or to the acquisition of objects. This implies not only a valuing of particular concrete objects or things, but a value orientation toward materiality, toward possession or striving for possession. Nichols finds, in contrast, that African Americans accord the highest value to interpersonal relationships. This implies not only a valuing of forming, honoring, and maintaining personal relationships, but a value commitment toward persons and relationships with them. Thus, African Americans reject isolationism and rugged individualism. Rather, they apprehend the individual person as person-in-community, rather than as individual striving over against community.

A second cultural difference concerns *epistemology*. Here, I want to situate Nichols's hypothesis in relation to the much more fundamental concern for the way in which the human mind knows. It will come as no surprise to some readers that I agree with Lonergan's basic proposals regarding human cognition. On Lonergan's account human knowing involves numerous distinct and irreducible activities: seeing, hearing, touching, smelling, tasting, inquiring, imagining, understanding, conceiving, reflecting, marshaling, and weighing the evidence; judging, deliberating, evaluating, and deciding. No single activity may be termed human knowing; rather, human knowing is a dynamic self-assembling and self-constituting structure. Sensible presentations stimulate inquiry, and inquiry is intelligence in action; it leads from experience through imagination to insight and from insight to concepts. Concepts call

cans. In addition, I have been the beneficiary of several informative conversations with Dr. Nichols on this issue.

For some useful discussions of implications of cultural difference on identity formation of blacks and whites, see John L. Hodge, et al., *Cultural Bases of Racism and Group Oppression: An Examination of Traditional "Western" Concepts, Values and Institutional Structures which Support Racism, Sexism, and Elitism* (Berkeley, Calif.: Two Riders, 1975); Benjamin P. Bowser and Raymond G. Hunt, eds., *Impacts of Racism on White Americans* (Beverly Hills, Calif.: Sage, 1981); J. Helms, *Black and White Racial Identity: Theory, Research, and Practice* (Westport, Conn.: Greenwood, 1989); W. Cross, *Shades of Black: Diversity in African-American Identity* (Philadelphia: Temple University Press, 1991).

forth reflection, and reflection is the requisite of rationality; it marshals and weighs the evidence, arrives either at judgment or doubt, and doubting renews the inquiry.[29]

Nichols's research indicates that Celtic, Anglo, European Americans approach and process knowing through counting and measuring, while African Americans approach and process knowing through symbolic imagery and rhythm. This hypothesis does not counter Lonergan's analysis of human knowing for, in fact, Lonergan's analysis of human cognition is just that—a transcultural analysis of *human* cognition. *There is, then, in the strict sense of the word, only human mind: there is neither a Celtic, Anglo, European American mind, nor an African American mind.* However, a correlation of Nichols's research with Lonergan's account of cognition indicates how data of sense are primary for Celtic, Anglo, European Americans in their process of knowing, while the imaginal, the symbolic, the rhythmic are primary for African Americans in their process of knowing. Unconsciously Celtic, Anglo, European Americans may be drawn to forms of empiricism and conceptualism, while unconsciously African Americans may be attracted to forms of intuitionism and idealism.

A third cultural difference highlighted in Nichols's account stems from the ways in which Celtic, Anglo, European Americans and African Americans express *logic*. Celtic, Anglo, European American culture fosters a notion of logic as dichotomous—"x" is *either* this *or* that. African American culture encourages a notion of logic as diunital—"x" is *both* this *and* that. Consider the following list of common adjectival dichotomies: good or bad, right or wrong, pure or impure, moral or immoral, truth or falsehood. When applied descriptively or connotatively or denotatively to *certain* premises, principles, objects, or actions, most would agree that these terms can only be exclusively determinate and dichotomous. At the same time, dichotomous logic's practice of exclusion may pattern human beings not only to rigidity and intolerance, but also to bias and dualistic thinking.

Dualism splits the world in two absolutely opposite and mutually hostile principles. It presupposes that what is not good is bad or evil, what is not true is patently false or a lie, what is not rational is nonrational or irrational. It is not difficult to grasp how dichotomous logic separates, isolates, segregates, closes off, and dissociates. Dualistic thinking splits reality into pairs of opposite parts, valuing one and disvaluing the other. What is valued is to be promoted and protected, what is disvalued is to be suppressed and destroyed. Insofar as dualistic thinking has become a mark of Western enlightened logic, then reason is valued over emotion, knowledge over opinion, science over religion, secular over sacred, the objective over the subjective, mind over body, male over female, private over public, divine over human, and so on.

To say that African Americans express logic in the union of opposites is to suggest that descriptive or connotative or denotative terms may exhibit so-

---

[29] B. Lonergan, "Cognitional Structure," *Collection*, 233. For a thorough presentation of Lonergan's account of human knowing see *Insight*.

called contradictory tendencies, yet, at the same time, those contradictory tendencies may be brought into unity. So, for example, African American culture's
expression of diunital logic approaches these tendencies, indeed the universe,
as complementary, interdependent pairs and quite necessary to one another.
Thus, African American culture not only tolerates ambiguity, but revels in it;
not only conjoins sacred and secular, but refuses to alienate them; not only
integrates knowing and doing, but contests such disconnection.

As a fourth cultural difference, Nichols identifies differences in *process*
between Celtic, Anglo, European Americans, and African Americans. I would
contend that the notion of process here is less a distinct category than a way
of expressing a world view. So to consider differences in process is to consider not only how Celtic, Anglo, European Americans and African Americans utilize, implement, and construct what they know and value, but also
how Celtic, Anglo, European Americans and African Americans incarnate what
they know and value. Process can be called the "determining mode" or basic
orientation of a culture, its people, and their world view. Thus, the "determining mode" or basic orientation of Celtic, Anglo, European American culture, its people and their world view is technological; the "determining mode"
or basic orientation of African American culture, its peoples, and their world
view is harmonious.[30]

If the basic orientation of the human person is directed toward objects or
the acquisition of objects, toward count-measure rationality, toward dichotomous and dualistic thinking and deciding, then the basic cultural orientation
is realized most fully through technological process and world view. Moreover, this process and world view focus on materiality, on the observable, on
the repetition, reproduction, and interchangeability of experiences, actions,
and things. The keenest projection of the technological world view is the
factory and its assembly line—even the global factory and its fragmented geo-
graphic diffusion of the assembly line.[31] In this world view, materiality and
dichotomy in production and in product as well as the empirical, the repeti-
tive, and the interchangeable assert control.

The term ntuology, which Nichols uses to refer to the process or basic

[30] Dona Richards, "The Implications of African-American Spirituality," *African Culture: The
Rhythms of Unity*, ed. Molefi Kete Asante and Kariamu Welsh Asante (Trenton, N.J.: Africa World,
1990), 211.

[31] Richard J. Barnet, *The Lean Years: Politics in the Age of Scarcity* (New York: Simon and
Schuster, 1980), 245. For some discussions of the impress of the factory on life in the United
States, see Richard J. Barnet and Ronald E. Müller, *Global Reach, The Power of the Multinational
Corporation* (New York: Simon Schuster, 1974); Daniel Bell, *The Coming of the Post-Industrial Soci-
ety* (New York: Basic Books, 1973), esp. 129-42. For some treatments of the history of technology
and its effect on human life, see Richard W. Fox and T. J. Lears, eds., *The Culture of Consumption:
Critical Essays in American History, 1880-1990* (New York: Pantheon, 1983); Thomas Hughes,
American Genesis: A Century of Invention and Technological Enthusiasm (New York: Viking, 1989);
John M. Staudenmaier, S.J., "The Politics of Successful Technologies," in *Context: History and the
History of Technology*, eds. Stephen Cutcliffe and Robert Post (Bethlehem, Pa.: Lehigh University
Press, 1989), 150-71; Langdon Wimmer, *Autonomous Technology: Technics-Out-of Control as a Theme
in Political Thought* (Cambridge, Mass.: MIT Press, 1977).

orientation of African American culture, is derived from the West African Bantu word NTU. Janheinz Jahn has made a study of the West African world view which is indispensable in understanding the meanings and import of NTU.[32] NTU is the first principle of African ontology and world order. That is to say, NTU is the first principle of African being and being African, of African making sense of and ordering the world and reality.[33] NTU is the principle of essential coherence and compatibility, of harmony among all things, even among those things that appear contradictory to one another. Yet, NTU is not to be confused with some power of absolute alignment or hegemonic violation of the integrity of what is disparate or contrary. Nor is NTU independent of the four categories *Muntu, Kintu, Hantu,* and *Kuntu.*[34] Rather, NTU is at once the dynamic manifestation of God as Being, human being, things, time-and-space, and modality. Jahn asserts: "NTU is what Muntu, Kintu, Hantu, and Kuntu all equally *are.* Force and matter are not being united in this conception; on the contrary, they have never been apart."[35]

If the basic orientation of the human person is directed toward human relationships, toward imaginal, symbolic, diunital, and associative thinking, then basic cultural orientation is realized most fully through ntuological process or world view. Moreover, this world view focuses on spirituality and spirit, on the fundamental and indissoluble unity of all life forces and their manifestations, on the numinous and the vital, and on change. The most obvious expression of the ntuological world view is found in African American worship. Here the spontaneous, the charismatic, and the unseen irrupt. Here saints and sinners sing and shout, and men and women yield to visitations of the Spirit. Here place and time are reconfigured by mystical ecstatic communion with the Spirit. Here the restless rhythms of blues and the moans and chants of the enslaved, gospel songs, jazz, and soul music weave healing and creating for life.

These differences between Celtic, Anglo, European American and Afri-

---

[32] Janheinz Jahn, *Muntu: African Culture and the Western World,* trans. Marjorie Grene (New York: Grove, 1990), esp. chap. 4. Jahn's analysis relies on the work of several African scholars including Alexis Kagame and Adebayo Adesanya, as well as French ethnologist Marcel Griaule's sustained interview with the Dogon sage Ogotemmeli. See Griaule, *Conversations with Ogotemmeli, An Introduction to Dogon Religious Ideas* (Oxford: African International Institute and Oxford University Press, 1965).

[33] The second principle is *Nommo.* Jahn writes: "The driving power ... that gives life and efficacy to all things is *Nommo,* the 'word,' ... which ... is word and water and seed and blood in one," *Muntu,* 101.

[34] Briefly: *Muntu* refers to human beings and to forces which are endowed with intelligence and integral agency (whether living, dead, orisha, or the Supreme Deity); the category *Kintu* is comprised of plants, animals, minerals, tools, etc.; the category *Hantu* embraces place and time; and *Kuntu* refers to the presence of a modal force, yet independent of its mediation (e.g., consider laughter—its timbre, infectious character, insinuation, but without the embodied woman or man laughing; or consider beauty—its force such that occurrences change themselves in its presence). See Jahn, *Muntu,* 99-104.

[35] Ibid., 101.

can American cultures are neither determinative, nor exhaustive of an individual man's or woman's personality or spirituality, decisions or choices; rather, they are suggestive of tendencies within cultures or cultural groups. Yet, these differences can provoke instances for shared learning and behavioral adaptation and change for Celtic, Anglo, European Americans, and African Americans. Consideration of cultural differences can be useful to criticisms of modernity and its grip on Celtic, Anglo, European American culture(s) and on life in the United States. For one thing, this analysis can uncover dispositions or tendencies or characteristics within Celtic, Anglo, European American culture(s) that are patient of or symbiotic with certain aspects of modernity. For instance, when the tendencies of modernity combine with the enforcement of the privileged use of binary oppositional logic, we find ourselves "habituated" to treating difference in derisive and negative ways.[36] We are habituated to racism: racist practices are encouraged and supported in this environment, and difference and change are feared and suspect. Another feature of this analysis is that it provokes questions about bias and responsibility with respect to our relation to modernity. After all, modernity is not some entity that exists apart from human experiences, understandings, judgments, and decisions—no matter how flawed. If the mass culture modernity generates leaves us "glutted by sensate gratification, ordered by benevolent governors," and renders us mere "creatures who have exchanged spiritual freedom and moral responsibility for economic and psychic security," then we must face up to instances of intellectual, religious, and moral deformation within our culture(s).[37]

Admitting, understanding, and grappling with these aspects of cultural difference is important for Catholic theological education, if Catholic theological educators are to teach African American students adequately and generously. *First,* if African American culture places value on interpersonal relationships, then we may need to revise our teaching styles to acknowledge this priority. The cultural situation of these students would call us to more human and personal engagement, more face-to-face and one-to-one encounter and conversation. Even in large lecture situations, regular meetings with individual students for conversation can go a long way toward meeting their needs. This will also mean a revision of our ideas about efficiency, for meeting student needs and helping them to become better theologians may be a very inefficient task vis-à-vis our ideas about how we use our time. This will have further implications for advising our African American students. As their teachers, perhaps, we will need to ask them more questions about themselves and their families, to understand and appreciate their culture's expres-

[36] My thanks to Dr. Christine Firer Hinze for the word "habituates" in this context. Our "corridor conversations" are stimulating opportunities for us to think together and aloud about some of these issues.

[37] T. J. Jackson Lears, *No Place of Grace* (New York: Pantheon, 1981), 300; see also James H. Evans, Jr., "African-American Christianity and the Postmodern Condition," *Journal of the American Academy of Religion* 58 (1990): 207-22.

sions in music and art, literature and theater, film and dance. And most importantly, as their teachers we will need to invite them to deeper intellectual engagement with theology. The next generation of African American Catholic theologians depends, in no small measure, on our willingness to invite African American Catholic students to theological study, to support their work in the wide range of the field, to nurture, challenge, and encourage them. Since our African American Catholic students are integral to the future of Catholic theology, especially in the United States, we must take them seriously, teach them rigorously, engage their questions thoughtfully and generously; we must love so as to demand and foster, to midwife their coming to theological speech.

Second, if it is the case that in cognition African Americans accord greater import to metaphor and symbolism, then Catholic theological educators will need to utilize a variety of media and styles in teaching so that African American students make the best use of this cognitive strength. At the same time, African American culture's preference for metaphor and symbolism ought to alert us to the potential of African American students to exploit metaphor and symbolism as theological categories and style. And, because symbol and metaphor ineluctably raise questions of metaphysics, we will be aiding African American students in charting foundational ground in theologizing the black experience.

Third, if Catholic theological educators seriously admit a multiplicity of cultures, if they take seriously the characteristics or orientations of African American culture, if they take the black human condition in the United States seriously, then they will be forced to grapple with their own avoidance and internalization of racism, their own deep and blinding enmeshment in bias. They will be forced to reconsider the sources, presuppositions, and tasks of Catholic theology in the United States.

Fourth, as Catholic theological educators, we must teach our African American students in such a way that they flourish as whole human beings. To do this is to resist racism. This pedagogical praxis expresses *humanity's essential humanness—our own and theirs.* For, in truth, as Fanon so compassionately insisted, "racism is not a constant of the human spirit."[38] This resistance to racism is rooted in a Christian anthropology that acknowledges, confesses, and testifies that all human beings are "one in Christ Jesus." Moreover, this same anthropology acknowledges, confesses, and testifies that our unity is incomplete unless we honor the riches of our differences.

Fifth, we Catholic theological educators value our students as "whole" persons. In educating our African American students, we must express this valuing in concrete practical ways. We must enlist the aid of elementary and secondary schools as well as colleges. A fully thematized theology is an extraordinarily high achievement of critical intellectuality, deep faith, and humility; still, much rests on chance. In this instance, the realization of such

---

[38] Fanon, "Racism and Culture," 41.

achievement begins in the thorough elementary and secondary school preparation of young black Catholic women and men. It continues in their recruitment and retention in superior baccalaureate programs in Catholic colleges and universities that provide solid grounding in the humanities, especially, history, literature, philosophy, and languages (e.g., Latin, Hebrew, Greek, Spanish, German, French) along with wide exposure to the natural and social sciences. Without such strenuous remote preparation, the participation of African American Catholic students in post-baccalaureate and doctoral study in theology is exceedingly difficult. Without our respect, regard, and support, their potential to make a contribution to Catholic theology is well nigh impossible.

The Irruption of Black Theology and Catholic Theological Education

As an exercise in Christian theology, black theology strives to discern, to understand, to interpret, and to impart the word of God and its meaning in various cultural and social contexts. However, black theology explicitly addresses the historical, cultural, and structural subordination of black peoples within social contexts dominated by white supremacist rule. Black theology explicitly contests the "heretical" use of the Hebrew and Christian Scriptures, Christian doctrine, and theology to justify that subordination. So, while it breaks with forms of Christian theology which overlook the particularities of historical social context and social praxis, black theology does not tear up its deep-rooted response to Christian revelation. Through critical biblical and doctrinal interpretation, black theology has retrieved the liberating dimensions of key Christian beliefs—God's abiding, compassionate, and profound love of black humanity; God's freeing and healing activity in history on behalf of the poor, oppressed women and men, the "wretched of the earth"; the intimate connection between divine reality and the historical struggles of suffering women and men against the powers and principalities of domination; the radical social character of Christian worship, work, and witness.

Although innovative, black theology has had a long period of incubation. Its hermeneutical antecedents can be located in powerful biblically rooted critiques of chattel slavery and Christianity's complicity with it by such advocates as David Walker, Henry Highland Garnet, Daniel Payne, Frederick Douglass, Maria Stewart, Sojourner Truth, and Anna Julia Cooper; in emancipatory antecedents in stalwart, even armed, resistance to racist assault by such activists as Denmark Vesey, Gabriel Prosser, and Nat Turner. The contemporary liberative provocation for black theology derives from a tensive encounter between (1) the weariness of the modern civil rights movement and its praxis of suffering love; (2) the explosive rebellions of frustrated black children, women, and men living in decaying inner cities—rebellions that were met with armed police and (local, state, federal) government response; and (3) pastoral reception and interpretation of the notion of black power.[39] Psychologically, morally, religiously, intellectually, this encounter prepared the way for the appearance of James Cone's angry polemic, *Black Theology and Black Power*.[40]

Under Cone's creative intellectual leadership, theologians of the black theology movement have sustained within Protestant Christianity for nearly thirty years one of the more innovative and fertile endeavors in North American Christian thought.[41] African American scholars not only provide role models for African American theological students, but also engage in active and critical research on neglected fields (e.g., African Americans in American church history, the Bible and slavery, conversion narratives of ex-slaves) and on new fields (e.g., the relation of African Traditional Religions and practices to the Christianity of the enslaved peoples, the religious cosmology and practices of the enslaved peoples). The presence of African American women and men as scholars and students provides the context for the following contributions of black theology to Catholic theological education.

1. *New voices and faces in history*. Prior to the emergence of black theology American church historiography displayed an incidental and casual attitude toward the history of Christianity among black people. Too often, this history was reduced to a special topic or was deemed interesting only when some crisis arose or was set aside for black eyes only.[42] Since the late 1960s, there has been an explosion of research and publication that has accorded mainstream legitimacy to the study of the black experience. This research has increased knowledge of the religious life and experiences of the enslaved Africans, of styles and strategies of slave preachers, of the role of Christianity in maintaining and abolishing slavery, of the long neglected struggles and contributions of black women. This research coincides with shifts in the framing and asking, answering and understanding of historical questions, with the advance of social, oral, and peoples' history.

2. *Defining new areas of research*. Approximately thirty years ago, with the

---

[39] The term "black power" may have originated with Adam Clayton Powell, who in an address at Howard University on May 29, 1966, declared that "Human rights are God given . . . to demand these God-given rights is to seek black power, the power to build black institutions." Quoted in Floyd B. Barbaus, *The Black Power Revolt* (Boston: Beacon, 1968), 189; see also Nathan Wright, Jr., *Black Power and Urban Unrest: Creative Possibilities* (New York: Hawthorne, 1967), 2-3, 13; Stokely Carmichael and Charles V. Hamilton, *Black Power: The Politics of Liberation in America* (New York: Vintage, 1967).

[40] James Cone, *Black Theology and Black Power* (New York: Seabury, 1969).

[41] Here, I am thinking of the work of Randall Bailey, Katie G. Cannon, Will Coleman, George Cummings, Riggins Earl, Jr., James H. Evans, Jr., Jacquelyn Grant, Robert Hood, Dwight Hopkins, Charles H. Long, Clarice Martin, Peter Paris, Marcia Riggs, J. Deotis Roberts, Cheryl Sanders, Emilie Townes, James M. Washington, Renita Weems, Cornel West, Delores S. Williams, Preston N. Williams, Gayraud S. Wilmore. For a relatively comprehensive bibliography of global black theology, see James H. Evans, Jr., compl., *Black Theology: A Critical Assessment and Annotated Bibliography* (Westport, Conn.: Greenwood, 1987).

[42] Robert T. Handy, "Negro Christianity and American Church Historiography," in *Reinterpretation in American Church History* 5, *Essays in Divinity*, ed. J. C. Brauer (Chicago: University of Chicago Press, 1968), 91; see August Meier and Elliot Rudwick, *Black History and the Historical Profession, 1915-1980* (Urbana and Chicago: University of Illinois Press, 1986).

collapse of the structures of legal segregation, the first programs in Black Studies were initiated at white universities and colleges.[43] Black Studies set the trajectory for change in content and method in studies in history, literature, artistic definition and expression, as well as in philosophy and religion. Since understanding black culture and history is formative for its meditation of Christian faith, black theology is advanced by Black Studies. Research on "black" or "slave" religion has lead to significant studies in music, aesthetics, anthropology, and theology.[44]

Another crucial and controversial area of inquiry is the study of Africanisms, persistent, identifiable remnants of language, custom, ritual, meanings and practices that carried as well as blended meanings, practices, and values of the various ethnic-cultural groups from among whom the enslaved peoples came.[45]

3. *New theological resources and models.* Black theology has provided us with new resources and models for thinking about anthropology, suffering, sin, Christology, spirituality, and community. For example, black theology's interrogation of the doctrine of humanity (theological anthropology) has gone a long way in disengaging the blackness (i.e., as an accident of pigmentation) of women and men from negative metaphorical, symbolic, even ontological

---

[43] Manning Marable, *Beyond Black and White: Transforming African-American Politics* (London: Verso/New Left, 1995), 109-17.

[44] As black studies became increasingly recursive, it became increasingly African-centered, thus, precipitating a change in paradigm—*Afrocentrism*. Despite deeply controversial, conflictual, and polemical usage, most basically Afrocentrism may be defined as a point of departure for asking and answering questions that place "African ideals at the center of any analysis that involves African culture and behavior," Molefi Kete Asante, *The Afrocentric Idea* (Philadelphia: Temple University Press, 1987), 8, 6. A "critical Afrocentricism" does not romanticize or exaggerate Africa or Africans or Africanity. Or, put provocatively: The histories and cultures of the peoples of West Africa are neither identical nor duplicative of the histories and cultures of the peoples of Northeast Africa. To collapse or conflate the history and culture of ancient Egypt into the history and culture of Ghana or Nigeria or Benin or the Gambia is inaccurate.

[45] Some representative works include Joseph E. Holloway, ed., *Africanisms in American Culture*; Albert J. Raboteau, *Slave Religion: The "Invisible Institution" in the Antebellum South* (New York: Oxford University Press, 1978); Sterling Stuckey, *Slave Culture: Nationalist Theory and the Foundations of Black America* (New York: Oxford University Press, 1987), esp., 3-97; Gayl Jones, *Liberating Voices: Oral Tradition in African American Literature* (New York: Penguin, 1991); John W. Blassingame, *The Slave Community: Plantation Life in the Antebellum South* (New York: Oxford University Press, 1979); Sidney W. Mintz and Richard Price, *The Birth of African American Culture: An Anthropological Perspective* (Boston: Beacon, 1992); Charles H. Long, *Significations: Signs, Symbols, and Images in the Interpretation of Religion* (Philadelphia: Fortress, 1986); Michael S. Harper and Robert B. Steptoe, eds., *Chant of Saints: A Gathering of Afro-American Literature, Art, and Scholarship* (Urbana and Chicago: University of Illinois Press, 1979); Alain Locke, ed., *The New Negro: An Interpretation* (New York: Albert and Charles Boni, 1925); John Lovell, Jr., *Black Song: The Forge and the Flame: How the Afro-American Spiritual Was Hammered Out* (New York: Macmillan, 1972); Lawrence Levine, *Black Culture and Black Consciousness: Afro-American Folk Thought from Slavery to Freedom* (New York: Oxford University Press, 1977); Henry H. Mitchell, *Black Belief: Folk Beliefs of Blacks Black Culture and Black Consciousness: Afro-American Folk Thought from Slavery to Freedom* (New York: Oxford University Press, 1977); Henry H. Mitchell, *Black Belief: Folk Beliefs of Blacks in America and West Africa* (New York: Harper and Row, 1975); Theophus H. Smith, *Conjuring Culture: Biblical Formations of Black America* (New York: Oxford University Press, 1994).

attribution. In this way, black theology questions the ideologization of doctrine. A case in point would be black theology's perceived neglect of critical inquiry into the existence of God, its philosophical naiveté. However when this question is situated within the matrix of African American religious experience, which is characterized by a preference for an affirmation of divine existence, the inquiry shifts to divine action. Thus, black theology consciously brings to the fore the role of religious experience in theological reflection. Or, consider black theology's probe of evil and suffering which contests tendencies toward Christian passivity or masochistic surrender.

4. *New models for learning and teaching.* Black theology rejects the hegemony of positivist, conceptualist, idealist, and empiricist epistemological and pedagogical approaches. And while black theology engages a "subjugated knowledge," that knowledge is never simplistic or naive, even if it has been made to appear so. Neither is the epistemological standpoint of black theology so particular that it is incapable of universals, nor is it only or exclusively oppositional. Rather, the epistemological standpoint of black theology identifies and differentiates human experience as criterion for meaning and engages and reverences dialogue (especially communal dialogue) in assessing knowledge claims. The epistemological standpoint of black theology is rooted in an ethic of care and compassion that values each human person as a "unique expression of a common spirit, power, or energy inherent in all life," that bridges the poisonous separation of thought and feeling, that requires the development of authentic capacities for empathic understanding and praxis, and that entails personal accountability for knowledge.[46]

Black theology offers a model of learning and teaching that values theological education as a communal, self-consciously critical activity. Black theology proposes an engaged pedagogy that addresses and relates differentiated human experiences and theoretical or theological learning that joins theory and praxis. An engaged pedagogy, moreover, is one that complexifies rather than simplifies the classroom—understanding is a communal goal; conversation and debate are prized; collaboration is intentional; difference, whether philosophic, racial, or cultural is valued; whatever offers insight and guidance for truth is engaged. The classroom is a site for grappling with questions that intend critical, creative, and responsible living. It is also a site for personal and collective transformation or conversion.

What might it mean to teach black theology in a Catholic context? Here are some questions that I have found useful in preparing and organizing courses. While there are no easy answers, these musings might facilitate the reader's reflection: Can I teach black theology without undergoing some personal transformation? Can I teach black theology without nudging and prodding my students, black and white, women and men, toward transformation or conversion? What sort of change will that transformation or conversion compel? If my nudging and prodding is inflammatory, do I not unwittingly

[46] Patricia Hill Collins, *Black Feminist Thought: Knowledge, Consciousness, and the Politics of Empowerment* (Boston: Unwin Hyman, 1990), esp. 206-20.

reinforce my students' biases? Am I not loitering too close to the edge of the cave? Does this course on black theology furnish a student's sole curricular contact with black theologians and black scholars and thinkers? If so, I must ask if marginalization is 'passing' as specialization? How do I facilitate an invigorating and demanding intellectual and personal encounter with black theology, when a dominant racist culture belittles black mind and black intelligence? How can I encourage my students, black and white women and men, to value materials and questions that a dominant racist culture ridicules by omission and studied oversight?

By questioning our engagement in the pedagogical process, we can make explicit our desire to convey to our students that theology is not only something to be read, but something that they must learn to do, that theology is not merely one intellectual exercise among others. Rather, theology demands a profound engagement of faith, mind, heart, of self-disposition, and life-orientation. At the same time, we can make explicit our desire to encourage and support our students in the criticism of her or his own horizon or world view.

Conclusion

To reflect on the Catholic theological education of African American women and men is to take the religious and social experiences of the African American Catholic faith community as data for theologizing. To take these experiences as data for theology is to call for a new style of teaching and doing Catholic theology in the United States. This will mean opening Catholic theology to new questions and new demands, new sources and new directions. And this opening will place urgent demands on black Catholic theologians and Church scholars—sustained research and writing, contributions to our advance in doctrinal understanding and pastoral practice, and the development of a sound body of theological literature (doctrinal and dogmatic, moral and ethical, constructive and systematic, foundational and philosophical) that will emerge from authentically engaging the Tradition from the perspective of being black and Catholic. This also will entail pressing tasks of a different sort for Celtic, Anglo, European American theologians and scholars—analysis of the social set-up in the United States, critical attention and response to the ways in which racist theories and racist practices are embedded in the social order, and reflection on the ambivalent participation of the Catholic Church in the United States in maintaining and colluding with those biased theories and practices, especially insofar as contemporary interpretations and discussions of Catholic social teaching in the United States, generally, have ignored or given scant attention to the nation's egregious racism.

These are some of the challenges and tasks to be met if the theological education of African American Catholics is to come to fruition in authentic African American expressions of Catholic theology—if Catholic theology is to bloom in the United States with the riches of diversity and difference.

26

Catholic Theological Education and U.S. Hispanics

Roberto S. Goizueta

I t is by now a commonplace that the future of the Catholic Church in the United States will be closely linked to the future of the Hispanic community. Approximately one-third of all baptized Catholics in the United States are Hispanic. By the year 2000, this number will increase to approximately 40 percent. By 2010, a majority of the Catholics in the United States will be Spanish-speaking. Already, Hispanics constitute a majority in numerous dioceses throughout the country.

Yet this population has been largely ignored by Catholic educational institutions, from parochial schools to seminaries and universities. The same institutions which so effectively educated and trained millions of Catholic immigrants from Europe have failed this "second wave" of immigrants. Despite the fact, for instance, that approximately three-fourths of U.S. Hispanics are Catholic, about three-fourths of Hispanic seminarians are Protestant.[1] In other words, the number of Catholics to Protestants in the general Hispanic population is exactly the reverse of that in the seminary population. One of the most dispiriting lessons I have learned in my work in the Latino community over the past decade is that, with rare exceptions, the possibility of attending a Catholic educational institution—whether a parochial school, seminary, or college—does not even cross the minds of most Hispanic young persons and their parents. Such a possibility is perceived as not only impossible, but, indeed, unthinkable.

Thus, when considering the question of Latinos and Latinas in Catholic theological education, we must place the question in this larger context. To do so is to recognize the deep cultural roots of the crisis: having become comfortably "American," the U.S. Catholic Church finds itself unable to respond to a Latino Catholicism which, in many ways, represents all that English-

---

[1] Allan Figueroa Deck, "At the Crossroads: North American and Hispanic," *We Are A People! Initiatives in Hispanic American Theology*, ed. Robert S. Goizueta (Minneapolis: Fortress Press, 1992), 7n.

speaking Catholics have, for generations, been struggling to escape. From the "superstition" and "Mariolatry" of popular religion to the emotional "excesses" of the liturgies, Latino Catholicism represents a dangerous memory, the memory of a Church uneasy with the modern world and, thus, a hindrance to the full assimilation of English-speaking Catholics in the melting pot of modern U.S. culture.

Anglo-Catholics fear Latino Catholics. Conservatives who dream of returning to a premodern Church fear the possibility—indeed, the inevitability—of a multicultural Church. In turn, liberals who would promote a multicultural Church fear and suspect that the "immature" forms of Catholicism prevalent in other cultures, such as Latino culture, might imply a return to a premodern Church. Latino Catholics are, thus, caught on the horns of a peculiarly modern dilemma: seek the approval of conservatives, and cease being Latino; or seek the approval of liberals, and cease being Catholic (at least in a form recognizable to Hispanics). Latino Catholics thus represent a challenge to a U.S. Church polarized between liberals and conservatives. Having been marginalized by both, we instinctively recognize their fundamental similarity. What the liberal and conservative Catholics have in common is a modern, dichotomous world view; and what they find unacceptable in Latino Catholics is precisely their refusal to fit neatly into that world view.

In this essay, three of the modern anthropological and epistemological dichotomies (there are many) which militate against the full participation of U.S. Hispanics in Catholic seminaries and theology departments will be addressed: (1) the dichotomy between individual and community, (2) the dichotomy between spirit and matter, and (3) the dichotomy between intellect and affect. Together, these are the marks of the modern rational individual, someone unacceptable to Latinos and Latinas. I will focus on the impact that these cultural differences have on theological education and will make a few practical suggestions about how Catholic seminaries and theology departments might respond to the challenge represented by these differences.

The Problem

For U.S. Hispanics, the self is intrinsically social; that is, the person is not primarily the basis but the product of communal relationships. To be a human being is to exist in relationship. This affects our understanding of both the Christian faith and the educational process. Religious faith is based on the family, of which the Church is perceived as an extension. Consequently, faith is never a private matter of the individual conscience, but is always formed by and manifested in community. Neither is education a purely private enterprise of personal betterment or achievement. Latino students have a deep sense of responsibility to their families, who support their educational efforts, and to their friends in school, who comprise their new "family." These, in turn, accompany the individual student.

Rarely, for instance, will one find a Hispanic student studying on his or her own; almost always, Latinos and Latinas will study in groups. The same is true of Latino scholars and teachers. When possible, we prefer to work in collaborative projects, whether jointly authored works, edited collections of essays, or professional symposia. The Academy of Catholic Hispanic Theologians of the United States structures its annual meetings in such a way as to foster dialogue from within which creative, new ideas may emerge. Indeed, this collaborative process is called for by our very constitution and by-laws. Individual papers and ideas are not the end but the beginning of the discussion.

This communal, or relational world view is our inheritance from our indigenous American, African, and Iberian Catholic roots. If these various cultures that have come together to produce the Latin American mestizaje are different from each other, they nevertheless have this in common: each reflects a relational, organic view of the self. Therefore, our Catholicism is not simply the "free choice" of one set of religious beliefs over others, but the foundation of our identity as people. "The Spanish-American Roman Catholic Church," observes the Cuban-American Methodist theologian Justo González, "is part of the common background of all Hispanics—if not personally, then at least in our ancestry.[2]

This common background shared by all Latinos and Latinas is becoming increasingly threatened by an Anglo-Catholic Church that is often perceived as individualistic and, therefore, alienating. The Latino experience of worship as a common celebration, involving and affirming the bonds of family and community, too often finds little sustenance in the U.S. Church. It should then come as no surprise that Latinos and Latinas are increasingly attracted to Protestant Evangelical and Pentecostal groups which emphasize these bonds in their worship services, their communal life, and their welcoming outreach to new immigrants. Consequently, these Protestant communities are, in some ways, more instinctively familiar to Latino Catholics than is the Catholicism we encounter in most U.S. Catholic parishes.

For Latino Catholics, religion and faith are identified with our human relationships; it is in and through these relationships that we celebrate the gift of life. Our relationships are the source of and reason for our celebration, the miracle for which we give thanks. A privatized religious faith is no more conceivable than is an isolated, autonomous individual; these are perceived not as reasons for celebration but as reasons for mourning.

The Latino reaction to this individualism is poignantly illustrated in an anecdote recounted by Virgilio Elizondo. He tells of an elderly Mexican woman who, upon seeing the architectural renovations made in her church, became dejected. To make the church more liturgically "correct" all the statutes had been removed, save a lone crucifix behind the altar. Asked why she had become so sad when she entered the renovated church, the elderly woman re-

---

[2] Justo González, *Mañana: Christian Theology from a Hispanic Perspective* (Nashville: Abingdon Press, 1990), 55.

sponded, "I know that Jesus is the most important one in the church, but that doesn't mean he has to be alone."

Even Jesus is not an autonomous individual; hence the important role of Mary. If to know a person is to know his or her family, then to know Jesus is to know Mary and the rest of Jesus' "family," the communion of saints. The special place of Mary and the communion of saints in Latino popular Catholicism should thus come as no surprise; if each person's identity is constituted by the relationships and communities which have birthed and nurtured him or her, then it is impossible to know Jesus truly without also knowing his family, especially his mother.

Heir to the Iberian, pre-Tridentine Catholicism of the Spanish conquest, Latino popular Catholicism embodies and makes present, in the modern Western world, the organic world view of a pre-Tridentine Catholicism itself rooted in popular rituals and devotions. This world view is evident to anyone visiting medieval European churches. As one approaches and enters these churches, the stained-glass windows, the many statues, and even the cemeteries so often placed at the entrance to the church, remind us of the great, trans-generational community of saints which has given us birth. With their many statues placed in every niche and photographs of loved ones hung on the walls or pinned to crucifixes and statues, Latino churches and homes convey the same sense of a world (both natural and supernatural) constituted by relationships.

This world is, in many ways, alien to the Catholicism of the dominant culture of the United States. It is the world which English-speaking Catholics thought they had left behind as they entered the "melting pot," pulled themselves up by their bootstraps, and climbed the socioeconomic ladder. It is the world which was so alien to post-Enlightenment Protestantism and which, thus, impeded the assimilation of Catholics into the Protestant mainstream in the United States—unless the former were willing to shed their "medieval superstitions." As Allan Figueroa Deck has pointed out:

> Anglo American Catholicism is rooted in the experience of the eighteenth century English Catholic settlers of Maryland. These people were truly English. They were also Catholic, yet imbued with the culture of modernity that Great Britain disseminated through its legal system, burgeoning commerce and industry, and its relatively democratic ideology . . . Even when huge waves of working-class or peasant-class immigrants began to swell the ranks of the U.S. Catholic church, its Anglo American character remained . . . These Catholics struggled throughout the nineteenth century to achieve recognition and status in an overwhelmingly Protestant land. In several important ways these Catholics *did* become American. They assimilated.[3]

---

[3] Deck, "At the Crossroads," 4-5.

This might be one reason, suggests Deck, why Hispanic Catholics in the United States have often (ironically) experienced greater support from Rome than from the U.S. bishops:

> It is interesting to review today the Americanist controversy of the late nineteenth century in light of the growing literature on inculturation. From today's vantage point it seems that North American progressives like Isaac Hecker and Archbishop Ireland may not have had a sufficient grasp of the difference between certain U.S. cultural values (which they championed) and countercultural gospel values. Perhaps Rome's views of American culture were informed not only by self-interest and restorationism but also by a certain intuitive awareness of the non-evangelical aspects of some of our most touted North American values. Some of the concerns and issues of importance to U.S. Hispanics (such as respect for a more symbolic, intuitive, ritualistic, and corporative faith) may well be better understood in Rome than in the United States.[4]

Indeed, in his November 14, 1988, address to the U.S. bishops, the apostolic pronuncio Archbishop Pio Laghi pressed the U.S. Church to respond more effectively to the Hispanic presence. The Church, he insisted, must provide

> for [Hispanics] the same supportive ecclesial environment that nurtured the faith of earlier generations of Catholics of other ethnic and cultural origins—Irish, German, Italian, Polish and the rest ... our success in this regard will be measured to the extent that Hispanic Catholics truly feel welcome in our parishes and institutions ... Much effort in recent years has been directed to the acculturation of the Spanish-speaking in the church and in American society. Perhaps now we need to give more thought to the possibility of encouraging non-Hispanics to understand and appreciate the richness of Hispanic culture.[5]

A second major characteristic of Latino popular Catholicism is, as Deck indicates above, its fundamentally incarnational, sacramental character. Here again, English-speaking Catholics—whether liberal or conservative—often respond ambivalently to Hispanics, for our religiosity looks too much like the devotionalism, or "piety" which, for successfully assimilated Anglo-Catholics, conjures up images of their own marginalized past.

Whether explicitly religious or not, Latinos and Latinas perceive the human person and the world as spiritual-material realities; the spiritual and the

---

[4] Ibid., 11.

[5] Archbishop Pio Laghi, Apostolic Pronuncio to the United States, "Stemming the Outflow of Hispanic Catholics," *Origins* 18 (November 24, 1988): 387-88.

material are inseparable. Once more, this holistic, organic world view reflects our Iberian Catholic past as much as it does our indigenous American and African past. In Latino popular religion, this sacramental, or incarnational world view is most evident in the sensuous, symbolic character of our worship. A typical Latino liturgical celebration envelops the participant in a cacophony of sounds, images, colors, and scents. Whenever possible, the persons with whom one worships are not just looked at out of the corner of one's eye, but are given a heartfelt embrace; the statue of Mary or the crucifix are not just looked at prayerfully, but are touched, kissed, caressed, and embraced. To be in relationship with another is to be in physical contact with him or her, whether that person is a neighbor or Jesus.

This very physical, sensuous quality of Latino Catholicism can only be suspect to a dominant culture which, as a Latino priest recently told me, "is afraid of the Incarnation." Influenced by the Enlightenment's reduction of the person to his or her mind, and of human existence to logical thinking, modern Anglo-Catholicism is very different from this very tactile and sensuous form of worship, so often perceived as, at best, exotic and, at worst, immature and un-Christian. Prayer to a statue is perceived as a sign of immaturity, while prayer to an immaterial Concept—itself, of course, a human product—is perceived as a sign of maturity. The suspicion of idolatry in the first case is rarely, if ever, extended to the second.

This prejudice against a faith mediated by physicality and bodiliness is manifested, further, in a certain suspicion of feelings as mediators of the sacred—this, at least, is what Hispanics usually experience in Anglo-Catholicism. Over and over again, U.S. Hispanics describe Anglo-Catholicism as "cold." If it is assumed that, because of the human tendency to become attached to material objects, matter is not to be trusted as a mediator of the sacred, then neither are the body and its feelings appropriate mediators of the sacred. Once again, this has had important consequences for Hispanics in the U.S. Catholic Church:

> The intellectual culture of North American Catholics was profoundly influenced by this American experience, imbuing U.S. Catholic leaders with concerns, interests, and perhaps even biases that would render the comprehension of things Hispanic problematic. Certainly one of those qualities was a predilection for more articulate, rational exposition of faith. Church historian Patrick Carey has contended that the importance placed on reason is a characteristic mark of United States Catholicism, but in the case of Hispanic Catholicism the opposite was true. What was stressed by the original Spanish missioners was the grafting of Catholic faith onto the rich vine of indigenous ritual, symbol, and myth.[6]

---

[6] Deck, "At the Crossroads," 5.

The modern dichotomy between reason and feelings has important ramifications for the theological education of Latinos and Latinas. U.S. Hispanics must constantly struggle against the stereotype of ourselves as physical, emotional people who (when seen through the dichotomous lenses of modernity) are incapable of and/or uninterested in rational thinking. In my years as a teacher, I have had to counsel many a Latino student who has been subjected to this type of humiliation. I have had very bright Hispanic undergraduates who, when asked why they do not consider going to graduate school, have responded that their faculty advisors had recommended against "setting your sights too high." In one case, a college professor's letter of recommendation on behalf of a Latino student's application for a graduate fellowship gave the student very high marks, adding that such academic achievement is especially noteworthy given the fact that this student came from a culture "that does not value intellectual achievement."

In Catholic seminaries, the "Hispanic issue" is treated—if at all—as a pastoral challenge demanding greater emotional sensitivity; rarely, if ever, is it treated as a theological challenge demanding intellectual conversion. Hispanics may challenge our hearts, but certainly not our minds (for that we have the Germans). Hispanics may represent a pastoral challenge to the Church, but certainly not an intellectual or theological challenge. Consequently, it is not at all uncommon for Latinos who enter U.S. seminaries to be encouraged to reject their supposedly "immature, pre-Vatican II" religious faith as a prerequisite for ordination. This prejudice places Latino seminarians in an unfair and impossible position: either abandon family, culture, and faith, or abandon the hope of becoming a priest.

Thus, as difficult as it is for Hispanics to find acceptance as priests and lay ministers, it will be even more difficult for Hispanics to find acceptance as theologians and scholars. The warmth, gentleness, and emotional effusiveness so often associated with Latinos and Latinas may, after all, lend themselves to pastoral work, but those same qualities will be perceived as obstacles to "sound scholarship."[7] Given the modern dichotomy between the intellect and affect, the affirmation of one implies the rejection of the other. Academic theology is rational and, thus, dispassionate. Hispanics are passionate and, thus, irrational.

Addressing the Problem

If Catholic educational institutions hope to attract the Latino or Latina to the ministry and the study of theology, those institutions must find ways to heal the epistemological and anthropological ruptures described above. Such

---

[7] As a youth, I was advised by my mother to avoid any display of emotion when in a discussion with *americanos*. While passionate discussions were a regular, accepted part of our lives as Cubans, she warned, in "American" culture, any display of emotion is interpreted as a sign that one has "lost control." At that point, an *americano* will stop listening to you.

a healing process would make possible, moreover, not only an opening to Hispanics and other marginalized groups, but also a retrieval of the Catholic intellectual and spiritual tradition, which has always rejected simplistic dichotomies. Indeed, the common denominator of those world views and theologies which, over the centuries, the Church has rejected as heterodox has been precisely their dichotomous epistemologies and anthropologies. How, then, might Catholic seminaries and theology departments begin to heal these divisions?

What I have meant to imply in the first section of this essay is that simply offering courses in U.S. Hispanic Theology, or integrating Hispanic concerns into the curricula, will not address the fundamental problem. While such steps are certainly welcome and necessary, they address the question of curricular content while ignoring the more basic questions of theological method and structure. For example, to invite Hispanic students into a graduate program because it offers courses in Hispanic theology while maintaining unchanged those curricular and professional structures which presuppose and embody the above mentioned epistemologies and anthropologies is to foreordain the failure of those students. The likelihood of long-term success would be about as great as the likelihood of creating a more pluralistic marine environment by introducing birds into the earth's oceans. In the long run, it is impossible to create pluralistic content without also creating pluralistic educational methods, structures, and environments.

As already mentioned, one of the most alienating aspects of education, in the eyes of Hispanics, is the radical individualism which it seems to presuppose and demand. Our Catholic institutions should thus take the lead in developing cooperative, or collaborative educational methods, structures, and environments. In research and scholarship, we should recognize, encourage, and reward collaborative projects. For example, rather than being perceived as somehow inferior to single authorship, joint and multiple authorship could be encouraged as a means of enriching and deepening one's own research. Other disciplines, such as the sciences and social sciences, have a long tradition of such collaborative research. Collaborative work is a part of the great Western intellectual tradition, from Plato to Thomas Aquinas—both of whom recognized the fundamental importance of *dialogue* as a methodology. The ancients drew freely from one another's ideas with astonishingly (for modern persons) little concern for ideological proprietorship. Indeed, predominantly oral peoples have no choice but to think collaboratively, in dialogue. It is with the invention of the printing press and the exaltation of individual reason that ideas come to be viewed as originating in the individual. Once that occurs, ideas are viewed as commodities that the scholar possesses and must, consequently, guard jealously lest they be appropriated by a competitor. This free market model militates against any scholarly collaboration; on the contrary, any dialogue or collaboration places in jeopardy one's most prized possessions.

This individualism also alienates the Hispanic student who is accustomed to working in groups and benefiting from the mutual support such group work entails. In my experience, it is not at all uncommon to find young Latinos or Latinas who fear excelling in their academic work because such achievement would marginalize them vis-à-vis their schoolmates. In a community-based culture, individual achievement will tend to be viewed with great ambivalence unless the entire group participates in and benefits from the achievement. Consequently, the current structure of academic programs, which fosters the student's acculturation into the individualistic world of the academy and promotes the virtues of individual research, functions to exclude many Hispanics. And, for Hispanic students already in colleges and universities, the successful completion of the degree is made much more difficult by the alienation often experienced in the process.

This alienation can be alleviated in a number of ways, for example: (1) effective faculty and student mentoring, (2) opportunities for community involvement, and (3) support for the student's family life. While the presence of other Latino students and Latino faculty in a graduate program would be ideal, even in their absence it is essential that a strong and effective structure be in place for providing mentoring from faculty and students, for it is the quality of the personal relationships developed in the academic environment which will, perhaps more than anything else, determine whether a Latino student will successfully complete a graduate program.

Faculty and peer mentoring may even begin prior to a student's matriculation in college, while he or she is still in high school. Hispanic students will be much more likely to consider matriculating at a Catholic college if they have already made friends and personal contacts in that institution. One promising example of such attempts at establishing relationships is the movement by several Catholic universities, including Marquette, the University of San Francisco, and Loyola of Chicago, to create structural and, especially, personal links between their own institutions and Latino high school students in the inner city.

Second, most Latino theology students come to their professional studies from a personal involvement in and commitment to the Church and the Latino community. Consequently, graduate theology programs should provide opportunities not only for developing friendships with other students and faculty, but also for participation in local church activities. This would require, above all, an acceptance of such community activity as an important, indeed, integral component of graduate theological work, whether in a seminary or a theology department. For the Latino and Latina, the Catholic theologian is, by definition, an active participant in the ecclesial community, both *qua* Catholic and *qua* theologian.

Theology is not simply an individual career but is, above all, an ecclesial vocation. Under the sway of modern liberal individualism, theology and ministry are seen as personal careers, or professions alongside law, medicine, accounting, management, etc. This professionalization presupposes precisely the kind of individual pursuit of excellence and achievement which, among Latino students, may be perceived as a betrayal of one's friends and family—

unless these are able to accompany the individual in that pursuit.

Like all Hispanics, the Hispanic theologian or minister also has deep roots in his or her own family. Perhaps the most difficult strain on Hispanic graduate students, and the one most deeply felt, is that placed on their family relationships. Latino culture does not accept a clear separation between private, "personal" relationships and public, professional relationships. These tend to be mingled and integrated, as symbolized by the daily "siesta" period which, more than merely a break from work, usually entails a break from one's professional relationships in order to take a long meal with one's family; family relationships are therefore integrated into the work day itself, rather than being relegated exclusively to the evening or weekend.

Thus, the individualism of the academic life in this country, which tends to remove the student from his or her friends and family in order to isolate him or her in the office or library for long periods of time, creates tremendous stress for all students but, because of the special place of the family in Hispanic culture, especially for Hispanic students and their families. This pressure is becoming increasingly acute with the laicization of theology and ministry.

Practically, an adequate response would thus involve an important personal dimension. Families of students—and especially children—must feel welcomed and respected in our schools. This would require not only the formation of structured programs, like day care, but also an openness to informal meetings and participation of families in school activities. Just as informal meetings (e.g., lunches) among students and faculty should be a part of the everyday life of a department or school, so should spouses and children feel routinely welcomed (within, of course, certain reasonable limits) to participate in the life of the school and department.

Similarly, informal meetings and conversations among faculty and students should be encouraged. For Hispanics, informal, ad hoc meetings and discussions are an integral part of work. The chat in the hallway, or the "discussion around the water fountain," which in this society is so often frowned upon as an unnecessary waste of time and a diversion from productive activity, or research, is, for Hispanics, a necessary element of work. Especially in the case of theological and ministerial studies, which purport to have humanistic ends, human relationships—whether professional or personal—are intrinsic to our self-understanding.

This relational world view yields, moreover, a profoundly incarnational, sacramental understanding of the theological task. For Latinos and Latinas, theology is inseparable from either praxis or spirituality. One of the most alienating and, indeed, incomprehensible structural obstacles for Hispanics in the modern U.S. Catholic university is the near total isolation of theology departments not only from other academic departments in the university but also from campus ministries and pastoral institutes. This isolation results from the refusal to take seriously the practical ground and end of theology, which is an intellectual, social, and ecclesial enterprise. It is, furthermore, a profoundly spiritual enterprise. These dimensions—the intellectual, the social, the ecclesial, and the spiritual—are all intrinsic to theology. In the modern U.S. Catholic university, the struggle to achieve "intellectual credibility" has led to an abandonment of the social, ecclesial, and spiritual tasks of theology since, in the modern academy, that credibility presupposes dichotomous epistemologies that marginalize these tasks. The irony is that, by isolating itself from each of these contexts, theology has made itself irrelevant to all four—to society (especially to the poor), to the Church (especially to the poor), and to the faith life of the people (especially the poor)—while nevertheless remaining thoroughly irrelevant to the academy.[8]

Our challenge as Catholic theologians and educators, then, is to begin to develop structures and institutions which will facilitate the integration of that which has been separated in modern Catholic education. Such an integration would not only make Catholic educational institutions more hospitable and attractive to Hispanics but would also represent a countercultural, liberating force for greater inclusivity in U.S. society and Church. For Hispanics, at least, a move toward such an organic, incarnational, and integral view of education would be a prerequisite for an authentic pluralism and cultural inclusivity. Ironically, one of the principal obstacles to such inclusivity is the very Anglo-Catholicism which has benefited from and now extols the "American" virtues of democracy and pluralism. To invite Hispanics into the modern fragmented university is to force us to choose between success in such a structure and our own cultural values, which abjure such fragmentation.

[8] These connections were very important during my own graduate studies. Marquette University afforded me the opportunity to integrate social science courses into my theological studies, thereby addressing my need to view theology as intrinsically related to the whole of human life. I was also afforded the opportunity to participate in several inner-city communities, such as the Catholic Worker and St. Benedict the Moor Parish, as well as numerous campus ministry activities. During my years at Marquette, serious attempts were also made—with varying success—to promote a communal life of prayer among students and faculty. All of this provided the personal and communal nurturance which gave meaning to and made possible my academic studies.

Afterword

Earl C. Muller, S.J.

This final offering gathers together some of the themes which surfaced during the conference and which deserve some final comment. These can be grouped together under the following overlapping themes: transitions which have brought Catholic theological education to its present position and which suggest agenda for the future; the present "disarray" within the discipline which, on the one hand, touches on issues of the proper methodology of theology and, on the other, finds many departments of theology undecided on appropriate educational and developmental goals; the place of departments of theology within their sponsoring institutions, within the Church, and within the academy; the correlative call for a theology that is accountable to and responsible for its various constituents; and the integrative claims made for and on theology in tension with the fragmentation that inevitably follows on specialization.

I

The present situation did not emerge overnight. While many aspects of that situation are adequately contextualized by considering what has happened in the wake of Vatican II, other issues are more neuralgic and have roots that extend back a century, indeed centuries. Some of the conference speakers touched on that history. I will attempt to avoid duplicating their presentations in my own comments but a brief sketch highlighting some of these long-term issues will provide useful perspectives and reminders for the discussion of the current situation to follow. This history touches particularly on the issues of the disarray within the discipline and the integrative character of theology.

Matthew Lamb in his paper points to the fragmentation "throughout twentieth-century Western cultures," focusing particularly on its academic and scientific aspects. Examining the millennial shifts that have taken place he concludes to the current need to integrate science and wisdom. He ranges the high Middle Ages with the second, scientific millennium which has led finally to the current fragmentation. The Scholastics would certainly have understood themselves as pursuing science but that period was also marked by an impressive synthesis between the faith (and its articulation in theology), philosophy, and culture. How thoroughgoing that synthesis in fact was is debatable; it did serve as a model for the Neo-Scholastic revival of the late nineteenth and early twentieth centuries as a specifically Catholic counter to the grand German idealistic systems of the nineteenth century. The medieval synthesis did not last; it began to unravel toward the close of that period. The Neo-Scholastic synthesis has likewise lost its dominance. Many of the causes, in both cases, remain with us.

Symptomatic, in the former case, was the rise of nominalism with its insistence on the concrete particular over and against either Platonic realism or Aristotelian conceptualism. The pathway from nominalism to empiricism or analytic philosophy is not straightforward but can nonetheless be discerned. Likewise, the shift of primary focus from the intellect to the will with the corollary focus on power and freedom adumbrated many of the emphases of the Enlightenment and subsequent developments in Western culture. This was the time of the rise of the *via moderna* in opposition to the *via antiqua* of Scotism and Thomism and of conciliarism as a counterbalance to papal power. Some of the similarities with the contemporary situation of the Church and of Catholic theological education are striking.

The real fragmentation of culture, however, followed on the Reformation. For all of the earlier intellectual turmoil there was still one faith which served publicly to unify the culture. Thomism, Scotism, and nominalism "were all equally accepted schools of Catholic thought."[1] The public character of faith was not at first challenged—both Catholics and Protestants sought to maintain the unity of society in terms of faith. The inevitable result of disunity in faith was disunity in society and a century of religious wars followed. The persistence of the commitment to the publicly unifying character of faith is seen in the Peace of Augsburg (1555) which codified the principle *cujus regio, ejus religio* for Catholics and Lutherans. This was extended to the Calvinists in the Peace of Westphalia (1648). The unity of society in faith was thus maintained in a geographically fragmented fashion.

The religious turmoil, however, had its effects in inculcating a general skepticism of religion among many intellectuals. This was reinforced by missionary reports of a great diversity of religions throughout the world and the practical successes of the nascent empirical sciences. The "father of English deism," Lord Herbert of Cherbury, died the same year as the Peace of Westphalia. René Descartes, who died two years later, set the critical agenda for the next century and beyond with his methodical doubt. His *cogito* foreshadowed the anthropological turn of modernity and postmodernity.

It is perhaps not surprising that deism took root first in England of the seventeenth century; it was a century of oscillation, at times bloody, between Catholic and Anglican monarchs. Nationalism, as a modern phenomenon, emerged in the same century in conjunction with the Puritan revolution. People ceased to look upon themselves so much as subjects of a monarch as citizens of a nation. Both developments served to break or reconfigure the relationship between faith and public life. John Locke, raised as a Puritan

---

[1] *New Catholic Encyclopedia*, s.v. "Nominalism" (G. Kung, vol. 10, 485).

and writing at the end of the century, captured a number of key themes of both movements and decisively influenced thought in France and America. In America, Locke inspired in the next century both the Puritan Jonathan Edwards, a graduate of Yale and the first president of Princeton, and Thomas Jefferson, a somewhat covert deist. In France deism, reaching influential expression in the works of Voltaire and Jean-Jacques Rousseau, joined with the devastating weaknesses of the *ancien régime* to lay the groundwork for the widespread opposition to the Church which characterized the later French Revolution.

By the time the Enlightenment was in full swing in the eighteenth century the unity of society was sought, not in a religious faith mired in superstition (often enough identified with Roman Catholicism), but in a rational faith in a common humanity, liberty and individual rights, and progress. Religion, as a force in the public arena, was restricted to what could be circumscribed by "reason alone," understood by Immanuel Kant in terms of the practical reason. Anything other than moral reasoning was consigned to the private sector. Christ became for many the great exemplar of the moral life and little more.

Reactions to the Enlightenment set in almost immediately. On the religious front rationalism was confronted with Wesley's emotional Methodism which had tremendous influence in Britain and America by the late eighteenth century in the latter. Germany spawned the analogous and earlier Pietist movement. Quietism bubbled to the surface in a number of places and forms of Jansenism remained quite active. Toward the end of the century there was the more secular reaction found in the rise of Romanticism whose "lyricism and transcendentalism" opposed "classicism and rationalism." Mozart and Hayden gave way to Beethoven and Berlioz. Transcendent feeling unified the world, not sterile logic-chopping. Romanticism found a fertile ground in Germany which, until Kant awoke from his dogmatic slumber, had maintained its metaphysical interest over and against the stark empiricism that was found elsewhere. By the seventies of the eighteenth century the *Sturm und Drang* was already thundering. If other countries emphasized reason in their nationalisms, Germany emphasized instinct.

The Enlightenment had had difficulty with the concept of history. It could not avoid the issue entirely since the idea of progress present in Enlightenment thought could scarcely overlook historical sequence. But reason was universal—if it served to unify a society it also served to unify history. Johann Gottfried Herder, late in the eighteenth century, had rejected the prevailing view that any group of people at any historical time could be judged by the same universalist principles, insisting rather, in good Romantic fashion, that each such group was utterly unique and needed to be judged in terms of its own context. The spirit of an age could only be captured by an intuitive breakthrough. The mood is that of the historicist. Taken to an extreme this insight fragments history and culture. Not only do other people, other cultures, other ages think uniquely, differently because of their particular historical contexts, they feel things in a unique, nonreproducible fashion.

Hegel (and for that matter Schelling) wanted to do for history what Kant had accomplished for reason. If reason threatened, under empirical assault, to crumble into disparate bundles of perceptions, then reason needed to be critiqued and the grounds for a sound metaphysics established. Likewise, if history threatened, under historicist assault, to fragment, then historical consciousness needed to be critiqued and the grounds for a sound metaphysics of history established, not in terms of the universalist principles of a naive Enlightenment, but in terms of an intuitive analysis of the dynamic of World Spirit.

Even as Hegel and Schelling were uniting history in Absolute Spirit the revolutions of the late eighteenth and the first half of the nineteenth century were firmly separating Church and state. If the American experience was rather benign, driven by the need to unite religiously diverse colonies, some of which had been founded explicitly as theocracies, the revolution in France, after initial attempts to reconcile the revolution and the Church had failed, turned markedly anti-clerical—the Church had been too closely allied with the *ancien régime*. It was the French Revolution which set the paradigm for Europe. The Church of the nineteenth century was, as one might expect, preoccupied with questions arising from the rationalism of the Enlightenment and from these revolutions: the relation between faith and reason, grace and nature, and the correlative relation between Church and state, questions which still exercise theologians.

"Enlightened" discourse, meanwhile, was taking its own course. Various forms of empiricism and positivism, principally in Europe but eventually also in America, were concluding to atheism or at least agnosticism and affected if not hostility to religion at least indifference. The "sacred canopy" has since then been stretched very thin to provide some sort of grounding for societal unity. Most Western societies are deeply fragmented as a consequence. By the end of the nineteenth century the left-wing descendants of Hegel had completed the critique of religion; their descendants in the present century enforced unified atheistic societies throughout Eastern Europe and large parts of Asia through massive repression. So much for the triumph of reason over faith.

Catholic theology in the nineteenth century, as Gerald McCool has noted, was marked by the quest for a unitary method.[2] The beginning of the century saw theology in considerable disarray. The Scholasticism that survived tended to be corrupted by Christian Wolff's deductive rationalism and, in any event, exerted very little influence at the turn of the century. In France clerical education was in shambles in the wake of the Revolution and the Napoleonic Wars—eclectic, unsystematic. The French tendency, in the face of philosophical confusion, was to insist on Catholic tradition over and against rationalism. In excess this led to various forms of fideism.

---

[2] Gerald A. McCool, *Catholic Theology in the Nineteenth Century: The Quest for a Unitary Method* (New York: Seabury/Crossroad, 1977), 29.

Gallicanism, already a problem in seventeenth-century France, took a German form in the Febronianism of eighteenth-century Germany and Austria. This lay behind the attempts of Maria Theresa and Joseph II to bring the Church under imperial control in the name of Church reform. Joseph's vision of clerical education, and that of his functionaries, was "strongly influenced by the rationalism of the Enlightenment."[3] Georg Hermes, educated in this system, had attempted a Kantian theology but failed to overcome its inevitable limitations with respect to Catholic faith.

Most other German theologians reacted against this reliance on the Enlightenment but the philosophical models available to them were considerably restricted. It is not surprising that the Romantic idealism of Schelling proved quite attractive, inspiring most notably the Tübingen school. The Romantic reaction lay behind many of the theological systems of the first half of the nineteenth century including the ontologism that became very popular in Italy, France, and Belgium and which exerted some influence in America. Augustine's doctrine of illumination was often appealed to as providing a way out of the Enlightenment impasse. Indeed, for a while this post-Kantian version of Augustinianism dominated Catholic theological thought and education.

It was not to last. Already under Gregory XVI the fideist traditionalism of Félicité de Lamennais and Louis Bautain as well as Hermes' rationalism had been condemned. Under Pio Nono, in the twelve years after Shelling's death, traditionalism and ontologism had been condemned as well as Anton Günther's dualism and Frohschammer's rationalism.[4] The only system not condemned was the renascent Scholasticism which had its most influential center in Rome; it was increasingly adopted as other systems were excluded.

Part of the reason for the turn from these systems had been political. If Lamennais had run afoul of Gallican bishops who denounced him to Rome, it was more often the case that the proponents of these systems had allied themselves with the forces of liberalism that Rome increasingly identified as "the enemy." Pius IX's initial sympathy for liberalism quickly soured under the press of events in Italy leading to the dissolution of the Papal States. But another part of the reason for the collapse of the tentative Augustinian, traditionalist, ontological synthesis was cultural. The "Romantic movement had run its course."[5] Even Schelling sensed that his time had passed. Dialectics had taken a materialistic turn, existentialism was in revolt against idealism, and many were increasingly seeking truth in a positivistic science. Aristotelian realism was replacing Platonic intuition throughout Europe. Thomism spoke to this cultural shift. A final reason for the collapse of the earlier consensus has to be laid at its own door. Whether semi-rationalists or traditionalists or ontologists, all had accepted some of the judgments of the Enlightenment without critique. The Neo-Thomists made the critique. For the most

[3] Ibid., 22-23.
[4] Ibid., 132.
[5] Ibid., 142.

part it turned on the issue of whether an adequate distinction was being made between natural knowledge and supernatural knowledge. It was not always clear, for instance, what difference there was between the vision of God necessary to ground any objective knowledge in these systems and the beatific vision.

The critique of the Enlightenment was not the only reason why Neo-Thomism succeeded. There was, in addition, the need to provide a unified theological and philosophical vision "that could stand comparison with the systems of Fichte, Schelling, and Hegel without compromising the supernaturality and the unique, historical character of positive Christian revelation."[6] It was not enough that strictly religious themes be made coherent. Something had been lost to the Church when the old medieval synthesis between theology, philosophy, and culture had broken down. The intervening attempts to bring unity out of the confusion and fragmentation had all failed. Further, within a brief span of time societal structures, the very culture, were undergoing radical changes. The Church needed not an eclecticism that could be conveniently ignored by the intellectual forces of the world but a new integrative vision for confronting the multiple crises of modernity. "It was precisely this systematic interrelation of epistemology, anthropology, metaphysics, and ethics" in philosophy that Neo-Thomism presented and presented better than any of the rival systems.[7] It was a synthesis that was to last in some measure for a hundred years and which provided the driving force for recovering and developing into modern instruments the inheritance of the Middle Ages and stands behind the monumental social teaching of the Church for which Leo XIII was particularly noted and the very successful Catholic Action movement of the first half of the twentieth century in America.

It very suddenly collapsed in the late 1950s. Philip Gleason in his paper has given a number of reasons for this collapse. They need not be rehearsed here in any detail. In some ways the most telling was the discovery, over the course of decades, that Thomism did not possess the systematic unity that had been claimed for it and which had been the justification for its imposition on the whole Church in the first place.[8] By the turn of the century the essentialist-Suarezian interpretation of Thomas which characterized the thought

---

[6] Ibid., 32.

[7] Ibid., 163.

[8] This is not to say that Matteo Liberatore or Joseph Kleutgen, who spearheaded the triumph of Neo-Thomism in the nineteenth century, were unaware of the differences of thought to be found in various expressions of medieval Scholasticism, though these difference were often glossed over: some simply made mistakes or the controversies were over less important aspects of the system. Nor, for all the resistance of their thought to the categories of history, were they unaware that Scholasticism itself had developed—it was precisely this awareness of development which allowed them to contend that underlying all these different systematic expressions there was a unified system that gradually emerged. St. Thomas provided a more perfect version of this system than did Augustine; Francisco Suarez, the Jesuit commentator on St. Thomas in the sixteenth century, had provided yet further development, perfecting the work of Thomas. Nor were Liberatore and Kleutgen unaware of the fact that sixteenth-century Thomism was not yet developed enough to handle all of the problems of modernity—hence their own efforts.

of the founders of the Neo-Thomist movement had given way to the existen-tialist-Cajetanist understanding of Réginald Garrigou-Lagrange, O.P., and later of Jacques Maritain. Étienne Gilson, more text and historically oriented, had made clear not only the differences between Suarez and Cajetan on the one hand and Thomas on the other but also the irreducible differences between the systems of Thomas, Bonaventure, and Duns Scotus. At the same time, exploiting a different aspect of Thomistic epistemology, Joseph Maréchal had worked out the basic lines of the rapprochement between Thomism and the subjectivism of modernity. By the time the fifties had arrived there were at least seven versions of Scholasticism vying for attention, each claiming (and still claiming) to provide the unitary system adequate to the modern needs of the Church.

Nor had Thomism been given the field unchallenged. France remained sympathetic to an Augustinian intuitionism which manifested itself at the turn of the century and in the decades after in the philosophy of Henri Bergson and Maurice Blondel's phenomenology of the human spirit. Nor did every-one give up the project of converting modern thought from within rather than retreating into Scholasticism. Modernism tended to be a set of attitudes more than any unified system but there was in it a general resistance to the rigid Neo-Thomism that dominated Church life and an openness to modern cul-ture and thought. To a certain extent there was an adherence to older liberal trends but also bitter attacks against ecclesial authority which led, in George Tyrrell's case, to his expulsion from the Society of Jesus. This was the time also when the historical-critical method was coming to the fore in Catholic scriptural studies. The more radical of the exegetes, among whom Alfred Loisy was notable, were all but losing their faith. Likewise, there were fresh attempts to defend the possibility of a post-Kantian Catholic theology as in the works of Albert Ehrhard.

A more effective movement began in the decades after the dust from the modernist crisis settled—the return to the sources of theology or ressourcement. This was occurring as well within Thomist circles as evidenced in the work of Gilson and the Dominicans at Saulchoir as Joseph Lienhard in his offering notes. But there was activity on a broader front, led by the liturgical move-ment, which spilled over into theology. For those of la nouvelle théologie there was the thought that it would be possible "for Catholic theologians to leap over the rigid scholasticism of the manuals and return to the Fathers."[9] The 1950s were a difficult time for these theologians in the wake of Pius XII's censure of the "advocates of novelty" in Humani Generis and the silencing of some, most notably Henri de Lubac. But this was quick in passing and it was clear in the Second Vatican Council that la nouvelle théologie had taken the field. It was no accident that the collapse of the hegemony of Thomism, as

Their conviction had been, however, that there was this development a unity which, with ap-propriate augmentation, could provide a more coherent philosophical and theological vision than could rival systems.

[9] McCool, Catholic Theology, 258.

Lienhard notes, coincided with "the high-water mark of Catholic historical theology."

This is not to say that Thomism has been superseded. The Thomism of a Maritain or a Gilson still has strong support in a number of circles and Transcendental Thomism, following on Karl Rahner and Bernard Lonergan, is currently the dominant theological methodology. But Augustinianism, even apart from the French, has found powerful advocates such as Hans Urs von Balthasar. Walter Kasper has sought to restore some of the leading ideas of the Tübingen School to Theology. Others are working inside the categories of existential phenomenology (including Rahner), American philosophy, various forms of process thought, and so on. The fundamental disarray of theology which characterized the first half of the nineteenth century has returned with only a different cast of characters. At the same time there is considerable interest in presenting to students a unitive vision capable of integrating faith and culture.

II

There are several points that emerge from this brief survey. The first is that the disarray that characterizes the present situation in theology is by no means a new phenomenon in the history of the Church and is unlikely to disappear anytime soon. A number of the methodological problems which confronted theology in the nineteenth century have still not been resolved a century and a half later. The oscillations between Augustinian and Aristotelian impulses which broke out in the early Middle Ages have continued down to the present day. Indeed, theological disagreement and even heresy has been present from the beginning.

Nor does it follow that this should be read negatively even if there are negative aspects that are attendant on this "diversity." A number of theologians are convinced that theological inquiry is essentially pluriform.[10] Gerald McCool provides an extended treatment of the development of this line of thought. He notes that the work of Henri Bouillard and Henri de Lubac began to establish a theoretical underpinning. The earlier Neo-Thomistic understanding of the evolution of theology had presumed a theory of progress, of elaboration from less explicit to more explicit understandings, which could not be historically substantiated. Indeed, the contingent notions of theology "change their meaning without logical necessity through being inserted into different historical contexts." They, in effect, "proposed an epistemology and metaphysics that introduced history and evolution into the very structure of

---

[10] That it was in practice pluriform even within a Scholastic framework was made clear by the work of Gilson who nonetheless held that it was united in "a unity of spirit, a unity in the way in which the medieval Christians did their philosophy," Gerald McCool, S.J., *From Unity to Pluralism: The Internal Evolution of Thomism* (New York: Fordham University Press, 1989), 170-73. More specifically, Gilson points out that "these masters all agreed on the truth of the Christian revelation received by faith," *The Philosopher and Theology* (New York: Random House, 1962), 177.

theology itself." To be sure, both held that "the fundamental affirmations of the Catholic faith are immutable" but "the contexts in which theologians attempt to elucidate them vary with time."[11]

The next development took place in the context of the defense of Bouillard in particular. Msgr. Bruno de Solanges argued that "the analogous character of human knowledge itself requires that there be such a plurality of systems," in effect "extending analogy from concepts and judgments to philosophical systems." This found considerable resonance among the Thomists trained in the tradition of Rousselot and Maréchal and echoed the approach already taken by Erich Przywara, not always classified as a Thomist, who took the analogy of being as embracing "the whole dynamic balance between the human and the divine in thought and action." He made the move of presenting Augustinian and Thomistic systems as fundamentally different in approach even if analogically united.[12] The Rousselot inspired Jesuit, Jean Marie Le Blond, made the case within a Thomistic context. This analogy is "based on the dynamic relation of the mind which refers its finite complex truths to God's infinite pure truth." It is an analogy of truth corresponding rather closely to the analogy of being. Philosophical systems are constructed "from limited, deficient, and historically conditioned concepts" and as such are not absolutely true but participate in the Truth.[13] It follows that there will be manifold such analogous systems which can be judged as more or less adequate to the divine mystery but never completely so.

This view of things has not gone unchallenged.[14] Aside from the critique brought to bear from the Maritainian Thomists who would resist the notion of theological pluralism, Donald J. Keefe, S.J., rejecting the traditional *analogia entis* as born of a necessitarian Neoplatonism that undermines the Christian discourse on the gratuity of creation and grace and which ultimately proves incompatible with the Aristotelian base of Thomism, proposes an analogy grounded, not in the relation of the mind to an ahistorical pure Truth, but in the relation of all created things and especially human beings to Jesus the Christ, through whom all things have been made and who is the very Truth of God. This analogy is thus grounded in the free presence of the eternal Son in history and looks to the integration of theology not in terms of some transcen-

---

[11] McCool, *Unity*, 206-11.

[12] Ibid., 214-16. "Augustinianism looks on the *analogia entis* as the immediacy of God's truth descending into the world. Thomism, on the contrary, considers the *analogia entis* the autonomous expression of human reason in its ascent from the world to God."

[13] Ibid., 217-18.

[14] Mary F. Rousseau, in her review of McCool's book in *Theological Studies* 52 (1991): 156-58, provides an important caveat: "Until recently, Thomistic pluralism was within a basic unity which accepted realism and metaphysics, used logic as its method, saw theology as the study of God, and required faith in the Scripture, interpreted by the Church, as the word of God for the starting-point of theology. Theologians who now take religion rather than God as their subject matter, who claim academic success rather than faith as their primary credential, who use various non-probative methods and welcome contradictory epistemological and metaphysical presuppositions, have created a pluralism beyond anything envisioned by Maritain, Gilson, de Lubac, or Aquinas himself."

dent Truth, in no real relation to human reality, but in the Eucharistic worship of the Church in which the Truth is really and historically present to the faithful throughout time and space. Every theology—and Catholic theology is essentially pluriform—is a hypothetical understanding of that Truth and will derive its truth value from the truth of the faith that is authentically proclaimed there.[15]

Even apart from Keefe's analysis there are an increasing number of theologians interested in a liturgical integration of theology, be it from the perspective of the sort of aesthetic proposed by von Balthasar or be it out of the renewal of interest in patristic theology. Several papers at the conference suggested such an integration. Needless to say, these matters need considerably more discussion if the current more eclectic and at times incoherent approach to theology is to yield eventually to a more coherent and broadly integrative vision. It seems clear, however, that some form of theological pluralism not only will persist but should persist. In the meantime theology programs will need to ensure that at least some students are encouraged to probe to these deeper methodological levels. But this cannot take place without a more general preparation; care must be taken to ensure that basic philosophical competence is developed throughout our programs.

Correlated with this theoretical task, further work needs to be done on establishing a broad consensus on the criteria of Catholic theology which could begin to bring some methodological order to the current disarray and allow professionalization to proceed in a way authentic to Catholic theology. Methodological coherence and integrative power are not enough; various atheistic, agnostic, pantheistic, and panentheistic systems are capable of this in some measure. What distinguishes the Christian vision from various non-Christian visions? What distinguishes a Catholic theological approach from Protestant approaches? General lines can be easily set out even if many would want to discuss the precise meaning and implications of each. Avery Dulles has provided a few indications in his paper. This sort of inquiry is appropriate to the academy quite apart from more properly ecclesial concerns. The respectability of theology departments vis-à-vis other academic departments depends in large measure on the establishment of disciplinary criteria and the construction of programs posited on those criteria. To the extent that these are left unarticulated to that extent it will be difficult to fashion coherent programs, a situation which can leave other departments questioning why disproportionate institutional resources are being channeled to such a department.

The methodological disarray has been sharpened by a common temptation to confuse faith and theology. In the period prior to Vatican II this tended to take the form of a rigid dogmatism on the part of some with regard to Neo-

---

[15] Keefe sets out two fundamental forms which transform Plato and Aristotle respectively into Augustinian and Thomistic style theologies. Cf. *Thomism and the Ontological Theology of Paul Tillich: A Comparison of Systems* (Leiden: Brill, 1971) and *Covenantal Theology: The Eucharistic Order of History*, rev. ed. with appendix, two volumes in one (Novato, Calif.: Presidio Press, 1996); orig. ed., 2 vol. (Washington, D.C.: University Press of America, 1991).

Thomism. That hegemony has been broken but it is all too easy to replace one methodological dogmatism with others. Our attempts to understand the faith remain precisely that—attempts that to a greater or lesser extent serve that purpose. The tendency to confuse the two has its ground in the relation between faith and reason. One expects a coherence between the fruits of rational reflection and the contents of the faith. It is, after all, the same God who reveals Himself through Christ to the first disciples who also created the heavens and the earth and whose light shines on human reason. It is natural to identify the "understandings" that one has reached with the truth, and thus, with the truth of the faith. The problem is that, as Thomas notes, the fruits of rational reflection are generally obtained only after much labor and even then are suffused with many errors. One cannot, in conflicts between the labor of reason and the faith, automatically assume that the faith must conform with the results that one has obtained through theological reflection.

The late medieval period held together, as noted above, because there was unity of faith. That unity of faith cannot be grounded in any of the theological methodologies that in point of fact are divided over and against each other. Either one methodology must come to dominate and drive out all the others, as happened in the late nineteenth century, or the unity must find its ground elsewhere than in theological methodology. In this latter case each methodology, however much it may be at odds with other methodologies, is freely associated with and subject to this extrinsic ground. The crucial issue is how one understands that extrinsic ground. The Reformation ultimately understood it in terms of the Word of God, Scripture, which was perspicacious, open to the individual reader; no magisterium could stand between the individual Christian and that Word. Catholicism, and this would be true also of Orthodoxy, sees the ground of unity in the Eucharist, the liturgical celebration in which the Word of God is proclaimed and in which the Lord becomes really present in the midst of the community. The reading (or hearing) of the Word of God by the individual Christian is inseparable from the proclamation of that Word in the midst of the community, it is inseparable from the hierarchy which presides at that Eucharist.

Given the communitarian focus of Catholic theology, the question refocuses on the relation of the bishop or the hierarchical magisterium to the Christian community. While Catholic theologians would generally acknowledge the need for coordination with the hierarchy, there is more discussion on the exact nature of priestly ordination and episcopal consecration and considerably more disagreement on the practical import of theoretical understandings of the role of the bishop with respect to theologians. The theoretical discussion in its more radical form turns on whether one is convinced that the bishop represents his church because he represents Christ or that the bishop represents Christ because he represents his church.[16] The former sort of view

---

[16] The former view underlies the thought of *Lumen Gentium* 18-27; Edward J. Kilmartin, S.J., "Apostolic Office: Sacrament of Christ," *Theological Studies* 36 (1975): 243-64, is representative of the latter view. Dulles and Komonchak provide comparable contrasts.

will ground the authenticity of the teaching office of the bishop directly in the mandate of Christ to the apostles to go teach all nations and not in "the consent of the Church"; the latter will tend to stress the reception by the faithful as determinative of the authenticity of hierarchical teaching. The former will insist on the essential difference between the representation of Christ by ordained ministers and that by all Christians; the latter will argue that the "apostolic office has an important though not exclusive role to play. All believers have . . . the task of representing Christ before each other and the world."[17] The former view presumes that there is a single magisterium and that the bishops have a duty to pass judgment on, among other things, the work of theologians; the latter view will sometimes insist on a double magisterium and that theologians will pass judgment on the hierarchy.

The polarizations in the Church, and in theology either as a cause of or a reflex of this, are serious. It is somewhat ironic that even as the polemical level is being lowered between divided Christian churches it has elevated within individual churches. However one assesses Cardinal Bernardin's recent Common Ground project, it testifies to the seriousness of the divisions between theologians and underscores the tension many experience between bishops and theologians. It also raises the question of how the Catholicity of our institutions is to be determined and assured in such a polarized climate. There are, here, a host of practical concerns over which there has been considerable disagreement even among those who share the same theoretical perspective.

A second point of interest follows on the privatization of faith that followed in the wake of the Enlightenment and the rise of critical and autonomous reason which underlie many of the presuppositions of the academy. There is in particular a tension between the doing of theology within the context of the ecclesial community and academic freedom as it is commonly understood. The Enlightenment presupposition of rational autonomy present in the notion of academic freedom can, but does not have to, run counter to the essentially communitarian character of the theological enterprise. The faith that the theologian is trying to understand is his or her own to be sure, but the faith of every individual is authoritatively and definitively shaped by the faith of the community which itself is formed by the faith of the Apostles. Catholic theology should resist the reductionism and fragmentation that can flow from an unchecked autonomy and it will do this, not on the level of rational argument which presumes the autonomy of reason, but on the level of revelatory authority found both at the origins of the faith and in its transmission. Ideally there will be no conflict between this authority and rational autonomy;[18] in a fallen world there is plenty of conflict. Although the discussions over *Ex corde Ecclesiae* have reached something of a plateau, for many they have not yet reached closure.

---

[17] Kilmartin, 264.

[18] Indeed, William Hoye's paper, "Origins of the Idea of Academic Freedom in the Medieval University," which unfortunately lay outside of the focus of the present volume and could not be included, argues that academic freedom was defended in its origins by the papacy.

But it also needs to be said that we cannot presume that the academy will recognize as legitimate every element or criterion which makes theology to be authentic; the acceptability of the oversight of theologians by the hierarchical magisterium, a reality which, as such, stands outside of the academy, is only the most obvious of such points. It is important for Catholic theology to be done in the context of the academy as it is to be done in the context of the culture, in the context of the world. But sometimes it will be necessary to refuse to be intimidated and to resist the demands of the academy, to refuse to allow our faith, which is the object of theology, to be reduced to the exigencies of autonomous reason which all too often bears the marks of fallenness. It is easy to state general principles in these matters; it is more difficult to decide concrete practices. Ongoing reflection is needed on the relation of theology to the academy.

There is, however, a second issue. The faith that theology tries to understand, rooted as it is in the gospel mandate to repent because the Kingdom of God is at hand, proclaims to the world and to the cultures it encounters the need to be transformed. It is a betrayal of that faith to accept privatization meekly. While theology, as an academic discipline, is conducted in the classroom and the study and not on the street, it cannot but articulate how this transformation of culture can be understood as it articulates that faith which calls for such transformation in the here and now.

A third point which emerges from the historical sketch outlined above is that the sort of integrative vision many wish to impart to our students may, in point of fact, have little impact on the culture as a whole. It is natural to desire that the work we do have a wider influence but, apart from striving to improve the quality of what we do and of what we demand from our students, there is little that we can do directly to effect this. American society, Western culture in general, is deeply fragmented, not simply in terms of divisions between believers and secularists who have little or no belief, but also among those who do affirm some religious perspective or other. It is unlikely that there will be any broad consensus on any number of important societal issues anytime soon. Dialogue with the culture is important but we cannot assume that the culture will be transformed simply because theologians are in dialogue with it. It is important that we do not lose our nerve in the face of indifference or even hostility. At times the vision we seek to impart will need to take on the character of a prophetic voice; we need to be sending our students into the world as innocent as doves, but as wise as serpents. In this it is particularly important to refuse to rely exclusively on those solutions to societal unity proposed since the Reformation. They are counterfeit. Authentic human unity will not be achieved apart from the action of God saving the world and the response of the world to God's action in faith. The prophetic call to any culture must at root be a call to faith.

A fourth point of interest is the recurring character of the drive to provide an integrative vision in the history of theology. In the conference itself this theme emerged constantly as well the correlative need to stress the integration of theology within itself, with other disciplines, with the culture. Thomas Aquinas had long ago pointed out the coextensive character of philosophy and theology. Philosophy, with its variety of disciplines, considers all of being. Theology considers God and everything that is related to God. In the older synthesis philosophy had had pride of place in the college curriculum for providing students with an integrative vision because theology had been understood to be a graduate discipline. The more profound (because rooted in the faith whose truth was guaranteed by God) theological vision embraced the philosophical vision. There was only one fundamental Christian vision.

This conviction implies several things which do characterize contemporary theological practice. First, a theological vision that is authentically all-encompassing will perforce be open to all cultures, not in the sense of naively taking on all of the presuppositions of fallen humanity in its myriad forms, but in the sense of taking up all that is good and noble in every culture. The gospel redeems cultures; it does not annihilate them. The gospel does not leave cultures antagonistic to one another but brings them together in a shared vision, in a symphony of praise where each note is heard distinctly but in unison with every other note. The challenge for theology is to articulate how this is possible and to articulate in the context of each culture the shared vision. Given the effective shrinkage of the world it becomes more and more crucial to provide to our students some sense of this world Church.

Second, a theological vision that is all-encompassing will perforce be open to all of the academic disciplines, not simply in the sense of incorporating them into the proper task of theology itself, as literary studies, or philosophy, or the historical disciplines are brought to bear on the faith and the texts and movements of that faith, but also in the sense of aiding each of the varied disciplines with the articulation of how the Christian faith can and should inspire the proper work of those disciplines. From both perspectives interdisciplinary studies are an important part of the mix of what students are introduced to and the sort of interactions that should take place within the context of a Catholic educational institution.

Third, although a department of theology will be primarily concerned with the academic component of a student's development it cannot so easily consign to other institutional structures (or to none at all) students' faith development. Theology as the articulation of an integrative vision will also have to articulate how its own articulation integrates with the rest of a person's life. One might expect, accordingly, collaboration between the department of theology and those other structural elements of an educational institution charged with broader aspects of student life, just as one expects collaboration between the department of theology and other academic disciplines.

Fourth, it follows that theology can ill afford to allow itself to be segmented into isolated areas. Again, the fundamental paradigm, one ultimately rooted in the Triune character of God, calls for a unity between the areas which enhances the distinctness of each.

Finally, given the call to Christian and religious unity, Catholic theology will seek to articulate that search for harmony rooted in the reconciliation that Christ has effected in the world. Full reconciliation, of course, requires addressing those issues that led to disunity in the first place. This will in part require a clarification of root issues and a clearing away of misunderstandings, tasks usefully addressed by theologians of all denominations and religious groups and addressed in the context of dialogue. In addition, each separate group has developed distinctive Christian or religious approaches that are in themselves authentic and which have become part of that rich diversity of faith vision that it is the proper object of theology to articulate and integrate. Again, as Paul first articulated in his vision of the unity between Jew and Gentile, what is in view is a unity that does not annihilate the distinctness of each. Such a unity can only be achieved in dialogue. It follows that Catholic departments of theology must seek out, in a manner appropriate to each institution, ecumenical contexts in which the bonds of unity as well as the distinctiveness of each party can be explored; modern Catholic theology is appropriately done in an ecumenical context.

A fifth consideration occasioned by the historical sketch given above is the explosion of knowledge and resources used in the modern theological context. No other age has been as rich in the recovery of the texts of the tradition and in the study of these texts as the present one. This recovery of the historical sources, the development of a historical consciousness, and the sea change that gave rise to *Divino Afflante Spiritu* were already well established by the time of Vatican II and, indeed, paved the way for it. Theology in this new climate is done, not only in the light of magisterial utterances, whether ecclesial or theological, but under the illumination of the broad range of the Christian tradition and the riches of the Scriptures. Moreover, if a previous age looked to reason to probe the faith, the present probes that same faith with the whole panoply of cultural resources—literary, sociological, psychological. If the prayer and the personal faith of the theologian always served as a source for his or her theology this has been expanded to embrace a broader range of experience, whether personal or communal or cultural. All of this fosters the emergence of a multiplicity of voices which, from time to time, do not all seem to be singing the same song. What can get communicated to the student is not a unified vision but something verging on a cacophony.

Theology today must mirror the rich diversity that comes from living, not simply in a local church, but in a world Church. Societies and cultures are multiple; none are monochromatic realities. Black theology or Hispanic theology or American theology or Euro-centered theology each offer a culture-based unitary vision. On the other hand each of these can be, and often are, themselves polyphonic: a Spanish theologian offers a different articulation from a Colombian theologian or from a German theologian. A black American as well as a Canadian theologian will have a very different appreciation for traditional American thinkers such as Dewey or Peirce or Edwards than will a white American theologian. The challenge is to search out points of contact and a unity that is not simply the reduction of these multiple voices to some a-historical, a-cultural scheme supposedly undergirding all these cultural articulations and that is implicitly understood to be the only "real" theology, or the averaging of these voices to some bland tenuous canopy. This challenge becomes quite difficult when, as is so often the case, these cultural and societal relations are marked by the fallenness of the world.

III

The Second Vatican Council conveniently marks not only the latest shift in the theological scene but also important transitions in Catholic theological education in the United States. That transition has been covered in the papers published in this volume and will not, for the most part, be repeated here. Instead I would suggest a few issues that remain with us in the wake of that transition.

Prior to the 1960s, theology was primarily understood to be a graduate discipline pursued after sufficient proficiency in philosophy, predominantly Thomism, had been achieved and one that was pursued primarily in the seminary context. Philosophy held pride of place in the task of imparting a unified vision to students attending Catholic colleges and universities. What religious instruction they received tended to be catechetical in nature. This changed in the 1960s when many departments of theology or religious studies were either being established or were being professionalized. Given the low esteem in which it had been held, the latter development in particular defined itself as doing something other than catechesis.

In addition to this, colleges and universities found themselves caught in the debate between theology and religious studies. There were two phases to this question. The earlier debate was whether theology or religion was appropriate in the collegiate context. The former was understood as scientific theology such as was done in the seminary context; the latter was oriented to the establishment of a way of life and was often understood to be more homiletic or catechetical in character. The push toward professionalization tipped the scales in the former direction but by this time the Neo-Scholastic scientific procedure of most seminary theology was no longer acceptable. In some places these shifts produced strange results which moved departments in the direction of religious studies rather than toward theology proper.

The second phase of the discussion has involved the encounter with the Enlightenment presuppositions which has undergirded modern academia in the United States and elsewhere. This engagement took place for a number of reasons, many laudatory but others quite problematic for Catholic theology. First, there has been the search for disciplinary methods that would make sense, not only to other departments in a Catholic college or university, but to the academy at large. One way this can be achieved is to embrace the methodologies of the secular disciplines. The positive side of this is that theology becomes a microcosm of the academic universe. It is precisely this character of theology and its faith-rooted vision which allows it to be an integrative force within our institutions and a potentially effective voice within the academy at large.

It can, on the other hand, also fall prey to the fragmentation which all too often characterizes the academy in which disciplines become isolated and insulated from other disciplines; it can fall prey to the turf wars which divide department from department and area from area within departments; it can fall prey to the polarizations which can afflict any department. Further, there are problems for Catholic theology when the secular disciplines become ends in themselves and supplant content. Quite apart from the subversion of the faith which this threatens, the question arises whether theologians in such a situation are able to compete qualitatively with other departments. That, broadly speaking, they often do not fare well in such comparisons is somewhat clear. Part of the problem is inbuilt. To the extent that a variety of secularist methodologies are pursued the theologian becomes jack of many disciplines, master of none. If an individual theologian narrows him- or herself down to one such methodology, the question arises why such a methodology is being pursued in a theology department rather than in a history or a sociology department and whether it can be as successfully pursued in a context effectively lacking methodological peers.

There is a another problem, however. A total reliance on secularist methodologies suggests that theology does not have its own proper methodology. To the extent that this is true, theology or religious studies departments will take on an eclectic character, consisting of a bundle of disciplines administratively brought together under some vague rubric such as Medieval Studies or Black Studies. Often such omnium-gatherums do not elicit the same level of respect as do other, more methodologically unified departments.[19] The problem, as noted in several of the papers, is exacerbated by the decatholicizing and secularizing shift in curricular offerings and by the tendency, certainly in secular universities, but even by some within Catholic universities, to view theology merely as opinion, as intellectually soft.

These problems sometimes can pit one area against another area within the same department. It has perhaps most acutely been felt, certainly in larger departments, between scriptural studies which perforce must rely extensively on secularist methodologies which require a high degree of specialization and systematic or moral theology where the referent to the Catholic tradition and magisterial pronouncements and the synthetic character of the attempt to articulate a theological vision presume commitments that run counter to the presuppositions of the academy at large and integrative interests that preclude extensive specialization.

Nor are these the only tensions that exist. Although colleges and universities understandably chose to orient their departments toward a scientific presentation of theology rather than toward fostering a way of life, the latter, as noted above, cannot so easily be dismissed as an improper concern of theol-

---

[19] Which is not at all to say that such programs do not have a raison d'etre and that what they accomplish could be accomplished as well in multiple contexts.

ogy departments or simply handed over to campus ministries or divisions of student life. All departments depend for their continued existence on conveying to a critical mass of their students an enthusiasm for the discipline which would encourage them to go on for further studies. One form of that enthusiasm is, of course, the pure love of learning and the discovery of an interesting subject matter on which to exercise that love; this motivation can be operative in departments of religious studies as well as in departments of theology. But, in point of fact, what motivates students to pursue studies in theology is rarely so "pure." Way-of-life issues play heavily in such decisions.[20] Seminaries and faculties with strong spirituality concentrations are perhaps a bit quicker to pick up the impossibility of divorcing the purely academic from the personal appropriation of the material by the students, though even these are not completely immune from this sort of tension.

Professionalization took a slightly different course in the seminaries. Prior to Vatican II they were the locus of professional theology. That theology, of course, was Neo-Thomist. Its collapse left the seminaries somewhat adrift though their fundamental purpose, the training of priests and other pastoral ministers, precluded their ever moving in the direction of religious studies. This clear purpose combined with the tendency of seminary faculty to be overworked and underpublished has led to a more recent stereotype of the seminaries as "pastoral shops" over and against the universities where "scientific" theology is done, a reversal from the pre-Vatican II situation. This view has rightly been challenged by those familiar with the seminary situation and the reforms that took place following Vatican II.[21]

At the same time these changes were taking place there were changes in Catholic family life and in the primary and secondary education of the last generation of students that importantly shape their readiness for theology. There are three major areas of concern. The first has to do with the grounding in the faith which students bring with them into undergraduate and seminary programs. Many have noted that there is considerable ignorance about the Catholic faith even among incoming seminarians. It is easy to point the finger at the shifts from the heavy memorization that characterized pre-Vatican II catechetical practice, which did leave students with a defined body of knowledge, to the stress after Vatican II on initiating students into Christian experience. But, perhaps more importantly, there has also been a shift in day-to-day

---

[20] Nor is this unique to theology departments. Psychology departments, to provide a secular example, while generally not interested in becoming counseling centers for their students, nonetheless are well aware that many come into their programs with personal agendas and of the usefulness to the discipline of encouraging students to internalize and even training them to apply the material presented in the course of studies. They do not simply hand the way-of-life issues over to counseling centers. Likewise, many students are brought into theology programs because of their own faith commitments or because they are attracted by the faith commitments of the faculty.

[21] Among the changes was the establishment of a mechanism for accreditation which has encouraged a professionalization proper to the seminary context. Indeed, by the time departments of theology were being established seminary reform was well under way.

Catholic life as the immigrant Church moved into the mainstream of American culture. Much of the earlier coherence of the Catholic community has been diluted and family life itself, following the culture, has become much more diffuse. This loss of Catholic culture cannot be easily replaced. The problem requires that special attention be given to the introduction that is given to students in undergraduate level courses. A couple of the conference presentations discuss this in more detail. Where an integrated core introduction to theology is not possible, creative use of the *Catechism of the Catholic Church* can provide a useful first or remedial course. This is not, however, a problem limited to theology; all departments must be concerned with bringing deficient students up to speed in their disciplines.

A second area of concern is philosophical or methodological readiness. With regard to the former, two factors have contributed to the problem. The first is the loss of the older Thomistic synthesis. Philosophical studies as preparation for theology tend today to be far more eclectic than formerly. Apart, perhaps, from logic courses, there is no longer a commonly assumed base available on which theological studies can be erected. The second factor is the shift of theology from the seminary context to the university. The shift in itself, and the correlate shift from clerical dominance in theology to a substantive lay presence, is not problematic. What is problematic is that the program sequence from philosophy to theology generally presumed, certainly in the pre-Vatican II seminary, has been lost. Undergraduate major programs in theology do not necessarily provide any sustained philosophical training and, for that matter, graduate programs will accept students from a variety of undergraduate programs which may or may not include a substantive philosophical component.[22] Needless to say, this situation needs to be addressed or intelligent theological discourse will become impossible.

The problem is not confined to philosophical background per se but encompasses the variety of methodologies that are brought to bear in theological discussions. Methodological facility in the secular disciplines cannot be presumed of incoming students and must be taught along with everything else. The proliferation of disciplines brought to bear in contemporary theological discourse has not ameliorated the problem.

A third area of concern is facility in languages. This is a peculiarly American problem. In the pre-Vatican II Church Catholic college preparatory schools usually included strong language components, including the classical languages. This has ceased to be the case. Pressure to provide more preparation in mathematics and the sciences has led to a corresponding deemphasis on languages. But further, there has been little incentive in the culture to stress language facility. Until recently most Americans would never even encoun-

---

[22] I often poll graduate classes on their philosophical readiness. In one recent class three-quarters had never had a course in ancient philosophy and had never otherwise encountered the basic texts. This, of course, rendered any intelligent reading of, for instance, the patristic texts on the trinitarian controversies quite difficult. Nor was this an unusual result. The situation in the seminaries has not been very different.

ter another spoken language and the world domination of English-speaking countries has left Americans generally complacent. For many academic disciplines this does not create problems but it does create severe problems for theology. Students acquire the requisite languages during graduate studies, but the lack of facility at the start severely limits their research capabilities until the end of their programs and the lack of funding for nonprogram skills such as language places yet added financial burdens on them.

IV

The ability of theology departments to respond adequately to these challenges is circumscribed by the multiple demands made on theology faculty and the limitation of resources. With regard to the former there is both the diversity of the student body and the variety of publics which institutions, and thus departments, attempt to serve. In addition to the distinct populations involved in graduate and undergraduate education on the one hand and the distinction between service courses and major courses which all academic departments have to wrestle with, theology departments must face additional relevant issues such as the Catholic/non-Catholic mix in their student population which will affect both decisions on course sequencing as well as how individual courses will be pitched. Departments may be faced with having to provide resources for the institution as a whole, for the local church, for specialized programs (catechist preparation, permanent deacon programs, lay ministry, service programs, etc.) all of which may or may not integrate well with the primary purpose of the faculty or which may stretch the faculty too thin.

At the same time there are constraints of time and money upon what can be accomplished. Catholic colleges and universities in general are underendowed though this situation has in recent decades been recognized and is gradually being addressed. There is, on top of this, comparatively little support coming in for theology departments. The reason is not hard to understand—theology graduates tend not to become very wealthy and are not in a position to support the theology programs of their alma mater to the same degree as graduates of other programs in the college or university. There will tend to be fewer chairs, scholarships, lectureships, and other research support, specified for theology, than is found in a number of other departments. This is further compounded by the relative lack of extra-institutional funds in the form of fellowships and the like earmarked for theological projects. There are a number of funds that will support liberal arts in general but some of these will not support "sectarian" projects. It can be counterproductive to formulate theology projects in the secularist terms that can attract this latter sort of support.

Institutions can and do try to redress this imbalance with funds at their disposal, but there is only so much that can be done. Theology faculty, charged with providing core courses to the entire student body, are typically burdened with large student loads and in larger institutions with heavy administrative duties. Budgetary constraints generally preclude the hiring of the additional full-time faculty necessary to address this problem. Where it is addressed, more and more of the teaching load falls on part-time faculty, often to the detriment of the cohesiveness of the overall program. Students may be able to obtain scholarship money but typically this money cannot be used to obtain the ancillary skills, such as language, which are essential to do theology competently.

Seminaries have different sorts of constraints. Although their programs are exclusively or predominantly oriented toward theology, the overall institutional support is more closely tied to tuition from a small student body and ecclesial subsidy. This will severely limit the sorts of resources available to faculty and students in some cases. Furthermore, faculty tend to be much more involved in overall student formation which leaves correspondingly less time for research.

What is being expected of theology in terms of the integration of society and culture is enormous. If the Middle Ages are any indication it is the task of centuries, not of decades. The obstacles are formidable and the resources are restricted. What is called for, if discouragement is to be avoided, is the development of broad strategies for dealing with "the impossible." It was our hope in convoking this meeting to stimulate this sort of broader thinking. Strategies, if they are successful, always deal with what is possible and with what is more important. Some suggestions have already been made above. I would suggest a few additional points for consideration by way of closing.

Although it sounds hackneyed it remains true that among the most valuable things an institution can do, if it has not already done so, is to clarify its mission statements and the values it wishes to encourage throughout the institution and to devise strategies allowing for a more effective use of limited resources. In this regard the publics which the institution seeks to serve will have to be kept firmly and concretely in view. They bring varied expectations which cannot be ignored. Certainly, whether in the colleges and universities or in seminaries, they look for that quality of education which will allow them to make their way in the world and expect to encounter challenging courses that will prepare them for this. On the other hand, students and their families generally make considerable financial sacrifices to attend Catholic institutions rather than secular ones and the motive generally is the conviction that such institutions offer something that cannot be reproduced in the secular environment—a faith-inspired vision. The same concern motivates many benefactors. To the extent that an institution allows this to be undermined it risks losing the support of those whose good will allows it to continue in existence. The challenge is to provide for this climate without compromising academic values.

The single most important factor in this regard is the hiring process. In general if compatibility with the institutional mission is not made a clear issue at this point it is virtually impossible to introduce it as an issue at the time of tenure and promotion. Without constant vigilance it is easy for our institutions to slide into an all too easy secularization that does not necessarily enhance academic quality but which does undermine the raison d'être of the institution as Catholic. The instances of institutions such as Harvard, which have largely lost any denominational adherence, sound a clear warning that needs to be heeded as our institutions close out their second century of existence. Beyond hiring, institutions are able to express their mission and values concretely through various forums which will on many occasions appropriately tap into the resources of the theology department—sponsored lectures and other series, interdisciplinary programs, and faculty assemblies. John Haughey provides an example of how funding choices can enhance the Catholic character of a university.

There is need here for ongoing institutional discernment with regard to what is appropriate and possible at a given time. There is a natural tendency to continue doing something that in some measure has been found to work. The problem is that other equally good options can be closed out indefinitely. This will be true with regard to hiring—the needs of the institution's clients in the nineties may not be the same as they were in the eighties or the sixties and this may well require rethinking the departmental focus—but this can be quite difficult to effect in practice. The same will be true also of institution-wide projects. It may well be the case that an institution will want to establish permanent forums for social justice or for interdisciplinary explorations. On the other hand every such permanent forum drains institutional resources of money and faculty time. A better strategy, certainly for smaller institutions, may be to shift the institutional focus periodically, always providing for some facet of the broad integrative vision which finds a reflection on the Catholic, Christian faith at its core.

Institutional resources may well dictate a more carefully focused department. Between the current eclectic scene in theology, the usefulness and appropriateness of ecumenical dialogue, the need to foster a number of distinct inculturations of theology, and the openness of theology to all of the other disciplines in the college or university, even the largest programs are hard pressed to provide other than superficial coverage of many legitimate areas. When a department tries to be all things to all constituencies the overall effort can end by being badly diffuse. Broad coverage usually comes at the expense of the sort of overlap of competencies which allow for deeper peer interaction. Some institutions have established centers of specialized study, the Lonergan center at Boston College or Augustinian Studies at Villanova, for instance, where this sort of deeper interaction is encouraged and supported by hiring policy and allocation of resources. Other institutions with the requisite resources may want to consider similar programs focusing on other figures or areas of theology: liberation theology, Rahner, Maritain, the Tübingen school, American theology, black or Hispanic theology, etc. Smaller programs may find it to their advantage to focus their programs in a similar way, calling on the resources of their various heritages, or in the case of newer programs, establishing basic theological orientations.

Among the disagreements that divide theology faculties, as William Shea noted in his paper, is whether theology is understood as a vocation or as a profession. It is certainly true that individuals will come down differently on this question and that these differences lead to sharp differences within departments on "questions such as spiritual formation of theologians and the aims of undergraduate education." I would suggest that Catholic institutions, in contrast to individuals, must understand themselves in terms of a call to serve the Church and from within an ecclesial matrix to serve the world. It was this sort of understanding which led to their being founded in the first place; it is only this sort of understanding which justifies an institution's advertising itself as Catholic. Students are thereby encouraged to expect that their faith will be served by that institution. This has several implications.

First, it will be in the interest of the institution to ensure that there is sufficient faculty who share this understanding of being called by God to the academic profession and more particularly that there is a critical mass of faculty in the theology department who share this conviction. Institutional values and mission are only concretized in flesh and blood. Related to this will be a concern for ongoing spiritual renewal within the institution. Part of the gospel that theologians reflect on is that the world is fallen and that Jesus is the Savior of the world. Purely secular solutions without genuine conversion of hearts will not really solve the problems of the world. It follows that purely secular solutions will not solve the problems facing theological education. It is clear enough to most that the best theology is that which flows from a lively faith. Lively faith requires growth in personal holiness; it requires a commitment to prayer and a refusal, as John Haughey has phrased it, to be "neighbor-numb." Mutual forbearance is a useful virtue in the present context. There is a continuing need for our institutions to manifest the holiness of the priestly people of God: celebrated in the same Eucharistic liturgy which serves as the point of integration for Catholic theology and worked out in an institutional discernment that is not simply the fruit of the light of reason but which is also properly spiritual, born of the faith and prayer and reflection of the academic community gathered together at that institution.

The conference was broadly conceived. As such it has risked superficiality. It was deeply gratifying that it was more than that. Still, there were many areas that could not be adequately covered and this should be summarily acknowledged. Master's programs and their special needs received relatively little attention. They have been multiplying in recent years and some examination needs to be given in future conferences to how they are accredited. The question of "accrediting" the Catholicity of our institutions has not reached any closure; indeed, we had deliberately avoided addressing this particular issue in any direct way, in part because of the complexity of the question, in part because there have been other forums for this. More needs to be done on the interface between theology and practice as well as on interdisciplinary opportunities. There were a number of papers at the conference on the lay presence in theology which could not be included in this collection; the infusion of other than clerical perspectives into theology is an important development that will need continued nurture. Practically every topic featured at the conference could be the subject of a future conference. Some thought needs to be given to ongoing forums for the sorts of discussions which this conference made possible. There is enough to do to keep us all busy for awhile.

Selected Bibliography on Theological Education in American Catholic Higher Education, 1881-1995

PAMELA C. YOUNG, C.S.J.

Published Sources:

A. Paul, Brother. "Panel Discussion: The Responsibility of the Sacred Doctrine Teacher Precisely as Such for the Catholic Formation of the Student—F. Discussion from the Floor." *Proceedings of the SCCTSD* 2 (1956): 69-75.

Alban of Mary, Brother. "Panel Discussion: The Responsibility of the Sacred Doctrine Teacher Precisely as Such for the Catholic Formation of the Student—B. Discussion." *Proceedings of the SCCTSD* 2 (1956): 51-56.

_____. "Presidential Address." *Proceedings of the SCCTSD* 5 (1959): 7-13.

Allemand, L. Edward. "The Division of Philosophy and Religion at De Paul University." *Living Light* 7 (winter 1970): 70-78.

Annarelli, James John. *Academic Freedom and Catholic Higher Education.* Westport, Conn.: Greenwood, 1987.

Ann Patrick, Sister. "Panel: College Teacher Training in Sacred Doctrine—A. The Program at 'Regina Mundi.'" *Proceedings of the SCCTSD* 4 (1958): 88-92.

Ann Rita, Sister. "Panel: College Teacher Training in Sacred Doctrine—B. The Program at St. Mary's School of Sacred Theology." *Proceedings of the SCCTSD* 4 (1958): 93-102.

Apczynski, John, ed. *Theology and the University.* Lanham, Md.: University Press of America, 1990.

"Are Our Colleges in Order?" *Journal of Religious Instruction* 4 (May 1934): 790-91.

Asbury, Beverly A. "Campus Ministry and Its Relationship to Religious Studies." In *Religion in the Undergraduate Curriculum: An Analysis and Interpretation,* edited by Claude Welch. Washington, D.C.: Association of American Colleges, 1972.

Ashley, Benedict M. "A New Curriculum of Christian Doctrine." *Religious Education* 56 (July-August 1961): 271-78.

Ashley, J. Matthew. "The Turn to Spirituality? The Relationship Between Theology and Spirituality." *Christian Spirituality Bulletin* 3 (fall 1995): 13-18.

_____. "Panel: The Integration of Sacred Doctrine and Specific Disciplines—A. Sacred Doctrine and Natural Science." *Proceedings of the SCCTSD* 3 (1957): 24-28.

Atsch, Lancelot G. "Panel Discussion: The Responsibility of the Sacred Doctrine Teacher Precisely as Such for the Catholic Formation of the Student—C. Discussion." *Proceedings of the SCCTSD* 2 (1956): 56-61.

"The Attitude of College Students." *Journal of Religious Instruction* 4 (January 1934): 392-93.

Bandas, R. G. "What Catholic Universities Are Doing to Help Prepare and Improve Teachers of Religion." *Journal of Religious Instruction* 9 (September 1938): 34-40.

Basil, Brother. "Re-appraising the College Religion Program." *Catholic Educator* 20 (May 1950): 473-74.

Beane, Marjorie Noterman. *From Framework to Freedom: A History of the Sister Formation Conference.* Lanham, Md.: University Press of America, 1993.

Benard, Edmund D. "Panel: College Teacher Training in Sacred Doctrine—D. Suggested Principles for Determining Future Programs." *Proceedings of the SCCTSD* 4 (1958): 108-12.

———. "Religion in the Curriculum." In *The Curriculum of the Catholic College*, edited by Roy J. Deferrari. Washington, D.C.: The Catholic University of America Press, 1952.

———. "Theology as Pivotal: Newman's Views." In *Integration in Catholic Colleges and Universities*, edited by Roy J. Deferrari. Washington, D.C.: The Catholic University of America Press, 1950.

Benson, Thomas L. "Study of Religion: Religious Studies as an Academic Discipline." In *The Encyclopedia of Religion* 14, edited by Mircea Eliade. New York: Macmillan, 1987.

Bischofberger, George. "Panel: Sacred Doctrine in Professional Schools—A. Special Problems of Teaching Sacred Doctrine in Professional Schools." *Proceedings of the SCCTSD* 3 (1957): 101-7.

Blumer, Frederick. "Academic Freedom at Church-Related Institutions: Two Views." *Academe* (January-February 1986): 50-51.

Bonachea, Rolando, ed. *Jesuit Higher Education: Essays on an American Tradition of Excellence.* Pittsburgh, Pa.: Duquesne University Press, 1989.

Bonée, John T. "Theology for the Undergrad: A Reply." *American Ecclesiastical Review* 136 (June 1957): 376-81.

Bonnette, D. "The Doctrinal Crisis in Catholic Colleges and Universities and Its Effect Upon Education." *Social Justice* 60 (November 1967): 220-36.

Bouwhuis, Andrew L. "Aims in College Evidences of Religion." *Journal of Religious Instruction* 1 (June 1931): 445-48.

———. "A Method of Teaching Religion in College." *Journal of Religious Instruction* 2 (September 1931): 66-70.

Bowdern, Thomas S. "A College Department of Religion." *Journal of Religious Instruction* 4 (April 1934): 740-47.

Boys, Mary C. "The Role of Theology in Religious Education." *Horizons* 11 (1984): 61-85.

Brady, Dominic. "The Responsibility for the Catholic Formation of the Student as Applied to the Marriage Course: Integration of Natural and Supernatural Principles in the Marriage Course." *Proceedings of the SCCTSD* 2 (1956): 87-94.

Brady, John M. "Christian Ethics in the College and University." *Journal of Religious Instruction* 3 (October 1932): 139-44.

Buckley, Michael J. "The Catholic University and Its Inherent Promise." *America* 168 (29 May 1993): 14-16.

_____. "The Catholic University and the Promise Inherent in Its Identity." In *Catholic Universities in Church and Society: A Dialogue on Ex corde Ecclesiae.* Washington, D.C.: Georgetown University Press, 1993.

_____. "A Collegiate Conversation: Father Buckley to Prof. O'Brien." *America* 169 (11 September 1993): 19-23.

Burghardt, Walter J. "Intellectual and Catholic? Or Catholic Intellectual?" *America* 160 (May 6, 1989): 424.

Burke, Eugene M. "Address of Welcome: First National Meeting of the Society." *Proceedings of the SCCTSD* 1 (1955): 5-9.

_____. "Catholic College Theology Looks to the Future." *Proceedings of the SCCTSD* 10 (1964): 88-104.

_____. "Panel Discussion: The Responsibility of the Sacred Doctrine Teacher Precisely as Such for the Catholic Formation of the Student—A. Statement of the Problem." *Proceedings of the SCCTSD* 2 (1956): 47-51.

_____. "Teaching of Theology to the Laity." *American Ecclesiastical Review* 114 (April 1946): 266-77.

Burns, J. A., and Bernard J. Kohlbrenner. *A History of Catholic Education in the United States.* New York: Benziger Brothers, 1937.

Burrell, David B. "Theology and Other Disciplines in Catholic Higher Education." *Occasional Papers on Catholic Higher Education* 3 (winter 1977): 9-12.

Burtchaell, James Tunstead. "The Decline and Fall of the Christian College" (I and II). *First Things* 12 and 13 (April and May 1991): 16-29; 30-38.

Cahill, P. Joseph. "Theological Education: Its Fragmentation and Unity." *Theological Studies* 45 (June 1984): 334-42.

Callahan, Daniel, William Scott, and F. X. Shea. *The Role of Theology in the University.* Milwaukee: Bruce, 1967.

Carlson, Sebastian. "Digest of the Discussion [of Charles E. Sheedy's 'The Problem of Theology for the Laity']." *Proceedings of the CTSA* 7 (1952): 117-24.

Carmody, John. "Professing Religion in the Classroom." *Horizons* 16 (spring 1989): 97-100.

Carr, Anne. "Evolution of a Program in College Theology." *Living Light* 5 (September 1968): 76-86.

_____. "Theology and Religious Studies: A Suggestion." *Horizons* 2 (spring 1975): 99-101.

Cassidy, Francis P. *Catholic College Foundations and Development in the United States (1677-1850).* Washington, D.C.: The Catholic University of America, 1924.

_____. "The Value of a Catholic College Education." *Catholic Educational Review* 23 (December 1925): 609-14.

The Catholic University of America School of Religious Studies. *A Century of Religious Studies: Faculty and Dissertations.* Washington, D.C.: School of Religious Studies,

The Catholic University of America, 1989.

"The Catholic University in the Modern World." In *American Catholic Higher Education: Essential Documents, 1967-1990*, edited by Alice Gallin. Notre Dame, Ind.: University of Notre Dame Press, 1992.

"The Catholic University in the Modern World." NCEA *College Newsletter* 35 (March 1973): 1-10.

"The Catholic University of Today." *America* 117 (12 August 1967): 154-56.

"The Changing World of Catholic Education." *Columbia College Today* 14 (fall 1966): 16-28.

Charles, Henry J. "Roman Catholics at Non-Catholic, University-Related Divinity Schools and Theologates." *Horizons* 20 (fall 1993): 311-23.

"College Department: Proceedings." NCEA *Bulletin* 27 (November 1930): 84-85.

"College Religion Courses." *Journal of Religious Instruction* 3 (February 1933): 510-16.

Collins, Jos. B. "Religious Education and CCD in the United States: Early Years (1902-1935)," *American Ecclesiastical Review* 169 (1975): 48-75 [reprinted in M. Warren, *Source Book*, 158-75].

_____. "Bishop O'Hara and a National C.C.D." *American Ecclesiastical Review* 169 (1975): 237-55.

Collins, Mary. "Theological Excellence in the Catholic University." *Current Issues in Catholic Higher Education* 12 (summer 1991): 57-60.

"Comprehensive Examinations." *Journal of Religious Instruction* 5 (June 1935): 837-38.

Connell, Francis J. "A New Theological Course." *Catholic University Bulletin* 13 (July 1945): 4-5, 12.

_____. "On Integrating Religion." In *Integration in Catholic Colleges and Universities*, edited by Roy J. Deferrari. Washington, D.C.: The Catholic University of America Press, 1950.

_____. "The Sacramental Apostolate as the Primary Source of Integration." In *Integration in Catholic Colleges and Universities*, edited by Roy J. Deferrari. Washington, D.C.: The Catholic University of America Press, 1950.

_____. "The Theological School in America." In *Essays on Catholic Education in the United States*, edited by Roy J. Deferrari. Washington, D.C.: The Catholic University of America Press, 1942.

_____. "Theology in Catholic Colleges as an Aid to the Lay Apostolate." In *Man and Modern Secularism*. New York: National Catholic Alumni Federation, 1940.

"The Content of Theology in the Curriculum of Catholic Colleges and Universities." *Journal of Religious Instruction* 11 (April 1941): 671-74.

Cooke, Bernard J. "College Theology and the Ecumenical Spirit." NCEA *Bulletin* 59 (August 1962): 166-70.

_____. "The Particular Aims of Teaching the Faith at the College Level." *Living Light* 1 (spring 1964): 64-70.

_____. "The Place of Theology in the Curriculum of the Catholic College." NCEA *Bulletin* 63 (August 1966): 210-13.

Cooper, John M. "The Apologetic Content of the Advanced Religion Course." *Catho-*

lic Educational Review 21 (April 1923): 207-13.

_____. "The Ascetic Content of the Advanced Religion Course." *Catholic Educational Review* 21 (June 1923): 349-56.

_____. "Catholic Education and Theology." In *Vital Problems of Catholic Education in the United States*, edited by Roy J. Deferrari. Washington, D.C.: The Catholic University of America Press, 1939.

_____. "Content and Credit Hours for Courses in Religion." NCEA *Bulletin* 23 (1926): 134-42.

_____. "The Dogmatic Content of the Advanced Religion Course." *Catholic Educational Review* 21 (February 1923): 80-88.

_____. "The Historical Content of the Advanced Religion Course." *Catholic Educational Review* 21 (March 1923): 153-60.

_____. "The Moral Content of the Advanced Religion Course." *Catholic Educational Review* 21 (January 1923): 1-13.

_____. "The Preparation of Teachers of Religion." *Journal of Religious Instruction* 10 (September 1939): 54-64.

_____. "Religion in the College Curriculum." In *College Organization and Administration*, edited by Roy J. Deferrari. Washington, D.C.: The Catholic University of America Press, 1947.

Coudreau, Francois. "The Layman's Responsibility in the Theological Mission of the Church." *Lumen Vitae* 38 (1973): 609-37.

"Courses in Religion at the University of Detroit and Xavier University." *Journal of Religious Instruction* 10 (December 1939): 341-48.

Cox, Ignatius W. "Religious and Moral Guidance of College Students." NCEA *Bulletin* 23 (1926): 143-52.

"Credit for College Courses in Religion." *Journal of Religious Instruction* 5 (October 1934): 99.

"Credit Recognition for Religion Courses." *Journal of Religious Instruction* 4 (June 1934): 881-82.

Creek, Sister Mary Immaculate. *A Panorama: 1844-1977; Saint Mary's College, Notre Dame, Indiana.* Notre Dame, Ind.: Saint Mary's College, 1977.

Crowe, Frederick E., S.J. "The Church as Learner: Two Crises, One Kairos." *Appropriating the Lonergan Idea*, edited by Michael Vertin. Washington, D.C.: The Catholic University of America Press, 1989.

C. Stephen, Brother. "Panel: Academic Training in Sacred Doctrine for Non-Clerical Religious—B. In the Training of the Teaching Brother." *Proceedings of the SCCTSD* 3 (1957): 90-100.

CTSA. "Report of the Committee on Ecclesiastical Academic Legislation" (April 18, 1980).

Cummins, Patrick. "Religious Training from the Standpoint of Philosophy." NCEA *Bulletin* 8 (November 1911): 276-89.

Cunningham, Lawrence S. "Gladly Wolde He Lerne and Gladly Teche: The Catholic Scholar in the New Millennium." *The Cresset* (June 1992).

Cunningham, William F. "The Catholic College Program of Religious Education." *NCEA Bulletin* 37 (August 1940): 187-97.

_____. "The Catholic College Program of Religious Instruction." *Journal of Religious Instruction* 10 (June 1940): 852-62.

_____. "Religious Education in the Catholic College." *Journal of Religious Instruction* 6 (October 1935): 131-37.

Cunningham, William T. "Administrative Coordination in a Catholic American University." *Catholic Educational Review* 26 (June 1928): 321-32.

Curran, Charles E. *Catholic Higher Education, Theology and Academic Freedom.* Notre Dame, Ind.: University of Notre Dame Press, 1990.

Cushing, Richard J. "The Necessity for Theology at the College Level." In *Theology, Philosophy, and History as Integrating Disciplines in the Catholic College of Liberal Arts,* edited by Roy J. Deferrari. Washington, D.C.: The Catholic University of America Press, 1953.

Dammann, Mother Grace. "The American Catholic College for Women." In *Higher Education for Catholic Women: An Historical Anthology,* edited by Mary J. Oates. New York: Garland, 1987.

_____. "Principles and Action in Catholic College Education." *NCEA Bulletin* 36 (1939): 173-85.

Deane, Charles J. "Religion in the Catholic College." *Journal of Religious Instruction* 4 (October 1933): 163-72.

_____. "Religion in the Catholic College." *NCEA Bulletin* 30 (November 1933): 133-42.

Deferrari, Roy J., ed. *College Organization and Administration.* Washington, D.C.: The Catholic University of America Press, 1947.

_____. *The Curriculum of the Catholic College: Integration and Concentration.* Washington, D.C.: The Catholic University of America Press, 1952.

_____. *Discipline and Integration in the Catholic College.* Washington, D.C.: The Catholic University of America Press, 1951.

_____. *Essays on Catholic Education in the United States.* Washington, D.C.: The Catholic University of America Press, 1942.

_____. *Guidance in Catholic Colleges and Universities.* Washington, D.C.: The Catholic University of America Press, 1949.

_____. *Integration in Catholic Colleges and Universities.* Washington, D.C.: The Catholic University of America Press, 1950.

_____. "Lay and Collegiate Interest in Theology." In *Theology, Philosophy, and History as Integrating Disciplines in the Catholic College of Liberal Arts,* edited by Roy J. Deferrari. Washington, D.C.: The Catholic University of America Press, 1953.

_____. *A Layman In Catholic Education: His Life and Times.* Boston: St. Paul Editions, 1966.

_____. *Memoirs of the Catholic University of America, 1918-1960.* Boston: Daughters of St. Paul, 1962.

_____. *The Philosophy of Higher Education.* Washington, D.C.: The Catholic University of America Press, 1948.

_____. *Some Problems of Catholic Higher Education in the United States.* Boston: Daughters of St. Paul, 1963.

_____. "Theology and the College Curriculum." NCEA *Bulletin* 49 (November 1952): 7-15.

_____. *Theology, Philosophy, and History as Integrating Disciplines in the Catholic College of Liberal Arts.* Washington, D.C.: The Catholic University of America Press, 1953.

_____. *Vital Problems of Catholic Education in the United States.* Washington, D.C.: The Catholic University of America Press, 1939.

Denty, Vera D. "Religious Education at American Catholic Colleges." *Lumen Vitae* 14 (1959): 549-54.

Dillon, David A. "Panel: The Integration of Sacred Doctrine and Specific Disciplines— C. Sacred Doctrine and Philosophy." *Proceedings of the SCCTSD* 3 (1957): 41-47.

Dillon, William T. "Adventure in Religion." *Journal of Religious Instruction* 14 (September 1943): 63-70.

_____. "Dreams Can Come True." *Journal of Religious Instruction* 14 (February 1944): 559-67.

_____. "An Ideal." *Journal of Religious Instruction* 14 (November 1943): 320-25.

"Does the Catholic College Teach Religion?" *Journal of Religious Instruction* 15 (September 1944): 6-7.

Donlan, Thomas C. *Theology and Education.* Dubuque, Iowa: Wm. C. Brown, 1952.

_____. "Theology and Higher Education." *CTSA Proceedings* 10 (1955): 222-50.

_____. "Theology as an Integrating Force in Catholic Higher Education." NCEA *Bulletin* 50 (August 1953): 183-92.

_____. "The Thomistic Approach in College Theology." *Proceedings of the SCCTSD* 1 (1955): 26-29.

Donovan, Charles F. "Newman on the College Religion Curriculum." *Journal of Religious Instruction* 16 (December 1945): 413-20.

Dowd, William A. "The Gospels in the College Course." *Journal of Religious Instruction* 3 (June 1933): 895-902.

Doyle, Sister Margaret Marie. *The Curricula of the Catholic Women's College.* Notre Dame, Ind.: University of Notre Dame, 1932.

Drinkwater, F. H. "Religious Instruction in Colleges and Secondary Schools." *Catholic Educational Review* 26 (December 1928): 592-98.

Dubay, Thomas. "Theology for the Undergrad." *American Ecclesiastical Review* 136 (February 1957): 95-99.

Dugan, D. "Sell-Out in College Theology." *America* 117 (18 November 1967): 605.

Dunn, E. Catherine, and Dorothy A. Mohler, eds. *Pioneering Women at The Catholic University of America.* Washington, D.C.: Department of Anthropology, The Catholic University of America, 1990.

"Eastern Unit Minutes." [Committee on Educational Problems, Eastern Unit, College and University Department, NCEA, Fordham University, 22 February 1940.] NCEA *College Newsletter* 3 (March 1940): 3-4.

Egan, James M. "Preparation of Theology Teachers." In *Theology in the Catholic College*, edited by Reginald Masterson. Dubuque, Iowa: The Priory Press, 1961.

"Electives in College Religion." *Journal of Religious Instruction* 4 (April 1934): 695-96.

Elias, John L. *Studies in Theology and Education*. Malabar, Fla.: R. E. Krieger, 1986.

Ellard, Gerald A. "The Liturgy Course in College: A Proposed Outline." *Journal of Religious Instruction* 3 (May 1933): 783-91.

_____. "The Liturgy Course in College: Its Present Content." *Journal of Religious Instruction* 3 (April 1933): 689-96.

Ellis, John Tracy. *The Formative Years of the Catholic University of America*. Washington, D.C.: American Catholic Historical Association, 1946.

_____. "American Catholics and the Intellectual Life." *Thought* 30 (autumn 1955): 351-88.

Endear, Philip. "Theology out of Spirituality: The Approach of Karl Rahner." *Christian Spirituality Bulletin* 3 (fall 1995): 6-8.

Euart, Sharon, writing for the NCCB. "Theologians and the Mandate to Teach." *Origins* 23 (December 16, 1993): 465.

Evans, John Whitney. *The Newman Movement: Roman Catholics in American Higher Education, 1883-1971*. Notre Dame, Ind.: University of Notre Dame Press, 1980.

Evans, J. "Theology at American Universities." *Tablet* 220 (December 1966): 1453-54.

Falque, Ferdinand G. "The Catholic College Administration and the Problem of Religious Training." *Journal of Religious Instruction* 2 (June 1932): 963-65.

Farley, Edward. "The Place of Theology in the Study of Religion." *Religious Studies and Theology* 5 (September 1985): 9-29.

Farrell, Alan P. *The Jesuit Code of Liberal Education: Development and Scope of the Ratio Studiorum*. Milwaukee: Bruce, 1938.

Farrell, Walter. "Argument for Teaching Theology in Catholic Colleges." NCEA *Bulletin* 43 (August 1946): 239-44.

_____. "Wisdom in the Colleges." *Catholic Educational Review* 48 (May 1950): 289-98.

Fenton, Joseph Clifford. "Theology and Religion." *American Ecclesiastical Review* 112 (June 1945): 447-63.

_____. "The Student and His Church." *Catholic Educational Review* 33 (March 1935): 129-39.

Fernan, John J. "The College Religion Course." *Lumen Vitae* 4 (1949): 301-5.

_____. "The Historical, Scriptural Approach in College Theology." *Proceedings of the SCCTSD* 1 (1955): 34-42.

_____. "Presidential Address." *Proceedings of the SCCTSD* 2 (1956): 98-105.

Fernan, John J., John Courtney Murray, and Eugene B. Gallagher. "A College Religion Course Panel Discussion." *Jesuit Educational Quarterly* 12 (October 1949): 79-97.

Fiorenza, Francis Schüssler. "Theology in the University." *Bulletin of the Council of Societies for the Study of Religion* (April 1993): 34.

Fitzpatrick, Edward A. "Report of the Committee on Educational Problems." NCEA

Bulletin 38 (August 1941): 218-28.

Fitzpatrick, Edward A., et al. "Report of the Committee on Educational Problems and Research: College Teaching of Religion." NCEA *Bulletin* 37 (August 1940): 123-86.

Ford, Charles E., and Edgar L. Roy, Jr. *The Renewal of Catholic Higher Education*. Washington, D.C.: NCEA, 1968.

Fowler, James W., Parker Palmer, and Barbara G. Wheeler, eds. *Caring for the Commonweal: Education for Religious and Public Life*. Macon, Ga.: Mercer University Press, 1990.

Francis Vincent, Brother. "Some Conditions and Practices in the Teaching of Religion in Some Catholic Colleges in the MiddleAtlantic and New England States." *Journal of Religious Instruction* 11 (November 1940): 264-70.

"Freshman Religion Placement Test." *Journal of Religious Instruction* 7 (November 1936): 261.

"The Freshman Religion Placement Test." *Journal of Religious Instruction* 9 (June 1939): 839-42.

Friel, George Quentin. "The Catholic College Looks at Its Product." *Journal of Religious Instruction* 14 (September 1943): 71-77.

From an Abundant Spring: The Walter Farrell Memorial Volume of the Thomist, edited by the Staff of *The Thomist*. New York: P. J. Kenedy & Sons, 1952.

Furey, Francis J. "Salvaging Permanent Values for the Women's Colleges in the Post-War Period." NCEA *Bulletin* 39 (August 1942): 195-204.

Gaffney, J. Patrick. "Let Theology Be Theology!" *Horizons* 1 (fall 1974): 91-94.

_____. "Theology Departments: Become Involved!" *Horizons* 2 (spring 1975): 87-89.

Gallagher, Eugene B., ed. *Proceedings of the National Jesuit Institute on College Religion*. College of the Holy Cross, Worcester, Mass., 2-14 August 1951.

Gallin, Alice. "The Place of Theology in the Liberal Arts Curriculum of the Catholic College and University." In *Theology and the University*, edited by John Apczynski. Lanham, Md.: University Press of America, 1990.

_____, ed. *American Catholic Higher Education: Essential Documents, 1967-1990*. Notre Dame, Ind.: University of Notre Dame Press, 1992.

Garraghan, Gilbert J. *Jesuits of the Middle United States*, 3 vols. New York: America Press, 1938.

Garvey, John D. "Theology in the American College: An Overview." *Lumen Vitae* 33 (1978): 367-76.

Gibbons, Edmund F. "Christian Doctrine in Our Schools. Who Teaches It? How Should It Be Taught?" Report of the Proceedings of the Seventh Annual Meeting. *The Catholic Education Association Bulletin* 7 (November 1910): 309-27.

Gleason, Philip. "The American Background of *Ex corde Ecclesiae*: A Historical Perspective." In *Catholic Universities in Church and Society: A Dialogue on Ex corde Ecclesiae*, edited by John P. Langan. Washington, D.C.: Georgetown University Press, 1993.

_____. *Contending with Modernity: Catholic Higher Education in the Twentieth Century*. New York: Oxford University Press, 1995.

_____. *Keeping the Faith: American Catholicism Past and Present*. Notre Dame, Ind.: University of Notre Dame Press, 1987.

Gottemoeller, Doris. "The Changing Mission of Religious Life." In *Starting Points: Six Essays Based on the Experience of U.S. Women Religious*, edited by Lora Ann Quiñonez. Washington, D.C.: Leadership Conference of Women Religious of the U.S.A., 1980.

"Graduate Apologetics for Laymen." *Journal of Religious Instruction* 7 (September 1936): 10.

"Graduate Courses in Religion." *Journal of Religious Instruction* 2 (June 1932): 911-12.

Greeley, Andrew M. *The Changing Catholic College*. Chicago: Aldine, 1967.

_____. *From Backwater to Mainstream: A Profile of Catholic Higher Education*. Berkeley, Calif.: The Carnegie Foundation for the Advancement of Teaching, 1969.

Grismer, R. "Christian Formation in the University." *Catholic Educational Review* 66 (November 1968): 523-32.

Grollmes, Eugene E., ed. *Guidelines for Jesuit Higher Education: The Consensus Statements, Recommendations, and Committee Reports of the J. E. A. Denver Workshop on Jesuit Universities and Colleges: Their Commitment in a World of Change*. Denver, Colo., 6-14 August 1969.

Haight, Roger D. "Theological Education as a Theological Problem—III: The Relationship Between Method in Theology and in Teaching Theology." *CTSA Proceedings* 40 (1985): 73-77.

Haley, Sister Marie Philip. "An Attitude Scale in Religion for Catholic Colleges." *Journal of Religious Instruction* 11 (June 1941): 919-27; and 12 (September 1941): 62-74.

Hamilton, Raphael N. *The Story of Marquette University: An Object Lesson in the Development of Catholic Higher Education*. Milwaukee: Marquette University Press, 1953.

Handren, Walter J. "The Responsibility for the Catholic Formation of the Student as Applied to the Marriage Course: Structure and Content of an Ideal Marriage Course." *Proceedings of the SCCTSD* 2 (1956): 76-86.

Hanley, Philip L. "Collegiate Theology for Catholic Living." In *From an Abundant Spring: The Walter Farrell Memorial Volume of The Thomist*, edited by the Staff of *The Thomist*. New York: P. J. Kenedy & Sons, 1952.

Harmless, J. William. "Theology as Hard-Won Wisdom." *Conversations* 5 (spring 1994): 20.

Hardon, John A. "A New Era in College Religious Instruction." In *Shaping the Christian Message: Essays in Religious Education*, edited by Gerard S. Sloyan. New York: Macmillan, 1958.

_____. "Panel: Fundamental Theology in the College Curriculum—B. The Magisterium." *Proceedings of the SCCTSD* 3 (1957): 67-75.

Hargrove, Katharine T., ed. *On The Other Side*. Englewood Cliffs, N.J.: Prentice-Hall, 1967.

Hart, Ray L. "Religious and Theological Studies in American Higher Education: A Pilot Study." *Journal of the American Academy of Religion* 59 (winter 1991): 715-827.

Hartnett, R. C. "Moral Theology for Juniors." *Journal of Religious Instruction* 12 (January 1942): 428-41.

Harvey, John F. "Panel: Fundamental Theology in the College Curriculum—A. Apologetics." *Proceedings of the SCCTSD* 3 (1957): 58-66.

_____. "The Problem of Training College Teachers of Theology: The Problem as It Concerns the Priest-Professor." *Proceedings of the SCCTSD* 1 (1955): 70-75.

Harvey, Van A. "On the Intellectual Marginality of American Theology." In *Religion and Twentieth Century American Intellectual Life*, edited by Michael J. Lacey. New York: Woodrow Wilson International Center for Scholars and Cambridge University Press, 1989.

Haughey, John C. "Theology and the Mission of the Jesuit College and University." *Conversations on Jesuit Higher Education* 5 (1994): 5-17.

Hearne, Brian. "Teaching Theology as Praxis and Experience." *Lumen Vitae* 37 (1982): 7-25.

Heft, James. "Academic Freedom and the Catholic Community." In *Theology and the University*, edited by John Apczynski. Lanham, Md.: University Press of America, 1990.

Heinz, Donald. "Re-Visioning Religious Studies: A Call to Come Home." *Horizons* 5 (fall 1978): 233-48.

Hellwig, Monika K. "Twenty-Six Years of Undergraduate Theology." *Conversations* 5 (spring 1994): 18.

Hennesey, James. *American Catholics: A History of the Roman Catholic Community in the United States.* New York: Oxford University Press, 1981.

Hesburgh, Theodore M., C.S.C., ed. *The Challenge and the Promise of a Catholic University.* Notre Dame, Ind.: University of Notre Dame Press, 1994.

Hogan, Peter E. *The Catholic University of America, 1896-1903: The Rectorship of Thomas J. Conaty.* Washington, D.C.: The Catholic University of America Press, 1949.

Holland, Clement. "Student Religious Guidance in Mid-Western Catholic Colleges." *Journal of Religious Instruction* 12 (June 1942): 879-87.

_____. "Student Religious Guidance in Mid-Western Catholic Colleges." *Journal of Religious Instruction* 13 (October 1942): 155-62.

Horan, Ellamay. "Accepting Credit in High School Religion Toward the Minimum Units Required for College Entrance." *Journal of Religious Instruction* 4 (October 1933): 180-84.

_____. "Data from an Administration of The Religion Placement Test for College Freshmen." *Journal of Religious Instruction* 8 (February 1938): 530-34.

_____. The Non-Catholic College and Credit for Courses in Religion." *Journal of Religious Instruction* 5 (October 1934): 158-71.

_____. "Recognizing Credit from Courses in Religion." *Journal of Religious Instruction* 5 (November 1934): 250-62.

Hughes, Dominic. "The Theologian and College Courses." In *Theology, Philosophy, and History as Integrating Disciplines in the Catholic College of Liberal Arts*, edited by Roy J. Deferrari. Washington, D.C.: The Catholic University of America Press, 1953.

Imbelli, Robert P. "Dual Loyalties in Catholic Theology." *Commonweal* 119 (April 24, 1992): 21.

Imbelli, Robert P. and Thomas Groome. "Signposts Towards a Pastoral Theology." *Theological Studies* 53 (1992): 127-37.

"Improving Religious Instruction at the College and High School Levels." *Journal of Religious Instruction* 6 (February 1936): 479.

"Inter-Faculty Program Inquiry Report." *Woodstock Letters* 95 (1966): 335-56.

"The Intellectual Element in College Religion." *Journal of Religious Instruction* 3 (January 1933): 384-85.

Jean Marie, Sister. "Panel: Academic Training in Sacred Doctrine for Non-Clerical Religious—Sacred Doctrine in the Training of the Religious Sister." *Proceedings of the SCCTSD* 3 (1957): 82-89.

_____. "The Religious Development of Women at the College of St. Catherine." *Journal of Religious Instruction* 3 (June 1933): 868-85.

Joel Stanislaus, Brother. "Religion and the College." *Journal of Religious Instruction* 12 (April 1942): 704-13.

John Paul II, Pope. *Ex corde Ecclesiae*. In *American Catholic Higher Education: Essential Documents, 1967-1990*, edited by Alice Gallin. Notre Dame, Ind.: University of Notre Dame Press, 1992.

Johnson, Luke Timothy. "The New Testament and the Examined Life: Thoughts on Teaching." *The Christian Century* (February 1-8, 1995): 108-11.

Jonsen, Albert R. "Moral Theology and the Modern Catholic College." *Religious Education* 65 (May-June 1970): 245-51.

Jordan, Edward B. "Some Problems of the Catholic College: I. The Teaching Staff." *Catholic Educational Review* 20 (June 1922): 321-29.

_____. "Some Problems of the Catholic College: II. The College and the High School." *Catholic Educational Review* 21 (March 1923): 129-39.

_____. "Some Problems of the Catholic College: The Number of Departments." *Catholic Educational Review* 22 (March 1924): 129-140.

Jungmann, Josef Andreas. "Christus, als Mittelpunkt religiöser Erziehung." *Stimmen der Zeit* 134 (1938): 218-33.

_____. *The Good News Yesterday and Today*. Translated (abridged) and edited by William A. Huesman. New York: W. H. Sadlier, Inc., 1962.

_____. *Handing on the Faith: A Manual of Catechetics*. New York: Herder and Herder, 1959.

Kaiser, Edwin G. "The Nature and Function of Courses in Sacred Theology and their Curricular Implications in Liberal Education." NCEA *College Newsletter* 20 (October 1956): 1, 14-18.

_____. "Theology and the Social Sciences." *Proceedings of the SCCTSD* 4 (1958): 70-87.

Kane, Joseph. "It's Time for Reveille." *Journal of Religious Instruction* 3 (September 1932): 49-53.

Kaufman, Gordon. "Critical Theology as a University Discipline." In *Theology and the University: Essays in Honor of John B. Cobb, Jr.*, edited by David Griffin and Joseph Hough, Jr. Albany, N.Y.: State University of New York Press, 1991.

Kauffmann, Bruce, and Berard L. Marthaler. "The Interdisciplinary Nature of Undergraduate Theology." *Occasional Papers on Catholic Higher Education* 1 (December 1975): 15-18.

Keating, Francis M. "The Finality of the College Course in Sacred Doctrine in the Light of the Finality of the Layman." *Proceedings of the SCCTSD* 2 (1956): 25-46.

Keeler, Sister Jerome. "A College Course in Liturgy." *Journal of Religious Instruction* 2 (October 1931): 171-75.

Kelly, Justin S. "Toward a New Theology: The Implications of Rockhurst." *Woodstock Letters* 95 (1966): 357-71.

Kennedy, Sister M. St. Mel. "The Faculty in Catholic Colleges for Women." *Catholic Educational Review* 59 (May 1961): 289-98.

Keogh, John W. "Credit and Non-Credit Courses in Religion at Secular and Non-Catholic Colleges and Universities." *Journal of Religious Instruction* 9 (March 1939): 577-84.

"Kinshasa Statement: The Catholic University in the Modern World." In *American Catholic Higher Education: Essential Documents, 1967-1990,* edited by Alice Gallin. Notre Dame, Ind.: University of Notre Dame Press, 1992.

Kolmer, Elizabeth. *Religious Women in the United States: A Survey of the Influential Literature from 1950 to 1983.* Wilmington, Del.: Michael Glazer, 1984.

Komonchak, Joseph A. "The Catholic University in the Church." In *Catholic Universities in Church and Society: A Dialogue on Ex corde Ecclesiae,* edited by John P. Langan. Washington, D.C.: Georgetown University Press, 1993.

_____. "The Magisterium and Theologians." *Chicago Studies* 29 (1990): 325.

Lacey, Michael J. "The Conflicted Situation of American Higher Education and the Contribution of Catholics." *Current Issues in Catholic Higher Education* 16 (summer 1995): 16-25.

_____. "The Backwardness of American Catholicism." *Proceedings of the Catholic Theological Society of America* 46 (1991): 1-15.

Lamb, Matthew L. "Will There Be Catholic Theology in the United States?" *America* 162 (26 May 1990): 523-25, 531-34.

"Land O'Lakes Statement: The Nature of the Contemporary Catholic University." In *American Catholic Higher Education: Essential Documents, 1967-1990,* edited by Alice Gallin. Notre Dame, Ind.: University of Notre Dame Press, 1992.

Landy, Thomas M. "Lay Leadership in Catholic Higher Education: Where Will It Come From?" *America* 162 (17 March 1990): 264, 266-68.

Langan, John P., ed. *Catholic Universities in Church and Society: A Dialogue on Ex corde Ecclesiae.* Washington, D.C.: Georgetown University Press, 1993.

Latourelle, René. "Lay Theologians." In *Theology: Science of Salvation,* translated by Sister Mary Dominic. Staten Island, N.Y.: Alba House, 1969.

Lavelle, Michael J. "What Is Meant by a 'Catholic' University?" *America* 170 (5 February 1994): 4-7.

Leahy, William P. *Adapting to America: Catholics, Jesuits, and Higher Education in the Twentieth Century.* Washington, D.C.: Georgetown University Press, 1991.

Le Beau, Walter. "Religious Instruction in College." *Journal of Religious Instruction* 6 (November 1935): 236-42.

Lee, James Michael. *The Shape of Religious Instruction*. Dayton: Pflaum, 1971.

Leimkuhler, Edwin M. "Religion Program for Catholic Students at the University of Dayton." *Journal of Religious Instruction* 11 (March 1941): 638-43.

Leonard, Joan. "The Non-Traditional Catholic College Student and Religious Studies." *Current Issues in Catholic Higher Education* 7 (winter 1987): 33-37.

Lonergan, Bernard. "Topics in Education." *Collected Works of Bernard Lonergan*, vol. 10. Edited by Robert Doran and Frederick Crowe. Toronto, Buffalo, London: University of Toronto Press, 1993.

_____. "The Role of a Catholic University in the Modern World." *Collection: Papers by Bernard Lonergan, S.J.*. Edited by F. E. Crowe. Montreal: Palm, 1967.

M. Charles Borromeo, Sister. "Panel Discussion: The Responsibility of the Sacred Doctrine Teacher Precisely as Such for the Catholic Formation of the Student—D. Discussion." *Proceedings of the SCCTSD* 2 (1956): 61-65.

_____, recorder. "Discussion of Papers on Teacher Training." *Proceedings of the SCCTSD* 1 (1955): 75-82.

M. Consilla, Sister, recorder. "Symposium: Sacred Doctrine for Student Sisters." *Proceedings of the SCCTSD* 5 (1959): 118-29.

M. Gregoria, Sister. "Summary of Study on Religion Curricula in Catholic Colleges and Universities." *Catholic Educational Review* 45 (December 1947): 611-13.

M. Romana, Sister. "The New Testament for College Freshmen." *Catholic Educational Review* 52 (May 1954): 525-33.

M. Rose Eileen, Sister. "Academic Preparation of College Teachers of Sacred Doctrine, 1953-1964." *Proceedings of the SCCTSD* 10 (1964): 51-85.

Mackin, Theodore J. "Theology's Disturbing Presence in the University." *Jesuit Educational Quarterly* 27 (January 1965): 149-61.

Madges, William. "Does Theology Belong in the University? The Nineteenth-Century Case in Ireland and Germany." In *Theology and the University*, edited by John Apczynski. Lanham, Md.: University Press of America, 1990.

Madgett, A. Patrick. "Institute of Religious Education." *Journal of Religious Instruction* 12 (November 1941): 254-60.

_____. "Institute of Religious Education, II." *Journal of Religious Instruction* 12 (December 1941): 358-61.

Maguire, J. J. "Religion in the Catholic College." *Commonweal* 67 (31 January 1958): 447-50.

Maher, Sister M. Gratia. *The Organization of Religious Instruction in Catholic Colleges for Women*. Washington, D.C.: The Catholic University of America Press, 1951.

Man and Modern Secularism. New York: National Catholic Alumni Federation, 1940.

Maria Renata, Sister. "After Twenty Years." *Holy Cross Courier* 38 (summer 1964): 10, 12.

Marie Carolyn, Sister. "Panel: The Integration of Sacred Doctrine and Specific Disciplines—B. Sacred Doctrine and History." *Proceedings of the SCCTSD* 3 (1957): 29-40.

Marie Therese, Mother. "The Problem of Training Teachers of Theology on the College Level." *Proceedings of the SCCTSD* 1 (1955): 49-64.

Markoe, John P. "College Religion Charts." *Journal of Religious Instruction* 2 (February

1932): 571-78.

Marr, George. "A College Course in Religion." CEA *Bulletin* 24 (November 1927): 157-65.

Marthaler, Berard L. "Catechesis and Theology." *Proceedings of the Catholic Theological Society of America* 28 (1973): 261-70.

_____. *The Catechism Yesterday and Today, The Evolution of Genre.* Collegeville, Minn.: The Liturgical Press, 1995.

_____. "The Department of Religion and Religious Education of the Catholic University of America." *Living Light* 9 (spring 1972): 19-22.

_____. "A Discipline in Quest of an Identity." *Horizons* 3 (fall 1976): 203-15.

_____. "To Teach Theology or to Teach the Faith." *Proceedings of the Catholic Theological Society of America* 31 (1976): 217-33.

Mary Eunicia, Sister. "Theology in the College Curriculum." *Journal of Religious Instruction* 8 (December 1937): 318-31.

Mary Genevieve, Sister. "An Annotated List of Books Based on a Suggested Outline for Religion Courses in Colleges." *Journal of Religious Instruction* 5 (April 1935): 675-85; 5 (May 1935): 779-89; 5 (June 1935): 888-902; 6 (September 1935): 56-59; 6 (October 1935): 143-48; 6 (November 1935): 243-50; 6 (December 1935): 326-32; 6 (January 1936): 410-16; 6 (February 1936): 524-31; 6 (March 1936): 622-26; 6 (April 1936): 713-17; 6 (May 1936): 801-15; 7 (September 1936): 61-67; 7 (October 1936): 160-68; 7 (November 1936): 262-64; 7 (January 1937): 426-29; 7 (March 1937): 644-52.

Mary Loyole, Sister. "Comprehensive Examinations in Religion as an Incentive to Scholarship." *Journal of Religious Instruction* 11 (October 1940): 171-75.

_____. "A Discussion of the Results of the Investigation: 'Analysis of the Range of Differences in Knowledge of Their Religion Among Catholic Students Entering Catholic Colleges as Freshmen.'" *Journal of Religious Instruction* 7 (February 1937): 552-62.

_____. "The 1935-36 Religion Placement Test for College Freshmen." *Journal of Religious Instruction* 7 (January 1937): 417-25.

Mary Loyole, Sister, and William F. Cunningham. "The 1937 Freshman Religion Placement Test." *Journal of Religious Instruction* 9 (September 1938): 41-48.

Mary Peter, Sister. "Comments of 'Religion in College.'" *Journal of Religious Instruction* 13 (May 1943): 730-32.

Masson, Robert. "Creative Teaching: Theology for the Head, Heart, Hands and Feet: An Approach to the First Course." *Horizons* 13 (1986): 90-103.

_____. "Taking the Pulse of an Emerging Genre: College Theology on the Catholic Campus." *Current Issues in Catholic Higher Education* 7 (winter 1987): 5-8.

Masterson, Reginald. Introduction to *Theology in the Catholic College,* edited by Reginald Masterson. Dubuque, Iowa: The Priory Press, 1961.

_____. "Panel: College Teacher Training in Sacred Doctrine—E. The Scope of Teacher Training Programs." *Proceedings of the SCCTSD* 4 (1958): 112-15.

McBrien, Richard. "Faith, Theology and Belief." *Commonweal* 101 (15 November 1974): 134-37.

_____. "The Pastoral Dimension of Theology Today." *America* 151 (28 July 1984): 25-28.

McCall, Raymond J. "At the College Level." *Commonweal* 31 (1 December 1939): 131.

McCluskey, Neil G. "America and the Catholic School." In *Catholic Education in America: A Documentary History,* edited by Neil G. McCluskey. New York: Teachers College, Columbia University, 1964.

_____, ed. *Catholic Education in America: A Documentary History.* New York: Teachers College, Columbia University, 1964.

_____. *The Catholic University: A Modern Appraisal.* Notre Dame, Ind.: University of Notre Dame Press, 1970.

McCool, Gerald A. "The Tradition of St. Thomas in North America: At 50 Years." *The Modern Schoolman* 65 (March 1988): 185-206.

McCormack, Stephen. "Panel Discussion: The Responsibility of the Sacred Doctrine Teacher Precisely as Such for the Catholic Formation of the Student—E. Discussion." *Proceedings of the SCCTSD* 2 (1956): 65-69.

McCormick, John F. *Marquette University.* Milwaukee: Marquette University Press, 1929.

McCrabb, Don. "Empowering the Spirit: Campus Ministry at Catholic Colleges and Universities." *New Catholic World* 231 (September/October 1988): 226-29.

[McDermott], Sister Maria Concepta. *The Making of a Sister-Teacher.* Notre Dame, Ind.: University of Notre Dame Press, 1965.

McDonnell, John F. "Panel: Fundamental Theology in the College Curriculum—C. Sacred Scripture." *Proceedings of the SCCTSD* 3 (1957): 76-81.

McFadden, William C. "'Catechism at 4 for all the Schools': Religious Instruction at Georgetown." In *Georgetown at Two Hundred: Faculty Reflections on the University's Future,* edited by William C. McFadden. Washington, D.C.: Georgetown University Press, 1990.

_____, ed. *Georgetown at Two Hundred: Faculty Reflections on the University's Future.* Washington, D.C.: Georgetown University Press, 1990.

McGinn, Bernard. "The Letter and the Spirit: Spirituality as an Academic Discipline." *Christian Spirituality Bulletin* 1 (fall 1993): 3-10

McGucken, William J. "The Renascence of Religion Teaching in American Catholic Schools." In *Essays on Catholic Education in the United States,* edited by Roy J. Deferrari, 329-51. Washington, D.C.: The Catholic University of America Press, 1942.

_____. "Report of the Committee on Educational Policy and Program." NCEA *Bulletin* 34 (1937): 88-91.

McIntosh, Mark. "Lover Without a Name: Spirituality and Constructive Christology Today." *Christian Spirituality Bulletin* 3 (fall 1995): 9-12.

McKenzie, John L. "Theology as an Integrating Factor in Jesuit Education." *Jesuit Educational Quarterly* 31 (June 1958): 19-26.

_____. "Theology in Jesuit Education." *Thought* 34 (autumn 1959): 347-56.

_____. "Training Teachers of College Theology." *Jesuit Educational Quarterly* 19 (1956): 94-108.

McMahon, Francis E. "Theology for the Layman." *Journal of Religious Instruction* 7

(March 1937): 630-40.

McNeill, Donald, and Karen Ann Paul. "Theology and Field-Based Learning." *Occasional Papers on Catholic Higher Education* 1 (December 1975): 35-41.

McNeill, Harry. "Integrating Religion." *Commonweal* 31 (10 November 1939): 75-77.

McQuade, James J. "Religious Education Association, 1942." *Journal of Religious Instruction* 13 (September 1942): 77-80.

McSweeny, Edward. "Is Religious Training as Necessary for the Student of the High School and College as it is for the Child of the Primary School?" NCEA *Proceedings* 3 (1906): 128-43.

Meilhac, Louis. "The Teaching of Religion in Catholic Universities: Results of a World Investigation by the Federation of Catholic Universities." *Lumen Vitae* 15 (1960): 417-32.

Meyers, Sister Bertrande. *The Education of Sisters: A Plan for Integrating the Religious, Social, Cultural and Professional Training of Sisters.* New York: Sheed & Ward, 1941.

_____. *Sisters for the 21st Century.* New York: Sheed & Ward, 1965.

Michel, Virgil G. "Religion for Credit." *Catholic Educational Review* 21 (October 1923): 465-70.

_____. "A Religious Need of the Day." *Catholic Educational Review* 23 (October 1925): 449-56.

Mooney, Christopher F. "College Theology and Liberal Education." *Thought* 34 (1959): 325-30.

_____. "The Role of Theology in the Education of Undergraduates." In *Catholic Colleges and the Secular Mystique,* edited by Eugene E. Grollmes. St. Louis: B. Herder, 1970.

_____. "Theology and the Catholic College—New Orientations." *Religious Education* 56 (May-June 1961): 218-23, 240.

Morrison, Bakewell. "An Interpretation of the Work of the Convention of Religion Teachers." *Jesuit Educational Quarterly* 1 (October 1938): 17-27.

_____. "Broadening Horizons: Meeting of the Institute of Religious Education." *Jesuit Educational Quarterly* 2 (December 1939): 138-41.

_____. "A Problem in Teaching College Religion." *Journal of Religious Instruction* 4 (May 1934): 826-31.

_____. "The Program of Religious Instruction at St. Louis University." *Journal of Religious Instruction* 10 (February 1940): 508-15.

_____. "Religion Teaching in the United States: College and University Level." *Lumen Vitae* 4 (October 1949): 767-88.

_____. "Some Remarks on the Fruits of Teaching Religion at St. Louis University." *Journal of Religious Instruction* 10 (March 1940): 590-96.

_____. "Teaching Religion at College." *America* 49 (22 April 1933): 62-63.

Mullaney, James V. "The General Principles of Integration of the Curriculum." *Proceedings of the SCCTSD* 3 (1957): 9-19.

Murray, John Courtney. "The Christian Idea of Education." In *The Christian Idea of Education,* edited by Edmund Fuller. New Haven: Yale University Press, 1957.

_____. "The Making of a Pluralistic Society—A Catholic View." In *Religion and the State University*, edited by Erich A. Walter. Ann Arbor: The University of Michigan Press, 1958.

_____. "Necessary Adjustments to Overcome Practical Difficulties." In *Man and Modern Secularism*. New York: National Catholic Alumni Federation, 1940.

_____. "On the Idea of a College Religion Course." *Jesuit Educational Quarterly* (October 1949): 80-81.

_____. "Towards a Theology for the Layman: The Problem of its Finality." *Theological Studies* 5 (March 1944): 43-75.

_____. "Towards a Theology for the Layman: The Pedagogical Problem." *Theological Studies* 5 (September 1944): 341-76.

Neal, Marie Augusta. Preface to *Religious Women in the United States: A Survey of the Influential Literature from 1950 to 1983*, by Elizabeth Kolmer. Wilmington, Del.: Michael Glazer, 1984.

Nouwen, Henri. "Theology as Doxology: Reflections on Theological Education." In *Caring for the Commonweal: Education for Religious and Public Life*, edited by Parker J. Palmer, Barbara G. Wheeler, and James W. Fowler. Macon, Ga.: Mercer University Press, 1990.

Novak, Vincent M. "A Report on Some Trends in Religious Education and Graduate Studies in the U.S.A." *Lumen Vitae* 30 (1975): 389-94.

Nuesse, C. Joseph. *The Catholic University of America: A Centennial History*. Washington, D.C.: The Catholic University of America Press, 1990.

_____. "Undergraduate Education at The Catholic University of America: The First Decades, 1889-1930." *U.S. Catholic Historian* 7 (fall 1988): 429-51.

Oates, Mary J. "The Development of Catholic Colleges for Women, 1895-1960." *U.S. Catholic Historian* 7 (fall 1988): 413-28.

_____, ed. *Higher Education for Catholic Women: An Historical Anthology*. New York: Garland, 1987.

O'Brien, David J. "The Church and Catholic Higher Education." *Horizons* 17 (1990): 7-29.

_____. "A Collegiate Conversation: Prof. O'Brien to Father Buckley." *America* 169 (11 September 1993): 18-23.

_____. *From the Heart of the American Church: Catholic Higher Education and American Culture*. Maryknoll, N.Y.: Orbis, 1994.

O'Collins, Gerald. "Catholic Theology (1965-1990)." *America* 162 (3 February 1990): 86-87, 104-5.

O'Connell, Laurence J. "The Role of Theology in the Liberal Arts Curriculum." In *Jesuit Higher Education: Essays on an American Tradition of Excellence*, edited by Rolando E. Bonachea. Pittsburgh, Pa.: Duquesne University Press, 1989.

O'Connor, Paul L. "Religion in the Undergraduate Jesuit Colleges." *Jesuit Educational Quarterly* 11 (June 1948): 41-48.

O'Donnell, Charles. "A Course in the History of Social Catholicism." *Journal of Religious Instruction* 9 (February 1939): 474-80.

O'Donnell, Luke. "The Teaching of College Theology." *American Ecclesiastical Review* 146 (1962): 167-73.

Ogden, Schubert M. "Religious Studies and Theological Studies: What Is Involved in the Distinction Between Them?" *Bulletin for the Council of Societies for the Study of*

Religion Bulletin 24 (February 1995): 3-4.

O'Hara, Charles M. "A Plan of Curricular Integration for the Catholic College." *Journal of Religious Instruction* 9 (October 1938): 143-50.

O'Hara, Edwin V. "Teaching Apologetics in Ecclesiastical Seminaries and in Catholic Colleges for Men and Women." *Journal of Religious Instruction* 1 (April 1931): 218-22.

O'Meara, Thomas F. "The Department of Theology at a Catholic University." In *The Challenge and Promise of a Catholic University*, edited by Theodore M. Hesburgh. Notre Dame, Ind.: University of Notre Dame Press, 1994.

_____. "Doctoral Programs in Theology at U.S. Catholic Universities." *America* 162 (3 February 1990): 79-80, 82, 84, 101-3.

O'Meara, Timothy. "The Evolution of a Catholic University—The Next Challenge." *New Catholic World* 231 (September/October 1988): 201-5.

O'Neil, Sister Mary Bernice. *Evaluation of the Curricula of a Selected Group of Catholic Women's Colleges*. Washington, D.C.: The Catholic University of America Press, 1942.

Ong, Walter J. "Yeast: A Parable for Catholic Higher Education." *America* 162 (7 April 1990): 347-49, 362-63.

Ostovich, Steven T. "Theology in the Postmodern University: Reflections from Political Philosophy and Theology." In *Theology and the University*, edited by John Apczynski. Lanham, Md.: University Press of America, 1990.

Padberg, John W. "Taking Theology Seriously." *Conversations on Jesuit Higher Education* 5 (1994): 3.

Palmer, Parker J. *To Know As We Are Known*. San Francisco: Harper and Row, 1983.

"Partial Mastery and College Students." *Journal of Religious Instruction* 4 (March 1934): 583-84.

Patterson, W. "College Theology: Career for Laymen." *America* 110 (28 March 1964): 412-16.

Pelikan, Jaroslav. "*Ex corde Universitatis*: Reflections on the Significance of Newman's 'Insisting Solely on Natural Theology'." In *Catholic Universities in Church and Society: A Dialogue on Ex corde Ecclesiae*, edited by John P. Langan. Washington, D.C.: Georgetown University Press, 1993.

Pheme Perkins. "Revisioning the Teaching of Scripture." *Current Issues in Catholic Higher Education* 7 (winter 1987): 29-32.

Phan, Peter C. "Multiculturalism, Church and the University." *Religious Education* 90 (winter 1995): 25.

Phelan, Gerald B. "Theology in the Curriculum of Catholic Colleges and Universities." In *Man and Modern Secularism*. New York: National Catholic Alumni Federation, 1940.

Pius, XI, Pope. *[Divini Illius Magistri.] Rappresentanti in Terra*. In *The Papal Encyclicals, 1903-1939*. Edited by Claudia Carlen. Wilmington, N.C.: McGrath, 1981.

Portier, William L. "The Mission of a Catholic College." In *Theology and the University*, edited by John Apczynski. Lanham, Md.: University Press of America, 1990.

"Postwar Planning for Jesuit Education: The Colleges—I. Review of Past Performance." *Jesuit Educational Quarterly* 7 (June 1943): 19-31.

Power, Edward J. *Catholic Higher Education in America: A History*. New York: Appleton-Century-Crofts, 1972.

_____. *A History of Catholic Higher Education in the United States.* Milwaukee: Bruce, 1958.

Prevallet, Elaine Marie. "Catholic College Theology: A Liberal Education?" *Living Light* 7 (summer 1970): 82-91.

"Providing for the Superior Student at the College Level." *Journal of Religious Instruction* 2 (January 1932): 419.

Pursley, Leo A. "Theology and the Laity." In *Theology and the Teacher: Three Addresses.* Notre Dame, Ind.: Saint Mary's College, 1953.

Quiñonez, Lora Ann, ed. *Starting Points: Six Essays Based on the Experience of U.S. Women Religious.* Washington, D.C.: Leadership Conference of Women Religious of the U.S.A., 1980.

Quiñonez, Lora Ann, and Mary Daniel Turner. *The Transformation of American Catholic Sisters.* Philadelphia: Temple University Press, 1992.

[Quirk], Sister Mary Richardine. "The Evolution of the Idea of Sister Formation, 1952-1960." *Sponsa Regis* 33 (April 1962): 223-33.

"Recommendations Made by the General Assembly, as Revised by the Executive Committee of the Jesuit Educational Association, and Approved by Its Board of Governors." In *Proceedings of the National Jesuit Institute on College Religion*, edited by Eugene B. Gallagher. College of the Holy Cross, Worcester, Mass., 2-14 August 1951.

"Religion Placement Test." *Journal of Religious Instruction* 6 (January 1936): 406-9.

"The Religion Placement Test for College Freshmen." *Journal of Religious Instruction* 6 (February 1936): 521-23.

"Religion Placement Test for College Freshmen." *Journal of Religious Instruction* 6 (March 1936): 619-21.

"The Religion Placement Test for College Freshmen." *Journal of Religious Instruction* 6 (April 1936): 707-12.

"The Religion Placement Test for College Freshmen." *Journal of Religious Instruction* 7 (September 1936): 60.

"The Religion Placement Test Study." *Journal of Religious Instruction* 6 (May 1936): 816.

"Religion Teaching: A Students' Viewpoint." *Ecclesiastical Review* 99 (November 1938): 439-47.

Rodgers, Rosemary T. *A History of the College Theology Society.* Villanova, Pa.: College Theology Society, 1983.

"Rome Statement: The Catholic University and the Aggiornamento." In *American Catholic Higher Education: Essential Documents, 1967-1990*, edited by Alice Gallin. Notre Dame, Ind.: University of Notre Dame Press, 1992.

Rooney, Edward B. "Editorial Comment: Postwar Planning for Education." *Jesuit Educational Quarterly* 5 (March 1943): 221-24.

Rousseau, R. W. "Theology and Culture in Catholic Colleges." *Perspectives* 5 (October 1960): 25-29.

Rowntree, Stephen C. "Ten Theses on Jesuit Higher Education." *America* 170 (28 May

1994): 6-12.

Rueve, Stephen J. "Non-Catholics in Catholic Colleges." *Journal of Religious Instruction* 8 (January 1938): 417-20.

_____. "Religion for Non-Catholics." *Journal of Religious Instruction* 6 (October 1935): 138-42.

Russell, William H. "The Case for Full-Time Teachers of Religion." *Journal of Religious Instruction* 11 (December 1940): 296-307.

_____. "Correspondence: Religion in College." *Journal of Religious Instruction* 14 (November 1943): 333-34.

_____. "The Department of Religious Education." *Catholic University Bulletin* 9 (March 1942): 4, 10.

_____. "The Nature and Function of Christo-centrism in the Teaching of Religion." *Journal of Religious Instruction* 12 (June 1942): 833-52.

_____. "The Priest and the Teaching of Religion." *Ecclesiastical Review* 99 (August 1938): 97-115.

_____. "Principles for a College Religion Course." *Journal of Religious Instruction* 8 (April 1938): 697-710.

_____. "Religion for College Students." NCEA *Bulletin* 43 (August 1946): 215-38.

_____. "Who May Teach Religion?" *Catholic Educational Review* 44 (February 1946): 78-85.

_____. "Why Not Religion for the Sisters and the Laity?" *Journal of Religious Instruction* 16 (October, November, December 1945): 220-25, 325-32, and 397-412.

_____. "Wisdom Derived from a Study of the Life of Christ and the Liturgy." *Catholic Educational Review* 48 (December 1950): 649-60.

Ruth, Sister Mary. "The Function of Religion in Character Formation." CEA *Bulletin* 25 (November 1928): 197-206.

Ryan, John K. "The Catholic College and the Catholic Mind." *Catholic Educational Review* 32 (December 1934): 577-86.

Ryan, Mary Perkins. "The Identity Crisis of Religious Educators." *Living Light* 5 (winter 1968-69): 6-18.

Salm, C. Luke. "The Le Moyne Plan." *Proceedings of the SCCSTD* 5 (1959): 112-16.

_____. "The Problem of Training Teachers of Theology at the College Level: The Problem as It Concerns the Religious Teaching Brother. *Proceedings of the SCCTSD* 1 (1955): 65-69.

_____. "The Status of Theology in the College." *Proceedings of the SCCTSD* 10 (1964): 38-50.

Schabert, Joseph A. "The Use of Objective Tests in the Teaching of Religion in College." *Journal of Religious Instruction* 1 (March 1931): 121-25.

Scharper, Philip. "The Relevance of Theology to the University." In *On The Other Side*, edited by Katharine T. Hargrove. Englewood Cliffs, N.J.: Prentice-Hall, Inc., 1967.

Schneiders, Sandra M. "Spirituality as an Academic Discipline: Reflections from Experience." *Christian Spirituality Bulletin* 1 (fall 1993): 10-15.

_____. "Spirituality in the Academy." *Theological Studies* 50 (1989): 676-97.

Schner, George P. *Education for Ministry: Reform and Renewal in Theological Education*. Kansas City, Mo.: Sheed & Ward, 1993.

Schubert, Frank D. *A Sociological Study of Secularization Trends in the American Catholic University: Decatholicizing the Catholic Religious Curriculum*. Lewiston, N.Y.: The Edwin Mellon Press, 1990.

Schumacher, Matthew. "Religion in College through Integration." In *College Organization and Administration*, edited by Roy J. Deferrari. Washington, D.C.: The Catholic University of America Press, 1947.

Schuth, Katarina *Reason for the Hope: The Futures of Roman Catholic Theologates*. Wilmington, Del.: Michael Glazier, 1989.

Schwehn, Mark R. *Exiles from Eden: Religion and the Academic Vocation in America*. New York: Oxford University Press, 1993.

_____. "Religion and the Life of Learning." *First Things* (August-September 1990): 34-43.

Shea, William M. "Beyond Tolerance: Pluralism and Catholic Higher Education." In *Theology and the University*, edited by John Apczynski. Lanham, Md.: University Press of America, 1990.

_____. "Dual Loyalties in Catholic Theology Finding Faith in Alien Texts." *Commonweal* 119 (January 31, 1992): 14.

_____. "Intelligence Shaped by Affection." *Conversations* 5 (spring 1994): 19.

_____. "Pluralism and the Challenge to Catholic Higher Education." *American Catholic Issues: A Newsletter* (spring 1994): 1.

Sheedy, Charles E. "The Problem of Theology for the Laity." *Proceedings of the Catholic Theological Society of America* 7 (1952): 111-17.

Sheehy, Maurice S. "An Advanced Religion Course: Content and Methods." *Journal of Religious Instruction* 1 (February 1931): 22-31.

_____. "A Postwar Religious Program for the Catholic College." In *College Organization and Administration*, edited by Roy J. Deferrari. Washington, D.C.: The Catholic University of America Press, 1947.

_____. "Religion and the College." *America* 45 (27 June 1931): 272-74

Sheldrake, Philip F. "Some Continuing Questions: The Relationship Between Spirituality and Theology," *Christian Spirituality Bulletin* 2 (spring 1994): 16.

Simonitsch, Roland G. "Observations on the Teaching of Religion at the College Level." *Journal of Religious Instruction* 13 (February 1943): 477-85.

_____. *Religious Instruction in Catholic Colleges for Men*. Washington, D.C.: The Catholic University of America Press, 1952.

Sloyan, Gerard S. "From Christ in the Gospel to Christ in the Church." *Proceedings of the SCCTSD* 1 (1955): 10-24.

_____. "The Good News and the Catechetical Scene in the United States." In Josef Andreas Jungmann, *The Good News Yesterday and Today*, translated (abridged) and edited by William A. Huesman. New York: W. H. Sadlier, 1962.

_____. "The New Role of the Study of Religion in Higher Education: What Does It Mean?" *Journal of Ecumenical Studies* 6 (winter 1969): 1-17.

_____. "Panel: College Teacher Training in Sacred Doctrine—C. The Program at The Catholic University of America." *Proceedings of the SCCTSD* 4 (1958): 103-8.

_____. ed. *Shaping the Christian Message: Essays in Religious Education.* New York: Macmillan, 1958.

_____. "Some Factors in the Teaching of Sacred Doctrine." *Catholic Educational Review* 53 (January 1955): 1-17.

_____. "Undergraduate Studies in Sacred Doctrine at One U.S. University." *Lumen Vitae* 15 (1960): 712-22.

Smith, Patricia. "Theological Education as a Theological Problem IV." *CTSA Proceedings* 40 (1985): 78-82.

Smith, Richard F. "How Theology Chairpersons View Their Task." *Occasional Papers in Catholic Higher Education* 1 (December 1975): 4-12.

"Some Data from Three Case Reports Made After Studying Students' Scores on 'The Religion Placement Test.'" *Journal of Religious Instruction* 7 (March 1937): 641-43.

"Some Desirable Trait-Actions in the College Teacher of Religion." *Journal of Religious Instruction* 2 (April 1932): 768-70.

Stanford, Edward V. "Religious Needs of College Freshmen: A Freshman Religious Survey." *Journal of Religious Instruction* 2 (January 1932): 462-72.

Stuhlmueller, Carroll. "Catholic Biblical Scholarship and College Theology." *Thomist* 23 (October 1960): 533-63.

"A Substitute for Credits." *Journal of Religious Instruction* 7 (May 1937): 783-85.

Suchocki, Marjorie. "Theological Education as a Theological Problem II: The One and the Many Revisited." *CTSA Proceedings* 40 (1985): 67-73.

_____. "Theological Foundations for Ethnic and Gender Diversity in Faculties or Excellence and the Motley Crew." *Theological Education* 26 (1990): 35-50.

Sullivan, C. Stephen. "The Dimensions of Theology in a Catholic College in the Light of Vatican II." In *On The Other Side*, edited by Katharine T. Hargrove. Englewood Cliffs, N.J.: Prentice-Hall, 1967.

Sullivan, William J. "The Catholic University and the Academic Study of Religion." In *Religion in the Undergraduate Curriculum: An Analysis and Interpretation*, edited by Claude Welch. Washington, D.C.: Association of American Colleges, 1972.

_____. "Theology for Undergraduates." *America* 121 (15 November 1969): 463-66.

Sutton, Donald. "The Role of Campus Ministry in a Jesuit College or University." In *Jesuit Higher Education: Essays on an American Tradition of Excellence*, edited by Rolando Bonachea. Pittsburgh, Pa.: Duquesne University Press, 1989.

Theology and the Teacher: Three Addresses. Notre Dame, Ind.: Saint Mary's College, 1953.

"Theology for Teachers." *Journal of Religious Instruction* 15 (October 1944): 163-64.

"Theology in the Curriculum of Catholic Colleges and Universities." *Journal of Religious Instruction* 11 (March 1941): 569-73.

"The Titles of Our College Religion Courses." *Journal of Religious Instruction* 3 (March

1933): 563.

Tracy, David. "Can Virtue Be Taught? Education, Character, and the Soul." In *Theology and the University*, edited by John Apczynski. Lanham, Md.: University Press of America, 1990.

"The University of Dayton's Reading List." *Journal of Religious Instruction* 7 (May 1937): 825-42.

Van Ackeren, Gerald. "The Finality of the College Course in Sacred Doctrine in the Light of the Finality of Theology." *Proceedings of the SCCTSD* 2 (1956): 10-24.

Van Heertum, J. A. "An Outline of Program for Religious Instruction in Catholic Academies and Colleges." CEA *Bulletin* 7 (November 1910): 145-56.

Vollert, Cyril. "The Origin, Development, and Purpose of the Society of Catholic College Teachers of Sacred Doctrine." NCEA *Bulletin* 51 (August 1954): 247-55.

_____. "Theology and University Education." *Modern Schoolman* 21 (1943): 12-25.

Ward, Ferdinand J. "A College Course in the Preparation for Marriage." *Journal of Religious Instruction* 9 (April 1939): 664-69.

_____. "Current Topics for Senior Religion." *Journal of Religious Education* 5 (February 1935): 535-38.

_____. "The Demonstration of Ceremonies in Senior Religion." *Journal of Religious Instruction* 5 (April 1935): 686-89.

_____. "The Lecture in Senior Religion." *Journal of Religious Instruction* 5 (December 1934): 320-23.

_____. "A Study of Comparative Religions in Catholic Colleges." *Journal of Religious Instruction* 9 (January 1939): 399-404.

_____. "The Questionnaire in Senior Religion." *Journal of Religious Instruction* 5 (May 1935): 790-95.

Weigel, Gustave. "American Catholic Intellectualism—A Theologian's Reflections." *Review of Politics* 19 (July 1957): 275-307.

_____. "The Meaning of Sacred Doctrine in the College." In *Shaping the Christian Message: Essays in Religious Education*, edited by Gerard S. Sloyan. New York: Macmillan, 1958.

Welch, Claude. *Graduate Education in Religion: A Critical Appraisal*. Missoula, Mont.: Council on the Study of Religion, 1971.

_____, ed. *Religion in the Undergraduate Curriculum: An Analysis and Interpretation*. Washington, D.C.: Association of American Colleges, 1972.

_____. "Theological Education as a Theological Problem I." *CTSA Proceedings* 40 (1985): 64-67.

Whalen, John P. "The Problem of College Theology." *Catholic Educational Review* 57 (December 1959): 583-90.

Wheeler, Barbara, and Edward Farley, eds. *Shifting Boundaries: Contextual Approaches to the Structure of Theological Education*. Louisville, Ky.: Westminster, 1991.

"When Is the Propitious Time?" *Journal of Religious Instruction* 6 (February 1936): 478-79.

White, Joseph M. *The Diocesan Seminary in the United States: A History from the 1780s to the Present*. Notre Dame, Ind.: University of Notre Dame Press, 1989.

_____. "Theological Studies at the Catholic University of America: Organization and Leadership before Vatican Council II." *U.S. Catholic Historian* 7 (fall 1988): 453-66.

Wister, Robert J. "The Teaching of Theology 1950-1990: The American Catholic Experience." *America* 162 (3 February 1990): 88, 90, 92-93, 106-7, 109.

Withey, Helen. "Panel: Sacred Doctrine in Professional Schools—B. Sacred Doctrine Courses in the Catholic School of Nursing." *Proceedings of the SCCTSD* 3 (1957): 108-13.

[Wolff], Sister M. Madeleva. "The Education of Our Young Religious Teachers." NCEA *Bulletin* 46 (August 1949): 253-56.

_____. *My First Seventy Years.* New York: Macmillan, 1959.

_____. "The Preparation of Teachers of Religion—College Viewpoint." NCEA *Bulletin* 46 (August 1949): 202-4.

_____. "Religion in College." *Journal of Religious Instruction* 13 (May 1943): 724-30.

_____. "Scholarship for Catholic Women." *Catholic Educational Review* 30 (January 1932): 21-32.

_____. "Theology and the Teacher." In *Theology and the Teacher: Three Addresses.* Notre Dame, Ind.: Saint Mary's College, 1953 (unpaged pamphlet).

Worgul, Jr., George S. *Issues in Academic Freedom.* Pittsburgh: Duquesne University Press, 1992.

Unpublished Papers and Dissertations:

Bull, George, S.J. "The Catholic Graduate School." 1938.

Carey, Patrick W. "Theology at Marquette University: A History." Unpublished monograph, 1987.

Carton, Sister M. Francis Regis. "An Inquiry into the Study of Sacred Doctrine and Faculty Preparation in Sixty-Three Catholic Colleges." Ph.D. diss., The Catholic University of America, 1963.

Charles, Henry J. "Roman Catholic Students and Graduates of Non-denominational University Related Divinity Schools." Report of a Lilly Endowment, 1991.

Hochwalt, F. G. "Status of Religious Education in Selected Catholic Colleges." Paper delivered at the Association of American Colleges Meeting, 9 January 1952.

Lucker, Raymond A. "The Aims of Religious Education in the Early Church and in the American Catechetical Movement." S.T.D. diss., Angelicum, 1966.

Mize, Sandra Yocum. "Saint Mary's Graduate School of Sacred Theology: The Theological Formation of Women Teaching Religion, 1943-1966." Paper delivered at the Notre Dame University Conference on Catholicism in the Twentieth Century, 1991.

Mountin, Susan M. "A Study of Undergraduate Roman Catholic Theology Education, 1952-1976." Ph.D. diss., Marquette University, 1994.

Quirk, Sister Mary Richardine. "Some Present-Day Problems in the Education of Teaching Sisters in the United States." Master's thesis, Marquette University,

1953.

Rodgers, Rosemary T. "The Changing Concept of College Theology: A Case Study." Ph.D. diss., The Catholic University of America, 1973.

Schneider, Mary. "The Transformation of American Women Religious: The Sister Formation Conference as Catalyst for Change (1954-1964)." Working Paper Series, Charles and Margaret Hall Cushwa Center for the Study of American Catholicism, University of Notre Dame, ser. 17, no. 1 (spring 1986).

[Wolff] Sister M. Madeleva. "Theology for Sisters." Address presented to the National Congress of Religious, Notre Dame, Ind., 10 August 1952.

Young, Pamela C. "Theological Education in American Catholic Higher Education, 1939-1973." Ph.D. diss., Marquette University, 1995.

Contributors

Fr. Lawrence E. Boadt, C.S.P., Washington Theological Union; Editor in chief, *Theological Inquires Series*; past Editor, *Catholic Biblical Quarterly*; Associate Editor, *New Catholic World*.

Dr. M. Shawn Copeland, Marquette University; past Bradley Fellow, The Institute for the Study of Politics and Religion, Boston College; Fellow, Society for Values in Higher Education; Co-director, Feminist Theology Series, *Concilium: Revue international de théologie*.

Dr. Lawrence S. Cunningham, Professor and Chair of Theology, University of Notre Dame; Founding Member, International Thomas Merton Society; Fellow of Society for Values in Higher Education; Editor, American Academy of Religion *Studies in Religion* monograph series; Associate Editor, *Journal of the American Academy of Religion, Horizons, Continuum, Dictionary of Religion, Encyclopedia of Catholicism*.

Fr. Austin Doran, St. John's Seminary, Camarillo; Assistant Professor and Spiritual Director, St. John's; member, Archdiocese of Los Angeles Spirituality Commission.

Fr. Avery Dulles, S.J., University Professor, Laurence J. McGinley Professor of Religion and Society, Fordham University; Woodrow Wilson International Center Fellow; Cardinal Spellman Award for Theology; Religious Education Forum Award, NCEA; past President, Catholic Theological Society of America; past President, American Theological Society.

Dr. Keith J. Egan, Professor and Chair of Religious Studies, Saint Mary's College, South Bend; Founder and Director of the Center for Spirituality, Saint Mary's; past President, College Theology Society; Senior Fellow, Lilly Fellows Program in the Humanities and the Arts; Associate Editor for Spirituality, *Encyclopedia of Catholicism*.

Most Rev. Francis E. George, O.M.I., Bishop of Yakima; member NCCB Committees on Missions, the Church in Latin America, Religious Life and Ministry; past member NCCB Committees on Doctrine and Nominations; USCC Administrative Board Alternate.

Dr. Philip Gleason, Professor, Department of History, University of Notre Dame; past President, American Catholic Historical Association; President-elect, Immigration History Society; Visiting Chairholder, Catholic Daughters of the Americas, Catholic University of America; Marionist Award, 1994; Honorary Doctorate, 1993, Loyola University.

Dr. Roberto S. Goizueta, Loyola University, Chicago; past President, Academy of Catholic Hispanic Theologians; past Program and Co-director, Aquinas Center of Theology, Emory University; Associate Editor, *Journal of Hispanic/Latino Theology*; Editorial Board, *Emory Theological Studies.*

Fr. John Haughey, S.J., Professor of Theology at Loyola University, Chicago.

Fr. James L. Heft, S.M., Provost, University of Dayton; past Chair, Religious Studies, Dayton; University of Toronto Scholar, 1969-77.

Dr. Monika K. Hellwig, Landegger Distinguished Professor of Theology, Georgetown University; Woodrow Wilson Research Fellow; past President, Catholic Theological Society of America; John Courtney Murray Award for Theology; General Editor, *Sacraments* and *Zachaeus* Doctrinal Series for Michael Glazier; Associate Editor, *Journal of Ecumenical Studies.*

Fr. Robert P. Imbelli, Associate Professor of Theology, Boston College; past Director, Institute of Religious Education and Pastoral Ministry, Boston College; past visiting Professor, Fordham, Princeton Theological.

Fr. Arthur L. Kennedy, past Chair, Theology Department, University of St. Thomas; Visiting Fellow, Institut für die Wissenshaften vom Menschen, Vienna; Editor, *Collected Works of Bernard Lonergan*; Director, Office of Ecumenism, Archdiocese of St. Paul and Minneapolis.

Fr. Joseph A. Komonchak, Catholic University of America; Woodrow Wilson Fellow, Smithsonian Institute; past Board Member Catholic Theological Society of America; Editor, *The New Dictionary of Theology* for Michael Glazier.

Fr. Thomas R. Kopfensteiner, Kenrick-Glennon Seminary; Young Scholars Award, ATS; Member, Committee to Revise the Ethical and Religious Directives for Catholic Health Care Services.

Fr. Matthew L. Lamb, Professor of Theology, Boston College; Universitätspreis from State University of Münster; past Board Member, Catholic Theological Society of America; Member, Editorial Board, *Communio: International Catholic Review*; Editorial Consultant, Fundamental Theology, *Concilium: Revue international de théologie.*

Most Rev. John J. Leibrecht, Bishop of Springfield-Cape Girardeau; past Superintendent of Schools, St. Louis Archdiocese; Chair, USCC *Ex corde Ecclesiae* Committee; past Chair NCCB Religious Life and Ministry Committee; past member of NCCB and USCC Administrative Boards, Committee on Education, Personnel.

Fr. Joseph T. Lienhard, S.J., Professor and Chair of Theology, Fordham University; Alexander von Humboldt Research Fellowship; Walter and Mary

Touhy Chair of Interreligious Studies, John Carroll University; Editor, *Patristic Monograph Series* for the North American Patristics Society.

Most Rev. Oscar H. Lipscomb, Archbishop of Mobile; past President, Alabama Historical Association; past Chair, Board of Governors, and member NCCB Committee on the North American College, Rome; NCCB Committees on Administration, Ecumenical and Interreligious Affairs, Mission and Structure of the NCCB; past Chair and Advisor, NCCB Doctrine Committee; USCC Administrative Board, *Ex corde Ecclesiae* Committee; past member USCC Committee of Bishops and Catholic College and University Presidents.

Fr. Berard L. Marthaler, O.F.M.Conv., Warren-Blanding Professor of Religion, Department of Religion and Religious Education, Catholic University of America; past Chair, Department of Religion, Catholic University; Executive Editor, *The Living Light*; General Editor, vols. 18 and 19, *New Catholic Encyclopedia*; General Editor, NCCB/USCC *Guidelines for Doctrinally Sound Catechetical Materials*.

Most Rev. Donald E. Pelotte, S.S.S., Bishop of Gallup; past Provincial Superior of the Congregation of the Blessed Sacrament; Chair, NCCB Committee on Native American Catholics; Advisor to NCCB Committees on Ecumenical and Interreligious Affairs and Vocations; past member of NCCB Committees on Missions, Pastoral Research and Practices, Permanent Diaconate; USCC Committee International Policy.

Sr. Katarina Schuth, O.S.F., Chair for the Social Scientific Study of Religion, University of St. Thomas; past Director, Lilly Endowment Study of the Futures of Catholic Theologates; Loras Lane Award for Outstanding Service to Seminaries, NCEA; Distinguished Catholic Leadership Award, FADICA.

Dr. William M. Shea, Professor and Chair, Department of Theology, St. Louis University.

Msgr. Robert J. Wister, Seton Hall University; past Executive Director of the Seminary Department of National Catholic Educational Association.

Sr. Susan K. Wood, S.C.L., St. John's University, Collegeville; Member, Joint Lutheran-Roman Catholic Planning Committee; Member, Advisory Board, Center for Theological Inquiry, Princeton.

Sr. Pamela C. Young, C.S.J., Vice-President, Sisters of St. Joseph of Wichita.

Index